Data Structures for Game Programmers

PREMIER PRESS
GAME DEVELOPMENT

Data Structures for Game Programmers

Ron Penton

© 2003 by Premier Press, a division of Course Technology. All rights reserved. No part of this book may be reproduced or transmitted in any form or by any means, electronic or mechanical, including photocopying, recording, or by any information storage or retrieval system without written permission from Premier Press, except for the inclusion of brief quotations in a review.

The Premier Press logo and related trade dress are trademarks of Premier Press and may not be used without written permission.

Publisher: Stacy L. Hiquet
Marketing Manager: Heather Hurley
Acquisitions Editor: Emi Smith
Project Editor: Karen A. Gill
Technical Reviewer: André LaMothe
Copyeditor: Stephanie Koutek
Interior Layout: LJ Graphics, Susan Honeywell
Cover Design: Mike Tanamachi
Indexer: Kelly Talbot
Proofreader: Jenny Davidson

Microsoft, Windows, and Visual C++ are trademarks of Microsoft Corporation. Wolfenstein, Doom, and Quake are trademarks of Id Software, Inc. Warcraft and Starcraft are trademarks of Blizzard Entertainment.

The artwork used in this book is copyrighted by its respective owners, and you may not use it in your own commercial works.

All other trademarks are the property of their respective owners.

Important: Premier Press cannot provide software support. Please contact the appropriate software manufacturer's technical support line or Web site for assistance.

Premier Press and the author have attempted throughout this book to distinguish proprietary trademarks from descriptive terms by following the capitalization style used by the manufacturer.

Information contained in this book has been obtained by Premier Press from sources believed to be reliable. However, because of the possibility of human or mechanical error by our sources, Premier Press, or others, the Publisher does not guarantee the accuracy, adequacy, or completeness of any information and is not responsible for any errors or omissions or the results obtained from use of such information. Readers should be particularly aware of the fact that the Internet is an ever-changing entity. Some facts may have changed since this book went to press.

ISBN: 1-931841-94-2

Library of Congress Catalog Card Number: 2002111226

Printed in the United States of America

03 04 05 06 07 BH 10 9 8 7 6 5 4 3 2 1

Premier Press, a division of Course Technology
2645 Erie Avenue, Suite 41
Cincinnati, Ohio 45208

To my family, for always being there for me.

Acknowledgments

I would first like to thank my family for putting up with me for the past nine months. Yes, yes, I'll start cleaning the house now.

I would like to thank all of my friends at school: Jim, James, Dan, Scott, Kevin, and Kelvin, for helping me get through all of those boring classes without falling asleep.

I would like to thank everyone at work for supporting me through this endeavor.

I especially want to thank Ernest Pazera, André LaMothe, and everyone else at Premier Press for giving me this tremendous opportunity and believing in me.

I would like to thank Bruno Sousa for opening the door to writing for me.

I want to thank the pioneers of Gamedev.net, Kevin Hawkins and Dave Astle, for paving the road for me and making a book such as this possible.

I would like to thank all of you in the #gamedev crew, specifically (in no particular order) Trent Polack, Evan Pipho, April Gould, Joseph Fernald, Andrew Vehlies, Andrew Nguyen, John Hattan, Ken Kinnison, Seth Robinson, Denis Lukianov, Sean Kent, Nicholas Cooper, Ian Overgard, Greg Rosenblatt, Yannick Loitière, Henrik Stuart, Chris Hargrove, Richard Benson, Mat Noguchi, and everyone else!

I would like to thank my artists, Steven Seator and Ari Feldman, who made this book's demos look so much better than they would have been.

And finally, I would like to thank the Pepsi Corporation, for making that wonderful "stay awake" juice known as Mountain Dew.

About the Author

Ron Penton's lifelong dream has always been to be a game programmer. From the age of 11, when his parents bought him his first game programming book on how to make adventure games, he has always striven to learn the most about how games work and how to create them.

Ron is currently finishing up his bachelor's degree in computer science at the State University of New York at Buffalo. He hopes to have a long career in game development.

Contents at a Glance

Introduction xxxii

Part One
Concepts. 1

Chapter 1	Basic Algorithm Analysis	3
Chapter 2	Templates	13

Part Two
The Basics. 37

Chapter 3	Arrays.	39
Chapter 4	Bitvectors.	83
Chapter 5	Multi-Dimensional Arrays	107
Chapter 6	Linked Lists	147
Chapter 7	Stacks and Queues	189
Chapter 8	Hash Tables	217
Chapter 9	Tying It Together: The Basics.	241

Part Three
Recursion and Trees. 315

Chapter 10	Recursion	317
Chapter 11	Trees	329
Chapter 12	Binary Trees	359
Chapter 13	Binary Search Trees.	389
Chapter 14	Priority Queues and Heaps	407

| Chapter 15 | Game Trees and Minimax Trees..... 431 |
| Chapter 16 | Tying It Together: Trees .... 463 |

Part Four
Graphs 477

Chapter 17	Graphs 479
Chapter 18	Using Graphs for AI: Finite State Machines................... 529
Chapter 19	Tying It Together: Graphs 563

Part Five
Algorithms 597

Chapter 20	Sorting Data................. 599
Chapter 21	Data Compression............. 645
Chapter 22	Random Numbers 697
Chapter 23	Pathfinding................. 715
Chapter 24	Tying It Together: Algorithms..... 769
Conclusion	 793

Part Six
Appendixes 799

Appendix A	A C++ Primer 801
Appendix B	The Memory Layout of a Computer Program..................... 835
Appendix C	Introduction to SDL........... 847
Appendix D	Introduction to the Standard Template Library..................... 879
	Index..................... 901

Contents

Letter from the Series Editor xxx

Introduction xxxii

Part One
Concepts 1

Chapter 1
Basic Algorithm Analysis 3
A Quick Lesson on Algorithm Analysis 4
   Big-O Notation 4
   Comparing the Various Complexities 9
Graphical Demonstration: Algorithm Complexity 10
Conclusion 11

Chapter 2
Templates 13
What Are Templates? 14
Template Functions 15
   Doing It the Old Way 15
   Doing It with Templates 17
Template Classes 19
Multiple Parameterized Types 24
Using Values as Template Parameters 27
   Using Values of a Specific Datatype 27
   Using Values of Other Parameterized Types 30

Problems with Templates	32
Visual C++ and Templates	34
Under the Hood	34
Conclusion	35

Part Two
The Basics ... 37

Chapter 3
Arrays ... 39

What Is an Array?	40
Graphical Demonstration: Arrays	41
Increasing or Decreasing Array Size	43
Inserting or Removing an Item	43
Native C Arrays and Pointers	43
Static Arrays	43
Dynamic Arrays	49
An Array Class and Useful Algorithms	59
The Data	59
The Constructor	59
The Destructor	60
The Resize Algorithm	60
The Access Operator	62
The Conversion Operator	63
Inserting an Item Between Two Existing Items	64
Removing an Item from the Array	65
A Faster Removal Method	66
Retrieving the Size of an Array	67
Example 3-3	67
Storing/Loading Arrays on Disk	68
Writing an Array to Disk	69
Reading an Array from Disk	70
Considerations for Writing and Reading Files	71

Application: Using Arrays to Store Game Data 71
  The Monster Class 72
  Declaring a Monster Array. 72
  Adding a Monster to the Game. 72
  Making a Better Insertion Algorithm 73
  Removing a Monster from the Game 74
  Checking for Monster Removal. 75
  Playing the Game. 76
Analysis of Arrays in Games 77
  Cache Issues 77
  Resizing Arrays 80
  Inserting/Removing Cells 80
Conclusion 80

Chapter 4
Bitvectors 83

What Is a Bitvector? 84
Graphical Demonstration: Bitvectors 85
  The Main Screen 86
  Using the Buttons 86
Creating a Bitvector Class. 86
  The Data. 87
  The Constructor. 87
  The Destructor. 87
  The Resize Algorithm 88
  The Access Operator 89
  The Set Function 91
  The ClearAll Function 93
  The SetAll Function 93
  The WriteFile Function 94
  The ReadFile Function. 94
  Example 4-1. 95

Application: The Quicksave	96
Creating a Player Class	97
Storing the Players in the Game	98
Initializing the Data Structures	98
Modifying Player Attributes	99
Saving the Player Array to Disk	100
Playing the Game	102
Bitfields	**102**
Declaring a Bitfield	103
Using a Bitfield	103
Analysis of Bitvectors and Bitfields in Games	**105**
Conclusion	**106**

Chapter 5
Multi-Dimensional Arrays 107

What Is a Multi-Dimensional Array?	108
Graphical Demonstration	111
Native Multi-Dimensional Arrays	112
Declaring a Multi-Dimensional Array	112
Accessing a Multi-Dimensional Array	115
Inside a Multi-Dimensional Array	116
Dynamic Multi-Dimensional Arrays	121
The Array2D Class	121
The Array3D Class	127
Application: Using 2D Arrays as Tilemaps	131
Storing the Tilemap	133
Generating the Tilemap	134
Drawing the Tilemap	135
Playing the Game	136
Application: Layered Tilemaps	136
Redefining the Tilemap	138
Reinitializing the Tilemap	139
Modifying the Rendering Algorithm	140

| Playing the Game.. 141
| Comparing Performance....................................... 142
| Comparing Size... 144
| Analysis of Multi-Dimensional Arrays in Games.................... 144
| Conclusion.. 145

Chapter 6
Linked Lists 147

What Is a Linked List?.. 148
Singly Linked Lists.. 149
    Graphical Demonstration: Singly Linked Lists................. 149
    Structure.. 150
    Example 6-4... 168
    Final Thoughts on Singly Linked Lists......................... 169
Doubly Linked Lists... 169
    Graphical Demonstration: Doubly Linked Lists................ 170
    Creating a Doubly Linked List................................ 171
    Doubly Linked List Algorithms................................ 172
Reading and Writing Lists to Disk................................. 174
    Writing a Linked List... 174
    Reading a Linked List... 175
Application: Game Inventories.................................... 176
    The Player Class.. 177
    The Item Class.. 177
    Adding an Item to the Inventory.............................. 178
    Removing an Item from the Inventory......................... 178
    Playing the Demo... 179
Application: Layered Tilemaps Revisited.......................... 180
    Declaring the Tilemap.. 181
    Creating the Tilemap... 182
    Drawing the Tilemap... 182
Analysis and Comparison of Linked Lists.......................... 184
    Algorithm Comparisons....................................... 184

Size Comparisons 185
Real-World Issues 187
Conclusion **188**

CHAPTER 7
STACKS AND QUEUES 189

Stacks 190
What Is a Stack? 190
Graphical Demonstration: Stacks 192
The Stack Functions 193
Implementing a Stack 193
Application: Game Menus 199
Queues 204
Graphical Demonstration: Queues 204
The Queue Functions 206
Implementing a Queue 206
Application: Command Queues 212
Conclusion 216

CHAPTER 8
HASH TABLES 217

What Is Sparse Data? 218
The Basic Hash Table 219
Collisions 221
Hashing Functions 221
Enhancing the Hash Table Structure 224
Linear Overflow 224
Quadratic Overflow 225
Linked Overflow 225
Graphical Demonstration: Hash Tables 226
Implementing a Hash Table 228

The HashEntry Class...228
The HashTable Class...229
Example 8-1: Using the Hash Table...........................233
Application: Using Hash Tables to Store Resources 235
The String Class..236
Using the Table...237
How the Demo Loads Resources................................237
Playing the Demo..238
Conclusion 239

Chapter 9
Tying It Together: The Basics ... 241

Why Classes Are Good 242
Storing Data in a Class 243
Hiding Data...245
Inheritance...248
Using the Classes in a Game.................................260
Making a Game 265
Adventure: Version One......................................266
Game 2—The Map Editor.......................................310
Conclusion 314

Part Three
Recursion and Trees............315

Chapter 10
Recursion 317

What Is Recursion? 318
A Simple Example: Powers....................................319
The Towers of Hanoi 320
The Rules...321
Solving the Puzzle..321

    Solving the Puzzle with a Computer 323
    Terminating Conditions 325
    Example 10-1: Coding the Algorithm for Real 325
Graphical Demonstration: Towers of Hanoi 327
Conclusion **328**

CHAPTER 11
TREES 329

What Is a Tree? 330
    The Recursive Nature of Trees 332
    Common Structure of Trees 332
Graphical Demonstration: Trees 333
    Tutorial 336
Building the Tree Class 338
    The Structure 339
    The Constructor 340
    The Destructor 340
    The Destroy Function 341
    The Count Function 342
The Tree Iterator 342
    The Structure 343
    The Basic Iterator Functions 343
    The Vertical Iterator Functions 345
    The Horizontal Iterator Functions 346
    The Other Functions 346
Building a Tree 347
    Top Down 347
    Bottom Up 347
Traversing a Tree 347
    The Preorder Traversal 348
    The Postorder Traversal 350
    Graphical Demonstration: Tree Traversals 351

Game Demo 11-1: Plotlines 352
    Using Trees to Store Plotlines 354
    Playing the Game 356
Conclusion 358

Chapter 12
Binary Trees 359

What Is a Binary Tree? 360
    Fullness 361
    Denseness 361
    Balance 362
Structure of Binary Trees 362
    Linked Binary Trees 362
    Arrayed Binary Trees 363
Graphical Demonstration: Binary Trees 366
Coding a Binary Tree 368
    The Structure 368
    The Constructor 369
    The Destructor and the Destroy Function 369
    The Count Function 370
    Using the BinaryTree Class 370
Traversing the Binary Tree 371
    The Preorder Traversal 372
    The Postorder Traversal 372
    The Inorder Traversal 372
    Graphical Demonstration: Binary Tree Traversals 373
Application: Parsing 374
    Arithmetic Expressions 376
    Parsing an Arithmetic Expression 376
    Recursive Descent Parsing 377
    Playing the Demo 386
Conclusion 388

Chapter 13
Binary Search Trees 389

What Is a BST? 390
    Inserting Data into a BST 391
    Finding Data in a BST 394
    Removing Data from a BST 394
    The BST Rules 394
    Sub-Optimal Trees 395
Graphical Demonstration: BSTs 395
Coding a BST 397
    The Structure 397
    Comparison Functions 397
    The Constructor 398
    The Destructor 398
    The Insert Function 399
    The Find Function 400
    Example 13-1: Using the BST Class 401
Application: Storing Resources, Revisited 402
    The Resource Class 402
    The Comparison Function 403
    Inserting Resources 403
    Finding Resources 403
    Playing the Demo 404
Conclusion 405

Chapter 14
Priority Queues and Heaps 407

What Is a Priority Queue? 408
What Is a Heap? 410
    Why Can a Heap Be a Priority Queue? 411
Graphical Demonstration: Heaps 417
Coding a Heap Class 418

The Structure 419
  The Constructor 419
  The Enqueue Function 420
  The WalkUp Function 420
  The Dequeue Function 422
  The WalkDown Function 422
Application: Building Queues 424
  The Units 426
  Creating a Factory 426
  The Heap 427
  Enqueuing a Unit 427
  Starting Construction 428
  Completing Construction 428
  Playing the Demo 429
Conclusion 430

Chapter 15
Game Trees and Minimax Trees . . . 431

What Is a Game Tree? 432
What Is a Minimax Tree? 434
Graphical Demonstration: Minimax Trees 437
Game States 439
More Complex Games 442
Application: Rock Piles 442
  The Game State 443
  The Global Variables 445
  Generating the Game Tree 446
  Simulating Play 452
  Playing the Game 454
More Complex Games 456
  Never-Ending Games 456
  Huge Games 459

Limited Depth Games 460
Conclusion 460

Chapter 16
Tying It Together: Trees 463
Expanding the Game 464
  Altering the Map Format 465
  Game Demo 16-1: Altering the Game 466
  The Map Editor 473
Further Enhancements 475
Conclusion 475

Part Four
Graphs 477

Chapter 17
Graphs 479
What Is a Graph? 480
  Linked Lists and Trees 480
  Graphs 482
  Parts of a Graph 482
Types of Graphs 482
  Bi-Directional Graphs 483
  Uni-Directional Graphs 483
  Weighted Graphs 484
  Tilemaps 485
Implementing a Graph 486
  Adjacency Tables 486
  Direction Tables 488
  General-Purpose Linked Graphs 489
Graphical Demonstration: Graphs 492
Graph Traversals 493

The Depth-First Search	493
The Breadth-First Search	495
A Final Word on Graph Traversals	499
Graphical Demonstration: Graph Traversals	500
The Graph Class	**501**
The GraphArc Class	501
The GraphNode Classes	502
The Graph Class	504
Application: Making a Direction-Table Dungeon	**512**
The Map	512
Creating the Map	513
Drawing the Map	514
Moving Around the Map	516
Playing the Demo	517
Application: Portal Engines	**518**
Sectors	519
Determining Sector Visibility	521
Coding the Demo	522
Playing the Demo	527
Conclusion	**528**

Chapter 18
Using Graphs for AI: Finite State Machines 529

What Is a Finite State Machine?	530
Complex Finite State Machines	533
Implementing a Finite State Machine	535
Graphical Demonstration: Finite State Machines	537
Even More Complex Finite State Machines	538
Multiplying States	538
Conditional Events	541
Representing Conditional Event Machines	542

Graphical Demonstration: Conditional Events 546
Game Demo 18-1: Intruder 547
    The Code 550
    Playing the Demo 559
Conclusion 560

Chapter 19
Tying It Together: Graphs 563

The New Map Format 564
    The New Room Entry Structure 565
    The File Format 566
Game Demonstration 19-1: Adding the New Map Format 567
    The DirectionMap 568
    Changes to the Game Logic 580
    Playing the Game 582
Converting Old Maps 583
The Directionmap Map Editor 584
    The Initial Map 585
    Setting and Clearing Tiles 586
    Loading a Map 588
    Saving a Map 590
    Using the Editor 593
Upgrading the Tilemap Editor 594
    The Save Function 594
    The Load Function 595
Conclusion 596

Part Five
Algorithms 597

Chapter 20
Sorting Data 599

The Simplest Sort: Bubble Sort 600
   Worst-Case Bubble Sort 601
   Graphical Demonstration: Bubble Sort 602
   Coding the Bubble Sort 604

The Hacked Sort: Heap Sort 609
   Graphical Demonstration: Heap Sort 611
   Coding the Heap Sort 613

The Fastest Sort: Quicksort 616
   Picking the Pivot 616
   Performing the Quicksort 618
   Graphical Demonstration: Quicksort 621
   Coding the Quicksort 623

Graphical Demonstration: Race 627

The Clever Sort: Radix Sort 630
   Graphical Demonstration: Radix Sorts 631
   Coding the Radix Sort 633

Other Sorts 637

Application: Depth-Based Games 638
   The Player Class 639
   The Globals 640
   The Player Comparison Function 640
   Initializing the Players 640
   Sorting the Players 641
   Drawing the Players 641
   Playing the Game 642

Conclusion 643

Chapter 21
Data Compression 645

Why Compress Data? 646
    Data Busses 647
    The Internet 649
Run Length Encoding 649
    What Kinds of Data Can Be Used for RLE? 650
    Graphical Demonstration: RLEs 651
    Coding an RLE Compressor and Decompressor 656
Huffman Trees 665
    Huffman Decoding 665
    Creating a Huffman Tree 667
    Coding a Huffman Tree Class 676
    Example 21-3 691
    Test Files 692
    Example 21-4 693
Data Encryption 693
Further Topics in Compression 694
Conclusion 694

Chapter 22
Random Numbers 697

Generating Random Integers 698
    Generating Random Numbers in a Program 699
    Using rand and srand 700
    Using a Non-Constant Seed Value 702
    Generating a Random Number Within a Range 702
Generating Random Percents 705
Generating Random Floats 706
Generating Non-Linear Random Numbers 707
    Probability Distribution Graphs 707
    Adding Two Random Numbers 709

    Adding Three Random Numbers 711
    Graphical Demonstration: Random Distribution Graphs 712

Conclusion 714

Chapter 23
Pathfinding 715

Basic Pathfinding 716
    Random Bouncing 718
    Object Tracing 719

Robust Pathfinding 721
    The Breadth-First Search 721
    Making a Smarter Pathfinder 739
    Making a Better Heuristic 746
    The A* Pathfinder 750
    Graphical Demonstration: Path Comparisons 753

Weighted Maps 754
    Application: Stealth 756

Thinking Beyond Tile-Based Pathfinding 762
    Line-Based Pathfinding 762
    Quadtrees 764
    Waypoints 765

Conclusion 767

Chapter 24
Tying It Together: Algorithms . . . 769

Making the Enemies Smarter with Pathfinding 770
    Adding Pathfinding to the TileMap Class 771
    Adding Pathfinding to the DirectionMap Class 780
    Visualizing the GetClosestCell Algorithm 785
    Is That All? 786
    Efficiency 790
    Playing the Game 791

Conclusion 791

Conclusion 793
Extra Topics 794
Further Reading and References 795
    Data Structure Books 795
    C++ Books 796
    Game Programming Books 797
    Web Sites 798
Conclusion 798

Part Six
Appendixes 799

Appendix A
A C++ Primer 801
Basic Bit Math 802
    Binary Numbers 802
    Computer Storage. 805
    Bitwise Math 807
    Bitwise Math in C++ 807
    Bitshifting. 809
Standard C/C++ Functions Used in This Book 811
    Basic Input/Output 811
    File I/O 814
    Math Functions 817
    The Time Function. 818
    The Random Functions 819
Exceptions and Error Handling. 820
    Assertions. 820
    Return Codes 820
    Exceptions. 821
Why C++?. 823

Class Topics 824
    Constructors 824
    Destructors 826
    Operator Overloads 827
    Conversion Operators 829
    The This Pointer 830
    Inline Functions 830
    Function Pointers 832
Conclusion 833

Appendix B
The Memory Layout of a Computer Program 835

The Memory Sections 836
The Code Memory 837
The Global Memory 838
    Global Variables 838
    Static Variables 839
The Stack 840
    Local Variables 840
    Parameters 842
    Return Values 843
The Free Store 844
Conclusion 845

Appendix C
Introduction to SDL 847

The Licensing 848
Setting Up SDL 849
    The Files 849
    Setting Up the Files 850
    Setting Up Visual C++ 851
Setting Up Your Project 853

Setting Up SDL_TTF 856
Distributing Your Programs 858
Using SDL 858
    SDL_Video 858
    SDL Event Handling 861
    SDL_Timer 863
    SDL_TTF 863
The SDLHelpers Library 865
The SDLFrame 867
The SDLGUI Library 869
    The SDLGUI Class 869
    The SDLGUIItem Class 874
    The SDLGUI Items 876
    The SDLGUIFrame 876
Conclusion 878

Appendix D
Introduction to the Standard
Template Library 879

STLPort 880
STL Versus This Book 882
Namespaces 883
The Organization of STL 885
Containers 889
    Sequence Containers 890
    Associative Containers 896
    Container Adaptors 896
    The Miscellaneous Containers 898
Conclusion 899

Index 901

Letter from the Series Editor

Dear reader,

I've always wanted to write a book on data structures. However, there is simply no way to do the job right unless you use graphics and animation, and that means a lot of work. I personally think that all computer books will be animated, annotated, and interactive within 10 years—they have to be. There is simply too much information these days to convey with text alone; we need to use graphics, color, sound, animation—anything and everything to try to make the complex computer science subjects understandable these days.

With that in mind, I wanted a data structures book that was like no other—a book using today's technology that could live up to my high standards. So I set out to find the perfect author and finally Ron Penton came along to take on the challenge. Ron, too, had my same vision for a data structures book. We couldn't do something that had been done—there are a zillion boring data structure books—but if we could apply gaming technology and graphics to teach the subject, we would have something unique. Moreover, this book is for anyone who wants to learn data structures and related important algorithms. Sure, if you're a game programmer then you will feel at home, but if you're not, then believe me, put down that hardbound college text and pick this book up because not only will you absolutely know this stuff inside and out by the time you're done, but you will have an image in your mind like you have never had before.

All right, now I want to talk about what you're going to find inside.

First, Ron has really outdone himself with the demonstrations in this book. I would have been happy with little dots moving around and some arrows, but he has created an entire system to build the book demos in so that you can see the data structures working and the algorithms processing them. It's simply amazing to actually see bubble sort, quick sort, heap sort, and so on all race each other, or the insertion and deletion of nodes in a tree. Only a game programmer could bring these and more to you—no one else would have the programming mastery of all the fields necessary to pull this off. On the other hand, if you are a game programmer, then you will greatly appreciate Ron's insight into applications of various data structures and algorithms for game-related programs. In fact, he came up with some pretty cool applications I hadn't thought of!

So what's inside? Well, the book starts off with an introduction, gets you warmed up with arrays, bit vectors, and simple stuff like that, and talks about the use of SDL (the simple direct media layer) used for the demos. Then the book drives a steak through the heart of the data structure dragon and covers asymptotic analysis, linked lists, queues, heaps, binary trees, graphs, hash tables, and the list goes on and on. After Ron has made you a believer that hash tables are the key to the universe, he switches gears to algorithms and covers many of the classic algorithms in computer science, such as sorting, searching, compression, and more. Of course, no book like this would be complete without coverage of recursion, and that's in here, too—but you will love it because for once, you will be able to *see* the recursion! Finally, the book ends with primers on C++, SDL, and the standard template library, so basically you will be a data structure god when you're done!

In conclusion, this book is for the person who is looking for both a practical and a theoretical base in data structures and algorithms. I guarantee that it will get you farther from ground zero than anything else.

André LaMothe
Series Editor

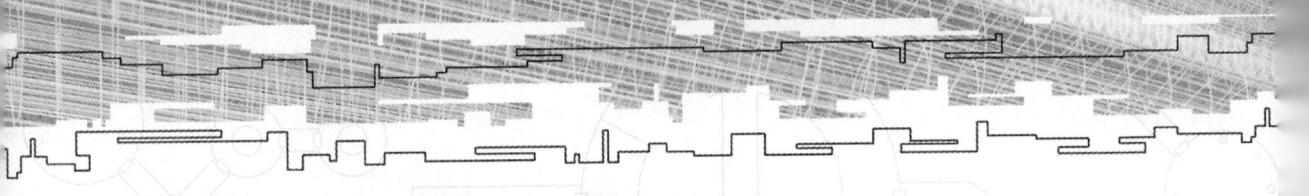

Introduction

What is a computer program? When you get down to the lowest level, you can separate a program into two main sections: the data and the instructions that operate on the data. These two sections of a program are commonly called the *data structures* and the *algorithms*.

This book will teach you how to create many data structures, ranging from the very simple to the moderately complex.

Understanding data structures and algorithms is an essential part of game programming. Knowing the most efficient way to store data and work with the data is an important part of game programming; you want your games to run as quickly as possible so you can pack as many cool features into them as you can.

I have a few goals with this book:

- Teach you how the most popular data structures and algorithms work
- Teach you how to make the structures and algorithms
- Teach you how to use the data structures in computer games

Mark Twain once said this:

> *It is a good thing, perhaps, to write for the amusement of the public. But it is a far higher and nobler thing to write for their instruction.*

I have always tried to help people whenever they need it. However, most of my help has been interactive—in chat rooms or in person. People ask me questions, and I answer them. If they don't understand, I can explain it better. A book is a different format for me because you cannot ask me a question if there is something you don't understand. So I have used the only method I can think of to prevent you from needing to ask questions: I explain *everything*. Well, not quite everything because that is pretty much impossible, but I have tried to explain as much as possible to help you understand things better.

Who Is This Book For?

If you're standing in the bookstore reading this Introduction and wondering, "Is this book good for me?", then read this section. If you've already bought the book, thank you! I am going to assume that you're reading this book because you want to learn more (unless some diabolical person is forcing you to read this as an arcane form of torture...).

This is a somewhat complex book because it deals with lots of concepts. However, I feel that I have included ample introductory material as well. Therefore, this book is for the game programmer who is just starting out at an *intermediate* level. So what do I expect you to know?

I expect you to know basic C++, but don't feel confused if you don't feel like an expert. Pretty much every complex topic I use in C++ is covered in Appendix A, so if you're unfamiliar with a concept or just forget how something works, take a few minutes to read that appendix.

The most complex feature of C++ that I use is *templates*, but you don't need to know about them before you read this book. Chapter 2 is an extensive introduction to templates, so don't worry if you don't know what they are just yet.

One advanced concept I use often in the later parts of the book is *recursion*, but you don't have to know about that, either. Chapter 10 is a small introduction to recursion.

This book is for anyone who wants to learn more about how a computer works, how to store data, and how to efficiently work on that data. All of this material is essential to game programming, so take a glance at the Table of Contents. If there is anything there that you don't already know about, this book is for you. Even if you know a little about the topics, this book is still good for you because every chapter goes in depth about these subjects.

Topics Covered in This Book

In this book, I cover many data structures and how to use them in games, ranging from the simple (arrays) to the complex (graphs and trees).

I have tried to make every chapter follow a certain format. First, I begin explaining the data structure or algorithm in theory so that you can see how it works and why it works. After that, I show you an interactive *Graphical Demonstration* of the structure, which is a demo on the CD that you can play around with to help you understand how it works. These demonstrations all use the *Simple DirectMedia Layer (SDL)* multimedia library, which I go more into depth on in just a little bit. All of these demonstrations are located in the \demonstrations\ directory on the CD.

After that, I show you how to actually code the structure or algorithm in C++. The code for these sections is mostly platform free, so it will usually compile on any compiler. I mention any sections that are platform-specific in the book. All of the code for the data structures and algorithms can be found on the CD in the directory \structures\ for your convenience. Copies of the files have also been placed in the directories of every demo that uses them. Whenever necessary, I have included console mode *Examples* on how these structures work in the \examples\ directory on the CD. All of the examples use pure C/C++, with no extra SDKs or APIs needed, so they use input and output to the text console window on your computer.

CAUTION

You are free to use any of the data structures included on the CD in any projects you use. However, be warned; they were designed to demonstrate the structures and are not super-optimized. Many functions can be made faster, particularly the small functions that can be inlined (see Appendix A). You cannot copy any of the structures because none of them implements proper copy constructors. Whenever you pass a structure into a function as a parameter, make absolutely certain that you pass-by-reference or use a pointer; otherwise, it will mess up your structure. If you don't know what this means just yet, look at the functions that use the data structures; they demonstrate how to use them correctly.

Finally, I show you an interactive *Game Demonstration*, which highlights the usage of the structure or algorithm in a game-like atmosphere. Most of these games are simple, but they prove a point. These demonstrations also use the SDL multimedia library and are located on the CD in the directory \demonstrations\.

Some chapters might deviate from the format to show you different versions of the structures.

I've separated this book into six main parts:

- Concepts
- The Basics
- Recursion and Trees
- Graphs
- Algorithms
- Appendixes

Concepts

In this part, I introduce you to some of the concepts used when dealing with data structures and algorithms. You might know some of them, or you might not.

- Basic Algorithm Analysis—This chapter is a little on the theoretical side, and it deals with topics that are usually taught in school. This chapter shows you how algorithms are rated for speed so that you can see how to choose the best algorithm for your needs.
- Templates—This is a somewhat advanced C++ concept. Some C++ books don't cover templates well, and because this book uses them extensively, I feel that it is a good idea to include a chapter on how to use them.

You can safely skip this section if you already know the material.

The Basics

In this part, I show you many of the basic data structures used within games and how to use them. These include

- Arrays—This chapter teaches you everything you ever needed to know about arrays. You might not think arrays need this much explaining, but they are an important structure in computing.
- Bitvectors—Bitvectors are an important part of space optimization. This chapter shows you how to store data in as small of a place as possible.
- Multi-Dimensional Arrays—This chapter expands on the array chapter and shows you how to use arrays with more than one dimension.
- Linked Lists—This chapter introduces you to the concept of linked data, which has many insertion and deletion benefits.

- Stacks and Queues—This is the first chapter that doesn't introduce you to a new structure. Instead, it shows you how to access data in certain ways.
- Hash Tables—This chapter shows you an advanced method of storing data by using both arrays and linked lists. It is the last structure covered in this part of the book.

In addition to those, the last chapter in this part (Chapter 9) is the first of the "Tying It Together" chapters. There are four of these chapters throughout the book, one at the end of Parts Two, Three, Four, and Five. In Chapter 9, I introduce you to the ideas of learning how to store custom game data and designing your own classes. After that, I show you how to design a basic game using many of the structures from this part of the book.

Recursion and Trees

In this Part, I introduce you to the ideas of recursion, recursive algorithms, and recursive data structures, namely *trees*. This Part includes the following chapters:

- Recursion—This is a small chapter introducing you to the idea of recursion and how it works. Recursion is a tough subject and isn't covered well in most C++ books, so I felt that I needed to include an introduction to the concept.
- Trees—This chapter introduces you to the idea of a linked tree data structure and how it is used.
- Binary Trees—This chapter shows you a specific subset of trees. Binary trees are the most frequently used tree structures in computing.
- Binary Search Trees—This chapter shows you how to store data in a recursive manner so that you can access it quickly later.
- Priority Queues and Heaps—Heaps are another variation of the binary tree. This chapter shows you how to use a binary tree to implement an efficient queue variation called the priority queue.
- Game Trees and Minimax Trees—Game Trees are a different kind of tree used to store state information about turn-based games.

In addition, Chapter 16 expands upon Chapter 9 and adds some tree-like properties to the game from Chapter 9.

Graphs

In this part, I introduce you to the graph data structure, which is another linked data structure that is somewhat like trees. This part of the book is broken down into the following chapters:

- Graphs—This chapter introduces you to the idea of the graph structure and its many derivatives. Graphs are used all over in game programming.
- Using Graphs for AI: Finite State Machines—This is an application of the graph data structure to the field of artificial intelligence—a way to make your games smarter.

Chapter 19 applies some concepts from the graph chapter and adds them to the game from Chapter 16.

Algorithms

Originally, I had planned to include these topics in the previous three parts, but they really fit better in a section of their own. Some of the topics use concepts from all three of the previous parts, and others don't. This part is composed of the following chapters:

- Sorting Data—This chapter covers four different sorting algorithms.
- Data Compression—This chapter shows you two ways to compress data.
- Random Numbers—This chapter shows you how to use the random number generator built into the C standard library and how to use some algorithms to get impressive results from generating random numbers.
- Pathfinding—This chapter shows you four different pathfinding algorithms to use on the maps you create in your games.

The final chapter, Chapter 24, expands on the game from Chapters 9, 16, and 19 by adding pathfinding support to the AIs in the game.

Appendixes

Finally, there are four appendixes in the book that cover a variety of topics:

- A C++ Primer—This appendix attempts to cover the features of C++ that are used in this book so you don't have to go running for a reference book every time I use something that you want to know more about.

- The Memory Layout of a Computer Program—To understand how to use a computer to its fullest extent, you must know about how it structures its memory. This appendix tells you this information.
- Introduction to SDL—This is a basic introduction to the Simple DirectMedia Layer library, which the book uses for all of the demonstrations. It also goes over the two SDL libraries I've developed to make the demonstrations in the book.
- Introduction to the Standard Template Library—This appendix introduces you to the C++ Standard Template Library, which is a built-in structure and algorithm library that should come with every compiler.

What's on the CD?

The CD for this book contains every Example, Game Demonstration, and Graphical Demonstration for the book. There are 33 Examples, 26 Game Demonstrations, and 34 Graphical Demonstrations. That is 93 examples and demonstrations! That should be enough to keep you busy for a while.

Just in case you end up wanting more, however, there's even more stuff on the CD. There are 19 code files full of the data structures and algorithms in this book, conveniently located in the directory \structures\, as well as the two SDL libraries I've developed for the book (see Appendix C).

In the \goodies\ directory, there are four articles—two dealing with trees and two dealing with SDL. They expand on the topics covered in this book.

In addition, the SDL, SDL_TTF, STLPort, and FreeType libraries (see Appendixes C and D for more information) are in that directory.

Figure I.1 shows you the layout of the CD.

Figure I.1

This is the way the CD is laid out.

The Simple Directmedia Layer

This is a game programming book, and as such, I had to choose an *Application Programming Interface (API)* to use that would allow me to graphically demonstrate the data structures and show them to you in real-world demos. At first, I thought I would use *DirectDraw*, but that idea was quickly laid to rest. *DirectX*, although a worthy API, is just a little too low level, and it would likely get in the way of describing the data structures. Also, I would have had to include a lengthy section telling you how to set up DirectX and all its hundreds of structures.

A friend of mine recently introduced me to a very simple API called *SDL: The Simple Directmedia Layer*. I think that the *S* part of the title should be emphasized because the API is simple. I was able to make a working SDL program (no, it wasn't "Hello World". It's the Array Demonstration from Chapter 3) in less than an hour after first looking at the header files. It truly is that simple.

Therefore, I decided that SDL was the API I wanted to use to demonstrate the concepts in this book. It's simple enough so that it will not get in the way of the theory, and I am confident that you will be able to pick it up in almost no time at all. I've provided a simple primer for SDL in Appendix C to get you started with it. So if you get confused by the graphics code, just take a peek at Appendix C. I promise, the book won't go anywhere until you return.

Coding Conventions Used in This Book

Although the point of this book is to demonstrate how to effectively organize your data, organizing your code is still somewhat important. Because of this, I will be adopting a simple coding standard.

In an effort to emphasize the scope of the different variables within the book, I have used a simple mutation of the popular Hungarian Notation:

- Global variables will be prefixed with g_.
  Examples: g_name, g_state
- Class/Structure member variables will be prefixed with m_.
  Examples: m_name, m_state
- Parameter variables will be prefixed with p_.
  Examples: p_name, p_state
- Local function variables have no prefix.
  Examples: name, state

Besides the prefix, all variables will be lowercase.

Class and function names will be title-cased, with each major word in the name capitalized.
Examples: ClassOne, ClassTwo, Function(), FunctionOne(), DoSomething()

Artwork

Two people provided the artwork used for the demos in this book. First and foremost, I would like to thank Steve Seator for making all of the person sprites and weapon icons in the game demos. He has an excellent Web site at http://www.spritedomain.net. If you're interested in his artwork, I urge you to visit the site.

The other artist is Ari Feldman, who provided most of the other sprites in the demos. His Web site is http://www.arifeldman.com.

I would like to thank both of them, because without them, my game demos would be even cheesier than they already are.

All of the artwork is copyrighted by them, so you cannot use it in your own game projects.

Are You Ready?

I suppose you're getting bored with all of this introductory stuff and anxious to get to the good stuff, so I'll stop blabbering on about all of this and let you read on. Have fun!

PART ONE

CONCEPTS

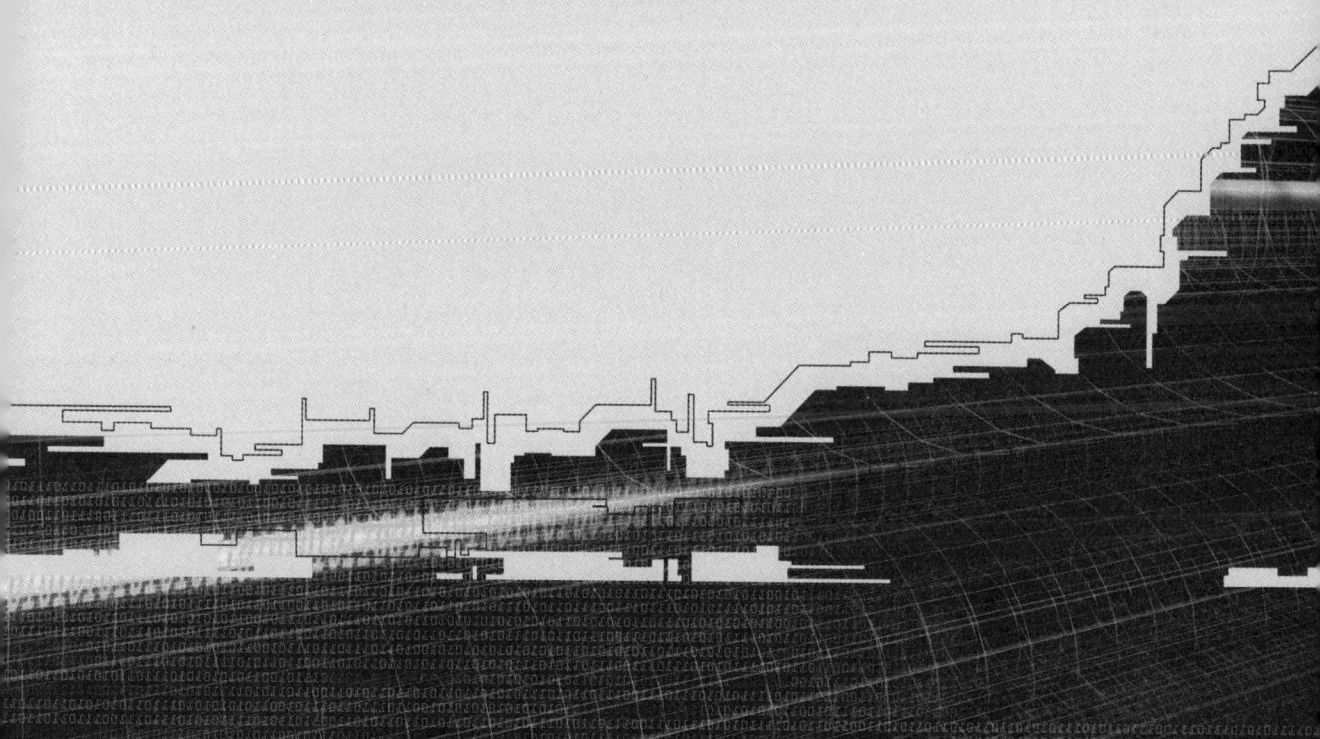

1 Basic Algorithm Analysis

2 Templates

CHAPTER 1

Basic Algorithm Analysis

1. Basic Algorithm Analysis

Almost any computer science teacher would probably kill me for including this topic as such a small chapter. After all, entire books are dedicated to this subject. But we're not computer science professors—we're game programmers! We don't care about all of this highly mathematical stuff, right? Well, that's only half right. We should at least pay some attention to the algorithms we write. In this chapter, you will learn

- How algorithms are rated for growth
- The most common complexity classes
- How each of the complexity classes compares to the others

A Quick Lesson on Algorithm Analysis

Some people spend their careers studying algorithms and data structures, and you should be thankful for them. These are the people who invented some of the nifty things you'll be using in this book. These things are used because people have proven that they work. For those of us who don't want to spend years proving that the efficiency of algorithm 1 is better than algorithm 2, this is a godsend.

However, I still think that at least some knowledge of how algorithms are analyzed is required. This section is meant to introduce you to the very basics of these concepts so that you can understand why some of the data structures and algorithms we use are better than others. Throughout the book, I refer to some of the terminology I've introduced here, so unless you already know a little about algorithm analysis, I beg you to please read this section.

Big-O Notation

Big-O notation is a helpful tool that computer scientists often use to help define the complexity of a function. Simply put, the Big-O of an algorithm is a function that roughly estimates how the algorithm scales when it is used on different sized datasets. Big-O notation is shown like this:

```
O(function);
```

The function is usually a mathematical formula based on the letters n and c, where n represents the number of data elements in the algorithm and c represents a constant number.

Imagine having a huge collection of action figures—at least 1,000 of them. But you're a very sloppy person, and you don't have them organized in any manner at all. (Okay, maybe you're not so sloppy, but just pretend.) Now, one of your friends comes over and wants to look at your exclusive Boba Fett action figure—the really rare one. In the worst-case scenario, you need to search through *every single one* of your figures because Boba Fett might be the 1000th figure in your collection.

In this example, the Big-O of the search would be $O(n)$, because the number of items to search is 1,000, and in the worst-case scenario, you have to search through every figure in the collection. (Technically, the worst case would be not finding him at all because your mom sold him for grocery money.) Of course, Boba Fett might be the first figure you look at or he might be the 500th, but when analyzing an algorithm, you don't (usually) care about the best case because the best case only occurs in optimal conditions, which almost never occur.

A number of different functions are typically used to examine the complexity of an algorithm, and these are (listed in order from the lowest complexity to the highest complexity) constant, $\log_2 n$, n, $n\log_2 n$, n^2, n^3, and 2^n. It's okay if you don't know exactly what these functions do. Just look at the graphs that follow; they will show you visually how the function looks as the number of data items increases.

O(c)

As I stated before, the C in a Big-O expression is a constant. Figure 1.1 illustrates the constant function. The graphs produced by the constant function are all horizontal, meaning that no matter how large the dataset is, the algorithm will take the same amount of time to complete. These functions are usually considered the fastest. Some of the structures in this book have algorithms associated with them that approach $O(c)$ as a best-case scenario.

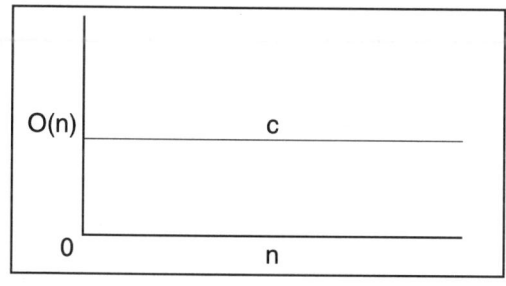

Figure 1.1

The constant function does not vary based on the size of the data. It operates at the same speed, no matter what the size of the data is.

O(Log₂n)

Figure 1.2 shows the logarithm base 2 function. In case you don't know, a logarithm function is the inverse of an exponential function. The best way to describe it is this: In a base 2 logarithm, the vertical component is increased by 1 whenever the dataset size is doubled. The log of 1 is 0, the log of 2 is 1, the log of 4 is 3, the log of 8 is 4, and so on. Logarithm-based algorithms are generally considered the most efficient algorithms in existence that depend on the size of the data. (Remember: $O(c)$ algorithms don't depend on the size of the data.)

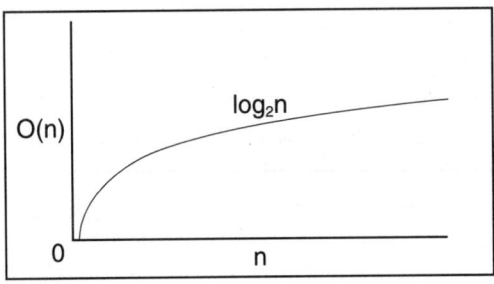

Figure 1.2

The Log_2n function varies with the size of the data, but becomes more efficient as more data is added.

O(n)

$O(n)$ is called the linear function. Figure 1.3 illustrates what this function looks like. Basically, an $O(n)$ algorithm grows at a constant rate with the data size. This growth rate means that if an $O(n)$ algorithm takes 20 seconds to operate on 1,000 data items, it would take roughly 40 seconds to operate on 2,000 data items. The scenario of trying to find the Boba Fett action figure is an example of an $O(n)$ algorithm.

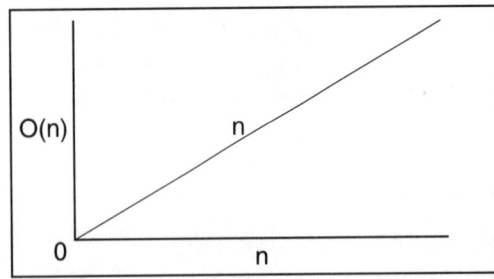

Figure 1.3

The linear function varies directly with the size of the data. Twice as much data will take twice as long to compute.

O(n log₂n)

This function, shown in Figure 1.4, is a popular lower-bound function for sorting algorithms. It is basically n multiplied by log_2n, so it is larger than any of the previous graphs, but compared to some of the more complex functions I discuss next, it is also considered a fairly efficient algorithm class.

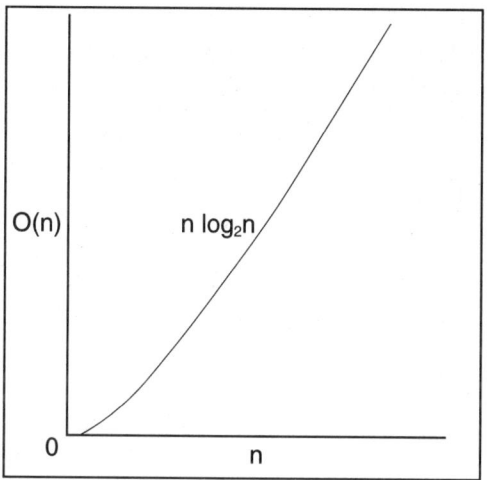

Figure 1.4

The n log_2n function varies with the size of the data, but has a relatively shallow curve, which makes functions that fall into this category seem efficient.

O(n^2)

This is where the more complex functions begin. An n^2 function (shown in Figure 1.5) is typically considered inefficient for most tasks because the function grows at an enormously high rate. For example, if it took 20 seconds to perform an algorithm on 1,000 data items, it would take 80 seconds for 2,000 items—4 times as long! In general, you should stay away from O(n^2) algorithms unless you have no other choice. An example of an O(n^2) function would be a for-loop with another for-loop nested inside.

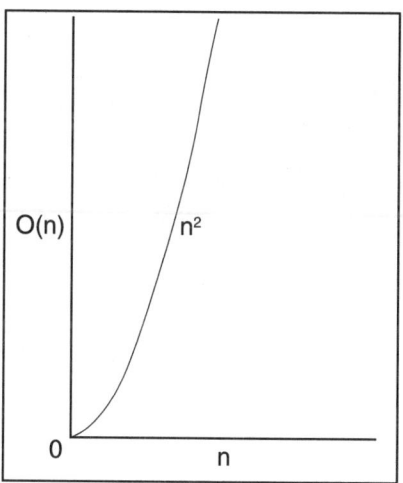

Figure 1.5

The n^2 function has a steep incline, which makes it undesirable.

O(n³)

If you thought O(n^2) was bad, O(n^3) is even worse! Even though the graph looks almost identical to O(n^2) (see Figures 1.5 and 1.6), it shoots up at a much higher rate. If it took 20 seconds to perform an algorithm on 1,000 items, it would take 160 seconds for 2,000 items! That's 8 times longer!

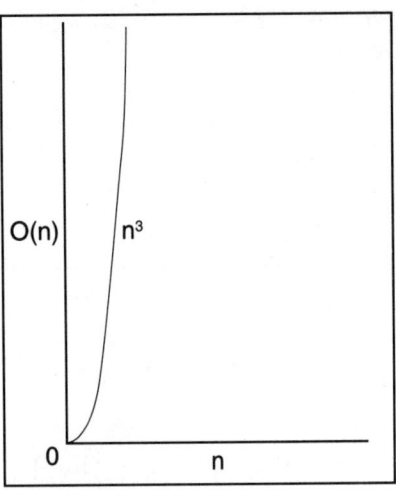

Figure 1.6

The n^3 function has an even steeper incline than the n^2 function.

O(2ⁿ)

The O(2^n) function is commonly called the *base-2 exponential function*. Every time the number of items in the algorithm increases by 1, the time it takes to complete the function doubles. See Figure 1.7 for the graph of this function. These are really inefficient algorithms—take care to avoid these at all costs!

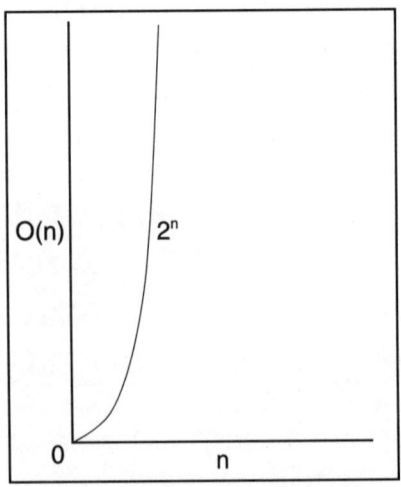

Figure 1.7

The base-2 exponential function is inefficient; every time you increase the size of the data by 1, the time it takes to complete the function doubles.

> **NOTE**
> $O(2^n)$ algorithms are actually faster than $O(n^3)$ algorithms for very small datasets. This has to do with the way an $O(2^n)$ algorithm slopes: It starts out slow, but shoots up quicker than all the other algorithms. For values of n that are less than 10, $O(2^n)$ is faster than $O(n^3)$.

Comparing the Various Complexities

The following table is a comparison of the various functions that gives you a better understanding of how the complexity functions affect the running time of an algorithm. (This is a generic algorithm prediction that assumes it takes exactly 1 second to process each item.)

TABLE 1.1 Running Time Comparisons

Complexity	16 Items	32 Items	64 Items	128 Items
$O(\log_2 n)$	4 seconds	5 seconds	6 seconds	7 seconds
$O(n)$	16 seconds	32 seconds	64 seconds	128 seconds
$O(n \log_2 n)$	64 seconds	160 seconds	384 seconds	896 seconds
$O(n^2)$	256 seconds	17 minutes	68 minutes	273 minutes
$O(n^3)$	68 minutes	546 minutes	73 hours	24 days
$O(2^n)$	18 hours	136 years	500,000 millennia	————*

* My calculator doesn't go this high.

As you can see, this table puts things in a better perspective. Even if you were to speed up a 2^n algorithm so that it spends a millisecond per item, it would still take millions of years to complete for 128 items. Isn't that insane? I hope you understand now why algorithms should be analyzed carefully for their complexity. You could accidentally create an algorithm that takes too much time to complete—and not even realize it!

There is one last thing to note about algorithm complexity. Let's say that you have an algorithm that performs a double-nested loop on n items and then performs a single loop on the same number of items. What would the complexity of this algorithm be? It is natural to assume that it would be $O(n^2 + n)$, but that is incorrect. Remember, when you measure the complexity of an algorithm, you really care only about how it grows as the data size increases. Eventually, the single n term will be overpowered by the much larger n^2 term and become insignificant. So the correct complexity of the algorithm is actually $O(n^2)$.

Also, keep in mind that dividing or multiplying by a constant has no effect on the complexity of an algorithm. If you had an algorithm consisting of a single for-loop and it only processed half of the items, the algorithm would not be $O(n/2)$. It would still be $O(n)$ because the growth of the algorithm is still linear; doubling the number of items that the algorithm works on still doubles the amount of time taken to complete the algorithm.

I'm sorry to lay down so much mathematical buzz-speak so early in the book, but I feel that it's important. If you walk away from this chapter having learned one thing, it should be the knowledge of which algorithm classes are generally faster than others.

Graphical Demonstration: Algorithm Complexity

I've included a demonstration of the different complexity graphs on the CD-ROM that comes with this book. It's a really simple program, and I encourage you to play around with it to gain an understanding of how the graphs of the functions look. The program is quite simple to understand, and you can find it in the \demonstrations\ch01\Demo01 - Algorithm Complexity\ directory on the CD.

Compiling the Demo

This demonstration uses the SDLGUI library that I have developed for the book. For more information about this library, see Appendix B, "The Memory Layout of a Computer Program."

To compile this demo, either open up the workspace file in the directory or create your own project using the settings described in Appendix B. If you create your own project, all of the files you need to include are in the directory.

When you start the program, as shown in Figure 1.8, you see a graph, six check boxes, and four arrows.

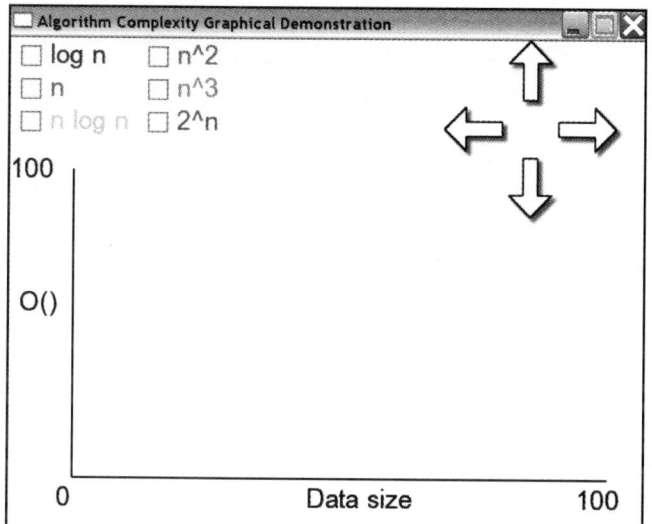

Figure 1.8

This is a screenshot of the demonstration in action.

You can click on any of the check boxes to make a graph appear. You can click any combination at the same time, which enables you to compare the different graphs.

The arrows adjust the graph axes. The up and down arrows increase and decrease the Y axis within a range of 10–5,000. The left and right arrows decrease and increase the X axis, also within a range of 10–5,000.

Conclusion

Algorithm analysis is a complex subject that many computer scientists spend a lot of time analyzing. Sometimes the topics in this chapter are called *asymptotic analysis*, which is the same thing. If you're confused by some of the stuff in this chapter, don't worry about it much; instead, just try to remember which running times are faster than others. Whenever I use Big-O notation in this book (which isn't frequently, by the way), I always take time to explain it.

CHAPTER 2

TEMPLATES

2. Templates

In this chapter, you learn about templates. Templates are a fairly important concept in computer programming when you are dealing with data structures because they allow you to easily maintain your code. If you already know about templates, you can safely skip this chapter, but if you are not very good at them (or have never even heard of them), I'd advise you to read on. In this chapter, you will learn

- What a template is
- How to create template functions
- How to create template classes
- How to use multiple template parameters
- How to use values as a template parameter
- The limitations and problems of templates
- How templates work under the hood

What Are Templates?

Templates are a relatively new concept in computer languages. A template is a software engineering tool that enables a programmer to reuse code on many different datatypes.

The best way to describe a template is as a pattern, or a mold, which will be reused over and over again. A real-world example would be the procedures of a company that manufactures figurines. First, the company produces a mold of the figure they want to produce. After that, they choose which material they want the figures made of, and then they use the mold to create the figure. With the same mold, they can make a figure out of plastic, pewter, iron, or even gold and silver.

A template in C++ is basically the same concept. A template is a mold for an algorithm or a class, and the programmers decide what type of material they want to use with it. This is a tremendously powerful tool, as you can see, because you can make a generic algorithm or a class that will theoretically operate on hundreds of different datatypes. The main advantage of using a template is that it allows you to stop copying and pasting code that operates on a specific datatype and changing it to a different datatype.

Say you want a specific algorithm to work on six different types of datatypes. Without templates, you would have to copy and paste the algorithm six times and manually change the datatypes in each copy! With templates, it is possible to make only one copy of the code and use that one copy over and over again. The algorithm on the right-hand side of Figure 2.1 is your mold, which allows you to make figurines of any type you want.

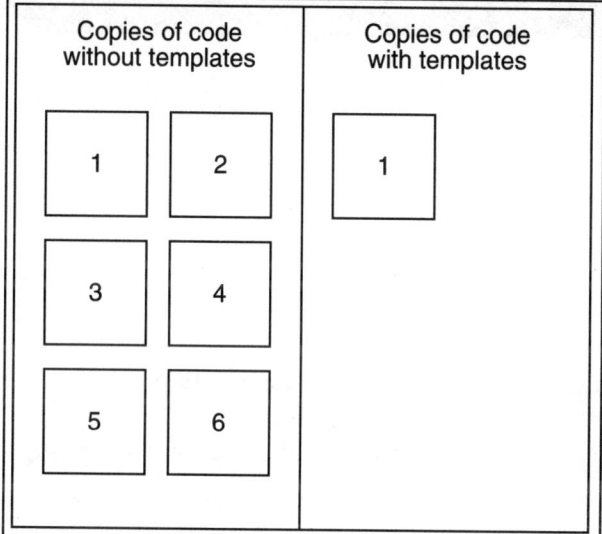

Figure 2.1

Using templates, you can make just one function that operates with many different datatypes.

C++ supports two kinds of templates: template functions and template classes.

Template Functions

A *template function* is a function that can operate on a generic datatype, which will allow you to use the same function on many different types of data.

Doing It the Old Way

Say that you want to make a function that performs an operation on an array of integers that sums up every item in the array and returns the result. Back in the bad old days, before templates, you would just make a function to do this, like so (the following functions are based on Example 2-1 on the CD, which you can find in the directory \examples\ch02\01 - Template Functions\):

2. Templates

> **NOTE**
> Although Chapter 3, "Arrays," discusses arrays, I am introducing them a little bit earlier here. If you're reading this book, you should probably know a little bit about arrays already. However, if you don't know about them, you may want to skip ahead and read the first part of Chapter 3 and then come back here.

```
1: int SumIntegers( int* p_array, int p_count )
2: {
3:   int index;
4:   int sum = 0;
5:   for( index = 0; index < p_count; index++ )
6:     sum += p_array[index];
7:   return sum;
8: }
```

Line 3 defines the `index` variable, which will be used to access each item in `p_array`. On line 4, I define the `sum` variable, which is initially empty, and on lines 5 and 6, we loop through the array, adding each index to the sum. Lastly, on line 7, the sum is returned.

A little further down the line, you might want to do the same thing, but with `float`s. Without templates, you would probably just copy the code and replace the `int`s with `float`s, like this:

```
1: float SumFloats( float* p_array, int p_count )
2: {
3:   int index;
4:   float sum = 0;
5:   for( index = 0; index < p_count; index++ )
6:     sum += p_array[index];
7:   return sum;
8: }
```

This is not too difficult, right? So what's the problem? What happens if you need to change the way the function sums the numbers? Although this situation is not very likely with the given example, it happens all the time in real code. You'd have to go back and change every copy of the code that you've made. What a pain in the butt!

Doing It with Templates

C++ comes to the rescue by allowing us to create template functions, which use the same algorithm but operate on different datatypes. The syntax for a template function is such:

```
template< class T >
returntype functionname( parameter list )
```

You first declare that you are creating a template by putting in the `template` keyword. You then put the `class` keyword and the name of the generic datatype after that, contained within the <> brackets. In the preceding example, T (which stands for "Template") is the name of the generic datatype, and whenever I want to use the class in the function, I refer to it as T. After that, you write the function declaration the same way you normally would. In my examples, I separate the template declaration and the function declaration into two lines, but you aren't required to do that. Technically, they can be on the same line, but I prefer separating them because it makes the code more readable.

> **NOTE**
> T is called a *parameterized type* in the world of software engineering.

Let's look at an example of a template function by condensing the two `sum` functions into one template function called `sum`:

```
1: template< class T >
2: T Sum( T* p_array, int p_count )
3: {
4:   int index;
5:   T sum = 0;
6:   for( index = 0; index < p_count; index++ )
7:     sum += p_array[index];
8:   return sum;
9: }
```

On line 1, I use the `template` keyword to tell the compiler that I am creating a template function that will have one generic datatype as a parameter, henceforth referred to as T. You can replace T with whatever name you want as long as it does not conflict with an existing class or type name. Some people would prefer to use more descriptive type names, such as `DataType` or `SumType`. Whatever name you choose should make sense and describe the usage of the datatype within the function.

2. Templates

> **CAUTION**
>
> It is essential, upon choosing a name for your generic datatype within the template, that you choose one that does not conflict with an existing class name. For example, if you have a template function that calls its generic class foo, but you also have a regular class named foo, the compiler won't like this and will barf error messages all over you.

On line 2, I declare the function signature. It will return an instance of type T, and it takes a pointer of type T as a parameter, which will be the array. Note how the count variable is an integer; there is no need to use a generic counting type because arrays are always indexed on discrete integer boundaries.

On line 4, I declare an integer index variable, which will be used to access the appropriate items in the array. On line 5, I declare the sum variable to be of type T, meaning that the sum will be the same datatype as the items in the array. I also initialize it to the value '0', which is important because the datatype T must have an overloaded assignment operator that takes a parameter of type int (because the compiler treats the constant '0' as an integer). If you are unfamiliar with operator overloads, please read about them in Appendix A, "A C++ Primer."

On line 6 and 7, I loop through the array and add every item in the array to the sum variable. Please note, however, that in order for line 7 to operate correctly, type T must have a working += operator. I go over the limitations of parameterized types in more detail in a later section.

On line 8, I simply return the sum variable.

Let's see this new function in action! Let's test it out on two different types of arrays!

```
1: void main()
2: {
3:     int intarray[10] = { 1, 2, 3, 4, 5, 6, 7, 8, 9, 10 };
4:     float floatarray[9] = { 1.1f, 2.2f, 3.3f, 4.4f, 5.5f,
5:                             6.6f, 7.7f, 8.8f, 9.9f };
6:
7:     // first sum the two arrays using the non-templated functions.
8:     cout << "Using SumIntegers, the sum of intarray is: ";
9:     cout << SumIntegers( intarray, 10 ) << endl;
10:    cout << "Using SumFloats, the sum of floatarray is: ";
11:    cout << SumFloats( floatarray, 9 ) << endl;
12:
```

```
13:        // now sum the two arrays using the templated function.
14:        cout << "Using Sum, the sum of intarray is: ";
15:        cout << Sum( intarray, 10 ) << endl;
16:        cout << "Using Sum, the sum of floatarray is: ";
17:        cout << Sum( floatarray, 9 ) << endl;
18: }
```

On lines 3 and 4, I declare the two arrays, one of type `int` and one of type `float`. On lines 8 through 11, I call the two non-templated `sum` functions `SumIntegers` and `SumFloats` and output the results to the console.

Lastly, on lines 13 through 17, instead of using the two separate `sum` functions, I use the templated `Sum` function on each array, even though they are of two totally different datatypes! Magic? Nope, it's one of C++'s niftier features.

Figure 2.2 shows Example 2-1 in action.

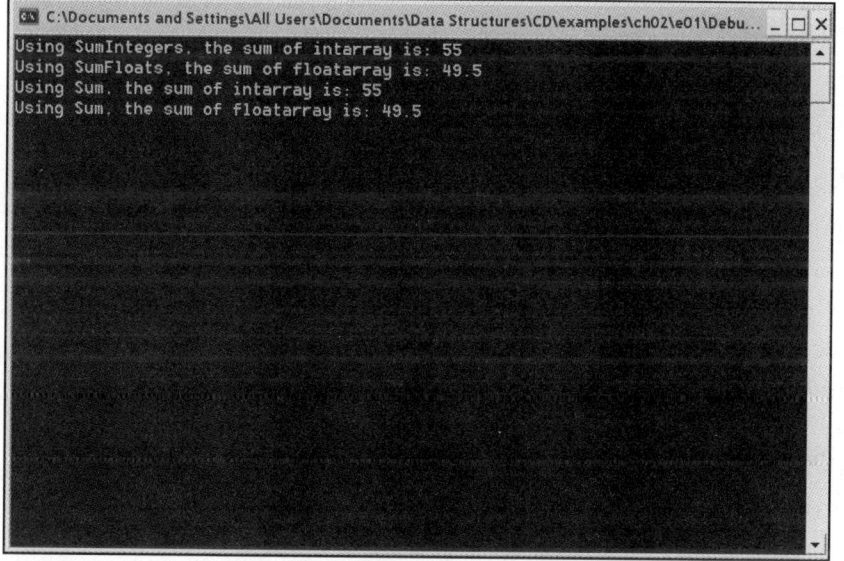

Figure 2.2

Screenshot for Example 2-1. The Sum function was used on two different arrays with no problems.

Template Classes

A *template class* is similar to a template function, except that a template class is an entire class that operates on a generic datatype. I base most of my data structures on templates within this book, so you need to understand what a template class is.

For example, say I want to create a class that is meant to retain a sum and have numerous types of data added to it. This is similar to the `sum` function I created in the previous section; however, it is based on a class instead. The following classes can be found on the CD in the directory \examples\ch02\02 - Template Classes\)

```
1: class IntAdder
2: {
3: public:
4:   // constructor
5:   IntAdder()
6:   {
7:     m_sum = 0;
8:   }
9:   // add function
10:  void Add( int p_number )
11:  {
12:    m_sum += p_number;
13:  }
14:  // get sum function.
15:  int Sum()
16:  {
17:    return m_sum;
18:  }
19: private:
20:   // sum variable.
21:   int m_sum;
22: };
```

In the previous section, I declared a local variable sum to maintain the sum of the numbers as the function looped through the array. This time, I let the class maintain a variable called m_sum (line 21) and keep track of it. On lines 5–8, I declare a constructor that initializes the m_sum variable to 0.

On lines 10–13 is the Add function, which takes an integer as a parameter and adds it to the m_sum variable.

The function Sum on lines 15–18 returns the current sum.

Say you now need the same functionality, but you need it to add floats instead of integers. You could copy and paste the entire class and create something that looks like this:

```
1: class FloatAdder
2: {
3: public:
4:   // constructor
```

```
5:    FloatAdder()
6:    {
7:      m_sum = 0.0f;
8:    }
9: // add function
10:   void Add( float p_number )
11:   {
12:     m_sum += p_number;
13:   }
14:   // get sum function.
15:   float Sum()
16:   {
17:     return m_sum;
18:   }
19: private:
20:   // sum variable.
21:   float m_sum;
22: };
```

In this class, there are three functions. The constructor clears the m_sum variable, Add adds a number to the current sum, and Sum returns the value of the current sum.

Look at how long the function is this time. It's no longer a simple 8-line function, but an entire 22-line class, almost three times as large! What happens if the class is responsible for doing even more things (like computing an average as well)? What happens when the class is changed *after* you have already copied it and modified it to work with floats? Now that you see the problem, you'll have to track down *every single copy* of the class that you've made and change each one! What a mess! Chances are likely that you won't have every function in an organized manner, and each one will probably be placed somewhere that seemed appropriate at the time you coded it. However, you have no reliable way of tracking each and every copy of the code, so the code will be thrown around and separated by chaos, as in Figure 2.3!

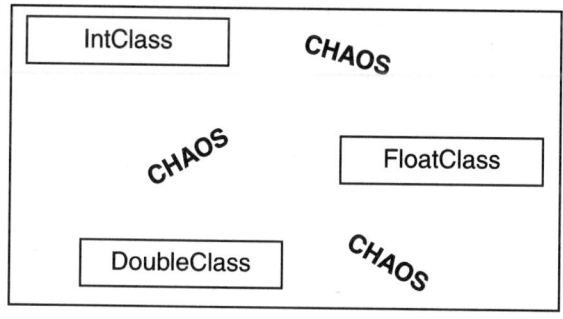

Figure 2.3

The organization of a non-templated class tends to be chaotic because you almost never have all of the classes in the same file.

So instead of copying the entire class every time you want it to operate on a different datatype, you can create a templated class that operates on a single generic type, like this:

```
1: template< class T >
2: class Adder
3: {
4: public:
5:   // constructor
6:   Adder()
7:   {
8:     m_sum = 0;
9:   }
10:  // add function
11:  void Add( T p_number )
12:  {
13:    m_sum += p_number;
14:  }
15:  // get sum function.
16:  T Sum()
17:  {
18:    return m_sum;
19:  }
20: private:
21:   // sum variable.
22:   T m_sum;
23: };
```

On line 1, I declare that I am creating a template that will operate on one generic datatype, named T. Starting at line 2, I declare the class just as I usually would, except that it operates on type T instead of a specific datatype.

On line 8, I set the initial value of m_sum to 0, which, as before, requires that the datatype have an assignment operator capable of accepting an integer parameter. On line 13, I increment the m_sum variable, which requires that datatype T have a += operator.

This is the syntax required to declare an instance of the adder class that operates on integers:

```
Adder<int> intadder;
```

The declaration of a template class instance is almost the same as declaring an instance of a normal class or datatype, except that a template class must have its parameterized types explicitly declared, within the arrow brackets, after the class name. In this example, I created an adder of type `int`, called `intAdder`. Here's how to use the adder class:

```
1:  void main()
2:  {
3:     IntAdder iadder1;
4:     Adder<int> iadder2;
5:     FloatAdder fadder1;
6:     Adder<float> fadder2;
7:     int i;
8:     float f;
9:     for( i = 0, f = 0.0f; i < 10; i++, f += 1.1f )
10:    {
11:       iadder1.Add( i );
12:       iadder2.Add( i );
13:       fadder1.Add( f );
14:       fadder2.Add( f );
15:    }
16:    cout << "The integer sum using an IntAdder: " << iadder1.Sum() << endl;
17:    cout << "The integer sum using an Adder: " << iadder2.Sum() << endl;
18:    cout << "The float sum using a FloatAdder: " << fadder1.Sum() << endl;
19:    cout << "The float sum using an Adder: " << fadder2.Sum() << endl;
20: }
```

On lines 3–6, I create four adders, which I'll use to keep track of sums.

On lines 7–11, I loop 10 times, telling the adders to add 10 different values, and then retrieve the final sums on lines 16–19. Neat, huh?

Figure 2.4 shows Example 2-2 in action.

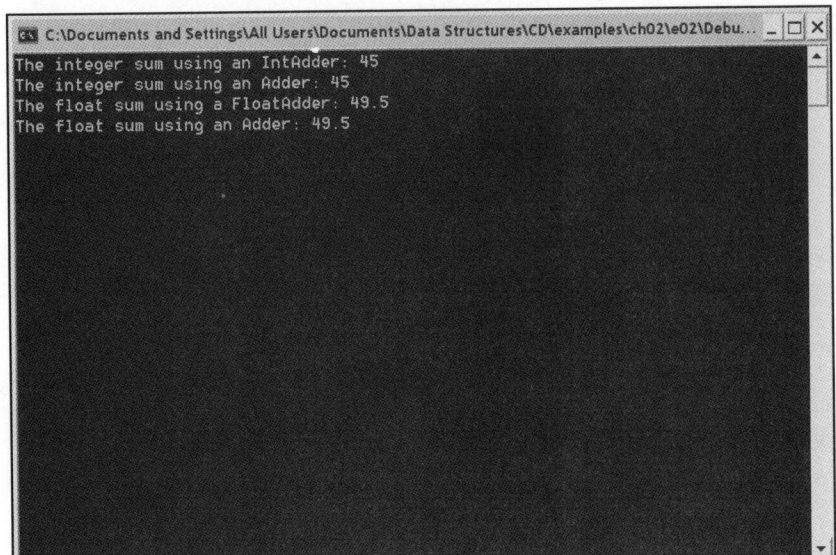

Figure 2.4

This is a screenshot for Example 2-2.

Multiple Parameterized Types

Templates do not have to be based on a single generic datatype. A template class or function can have any number of parameterized types! You declare each type within the arrow brackets as such:

```
template< class one, class two, class three >
```

You must separate each datatype name by a comma within the brackets. This scenario is an example of a time when naming your generic datatypes with descriptive names becomes important because each generic type usually has a different purpose.

Functions and classes that have multiple template parameters are usually chunks of code in which you want to modify more than one datatype to suit different purposes. Without templates, it is even easier for your code to degenerate into pure chaos, as shown in Figure 2.5.

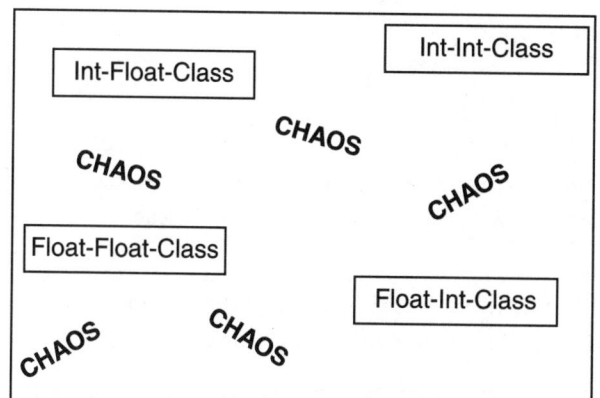

Figure 2.5

This demonstrates the chaos separating all the different kinds of classes without using templates.

Next, I'll create a template function that determines the average of an array of arbitrary datatypes. (This class can be found on the CD in the directory \examples\ch02\03 - Multiple Parameters\.)

```
1: template< class Sumtype, class Averagetype >
2: Averagetype Average( Sumtype* p_array, Averagetype p_count )
3: {
4:   int index;
5:   Sumtype sum = 0;
6:   for( index = 0; p_count > index; index++ )
7:     sum += p_array[index];
8:   return (Averagetype)sum / p_count;
9: }
```

On line 1, I declare that I will be making a template that has two generic datatypes: a Sumtype and an Averagetype. The Sumtype is the datatype I will be summing, and the Averagetype is the datatype that I will be returning from the function.

On line 2, I declare that I am returning a value of type Averagetype and receiving an array of Sumtypes. Note also that the count is of type Averagetype because the average of a list is defined as the sum over the count.

On lines 6 and 7, I loop through the list, just like the Sum template function I defined earlier, except for one small difference. Because the p_count variable is no longer of definite type, it must support a > (greater-than) operator that compares itself to an int.

The rest of this function is the same as the Sum template function I created earlier, with one exception: On line 8, I convert the local variable sum into an Averagetype, divide the sum by the count, and return the result. This line assumes that it is possible to convert an instance of Sumtype into an Averagetype.

Here, you can see this function in action:

```
1: void main()
2: {
3:   int array[10] = { 1, 2, 3, 4, 5, 6, 7, 8, 9, 10 };
4:   cout << "Average( array, 10 ) = " << Average( array, 10 ) << endl;
5:   cout << "Average( array, 10.0f ) = " << Average( array, 10.0f ) << endl;
6: }
```

An array of integers is defined on line 3. On lines 4 and 5, the Average function is called with two different sets of parameters. The first one is called with 10 as the second parameter, and the second one is called with 10.0f as the second parameter. Because C++ treats 10 as an int and 10.0f as a float, the two functions are called with two different sets of template parameters: <int, int> and <int, float>.

The compiler determines which datatypes to use at compile time by analyzing the parameters of the function. Because 10.0f is passed in on line 5, the compiler treats that as a float, calls the <int, float> version, and returns the average as a float.

NOTE
The compiler determines the types of a template function *implicitly*. In plain English, the compiler analyzes the datatypes that are passed into the function and creates the appropriate template. The type of a template function is never determined by its return value, only by the parameters.

The results of the example are shown in Figure 2.6.

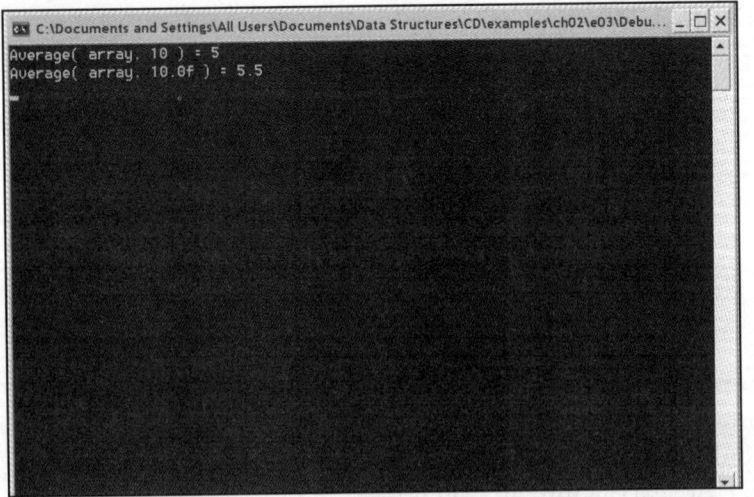

Figure 2.6

This is a screenshot for Example 2-3.

Using Values as Template Parameters

Until now, you've only seen me using *datatypes* as parameters for a template function or class. However, you don't necessarily need to use datatypes as parameters; C++ allows you to use *values* of a particular datatype. C++ is so flexible that it even allows you to use a value of a generic datatype as a template parameter.

Using Values of a Specific Datatype

First, let me show you how to declare a template parameter with a value of a specific datatype. Templates of this type are declared as such:

```
template< datatype value >
```

where `datatype` is a datatype and `value` is a specific value of that type. Note that because templates are a compile-time feature, the value in a template parameter must be resolved at compile time; that is, you cannot create a template based on a variable.

Try using this feature by creating a simple fixed-length array class. (You can find this class in the directory \examples\ch02\04 - Values as Parameters\ on the CD; don't confuse it with the `Array` class of the same name found in the \structures\ directory. Arrays will be discussed in far more detail in Chapter 3.)

```
 1: template< class Datatype, int size >
 2: class Array
 3: {
 4: public:
 5:   // set function, sets an index
 6:   void Set( Datatype p_item, int p_index )
 7:   {
 8:     m_array[p_index] = p_item;
 9:   }
10:   // get function, gets an index
11:   Datatype Get( int p_index )
12:   {
13:     return m_array[p_index];
14:   }
15: private:
```

```
16:    // the array.
17:    Datatype m_array[size];
18: };
```

On line 1, I declare that I am creating a template that will have one generic datatype, `Datatype`, and one integer value, `size`. On lines 6–14, define the `Set` and `Get` functions, which set an item in the array or get an item in the array.

The most important part of this class declaration is on line 17: I declare an array of `Datatype` with a size of `size`, which will never change.

Figure 2.7 shows how three different `Array` classes are created, using different parameters.

> **NOTE**
> Note that template classes with different value parameters are considered totally different types. For example, if you create a function that takes an `Array<int,5>` as a parameter and you try passing an `Array<int,4>` into it, the compiler will give you an error.

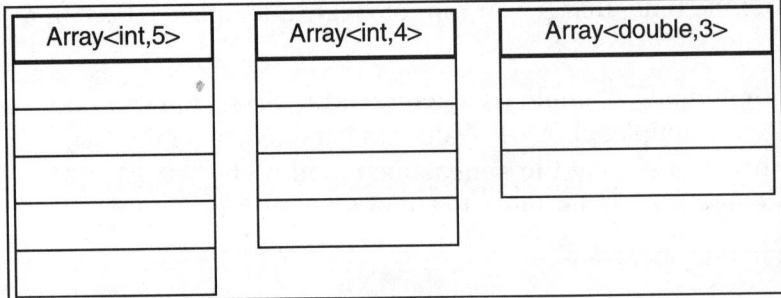

Figure 2.7
The `Array` class with three different parameter configurations. Remember that `double`s are twice as large as `int`s.

Here it is in action:

```
1: void main()
2: {
3:    Array<int, 5> iarray5;
4:    Array<int, 10> iarray10;
5:    Array<float, 15> farray15;
6:    iarray5.Set( 10, 0 );
7:    iarray5.Set( 3, 1 );
8:    iarray10.Set( 11, 9 );
9:    iarray10.Set( 2, 4 );
10:   farray15.Set( 10.1f, 3 );
```

```
11:    farray15.Set( 3.1415f, 14 );
12:    cout << "iarray5.Get( 0 ) = " << iarray5.Get( 0 ) << endl;
13:    cout << "iarray5.Get( 1 ) = " << iarray5.Get( 1 ) << endl;
14:    cout << "iarray10.Get( 9 ) = " << iarray10.Get( 9 ) << endl;
15:    cout << "iarray10.Get( 4 ) = " << iarray10.Get( 4 ) << endl;
16:    cout << "farray15.Get( 3 ) = " << farray15.Get( 3 ) << endl;
17:    cout << "farray15.Get( 14 ) = " << farray15.Get( 14 ) << endl;
18: }
```

On lines 3–5, I declare three arrays: one of type `int` which will hold 5 items, another one of type `int` which will hold 10 items, and an array of type `float` which will hold 15 items. Lines 6–17 just set various items in the arrays and then retrieve them again. Figure 2.8 shows Example 2-4 in action.

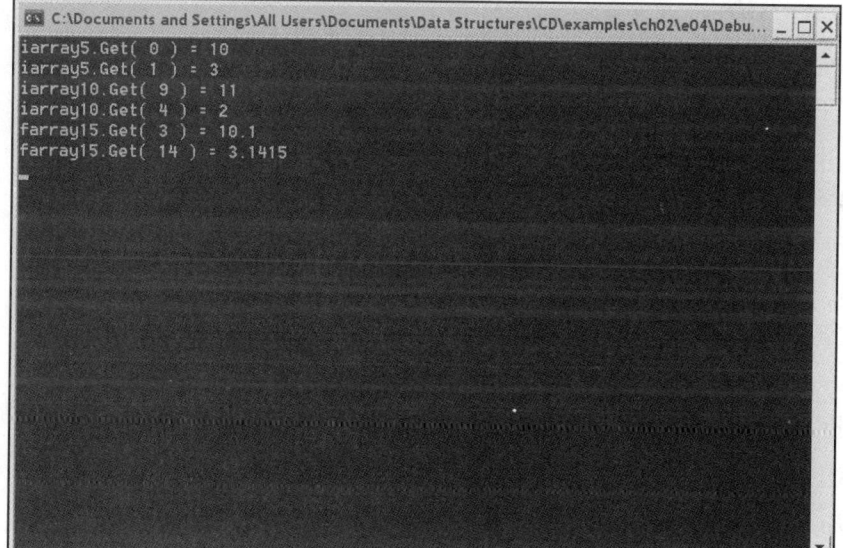

Figure 2.8

This is a screenshot from Example 2-4.

You might be saying to yourself, "Well, that was pretty cool, but I could do the same thing without as much code." You would be absolutely correct, but keep something in mind: Because you're encapsulating the array into a class, you could add functions or even *bounds checking*, which checks to make sure that you are reading and writing data in the valid parts of the array. In the `Set` and `Get` functions, you could add some code that compares the index variable to see if it is within the range of 0 to `size-1` and then take action depending upon whether or not it is. Besides, the point of this demonstration was to show how to use value parameters in a template.

Using Values of Other Parameterized Types

You don't necessarily need to use a value of a specific datatype as a parameter, however. A value parameter could be of a generic datatype, like so:

```
template< class T, T value>
```

This code declares a template of a generic datatype T, which will also have a value of the same type. This can be useful in several respects. What if you wanted to modify the array class so that it had a Clear function? This function clears a particular index to a value that is considered to be 'zero' by the parameterized class. The simplest way would be to add a Clear function to the array class, like this:

```
1: void Clear( int p_index )
2: {
3:   m_array[p_index] = 0;
4: }
```

This code certainly looks harmless, but it is flawed nonetheless. Line 3 assumes that Datatype has an assignment operator that is capable of accepting a right-hand value of the integer 0. If you decide to make a custom class which does not have an assignment operator and then create an array of that class, the Clear function will cause a compiler error. In fact, the *only* types that you can safely use this function with are the C built-in types: int, float, char, and double.

The easy solution would be to define the zero value of Datatype within the template parameter list, like this:

```
1: template< class Datatype, int size, Datatype zero >
```

The clear function can now be safely modified to look like this (this function is added to the Array class from Example 2-4 and can be found in Example 2-5 on the CD):

```
1: void Clear( int p_index )
2: {
3:   m_array[p_index] = zero;
4: }
```

Now, on line 3, instead of setting the item at the index to the integer value 0, you set it to the specific instance of the zero value for the given class! These changes can easily be made to the previous templated `Array` class from this section.

So how would you declare an instance of the modified `Array` class? It is the same as declaring the previous `Array` class, with the inclusion of one template parameter:

```
Array< int, 10, 0 > intarray10;
```

This declares an `Array` of type `int` whose size will be 10, which will treat the number 0 as its zero value. You can declare a floating-point array in the same way:

```
Array< float, 10, 0.0f > floatarray10;
```

In an interesting side effect, you can also have your array clear indexes to a value other than zero by defining an array like this:

```
Array< int, 15, 42 > intarray15;
```

This `Array` will clear the specified index to 42 instead of 0 whenever the `Clear` function is called. The full effect is demonstrated in this code snippet:

```
1: Array< int, 5, 0 > array1;
2: Array< int, 10, 42 > array2;
3: Array< float, 5, 0.5f > array3;
4: array1.Clear( 0 );
5: array2.Clear( 0 );
6: array3.Clear( 0 );
7: cout << "array1.Get( 0 ) = " << array1.Get( 0 ) << endl;
8: cout << "array2.Get( 0 ) = " << array2.Get( 0 ) << endl;
9: cout << "array3.Get( 0 ) = " << array3.Get( 0 ) << endl;
```

I declare three arrays on lines 1–3: a 5-index integer array that clears to 0, a 10-index integer array that clears to 42, and a 5-index float array that clears to 0.5f. Then, on lines 4–6, I call the `Clear` function on each array at index 0. Lines 7–9 print out the values of the cleared indexes: 0, 42, and 0.5. Figure 2.9 shows Example 2-5 in action.

As you can see, templates open up a whole new world of possibilities.

Figure 2.9

This is a screenshot of Example 2-5.

Problems with Templates

Templates, like all good things, have a few "gotchas." Because a template function or class is designed to work with a broad range of datatypes, the number of things you can do with a template is somewhat limited. Sure, you can use certain functions of a parameterized datatype if you assume that the datatype has that function. For example, look at the following template function. (All the functions and classes in this section can be found on the CD in Example 2-6.)

```
1: template<class T>
2: void Function( T p_item )
3: {
4:   p_item.DoSomething();
5: }
```

On line 1, I state that I am creating a template of one generic type, T. Line 2 defines the function name, Function, which will take one instance of datatype T and return nothing. On line 4, the function calls the DoSomething function of the item that was passed into Function.

Problems with Templates   33

The function in this example assumes that datatype T has a function called DoSomething and will work fine if Function is called with ClassOne as a parameter:

```
1: class ClassOne
2: {
3: public:
4:   void DoSomething()
5:   {
6:     return;
7:   }
8: };
```

But what happens when ClassTwo is passed in? ClassTwo doesn't have a DoSomething function, but it has a DoSomethingElse function:

```
1: class ClassTwo
2: {
3: public:
4:   void DoSomethingElse()
5:   {
6:     return;
7:   }
8: };
```

See what happens when you try to run this code using the two classes defined previously:

```
1: void main()
2: {
3:   ClassOne a;
4:   ClassTwo b;
5:   Function( a );
6:   Function( b );
7: }
```

Microsoft Visual C++ 6.0 spits out this error message: error C2039: 'DoSomething' : is not a member of 'ClassTwo'. If you're using a different compiler, it should give you an error similar to that.

> **NOTE**
> Take care to always document which operators, conversion operators, and functions of a parameterized datatype you use so that people who use this class or function know what is expected of the datatypes they use with it.

Visual C++ and Templates

Another thing I must warn you about is Microsoft Visual C++ 6.0's method of implementing templates. Templates are a relatively recent addition to the C++ standard, and Microsoft's implementation of them is not exactly standard. There is one tiny problem with the way MSVC6 handles templates. (In fact, most compilers have the same flaw.)

Normally, when programming a non-template class, you would separate the class header and the class implementation into two files: an .h file and a .cpp file. The function declarations and data declarations go in the header file, and the implementations of each of the functions go into a .cpp file.

If you try programming a template class in this way, MSVC6 will give you errors. It has to do with the way template classes are implemented (see the next section). You'll notice that in every implementation of a template class, I've defined the functions inline, within the header files. This is to get around the problem in MSVC6, which happens to be my main compiler.

It took me a long time to figure this out, so hopefully I'm saving you a bit of trouble if you decide to do this on your own.

Under the Hood

This section is strictly optional and is intended for those of you who wonder how a template works. Remember when I said that the alternative to copying and pasting lots of code was to use a template? Well, that's exactly how C++ implements a template. C++ goes through the template definition, copies the code, and replaces every instance of the parameterized type name with the actual type name. Figure 2.10 shows how C++ basically takes one copy of the code and converts it into as many copies as are needed.

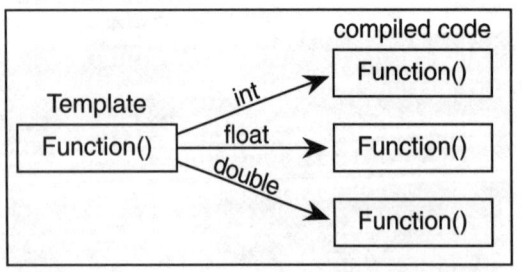

Figure 2.10

The compiler performs the copying for you automatically when you compile the program so that you don't have to do it manually.

The beauty of template implementation is that instead of managing all the copying and pasting yourself, you make the compiler do it instead, allowing you to maintain only one copy of the code.

Take a look at the `Sum` function from earlier, for example. When I compiled the code that called the function, once for an integer array, and once for a float array, the compiler actually made two copies of that function. In the first copy, it replaced every instance of `T` with `int` (creating an exact replica of the `SumIntegers` function from the "Doing It the Old Way" section), and it replaced every instance of `T` with `float` in the second copy (creating an exact replica of the `SumFloats` function).

> **NOTE**
> C++ often gets a bad rap as being "slow." This accusation is false, and templates demonstrate this fact perfectly. A template is nothing more than a copied-and-pasted bunch of code—the compiler does all the work for you. Therefore, you can write a really fast algorithm and have it run at full speed for every datatype you want! Isn't that cool?

Essentially, this means that a template is very similar to a `#define` macro. The main difference is that `#define` is done with the pre-processor, whereas templates are done by the compiler with complete type-safety. This difference is the reason why MSVC6 requires template functions and classes to be defined inline; if they aren't, it cannot find the code, and it will give you a compiler error.

Of course, templates rarely need to be so complex that you need to modularize the code. Writing template functions and classes entirely inline is generally acceptable, at least until the problem is fixed.

Conclusion

I hope by now you can see why templates are tremendously powerful. I must admit, when I first saw something about templates in a book, I skipped the chapter because it sounded boring, but after getting tired of making a different sorting algorithm for every different kind of data that I wanted to sort, I decided to look into templates.

I'm glad I did learn about templates because I don't know how I ever lived without them before. Granted, the syntax can get a little ugly here and there, but that is just a minor problem when compared with how useful they are.

It is important that you gain at least a little working knowledge of how templates work because almost all of the data structures in this book use templates.

There is one final thing that I feel should be mentioned: Some people love to abuse templates and make really strange-looking code that is almost impossible to read or understand, which is why a lot of new programmers tend to dislike templates. I have not done this at all. Every template class or function in this book uses simple template features so that you can understand them better.

PART TWO

THE BASICS

3 **Arrays**

4 **Bitvectors**

5 **Multi-Dimensional Arrays**

6 **Linked Lists**

7 **Stacks and Queues**

8 **Hash Tables**

9 **Tying It Together: The Basics**

CHAPTER 3

ARRAYS

3. Arrays

Arrays are perhaps the most basic data structures in existence; they have been around since the very first computers. Some of you might already know all there is to know about arrays, and you can safely skip this chapter. Those of you who aren't so keen as to how arrays work might want to read on, though. In this chapter, you'll learn

- What an array is
- How to create native static arrays
- How to create native dynamic arrays
- How to delete dynamic arrays to prevent memory leaks
- How to resize dynamic arrays
- What a string is
- How to create your own robust array class
- How to insert and remove cells from an array
- How to load and store arrays to disk
- How to use arrays to store data in a game

What Is an Array?

In computer terms, arrays have been around forever. The array is perhaps the most basic data structure in a computer, and it's still the most widely used.

You can think of an array as a jail block. It is a long one-dimensional structure containing numerous cells. Each cell can contain exactly one item, and an index number is used to access each cell.

Typically, when we represent an array in figures, we use squares to represent the cells, as in Figure 3.1.

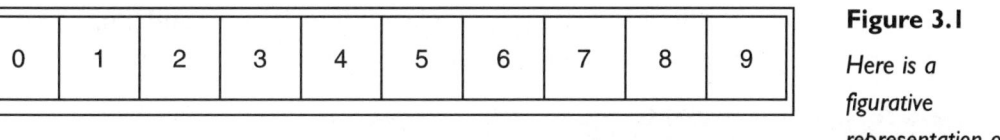

Figure 3.1
Here is a figurative representation of an array.

When dealing with arrays, each cell has its own index number. Typically, the very first cell has an index of 0 (zero), but that doesn't always have to be the case, as you shall see later on.

An array is called a *linear* data structure, as opposed to some of the more advanced *branching* data structures, which I go over in the later chapters of the book. Arrays are also called *random-access* structures because it is possible to instantly access any item within an array if you know its index. Accessing items within an array is an $O(c)$ algorithm; no matter how many items are in an array, it will still take the same amount of time to access any index.

Graphical Demonstration: Arrays

The graphical demonstration for arrays is located on the CD in the directory \demonstrations\ch03\Demo01 - Array. This demonstration is designed to be a helpful tool for you to use to augment your understanding of the array data structure. If any of the algorithms that are explained in the chapter don't make immediate sense to you, I highly recommend checking out this graphical demonstration.

Compiling the Demo

This demonstration uses the SDLGUI library that I have developed for the book. For more information about this library, see Appendix B, "The Memory Layout of a Computer Program."

To compile this demo, either open up the workspace file in the directory or create your own project using the settings described in Appendix B. If you create your own project, all of the files you need to include are in the directory.

When you start the program, you will be greeted with four buttons and a pictorial representation of a ten-cell array. Figure 3.2 is a screenshot of the program in action.

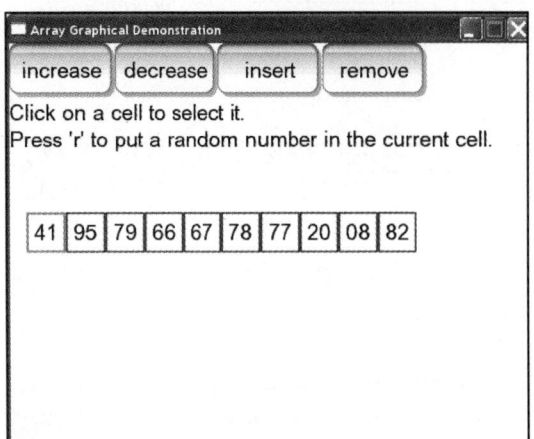

Figure 3.2

This is the starting screen for the array demo.

Each of the four buttons performs a different function upon the array. I explain them in the following sections.

Use the mouse to select a cell, which then turns red.

Press the R button to insert a random number from 0–99 into the current cell.

When you press any of the buttons, an animation starts and text relating to the algorithm appears. When an animation is complete, a button with the caption "Continue" appears. Press this button to continue the algorithm.

Occasionally, you might notice that some cells contain a red X instead of a number. Figure 3.3 shows an array with a red X in it.

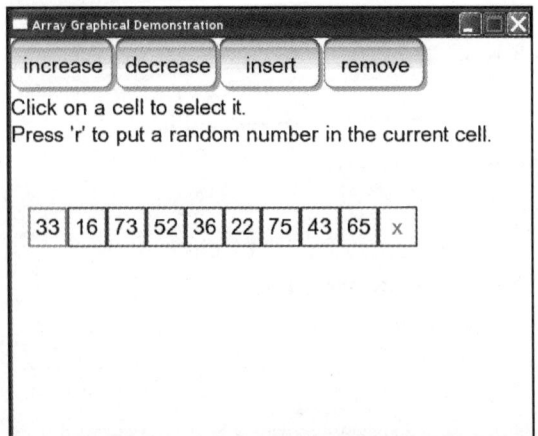

Figure 3.3

The array has a red X, which means that the data in that cell is undefined garbage.

The red X signifies that the contents of the cell are undefined. See the section on resizing arrays later in this chapter.

Increasing or Decreasing Array Size

These two buttons increase or decrease the array size by one cell. The demo goes through the algorithm step by step and shows you the process that occurs. When an array is increased in size, the extra cell at the end contains a red X because the value of that cell is undefined.

Inserting or Removing an Item

These two buttons either insert a new random number into the current cell or remove the item in the current cell. The demo shows you the step-by-step process that occurs.

Native C Arrays and Pointers

I'm sure you've used an array of some sort before. However, more advanced array tricks in C and C++ always tend to trip up beginner programmers. I certainly had some problems with arrays when I first started using C. My problem was that I came from BASIC programming, where arrays are much more user-friendly.

Arrays in C are closely bound to pointer tricks. Therefore, it is very important that you know how to use pointers to your own advantage before we go much further.

Static Arrays

An array is called *static* when its size cannot be modified. These are the easiest types of arrays to create and manipulate.

Declaring a Static Array

The easiest way to create a static array in C is to use the bracket notation:

```
int array[10];
```

This code creates an integer array with 10 items in it. Because native C arrays are numbered starting with 0, the range of valid indexes for this array is 0–9. Trying to access index 10 in this array is considered a *fencepost* error. If you look at a fence, you'll see that there are more fenceposts than there are parts of the fence. Figure 3.4 shows how you can easily confuse the number of fence sections and the number of fenceposts.

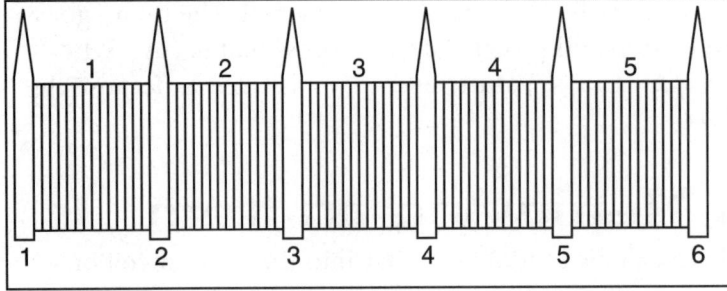

Figure 3.4

There are more fence posts than fence sections. This is the same situation with arrays, where you can easily read or write past the end of the array because you think there are more cells than there really are.

Normally, you would expect that the tenth index in an array would have the index 10, but it is really 9. Remember, this is due to the arrays being counted up from 0, not 1. I cannot stress enough the importance of keeping this fact in mind. Perhaps my most frequent source of bugs is fencepost errors, or being off by one.

> **NOTE**
>
> This is the same reason that many mathematicians say that the third millennium started in 2001 and not 2000. Because the calendar starts at year 1 and not 0, the year 2000 was the 2000th year and thus the last year of the second millennium. If they had started counting at 0 instead, 2000 would have been the start of the third millennium, not the end of the second.

Accessing an Array

Accessing the array is as simple as placing the index of the cell you want to view or modify within the brackets when referring to the array:

```
1: array[0] = 5;
2: array[1] = array[0];
```

Line 1 sets cell 0 to hold the integer 5, and line 2 sets cell 1 to hold the same integer as cell 0. Figure 3.5 shows a picture of what the array should look like after executing the previous code snippet.

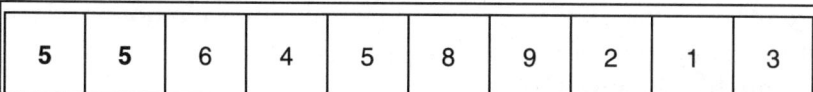

Figure 3.5
Here are the contents of the array after executing the simple 2-line code segment.

Cells 0 and 1 both hold 5, but what the heck happened to all the other cells? Why do they hold all those weird numbers? When you create an array in C/C++, the array is not initialized. So what happens is that the array holds junk, and you have no idea what is in the array right after you create it.

What happens when an array is accessed past the end? One of several things, actually. If you are just reading memory, there might not be a problem. One thing that could happen would be that your program would crash because your compiler has code that detects if you are reading memory out of bounds and the code throws an error.

Another thing could happen, and this is usually more devastating. Your program could read a value that was total junk and not crash at all. I say that it's more devastating because it is a source of some very nasty and undetectable bugs. Your program reads a junk value, and for all intents and purposes, it thinks the value is valid. Nasty little things like this can be very difficult and time consuming to track down.

> **NOTE**
> You must take care to initialize arrays after you declare or create them because you might end up with nasty bugs if your code assumes that the array contains valid information.

> **NOTE**
> Microsoft's Visual C++ sets all byte memory it uses to the hex value `0xcd` when it is in debug mode, so each item in the integer array will contain `0xcdcdcdcd` (integers are 4 bytes), which is equivalent to the base 10 number $-842,150,451$. Whenever you're looking at memory and it contains that number, you can be certain that you forgot to initialize the memory with a value.

What if you are writing past the end of an array? The end effect of this is usually worse than reading past the end of an array. This time, you might manage to change memory that isn't even yours to touch. This is usually referred to as an *access violation* and results in *damaging* data. Sometimes it messes up important data and sometimes it doesn't, but you can never be sure. Bugs of this type are even more deadly because the bug is caused by code that you wouldn't even suspect of causing the bug in the first place! Another possibility would be that the program just crashes. Either way, the end result is undesirable, and you should avoid it at all costs.

> **CAUTION**
> Never read or write past the end of an array, even if you think it is safe.

Passing an Array into a Function

So how do you pass this array into a function? There are several ways to do this. The first way is to declare the function parameter using the bracket notation, like this:

```
1: void ArrayFunction( int p_array[] )
2: {
3:   p_array[0] = 10;
4: }
```

On line 1, I declare that the function will be taking an integer array as a parameter. Line 3 sets the first index to 0. Now, all I have to do if I want to pass the array into this function is to do this:

```
ArrayFunction( array );
```

Note that you can put a number within the brackets of the function definition, but the compiler will ignore the numbers within the brackets.

The other way to declare that an array is being passed into a function is to use the pointer symbol, like this:

```
1: void ArrayFunction( int* p_array )
2: {
3:   p_array[0] = 10;
4: }
```

This function works the same as the first `ArrayFunction`, except that I use the pointer symbol instead of the brackets. I'm sure many of you are now sitting there with question marks above your heads, wondering, "Why does that work?"

Inside an Array

The simple answer is that it works because p_array is a pointer. When C/C++ creates an array, it does two things: It makes enough room for the array in memory, and it treats the name of the array as a pointer to the block of memory where the array is stored.

So, what you end up with is something like Figure 3.6.

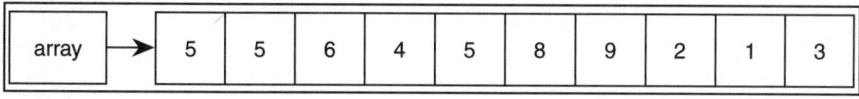

Figure 3.6
An array is just a large chunk of continuous memory, internally.

Why is an array a pointer? Well, an array is a pointer because of the way an array is accessed. Remember when I said that an array is random-access and that the algorithm to access any cell within the array is an O(c) algorithm? What your compiler is essentially doing is taking the pointer to the start of the array and calculating the position in memory of the cell you want to access. Here's what happens when you want to get the fifth cell of the array:

1. The compiler multiplies 5 by the size of the data.
2. The compiler adds that to the pointer.
3. The compiler treats that as a new pointer and returns the value at that address.

Isn't that cool? Playing around with an array is all about playing around with pointers. The compiler literally turns the line

x = array[5];

into

x = *(array + 5);

Now, lucky for us, the compiler does the multiplication automatically, so we don't even need to multiply. It adds 5 to the array pointer and then retrieves

TIP

Because the compiler does the multiplication automatically, you can actually reverse the order of the pointer and the subscript like this: x = 5[array];, and it will still work! You can amaze your friends by writing totally unreadable code like this! I wouldn't recommend doing anything like this in serious code, however. I only include it here to show you how it works.

the value at that index. You can replace 5 with any index you want, and the algorithm will take the same exact amount of time. Figure 3.7 shows how this algorithm is performed.

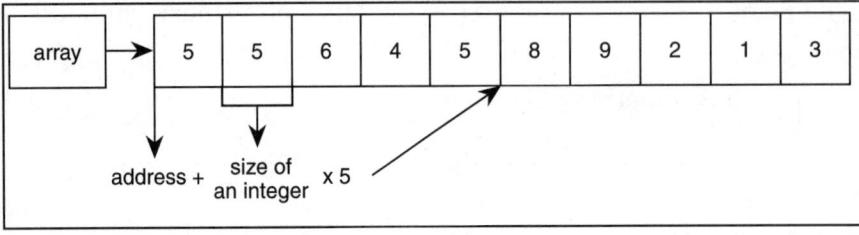

Figure 3.7
The address of the data you want to access is calculated by adding the starting offset pointer to the size of the data multiplied by the index you want to get.

Initializing a Static Array

C++ allows you to initialize a static array with a pre-determined number of values so that the array contains valid information from the very start. For example, to initialize a five-cell integer array with the numbers 1 through 5, you would code this:

```
int array[5] = { 1, 2, 3, 4, 5 };
```

C++ also allows you to leave out the length of the array and determine it automatically by counting the number of items contained within the initializing list:

```
int array[] = { 1, 2, 3, 4, 5, 6 };
```

This time, the array is created and automatically sized to hold six cells. The only difficult part about doing something like this is figuring out the size of the array after it is created, but you can do that by using the sizeof operator. Note that the sizeof operator returns the number of bytes contained within the array, so you'll need to divide the answer by the size of the datatype that was used in the array:

> **NOTE**
> The sizeof operator only works on a static array within the same scope in which it was defined. If you pass the array to a function or return it from a function, the sizeof operator will no longer return the actual size of the array.

```
int size = sizeof( array ) / sizeof( int );
```

Example 3-1

Here is the listing of Example 3-1, which demonstrates all of the major concepts of static arrays. It is on the CD in the directory \examples\ch03\01 - Static Arrays\.

```
void main()
{
    // declare an array with 10 cells.
    int array1[10];
    // declare x
    int x;
    // set the first cell to 5, then set the second
    // cell to the first cell.
    array1[0] = 5;
    array1[1] = array1[0];
    // DONT EVER DO THIS:
    // this next line of code writes past the end
    // of the array, potentially causing harm.
    // array1[10] = 0;
    // pass the array to a function.
    ArrayFunction( array1 );
    // set cell 5 to 42.
    array1[5] = 42;
    // retrieve the value of cell 5 using 3 different methods.
    // x should be 42 after each operation.
    x = array1[5];
    x = *( array1 + 5 );
    x = 5[array1];
    // declare a second array and initialize it.
    int array2[5] = { 1, 2, 3, 4, 5 };
    // declare a third array and initialize it without a specific size
    int array3[] = { 1, 2, 3, 4, 5, 6 };
    // retrieve the number of cells in array3:
    int size = sizeof( array3 ) / sizeof( int );
}
```

This example has no output.

Dynamic Arrays

Dynamic arrays are more complex than static arrays. You cannot create a dynamic array as easily as a static array. Instead, you must use the pointer notation to create and manage a dynamic array. There are two main ways of creating a dynamic array: By using C's `malloc`/`calloc` (memory allocate and clear allocate) or by using C++'s `new`. Both `malloc` and `calloc` require the inclusion of the `malloc.h` header file, but `new` is a built-in language feature and doesn't need a header. Each method has its strengths and weaknesses, and both of them allocate memory on the heap. (See Appendix B for an explanation of the memory layout.) Whichever method you use to create a dynamic array, the arrays are declared the same way.

When you declare a dynamic array, you declare it just like you would declare a pointer. (Note that it is not an array yet.)

```
int* array = 0;
```

Note that I've initialized the array pointer to 0. When you declare a basic type in C++, it is almost always filled with random data, so the pointer will be pointing somewhere in memory that you shouldn't be pointing to. The value 0 is considered to be the universal value for an uninitialized pointer. It is mostly a safety precaution so you know that the array has not been initialized yet.

Allocating a Dynamic Array

There are three different ways you can allocate memory for a dynamic array: `malloc`, `calloc`, and `new`.

Malloc

To use `malloc`, you must tell it how many bytes you want it to allocate. If you know the size of the datatype you want to create, multiply that by the number of cells you want in the array. However, most of the time you don't know the size of the structure (or it is a pain in the butt to figure it out manually), so you should let the compiler figure it out for you. To do this, you must use the `sizeof` operator multiplied by the number of cells you want in the array. Malloc then returns a void pointer to the memory that it has just allocated on the heap.

```
array = (int*)malloc( sizeof(int) * 10 );
```

Look at the parameter of `malloc` first. You retrieve the size of an integer (which is usually four bytes, but some compilers use different-sized integers) and multiply that by 10. This should give you enough space for an array that will contain ten integers. Now, look in front of the `malloc` call; you see the `int` keyword followed by a pointer symbol, all within parentheses. This part is only needed if you are using C++. Remember, `malloc` returns a `void` pointer, which means that it has no type. C was lax and allowed you to *implicitly* cast the pointer into an integer pointer, but

C++ doesn't allow you to do that. Implicit conversion means that it will automatically convert the `void` pointer that `malloc` returns into an `int` pointer. C++ will complain about the line without that conversion.

Now, if everything goes as planned, `array` should now point to a valid array. There is a chance that `array` doesn't point to a new array, however. It might still be 0. If the amount of memory you ask for is not available, `malloc` returns 0.

Now that you have your array, you can use it exactly like you used the static array.

> **NOTE**
> C++ has a new feature called *strong type-checking*. It does not allow you to convert pointers of one type into a pointer of another type unless you *explicitly* tell it to.

> **NOTE**
> Make sure you always check to see if your calls to `malloc` return a non-zero value. If it does return 0, then you should take an appropriate action from there, such as displaying an error message to the user or propagating the error to a higher level and exiting with an error code.

Calloc

Whenever you get memory from `malloc`, the memory you get is mostly junk. Most of the time you will have to manually reset the memory to the values you want. Usually the most popular initial value is 0. This is what `calloc` is for. `Calloc` is exactly like `malloc`, except that it goes one step further and resets every byte that it allocates to 0.

```
array = (int*)calloc( 10, sizeof(int) );
```

Note that `calloc` has 2 parameters instead of 1. Whereas `malloc` accepts the number of bytes you want to allocate as the only parameter, `calloc` wants the number of cells as the first parameter and the size of each cell in bytes as the second parameter.

Figure 3.8 shows an array created by `calloc`.

| 0 | 0 | 0 | 0 | 0 | 0 | 0 | 0 | 0 | 0 |

Figure 3.8
An array created by `calloc` has all of its memory cleared to 0.

New

C++ uses a different method of creating dynamic arrays, but the end result is the same. The new operator places all memory it allocates on the heap, just like malloc does. The new operator, however, doesn't return a void pointer. Instead, it returns a pointer to whichever datatype you request from it, thus removing the requirement to cast the pointer to the appropriate datatype. The new operator also automatically determines the datatype's size, so you don't have to use the sizeof operator at all. Here's an example of how to create a 10-cell integer array using new:

```
1: int* array = 0;
2: array = new int[10];
```

On line 1, I declare the array just like I did before and set it to 0. On line 2, I tell new to give me an array with ten integers.

Unlike malloc, there is some confusion as to what happens when a call to new fails. Before the C++ standard was actually standardized, new used to act just like malloc when it failed and return 0. However, when *exceptions* (a new error-handling feature) were added to the C++ standard, new was changed to throw an exception whenever it failed. (See Appendix A, "A C++ Primer," for more information about exceptions.) In the official standard, new throws an exception of type bad_alloc. However, most compilers just return 0 anyway and don't throw the exception. This is because the makers of the compilers want to be able to let people compile code that was made prior to the standard. You should check your compiler documentation to determine which event happens. MSVC6 currently returns 0 whenever a call to new fails.

The new approach looks a lot cleaner than the malloc approach, and it's generally more understandable. There is one major difference between this approach and malloc, however: malloc returns memory that will contain junk, but new executes the default constructor for each item in the array. (See Appendix A if you are unfamiliar with constructors.) In this example, both methods are the same because ints don't have constructors and will contain junk no matter which method you use, but if you used new to create an array of classes, each class will be constructed properly.

This approach can either be a good thing or a bad thing, depending on how you use it. Logic tells us that if a constructor is called on every item, it will take longer to create the array, so malloc should be faster. However, constructors are meant to initialize a class so that it contains useful information. Most of the time, you'll find yourself manually initializing your arrays after using malloc anyway, so the loss of speed from using new is usually minimal. Personally, I recommend using new over malloc because it is cleaner and safer.

Deleting a Dynamic Array

When you are using a static array, it is automatically created for you when it goes in scope and destroyed when it goes out of scope. This is not so with a dynamic array. Because you have to manually create a dynamic array yourself, you also have to manually destroy the array as well. If you don't destroy it, you will have a memory leak.

The way you destroy a dynamic array depends on the method you used to create it. If you used `malloc` to create the array, then you need to use the `free` function to destroy it. If you used `new` to create the array, then you need to use the `delete` operator to destroy it.

> **CAUTION**
> Be sure to destroy every dynamic array that you create, or you will have a memory leak.

Free

When you use `malloc` or `calloc` to create an array, you must use `free` to destroy it. The `free` function is fairly simple and accepts a single pointer, which should be a pointer to your array. It is used like this:

```
free( array );
```

The `free` function accepts a void pointer, but unlike `malloc` and `calloc`, `free` doesn't require that you cast the pointer first. C++ allows you to cast any pointer to void without explicitly saying so. The end result is that the program tells the computer that you are no longer using the memory and it is free to use it for other purposes.

Unfortunately, your array pointer has not changed. It still points to the same place in memory that it pointed to before, but that memory is no longer yours to touch. It is generally considered a good idea to clear the pointer to 0 right after you call `free`. Otherwise, you have what is called a *stray pointer*. Stray pointers are dangerous, because using them will give the same effects as reading or writing past the end of an array: unpredictable.

> **CAUTION**
> Always reset your pointers to 0 after freeing them, even if you don't plan on using them again. If you end up adding code later on, you might accidentally forget to reset the pointer.

Delete

If you've created an array with new, then you must destroy it using the delete keyword. Using delete on an array is different from deleting a normal pointer, however: You must be sure to use the brackets after the keyword, like this:

```
delete[] array;
```

If you don't use the brackets when you delete an array, delete will only destroy the first cell and nothing else. This will lead to a memory leak.

> **CAUTION**
> When deleting an array, *always* use the bracket notation.

The main difference between delete and free is that delete calls the destructor of every item in the array, whereas free doesn't. This can be quite a helpful feature if the items in the array need to be destructed. This way, you don't have to manually call a cleanup function for each item in the array before you delete the array. You will see how useful destructors are when you learn about the Array class later in this chapter.

Resizing a Dynamic Array

Perhaps the most important part of using a dynamic array is having the ability to resize it. Depending upon the method you used to create the array, you can use one of two methods.

Realloc

You would use realloc when you have created an array using malloc. Realloc is a really nice function that tries to resize the array without moving it, if possible. You pass in a pointer the old array and the size of the new array, and it will return a pointer to the resized array. Here's how you would resize an array from 10 cells to 20 cells:

```
1: int* array = 0;
2: array = (int*)malloc( 10 * sizeof(int) );
3: array = (int*)realloc( array, 20 * sizeof(int) );
```

Lines 1 and 2 should be nothing new; they declare and allocate a 10-cell integer array. On line 3, you pass the array pointer as the first argument to realloc and indicate the size of the new array in bytes as the second argument. Just as you did for malloc, you must cast the result of realloc to an integer pointer. If everything went all right, you now have a 20-cell array.

There is one little catch, however. The call to `realloc` might not be able to find enough memory for the new array and thus will return 0. But what happened to the old array, you ask? It's gone. It was not destroyed, and you now have a memory leak.

What happens is that it tries to create enough memory for the new array, and if it can't, then it returns 0 and leaves the original array alone. Unfortunately, in the previous example, you overwrote the pointer to the 10-cell array, and you now have no way to get that back.

> **CAUTION**
> Never write over a pointer to an array that you have not destroyed unless you've stored the address of the array somewhere else first. You will end up with memory leaks.

So how can you fix this problem? You need to create a temporary variable to hold the address of the array:

```
1: int* array = 0;
2: int* temp = 0;
3: array = (int*)malloc( 10 * sizeof(int) );
4: temp = array;
5: array = (int*)realloc( array, 20 * sizeof(int) );
6: if( array == 0 )
7: {
8:    array = temp;
9:    // insert error handling code here.
10: }
```

As you can see, this code is much more complex than the first `realloc` example, but it is a necessity. Checking for errors when resizing arrays is an absolute must.

The great thing about `realloc` is that it automatically copies over everything from the old array into the new array. This saves you a lot of hassle. Another good thing about `realloc` is that it might not move the array at all; it might be able to find out if there is unused space after the current array and just tell the memory manager that it's taking

> **NOTE**
> Always check to see if your memory allocations have not failed. Nothing ticks off a gamer more than working for hours on a game and then having the game crash on them for no apparent reason. You should at least be able to implement an error checking system that saves the current game state and exits with an error message, keeping the game player from going crazy and hunting you down.

over that memory as well. If this happens, then the function doesn't even move any data over to a new array, because there is no new array! It just returns a pointer to the same array! As you can imagine, this is really fast. Figure 3.9 shows how a larger array is created using `realloc`.

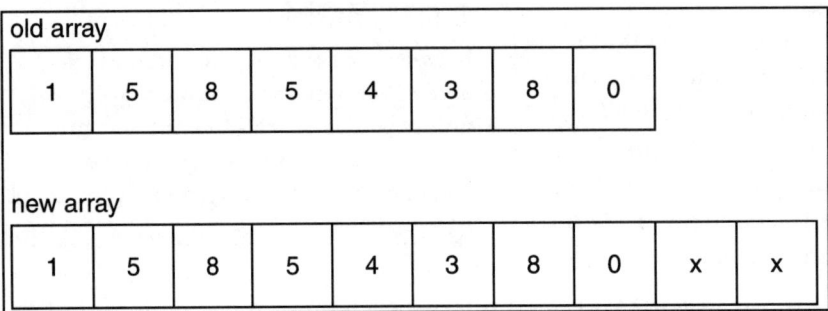

Figure 3.9

This shows a call to `realloc` to a bigger array without moving data. There is no way to determine beforehand what will be contained in the extra indexes added at the end.

Another thing you should note is that you might lose data if you make the array smaller. If you go from 20 cells to 10 cells, the first 10 cells will be preserved, but the last 10 cells will be lost, because there is not enough room for them in the new array. Figure 3.10 demonstrates what happens when you make an array smaller.

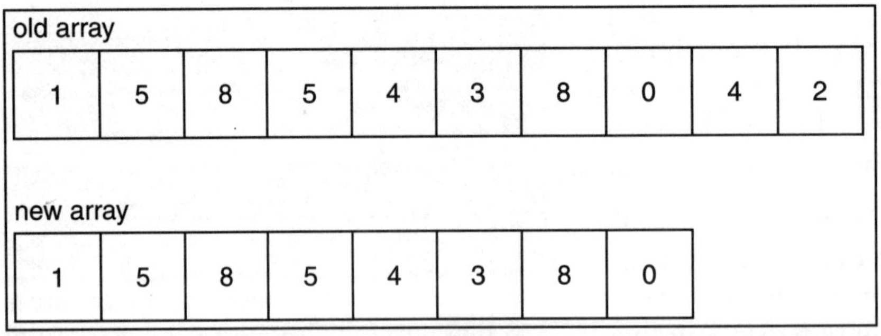

Figure 3.10

This shows a call to `realloc` to a smaller array. The items at the end that were chopped off are now lost.

Resizing Arrays Created with new

Unfortunately, the process of resizing arrays created with the `new` operator is its main weakness. There is no C++ equivalent to the `realloc` function. Instead, you must resize the array manually. Yes, this is usually a big pain in the butt, but if you encapsulate this functionality into an array class, you almost never need to worry about it.

Resizing a dynamic array created with new is a three-step process:

1. Create a new array with the new size.
2 Copy over all possible data.
3. Delete the old array.

Here's the algorithm in action:

```
1: int* array = 0;
2: int* temp = 0;
3: int index;
4: array = new int[10];
5: temp = new int[20];
6: for( index = 0; index < 10; index++ )
7:   temp[index] = array[index];
8: delete[] array;
9: array = temp;
10: temp = 0;
```

In this example, the array is declared on line 1 and allocated on line 4, just like in the previous examples using new. A temporary array, named temp, is also used. This array is defined on line 2 and allocated on line 5. This temporary array will hold the resized array so you can copy over all the data before you delete the old array. So, by line 6, there are two arrays in memory, occupying a total of 30 cells.

On line 6 and 7, you loop through the first 10 cells and copy them over from array to temp. Note that you cannot copy any more than that, because the original array is only 10 cells long.

After the array is copied over, the old array is destroyed by using the delete[] operator and the new array is assigned over to the old pointer (line 9). Last, the temp pointer is cleared to 0 as a precautionary measure.

This method does not use any error checking code, however. In this example, you would have to add a line after line 5 that checks to see if the new array that temp points to is valid or not. If temp contains 0, then you would have to handle the error somehow—most likely by saving all valid data, telling the user there was an error, and quitting out gracefully.

Example 3-2

Here is the code listing for Example 3-2, which demonstrates creating, clearing, resizing, and deleting an array. The code is on the CD in the directory \examples\ch03\02 - Dynamic Arrays\.

```
void main()
{
    // declare 3 array pointers, and set them to 0.
    int* array1 = 0;
    int* array2 = 0;
    int* array3 = 0;

    // allocate an array with 10 cells using malloc.
    array1 = (int*)malloc( 10 * sizeof(int) );

    // allocate an array with 10 cells using calloc.
    array2 = (int*)calloc( 10, sizeof(int) );

    // allocate an array with 10 cells using new.
    array3 = new int[10];

    // resize array1 and array2 using realloc.
    // note that the end of array2 will not have 0s in it.
    array1 = (int*)realloc( array1, 20 * sizeof(int) );
    array2 = (int*)realloc( array2, 20 * sizeof(int) );

    // resize array3 using the resize algorithm.
    int* temp = 0;
    int index;
    temp = new int[20];
    for( index = 0; index < 10; index++ )
        temp[index] = array3[index];
    delete[] array3;
    array3 = temp;
    temp = 0;

    // free the first two arrays using free.
    free( array1 );
    free( array2 );
```

```
        // free the third array using delete[]
        delete[] array3;
}
```

Example 3-2 has no output.

An Array Class and Useful Algorithms

By this point, you have seen how an array works and how to resize them. The question remains, however, if there is a way to make the process of creating, resizing, and deleting arrays easier. Yes, there is.

It turns out that you can easily encapsulate the common array algorithms into a class of its own. What's even better is that you can make it templated, so you can create an array based on any datatype that you want.

This data structure is located on the CD in the file \structures\array.h.

The Data

First, you need to think about the things you want in the array class. Two things pop immediately into mind: a pointer to the array and the length of the array. I put them into a template array class like this:

```
1: template<class Datatype>
2: class Array
3: {
4: public:
5:   Datatype* m_array;
6:   int m_size;
7: };
```

On lines 1 and 2, I declare a template class named Array, which will have one parameterized type, named Datatype. This is the type of data that will be stored within the array.

The Constructor

Now, I want to make a constructor that initializes the array automatically. The constructor of the Array class will take one parameter: the size of the array.

```
1: Array( int p_size )
2: {
3:   m_array = new Datatype[p_size];
4:   m_size = p_size;
6: }
```

The constructor first allocates enough space for the array using `new`, and then it makes `m_array` point to the memory and sets the size of the array.

This line of code constructs an integer array to contain 10 cells:

```
Array<int> intarray( 10 );
```

> **NOTE**
> Note that it is possible to construct the `Array` with negative values for the size, which will cause the array to not get created (on your own, you might want to add that kind of protection). It is also possible to create an array with a size of 0. The C++ `new` operator will return a valid pointer to an array with no cells! The worst part is that if you don't delete the empty array when you're done with it, you get a memory leak anyway! Don't look at me—I didn't make the C++ standard!

The Destructor

Now, perhaps the coolest thing about creating your own array class is that you can make it manage your memory for you automatically. Now you don't have to worry about deleting your array; the array class does this for you in the destructor!

```
1: ~Array()
2: {
3:   if( m_array != 0 )
4:     delete[] m_array;
5:   m_array = 0;
6: }
```

Pay close attention to line 3: I check to see if the array pointer is not 0 before I delete the array. This is because the array is assumed to be invalid if the pointer is 0, and deleting it will cause errors.

The Resize Algorithm

I now need to add a method to resize the array by using the algorithm I discussed earlier. Remember, this algorithm creates a new array, copies everything it can over, and then deletes the old array.

```
1: void Resize( int p_size )
2: {
```

```
3:  Datatype* newarray = new Datatype[p_size];
4:  if( newarray == 0 )
5:    return;
6:  int min;
7:  if( p_size < m_size )
8:    min = p_size;
9:  else
10:   min = m_size;
11: int index;
12: for( index = 0; index < min; index++ )
13:   newarray[index] = m_array[index];
14: m_size = p_size;
15: if( m_array != 0 )
16:   delete[] m_array;
17: m_array = newarray;
18: }
```

On line 1, I accept a single integer as a parameter, which will be the new size of the array, named p_size. On line 3, I declare a new array pointer named newarray. This pointer will hold the new array.

On line 4, I check to see if I was able to allocate enough memory for the new array. If new failed, then either newarray will contain 0 (on most compilers) or a bad_alloc exception will have been thrown (on ISO-standard compilers). Because most compilers return 0, I handle that case only and just return without modifying anything. This way, when you cannot allocate enough memory, your array will still contain all of its data. You should make sure that the routine didn't fail when you resize the array so you can handle the error as you deem necessary.

On line 6, I declare the min variable. This variable is quite important when copying data from the old array to the new array. If p_size is smaller than the current size, then you can only copy p_size items over to the new array, and everything in the old array past that will be lost. If p_size is larger than the current size, you can only copy the entire array over and nothing more. So, on lines 7–10, I determine which is smaller, m_size or p_size, and set min to that value.

On lines 11 and 12, I loop through from index 0 to min and copy every item from the old array to the new array. Note that if the old array doesn't exist (i.e. m_size is 0 and so is min), the loop doesn't copy anything.

On line 13, I set the current size to the new size of the array, and on line 14, I check to see if the old array existed. If so, I delete the old array on line 15 and finally make the m_array pointer point to the new array.

The Access Operator

I'm well on my way to having a fully functional array class, with one exception: I have yet to add a feature that allows me to access and modify the array contents. I think that one of the coolest features of C++ is its ability to overload operators. In this case, I will overload the offset (square bracket) operator so I can use the array just like a normal array! If you are unfamiliar with operator overloads, see Appendix A.

This routine will allow the client of the class to access or modify the contents of the array, but also allow you to have access protections built in.

```
1: Datatype& operator[] ( int p_index )
2: {
3:   return m_array[p_index];
4: }
```

You need to pay particular attention to the return type of this function: It returns a *reference* to a Datatype. Why does it return a reference? It returns a reference so that you can do something like this:

```
1: Array<int> intarray(10);
2: intarray[5] = 42;
```

On line 1, I declare an integer array using the array class, and I make it 10 cells large.

So what happens on line 2? The offset operator is called, and it returns a reference to the item at index 5, which is then set to 42. So what ends up happening is that the value 42 is physically placed inside the array. If the offset operator function only returned a value, then that line of code would accomplish absolutely nothing: It would load the value at index 5 onto the stack, set the value on the stack to 42, and then totally discard the value.

So why would you prefer to have a function that accesses cells of an array, instead of just using the regular offset operator on the m_array variable? One reason has to do with error checking. Most programmers like to put error-checking code in the access routine. This way, we can be sure that the client never touches memory that they aren't allowed to touch.

It also makes it much cleaner and clearer to access the array. Tell me, which way do you prefer:

```
1: intarray.m_array[5] = 42;
2: intarray[5] = 42;
```

An Array Class and Useful Algorithms

Line 1 looks like an ugly mess. Line 2 is nice and pretty, and it is safer to use if the class has built-in bounds checking.

The nice thing about the offset operator algorithm I made up is that I can use it to retrieve items within the array too, like this:

```
int temp = intarray[5];
```

The Conversion Operator

Now that you've got a flexible and working array class, you can start to use it in your programs. You might notice a problem with it, however.

If you have a function that accepts a standard array pointer as a parameter, and you try passing in this array class, the compiler will tell you that you cannot do that. This seems a bit awkward because you want to use the nifty features of the Array class, but you don't want to spend weeks updating all of your code to use the new Array class. The inside of the array is a pointer anyway, so why should this incompatibility exist?

C++ offers a really neat feature to fix this problem: a *conversion operator*. A conversion operator allows you to *implicitly* convert a class into a different data type. For example, when the function process expects an int* and you pass in an Array<int>, you want the compiler to treat the array as an int*.

Here is how you would code the conversion operator for the Array class:

```
operator Datatype* ()
{
    return m_array;
}
```

The first line declares that this conversion operator will be returning a pointer to a Datatype. Conversion operators do not have parameters. This operator is simple because the internal representation of the array is already in the form that you want it to be, so it just returns the pointer to the array.

If you have a function that takes an integer array pointer like this:

```
void Process( int* p_array );
```

you can easily use the function like this:

```
// declare 3 different types of arrays
Array<int> array1( 16 );
int array2[16];
```

```
int* array3 = new int[16];
// call the function on the three arrays
Process( array1 );
Process( array2 );
Process( array3 );
```

The conversion operator for the `Array` class automatically treats the class as a standard pointer. This makes the two different ways of representing arrays interchangeable.

Inserting an Item Between Two Existing Items

One thing I haven't covered yet is how to insert an item into an array in between two existing items. The reason for this is that it is not a straightforward operation. To insert an item into the array, you need to first move everything after the desired index up one cell. Figure 3.11 shows what happens when you insert an item at index 3.

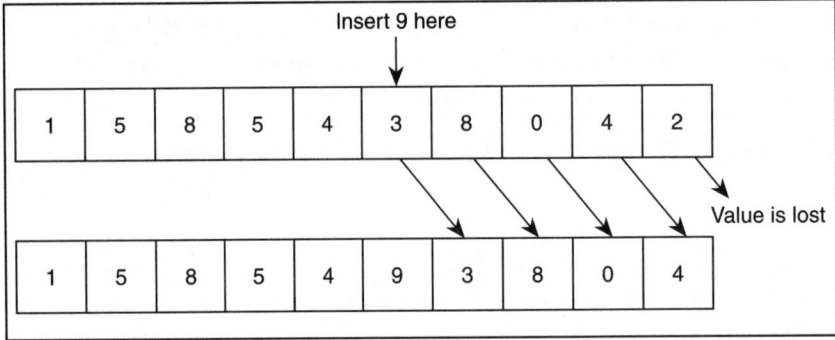

Figure 3.11

Inserting into an array involves moving everything up to the next cell and then inserting the new value.

Everything from index 4 through index 8 must be moved up one cell. The item in cell 9 cannot be moved up, so it is overwritten. Therefore, this algorithm will only work on arrays that aren't full: You don't want to be writing over anything in your array. Here's the algorithm:

```
1: void Insert( Datatype p_item, int p_index )
2: {
3:     int index;
4:     for( index = m_size - 1; index > p_index; index-- )
5:         m_array[index] = m_array[index - 1];
```

```
6:    m_array[p_index] = p_item;
7:  }
```

On line 1, I take two parameters: `p_item`, which is the item I want to insert into the array, and `p_index`, the index at which I want to insert `p_item`. I declare an index variable on line 3, which will count from the end of the array downwards in the for-loop on lines 4 and 5.

Why do you count backwards? The reason has to do with the way that data is copied over: Say you have a 10-cell array and you want to insert something into cell 3. If you copied cell 3 over to cell 4, and then cell 4 over to cell 5, and so on, you would end up with everything in cells 4-9 being the same. This is because you'd have written over the data in cell 4 before you were able to copy it over to cell 5—and in actuality, you'd copy cell 3 over into every cell after it. So instead, the algorithm would start at cell 9 and copy cell 8 into it, and then copy cell 7 into cell 8, and so on.

Lastly, on line 6, I copy `p_item` into the array at cell `p_index`.

Removing an Item from the Array

Removing an item from an array is almost the same algorithm as inserting one, but there are a few differences. First of all, if an item is removed, everything above the index is moved down one index, and the last item in the array is duplicated. Figure 3.12 shows how this is accomplished.

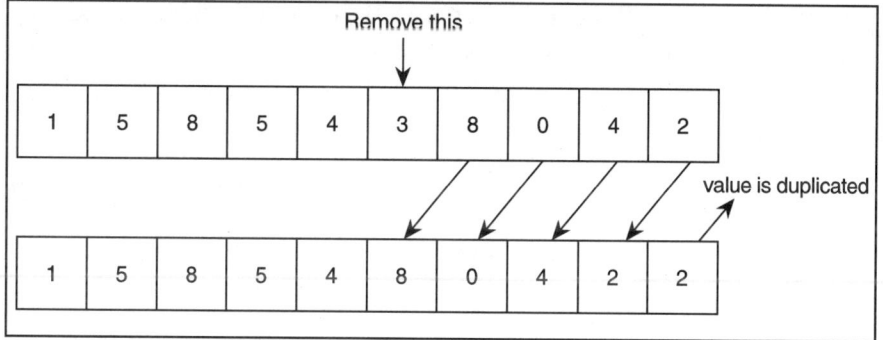

Figure 3.12

Removing an item from an array involves moving everything down by one index.

It is important to note that the loop algorithm is normal (as opposed to a reversed loop for item insertion) for item removal because you are moving data down the array instead of up the array. You end up with the following algorithm:

```
1: void Remove( int p_index )
2: {
3:   int index;
4:   for( index = p_index + 1; index < m_size; index++ )
5:     m_array[index - 1] = m_array[index];
6: }
```

This time, the only parameter is the index that you want to remove, p_index. On line 3, I declare an index variable to loop through the array, and I move every item down one index on lines 4 and 5.

A Faster Removal Method

There is a faster removal algorithm, but it only works when the order of items in your array doesn't matter. In addition, it requires you to constantly keep track of the number of items actually in the array, as opposed to just the capacity.

For example, you have a 10-cell array in which you have 8 items stored in indexes 0–7. If the order of your items in your array doesn't matter and you want to remove the item at index 3, you can move the item at index 7 into index 3. The order of your array is altered, but the removal algorithm moved only one item, a significant savings of speed.

Unfortunately, the array class doesn't keep track of how many items you've put into the array, so to use this algorithm, you would need to keep track of this information yourself. The good thing is that the algorithm is so simple, it's not too difficult to implement. For this example, I'll assume that count is a variable that maintains the current count of items in the array, and intarray is the actual array.

```
1: count--;
2: intarray[3] = intarray[count];
```

In this example, I removed index 3 from the array by overwriting it with the item in the last index. If there are 8 items in the array, then count will contain 8, but the last item is in cell 7. So in line 1, I decrement the count from 8 to 7 and move cell 7 into cell 3 on line 2.

Pretty neat, huh? Figure 3.13 shows how this algorithm works.

An Array Class and Useful Algorithms 67

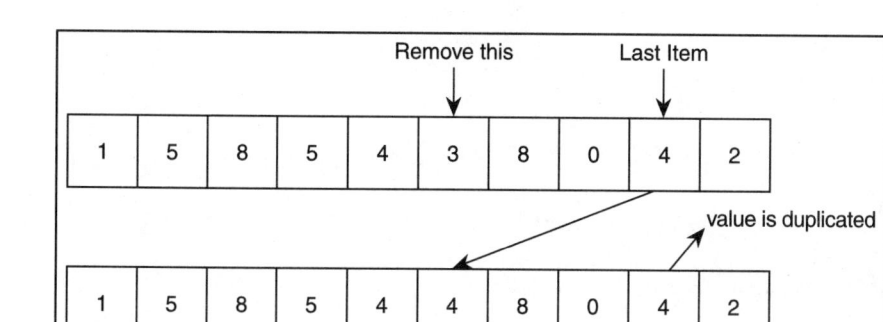

Figure 3.13

This figure shows how to remove an index using the fast removal algorithm. The last item is moved down into the index of the item that is being removed.

In the figure, the array contains 9 items and 10 cells. The last cell, although conceptually empty, still has a value in it. (Memory has a value in it at all times.) When the fast-remove algorithm is performed, the 4 from the last cell is copied into the cell that you are removing, and the last item pointer is decremented so that it points to the cell with 0 in it. Note how the last two indexes, although conceptually empty, still have data in them, and the value 4 is duplicated in the array.

Retrieving the Size of an Array

The great thing about having your own array class is that it remembers the size of the array for you, unlike native arrays. Here is a function to retrieve the size of the array:

```
1: int Size()
2: {
3:   return m_size;
4: }
```

Example 3-3

Here is the code listing for Example 3-3. It uses the Array class, which you can find in the \structures\ directory on the CD, and demonstrates the major features of the class:

```
void main()
{
    // create two arrays, one for an integer array
    // and one for a float array.
```

```
    Array<int> intarray( 10 );
    Array<float> floatarray( 5 );

    // use the access operator to store values.
    intarray[0] = 10;
    floatarray[0] = 3.1415f;

    // use the access operator to retrieve values.
    int i = intarray[0];
    float f = floatarray[0];

    // store values at index 1 in both arrays.
    intarray[1] = 12;
    floatarray[1] = 6.28f;

    // insert values between cells 0 and 1 in both arrays.
    intarray.Insert( 11, 1 );
    floatarray.Insert( 4.2f, 1 );

    // remove the items at cell 0 in both arrays.
    intarray.Remove( 0 );
    floatarray.Remove( 0 );

    // resize both arrays
    intarray.Resize( 3 );
    floatarray.Resize( 4 );

    // both arrays are automatically deleted by the Array
    // class destructor.
}
```

Example 3-3 has no output.

Storing/Loading Arrays on Disk

Quite often, you will want to store the contents of your arrays onto a more permanent medium, such as a hard disk. In this way, you can easily store and retrieve information for a game, which will make it easy for you to implement a save/load feature.

Storing/Loading Arrays on Disk

For saving and loading, I will use the standard C file functions (I like them better than C++'s): `fopen`, `fread`, `fwrite`, `fclose`. If you are unfamiliar with them, please see Appendix A.

Luckily, C's file IO functions operate on arrays! This means that you have to do very little work to read or write an array. I'll be adding these functions to the array class I just created.

Writing an Array to Disk

You want a routine that writes an array to disk first. It will be straightforward and write the entire array to a single file.

```
1:  bool WriteFile( const char* p_filename )
2:  {
3:    FILE* outfile = 0;
4:    int written = 0;
5:    outfile = fopen( p_filename, "wb" );
6:    if( outfile == 0 )
7:      return false;
8:    written = fwrite( m_array, sizeof( datatype ), m_size, outfile );
9:    fclose( outfile );
10:   if( written != m_size )
11:     return false;
12:   return true;
13: }
```

On line 1, I declare the function to take one parameter: the name of the file I am writing the array to. On line 3, I declare a `FILE` pointer, which will point to the open `FILE` in memory. I declare an integer on line 4, which will keep track of how many items were actually written to disk.

One line 5, I open the file in `"wb"` mode. This mode tries to open the given file for writing and destroys its contents, essentially emptying the file. This mode also opens the file in binary mode, which is the mode in which all non-text data is stored.

On line 6, I check to see if the file was actually opened. There are numerous reasons why opening a file for writing

> **CAUTION**
>
> Please be careful when dealing with files. The `WriteFile` algorithm will *destroy* any file that already exists because it uses `"wb"` mode, and if you accidentally tell it to write to an important file, there is absolutely *no way* to get the file back.

might fail, so it's a good idea to check for this. If the file hasn't been opened, the function returns false.

The array is written to disk on line 8 by using `fwrite`. This function tries to write the entire array to disk by first passing a pointer to the array, and then the size of the items in the array, and then the number of items in the array, and finally the file that the array should be written to. `fwrite` returns the number of full items that were actually written to disk, which I store in the `written` variable.

On line 10, I check to see if the entire array was written. If not, the function returns `false` on line 11. If all went well, however, the function reaches line 12 and returns `true`.

If this function returned `true`, then your array is now safely stored on disk.

Reading an Array from Disk

Now, there really isn't much use in writing an array to disk if you don't have some way to retrieve the array. Luckily (again), C's `fread` function works really well with arrays, so I'll create a `read` function just like my `write` function:

```
 1: bool ReadFile( const char* p_filename )
 2: {
 3:    FILE* infile = 0;
 4:    int read = 0;
 5:    infile = fopen( p_filename, "rb" );
 6:    if( infile == 0 )
 7:      return false;
 8:    read = fread( m_array, sizeof( datatype ), m_size, infile );
 9:    fclose( infile );
10:    if( read != m_size )
11:      return false;
12:    return true;
13: }
```

This function is almost exactly like the `WriteFile` function. This time, instead of opening the file in `"wb"` mode, I open it in `"rb"` mode, which means that I'll be reading binary information from the file. If the file doesn't exist, the call to `fopen` will fail, and the `ReadFile` function will return `false` (lines 6–7).

On line 8, you read in the same number of items as there are cells in the array, which means that you must resize the array to the number of items you want to load from the file.

If you could not read in all the items from disk, then the routine returns false. Lastly, it returns true if the function was able to read everything it expected.

Considerations for Writing and Reading Files

You must take some things into consideration when writing an array of objects to a file. Mainly, you must be sure that the object contains only values and no pointers.

For example, if you have a class that contains a pointer to another class and you write that class to disk using `fwrite`, the pointer value is stored on disk, but not what it points to. This could get quite messy later on when you attempt to load the class from disk; you'll end up with a class pointing to a place in memory that was valid when you saved the class but isn't valid anymore.

You can see how to fix these kinds of problems in Chapter 9, "Tying It Together: The Basics."

Application: Using Arrays to Store Game Data

This is Game Demonstration 3-1, which can be found on the CD in the directory \demonstrations\ch03\Game01 - Monsters\.

> ### Compiling the Demo
>
> This demonstration uses the SDLGUI library that I have developed for the book. For more information about this library, see Appendix B.
>
> To compile this demo, either open up the workspace file in the directory or create your own project using the settings described in Appendix B. If you create your own project, all of the files you need to include are in the directory.

Games need to keep track of great amounts of information. Games also need to be able to access and modify this information rather quickly; no one likes a slow game. Arrays offer both of these advantages and are thus used quite often within games.

This section shows you a very simple demonstration game to help you understand how to store objects within a game. I'll be storing monsters in an array.

The Monster Class

I begin by first defining the `Monster` class:

```
class Monster
{
public:
  int m_x;
  int m_y;
  int m_hitpoints;
};
```

This is a very simplistic monster class—all it has is three variables: The x and y coordinates of the monster in the game world and its hit points. Obviously, a real monster would have much more information associated with it in a real game, but this is just for demonstration purposes.

Declaring a Monster Array

In the game, you want to declare an array of monsters. Where you put the array is up to you, but for this simple demonstration, I will make it global. I will also have a separate integer that will keep track of how many monsters are currently in the game. Remember, arrays do not need to be packed full, and initially there will be no monsters.

In this demo, I am going to limit myself to 32 total monsters, so I will initialize the array to 32 cells and reset the monster count to 0:

```
Array<Monster> g_monsterarray( 32 );
int g_monsters = 0;
```

These are both global variables, which I don't recommend for a real game, but it increases the readability of this simple example.

Adding a Monster to the Game

So, now that I have my array of monsters, I want to be able to create a monster and put it into the game, right? For this, I will make an `AddMonster` function, which will try to add a random monster to the game. (See Chapter 22, "Random Numbers," and Appendix A for information on random numbers.)

```
 1: bool AddMonster()
 2: {
 3:   if( g_monsters == 32 )
 4:     return false;
 5:   g_monsterarray[g_monsters].m_x = rand() % 640;
 6:   g_monsterarray[g_monsters].m_y = rand() % 480;
 7:   g_monsterarray[g_monsters].m_hitpoints = 11 + (rand() % 10);
 8:   g_monsters++;
 9:   return true;
10: }
```

First, note the return type on line 1. The function returns a Boolean. If the function returns `false`, then the function failed and could not add a monster. If the function returned `true`, then it placed a new monster in the array.

On line 3, I check to see if there are 32 monsters in the game. If so, I return `false`, because I can't fit any more monsters in the array.

On lines 5–7, I set the information for the new monster, which is at the same index as the `g_monsters` variable. For example, if there are 0 monsters, then the new monster should be placed at index 0, and if there is 1 monster, then the new monster should be placed at index 1.

As for the variables, I simply set the x position of the monster to a number between 0 and 639 and the y position to a number between 0 and 479 because the screen is in 640 × 480 resolution. On line 7, I set the monsters hitpoints to a value between 11 and 20.

On line 8, I increment the monster count to signify that I have added a monster, and I return `true` on line 9, telling the caller that the routine has finished successfully and the monster has been added to the array.

Making a Better Insertion Algorithm

I bet many of you are looking at the `AddMonster` algorithm and saying to yourselves, "Why should I limit myself to only 32 monsters?" Well, you shouldn't. Because the `Array` class supports dynamic resizing, you can easily adapt the algorithm so that it increases in size when you need to add more monsters.

When do you resize the array, though? Do you resize it by one cell if you determine that the array is full? No! Doing it that way is wasteful and slow. Remember, when you resize an array, the algorithm first needs to allocate new memory. Then it needs to copy everything over, and then it needs to delete the old array. This is quite wasteful in terms of speed.

So what do you do instead? The most popular approach is to increase the size of the array in "chunks." Because the array originally carries 32 monsters, when you try to insert the 33rd monster, you should make enough room for future expansion and resize it to 64 cells. That way, you can insert 32 more monsters before you need to resize again!

This method of resizing is pretty efficient in real-world use. Some people prefer to double the size of the array each time it is expanded. STL's `vector` does this. In most cases, that method is wasteful in terms of space. What happens if you have a 1024-cell vector and you insert 1025 monsters? Then the vector resizes itself to 2048 cells, which is almost twice as many as you need.

I find that increasing the size of an array by a constant amount is much more efficient in the long run, so in the revised algorithm, I'll increase the monster array by 32 cells each time I reach the limit:

```
1: bool AddMonster()
2: {
3:   if( g_monsters == g_monsterarray.Size() )
4:     g_monsterarray.Resize( g_monsterarray.Size() + 32 );
5:   g_monsterarray[g_monsters].m_x = rand() % 640;
6:   g_monsterarray[g_monsters].m_y = rand() % 480;
7:   g_monsterarray[g_monsters].m_hitpoints = 11 + (rand() % 10);
8:   g_monsters++;
9:   return true;
10: }
```

This algorithm is identical to the previous one, with one exception: Lines 3 and 4 are different. On line 3, I first check to see if the monster array can hold enough monsters. If not, line 4 resizes the array to `g_monsterarray.Size() + 32`, adding 32 cells.

Removing a Monster from the Game

You want it to be possible to remove monsters from the game. You also want it to be possible to remove any monster in the array at any time from the game, and there are two approaches you can take to do this.

The first method uses the `Remove` function of the array class. It would look like this:

```
void RemoveMonster( int p_index )
{
  g_monsterarray.Remove( p_index );
  g_monsters--;
}
```

The game demo won't use this method, however. The problem with this method is that it takes too long. Sure, in the demo I won't be creating more than a few dozen monsters at most. That doesn't seem like a lot right now, but what happens when you eventually get hundreds or thousands of monsters in a game? This algorithm slows things down considerably.

Lucky for me, the order of the monsters in the array doesn't matter in this simple demo, and I'll be using the fast removal algorithm instead:

```
void RemoveMonster( int p_index )
{
  g_monsters--;
  g_monsterarray[p_index] = g_monsterarray[g_monsters];
}
```

With this approach, I take the last monster in the array and move it into the cell that the monster I want to remove previously occupied. Instead of moving many monsters down the array, I only move one monster.

> **NOTE**
>
> The `RemoveMonster` algorithm does not resize the array at all, but the `AddMonster` algorithm does. Why is this? Well, I generally consider it wasteful to downsize arrays unless I *absolutely* need the extra space that is being cleared up. So what ends up happening in the game is that the monster array will eventually reach the worst-case size and then stay at that size forever, allowing you to add many monsters rapidly after the array has reached its optimum. This is also helpful for profiling your game because after you are done running it, you can see how large your monster array is and have an estimate of the maximum number of monsters you had in the game at any point in time.

Checking for Monster Removal

In this little game, there is only one condition which must be true in order for a monster to be removed: The monster's hitpoints must be 0 or less. To check for this condition, I need to have a function that loops through the monster array and checks each monster. If a monster is found to have 0 or fewer hitpoints, it is then removed:

```
1: void CheckMonsters()
2: {
3:   int index = 0;
4:   while( index < g_monsters )
5:   {
6:     if( g_monsterarray[index].m_hitpoints <= 0 )
7:       RemoveMonster( index );
8:     else
9 :      index++;
10:  }
11: }
```

On line 3, I declare an `index` variable. This variable will be used to loop through every index in the `g_monsterarray`. It is initially set to 0. Lines 4-10 are one large `while` loop, which continues looping while `index` is less than `g_monsters`. On line 6, I check to see if the current monster is dead (`m_hitpoints <= 0`). If so, I remove the monster using the `RemoveMonster` function. If the monster isn't dead, I skip it and go on to the next monster by incrementing `index` (line 9).

The reason I don't increment `index` if I remove the monster is because a new monster is moved into the same index I just removed. If I incremented `index` anyway, I'd totally skip over a monster, which might be dead. That would be a very interesting bug.

Playing the Game

When you start up the game, you are faced with a blank screen. You can add monsters to the screen by pressing any key on the keyboard except Escape, which causes the game to exit.

After you've added monsters to the screen, you can click on them to "hit" them, causing their hitpoints to decrease. Once a monster's hitpoints reach 0, the monster is removed from the game using the `CheckMonsters` function defined in the previous section, which is called once every frame.

Figure 3.14 shows a screenshot of this game demo in action.

Figure 3.14

This is a screenshot of the Array Game Demonstration in action.

Analysis of Arrays in Games

Arrays are the most common data structure. I've never seen a complicated program that doesn't use arrays. Let's face it, arrays are great to use for several reasons:

- They are easy to create.
- They are fast to access.
- They are easy to maintain and destroy when needed.

So if arrays have all these good attributes, why aren't they used for everything? Simple: Arrays aren't perfect—they do have some flaws.

Cache Issues

Arrays are great for being able to access every item in the array randomly... in theory. In reality, arrays aren't actually randomly accessible. This has to do with the way computers actually work.

A computer is a complex machine with many layers of memory. The lowest of these layers is called the *registers*. Data needs to be loaded into these registers in order for the processor to actually do anything with them. The good thing is that registers are the fastest blocks of memory in the entire computer. The bad thing is that there aren't very many registers. The x86 and x87 architecture only has (8) 32-bit registers and (8) 80-bit floating point registers, so only a very small amount of data can be manipulated at the same time.

Luckily for us, all processors have a larger memory area almost as fast as the registers called the *level 1 cache* (L1 cache). This cache is where the computer puts important data that it will need to access often (the actual binary code of each program is stored in this cache, too). There might be other levels of cache as well, but the most important is the level 1 cache. The size is usually around 32–128 kilobytes of memory, which doesn't seem too large, but it's a great deal larger than the registers. Figure 3.15 shows the speed/size relationship between the various memory levels.

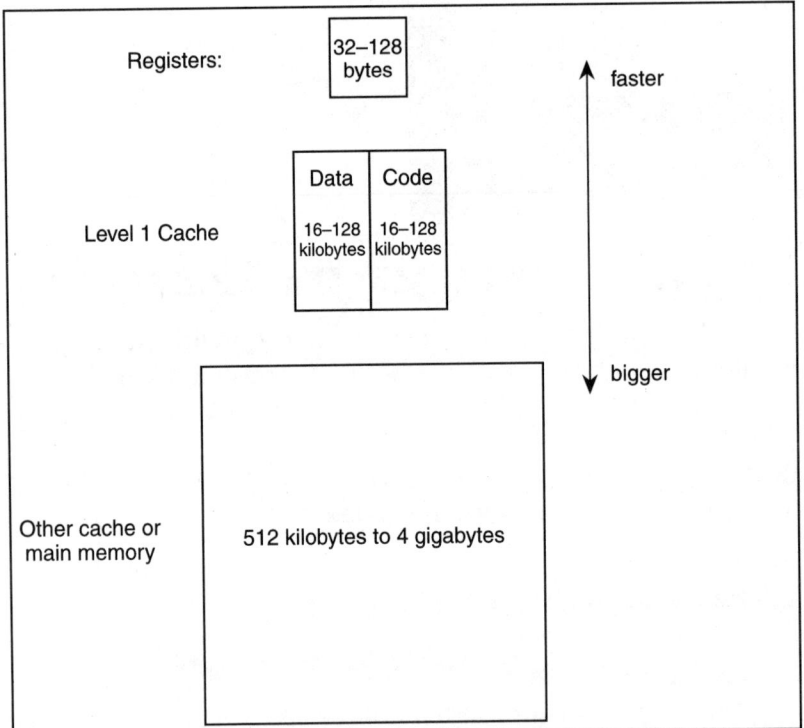

Figure 3.15

This shows the speed/size relationship between different memory levels. Generally, larger memory is slower, and smaller memory is faster.

So whenever data needs to be accessed, the processor needs to search for it in one of the memory levels. If it's already in the registers, it just performs the operation on it. If the data is in the L1 cache, it makes space in the registers by saving whichever data was in the registers previously and moving the new data into the registers. If the data isn't in the L1 cache, the processor needs to find it in one of the other memory levels, which can become a slow process.

What does this have to do with arrays? When the memory is moved from level to level (except from the L1 to the registers), a large chunk is always moved at one time because it is more efficient to move chunks. When you access a cell of an array, the processor actually loads a chunk of your array into the L1 cache.

Say you're working on a simple system that has a cache of 8 cells and you are accessing a 16-cell array. Figure 3.16 shows the described system. When you access the first cell in your array, the processor loads the first 8 cells of the array into the cache. After that, you can access cells 1–7 really quickly because they are already in the cache. You can change them and do whatever you want to them.

Now, say you want to access the last cell of the array. Well, because you've modified some cells in the first half of the array, the processor needs to move those back into memory, and then it needs to load the second half of the array into the cache. This whole process took a lot longer than the supposed "instant access" an array theoretically has.

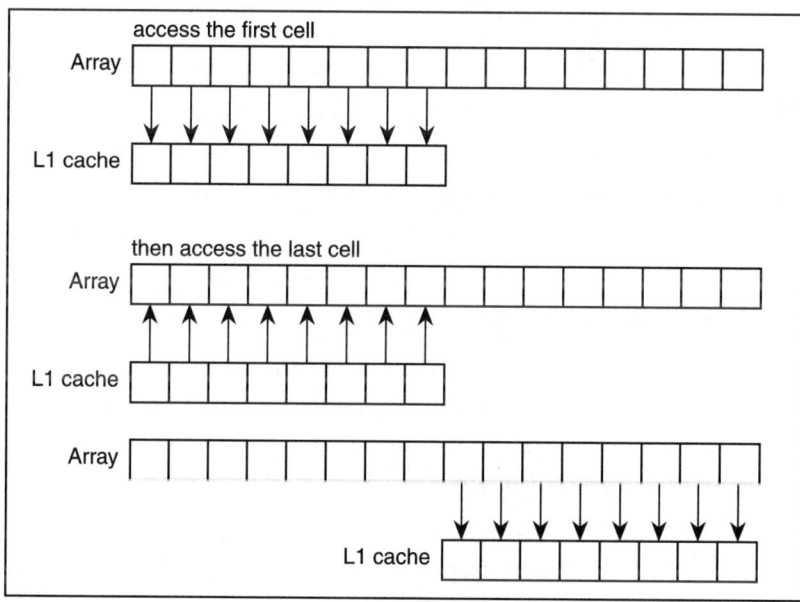

Figure 3.16

When the first part of the array is accessed, it is stored in the cache. When the second part is accessed, the first part is written back out to memory, and the second part is stored in the cache.

So that's one thing you have to pay attention to when dealing with arrays. Looping through them in a single loop is nice and fast because you use as much of the array as possible at one time. However, an algorithm that randomly jumps to different cells that are far away from each other will be slow because you're causing the processor to move around a great deal of memory. Profiling programs have shown that the processor spends most of its time moving memory around, which is a major optimization concern.

Try to keep this in mind when working with arrays. After all, if something appears to be too good to be true, it probably is.

Resizing Arrays

Perhaps the largest problem with arrays is that they are mostly inflexible in size. When you have really large arrays containing mounds of data and all of a sudden you want to resize it, it's going to take a while. The reason for this is that the array resize algorithm is $O(n)$, and that's not even counting the compiler's implementation of `new` and `delete`.

First, the compiler must find enough memory to contain the old array *and* the new array at the same time, which can be quite difficult to do if you're low on memory. Then you need to copy every item that you can from the old array into the new array and delete the old array. This is not something you want to be doing too often in a real-time game.

Here are the downsides:

- Resizing an array takes as much memory as the old array plus the new array.
- Resizing an array is an $O(n)$ algorithm—the larger the array, the longer it takes.

Inserting/Removing Cells

Another downside to arrays is that it is not very easy to insert and remove items while preserving the order of the array. To do this, you must physically move every item past the cell where you want to insert/remove up or down one cell. This algorithm is also $O(n)$, and it takes longer as the size of the array increases.

There is, of course, the fast removal algorithm if you don't care about preserving the order of the array, but that doesn't help if you need the order to stay the same.

Conclusion

You might have read this chapter not knowing anything about arrays, or you might not have. Either way, I hope this chapter presented some new information that you can use to better your programming.

There is a weird cycle in game programming that is often used. A programmer starts off learning how to use arrays and uses them almost exclusively. Then, later on, he learns about the nifty advanced data structures such as *linked lists* (see Chapter 6, "Linked Lists"). Eventually, though, he ends up using arrays again. Simply put, arrays are the most often used data structures in game programming simply because processors are optimized to process arrays. With the advent of *vector processing* features in the x86 microprocessors (MMX, 3DNow, SSE, and SSE2), arrays have become even more important because these new features operate even more efficiently on arrays.

My advice is to become as familiar with arrays as humanly possible. You will be using them for the rest of your life. You will see that almost all of the chapters in this book use arrays in one form or another.

CHAPTER 4

BITVECTORS

4. Bitvectors

Bitvectors are an important part of optimizing small data items, yet they are so frequently missing from data structures books. Because they are fairly easy to understand, I have included them in this book. Bitvectors have many names, and you might have used something similar before, in which case you can skip this chapter. In this chapter, you will learn

- What a bitvector is
- How to create a bitvector
- How to access the bits inside a bitvector
- How to rapidly set and clear every bit within a bitvector
- How to read and write a bitvector to disk
- How to apply bitvectors to games using the quicksave method
- What a bitfield is
- How to declare and access bitfields

What Is a Bitvector?

A *bitvector* is a specialized kind of array. Basically, a bitvector is meant to condense bit values (or booleans) into an array so that no space is wasted.

So why not just create a Boolean array? The reason is not so simple: Most compilers use a larger datatype, such as an integer, in place of a Boolean. They do this because most computers can only send a fixed amount of bits at a time through memory and to the processor. Every x86 machine from the 386 upwards can only send data in packs of 32 bits.

Unfortunately, this is inefficient on a size basis. You often want data to take up the smallest amount of size possible, especially when you're dealing with network transfers and saving massive virtual worlds to disk.

Enter the bitvector, designed to pack the data as closely as possible.

Designing a bitvector is a tricky task, however, because you need to use bit manipulation (see Appendix A if you are unfamiliar with bit manipulation). The method I use is to create an array of long integers, which are usually 32 bits long (see Figure 4.1). You should check your compiler documentation—if your compiler doesn't support 32-bit integers, you can easily modify the bitvector class to work on larger or smaller integer sizes.

Now, for each index in the array, you should be able to access 32 individual bits.

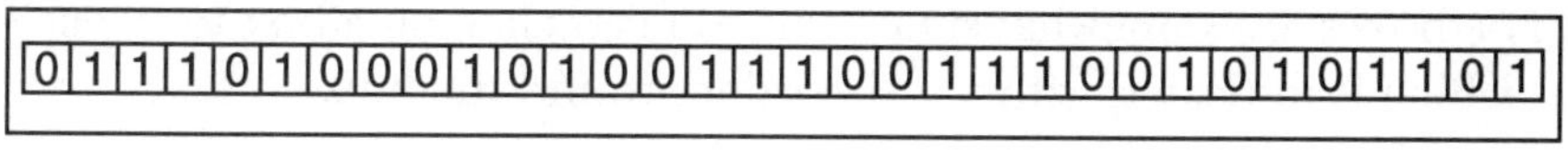

| 0 | 1 | 1 | 1 | 0 | 1 | 0 | 0 | 0 | 1 | 0 | 1 | 0 | 0 | 1 | 1 | 1 | 0 | 0 | 1 | 1 | 1 | 0 | 0 | 1 | 0 | 1 | 0 | 1 | 1 | 0 | 1 |

Figure 4.1

Here is a bitvector containing 32 indexes. On most machines, these 32 indexes take up the same amount of room as a single integer.

Graphical Demonstration: Bitvectors

The graphical demonstration for bitvectors is located on the CD that comes with this book in the directory \demonstrations\ch04\Demo01 - Bitvectors\. This demonstration shows you how to set and clear the bits within a bitvector. The other common operations on a bitvector, such as resizing, creating, and deleting, are not shown in this demo because they are the same as the array algorithms that I have already demonstrated.

> **Compiling the Demo**
>
> This demonstration uses the SDLGUI library that I have developed for the book. For more information about this library, see Appendix B, "The Memory Layout of a Computer Program."
>
> To compile this demo, either open up the workspace file in the directory or create your own project using the settings described in Appendix B. If you create your own project, all of the files you need to include are in the directory.

The Main Screen

When you run the program, you are presented with the main screen, as shown in Figure 4.2. There are two buttons and a long bar containing white or grey boxes. This represents a bitvector that is two cells large, and each cell has 32 bits, giving you a total of 64 bits. White boxes mean that the cell has a value of 0, and grey boxes contain a value of 1. The boxes are somewhat small, but you can click on a box to select the current index, which is indicated with a red border around the box.

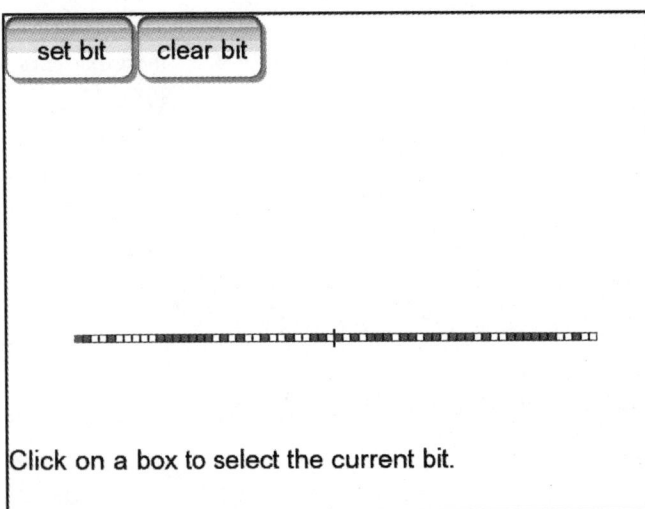

Figure 4.2

This is the main screen of the Bitvector Graphics Demonstration.

Using the Buttons

When you have selected the index that you want to set or clear, you must click on the Set Bit or Clear Bit buttons. After you do this, the demo goes through the procedure to set or clear a bit. I cover the algorithm for these functions in the next section, and you can follow along using the demo.

Creating a Bitvector Class

In this section, I'm going to build a bitvector class. This class will assume that an `unsigned long int` is 32 bits, which should work on the majority of systems out there. If not, it can easily be modified so that it works on integers of any bit size.

The bitvector class is contained on the CD in the file \structures\bitvector.h.

The Data

First, I begin by creating the data members of the class:

```
class Bitvector
{
protected:
    unsigned long int* m_array;
    int m_size;
};
```

You'll notice that the data members look almost exactly like the ones I used in the Array class (see Chapter 3, "Arrays"), with the exception of the type of m_array. This time, it is an unsigned long int instead of a generic datatype, because a bitvector is only suitable for storing booleans.

The size variable keeps track of the number of integers within the array. Note that because I am using 32-bit integers to store the bitvector, the number of bits in the vector must be a multiple of 32 (32, 64, 96, and so on). Therefore, to find out how many bits are in the vector, you simply multiply the number of integers by 32. A 1-integer array can hold 32 bits, a 2-integer array can hold 64 bits, and so on.

The Constructor

The constructor for this class is the same as the array constructor:

```
Bitvector( int p_size )
{
    m_array = 0;
    m_size = 0;
    Resize( p_size );
}
```

This piece of code clears the array pointer to 0, sets the size to 0, and then calls the Resize algorithm to resize the array to the correct size.

The Destructor

Again, this part is the same as the array destructor:

```
~Bitvector()
{
    if( m_array != 0 )
```

```
    delete[] m_array;
  m_array = 0;
}
```

This deletes the array if it exists.

The Resize Algorithm

The bitvector resize algorithm is similar to the array resize algorithm, with one exception: Instead of resizing the array to a certain number of integers, I perform a few calculations and resize the vector to the given number of bits. This change allows users of the class to request a certain number of bits without having to figure out how many integers they will turn into.

```
1:  void Resize( int p_size )
2:  {
3:    unsigned long int* newvector = 0;
4:    if( p_size % 32 == 0 )
5:      p_size = p_size / 32;
6:    else
7:      p_size = (p_size / 32) + 1;
8:    newvector = new unsigned long int[p_size];
9:    if( newvector == 0 )
10:     return;
11:   int min;
12:   if( p_size < m_size )
13:     min = p_size;
14:   else
15:     min = m_size;
16:   int index;
17:   for( index = 0; index < min; index++ )
18:     newvector[index] = m_array[index];
19:   m_size = p_size;
20:   if( m_array != 0 )
21:     delete[] m_array;
22:   m_array = newvector;
23: }
```

The only part of this algorithm that is different from the array resize algorithm is within lines 4–7. When a size is passed into this routine, it is assumed to be in bits, so I need to take that number and figure out how many cells to make. On line 4, I check to see if the number of bits is divisible by 32. If so, then the size of the array is the number of bits required divided by 32. Hence, passing in 32 will result in 1 cell, 64 will result in two cells, and so on.

However, if the user passes in a number that is not divisible by 32, I need to do a little work. If the user passes in 31, for example, 31 divided by 32 will result in 0, because it is an integer division. 0 cells is obviously an incorrect amount, so I need to add 1 to the cell count, which is what happens on line 7. The end result of this algorithm is that you will always end up with a bitvector that contains as many bits as you need, plus some additional bits if the number isn't divisible by 32.

If the integer you are using to store the bits isn't 32 bits long, it is a simple task to change it. In lines 4–7, all you need to do is change all occurrences of 32 into the size of the integer you are using. If, for example, you are using an older 16-bit system, those four lines would look like this:

```
4:   if( p_size % 16 == 0 )
5:     p_size = p_size / 16;
6:   else
7:     p_size = (p_size / 16) + 1;
```

The same goes for 8 bits, or 64 bits, or however many bits your integers use.

The Access Operator

This is one part of the bitvector class that deviates from the array class. In the array, I was able to make the access operator act in two ways: It could retrieve the value at an index and at the same time allow you to modify the item. You cannot do that with a bitvector.

The array access operator returned a reference to the item in the given cell, but because I am playing around with individual bits and not actual datatypes, I am not allowed to return a reference to a specific bit. So the access operator is limited to retrieving the value at a given index.

There are several parts to retrieving an individual bit within a bitvector:

1. Find the cell that the bit is in.
2. Find which bit in the cell is the required one.
3. Retrieve the bit.
4. Shift it down so it has a value of 0 or 1.

Step 1 is easy: To find out which cell a bit is in, divide the index by 32. If you want to find any bit from 0–31, it will be in the first cell; any bit from 32–63 will be in the second cell, and so on.

The next step is a little tricky. To figure out which bit in the cell you want to access, you need to take the original index and modulo it by 32. Any index from 0–31 modulo 32 will give you the same number, so if you want bit 5, you will need to retrieve the 5th bit of cell 0. What happens when you want to get bit 34? 34 modulo 32 is 2, so you access bit 2 of cell 1.

```
1: bool operator[] ( int p_index )
2: {
3:   int cell = p_index / 32;
4:   int bit = p_index % 32;
5:   return (m_array[cell] & (1 << bit)) >> bit;
6: }
```

Lines 3 and 4 find the cell and bit-index that you want to retrieve, which parallel steps 1 and 2 of the algorithm, but line 5 needs some explaining. First of all, you access the integer at index `cell`. This returns an integer. Next, you take 1 and shift it up `bit` spaces. Now, this should give you a 1 at the same bit position as the bit you want to retrieve, right? Take a look at Figure 4.3 to see how this works.

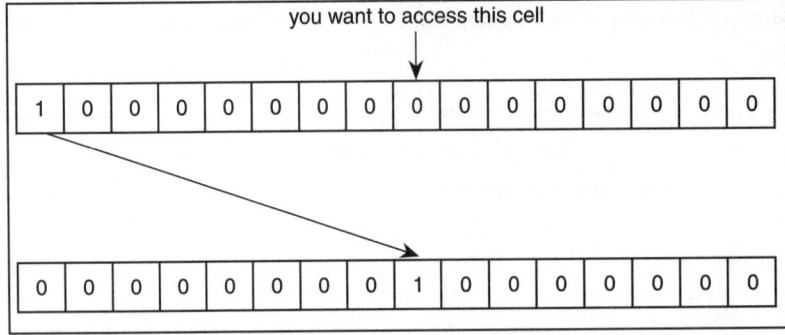

Figure 4.3

This shows the 1 being shifted up into the correct position.

If you want to retrieve bit 0, then 1 shifted up 0 places is still 1. If you want to access bit 5, then 1 shifted up 5 places is 32, which, represented in binary, is 100000. The 1 is in index 5.

Now that you have shifted a 1 into the appropriate place, you need to retrieve the bit in the cell. This step is easy—all you need to do is `binary` and the two numbers together. Remember the binary rules:

    1 & 1 = 1
    1 & 0 = 0

So when you take that 1 and `binary and` it with the given cell, you essentially retrieve the bit in the array at the correct bit-position. However, the result of the `binary and` isn't a 1 or a 0. If bit 5 had a 1 in it, then the result of the operation would be 32, or 100000. You need to shift this number back down so that it is either a 1 or a zero. So you shift it down 5 bits, and voila! You have a 1!

Note that you can modify the access algorithm for any size integer by replacing all occurrences of 32 with whatever integer size your platform uses.

The Set Function

Setting a bit within the bitvector is a slightly more complicated task. Because there is no single way to set an individual bit within an integer, you need to rely on the binary math rules: Use the *and* operator to clear bits and use the *or* operator to set bits.

```
1: void Set( int p_index, bool p_value )
2: {
3:   int cell = p_index / 32;
4:   int bit = p_index % 32;
5:   if( p_value == true )
6:     m_array[cell] = (m_array[cell] | (1 << bit));
7:   else
8:     m_array[cell] = (m_array[cell] & (~(1 << bit)));
9: }
```

Lines 3 and 4 are the same from the access operator; they retrieve the cell number and the bit number. At this point, you need to make a choice: If the value you want to set is true, then you want to set the correct bit within the vector; if the value you want to set is false, then you want to clear the correct bit within the vector. To do this, you rely on four binary math rules:

1. *x* and 1 = *x*
2. *x* and 0 = 0
3. *x* or 1 = 1
4. *x* or 0 = *x*

Rules 1 and 4 are known as *identity* functions, which just return the same value as *x*. Rule 2 is the *clear* function—no matter what *x* is, the result is 0. Rule 3 is the *set* function—the result is 1, no matter what *x* is.

For the set function to work (line 6), you shift a 1 into the bit position that you want to set, and you *logically or* that with the correct cell. This process is demonstrated in Figure 4.4.

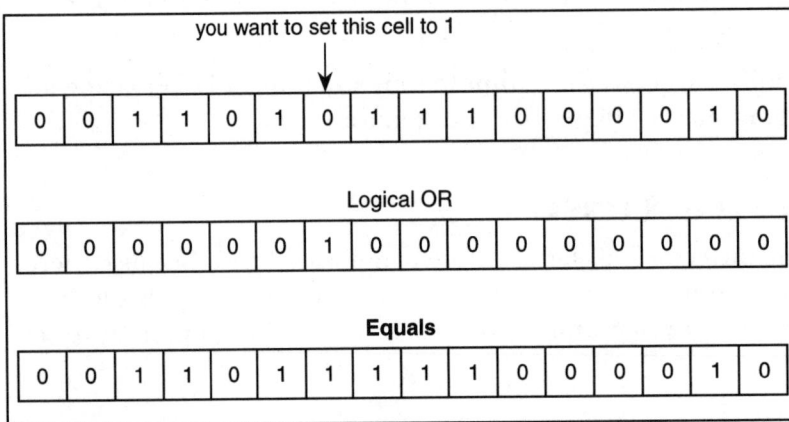

Figure 4.4

This shows how to set a bit. Note that every bit in the final result is the same except for the one bit that I wanted to set, which became 1.

Once you are done with the operation, the correct bit is set.

For the *clear* function to work, you need to do a little more work. This time, to clear the correct bit and keep all the other bits the same, the bit you want to clear needs to be 0, and every other bit needs to be 1. Remember, using the *logical and* operator with a 1 is the identity function. Figure 4.5 demonstrates this algorithm.

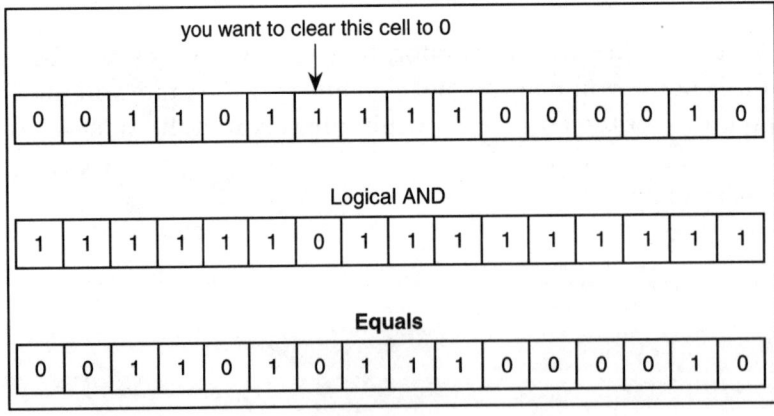

Figure 4.5

This shows how to clear a bit. Note that every bit in the final result is the same except for the one bit that you wanted to clear, which became 0.

So you use the shift operator to first shift a 1 into the desired position that you want to clear. Then, the *logical not* operator reverses every bit so that there is a 0 where the 1 was, and everything else is now 1. After using the logical and operator on the cell, the desired bit is now cleared.

If you want to convert the algorithm to an integer size different from 32 bits, just change all instances of 32 to the desired bit size.

The ClearAll Function

There are times when you will want to clear the entire contents of a bitvector quickly, and as you might guess, looping through every bit and clearing it doesn't seem to be efficient. Instead, there is a better method, where you set each integer in each cell to 0. On a 32-bit system, you've just set 32 bits to 0 at once.

```
1: void ClearAll()
2: {
3:   int index;
4:   for( index = 0; index < m_size; index++ )
5:     m_array[index] = 0;
6: }
```

The algorithm loops through and sets every cell to 0. Figure 4.6 shows how the clear function works.

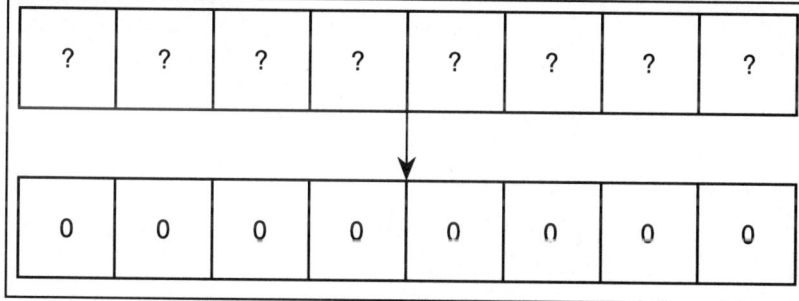

Figure 4.6

This figure represents an 8-celled bitvector. If each cell had 32 bits, then there would be 256 bits. The algorithm sets each cell to 0, clearing 32 bits at a time.

The SetAll Function

There might also be times when you need to set every bit in the bitvector to 1. Luckily, the procedure is just as easy as the ClearAll function—instead of replacing each integer with 0, you replace each integer with a number that is all 1s. On a 32-bit system, this number would be hexadecimal FFFFFFFF, or decimal 4,294,967,295. Each F in the hex representation is 4 bits, so you need 8 of them for 32 bits.

```
1: void SetAll()
2: {
3:   int index;
4:   for( index = 0; index < m_size; index++ )
5:     m_array[index] = 0xFFFFFFFF;
6: }
```

If you were to use this algorithm for a different integer size, you would need to replace 0xFFFFFFFF with the hex equivalent for the correct size. 8 bits would be 0xFF, 16 bits would be 0xFFFF, and so on.

The WriteFile Function

Because a bitvector is an array of integers, saving a bitvector to disk is the same as the way you save arrays to disk.

```
1: bool WriteFile( const char* p_filename )
2: {
3:   FILE* outfile = 0;
4:   int written = 0;
5:   outfile = fopen( p_filename, "wb" );
6:   if( outfile == 0 )
7:     return false;
8:   written = fwrite( m_array, sizeof(unsigned long int), m_size, outfile );
9:   fclose( outfile );
10:  if( written != m_size )
11:    return false;
12:  return true;
13: }
```

The only change in the algorithm is on line 8—instead of passing the size of a generic datatype, you pass the size of an unsigned long integer.

The ReadFile Function

Like the WriteFile function, the ReadFile function is almost the same as the Array::ReadFile algorithm:

```
 1: bool ReadFile( const char* p_filename )
 2: {
 3:   FILE* infile = 0;
 4:   int read = 0;
 5:   infile = fopen( p_filename, "rb" );
 6:   if( infile == 0 )
 7:     return false;
 8:   read = fread( m_array, sizeof(unsigned long int), m_size, infile );
 9:   fclose( infile );
10:   if( read != m_size )
11:     return false;
12:   return true;
13: }
```

The only change is on line 8, where you change the generic datatype to an `unsigned long int`.

Example 4-1

This is Example 4-1, which can be found on the CD in the directory \examples\ch04\01 - The Bitvector Class\.

Here is the code listing for Example 4-1, which covers all of the basic features of the `Bitvector` class:

```
void main()
{
    // create a bitvector with 32 bits.
    Bitvector bitv( 32 );
    bool b;

    // set index 0 to true and retrieve it again.
    bitv.Set( 0, true );
    b = bitv[0];

    // set index 31 to false and retrieve it again.
    bitv.Set( 31, false );
    b = bitv[31];

    // set all the bits in the vector to 0
    bitv.ClearAll();
```

```
    // set all the bits in the vector to 1
    bitv.SetAll();

    // resize the bitvector to 48 bits
    bitv.Resize( 48 );

    // get the size of the bitvector.
    int s = bitv.Size();

    // Why is s = 64? Remember, because you are on a 32-bit system,
    // you can only have multiples of 32. Because you asked for 48
    // bits, the resize algorithm had to make enough room for 48 bits,
    // so it jumped up to the next level and made 64.
}
```

This example has no output.

Application: The Quicksave

This is Game Demonstration 4-1, which can be found on the CD in the directory \demonstrations\ch04\Game01 - Saving Players\.

> ### Compiling the Demo
>
> This demonstration uses the SDLHelpers library that I have developed for the book. For more information about this library, see Appendix B, "The Memory Layout of a Computer Program."
>
> To compile this demo, either open up the workspace file in the directory or create your own project using the settings described in Appendix B. If you create your own project, all of the files you need to include are in the directory.

Games these days are huge. They take up hundreds of megabytes of memory at any given time and simulate many things all at once. Games are usually so large that saving the entire state of the game is a big pain in the butt. However, games are also pretty much useless if they don't have a save feature. What's the point of playing a long and complex game without being able to start up where you left off the last time?

Unfortunately, a *ton* of data usually needs to be stored whenever you save a game. Almost all the time, this data is going to be stored on some kind of hard disk, which is significantly slower than system memory. The larger the game gets, the longer it will take to save the game.

If you've played some of the more recent games, you'll notice that many of them have a *quicksave* feature, which seems to instantly save the game without lagging up the game at all. It's a pretty neat trick, and it can be accomplished by using bitvectors.

For most games, most of the actual game world doesn't change much in the matter of a few minutes, especially if the game is single player. Typically, a player can only be in one place at a time, and there is a limited amount of things that the person can modify in the time between saves. So if a player saves the game and moves around for a little bit and then saves the game again, instead of re-saving everything to disk, you just need to save the things that have changed! This is the reasoning behind the quicksave.

Creating a Player Class

In this demonstration, you will be keeping track of a number of players within the game. They aren't necessarily actual people, but might also represent monsters and computer-controlled players as well.

```
class Player
{
public:
  int m_life;
  int m_money;
  int m_experience;
  int m_level;
};
```

This is an overly simplistic player class that only has four statistics: life, money, experience, and level. Their purpose is not very important here; you only need to know that these variables will be changed within the game.

Storing the Players in the Game

For this demonstration, I'll use my good old friend, the array, to store the players in the game. This is somewhat important for this demonstration because each player in the game is assigned an ID number that corresponds to his index in the array. I'll also define a bitvector, which will keep track of which players have been modified.

For this demonstration, you have 64 players, so the array and the bitvector are initialized to hold 64 items:

```
Array<Player> g_playerarray( 64 );
Bitvector g_modifiedstates( 64 );
```

These variables are global in the demo so that you can always easily access them. The g_modifiedstates vector will be the same size as the g_playerarray. Each index in the vector will correspond to the same index in the playerarray. If any given bit is zero, that means that the corresponding player has not been modified since the last game save, but if the bit is 1, then the corresponding player *has* been modified since the last game save and thus needs to be written to disk.

Initializing the Data Structures

You need to initialize the array and the bitvector somehow, so create a loop inside a GameInit function and use random numbers for the player statistics:

```
1: void GameInit()
2: {
3:   int index;
4:   for( index = 0; index < 64; index++ )
5:   {
6:     g_playerarray[index].m_life = 11 + rand() % 10;
7:     g_playerarray[index].m_money = rand() % 100;
8:     g_playerarray[index].m_experience = 0;
9:     g_playerarray[index].m_level = 1 + rand() % 5;
10:  }
11:  g_modifiedstates.SetAll();
12: }
```

On lines 4–10, the algorithm loops through and initializes all the players, giving them 11–20 life, 0–99 money, and 0 experience and making them level 1–5.

Lastly, on line 11, I call the SetAll function of the bitvector, setting every item in the vector to 1. The reason I do this is because every player has just been initialized and has not been saved to disk yet.

Modifying Player Attributes

Now, whenever you modify the attributes of a player, you need to make sure that the modified bit is set in the g_modifiedstates bitvector. The best way to assure this is to use specialized functions that set the values of the player variables:

```
void SetLife( int p_player, int p_life )
{
 g_playerarray[p_player].m_life = p_life;
 g_modifiedstates.Set( p_player, true );
}
```

This sets the new life of the player and sets the corresponding g_modifiedstates flag at the same time. The other three functions are alike:

```
void SetMoney( int p_player, int p_money )
{
 g_playerarray[p_player].m_money = p_money;
 g_modifiedstates.Set( p_player, true );
}
void SetExperience( int p_player, int p_experience )
{
 g_playerarray[p_player].m_experience = p_experience;
 g_modifiedstates.Set( p_player, true );
}
void SetLevel( int p_player, int p_level )
{
 g_playerarray[p_player].m_level = p_level;
 g_modifiedstates.Set( p_player, true );
}
```

Each of the functions modifies the player class and updates the modified flag in the g_modifiedstates bitvector.

Saving the Player Array to Disk

Now, to save the player array to disk, you're going to need a more complicated algorithm than just saving the entire array to disk. The algorithm you're going to use is to iterate through the entire array and check the modified flag for each player. If the flag is true, you write the player to the appropriate place on the disk.

```
1: bool SavePlayers( const char* p_filename )
2: {
3:   int index;
4:   FILE* savefile = fopen( p_filename, "wb" );
5:   if( savefile == 0 )
6:     return false;
7:   for( index = 0; index < 64; index++ )
8:   {
9:     if( g_modifiedstates[index] == true )
10:    {
11:      fseek( savefile, sizeof(Player) * index, SEEK_SET );
12:      fwrite( &(g_playerarray[index]), sizeof(Player), 1, savefile );
13:    }
14:  }
15:  g_modifiedstates.ClearAll();
16:  return true;
17: }
```

On line 1, you declare the `SavePlayers` function. This will take a string, which is the name of the file you want to save the players in. On line 4, you open that file for writing. You check to see if the file cannot be opened on line 5, and if not, return failure on line 6.

On lines 7–14, you loop through all 64 players in the game. First, you check to see if the player has been modified since the last save (line 9). If the player hasn't been modified, you skip over him and go on to the next player.

If the player *has* been modified, then you need to do two things: find the right place in the file to write the player and then actually write the player. These things are accomplished, respectively, on lines 11 and 12.

On line 12, you use the `fseek` command to move the file pointer to the appropriate place in the file. Because the file is basically just an array of `Player`s, the position of the current player is the size of the `Player` class times the current index. Remember, files are byte-based, so you need to multiply by the size of the player yourself.

Application: The Quicksave

After that, you write the individual player to file by first getting the player and then using the address-of operator (&) to pass a pointer into `fwrite` (if you'll recall, `fwrite` requires a pointer to the data you want to write).

Finally, after all the players have been written, you call the `ClearAll` function of the `g_modifiedstates` bitvector, clearing every bit to 0. This signifies that every single player is now up to date and written to file. If you were to call the `SavePlayers` function twice in a row, the second call would do nothing, because none of the players have changed since they were last saved to disk. Figure 4.7 demonstrates how the algorithm writes players to disk.

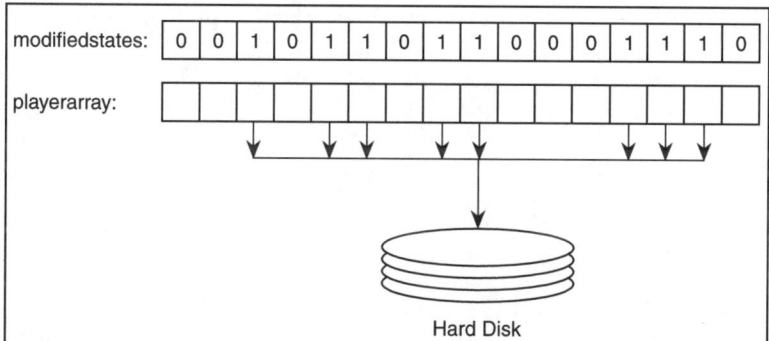

Figure 4.7

The `g_modifiedstates` *bitvector determines which players are written to disk.*

> **NOTE**
> This method in this particular example is probably slower than writing the entire array to disk, or at least not any faster. This is because of the way computers write data to disk today: They use a caching system. When you write something to disk, it isn't written immediately; it goes in a memory chip in the hard drive called the *cache buffer*. When the cache buffer is full enough, the hard drive then writes all the data in the buffer to the disk. In the previous example, the data you were saving wasn't large enough to fill a disk cache and you probably didn't save any time by only writing the things that didn't change. However, this is only because the data is small. Once you start working on large projects in which many megabytes of data need to be written to a file, the method of writing only what has changed becomes a very efficient method of saving data.

Playing the Game

When you start the game up, 64 "players" will be shown on the screen, each one with a box around it. The boxes signify that the players haven't been saved to disk yet, and the boxes will disappear when you press the S key on the keyboard. Clicking on a player will randomize their attributes and cause a box to appear around the player, signifying that the player has been modified since the last time it was saved to disk.

Figure 4.8 shows a screenshot of the game in action.

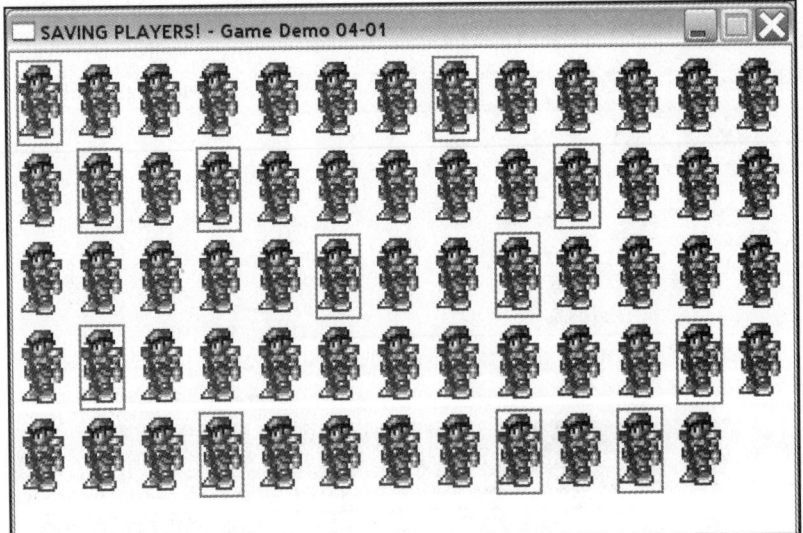

Figure 4.8

This is a screenshot of the Bitvector Game Demo in action.

Bitfields

Bitvectors are great for packing Boolean variables into as small a space as possible, but what if you need something larger than a Boolean? Imagine a system in which a player can be in one of four states: walking, attacking, sleeping, or dead.

Because a boolean can only hold two values, it is not going to be large enough for these four states, but an integer which can store four billion values is clearly too large.

The number of bits needed to hold four values is two, because $2^2 = 4$. C++ doesn't come with a 2-bit datatype, though, so the smallest you could use would be an 8-bit char, which wastes 6 bits. Although this might seem small, when you're talking about saving or sending the states of hundreds of players over a network, that means you're sending 4 four times as much data that you need to be transmitted. This is obviously a large waste.

Luckily, C++ introduces the notion of *bitfields*, individual integer variables within a class or structure that contain a certain number of bits.

Declaring a Bitfield

As the name implies, a *bitfield* is simply a small field within a class or structure that has a specific size in bits. There are only two types of bitfields: signed and unsigned. Both types are assumed to be integers.

Here is how you declare a bitfield:

```
signed a : 4;
```

This declares a signed bitfield named a with a size of 4 bits. Because it is 4 bits, it can hold a total of 16 values. Because this is a signed field, the range of valid numbers is –8 through 7.

> **NOTE**
> A bitfield cannot be declared outside of a class or a structure; they can only exist within a class or a structure.

> **NOTE**
> Because of the way signed integers are encoded, there is always one more negative value than positive value. The exact formula for the minimum value is: -2^{n-1}, where n is the size of the bitfield. The formula for the maximum value is: $2^{n-1}-1$.

Using a Bitfield

A bitfield can be used exactly like a normal integer. Here it is in action first:

```
class Player
{
public:
 unsigned m_state : 2;
 unsigned m_haskey : 1;
};
```

First, this declares a very simple player class that has two variables, a 2-bit state and a 1-bit flag determining if the player has a key. You can access each of the fields in the same way you access any integer:

```
Player bob;
bob.m_state = 0;
bob.m_haskey = 1;
```

From now on, you can do anything you want to the bitfield that you can do with an integer, with one exception: the address-of (&) operator doesn't work on bitfields. This is because bitfields are not variables; they are just small parts of one larger variable.

One cool thing about bitfields is that they can be used in conjunction with other variables seamlessly. You can mix bitfields and regular variables easily within the same structure or class.

```
class Player
{
  unsigned m_state : 2;
  unsigned m_haskey : 1;
  int m_hitpoints;
};
```

In the preceding example, I've combined two bitfields with an integer. On MSVC6, the size of this class would be 8: 4 bytes for the integer, and 4 bytes for the two bitfields.

Some compilers aren't too smart, though. For example, what happens if you were to adjust the order of the variables so that they were in this order: `m_state`, `m_hitpoints`, `m_haskey`? MSVC6 creates the structure, but this time it takes up 12 bytes: 4 for `m_state`, 4 for `m_hitpoints`, and 4 for `m_haskey`. Figure 4.9 shows how the two different structures are created in memory.

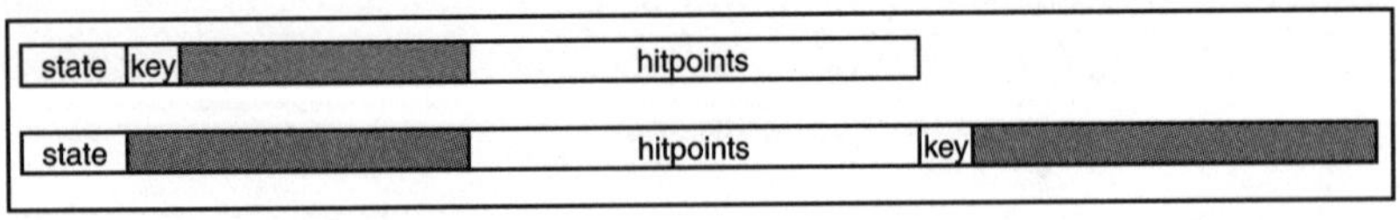

Figure 4.9

This figure represents the two different structures that are possible by rearranging the declarations of bitfields.

> **NOTE**
> Make sure that you keep all of your bitfields together when you define them. You cannot rely on the compiler to optimize the structure automatically for you.

> **NOTE**
> Also keep in mind that a single bitfield is useless on its own. The reason for this is that most compilers put the bitfields into a padded structure. So a bitfield of size 1 in MSVC6 will still take up a full 32 bits if there are no other bitfields around.

Analysis of Bitvectors and Bitfields in Games

Bitfields and bitvectors are really useful for efficient memory usage. Unfortunately, this comes at a cost: Compared to normal booleans and integers, bitvectors and bitfields require more processing time to retrieve and store values.

Most computers these days come with so much memory, however, that we don't know what to do with all of it. So this begs the question: Is the amount of memory that you have saved worth the extra processing power? There is no correct answer to this question, and whatever choice you make depends on your circumstances.

In most cases, the amount of space you save using bitvectors and bitfields is really negligible, but I wouldn't rule them out quite yet. Within the past few years, *Massively Multiplayer Online* (MMO) games have become hugely popular. In these types of games, many thousands of players could theoretically be playing at any given moment. As these games get larger and more complex, the strains that these games will place on the network will be tremendous. Storing data as efficiently as possible is a major focus in these games, and the technologies behind bitvectors and bitfields helps quite a bit.

In the end, it comes down to the most popular tradeoff in computer programming: Should you sacrifice speed for memory or memory for speed? If memory is more important, then you should use bitvectors and bitfields.

Conclusion

In this chapter, you learned how to store bits into a larger integer structure, how to read them back out again, and how to create a class that automates these procedures for you. In addition, you learned how to use bitvectors to implement a simple quicksave system.

You also learned how to use bitfields as an alternative to bitvectors to save data that doesn't need large amounts of memory but requires more than a single bit.

Bitvectors and bitfields are topics that I see neglected in a lot of books. In fact, I have only seen one book that even mentions bitfields; I had to do most of the research on them by experimentation. Perhaps it is because they aren't generally as useful as other data structures, or perhaps it is because they are somewhat awkward to work with. Either way, I still consider it important to at least know about them and know when to use them. This chapter introduced a major point in game programming: the speed versus memory tradeoff.

In almost every program, there is a place where you must decide whether it is better to have a faster algorithm or to take up less memory. This problem will show up a few times later in this book as well, so keep a lookout for it.

CHAPTER 5

Multi-Dimensional Arrays

5. Multi-Dimensional Arrays

Previously, I've only talked about linear array structures—those with only one dimension. This chapter will introduce you to the more complex class of arrays named multi-dimensional arrays. You will find that multi-dimensional arrays are more specific in their nature and cannot be applied to as many situations as regular arrays can be. In this chapter, you will learn:

- What a multi-dimensional array is
- How to declare native multi-dimensional arrays
- How to initialize multi-dimensional arrays
- How to pass multi-dimensional arrays into functions
- How to access multi-dimensional array cells
- How a multi-dimensional array is structured internally
- How to create a dynamic 2D array class
- How to create a dynamic 3D array class
- How to make a tilemap using 2D arrays
- How to make a layered tilemap using 3D arrays

What Is a Multi-Dimensional Array?

By now, you should know quite a bit about arrays. If not, you can read all about them in Chapter 3, "Arrays." The arrays I describe in Chapter 3 are more formally known as *single-dimension* arrays, but no one actually calls them that. They are called that because they can be thought of in a single dimension.

If you think about graphs for a moment, the single-dimension universe has only one axis (traditionally called the *x* axis), often referred to as *length*. Any item in a single-dimension universe can only have one coordinate. What you end up with is a long one-dimensional line for the entire universe. See Figure 5.1 for a pictorial representation of the different dimensions.

Now, imagine expanding that universe into two dimensions by adding another axis: *height* (traditionally called the *y* axis). Instead of just a line, this time you have a plane, and any point on the plane can have *two* coordinates instead of just one.

And finally, there is the three-dimensional universe, in which the third axis is *depth* (traditionally called the *z* axis). All points in the three-dimensional universe have three coordinates.

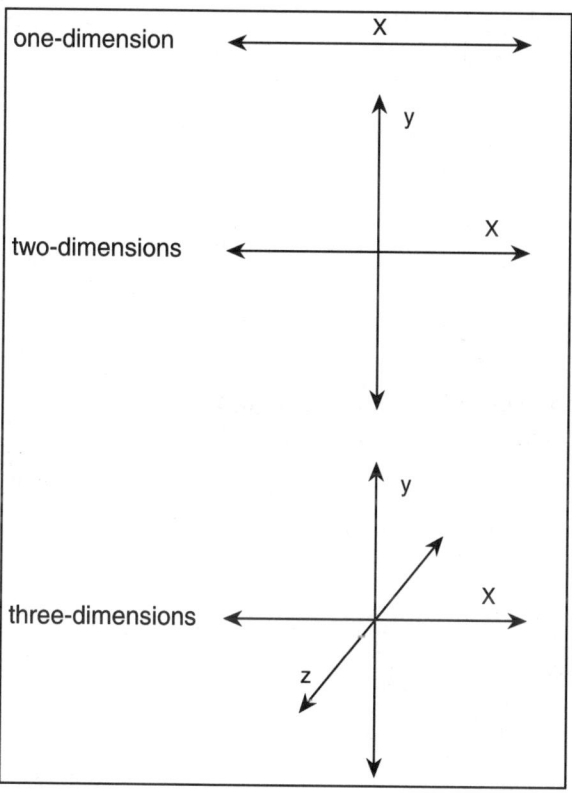

Figure 5.1

The three common universes. The z axis for the third dimension can be thought of as coming out of the paper, toward you.

Now, there are other dimensions past the third dimension, but they are pretty much impossible to draw in a way you could understand. Therefore, this chapter will mainly be concerned with two- and three-dimensional arrays.

If a one-dimensional array looks like a plain line, then a two-dimensional array looks like a grid. Figure 5.2 shows how a two-dimensional array is usually represented.

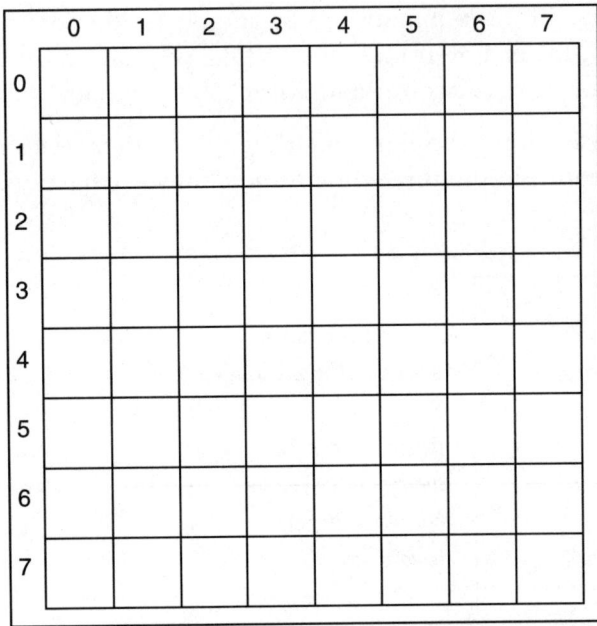

Figure 5.2

This is a two-dimensional array of size (8,8).

A two-dimensional array has two dimensions, a length and a height. In Figure 5.2, both of these dimensions are 8 cells, giving us a total of 64 cells.

A three-dimensional array uses all three dimensions, as demonstrated by Figure 5.3. As you can see, it's difficult to represent a 3D array because half of the information is hidden. After all, the paper is only 2D. The 3D array shown in Figure 5.3 has a size of (4,4,4), giving us 64 cells.

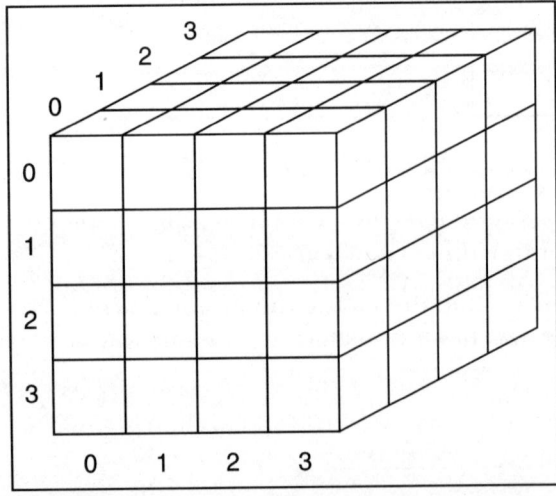

Figure 5.3

This is a three-dimensional array of size (4,4,4).

Graphical Demonstration

The graphical demonstration for this chapter can be found in the directory \demonstrations\ch05\Demo01 - 2D Array\. Because it is very difficult to represent arrays with more than two dimensions graphically, this demonstration only shows 2D arrays and the algorithm to resize them.

> ## Compiling the Demo
>
> This demonstration uses the SDLGUI library that I have developed for the book. For more information about this library, see Appendix B, "The Memory Layout of a Computer Program."
>
> To compile this demo, either open up the workspace file in the directory or create your own project using the settings described in Appendix B. If you create your own project, all of the files you need to include are in the directory.

When you start the program, you will be presented with a screen like the one shown in Figure 5.4.

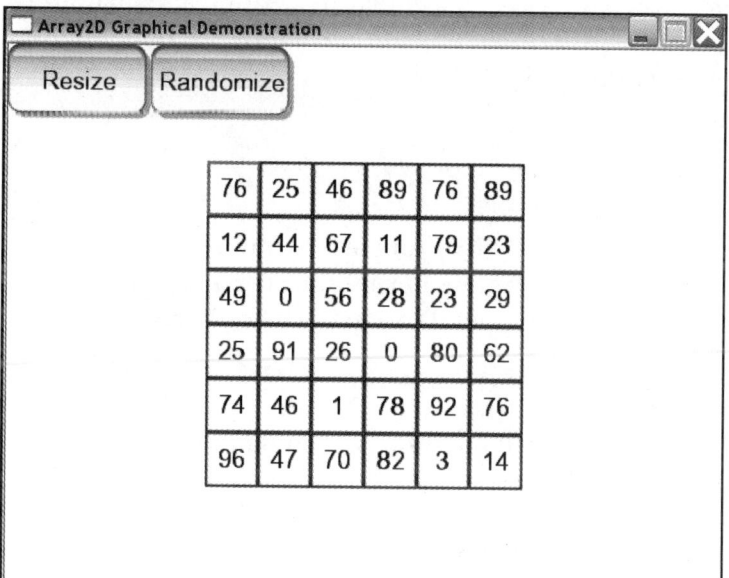

Figure 5.4

This is a screenshot for the Array2D Graphical Demonstration.

There are two buttons shown on the screen, one that will let you resize the array and one that will let you randomize the number in every cell.

The demonstration will show the exact algorithm used to resize a 2D array and will show red Xs in cells whose value is "invalid." I used this same approach in the Array Graphical Demonstration from Chapter 3. When resizing an array, four arrows appear on the upper-right side of the screen—use these to change the size of the new array, which will be shown in gray boxes. After you have attained the size that you want, press the Continue button, and the program will illustrate how it copies cells over into the new array.

Native Multi-Dimensional Arrays

C++ has native support for static multi-dimensional arrays. This is usually the most common way of using a multi-dimensional array because resizing one of these arrays is a rarely needed occurrence.

Declaring a Multi-Dimensional Array

Creating a multi-dimensional array in C++ is very similar to creating a regular array. Instead of just one dimension being specified, you add the additional dimensions in square brackets after the other dimensions:

```
int array2d[5][5];
int array3d[4][4][4];
int array4d[3][3][3][3];
```

These declarations declare a 2D array, a 3D array, and a 4D array, respectively. The number of cells each array contains is determined by multiplying all of the dimensions together, so the 2D array has 25 cells, the 3D array has 64 cells, and the 4D array has 81 cells.

Even though I only talk about 2D and 3D arrays in the beginning of this chapter, in reality you can have an array with as many dimensions as you want, depending on the limitations of your compiler. The problems with arrays with more than three dimensions are numerous though. First of all, they are impossible to visualize, unless you come from an alternate dimension where you can see more than three dimensions. Second, arrays with large dimensions tend to get much larger quickly due to the fact that their dimensions are multiplied to get the size. For example, even though each dimension in `array4d` in the previous code segment is only three cells large, the entire array takes up 81 cells. Compare this to `array3d`, however, in which each dimension is four cells large, yet the entire array only takes up 64 cells.

Initializing a 2D Array

Initializing a multi-dimensional array is just like initializing a normal array, except that it involves a lot more curly brackets. For example, if you want to initialize a 3x3 array to contain the numbers 1 through 9, you would declare it like so:

```
int array[3][3] = { { 1, 2, 3 },
                    { 4, 5, 6 },
                    { 7, 8, 9 } };
```

Because a 2D array can be thought of as an array of arrays, each row in the array is defined like a normal array. Outside, each row is combined together again, separated by commas and enclosed in brackets.

Initializing Arrays with More Than Two Dimensions

Using the logic from the previous section, you can extend the idea into three dimensions:

```
int array[2][2][2] = { { { 1, 2 },
                         { 3, 4 } },
                       { { 5, 6 },
                         { 7, 8 } } };
```

That looks bad and difficult to understand, but you can see the structure if you stare at it long enough. Lines 1 and 2 form a 2 × 2 2D array, and so do lines 3 and 4, so you're looking at two 2D arrays put together, forming a 3D array.

For the particularly devious people out there, here is a 2 × 2 × 2 × 2 4D array initialization:

```
int array[2][2][2][2] = { { { { 1, 2 },
                              { 3, 4 } },
                            { { 5, 6 },
                              { 7, 8 } } },
                          { { { 9, 10 },
                              { 11, 12 } },
```

```
              { { 13, 14 },
                { 15, 16 } } };
```

I do not recommend initializing arrays like this often. As you can see, the definition gets quite messy, and it becomes almost impossible to keep track of all the little brackets. It is not intuitive to initialize arrays with more than two dimensions in code because code is represented on a 2D plane (your screen or paper).

Initializing Non-Symmetrical Multi-Dimensional Arrays

Now you need to figure out which dimensions are initialized first. Due to C++'s notational conventions (see the "Inside a Multi-Dimensional Array" section for a more in-depth examination), the first dimension defined represents the number of rows in a 2D array. So, to initialize a 3x2 array, you would write this:

```
int array[3][2] = { { 1, 2 },
                    { 3, 4 },
                    { 5, 6 } };
```

In other words, the array is in *row major* form. Each row consists of two columns. The layout in memory is linear starting with row 0, followed by row 1, and lastly by row 2. Due to this arrangement, defining the array with three items in each innermost bracket will cause a compiler error. Arrays with more than two dimensions follow the same pattern. For example, a 3D array with dimensions $3 \times 2 \times 1$:

```
int array[3][2][1] = { { { 1 },
                         { 2 } },
                       { { 3 },
                         { 4 } },
                       { { 5 },
                         { 6 } } };
```

All multi-dimensional arrays follow the same pattern: The last dimension defined determines the number of items that are placed in the innermost brackets.

Initializing Variable Length Multi-Dimensional Arrays

Last, like regular arrays, it is possible to define a multi-dimensional array in which you let the compiler determine the size of the array automatically, depending on how many items are in the initializer list.

There is one catch, however: Only the first dimension can be left out. Every other dimension must be explicitly defined. I explain the reasons for this in the section entitled "Inside a Multi-Dimensional Array" later on.

For example, this is invalid:

```
int array[][] = { { 1, 2 },
                  { 3, 4 } };
```

Even though it is obvious to us that this is a 2 × 2 array, the compiler will not accept this. The proper declaration is this:

```
int array[][2] = { { 1, 2 },
                   { 3, 4 } };
```

The same applies to every array of any dimension—only the first dimension can be left blank.

Accessing a Multi-Dimensional Array

Accessing the items in a multi-dimensional array is just as easy as accessing items in a regular array.

```
array2d[4][3] = 10;
array3d[3][1][0] = 15;
array4d[2][2][1][0] = 20;
```

These operations put numbers into the arrays at different indexes. `array2d` puts the value 10 into the array at (4,3), which on a 2D grid would look like Figure 5.5. 15 is put into `array3d` at index (3,1,0), which would look like Figure 5.6. Of course, it is impossible to visualize where the 20 is put within `array4d`, so I cannot show a figure of that here.

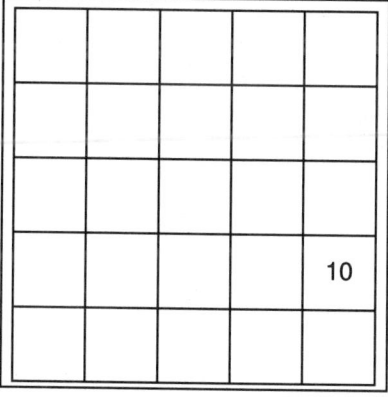

Figure 5.5 *This figure shows where the 10 is put within* array2d.

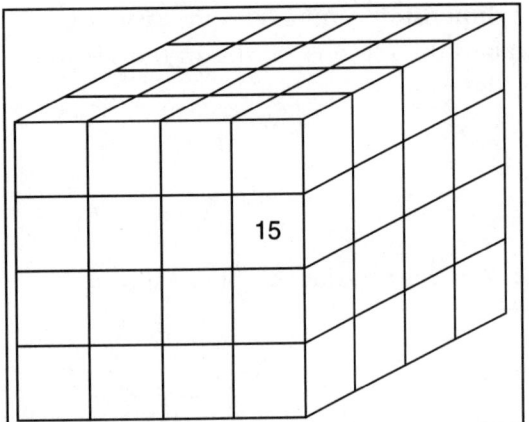

Figure 5.6

This figure shows where the 15 is put within `array3d`.

Inside a Multi-Dimensional Array

So how does C++ represent a multi-dimensional array internally? Remember how a normal array works, first of all. You hand it an index, and it figures out the correct place in memory by multiplying the size of an item and adding that to the array offset. Hold on to this thought for a moment.

Inside 2D Arrays

When you think of a two-dimensional array, isn't it really just an array of arrays? Look at Figure 5.7 for a moment.

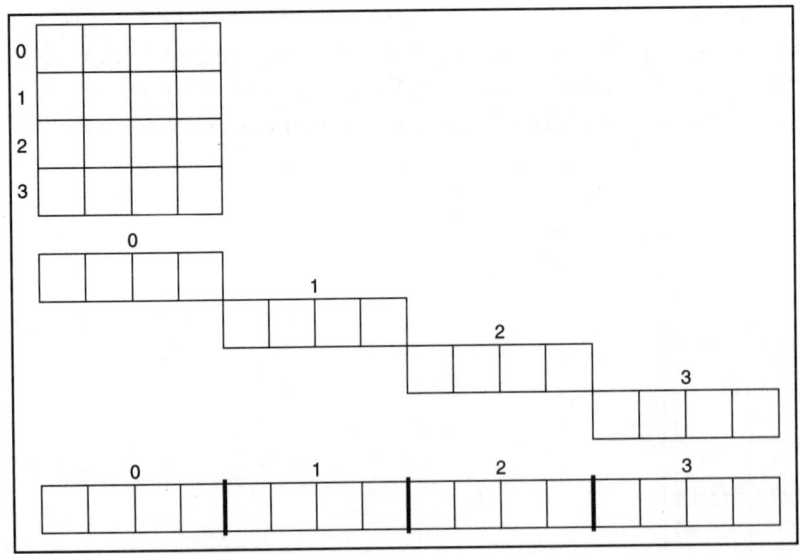

Figure 5.7

This is how you convert a 2D array into a 1D array.

You see, if you treat each row in the 2D array as a single item, you can view the 2D array as a 1D array of arrays. Figure 5.7 shows how you slide each row out to the right and combine all four rows into a single array.

The general formula for converting a 2D coordinate into a 1D coordinate is then:

```
y * width + x
```

Therefore, if you wanted the cell at row 2, column 3 in a 4 × 4 array, the result would be 2 * 4 + 3, which turns out to be 11.

This is how C++ stores and accesses 2D arrays. It stores the array data as a single array and uses the formula for getting indexes.

Expanding to Higher Dimensions

If a 2D array can be thought of as a 1D array of arrays, then a 3D array can be thought of as an array of 2D arrays. (See Figure 5.8.) Expanding upon this, a 3D array is really just an array of arrays of arrays (say that ten times fast!). How about a 4D array? Isn't that just an array of 3D arrays? Of course, after your dimensions get larger than 3, it becomes very difficult to imagine how an array is stored visually.

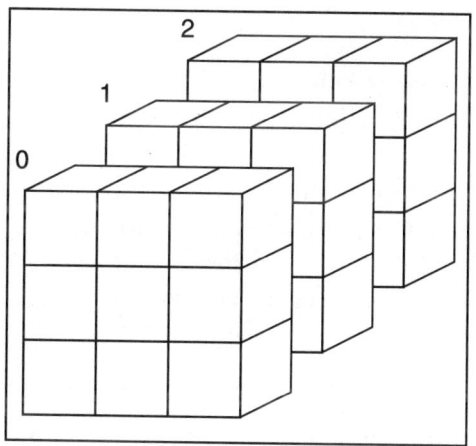

Figure 5.8

A 3D array is just an array of 2D arrays.

So now you want to figure out how to access a cell within a 3D array. Because a 3D array is essentially an array of 2D arrays, you need to figure out which 2D array you want to access first. To do that, you need to know the size of each 2D array, which is simply the width times the height. After that, the algorithm is exactly like accessing a 2D array:

```
(z * width * height) + (y * width) + (x)
```

The first term, *z* * *width* * *height*, finds which 2D array you want to access first. If *z* was 2 in a 3 × 3 × 3 array, then this would give you 2 * 3 * 3, which is 18. The second term determines which row within the 2D array you want to access. If *y* was 1, then you would have 1 * 3, which is 3. Then the third term is simply the index of the 1D array that you now have the address of. If *x* is 1, then you simply add 18, 3, and 1, and the final index is 22.

A Note on Conventions

Up until this point, I've used the standard mathematical convention for representing the axes of 2D and 3D arrays. The *x* dimension (width) is always represented as the horizontal axis, the *y* dimension (height) is always represented as the vertical axis, and the *z* dimension (depth) is always represented as going into or out of the paper.

Unfortunately, C++ uses a different convention and reverses the ordering of the axis. When you define a 1D array, there is no confusion, because there is only one dimension. Here is how C++ arrays are defined:

```
int array1d[width];
int array2d[height][width];
int array3d[depth][height][width];
```

This doesn't look like such a large deal on the surface. This is because when dealing with multi-dimensional arrays, the axes are largely arbitrary to the users' needs. For example, you could create a simple 2D array that keeps track of the different types of monsters in a game. One axis of the array represents the size of the monsters (small, medium, large), and the other axis represents the types of monsters (goblin, orc, troll). Does it matter which axis is defined first? In this case, it doesn't seem to matter. Declaring the monster array either way seems to be acceptable:

```
int monsters[SIZES][TYPES];
int monsters[TYPES][SIZES];
```

So as long as your axes are always the same for the arrays, it should cause no problems. The only time the ordering of your axes matters is when you use static multi-dimensional arrays and you pass them into functions, which I discuss in the next section.

Passing Multi-Dimensional Arrays to Functions

Multi-dimensional arrays can be passed into functions just like normal arrays can. There are several ways to do this.

The most popular way is to have the function assume that it will be receiving an array of a specific size, like this:

```
void Function( int p_array2d[4][5], int p_array3d[2][4][2] );
```

This function can accept a 2D array with dimensions 4 × 5 and a 3D array with dimensions 2 × 4 × 2 (technically, in both cases, the compiler ignores the first dimension, so passing a 6 × 5 and a 3 × 4 × 2 array would work perfectly fine as well. You'll see why this is later on). If you try passing in a 2D array or 3D array with different dimensions, it won't work and will give you a compiler error.

That works fine, but what happens when you want to pass arrays that don't have specific sizes? You could easily do this with a 1D array by neglecting the number in the function call, but you have no such luck with multi-dimensional arrays. The following line of code is invalid in C++:

```
void Function( int p_array2d[][] );
```

In MSVC6, this will generate an error message: `error C2087: '<Unknown>' : missing subscript`. Of course, if you had no idea that this code was invalid, that error would make no sense.

So why can't you do this in C++? Remember how the compiler accesses an element within the 2D array: it multiplies the row number times the width of each row and then adds the column number. Trying to pass in a 2D array without a specified width causes a problem, because then the compiler will not have any idea how to access a particular row. So to pass a 2D array into a function, you are required to at least give the width of the array as a parameter, like this:

```
void Function( int p_array[][4] );
```

This function accepts any 2D array with a width of 4. You can pass in a 1 × 4 array or a 2 × 4 array or a 100 × 4 array. However, you cannot pass in an array with a different width. C++ will not let you.

Note that reversing the order of the subscript will cause a compiler error. This is invalid:

```
void Function( int p_array[4][] );
```

5. Multi-Dimensional Arrays

The same applies to 3D arrays, too, except with 3D arrays, you need to know the width and the height to access any given cell, so you can only pass in 3D arrays with a fixed width and height.

```
void Function1( int p_array[][][] );
void Function2( int p_array[][][5] );
void Function3( int p_array[][4][5] );
```

Functions 1 and 2 are both invalid; they will not compile. Function 2 will not compile for the same reason a 2D array with no sizes won't compile: you need both a height and a width to access a 3D array. Function 3 is the only function that will compile, and it only accepts arrays with a height of 4 and a width of 5, such as 1 × 4 × 5 or 3 × 4 × 5 or 100 × 4 × 5.

As it turns out, any multi-dimension array with N dimensions requires $N\text{-}1$ dimension sizes to access any element within the array. Therefore, a 4D array will require three static dimension sizes, and a 5D array will require four static dimension sizes, and so on:

```
void Function4( int p_array[][3][2][3] );
void Function5( int p_array[][4][5][4][3] );
void Function6( int p_array[][3][6][7][4][5] );
```

This basically means that for any array, no matter how many dimensions it has, you can only have one dimension that varies in size when you pass it into a function.

Take a look back at the monster array example from the previous section. In your game, you only plan on having three different sizes of monsters (small, medium, large), and you don't plan on having different sizes in the future. Right now you only have three different monster types as well (goblin, orc, troll), but you think you might add different monster types in the future (such as a skeleton or even a dragon). You also have a function that is designed to process the monster array somehow. You could do it this way:

```
void Process( int p_monsters[3][3] );
```

But there is a problem. This function needs to be changed every time you add another monster. What you want to do is make it more flexible so that it can accept arrays with any number of monster types:

```
void Process( int p_monsters[][3] );
```

This is where the order of your axes becomes important. Because you want to be able to process any number of monster types but have a fixed number of monster sizes, you need to declare the array with the variable dimension first:

```
int monsters[TYPES][SIZES];
```

I need to say one more thing about passing arrays into functions. If you pass in an array with a variable dimension size, there is no way for C++ to determine the size of that dimension. With the previous example, if you passed in a 5 × 3 array to Process, there is really no way for the function to tell that the array has a height of 5. Instead, it is usually a good idea to pass in another variable to the function telling it how large the variable dimension is. For example, it would be better to redefine the Process function to look like this:

```
void Process( int p_monsters[][3], int p_monstertypes );
```

This way, when you do anything with the p_monsters array, you know exactly how large it is.

Example 5-1

Example 5-1 can be found on the CD in the directory \examples\ch05\01 - Static XD Arrays\. It combines most of the code snippets from this section into one file to demonstrate how static multi-dimensional arrays work. There is no need for a code listing here.

Dynamic Multi-Dimensional Arrays

Sometimes in game programming, you will need to have a dynamically sized multi-dimensional array. This usually happens when you don't know the dimensions of the array you need at compile time (this happens very frequently with bitmap and game-map loading), so you need some way to create a dynamic multi-dimensional array.

If you remember from the last section, C++ stores multi-dimensional arrays in a normal array and uses a formula to access each cell. You use this same method to create 2D and 3D array classes.

The Array2D Class

You can find the source for the Array2D class on the CD in the file \structures\Array2D.h.

The Template Parameters

Because you want your class to be able to work with many different types of datatypes, you'll be making it templated just like the Array class from Chapter 3. The Array2D class only needs one template parameter: the datatype of the items that will be stored in the array, which I'll call Datatype:

```
template <class Datatype>
class Array2D
```

The Data

The first thing you need to determine is what kind of data your Array2D class requires. You know that you need a pointer to Datatype, just like the Array class. Because this is going to be a 2D array, though, you need more than just a size variable. This time, you need a width and a height:

```
Datatype* m_array;
int m_width;
int m_height;
```

The Constructor

The Array class took a single integer as a parameter for its constructor, which was the size of the array. For a 2D array, because you need two dimensions, you'll take two parameters as well:

```
1: Array2d( int p_width, int p_height )
2: {
3:   m_array = new Datatype[ p_width * p_height ];
4:   m_width = p_width;
5:   m_height = p_height;
6: }
```

On line 3 you create the new array with a size of p_width * p_height, which is the formula for the total number of cells in a 2D array (5 × 5 = 25 cells, 3 × 4 = 12 cells, and so on).

On lines 4 and 5, you just set the width and height member variables.

The constructor is used just like the Array constructor:

```
Array2D<int> intarray( 10, 10 );
Array2D<float> floatarray( 5, 7 );
```

The Destructor

Remember how the `Array` class was able to automatically delete the memory of the array for us? You'll be doing the same exact thing with the `Array2D` class:

```
1: ~Array2D()
2: {
3:   if( m_array != 0 )
4:     delete[] m_array;
5:   m_array = 0;
6: }
```

On line 3 you check to make sure the pointer is valid, just in case it isn't, and on line 4 you delete the array.

The Get Function

Unfortunately, you cannot overload the double bracket operators (`[][]`), because C++ will not allow it. Therefore, you need to use your own function to be able to access items within the 2D array. I call it the `Get` function because it gets an item within a cell.

The function will take 2 arguments, the *x* and the *y* coordinates of the cell to retrieve:

```
1: Datatype& Get( int p_x, int p_y )
2: {
3:   return m_array[ p_y * m_width + p_x ];
4: }
```

Remember the algorithm used to access a cell in a 2D array from the section on static 2D arrays? That's the same algorithm you'll find within the brackets!

The `Get` function works two ways. It can retrieve a value from an array, and it can also store a value back into the array:

```
intarray.Get( 4, 5 ) = 10;
int value = intarray.Get( 4, 5 );
```

The Resize Function

Sometimes you might want to resize the array to a different size and keep everything that already exists within the current array. Although this was a simple task to complete with a 1D array, it is a bit more complex with a 2D array.

This time, because it is possible to resize two dimensions at the same time (requiring the user to only resize one dimension at a time is easier to code, but it is wasteful in terms of processing power), you need to keep track of only the cells that will exist in both arrays. Figure 5.9 shows which cells need to be copied over when resizing a 4 × 5 array to a 6 × 4 array. The size of the sub-array that needs to be copied is 4 × 4.

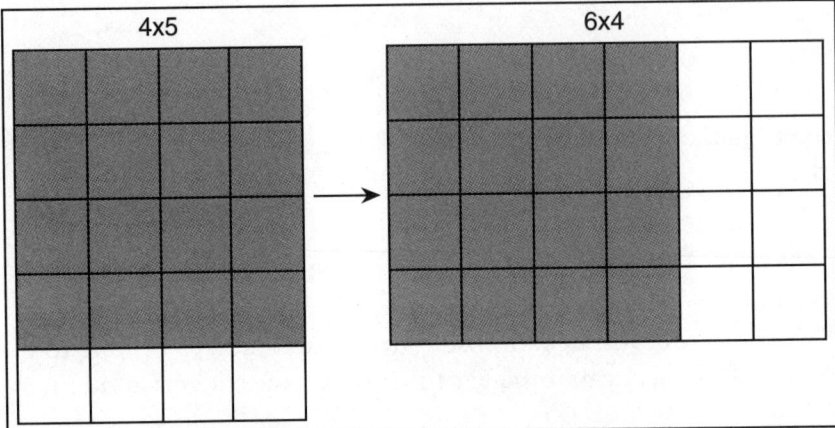

Figure 5.9

The shaded cells are the cells that will be copied from the old array to the new array.

Remember the algorithm used to resize a 1D array? You choose the smaller of the two dimensions and only copy over that many cells. For a 2D array, you need to do that for each dimension. For example, for the array in Figure 5.9, the first dimension changes from 4 to 6, so 4 is chosen because it is the smaller of the two. The second dimension changes from 5 to 4, so 4 is also chosen.

In this manner, you can code the 2D array resize function:

```
1: void Resize( int p_width, int p_height )
2: {
3:    Datatype* newarray = new Datatype[ p_width * p_height ];
4:    if( newarray == 0 )
5:       return;
6:    int x, y, t1, t2;
7:    int minx = (p_width < m_width ? p_width : m_width);
8:    int miny = (p_height < m_height ? p_height : m_height);
9:    for( y = 0; y < miny; y++ )
10:   {
11:      t1 = y * p_width;
12:      t2 = y * m_width;
13:      for( x = 0; x < minx; x++ )
```

```
14:    {
15:      newarray[ t1 + x ] = m_array[ t2 + x ];
16:    }
17:  }
18:  if( m_array != 0 )
19:    delete[] m_array;
20:  m_array = newarray;
21:  m_width = p_width;
22:  m_height = p_height;
23: }
```

If you look closely, this is nothing more than a 2D extension of the `Array::Resize` algorithm. On line 3, you allocate the new array and check to see if it was allocated correctly on line 4. If not, the routine just exits on line 5, without changing anything.

On line 6, you declare four variables, `x`, `y`, `t1`, and `t2`. The first two, `x` and `y`, will be used as coordinates when moving items from the old array to the new array. The second two, `t1` and `t2`, are temporary variables which will be used for optimizing the algorithm a little bit.

On lines 7 and 8, you simply find the smallest x dimension and the smallest y dimension and store those values in `minx` and `miny`.

On lines 9–17, there is a doubly-nested `for`-loop. The outer loop goes through all the *y*-coordinates first and the inner loop goes through all the *x*-coordinates, so you end up copying the items over in this order (for a 3 × 2 array): (0,0), (1,0), (2,0), (0,1), (1,1), (2,1). The top row is copied first, and then the bottom row is copied.

Lines 11 and 12 contain a special optimization. Remember how the algorithm for getting the index of a cell is y * w + x? Well, in the innermost loop, the y doesn't change at all; only the x does. So this means that you can move the multiplication out of the inner loop and store the result in `t1` and `t2`. When reading line 15, just replace `t1` with y * p_width and `t2` with y * m_width in your mind. There are other optimizations that can be made as well, but I've opted to leave them out, because this method is more readable.

After the loop is done, lines 18–22 just delete the old array and set the new variables.

Getting the Size of the Array

Because this is a 2D array, there isn't just one size now; three different sizes can be associated with the array: the number of cells in the array, the width, and the height. The width and the height are easy sizes to retrieve:

```
int Width()
{
  return m_width;
}
int Height()
{
  return m_height;
}
```

These functions just return the associated variables.

To retrieve the number of cells, you need to do a little more work:

```
int Size()
{
  return m_width * m_height;
}
```

This multiplies the width and the height.

Example 5-2

Example 5-2 demonstrates how to use the `Array2D` class. Here is a code listing of the example:

```
void main()
{
    // declare the arrays.
    Array2D<int> iarray( 5, 5 );
    Array2D<float> farray( 4, 4 );
    int i, x, y;
    float f;
    // We cannot do this with the Array2D class:
    // iarray[4][4] = 10
    // do this instead:
    iarray.Get( 4, 4 ) = 10;
    // set a cell in farray.
    farray.Get( 3, 2 ) = 0.5f;
```

```
    // retrieve the cells that we just set.
    i = iarray.Get( 4, 4 );
    f = farray.Get( 3, 2 );
    // get the size of each array.
    i = iarray.Size();
    i = farray.Size();
    // fill the integer array with consecutive numbers
    for( y = 0; y < 5; y++ )
    {
        for( x = 0; x < 5; x++ )
        {
            iarray.Get( x, y ) = y * 5 + x;
        }
    }

    // resize the array to make it larger:
    iarray.Resize( 6, 6 );
    // resize the array to make it smaller:
    iarray.Resize( 3, 3 );
}
```

The Array3D Class

The most commonly used arrays are one, two, and three dimensions, in order from the most popular to the least. Arrays with more than three dimensions are somewhat rare and thus do not warrant having their own classes in this book, but I did create an Array3D class for you to play around with as well.

Code Listing

Because the Array3D class is another extension of the Array2D class, and I have explained all the major concepts, here is a code listing of the class:

```
template <class Datatype>
class Array3D
{
public:
    // constructor
    Array3D( int p_width, int p_height, int p_depth )
    {
```

5. Multi-Dimensional Arrays

```cpp
    m_array = new Datatype[ p_width * p_height * p_depth ];
    m_width = p_width;
    m_height = p_height;
    m_depth = p_depth;
}
// destructor
~Array3D()
{
    if( m_array != 0 )
        delete[] m_array;
    m_array = 0;
}


Datatype& Get( int p_x, int p_y, int p_z )
{
    return m_array[ (p_z * m_width * m_height) +
                    (p_y * m_width) +
                    p_x ];
}


void Resize( int p_width, int p_height, int p_depth )
{
    // create a new array.
    Datatype* newarray = new Datatype[ p_width * p_height * p_depth ];
    if( newarray == 0 )
        return;
    // create the three coordinate variables and the four temp
    // variables.
    int x, y, z, t1, t2, t3, t4;
    // determine the minimum of all dimensions.
    int minx = (p_width < m_width ? p_width : m_width);
    int miny = (p_height < m_height ? p_height : m_height);
    int minz = (p_depth < m_depth ? p_depth : m_depth);
    // loop through each cell and copy everything over.
    for( z = 0; z < minz; z++ )
    {
        // precalculate the outer term (z) of the
        // access algorithm
        t1 = z * p_width * p_height;
        t2 = z * m_width * m_height;
```

```cpp
            for( y = 0; y < miny; y++ )
            {
                // precalculate the middle term (y) of the
                // access algorithm
                t3 = y * p_width;
                t4 = y * m_width;
                for( x = 0; x < minx; x++ )
                {
                    // move the data to the new array.
                    newarray[ t1 + t3 + x ] = m_array[ t2 + t4 + x ];
                }
            }
        }
        // delete the old array.
        if( m_array != 0 )
            delete[] m_array;
        // set the new array, and the width, height, and depth
        m_array = newarray;
        m_width = p_width;
        m_height = p_height;
        m_depth = p_depth;
    }

    int Size()
    {
        return m_width * m_height * m_depth;
    }

    int Width()
    {
        return m_width;
    }

    int Height()
    {
        return m_height;
    }

    int Depth()
    {
```

```
            return m_depth;
    }

private:
    Datatype* m_array;
    int m_width;
    int m_height;
    int m_depth;
};
```

The entire class is virtually identical to `Array2D`, except that there is a new dimension, the depth, and the `Constructor`, `Get`, and `Resize` functions have been modified to take this into account.

Example 5-3

Example 5-3 on the CD is an almost exact copy of Example 5-2, except that it has been modified to work with three dimensions rather than two.

```
void main()
{
    // declare the arrays.
    Array3D<int> iarray( 2, 5, 3 );
    Array3D<float> farray( 3, 4, 5 );
    int i, x, y, z;
    float f;
    // set a few cells
    iarray.Get( 1, 4, 0 ) = 10;
    farray.Get( 3, 2, 3 ) = 0.5f;
    // retrieve the cells that we just set.
    i = iarray.Get( 1, 4, 0 );
    f = farray.Get( 3, 2, 3 );
    // get the size of each array.
    i = iarray.Size();
    i = farray.Size();
    // fill the integer array with consecutive numbers
    for( z = 0; z < 3; z++ )
    {
        for( y = 0; y < 5; y++ )
        {
            for( x = 0; x < 2; x++ )
            {
```

```
                    iarray.Get( x, y, z ) = (z * 2 * 5) + (y * 2) + (x);
                }
            }
        }
        // resize the array to make it larger:
        iarray.Resize( 3, 6, 4 );
        // resize the array to make it smaller:
        iarray.Resize( 2, 2, 2 );
}
```

Application: Using 2D Arrays as Tilemaps

This is Game Demonstration 5-1, which you can find on the CD in the directory \demonstrations\ch05\Game01 - Tilemapping\.

> ### Compiling the Demo
>
> This demonstration uses the SDLHelpers library that I have developed for the book. For more information about this library, see Appendix B.
>
> To compile this demo, either open up the workspace file in the directory or create your own project using the settings described in Appendix B. If you create your own project, all of the files you need to include are in the directory.

When you look at an image on your computer screen, you're seeing a 2D array of pixels. A graphical computer game, then, is nothing other than a 2D array of pixels that changes at 30 to 60 times per second. Obviously, it is very difficult to control every single pixel on the screen at that high of a framerate, so the idea of *tilemaps* surfaced. A tilemap is a 2D array of *tiles*, in which each tile acts like a pixel on its own. Tilemaps are used quite often in games, and they still have applications in newer 3D games (they are usually called *terrain maps* in 3D, a 2D array represents the height of each tile in a level).

Because tilemaps allow you to abstract the idea of pixels to a higher level, this significantly simplifies a drawing engine. For example, without tilemaps, a large game would have a huge bitmap representing the entire game world. Using tilemaps, you can have your artists draw up a few tiles and then use a map editor to arrange the tiles so that they form a complete picture. See Figure 5.10 for a pictorial representation of both of these methods.

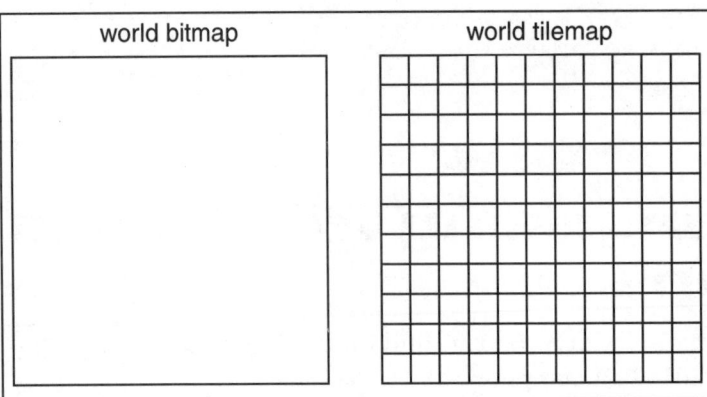

Figure 5.10

This is a comparison of the two image storing methods.

Now, when you want to design your tilemap, you'll have a palette of tiles (grass, stone path, snow, and so on), and you can design your map using these tiles, as Figure 5.11 shows.

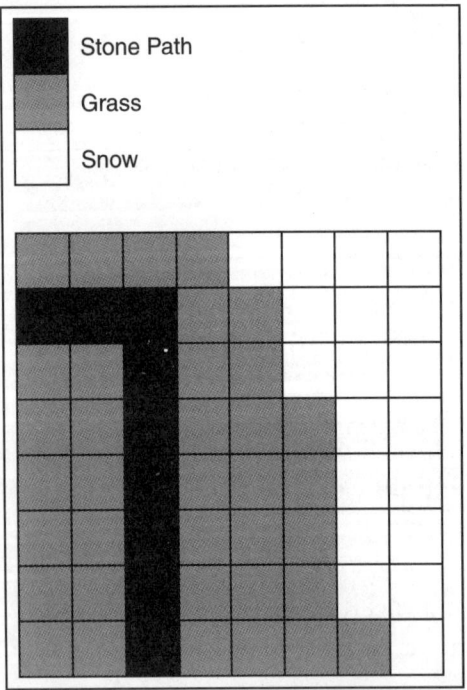

Figure 5.11

Here is a sample tilemap showing grass, snow, and a stone path.

Now, instead of drawing every pixel of the entire map, you only have three different tiles.

Storing the Tilemap

In the demo, I will need some way to store the tilemap. Naturally, because this chapter is about multi-dimensional arrays, I'll use one of those. In this case, a 2D array looks like it is optimal for the task, because a tilemap is just a simple 2D array of tiles, so I'll use the `Array2D` class. The simple demo will use a map of 16 tiles by 16 tiles, so I'll need declarations for those, too:

```
const int MAPWIDTH          = 16;
const int MAPHEIGHT         = 16;
Array2D<int> g_tilemap( MAPWIDTH, MAPHEIGHT );
```

I defined the width and height as global constants so that it will be easy to change them in the future. So the game demo creates a 16x16 array of integers, which will be the tilemap. The integers in each cell of the tilemap will then reference a tile number. When the tiles are loaded into the game, each one is given a number in the tile bitmap array:

```
SDL_Surface* g_tiles[TILES];
g_tiles[0]  = SDL_LoadBMP( "grass1.bmp" );
g_tiles[1]  = SDL_LoadBMP( "grass2.bmp" );
g_tiles[2]  = SDL_LoadBMP( "grass3.bmp" );
g_tiles[3]  = SDL_LoadBMP( "grass4.bmp" );
g_tiles[4]  = SDL_LoadBMP( "roadh.bmp" );
g_tiles[5]  = SDL_LoadBMP( "roadv.bmp" );
g_tiles[6]  = SDL_LoadBMP( "roadtopleft.bmp" );
g_tiles[7]  = SDL_LoadBMP( "roadtopright.bmp" );
g_tiles[8]  = SDL_LoadBMP( "roadbottomleft.bmp" );
g_tiles[9]  = SDL_LoadBMP( "roadbottomright.bmp" );
g_tiles[10] = SDL_LoadBMP( "snow1.bmp" );
g_tiles[11] = SDL_LoadBMP( "snow2.bmp" );
```

The `g_tiles` array is just an array of `SDL_Surfaces`. The four grass bitmaps are given the indexes 0–3, the road bitmaps are given indexes 4–9, and the snow bitmaps get indexes 10 and 11.

Generating the Tilemap

Now I need an algorithm to generate the tilemap. For this demo, I've used a simple method: Randomization of the grass and snow and a pre-set loop to create the road.

First, take a look at the grass and snow:

```
for( y = 0; y < MAPHEIGHT; y++ )
{
    for( x = 0; x < (MAPWIDTH / 2); x++ )
    {
        g_tilemap.Get( x, y ) = rand() % 4;
        g_tilemap.Get( x + (MAPWIDTH / 2), y ) = (rand() % 2) + 10;
    }
}
```

This is a simple doubly-nested `for`-loop that iterates through all 16 tiles on the vertical axis but only 8 tiles on the horizontal axis. This is because the left 8 columns of the map are grass and the right 8 columns are snow. For each grass tile, I generate a number 0–3, which is a grass tile, and for each snow tile, I generate the number 10 or 11, which matches the snow indexes.

Now I generate the road, which will be a rectangle:

```
for( x = 4; x < 10; x++ )
{
    g_tilemap.Get( x, 2 ) = 4;
    g_tilemap.Get( x, 6 ) = 4;
}
for( y = 3; y < 7; y++ )
{
    g_tilemap.Get( 4, y ) = 5;
    g_tilemap.Get( 9, y ) = 5;
}
g_tilemap.Get( 4, 2 ) = 6;
g_tilemap.Get( 9, 2 ) = 7;
g_tilemap.Get( 4, 6 ) = 8;
g_tilemap.Get( 9, 6 ) = 9;
```

The road will be a rectangle from (4,2) to (9,6). The first `for`-loop places horizontal road tiles from (4,2) to (9,2) and from (4,6) to (9,6). The second `for`-loop places vertical road tiles from (4,3) to (4,6) and from (9,3) to (9,6).

The last four lines of code place the corner tiles at each corner.

Drawing the Tilemap

In this demo, you will be using a tilemap drawing algorithm that will draw the tilemap with the upper-left tile being drawn at the given coordinates.

```
1: void DrawTilemap( int p_x, int p_y )
2: {
3:      int x, y;
4:      int bx = p_x;
5:      int by = p_y;
6:      for( y = 0; y < MAPHEIGHT; y++ )
7:      {
8:          for( x = 0; x < MAPWIDTH; x++ )
9:          {
10:             SDLBlit( g_tiles[g_tilemap.Get( x, y )], g_window, bx, by );
11:             bx += TILESIZE;
12:         }
13:         bx = p_x;
14:         by += TILESIZE;
15:     }
16: }
```

On line 3, you declare x and y, which will keep track of the current tile that is being drawn. On lines 4 and 5, you declare bx and by, which will keep the current drawing coordinates of the algorithm.

On line 6, you start the drawing algorithm by looping through all the Ys on the outside, and the Xs on the inside, so you draw horizontally, left to right. Line 10 is important because it demonstrates how you use the 2D array. The code g_tilemap.Get(x, y) retrieves the bitmap number of the current tile, which is then used to access a bitmap within the g_tiles array, which is passed into the SDLBlit function (using my SDLHelpers library, see Appendix C, "Introduction to SDL," for more information) using the bx and by values. After every tile is drawn, the bx value is increased by TILESIZE, which in this program is 64. After each row is completed, the bx value is reset to p_x and by is incremented by TILESIZE, moving the rendering down one row.

Playing the Game

When you launch the game, you are greeted with the tilemap! Hooray! It should look like Figure 5.12.

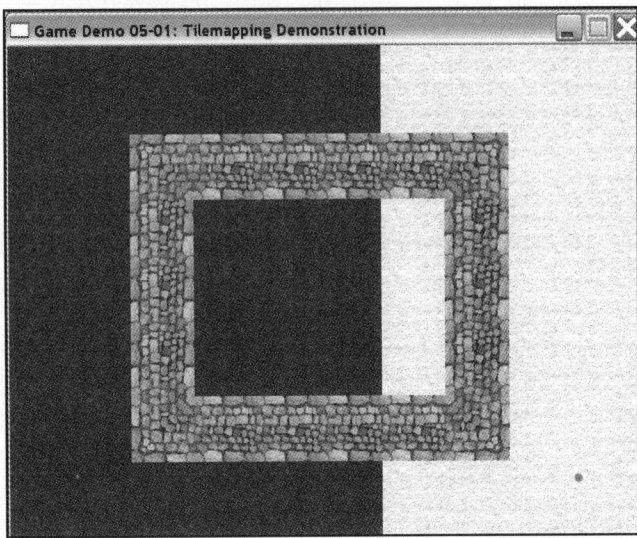

Figure 5.12

Here is a screenshot of Game Demo 5-1.

You can use the arrow keys on your keyboard to move the map around. Don't worry about going off the edges of the map; the algorithm still works fine.

Application: Layered Tilemaps

This is Game Demonstration 5-2, and you can find it on the CD in the directory \demonstrations\ch05\Game02 - Layered Tilemapping\.

Compiling the Demo

This demonstration uses the SDLHelpers library that I have developed for the book. For more information about this library, see Appendix B.

To compile this demo, either open up the workspace file in the directory or create your own project using the settings described in Appendix B. If you create your own project, all of the files you need to include are in the directory.

Application: Layered Tilemaps

If you look at the line separating the snow and the grass tiles from the previous example, you immediately notice that it doesn't look right. Snow just doesn't fall in a solid line like that. The easiest solution would be to draw a "transition" tile, in which you would draw some snow on the grass tile to make it look more natural. This method is fine for your small demo, but it has some problems in real life. What happens when you want to create an overlapping snow tile on other terrain types as well? You'll have to create a transition tile for each type of different tile that you want snow to be on top of, which quickly takes up lots of memory and might even anger your artists.

So, a more efficient system was devised, called *layered* tilemaps. This method allows you to have two or more layers on your tilemap. Figure 5.13 shows an example of a two-layer tilemap.

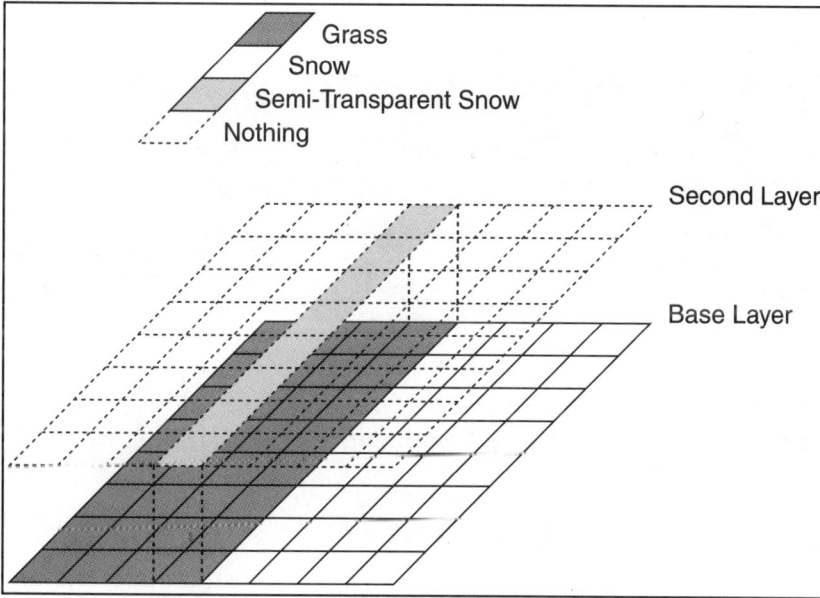

Figure 5.13

This is a two-layer tilemap, with a semi-transparent tile on the second layer.

Notice something about the figure? That's right, it's really a 3D array! So you'll be using the `Array3D` class to store your layered tilemap.

In the figure, the bottom (base) layer is composed of pure grass and snow tiles. The second layer is more interesting, though. First of all, you might notice that most of the tiles are blank. This is frequently the case with multi-layer tilemaps, because not every tile needs to have more than one layer. Second, the only bitmap on the second layer is described as "semi-transparent snow," and it is layered right over the grass tiles that are adjacent to the snow tiles. This means that the tile should be transparent in some places, letting the renderer show some of the tiles underneath. Figure 5.14 shows the bitmap you will use for the second layer. Every pure black pixel on the bitmap is treated as a transparent pixel and won't be drawn. This means that the grass texture from the base layer will show through the snow texture.

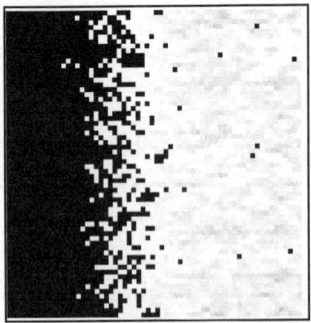

Figure 5.14

This is a semi-transparent snow bitmap. The black pixels are ignored by the drawing function, so that anything below it shows through.

> **NOTE**
>
> The bitmap in Figure 5.14 is relatively simple and causes harsh contrasts between the snow pixels and the grass pixels. If you are using a more complex API with support for *alpha blending*, you can create some cool smooth transition effects from the snow to the grass.

The implications of this method are numerous. You can easily replace the grass textures with something else, perhaps gravel, road, or dirt, and make it look like the snow is covering it without needing to create a whole new set of transition tiles.

Redefining the Tilemap

I need to use a 3D array instead of 2D for this game demo. Almost nothing else in this demo is changed from the 2D tilemap demo.

```
const int LAYERS              = 2;
Array3D<int> g_tilemap( MAPWIDTH, MAPHEIGHT, LAYERS );
```

You might note the addition of another variable, LAYERS. This is just to determine how many layers the tilemap should have. This particular demo uses two layers, although you might find uses for more than two.

Reinitializing the Tilemap

Because the tilemap now has two layers instead of just one, you need to determine which tiles go on which layer. You'll be using the same half-grass/half-snow design of the previous demo for layer 0 (the base layer). There is absolutely no change in the code except for the addition of the number 0 in the third parameter of the `Get` function.

The road is created on the base layer as well, with no changes.

For this demonstration, I've decided to add another road below the first one, which only goes halfway through the map horizontally. The reason it only goes halfway will become apparent when you see the demo; it looks like this road was snowed on and not cleared off.

```
// create another road
for( x = 0; x < (MAPWIDTH / 2); x++ )
{
    g_tilemap.Get( x, 8, 0 ) = 4;
}
```

Now, you will clear the second layer and initialize it all to -1, which is the value that the tile renderer uses to show that the tile doesn't exist.

```
// clear the second layer
for( y = 0; y < MAPHEIGHT; y++ )
{
    for( x = 0; x < MAPWIDTH; x++ )
    {
        g_tilemap.Get( x, y, 1 ) = -1;
    }
}
```

After that, you need to create one long vertical line of partially transparent snow tiles to cover up the grass, like Figure 5.13 shows.

```
// add the transparent snow tiles over the grass.
for( y = 0; y < MAPHEIGHT; y++ )
{
    g_tilemap.Get( (MAPWIDTH/2) - 1, y, 1 ) = 12;
}
```

This runs vertically down the grass line, which is located at *x* coordinate `MAPWIDTH/2`, and sets all the tiles to 12, the transparent snow sprite.

Because the rectangular road path goes over both the snow and the grass, the transparent snow tiles will overlap with the road, which will make it look weird. So you need to clear off the snow tiles that lie on top of the first road.

```
// clear the snow off of the path tiles.
g_tilemap.Get( (MAPWIDTH/2) - 1, 2, 1 ) = -1;
g_tilemap.Get( (MAPWIDTH/2) - 1, 6, 1 ) = -1;
```

Modifying the Rendering Algorithm

To draw multiple layers, you need to change the rendering algorithm into a triply-nested for-loop instead of just a doubly-nested one. This doesn't pose much of a problem; you simply add an outer loop that goes through each layer:

```
 1: void DrawTilemap( int p_x, int p_y )
 2: {
 3:     int x, y, z;
 4:     int bx = p_x;
 5:     int by = p_y;
 6:     int index;
 7:     for( z = 0; z < LAYERS; z++ )
 8:     {
 9:         bx = p_x;
10:         by = p_y;
11:         for( y = 0; y < MAPHEIGHT; y++ )
12:         {
13:             for( x = 0; x < MAPWIDTH; x++ )
14:             {
15:                 index = g_tilemap.Get( x, y, z );
16:                 if( index != -1 )
17:                 {
18:                     SDLBlit( g_tiles[index], g_window, bx, by );
19:                 }
20:                 bx += TILESIZE;
21:             }
22:             bx = p_x;
23:             by += TILESIZE;
24:         }
25:     }
26: }
```

This time, I've added a third looping variable, z. This will loop through each layer of the tilemap.

On line 6, I've added an `index` variable, which will be used to cache the bitmap index of the current tile. You will see the reason for it in a little bit.

The outermost loop, starting on line 7, loops through each layer, starting with the base layer. Every time a new layer is started, the loop resets `bx` and `by` to the original values because each layer is drawn directly on top of the previous layer.

Starting at line 15, I determine if the tile should be drawn and then draw it. In the first tilemap demonstration, I assumed that every tile will be a valid tile. However, I cannot do that this time, because many of the tiles on some of the layers might be −1, which is invalid. So on line 15, I get the index of the current tile, and if it isn't invalid, I continue to draw it. If it is invalid, I don't draw anything.

The rest of the algorithm is the same as the original.

Playing the Game

The game demo plays the same way as the first one. The arrow keys move the map around on the screen. Figure 5.15 shows a screenshot from the game demo.

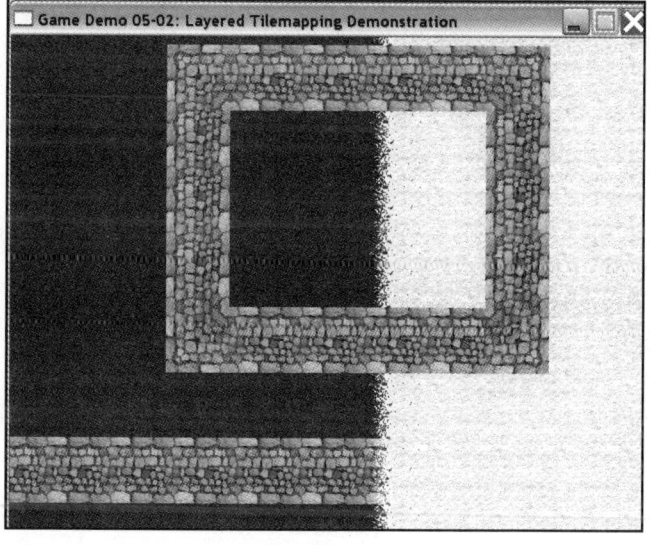

Figure 5.15

This is a screenshot from the Layered Tilemap demo.

Notice how the second road disappears into the snow? That's the power of layered tilemaps.

Comparing Performance

There is one important note that I feel I must make about the layered tilemap demo. It will be significantly slower than the single-layer tilemap version. The reason for this is because the rendering routine now adds an `if` statement for every tile to check if it is valid. Although this might not seem to be a lot of overhead, it adds up. However, there is another problem with many `if` statements: They mess with the processor's branch prediction unit.

Modern processors don't actually compute one instruction at a time. They are actually working on many instructions all at once! The processors use a feature called *pipelining*, in which each instruction is entered into a large pipeline and processed at different stages, all in the same clock cycle. The Pentium 3 and the Athlon each have 10 pipeline stages, and the Pentium 4 has 20 stages! That means that these processors are working on 10 to 20 instructions at the same time! The big problem is that the processor always tries to keep the pipeline full at all times, and so when it puts a conditional instruction (`if`, `while`, `for`, `else if`) into the pipeline, it has no way to know if the statement will return true or false until 10 to 20 instructions later. So how does it determine which instructions to put in the pipeline after a conditional instruction? It guesses. The processor uses a special unit called the *branch predictor* to determine which instruction is placed into the pipeline next. If it guesses wrong, the pipeline needs to be flushed, and everything the processor has done since it made the wrong guess needs to be ignored.

For example, Figure 5.16 shows a simple four-stage pipeline, with five instructions being processed. A four-stage pipeline means that every instruction can be separated into four different parts (such as loading the instruction, decoding the instruction, and so on). You can think of this as an assembly line in a car factory; each one of the stages in the pipeline performs one dedicated task on a car (or piece of data in a computer). After the current stage is complete, it passes the instruction onto the next stage and gets a new instruction from the previous stage.

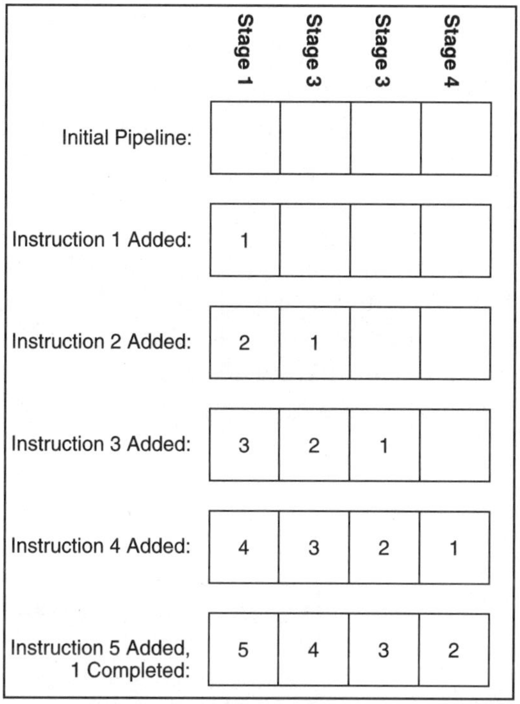

Application: Layered Tilemaps

	Stage 1	Stage 3	Stage 3	Stage 4
Initial Pipeline:				
Instruction 1 Added:	1			
Instruction 2 Added:	2	1		
Instruction 3 Added:	3	2	1	
Instruction 4 Added:	4	3	2	1
Instruction 5 Added, 1 Completed:	5	4	3	2

Figure 5.16 *This is a four-stage pipeline, with five instructions being computed.*

In the first part, all four stages are empty, and the processor isn't doing anything. After an instruction is executed, it takes four clock cycles to complete because each stage in the pipeline takes one cycle to complete. When one cycle has passed, the first instruction moves on to stage 2, and instruction 2 is added into the pipeline. This process continues until three cycles later, when the first instruction is finally finished.

> **NOTE**
> This pipeline has a *latency* of four cycles, which means that it takes four cycles for any single instruction to complete. This pipeline has a *throughput* of one cycle, though, because after every cycle, another instruction is completed. When the amount of work per cycle is decreased, the processor runs more quickly. This is why the Pentium 3 and Athlon processors are faster than the Pentium 4 processor at the same speed. The Pentium 4 has a larger pipeline and does less work per clock cycle, so it can run at a faster clock speed. An Athlon can calculate one instruction in 10 cycles, whereas a Pentium 4 needs 20 cycles for that one instruction. Although theoretically the Pentium 4 should be faster because it has a larger *throughput*, that benefit rarely appears in real life due to frequent pipeline flushes.

When you have lots of `if` statements in your code, the chances that the processor will make a correct guess on the result of the conditional are lowered, and you end up with code that is significantly slower as a result. These problems are very large for processors that have huge pipelines (such as the P4), but don't cause quite as many problems on smaller pipelines (P3 and Athlon).

Comparing Size

Another problem with using a 3D layered tilemap is the waste of space. In the first tilemap demo, the tilemap used 256 tiles (16*16). In this demo, the tilemap can store 512 tiles, but I only use 270 of them, which means that I waste 242 tiles! 47 percent of all the tile space is wasted on blank tiles! This is just one thing you need to think about when dealing with tilemaps.

Analysis of Multi-Dimensional Arrays in Games

Multi-dimensional arrays are not as "general-purpose" as 1D arrays and thus are more suited to specific problems. You'll find, more often than not, that if a problem requires a 2D or 3D array, there probably isn't any other way to solve the problem. This puts you into a predicament because you've seen how multi-dimensional arrays can easily become huge very quickly. Although memory concerns are no longer a primary concern with game programming, don't forget that multi-dimensional arrays do not increase in size linearly, especially if you increase more than one dimension at a time.

Perhaps the largest thing you should be concerned with when dealing with multi-dimensional arrays is how to iterate through them. If you are not familiar with how computer cache systems work, take a look back to Chapter 3 for a moment and read the section on caches.

When you iterate through a multi-dimensional array, you need to keep track of which dimension you iterate through on the innermost loop. For example, when you iterate through a 2D array with the horizontal x coordinate as the inner loop, you visit the cells in the order shown in Figure 5.17 in the top 1D array. The order goes in a straight line from left to right.

However, when you iterate with the vertical y coordinate as the inner loop, you visit the cells in the order shown in the second 1D array. The order jumps around on every access to the array. For large arrays, this will wreak havoc with the cache.

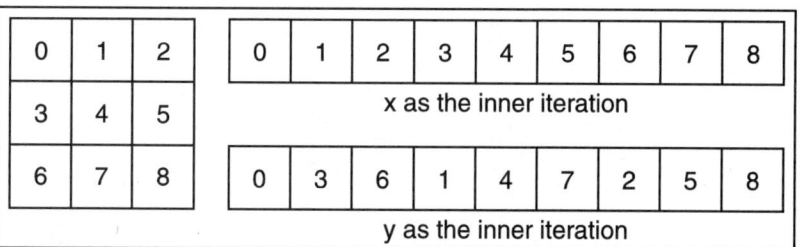

Figure 5.17

This figure shows the order of visitation using two different loops on a 2D array.

Conclusion

In this chapter, you learned everything a normal human being should know about multi-dimensional arrays, such as how to declare them, initialize them, access their cells, and pass them into functions. You also learned how to encapsulate 2D and 3D arrays into a class by using a 1D array and how to resize them.

Although the two game demos in this chapter only taught you how to use multi-dimensional arrays in relation to tilemaps (a subject that will be expanded in Chapters 6, "Linked Lists," 17, "Graphs," and 23, "Pathfinding"), there are still plenty of uses for multi-dimensional arrays. If you work with bitmapped graphics, you will use 2D arrays quite often.

Of course, multi-dimensional arrays are not nearly as universally usable as 1D arrays; multi-dimensional arrays are designed to store data that is ordered in a complex manner, whereas 1D arrays can store anything.

CHAPTER 6

LINKED LISTS

6. Linked Lists

I'm sure you've wished many times when you've been programming that you could use a more flexible data structure than an array. Perhaps you've wanted to conserve memory or be able to insert and remove data quickly. If so, then the *linked list* is the answer to your problems. In this chapter, you will learn

- What a linked list is
- How to create two different versions of linked lists
- How to insert and remove data from linked lists
- How to write linked lists to disk
- How to use linked lists in games
- How the two linked list versions compare to each other, and also to arrays

What Is a Linked List?

In Chapter 3, "Arrays," I introduced you to arrays. I went over the downsides of using arrays: You cannot insert or remove data into them quickly (at least in the middle), and they are fixed at a certain size. Now, imagine that you have a container that acts similarly to an array, but fixes those problems. The data structure that does this is called a *linked list*, sometimes known as just a *list*.

Like an array, a linked list is composed of many cells that contain data, although they are called *nodes* when referring to linked lists. In an array, cells are packed right next to each other in memory, and cells contain nothing but the data in the array. A node is different, however. The nodes in a linked list are not packed together like cells.

Instead, each node in a linked list points to the next node in the list. Figure 6.1 shows a graphical representation of a linked list with four nodes. Each node in a linked list is actually a class on its own and contains a pointer to the next node in the list.

Singly Linked Lists 149

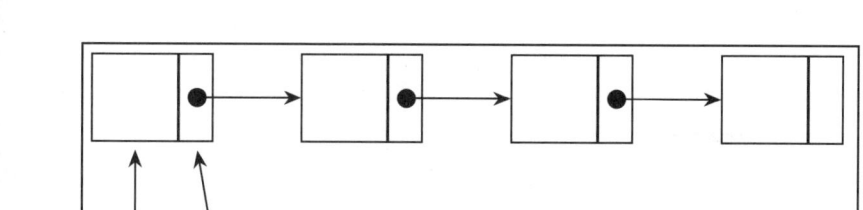

Figure 6.1

Here is a pictorial representation of a four-node linked list. Each node points to the next node in the list.

Because of the way that linked lists are structured, you can easily add or remove nodes at the beginning or the end of a list, or even in the middle of the list.

Many different linked list variations exist, but I only cover two of them here.

Singly Linked Lists

Singly linked lists are the simplest types of linked lists. Each node in the list points only to the next node. Figure 6.1 is an example of a singly linked list.

Graphical Demonstration: Singly Linked Lists

You can find the singly linked list graphical demo on the CD in the directory \demonstrations\ch06\Demo01 - Linked List\. This demo shows you how to iterate through singly linked lists and how to insert and remove nodes from them.

Compiling the Demo

This demonstration uses the SDLGUI library that I have developed for the book. For more information about this library, see Appendix B, "The Memory Layout of a Computer Program."

To compile this demo, either open up the workspace file in the directory or create your own project using the settings described in Appendix B. If you create your own project, all of the files you need to include are in the directory.

When the program starts, you are presented with four buttons and a five-node singly linked list. Figure 6.2 shows a screenshot of this scenario.

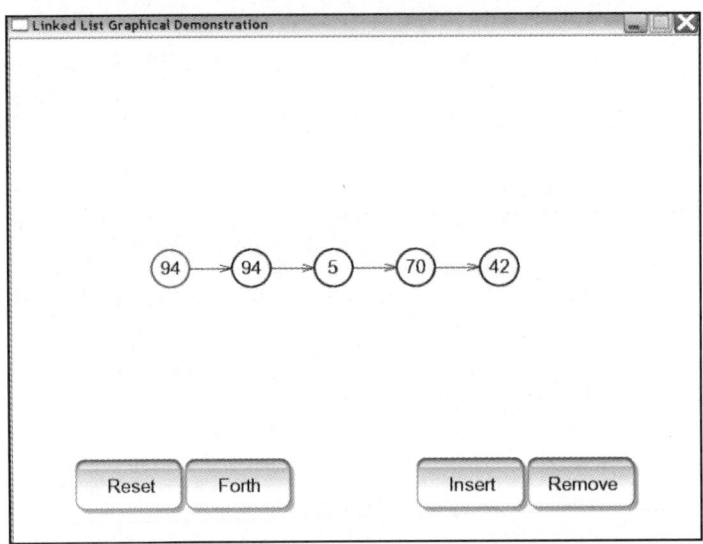

Figure 6.2

Here is a screenshot from the Singly Linked List graphical demonstration.

The very first node on the left will be colored red to indicate that it is the current node. In the Chapter 3 array demo, you could click on any cell in the array to select it. You cannot do that here, for reasons that I explain later on. Instead, you must select the nodes using the two buttons on the left side: Reset and Forth.

The Reset button makes the very first node in the list the current node. The Forth button selects the next node in the list. These two controls are called the *iteration* controls.

On the right-hand side, you have two more buttons, Insert and Remove. The Insert button starts an animation that demonstrates how to insert a node into the list, and the Remove button demonstrates how to remove a node from the list. When I describe these algorithms later on, I think it will help you a lot to see the demo in action.

Structure

This section deals with the code of the singly linked list class, which can be found on the CD in the \structures\ directory in the file SLinkedList.h.

Even though a singly linked list is in theory a specific type of structure, it turns out that there are many ways of implementing this type of list. I start off by looking at the simplest way to implement a singly linked list: with a plain node class.

The SListNode Class

I call this class the SListNode. It is simple and contains only two data members:

```
template<class Datatype>
class SListNode
{
public:
    Datatype m_data;
    SListNode<Datatype>* m_next;
};
```

The first member is m_data, which holds the data that is going to be stored in the node. The second member is m_next, which is a pointer to another SListNode class. Using this, it is possible to create a linked list, like Example 6-1 shows (this can be found on the CD in the directory \examples\ch06\01 - Building a simple List\):

```
1: SListNode<int>* list = new SListNode<int>;
2: list->m_data = 10;
3: list->m_next = new SListNode<int>;
4: list->m_next->m_data = 20;
5: list->m_next->m_next = new SListNode<int>;
6: list->m_next->m_next->m_data = 30;
```

On line 1, I declare a pointer to the SListNode class, list, and create a new node for it. Line 2 sets the data inside the node to the value 10.

Now, on line 3, I create a new node and tell list to point to it. Then, on line 4, I set the data inside the second node to 20. Finally, I repeat this process again and create a third node. On line 5, I tell the second node to point to the third node and set the third node to 30. Figure 6.3 shows this process.

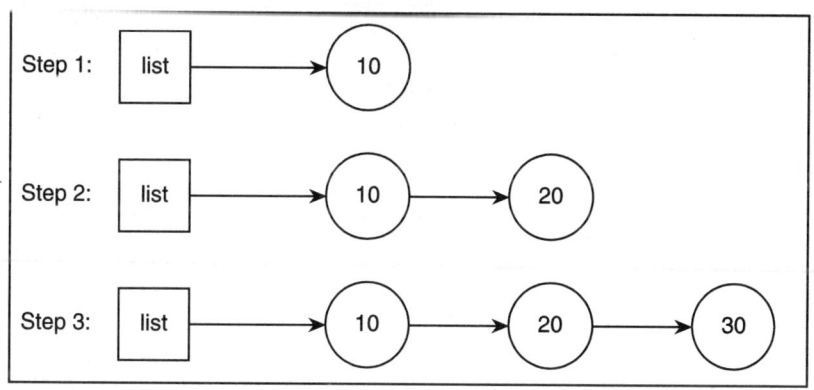

Figure 6.3

This is how you create a new linked list without a container class, as in Example 6-1.

As you can imagine, this method tends to become a little cumbersome. Adding items to the list becomes very difficult as the size increases. Accessing items becomes just as difficult. Because of this, you should find a better way to access the list.

The InsertAfter Function

First of all, you need a better method of inserting nodes. I'll build this into the `SListNode` class and call it `InsertAfter` because I am inserting a node after the current node.

The purpose of this function is to insert a new node after an existing node. However, if there is already a node after the current node, you need to move that node over. Figure 6.4 shows what I want to do. If `InsertAfter` is called on node 10, then I want to insert the new node immediately after 10, but before 30.

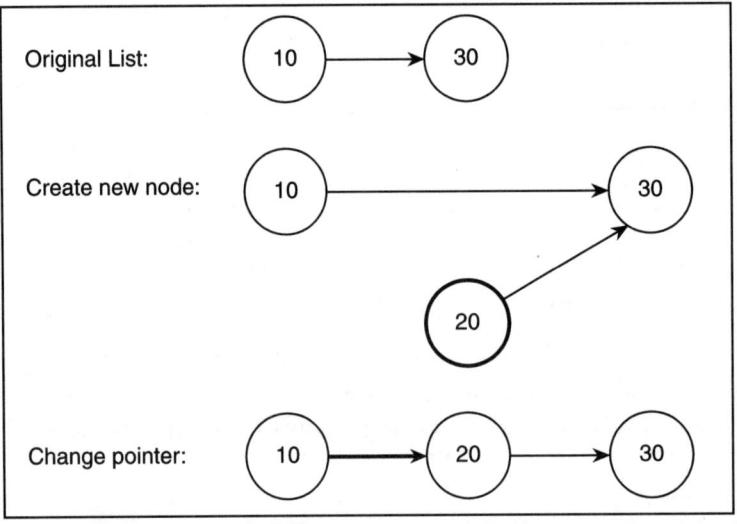

Figure 6.4

This shows the process of inserting a new node into a linked list.

This process has two steps:

1. Create a new node that points to 30.
2. Make 10 point to the new node.

This process can also be viewed graphically using the Singly Linked List graphical demonstration, which I introduced earlier.

The code looks like this:

```
void InsertAfter( Datatype p_data )
{
```

```
    // create the new node.
    SListNode<Datatype>* newnode = new SListNode<Datatype>;
    newnode->m_data = p_data;
    // make the new node point to the next node.
    newnode->m_next = m_next;
    // make the previous node point to the new node
    m_next = newnode;
}
```

The first step is to create a new node and set its data. You then take that new node and make it point to the next node in the list. Finally, you make the current node point to the next node.

This is a very simple process, as you can see, which makes linked lists a powerful and flexible tool.

Iterators

Now that you've automated the insertion process, you need to have some way of moving through a linked list and accessing all of the nodes. Obviously the method used in Example 6-1 is too cumbersome to use with ease, so you need a new concept, called *iterators*.

An *iterator* is simply a structure that allows you to move through a linked list from start to finish, for singly linked lists, at least. The definition of an iterator becomes more general when you go on to different kinds of lists.

An iterator basically points to a specific node in a list. Figure 6.5 shows four different iterators, named itr1 through itr4, pointing to various nodes in a three-node linked list. Note that any number of iterators can point to the same node in a list.

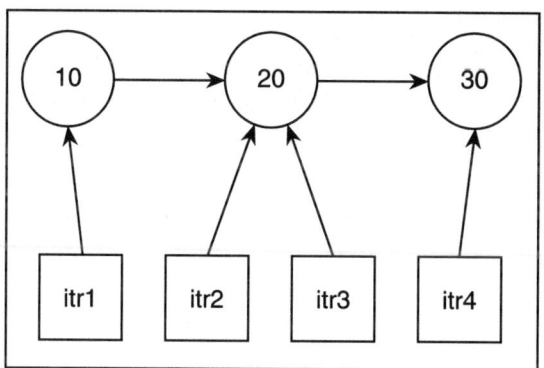

Figure 6.5

The structures on the bottom are iterators, pointing to nodes in a list. Many different iterators can point to the same node.

For this simple iteration example, I'll just use a `SListNode` pointer as the iterator. This is Example 6-2:

```cpp
// create a new linked list.
SListNode<int>* list = new SListNode<int>;
list->m_data = 10;
// insert 30 and then 20 before that, so the list is 10, 20, 30.
list->InsertAfter( 30 );
list->InsertAfter( 20 );
cout << "the list contains: ";
// create a new iterator and make it point to the
// beginning of the list.
SListNode<int>* itr = list;
cout << itr->m_data << ", ";
// move the iterator to the next node in the list.
itr = itr->m_next;
cout << itr->m_data << ", ";
// move the iterator forward again.
itr = itr->m_next;
cout << itr->m_data << ", ";
// reset the iterator to the beginning again.
itr = list;
```

In this example, the iterator can only move forward. This is one of the limitations of a singly linked list. To get to a previous node in the list, you need to reset the iterator all the way back to the beginning and move it forward again.

> **NOTE**
> Because of the forward-only motion of singly linked list iterators, these types of lists are rarely used in the real world.

Encapsulating a Linked List

Up until now, you've only been dealing with the linked list node structure and not any specific linked list class. I have always preferred to wrap the node structure into another class, however, because it makes working with the linked list much easier.

So I'll begin by creating the `SLinkedList` class, which will contain pointers to the front and back nodes of the list. I call these the *head* and the *tail*.

```cpp
template<class Datatype>
class SLinkedList
{
public:
```

```
    SListNode<Datatype>* m_head;
    SListNode<Datatype>* m_tail;
    int m_count;
};
```

So what you end up with is a class that contains three things, as Figure 6.6 depicts: a pointer to the first node in the list, a pointer to the last node in the list, and the total number of nodes in the list. This class will make working with linked lists much easier.

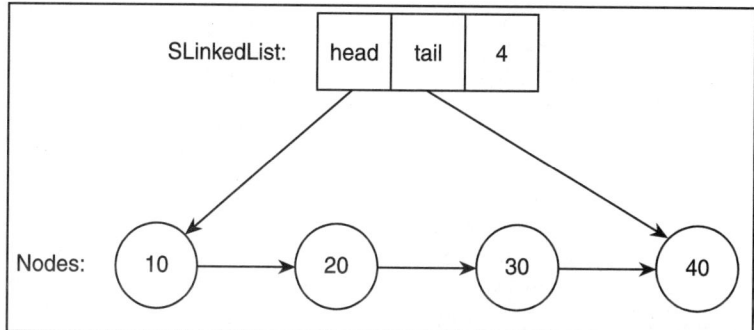

Figure 6.6

When a linked list is encapsulated into a container class, it is easier to work with. The class manages the pointers for you.

The Constructor

The first function I'll give to the SLinkedList class is a constructor. This function sets the pointers and the count to 0 so you know that the list has nothing in it and doesn't point to any nodes.

```
SLinkedList()
{
    m_head = 0;
    m_tail = 0;
    m_count = 0;
}
```

Whenever the head or the tail is 0, the list is empty.

The Destructor

After you are done using the list, you want it to be able to delete all the nodes that it has created automatically so you don't have to manually clean them up yourself. You can do this by using the same kind of iterators I used earlier to iterate through the list and delete each node.

```cpp
~SLinkedList()
{
    // temporary node pointers.
    SListNode<Datatype>* itr = m_head;
    SListNode<Datatype>* next;
    while( itr != 0 )
    {
        // save the pointer to the next node.
        next = itr->m_next;
        // delete the current node.
        delete itr;
        // make the next node the current node.
        itr = next;
    }
}
```

This method uses two iterators: `itr` and `next`. When this code starts out, it initializes `itr` to point to the first node in the list and then enters a loop. The next pointer points to the node directly after `itr`. I do this for a reason: When `itr` is deleted, you have no way of telling where the next node is going to be.

So you delete the node that the iterator points to and then move it forward. You do this until the iterator is 0. Because the last node in the list points to nothing, its `m_next` pointer will contain 0. Therefore, when `itr` is 0, every node in the list has been deleted.

The Append Function

After that, you want to give the `SLinkedList` class a function to add nodes. This is the `Append` function. This function adds a new node to the end of the list.

```cpp
void Append( Datatype p_data )
{
    if( m_head == 0 )
    {
        // create a new head node.
        m_head = m_tail = new SListNode<Datatype>;
        m_head->m_data = p_data;
    }
    else
    {
        // insert a new node after the tail and reset the tail.
```

```
        m_tail->InsertAfter( p_data );
        m_tail = m_tail->m_next;
    }
    m_count++;
}
```

To append an item to the end of the list, you could simply call `InsertAfter` on the last node of the list, right? Well, it's not quite that simple. What happens if there is no last node? This is why the `if/else` block exists.

If m_head is 0, the list is empty and you need to create a new head node. In this case, you simply create a new node and make the m_head and the m_tail pointers point to that node.

If m_head isn't 0, you can call `InsertAfter` on the tail node. The thing you have to remember in this case is that because you've added another node to the back, you need to update the m_tail pointer so that it points to the new node.

Figure 6.7 shows the process of appending a new node.

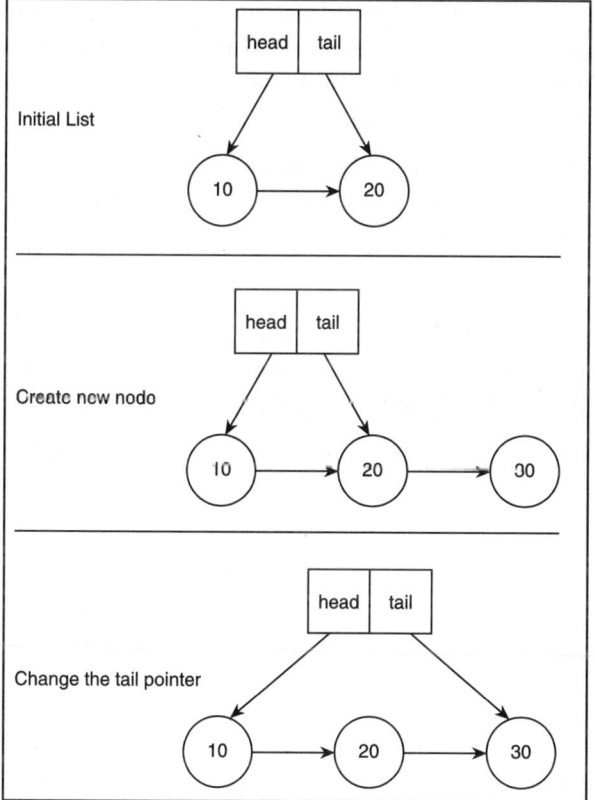

Figure 6.7

This is the process of adding a new node at the end of a singly linked list.

The Prepend Function

Now that you can add items to the end of a linked list, wouldn't it be cool to be able to add items to the beginning? This method is called *prepending*.

```
void Prepend( Datatype p_data )
{
    // create the new node.
    SListNode<Datatype>* newnode = new SListNode<Datatype>;
    newnode->m_data = p_data;
    newnode->m_next = m_head;
    // set the head node and the tail node if needed.
    m_head = newnode;
    if( m_tail == 0 )
        m_tail = m_head;
    m_count++;
}
```

This method is actually a little bit simpler. First, you create a new node and initialize it. Then, you tell it to point to the head node in the list. Now the m_head pointer is still pointing to the old head node, so you need to update it to point to the new node. Note that this algorithm works even if the list is empty because m_head was 0 and the new nodes' m_next pointer will also end up being 0.

You still need to check if the list was empty, though. If the list was empty, then m_tail will also be 0, so you need to update it to point to the head. Figure 6.8 shows the process.

The RemoveHead Function

As you can see with the Append function, adding nodes to the beginning of a linked list is easy to do. Removing nodes from the beginning of a list is easy as well.

```
void RemoveHead()
{
    SListNode<Datatype>* node = 0;
    if( m_head != 0 )
    {
        // make node point to the next node.
        node = m_head->m_next;
        // then delete the head and make the pointer
        // point to node.
```

```
        delete m_head;
        m_head = node;
        // if the head is null, then you've just deleted the only node
        // in the list. set the tail to 0.
        if( m_head == 0 )
            m_tail = 0;
        m_count--;
    }
}
```

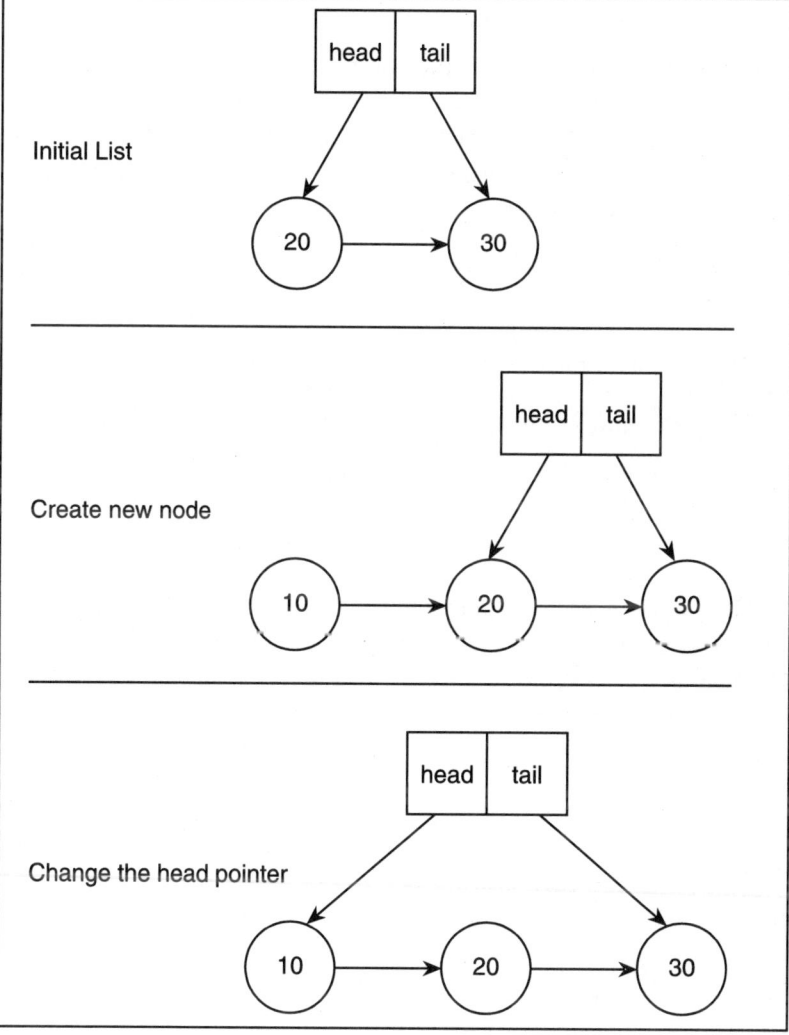

Figure 6.8

This is the process of adding a new node to the front of a singly linked list.

All you need to do is delete the first node and move the head pointer up to point to the next node in the list. There are two special cases, though. First of all, the list might be empty. In that case, do nothing. In the second case, there might be only one node left in the list. In that case, delete the node and set the head and tail pointers to 0.

The RemoveTail Function

Unfortunately, removing the tail of a singly linked list is much more difficult than removing the head. When you remove the head of the list, all you need to do is update the head pointer to point to the next node. This task is easy because the head node already has a pointer to the next node.

When you remove the tail node, you want to make the tail pointer point to the previous node in the list. This is a problem because a singly linked list node doesn't point to the previous node. Instead, you need to go through the entire list and find the previous node. This makes the `RemoveTail` algorithm much slower than the `RemoveHead` algorithm because it needs to do searching.

```cpp
void RemoveTail()
{
    SListNode<Datatype>* node = m_head;
    // if the list isn't empty, then remove a node.
    if( m_head != 0 )
    {
        // if the head is equal to the tail, then
        // the list has 1 node, and you are removing it.
        if( m_head == m_tail )
        {
            // delete the node and set both pointers
            // to 0.
            delete m_head;
            m_head = m_tail = 0;
        }
        else
        {
            // skip ahead until you find the node
            // right before the tail node
            while( node->m_next != m_tail )
```

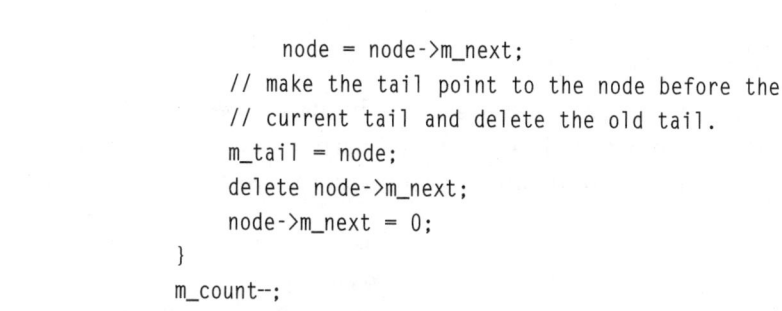

```
            node = node->m_next;
        // make the tail point to the node before the
        // current tail and delete the old tail.
        m_tail = node;
        delete node->m_next;
        node->m_next = 0;
    }
    m_count--;
}
```

Figure 6.9 shows the process of removing the tail node.

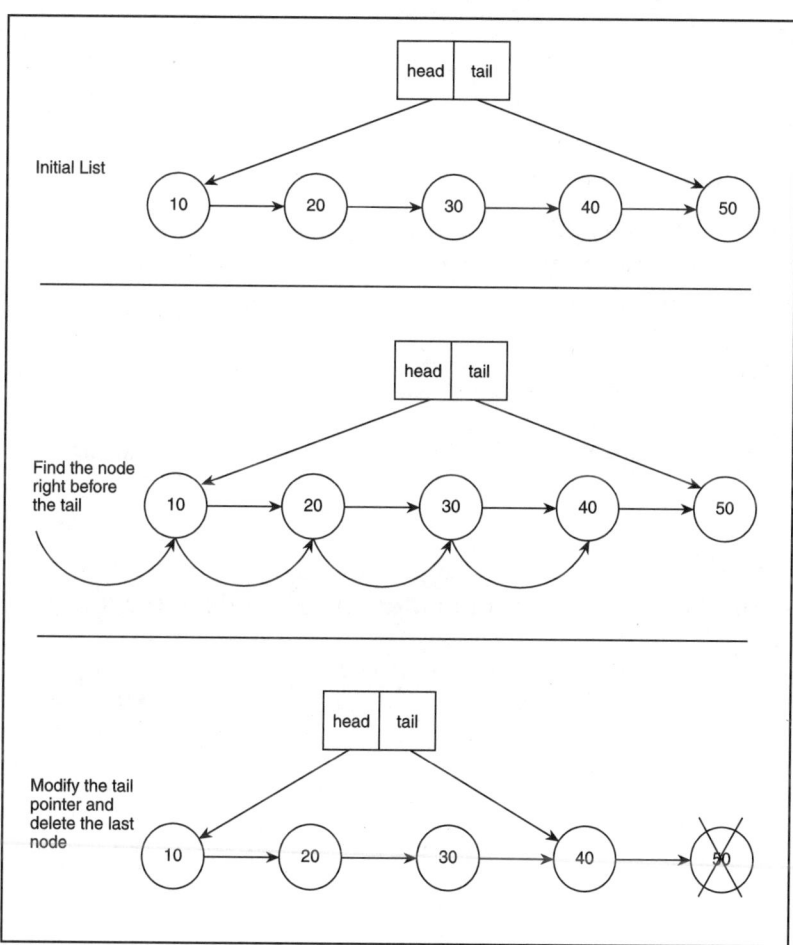

Figure 6.9

This is the process of removing the tail node of a linked list. Note how it is a more involved process than removing the head node.

The SListIterator Class

Now, to interface with your new `SLinkedList` class, you should create an iterator class, which automates the iterator functions I covered earlier. This class contains two things: A pointer to the current node and a pointer to the list that the node is in. You'll see why in a little bit.

```
template<class Datatype>
class SListIterator
{
public:
    SListNode<Datatype>* m_node;
    SLinkedList<Datatype>* m_list;
};
```

The Constructor

The constructor for the `SListIterator` takes two parameters: The list that the iterator is for and the current node of the iterator.

```
SListIterator( SLinkedList<Datatype>* p_list = 0,
               SListNode<Datatype>* p_node = 0 )
{
    m_list = p_list;
    m_node = p_node;
}
```

If the parameters are missing, then they default to 0, making the iterator somewhat worthless.

The Start Function

The `Start` function resets the iterator to point to the very first node in the list.

```
void Start()
{
    if( m_list != 0 )
        m_node = m_list->m_head;
}
```

This is very straightforward: If the list is valid (not 0), then make the iterator point to the head.

The Forth Function

The Forth function moves the iterator to the next node in the list.

```
void Forth()
{
    if( m_node != 0 )
        m_node = m_node->m_next;
}
```

The only time this function does nothing is when the current node is 0. When the current node is 0, then this iterator isn't pointing at anything and is invalid.

The Item Function

This function returns a reference to the item stored in the node that the iterator is pointing to.

```
Datatype& Item()
{
    return m_node->m_data;
}
```

The Valid Function

This function checks to see if the iterator is pointing to a non-0 node. If so, then it returns true; otherwise, it returns false.

```
bool Valid()
{
    return (m_node != 0);
}
```

The GetIterator Function

Now that you've created a basic iterator class, you need a way to be able to generate iterators.

```
SListIterator<Datatype> GetIterator()
{
    return SListIterator<Datatype>( this, m_head );
}
```

This function creates a new iterator pointing to the head of the current list.

Using Iterators

Now that you have the basic functions set, try rewriting Example 6-2 so that you use the SLinkedList and SListIterator classes. This is Example 6-3:

```
// create a new linked list.
SLinkedList<int> list;
// insert 10, 20 and 30.
list.Append( 10 );
list.Append( 20 );
list.Append( 30 );
cout << "the list contains: ";
// create a new iterator and make it point to the
// beginning of the list.
SListIterator<int> itr = list.GetIterator();
// loop through the list while the iterator is valid.
for( itr.Start(); itr.Valid(); itr.Forth() )
{
    cout << itr.Item() << ", ";
}
// reset the iterator to the beginning again.
itr.Start();
```

You should immediately notice that this version of the program is much easier to read and understand than Example 6-2.

The iterator functions make it easy to use a linked list in a for-loop. In the first part of the for-loop, the iterator is reset to the beginning of the list. Then it loops while the iterator is valid and moves the iterator forward by one node each time.

The Insert Function

Now that you have iterators working, you can move on to the more advanced linked list routines. The first is the Insert function, which inserts a node after an iterator. This function allows you to insert nodes into the list at any position you like.

```
// inserts an item after the current iterator or appends
// data if iterator is invalid.
void Insert( SListIterator<Datatype>& p_iterator, Datatype p_data )
{
    // if the iterator doesn't belong to this list, do nothing.
    if( p_iterator.m_list != this )
```

```
            return;
    if( p_iterator.m_node != 0 )
    {
        // if the iterator is valid, then insert the node
        p_iterator.m_node->InsertAfter( p_data );
        // if the iterator is the tail node, then
        // update the tail pointer to point to the
        // new node.
        if( p_iterator.m_node == m_tail )
        {
            m_tail = p_iterator.m_node->m_next;
        }
        m_count++;
    }
    else
    {
        // if the iterator is invalid, just append the data
        Append( p_data );
    }
}
```

The first thing you need to do is to make sure that the iterator that was passed in is an iterator for this list. You don't want an iterator belonging to a different list to be passed into this list, right? So if the iterator doesn't match, the function just returns and doesn't do anything. A more complex system would probably return an error code or throw an exception, but that is outside the scope of this book.

When you are sure that the iterator belongs to this list, there are two major conditions for this function: The iterator can be valid, or it can be invalid.

If the iterator is valid, then all you need to do is insert the node after the iterator. Because the function only inserts nodes *after* the iterator, the function can never insert a node in front of the head node. However, because the function can put a node at the end of the list, you need to check if it did so and update the tail pointer accordingly.

If the iterator isn't valid, I prefer to append the node at the end of the list, so you just call the Append function.

The Remove Function

The Remove function is the most complicated of all of the singly linked list functions. The reason for this is because of the nature of a singly linked list node: It only points to the next node. If you want to remove any node within a list, you need to find the previous node first and link that up to the next node in the list, like the Singly Linked List demo shows you.

```cpp
void Remove( SListIterator<Datatype>& p_iterator )
{
    SListNode<Datatype>* node = m_head;
    // if the iterator doesn't belong to this list, do nothing.
    if( p_iterator.m_list != this )
        return;
    // if node is invalid, do nothing.
    if( p_iterator.m_node == 0 )
        return;
    if( p_iterator.m_node == m_head )
    {
        // move the iterator forward and delete the head.
        p_iterator.Forth();
        RemoveHead();
    }
    else
    {
        // scan forward through the list until you find
        // the node prior to the node you want to remove
        while( node->m_next != p_iterator.m_node )
            node = node->m_next;
        // move the iterator forward.
        p_iterator.Forth();
        // if the node you are deleting is the tail,
        // update the tail node.
        if( node->m_next == m_tail )
        {
            m_tail = node;
        }
        // delete the node.
        delete node->m_next;
        // re-link the list.
        node->m_next = p_iterator.m_node;
    }
```

```
        m_count--;
    }
```

The first thing you check is to see if the iterator is valid. If it isn't, then you just return and don't do anything.

One thing I want to call attention to is the behavior of the iterator. When you inserted a node using an iterator, the iterator stayed pointing to the same node. However, you can't do that when you are removing nodes. You are left with two options. You can either invalidate the iterator or move the iterator to the next item in the list. I prefer the second method, so whenever you remove a node, the iterator will be moved forward to the next node.

Figure 6.10 illustrates this process.

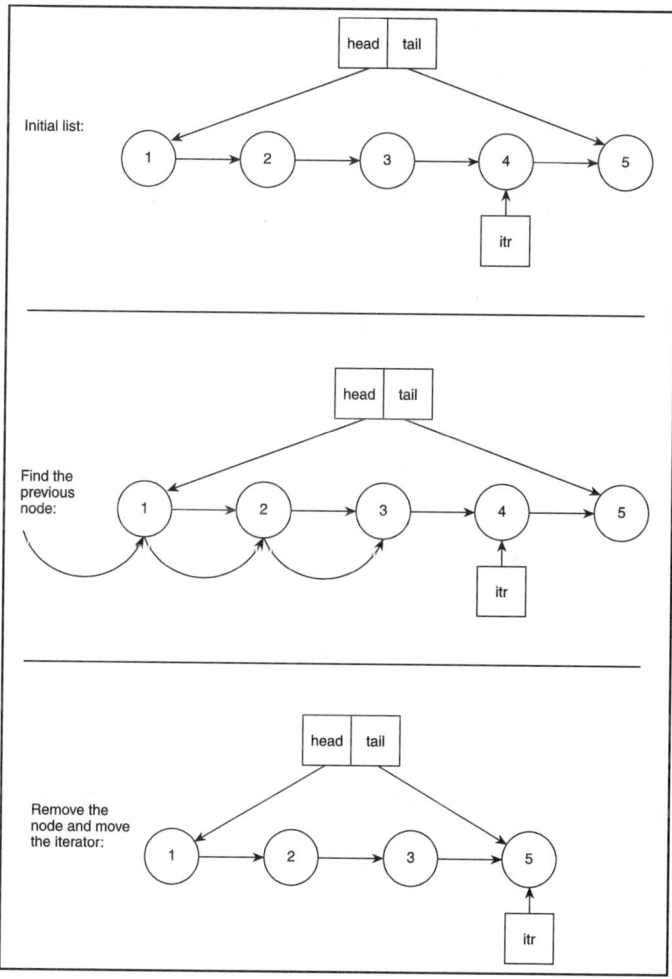

Figure 6.10

This shows how to remove a node that an iterator is pointing to. It is similar to removing the tail of a list.

The algorithm then loops through the list until you find the node prior to the node you want to remove. Remember, you did this with the `RemoveTail` function as well, because the node doesn't point back to the prior node.

So before you actually delete the node, you move the iterator forward and make it point to the next node in the list. This method is nice because it allows you to iterate through a list and remove selected items at a whim, and you don't have to reset the iterator every time you delete an item.

Finally, you delete the node and tell the node prior to it to point to the node after the node you just removed.

> **CAUTION**
> The last step in the Remove algorithm is very important. If you don't relink the list, the last half of the list will essentially be lost. Not only can you not access the data anymore, but it is a memory leak as well because you cannot delete it.

Example 6-4

Now that you've completed the `SlinkedList` class, I can demonstrate the advanced features of the iterators. This is Example 6-4. (It can be found on the CD in the directory \examples\ch06\04 - Using SLinkedList\.)

```
// create a new linked list.
SLinkedList<int> list;
SListIterator<int> itr;
// insert 10, 30 and 40.
list.Append( 10 );
list.Append( 30 );
list.Append( 40 );
PrintList( list );
// use the iterator to insert 20 between 10 and 30.
itr = list.GetIterator();
list.Insert( itr, 20 );
PrintList( list );
// use the iterator to remove 30.
itr.Forth();
itr.Forth();
list.Remove( itr );
PrintList( list );
```

`PrintList` is a simple function that just iterates through the list and prints out what it contains. It really isn't much more than the `for`-loop that was used in Example 6-3, so I do not list it here.

In the first code block after the list and the iterator declarations, you append 10, 30, and 40 to the list in that order and print it out. That was simple—you've seen the Append function before.

In the second code block, you get an iterator and reset it to the beginning of list. At this point, itr should be pointing to 10. Now you call the Insert function on the list and insert 20 right after 10, making the list 10, 20, 30, 40.

Finally, in the third code block, you move the iterator forward by two places so that it points to 30 and then remove it. This gives you 10, 20, 40.

Final Thoughts on Singly Linked Lists

Now that you've seen the structure and the usage of singly linked lists, I can make a few observations about them.

First of all, the most obvious strength is that you can insert and delete items from a singly linked list quite quickly. With an array, you are forced to move lots of data around to insert an item, but you don't have to do any of that with a linked list.

Another strength is the ability to expand to indefinite sizes. You can store as many items within a linked list as you want to, as long as you have enough memory to do so.

The major downside is that you cannot access items within the list like you can with an array. You can only use an iterator to go through the list, and you can only go from start to finish. This limitation makes linked lists somewhat less useful than arrays in some instances.

Doubly Linked Lists

Now you can move on to the most common linked lists: *doubly linked lists*. Whereas a singly linked list only had one pointer per node, a doubly linked list has two pointers per node. (Bet you didn't see that one coming!) The second pointer in a doubly linked list node is a pointer to the previous node in the list. Figure 6.11 shows a four-node doubly linked list.

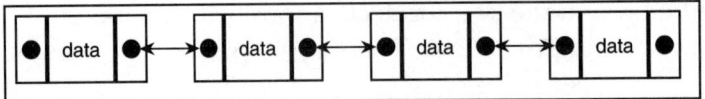

Figure 6.11

A four-node doubly linked list is a more complex version of a singly linked list. Each node now has two pointers, instead of just one.

Most of the algorithms involving a doubly linked list are very similar to the singly linked versions, so we won't spend much time discussing them. I'll mainly go over the important additions or differences between the algorithms, because the concepts are all basically the same for both types of lists.

Graphical Demonstration: Doubly Linked Lists

You can find the graphical demonstration for doubly linked lists on the CD in the directory \demonstrations\ch06\Demo02 - Doubly Linked List\. This demo is very similar to the singly linked list demo. It has a few new buttons, though, as Figure 6.12 shows.

> ### Compiling the Demo
>
> This demonstration uses the SDLGUI library that I have developed for the book. For more information about this library, see Appendix B.
>
> To compile this demo, either open up the workspace file in the directory or create your own project using the settings described in Appendix B. If you create your own project, all of the files you need to include are in the directory.

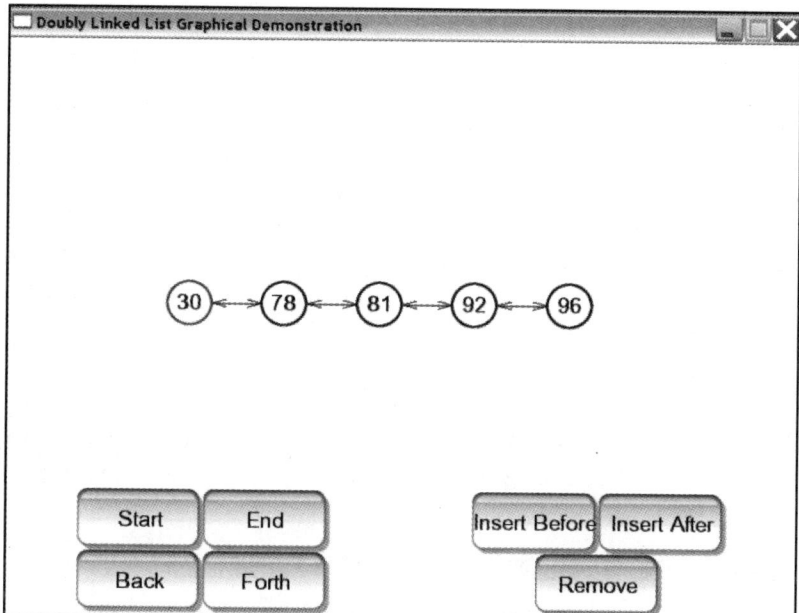

Figure 6.12

This is a screenshot from the Doubly Linked List Graphical Demonstration.

On the left are two new buttons: Back and End. The Back button moves the iterator to the previous node in the list, and the End button moves the iterator to the end of the list.

On the right is one new button: Insert Before. This button inserts a new node before the current node.

Creating a Doubly Linked List

The classes used for doubly linked lists are the same as those used for the singly linked lists, with minor changes. You change the S to a D to denote that the list is doubly linked. The classes are all located in \structures\DLinkedList.h.

Because the two different lists are so similar in nature, I describe doubly linked lists differently, without code, instead of just pasting all the code into the book. If you really must see the code, then please follow along by reading the code from the CD, but it shouldn't be necessary.

The Node Structure

As I stated earlier, each linked list node has two pointers instead of just one. The additional pointer points to the previous node on the list. Figure 6.13 shows a doubly linked list node.

6. Linked Lists

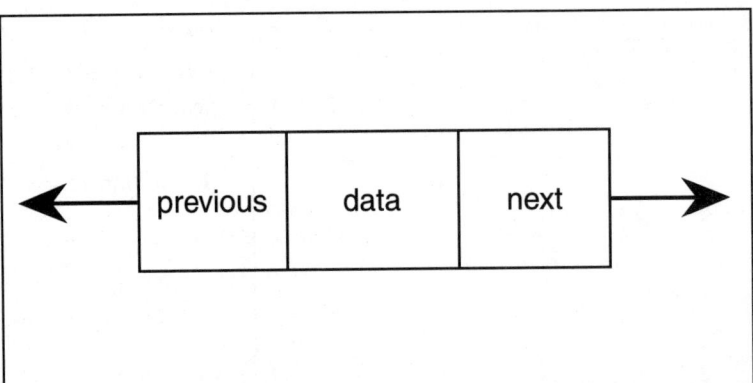

Figure 6.13

This is a doubly linked list node.

Because a doubly linked list node has two pointers, it is a little more complicated to add and remove nodes from the list because there are more pointers to rearrange.

Doubly Linked List Algorithms

I'll now briefly cover the most common algorithms used on doubly linked lists: insertion and removal of nodes. All of the other algorithms (remove head or tail, append, prepend) are based on the same concepts. As with the SLinkedList class, all the code is on the CD if you need to see these algorithms in action.

Inserting a Node

The method for inserting a node into a doubly linked list is slightly more complex than the singly linked list method. If you are inserting node *N* between nodes *L* (left) and *R* (right), the basic algorithm follows these steps:

1. Create a new node, *N*.
2. Make *N*'s previous pointer point to *L*.
3. Make *N*'s next pointer point to *R*.
4. If *L* exists, make *L*'s next pointer point to *N*.
5. If *R* exists, make *R*'s previous pointer point to *N*.

Figure 6.14 shows this process.

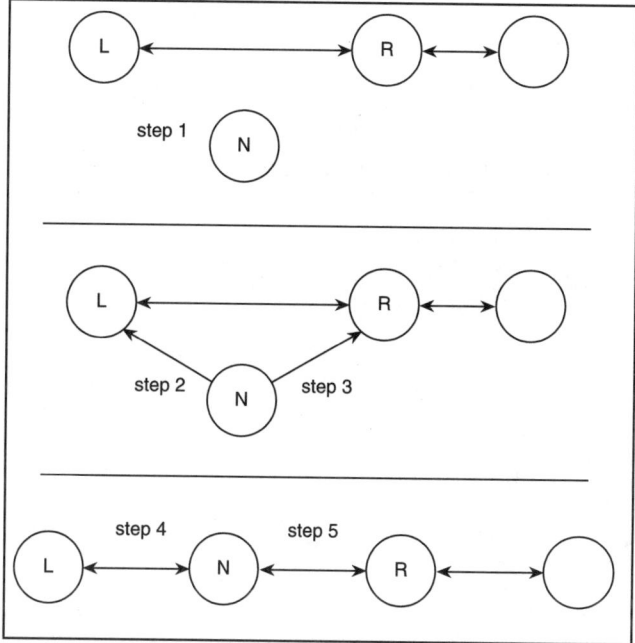

Figure 6.14

This is how you insert a node into a doubly linked list.

Because you might be inserting a node at the front or the end of the list, the `if` statements in Steps 4 and 5 are important. If you're inserting a node at the front of the list, then node *L* doesn't exist. The same applies with the end, in which case *R* doesn't exist.

If you compared this algorithm to the singly linked version, Steps 2 and 5 wouldn't exist.

Removing a Node

This algorithm differs the most from the singly linked list version. In a singly linked list, you had to search the list for the node prior to the node you wanted to remove because the node didn't know which node was behind it. Because each node in a doubly linked list points back to the prior node, you can use that information and simply remove the node without searching through the list.

If you are removing node *N*, which is in between nodes *L* and *R*, the algorithm is as follows:

1. If *L* exists, make *L*'s next pointer point to *R*.
2. If *R* exists, make *R*'s previous pointer point to *L*.
3. Delete *N*.

This process is demonstrated in Figure 6.15.

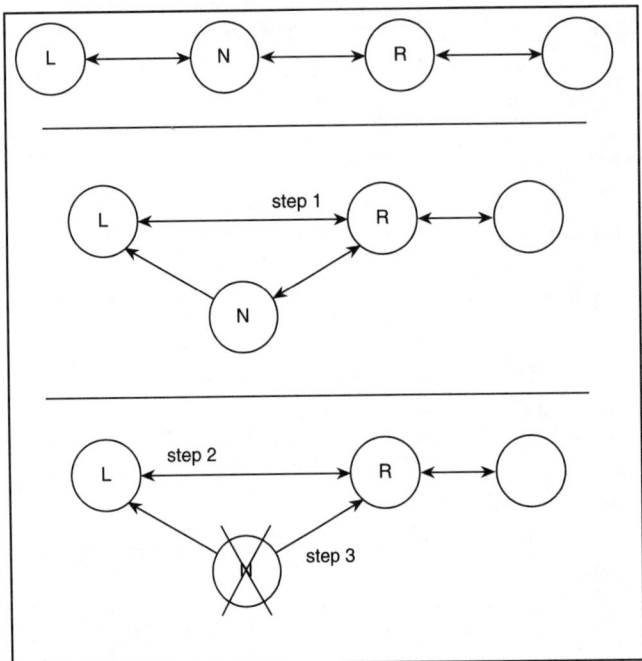

Figure 6.15

This is how you remove a mode from a doubly linked list.

As you can see, removing a node from a doubly linked list is much easier.

Reading and Writing Lists to Disk

In Chapter 3, when I showed you how to read and write arrays onto disk, it was nice and easy because C file functions work directly with arrays. With linked lists, you have no such luck; you have to make your own. Luckily, it is not that difficult to read and write linked lists. I'll show you how to read and write SLinkedLists to disk but not DLinkedLists. Don't worry, though; the algorithms are virtually identical for each list type.

Writing a Linked List

The process for writing the contents of a linked list to disk is simple: You create an iterator, iterate through the list, and store the contents of every node into the file.

Because lists have a variable size, it is often a good idea to store the number of nodes that are being written to the file first. This way, when it comes time to read the list back in, the algorithm first reads the number of nodes stored in the file and then reads all the nodes in.

Here is the `SaveToDisk` function in `SLinkedList`:

```
1:  bool SaveToDisk( char* p_filename )
2:  {
3:      FILE* outfile = 0;
4:      SListNode* itr = m_head;
5:      outfile = fopen( p_filename, "wb" );
6:      if( outfile == 0 )
7:          return false;
8:      fwrite( &m_count, sizeof( int ), 1, outfile );
9:      while( itr != 0 )
10:     {
11:         fwrite( &(itr->m_data), sizeof( Datatype ), 1, outfile );
12:         itr = itr->m_next;
13:     }
14:     fclose( outfile );
15:     return true;
16: }
```

You open the file, like you did last time, in "write binary" mode. However, instead of just writing the list, you first write the size of the list on line 8. After that, you loop through the list on lines 9–13 and write the data at each node.

Line 11 is where the actual writing is accomplished. The first parameter to `fwrite` is a pointer to the data that you want to write. Because you want to write the data in the iterator, you use the & operator to get a pointer to the data. The second parameter is the size of the data. Because you don't know the size of the datatype, you use the `sizeof` operator to calculate that automatically. The next parameter is the number of items you are writing to disk, which is 1, because you can only write one node at a time. The last parameter is a pointer to the file.

Reading a Linked List

Reading a linked list is a little more involved than writing one. First, you need to read in the number of nodes that were saved to the file. Then you need to read in each of the nodes from the disk into a temporary buffer. Finally, you append that buffer to the list and repeat the process.

Here is the code:

```
1:   bool ReadFromDisk( char* p_filename )
2:   {
3:       FILE* infile = 0;
4:       Datatype buffer;
5:       int count = 0;
6:       infile = fopen( p_filename, "rb" );
7:       if( infile == 0 )
8:           return false;
9:       fread( &count, sizeof( int ), 1, infile );
10:      while( count != 0 )
11:      {
12:          fread( &buffer, sizeof( Datatype ), 1, infile );
13:          Append( buffer );
14:          count--;
15:      }
16:      fclose( infile );
17:      return true;
18:  }
```

The first thing you do is read in the size of the list on line 9. Then you enter a loop which decrements the count variable until it is zero, reading in a node at a time. The function reads each node into the buffer and appends the buffer to the end of the list.

It is a little more work to read and write linked lists, but it is still pretty easy. The DLinkedList file algorithms are literally exactly the same, and there is no need to show them here.

> **NOTE**
> The beauty of these methods is that you can swap the different containers at will. Data saved from a singly linked list can be loaded into an array (you need to ignore the leading size variable, though) or a doubly linked list, and vice versa.

Application: Game Inventories

This is Game Demonstration 6-1, and it can be found on the CD in the directory \demonstrations\ch06\Game01 - Inventories\.

Application: Game Inventories

> ### Compiling the Demo
>
> This demonstration uses the SDLHelpers library that I have developed for the book. For more information about this library, see Appendix B.
>
> To compile this demo, either open up the workspace file in the directory or create your own project using the settings described in Appendix B. If you create your own project, all of the files you need to include are in the directory.

The main use of a linked list in games involves things for which you don't want to have a finite limit. For example, in a role-playing game, you could make it so that the player can only carry 32 items and give him a 32-item array, but why would you want to? Why should he be limited to 32 items? What happens if your game has different types of characters that can gradually carry more items as they grow stronger?

For a solution to this problem, I look at linked lists, which are good at storing any number of items.

The Player Class

Your simple game player will only have two attributes: the weight of all the items he can carry and the weight of all the items he is currently carrying. For the inventory, you'll use a doubly linked list.

```
class Player
{
public:
    int m_weightMax;
    int m_currentWeight;
    DLinkedList<Item> m_inventory;
};
```

The Item Class

The Item class will also be very simple and will only have two attributes: the type of the item and the weight of the item. The type will be a number from 0–7 because I have 8 different kinds of items in this demo. The weight will be a randomly generated number from 10–20. (See Chapter 22, "Random Numbers," for more information about random numbers.)

```
class Item
{
public:
    int m_type;
    int m_weight;
};
```

Adding an Item to the Inventory

Whenever the player picks up a new item, you want to add that to the inventory. In this demo, I use an algorithm that randomly generates a weight for a given item type and adds it to the player's inventory:

```
 1: void AddItem( int p_type )
 2: {
 3:     Item item;
 4:     item.m_type = p_type;
 5:     item.m_weight = rand() % 11 + 10;
 6:     if( item.m_weight + g_player.m_currentWeight < g_player.m_weightMax )
 7:     {
 8:         g_player.m_inventory.Append( item );
 9:         g_player.m_currentWeight += item.m_weight;
10:     }
11: }
```

The user passes in an item type as a parameter, which is set on line 4. A random weight from 10–20 is generated on line 5.

On line 6, you see if the item is too heavy to pick up or not. If it is too heavy, then you do nothing. If it isn't, you add the item to the inventory list. You also update the player's current weight on line 9.

Not too difficult, is it? The easiest part is using the Append function—it adds the item to the inventory automatically, and you don't have to worry about overflowing anything!

Removing an Item from the Inventory

Removing an item is somewhat more difficult than adding an item because you can remove any item in your inventory at any time. Therefore, you need some method of specifying which item to remove.

In the demo, you keep track of a *current* item, and you can only remove the current item. You keep track of it by using an iterator. Whenever you want to remove the item, you pass the iterator into the function:

```
1: void RemoveItem( DListIterator<Item> p_itr )
2: {
3:     if( p_itr.Valid() )
4:     {
5:         g_player.m_currentWeight -= p_itr.Item().m_weight;
6:         g_player.m_inventory.Remove( p_itr );
7:     }
8: }
```

So the user passes in an iterator pointing to the player's linked list. The algorithm then determines if the iterator is valid on line 3, and if so, it proceeds to subtract the items weight from the player's weight and then removes the item from the list.

Playing the Demo

When the demo starts out, you are given one sword in your inventory. Figure 6.16 shows a screenshot of the program. The icons at the bottom represent the eight different items you can add to your inventory. The line of items in the middle of the screen represent your inventory. The item within the black box represents the current item in your inventory.

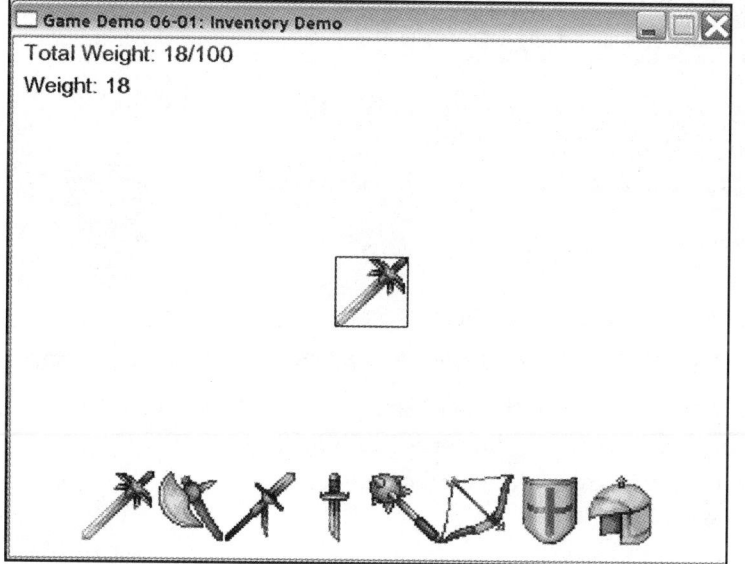

Figure 6.16

This is a screenshot from Game Demonstration 6-1.

The demo is compiled so that you can only hold a weight of 100, so you can add up to 10 items to your inventory if they each weigh 10 units.

Table 6.1 lists the commands that are used in the game.

Table 6.1 Inventory Demo Controls

Action	Effect
Clicking on icons on bottom	Adds item to inventory
Clicking in black box	Removes current item from inventory
Pressing left arrow key	Moves focus to previous inventory item
Pressing right arrow key	Moves focus to next inventory item
Pressing up arrow key	Increases player's capacity by 50
Pressing down arrow key	Decreases player's capacity by 50

The game is pretty simple and is meant to just demonstrate having a flexible number of items in your inventory.

Application: Layered Tilemaps Revisited

This is Game Demo 6-2, and the files for it are located on the CD in the directory \demonstrations\ch06\Game02 - Layered Tilemapping\.

Compiling the Demo

This demonstration uses the SDLHelpers library that I have developed for the book. For more information about this library, see Appendix B.

To compile this demo, either open up the workspace file in the directory or create your own project using the settings described in Appendix B. If you create your own project, all of the files you need to include are in the directory.

Application: Layered Tilemaps Revisited

In Chapter 5, "Multi-Dimensional Arrays," I showed you how to use 3D arrays to represent a layered tilemap. The biggest flaw with that method, however, was that it wasted space for layers that are mostly blank.

Using a 2D array of linked lists can solve this problem.

For example, say you have an 8 × 8 map. You want the top row of the map to have another layer on top of that. Using a 3D array, you'd need to make it 8 × 8 × 2, which is 128 cells. To make things even worse, what if half of those tiles needed another layer on top of them? Then you would need an 8 × 8 × 3 array, which takes up 192 cells, when you're only using 64 + 8 + 4 of them, which is 76 cells. That means you're only using 40 percent of the cells that are in the array for anything useful, which is a big waste of space.

Now, what would happen if you made a 2D array and stored a linked list in each of the cells in the array? If you wanted to create the map that I just described, it would look something like Figure 6.17.

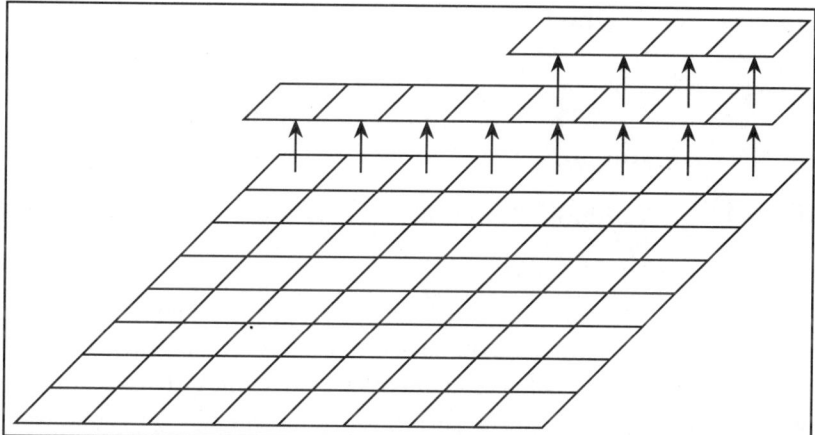

Figure 6.17

Here is a 2D array of linked lists. This allows you to have an infinite number of layers on each tile, without wasting space.

As you can see, you use the linked list structure to conserve space that would otherwise be wasted. Any cell that only has one layer only has one node in its linked list. The top right cell has three nodes in its linked list.

Declaring the Tilemap

Take a look at how this tilemap would be defined:

```
Array2D< SLinkedList<int> > g_tilemap( MAPWIDTH, MAPHEIGHT );
```

This definition creates a 2D array of singly linked lists. The 2D array has dimensions `MAPWIDTH` and `MAPHEIGHT`, which are constants defined in the demo program.

As before, each tile will be an integer, which will determine which tile graphic is drawn.

> **NOTE**
> Please take notice of the space between the two > brackets. It is very important that you place the space there. Otherwise, the compiler will see the >> operator, which will cause a compiler error.

Creating the Tilemap

Now that you've defined the tilemap, you need to fill it with values. You'll use the same map that you used in Game Demonstration 5-2, so you can see how similar this method is to the 3D method.

Remember back to the 3D array method:

```
g_tilemap.Get( x, y, 0 ) = rand() % 4;
```

This line set the tile at (x, y, 0) to a random number from 0–3. Layer 0 was the lowest layer, and tiles 0–3 are grass tiles.

Using an array, the line looks only slightly different:

```
g_tilemap.Get( x, y ).Append( rand() % 4 );
```

Because you're using a 2D array this time, you don't access a specific layer number; instead, you just access a cell within the 2D array at coordinates (x, y) and add a new node to the list stored in that cell. This isn't really an earth-shattering change; it's actually quite cool.

So whenever you want to add another layer on top of a given tile, all you need to do is append another tile to the list! This way, some tiles can have as many layers as you want, and others will only have one, and no space will be wasted!

Drawing the Tilemap

Drawing the tilemap in this layout is a little different than drawing it with a 3D array. When you used a 3D array, you drew the entire bottom layer first, and then the next layer up, and so on until all layers were drawn.

Because you're using linked lists now, you can't really draw each layer individually. This time, you loop through each x and y coordinate in the map and draw every layer for the current tile. Here is the algorithm used with linked lists:

```
1:  void DrawTilemap( int p_x, int p_y )
2:  {
3:      int x, y;
4:      int bx = p_x;
5:      int by = p_y;
6:      int index;
7:      SListIterator<int> itr;
8:      for( y = 0; y < MAPHEIGHT; y++ )
9:      {
10:         for( x = 0; x < MAPWIDTH; x++ )
11:         {
12:             itr = g_tilemap.Get( x, y ).GetIterator();
13:             for( itr.Start(); itr.Valid(); itr.Forth() )
14:             {
15:                 index = itr.Item();
16:                 SDLBlit( g_tiles[index], g_window, bx, by );
17:             }
18:             bx += TILESIZE;
19:         }
20:         bx = p_x;
21:         by += TILESIZE;
22:     }
23: }
```

The main difference with this algorithm when compared to the 3D array version is that the x and the y loops are on the outside and the layer loop (previously z) is on the inside. The important changes are in bold; the rest of the algorithm is unchanged.

Instead of a z coordinate, I now have an iterator, `itr`. For every tile, I get an iterator pointing at the list in that tile (line 12). On the next line, I start a for-loop that loops through each layer on the current tile.

Remember in the 3D array version when I checked to see if the current tile number was -1? I did this because some tiles might be invalid, and I did not draw them if they were. This time, I don't need to check for that because there are no invalid tiles. The linked list structure only stores valid tile numbers, so I can assume that every tile is valid.

Analysis and Comparison of Linked Lists

This was a long chapter, but it was packed full of information. You learned about two variations of the linked list data structure and two uses of them in game programming. You might, however, be surprised to learn that this is nowhere near the end of it. There are many more variations of lists, but most of them serve very specific purposes, so they aren't used too often in the real world. My favorite variation is the *circular doubly linked list*, and I would advise you to look further into that if you are interested.

Algorithm Comparisons

I would like to now show you a chart that details the strengths and weaknesses of the three general linear structures I've analyzed: arrays, singly linked lists, and doubly linked lists. This is Table 6.2.

Table 6.2 The Linear Data Structures Compared

Algorithm	Array	Singly Linked	Doubly Linked
Resize	$O(n)$	*	*
Insertion	$O(n)$	$O(c)$	$O(c)$
Removal	$O(n)$	$O(n)$	$O(c)$
Fast Removal	$O(c)$	**	**
Append	$O(c)/O(n)$***	$O(c)$	$O(c)$
Prepend	$O(n)$	$O(c)$	$O(c)$
Remove Tail	$O(c)$	$O(n)$	$O(c)$
Remove Head	$O(n)$	$O(c)$	$O(c)$
Access Random Index	$O(c)$	$O(n)$	$O(n)$

* Resize for lists is not a specific algorithm, it is automatically performed in the Insertion and Removal algorithms.

** Lists do not need the Fast Removal algorithm.

*** With arrays, if there isn't enough room to store the new item, Append becomes $O(n)$ but Prepend stays the same. Technically, the prepend algorithm will take twice as long, but the constant 2 is ignored.

If the $O(n)$ and $O(c)$ notation doesn't look familiar, please go back and read Chapter 1, "Basic Algorithm Analysis"; it has all the information you need about algorithm analysis.

Basically, $O(c)$ means that the algorithm completes itself quickly and doesn't depend on the number of items in the array or list. $O(n)$ is slower than $O(c)$, however, because the amount of time that it takes to complete depends on the number of items in the array or list.

The first thing that you should notice from Table 6.2 is that the different structures have different strengths and weaknesses. You can access any given index in an array instantly, which you cannot do with a list. On the other hand, inserting an item into an array is slower than inserting an item into a list. Finally, the two types of lists themselves have differences; removing a node from a doubly linked list is far faster than removing a node from a singly linked list.

Size Comparisons

Another downside that isn't apparent from looking at Table 6.2 is the size of the structure. You might think that an array, a singly linked list, and a doubly linked list all holding 2,000 integers would all be the same size, but that is not the case.

An array that has a capacity of 2,000 cells will take up 8,000 bytes of memory (assuming you are using 32-bit integers, which are 4 bytes each).

A singly linked list will take up 16,000 bytes of memory, though! Why is this? Remember that each node in a linked list has two items: the data and the pointer. On 32-bit systems, the pointers are 32 bits, and if you are using integers, so is the data. So you end up using 2 * 4 * 2,000 bytes of memory, or twice as much as an array of the same size!

If that wasn't bad enough, a doubly linked list takes three times as much memory as the array because it has two pointers per node. That puts it at 24,000 bytes of memory!

This concept in linked lists is called *overhead*. Table 6.3 shows how much overhead each of the structures has, based on the number of items in the structure.

Table 6.3 Data Structure Overhead

Structure	Overhead (Bytes)
Array	x * s
Singly Linked List	n * 4
Doubly Linked List	n * 8

x is the number of cells that are unused in an array. s is the size of the data structure in bytes. n is the number of items in the data structure.

Just to get an idea of how overhead is measured, let's compare the different structures with two different datatypes. The first datatype is a plain integer, which is 4 bytes. The second datatype is an imaginary complex character within a computer game, which takes up 1,024 bytes. Table 6.4 shows the overhead of the node pointers in each of the lists.

Table 6.4 Overhead Comparison

Datatype	1L-List Size	1L-List %	2L-List Size	2L-List %
int	n * 8	50%	n * 12	66%
player	n * 1,028	0.39%	n * 1032	0.78%

As you can see from the table, 50 percent of the space in a singly linked list of integers is wasted on the nodes. That's half of the entire space! It gets even worse with a doubly linked list—66 percent of the space used is for nodes in a list of integers!

This isn't so bad, though. Look at the second row now, where you use a list of players instead of integers. The size of the player far outweighs the size of the node pointers, so the amount of space in a list of players that is dedicated to the nodes is much less. In a singly linked list, this turns out to be 0.39 percent. In a doubly linked list, the number is larger, but still relatively small at 0.78 percent.

What kind of conclusion can you make from this? It is far more efficient to store large data structures in linked lists than to store small ones. Of course, you might not care about all of this if you have lots of memory at your disposal.

Real-World Issues

What I'm going to tell you in this section will probably make you want to hit me—hard. Linked lists in games don't have many uses if you want to make your game super fast. The reason for this is caching. Remember when I told you in Chapter 3 about how caches work? They load entire chunks of memory into ultra-fast memory so it can work with the memory quickly. This method works great with arrays, because an array is a chunk of memory.

A linked list is not a chunk of memory, though. Because of the linked nature of lists, the nodes can be anywhere in memory. Figure 6.18 shows an example of linked list nodes in memory. In this figure, each block represents one of the nodes in a seven-node singly linked list. Each one of the shaded blocks represents any number of memory positions separating the nodes in memory.

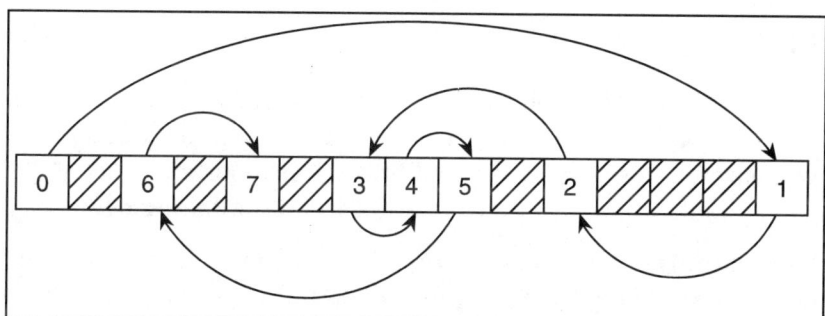

Figure 6.18

The location of nodes in memory isn't continuous. They might be all over the place in memory.

As you can see, the nodes aren't in order. The first node is at the beginning, but the next one is way over at the end of the memory, and the next jumps back again, and the nodes jump all over the place in memory. This isn't like an array at all.

So what ends up happening when you process a linked list is that the cache is constantly swapping blocks of memory in and out, giving the same effect of randomly accessing elements in an array. For this reason, lists are generally slower than arrays when performing small algorithms on every item in the list.

If, on the other hand, you have a large algorithm that does a lot of work on each node in the list, then the overhead of the cache swapping is diminished greatly.

You also must remember that every time you create a new node, you tell the computer to allocate more memory for you, which is slow.

The end result? Don't use linked lists for things that require little processing or things that will be created and destroyed quickly.

For example: Using a linked list to maintain information about the number of bullets flying around in a game at any given time is not worthwhile. The lifetime of a bullet is a few frames at most (1/10 of a second?), so you would have to delete it almost immediately after creating it! You're much better off creating a large array to store all these bullets instead, even if you are limiting yourself to a certain number of bullets in the game at a given time. (Honestly, though, when was the last time you played a game where there were more than 1,000 bullets in the air at any given time?)

Always remember: When you are not sure which data structure you should use, try all the options and benchmark them. If one method slows your game down to a crawl, then it is no good for you. If another structure causes you to code massive amounts of code just to do one thing, you should consider using a different structure.

Conclusion

Most programming books only briefly cover data structure topics, usually ending with a simple introduction to linked lists. Chances are, you've already seen linked lists before. But even if you haven't, this chapter covered linked lists in far more detail than other programming books do, so I hope you have learned something new.

From now on, you'll be learning about data structures that aren't usually seen in general programming books, so there is a lot more you can learn from this book.

CHAPTER 7

STACKS AND QUEUES

The chapters before this one have only been concerned with methods of storing data within a program. This chapter will introduce you to two new abstract structures, which, instead of specifying how data is *stored*, will specify how data is *accessed*. They are the *stack* and the *queue* data structures. Because these structures are very similar in nature, they are both in the same chapter.

In this chapter, you will learn

- What a stack is
- How to implement a stack as a linked list
- How to implement a stack as an array
- How to create a simple menu system using stacks
- What a queue is
- How to implement a queue as a linked list
- How to implement a queue as an array
- How to create a command queue

Stacks

Even if you've never heard of a stack, you've most likely used one. In fact, pretty much every program you've ever written has used a stack. After you have learned what a stack is, check out Appendix B, "The Memory Layout of a Computer Program." That Appendix shows you how stacks are used in all programs.

What Is a Stack?

I'm sure you've eaten at a buffet restaurant before. If not, then let me explain what happens: You go up to the counter, grab a plate from the top of a *stack* of plates, and serve yourself some food. Whenever the restaurant cleans a dish, they put it back onto the stack. Figure 7.1 shows a stack of dishes.

Stacks

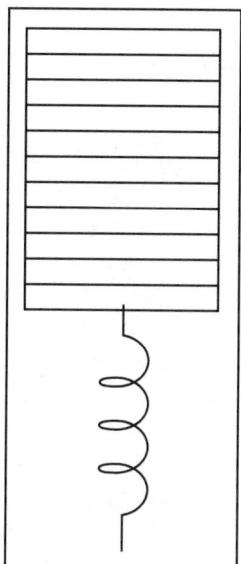

Figure 7.1

A stack of dishes. You can only take a dish from the top or place a new dish on top. The dishes on the bottom are not accessible to you.

There are only two things that you can do with a stack of dishes: You can put a dish on top of it, and you can take a dish off of the top. With computer stacks, putting something on top of the stack is called *pushing*. When you take something off of the top, it is called *popping*.

Stacks are commonly known as *LIFO* structures, which stands for *Last In, First Out*. (Some people call them *FILO* structures—*First In, Last Out*. It means the same thing.) It is called LIFO because the last item that you put into a stack is the first item that is removed. Figure 7.2 shows what happens when you push 3 numbers onto a stack, and then pop them off. The number 10 is pushed first, and then 20, and then 30. Then 30 is popped off, and then 20, and then 10. 30 is the last number put into the stack and the first one removed. This is why a stack is often called LIFO.

> **NOTE**
> In a theoretical stack, the only item that is ever visible is the item at the top of the stack. However, in the real world, you often look at more than just the top of the stack. The computer accesses items below the top of the stack all the time, in fact. (See Appendix B.) For this reason, all of the stack implementations in this book provide ways for you to access more than just the top of the stack.

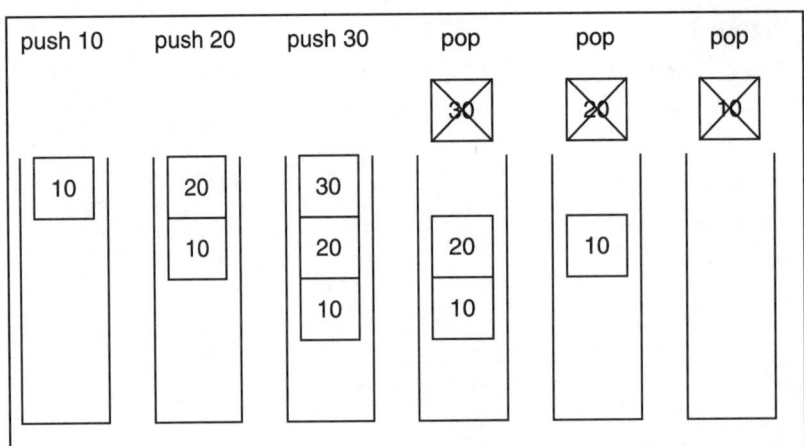

Figure 7.2

This figure shows how to push and pop numbers onto and from a stack.

Graphical Demonstration: Stacks

The graphical demonstration for the stack data structure is on the CD in the directory \demonstrations\cd07\Demo01 – Stacks\. This demo is quite simple and only has two functions: You can push a number onto the stack or you can pop a number off of the stack.

Compiling the Demo

This demonstration uses the SDLGUI library that I have developed for the book. For more information about this library, see Appendix B.

To compile this demo, either open up the workspace file in the directory or create your own project using the settings described in Appendix B. If you create your own project, all of the files you need to include are in the directory.

When the program starts, you are presented with two buttons and an empty stack. You can press the Push button to push numbers into the stack and the Pop button to pop numbers off of the stack. Like I said, it really is simple. Figure 7.3 shows a screenshot from the demo.

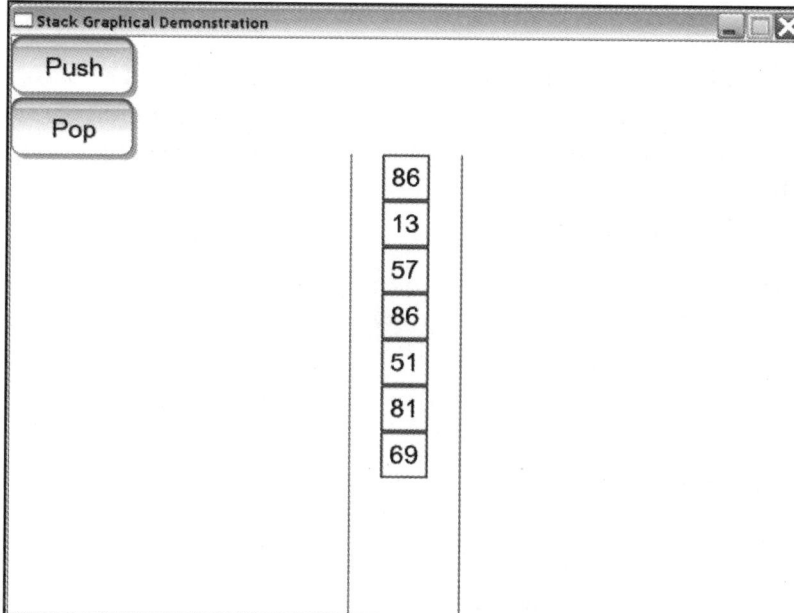

Figure 7.3

Here is a screenshot from the Stack demo.

The Stack Functions

Table 7.1 shows the functions that the stack classes in this book have. All of the stack classes are on the CD in the \structures\stack.h file.

Table 7.1 Stack Functions

Name	Description
Push	This places an item on the top of the stack.
Pop	This removes the item at the top of the stack.
Top	This accesses the item at the top of the stack.
Count	This returns the number of items in the stack.

Implementing a Stack

As I stated before, a stack doesn't define how you *store* data, but rather how you *access* it. Because of this, you can implement a stack in many ways. I show you two ways here, one using linked lists and one using arrays.

Linked Stacks

A *linked stack* uses a linked list to store the data in the stack. Your linked stack class will be called `LStack`. To gain the capabilities of the `DLinkedList` class, your `LStack` class will inherit it. If you are unfamiliar with inheritance, the first section of Chapter 9, "Tying It Together: The Basics," discusses inheritance.

The `LStack` definition (without function definitions) will look like this:

```
template<class Datatype>
class LStack : public DLinkedList<Datatype>
{
public:
};
```

You don't need to add any data at all for this implementation.

If you look at a linked list, you can easily see how you can turn it into a stack. Figure 7.4 shows how you can look at a linked stack. The head of the list points to the bottom of the stack, and the tail of the list points to the top of the stack.

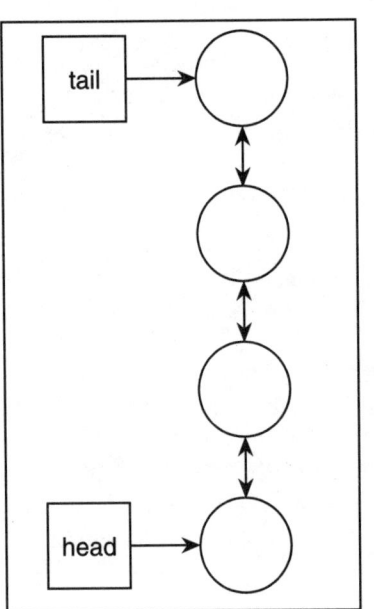

Figure 7.4

You can use a linked list as a stack if you treat the head of the stack as the bottom and the tail as the top of the stack.

The Push Function

Because the `Push` function only places a new item at the top of the stack, all you need to do is call the `Append` function of the linked list, and it will add a new node to the top of the list.

```
void Push( Datatype p_data )
{
    Append( p_data );
}
```

The Pop Function

To pop an item off the top of the stack, all you need to do is remove the tail of the list:

```
void Pop()
{
    RemoveTail();
}
```

The Top Function

Now you need a function that makes it easy to access the top of the stack. This is easy—just return the item that the tail points to:

```
Datatype Top()
{
    return m_tail->m_data;
}
```

> **CAUTION**
> The Top function will not work correctly if the stack is empty. In all likelihood, it will cause the system to crash because you are trying to access an item that doesn't exist. Be careful and make sure that the stack is not empty before you call this function.

The Count Function

Last, you need some way to figure out how many items are in the stack:

```
int Count()
{
    return m_count;
}
```

This just returns the count of the nodes in the linked list.

Using the DLinkedList Functions

Because the LStack class inherited the DLinkedList class, you are able to use any instance of a LStack as a DLinkedList as well. This means that you can create iterators and iterate through the entire stack like a linked list and even remove items from the middle of the stack.

Granted, that is not very stack-like behavior, but it makes the class more flexible. A computer science teacher would probably yell at me for telling you that, though.

Why Use a Linked Stack?

As you can see, a linked list is a nice structure to use when implementing a stack. In fact, I listed it first because it is so easy to implement.

The advantages are that you can push as many items as you want onto the stack without having to worry about running out of room. Also, because every operation is performed at the end of the list, pushing and popping are both O(c) algorithms.

Arrayed Stacks

You can also implement a stack as an array. *Arrayed stacks* are a little bit more difficult to work with than linked stacks, but not by much. The only real limitation they introduce is that they are of a fixed size, but you can use the array's Resize function to make it bigger or smaller as you desire. This class is called the AStack class.

Like the LStack, the AStack will inherit its base structure, which will be an array this time. Unlike the LStack, however, this time a new variable needs to be added. This variable will keep track of the current top of the stack.

```
template<class Datatype>
class AStack : public Array<Datatype>
{
public:
    int m_top;
};
```

If you flip an array so that it is drawn vertically, you can see how it looks like a stack. Figure 7.5 shows how an arrayed stack would look. In an eight-cell array, index 0 is the bottom of the stack, and the top of the stack varies depending on how many items are in the stack. In the stack in the figure, there are five items in the stack, and the m_top index points to the first empty index, which is 5 in this case.

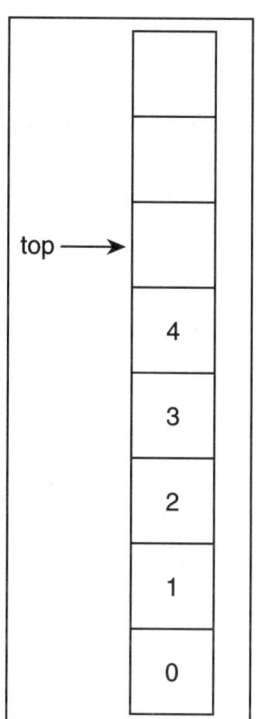

Figure 7.5

You can use an array as a stack by using the lowest index as the bottom of the stack and the higher indexes as the top of the stack.

The Constructor

Because the `Array` class constructor requires an integer as a parameter, so does the `AStack` class. The constructor will also clear the `m_top` variable to 0 because the initial stack will be empty.

```
AStack( int p_size ) : Array<Datatype>( p_size )
{
    m_top = 0;
}
```

The first line uses the standard C++ inherited class constructor notation. It basically says, "I am an `Array`; construct me with size `p_size`." The syntax looks funny, but it's really simple. Then `m_top` is initialized to 0.

An instance of `AStack` is declared like this:

`AStack<int> stack( 10 );`

That creates a stack of integers with 10 cells.

The Push Function

Because the `m_top` index always points at the first empty index, the `Push` function can simply place the new item into that index. After the item is inserted, the `m_top` index can be incremented.

```
bool Push( Datatype p_data )
{
    if( m_size != m_top )
    {
        m_array[m_top] = p_data;
        m_top++;
        return true;
    }
    return false;
}
```

Note that this function returns a bool. The `LStack` class didn't return anything because it never runs out of room, but it is possible for the `AStack` to run out of room. Therefore, when it does run out of room, it returns `false`.

The Pop Function

The `Pop` function is simpler than the `Push` function. Whenever something is popped off the stack, all you need to do is decrement the `m_top` index. You don't need to physically remove the item at all.

```
void Pop()
{
    if( m_top > 0 )
        m_top--;
}
```

However, you do need to check to see if the stack is empty. If `m_top` is 0, then it is empty, and you shouldn't do anything or else you'll end up with a negative `m_top` index. This is a good place to add some error-checking code. You can make the function return an error value.

The Top Function

Because the `m_top` index always points to the first empty cell, subtracting 1 from it will give you the index of the top item in the stack.

```
Datatype Top()
{
```

```
    return m_array[m_top - 1];
}
```

The Count Function

The `m_top` function also tells us how many items are stored in the stack. For example, if `m_top` is 0, the first open index is the very first index in the array, which means that the stack is empty.

```
int Count()
{
    return m_top;
}
```

Why Use an Arrayed Stack?

As you can see, an arrayed stack requires a little more code to implement, but it really isn't a big deal. An arrayed stack is nice because it doesn't have the overhead that a linked stack does.

One of the major disadvantages is the amount of time it takes to resize an arrayed stack because the array resize algorithm is $O(n)$. If you never need to resize the stack, you don't have to worry about this.

Application: Game Menus

This is Game Demo 7-1, which is located on the CD in the directory \demonstrations\ch07\Game01 – Menus\.

> ### Compiling the Demo
>
> This demonstration uses the SDL Helpers library that I have developed for the book. For more information about this library, see Appendix B.
>
> To compile this demo, either open up the workspace file in the directory or create your own project using the settings described in Appendix B. If you create your own project, all of the files you need to include are in the directory.

I'm sure you've played a game that has menus before. Games like *Quake3*, *Half-Life*, and *Doom* all have the menus that I am talking about. If you are unfamiliar with these types of menus, let me explain them a little bit.

During the game, you usually press Escape to bring up an options menu. From this main menu, several options are displayed. Typically, the options allow you to create a new game, save the game, load a new game, or configure game options. Figure 7.6 shows an example of one of these menus.

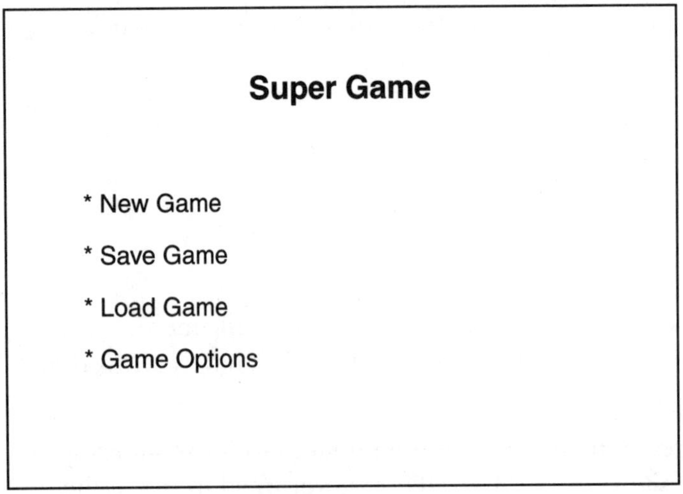

Super Game

* New Game

* Save Game

* Load Game

* Game Options

Figure 7.6

This is a sample game main menu that allows you to perform functions related to the game management or options.

Now that you're at the main menu, you can select one of the options listed, and it will bring up a new menu based on your selection. These are sometimes called *sub-menus*. For example, if you selected Game Options from the main menu, it would bring up something like Figure 7.7.

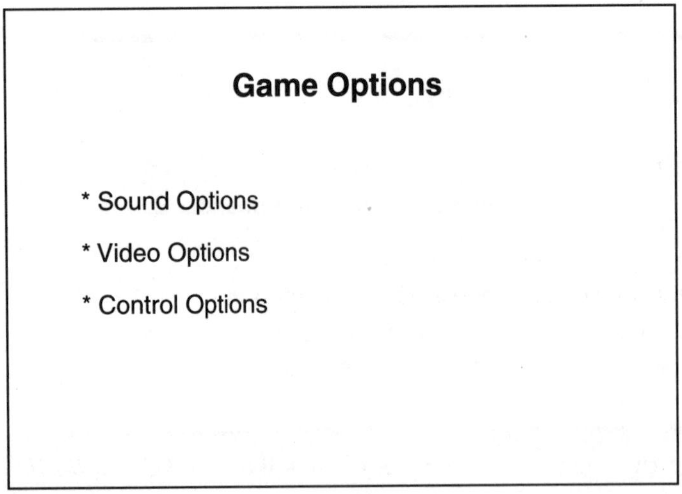

Game Options

* Sound Options

* Video Options

* Control Options

Figure 7.7

This is a sample sub-menu from the main menu.

Now you have several options from this menu: You could press Escape and go back to the main menu or you could choose one of the three options listed, each of which brings up another menu.

It turns out that a stack can model a menu system like this quite easily. Every time you go to a sub-menu from an existing menu, the new menu is created and pushed onto the stack. Every time you press Escape, the current menu is popped off of the stack and you go back to the previous menu. The current menu is always on the top of the stack.

The Stack and the Array

For this demo, I will create a simple Menu class to use, which I go over in the next section. Right now, all you need to know is that is exists.

The demo will use 10 total menus, and the maximum number of menus that can be open at a time is 3. I create an array to store 10 menus and a stack that stores 3 menu pointers:

```
Array<Menu> g_menus( 10 );
AStack<Menu*> g_stack( 3 );
```

When the demo begins, the main menu should be showing, so it is added to the menu stack using the Push function before any menu drawing is done. The main menu is in the g_menus array at index 0.

```
    g_stack.Push( &(g_menus[0]) );
```

Note how the address of the menu is pushed onto the stack because the stack holds menu pointers. This is done to conserve memory; there is no point in copying the menu over.

Creating a Menu Class

You'll be using a very simple menu class for this demo. It will only contain coordinates, a background color, three text strings representing the options, and three indexes of the menus that are spawned from each of the options.

Here is the class listing:

```
class Menu
{
public:
    char* m_options[3];
    int m_optionSpawns[3];
```

```
    int m_x;
    int m_y;
    int m_w;
    int m_h;
    SDL_Color m_color;
};
```

The `m_options` array holds pointers to strings, and the `m_optionsSpawns` array holds indexes. For example, if `m_options[0]` was "Sound Menu" and the sound menu is at index 1 in the `g_menus` array, then the menu will be initialized like this:

```
menu.m_options[0] = "Sound Menu";
menu.m_optionSpawns[0] = 1;
```

This simply means that if the "Sound Menu" option is selected, the sound menu will be pushed onto the stack.

The other options are all cosmetic.

Here is the initialization of the main menu:

```
// main menu
g_menus[0].m_options[0] = "1 - Sound";
g_menus[0].m_optionSpawns[0] = 1;
g_menus[0].m_options[1] = "2 - Graphics";
g_menus[0].m_optionSpawns[1] = 2;
g_menus[0].m_options[2] = "3 - Controls";
g_menus[0].m_optionSpawns[2] = 3;
g_menus[0].m_x = 16;
g_menus[0].m_y = 16;
g_menus[0].m_w = 768;
g_menus[0].m_h = 568;
g_menus[0].m_color = LTGREY;
```

The main menu has three options: Sound, Graphics, and Controls. These menus have indexes of 1, 2, and 3, respectively.

Adding a Menu to the Stack

The program detects which option you've selected at each menu and pushes the selected menu onto the menu stack:

```
x = g_stack.Top()->m_optionSpawns[0];
if( x != 0 )
{
```

```
        g_stack.Push( &g_menus[x] );
}
```

Because not all options are valid in every menu, the value 0 is used to denote that an option doesn't spawn a new menu. The top of the stack is accessed, and if option 0 spawns a new window, the appropriate menu is retrieved and pushed onto the stack.

Removing a Menu from the Stack

Whenever you go back to a previous menu in the demo, the current menu is popped off the stack.

```
if( g_stack.Top() != &g_menus[0] )
    g_stack.Pop();
```

This code checks to see if you are trying to pop off the main menu (index 0). If you are, then it does nothing, because you cannot remove the main menu in this demo.

If you are removing another menu, it pops the menu off the stack. It's that simple.

Playing the Demo

The commands for this demo are fairly simple and are shown in Table 7.2.

Table 7.2 Menu Demo Controls

Key	Action
Esc	Quits the demo at any time
0	Goes back to the previous menu
1	Goes to sub-menu 1
2	Goes to sub-menu 2
3	Goes to sub-menu 3

Figure 7.8 shows a screenshot from the demo in action.

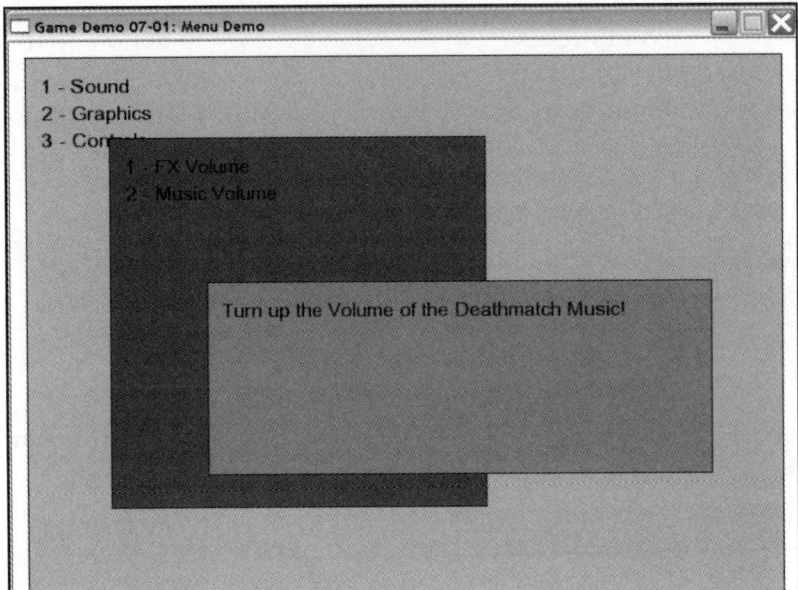

Figure 7.8

This is a screenshot from the menu game demo.

Queues

I'm sure that you know what a queue is. If you've never heard of the term before, you probably still know what they are. If you've ever been to a grocery store, you stand in a queue when you are checked out.

Basically, a queue is a *FIFO* structure (*First In, First Out*). The person who gets into line first will be checked out first.

Queues, like stacks, only have two functions: Enqueue and Dequeue. You can add items to the end of a queue, and you can remove items from the front of a queue.

Graphical Demonstration: Queues

This demonstration can be found on the CD in the directory \demonstrations\ch07\Demo02 – Queues\.

Compiling the Demo

This demonstration uses the SDLGUI library that I have developed for the book. For more information about this library, see Appendix B.

To compile this demo, either open up the workspace file in the directory or create your own project using the settings described in Appendix B. If you create your own project, all of the files you need to include are in the directory.

This demo is very similar to the stack demo, and you only have two buttons: Enqueue and Dequeue. The queue starts on the left side of the screen and ends at the right side.

Figure 7.9 shows the demo in action.

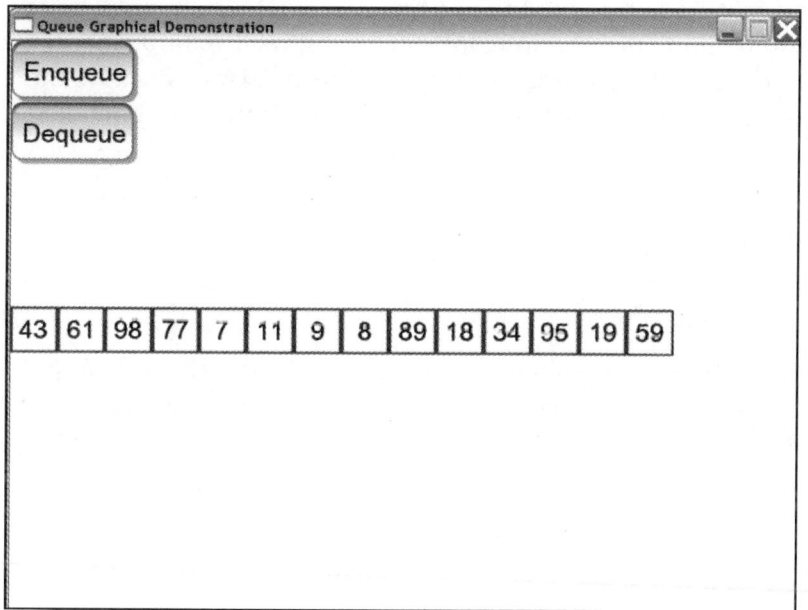

Figure 7.9

This is a screenshot from the queue demo.

The Queue Functions

Table 7.3 shows the functions that the queue classes in this book will have. All queue classes are located on the CD in the \structures\queue.h file.

Table 7.3 Queue Functions

Name	Description
Enqueue	Puts a new item at the end of the queue
Dequeue	Removes the item at the front of the queue
Front	Returns the item at the front of the queue
Count	Returns the number of items currently in the queue

Implementing a Queue

Like stacks, queues can be implemented in many different ways. I've implemented two of them for you, one using linked lists and the other using arrays. Because the linked queue is very similar to the linked stack, I only show you the two functions that change.

The arrayed queue is very different from an arrayed stack, however, and needs to be explained in detail.

Linked Queues

As I stated previously, *linked queues* are almost identical to linked stacks, so I only need to cover the two functions that have changed. Both stacks and queues use the `Append` function to add an item to the structure, so the `Push` and the `Enqueue` functions are identical, but where a stack removes the *last* item that was inserted, a queue instead removes the *first* item that was inserted.

The Dequeue Function

This function is similar to the stack's `Pop` function. Because a queue removes the first item instead of the last, you just need to switch the `RemoveTail` function to the `RemoveHead` function.

```
void Dequeue()
{
    RemoveHead();
}
```

The Front Function

Again, because the queue reads the front item instead of the last, the `m_tail` pointer in the Top function needs to be changed to the `m_head` pointer.

```
Datatype Front()
{
    return m_head->m_data;
}
```

Arrayed Queues

Arrayed queues are the most complex implementation of all of the structures I cover in this chapter. They are sometimes known as *circular queues*.

First, to see why these are more difficult to implement than the others, I need to show you how they work. Imagine an empty array with eight cells. This will be the queue. When an item is first placed into the queue, it will go into index 0. Then the next item will be placed into index 1, and the next one into index 2, and so on.

After five items have been inserted, they take up indexes 0 through 4, as in Figure 7.10.

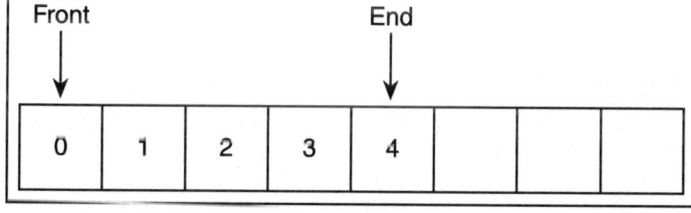

Figure 7.10

This is an arrayed queue with five items.

Now, you could do one of two things if you wanted to dequeue an item from the arrayed queue.

The first option you could do is move everything down, like Figure 7.11 shows. This option seems nice and simple, but it has a major flaw: It uses the array's `Remove` function, which, as you saw in Chapter 3, "Arrays," is an O(*n*) algorithm. This means that removing an item from the queue like this will take some time, and it will take longer amounts of time on larger queues. Plus, it involves physically moving around lots of data, which is slow.

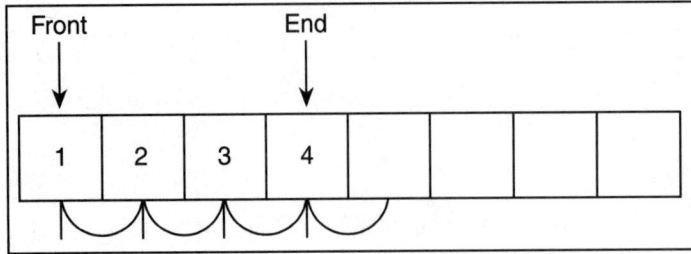

Figure 7.11

This is the slow method of dequeuing something by moving everything down by one index to remove the first item.

Because you naturally want everything to run as fast as possible, you need to find a faster way to do this.

The second method is somewhat simple, but you need a new variable to implement it. Instead of having index 0 at the front of the queue, a variable index points to the front of the queue. So when the first item in the queue from Figure 7.10 is removed, the front index will be incremented, and it will end up looking like Figure 7.12.

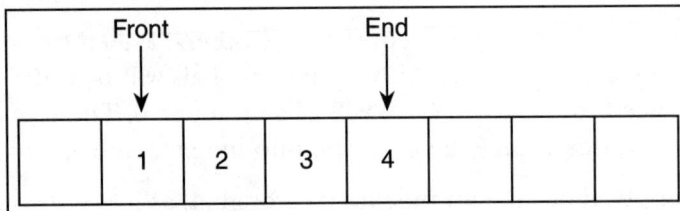

Figure 7.12

This is the fast method of dequeueing something. The front index is incremented when the front of the queue is removed.

While this method seems really cool when you first start out, you quickly realize that there is a problem. You can insert three more items into this queue, but what happens when you try to insert a fourth item?

The fourth item is wrapped around the end of the array and is placed into index 0 again. This is where the term *circular queue* comes from—you need to treat this array like it is a circle. Figure 7.13 shows what the queue looks like as a circle if you insert 5, 6, 7, and 8 into the queue from Figure 7.12.

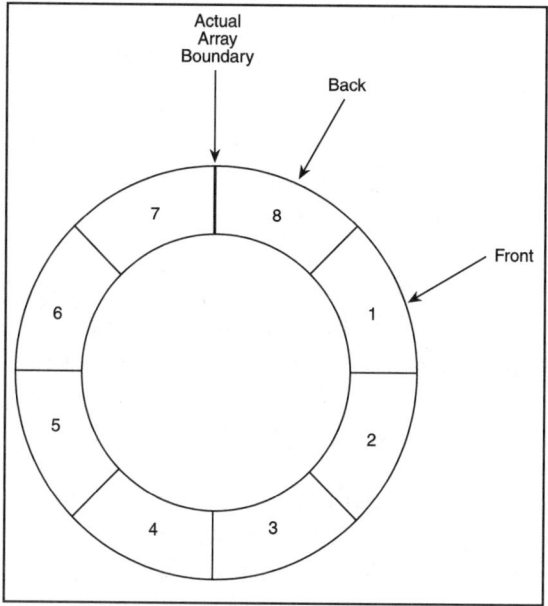

Figure 7.13

A full circular queue: The items wrap around the boundary and start at the beginning when you go past the end.

The Structure

For a circular queue, you need to have two new variables: the index of the front of the queue and the number of items within the queue.

```
template<class Datatype>
class AQueue : public Array<Datatype>
{
public:
    int m_front;
    int m_count;
};
```

The Constructor

Because the AQueue class is inherited from the Array class like the AStack class is, you need to use a constructor that constructs the array and initializes the variables.

```
AQueue( int p_size ) : Array<Datatype>( p_size )
{
    m_front = 0;
    m_count = 0;
}
```

The queue calls the Array constructor to tell it the size it wants to be, and the front index and the count variable are both reset to 0 because the queue is empty.

AQueues are constructed the same way AStacks are:

AQueue<int> queue(10);

This creates a queue of integers with a size of 10.

The Enqueue Function

The Enqueue function is fairly straightforward: You need to find the first empty index and put the new item into it. You can find the first open index by using the following formula:

index = m_first + m_count;

However, that line of code has a problem. Remember when I inserted 8 into the queue from Figure 7.12? In that figure, m_first was 1 and m_count was 7. 7 + 1 is 8, but 8 is an invalid index for that array because the only valid indexes are 0–7. Oops.

You need to take an extra step: Use the modulo operator to wrap the index around to the other end of the array:

index = (m_first + m_count) % m_size;

In the example queue, m_size is 8. 8 modulo 8 is 0, which is the correct index!

Here is the function:

```
bool Enqueue( Datatype p_data )
{
    if( m_size != m_count )
    {
        m_array[(m_count + m_front) % m_size] = p_data;
        m_count++;
        return true;
    }
    return false;
}
```

Also note that the size of the array is checked against the number of items in the queue. If they match, there is no room left, and false is returned. The important algorithm is in bold in the code snippet.

The Dequeue Function

The Dequeue function is much simpler. If there are items left in the queue, the front index is incremented by 1. If the front index passes the end of the array, it is reset to 0 again.

```
void Dequeue()
{
    if( m_count > 0 )
    {
        m_count--;
        m_front++;
        if( m_front == m_size )
            m_front = 0;
    }
}
```

The Front Function

The Front function is the simplest of them all. You just need to return the item at the index that m_front points to.

```
Datatype Front()
{
    return m_array[m_front];
}
```

The Access Operator

There is one more thing that needs to be changed to make this class useful. Because this class inherits from the Array class, it can use all of the functions that came with the Array class. This includes the access operator, which allows you to access any item in the array given an index. So how should this operator work with a queue? Should it return the correct index all of the time? Or should it return an index based on the front of the queue?

I prefer the second method. I like the idea of accessing the queue and having index 0 always return the front of the queue and index 1 return the second item in the queue, and so forth. To do this, all I need to do is redefine the access operator function so that it calculates the index based on the front of the queue.

```
Datatype& operator[] ( int p_index )
{
```

```
        return m_array[(p_index + m_front) % m_size];
}
```

The code in bold is the important part of the algorithm. Do you notice anything about it? It is almost exactly the same as the code I used to access the end of the array! All I do is add the front index to the index I want and then wrap the result around using the `modulo` function.

Resizing

Resizing a circular queue is a complicated procedure, which I have not implemented here because I am running out of room for this chapter. If you use the array's `Resize` function, the queue will be corrupted, so you really should not use it with a circular queue. If you decide that you really want to resize circular queues, the process goes like this: Create a new array and start copying the items over so that the front of the queue gets placed into index 0 in the new array.

Application: Command Queues

This is Game Demo 7-2, located on the CD in the directory \demonstrations\ch07\Game02 - Command Queues\.

> ### Compiling the Demo
>
> This demonstration uses the SDLHelpers library that I have developed for the book. For more information about this library, see Appendix B.
>
> To compile this demo, either open up the workspace file in the directory or create your own project using the settings described in Appendix B. If you create your own project, all of the files you need to include are in the directory.

I'm sure you've played some sort of *Real Time Strategy* (*RTS* for short) game before. Some of the games that fall into this category are *Command & Conquer*, *Warcraft*, and *Starcraft*. If not, then let me briefly explain them for a moment. In these games, you are presented with an overhead view of a map, and you are supposed to move different *units* around on the map so that they do various things. Most of the time they end up waging war with the computer players or other humans.

In some of these games, it is possible to tell your units to move to one place and then move to another place after they are done making the first move. This is called *command queuing*.

For this demo, you will use a queue to implement the movement of a spaceship flying around the screen.

The Player and the Coordinates

To make things easier, a simple coordinate class is used. There is nothing special about it; it contains *x* and *y* coordinates:

```
class Coordinates
{
public:
    int x;
    int y;
};
```

Now, a class for the player needs to be created. The player will have three variables: the current *x* and *y* positions and a queue of all movement commands.

```
class Player
{
public:
    int x;
    int y;
    LQueue<Coordinates> m_queue;
};
```

I used a linked queue here because it is flexible. You can issue as many commands as you want.

The queue holds coordinates. If the queue is empty, the player isn't moving at all. If there are coordinates in the queue, the player is currently moving toward the first pair of coordinates.

For example, if the spaceship starts out at coordinates (20,10), and you were to add (30,30), (50,20), (40,10), and (10,30) coordinates to the queue, the spaceship would move in a path like the one shown in Figure 7.14.

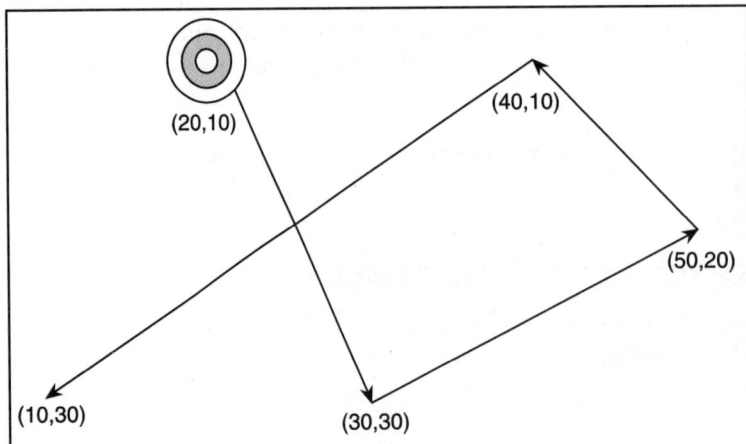

Figure 7.14

The figure shows the path of the spaceship. Each pair of coordinates was stored in a queue.

Adding a Command to the Queue

In the demo, a set of coordinates is added to the players queue whenever the mouse is clicked. Here is how it is accomplished:

```
SDL_GetMouseState( &c.x, &c.y );
g_player.m_queue.Enqueue( c );
```

The c variable is an instance of the Coordinate class. The g_player variable is an instance of the Player class.

Whenever the mouse is clicked, the coordinates of the mouse are retrieved by using the SDL_GetMouseState function and placed into c. The c variable is then added to the player queue.

The beauty of this is that it is a *fire and forget* method. You don't care what the player is currently doing; you just add the command to the players queue, and he will eventually get to it.

Removing a Command from the Queue

This is a little more difficult than adding a command to the queue because you need to be able to detect if a command has been completed or not. Because this demo only involves the movement of a spaceship, it is easy to detect if the spaceship has reached its destination.

```
if( g_player.x == g_player.m_queue.Front().x &&
    g_player.y == g_player.m_queue.Front().y )
{
```

```
    g_player.m_queue.Dequeue();
    if( g_player.m_queue.Count() > 0 )
        Calculate();
}
```

This code snippet checks to see if the current position of the spaceship is equal to the position of the current command in the queue. If it is, then the spaceship has completed the movement command, and the command should be removed.

After the command is removed, you still have some work to do. You need to start processing the next command in the queue. The second `if` statement in the code snippet checks to see if there are any more commands in the queue. If so, then it calls the `Calculate` function, which is a helper function that calculates some variables that determine the direction that the spaceship flies.

What the `Calculate` function does exactly is not important for this demo. Instead, you should see that after a command is completed, you need to start processing the next command in the queue. In a more complicated system with more than one command type, you would call a function that does even more than `Calculate` does.

Playing the Game

This game is very simple. All you need to do is move the mouse around and click on the window where you want the spaceship to go. The spaceship will then move to that place in one second. If you're fast enough, you can enqueue many different coordinates. Figure 7.15 shows a screenshot from the game in action.

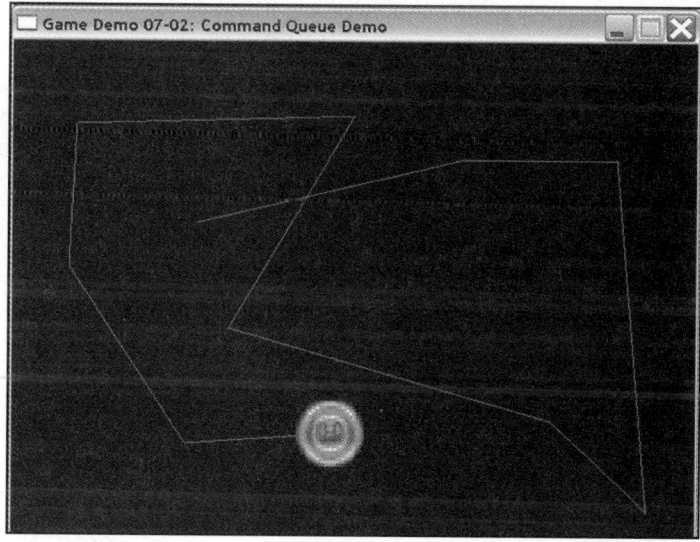

Figure 7.15

This is a screenshot from the command queue demo.

As the figure shows, the ship will follow the line on the screen. The line represents all of the coordinates that are in the queue.

Conclusion

After reading this chapter, you should see that not all data structures have a specific implementation. As this chapter showed, the stack and the queue data structures really don't specify how the data is stored underneath.

This freedom means that you should take time to analyze what your program needs. If expandability is more important than speed, use linked stacks and queues. If speed is more important than expandability, use arrayed stacks and queues.

Everything in game programming is a tradeoff, and you should always try to spend time analyzing exactly what you want your game to do before you jump right in and start coding.

CHAPTER 8

Hash Tables

8. Hash Tables

This chapter covers the most advanced of what I like to call the *basic* data structures. I must warn you, though; this chapter isn't very basic. In fact, most people I know who like computer programming absolutely hate the topics I cover in this chapter.

However, I feel that this hatred exists because no one ever teaches this material in a way that makes it easy to understand. I hope to fix that and give you an enlightening and educational look at these topics so you can see how useful they are in real life.

In this chapter, you will learn

- What sparse data is
- What key-based data is
- What a hash table is
- How to store data into a hash table
- What a hash table is
- What a hash collision is
- How to solve hash collisions
- How to create a linked hash table
- How to store and retrieve string-based game resources quickly

What Is Sparse Data?

Most books and classes that teach *hash tables* jump right into their implementation and give no background on what they are meant to do. Instead of taking that route, I give you a little background information.

The first thing you should know about is *sparse* data. Imagine that you are implementing a complex game world in which each player in the game is accessed by an *identification number*. This number is often called a *key* in programming. Each key will be unique, and no two players will have the same key. Now, imagine that these keys are not contiguous; they are instead generated by a complex algorithm that produces seemingly random numbers from 0 to 1,000,000. For example, in a system with three players, the players might have these keys:

Player 1: 945,253

Player 2: 433,455

Player 3: 36,549

These numbers are *sparse*; they are far away from each other.

Now what happens when you want to store the players in a data structure so that you can easily access a player by their key? Your first instinct should be to use an array so you can access them quickly, but you will end up with an array looking like Figure 8.1.

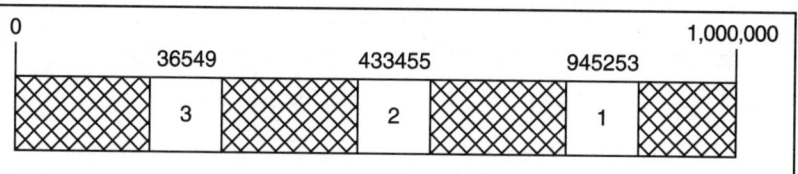

Figure 8.1

Sparse data stored in an array. Note how much space is wasted when these players are stored in the same indexes as their keys.

Only three indexes out of 1,000,000 are used, which is a waste of memory.

The other option is to store the data in a linked list. Although a linked list works great for only three pieces of data, what happens if the game needs 10,000? Searching through a linked list of 10,000 players just to find one is a waste of time. Note that even with 10,000 players, the array option is still out of the question, because for every player there will be 100 empty cells, which is a waste of memory.

The Basic Hash Table

The hash table data structure turns out to be the perfect solution to the problem. It allows you to do the following:

- Quickly store sparse key-based data in a reasonable amount of space
- Quickly determine if a certain key is within the table

The important word here is *quickly*. You'll begin to see why as you read on.

For right now, you can think of a hash table as just an array. If you want to store 10 players, you should create an array with 10 cells. Figure 8.2 shows a very basic hash table.

8. Hash Tables

> **TIP**
>
> It is actually more efficient to make your hash table sizes prime numbers. I can't really explain why this is without going into a whole discussion about discrete mathematics, but you should generally try to find a prime number above the desired number of items you store in the table. For example, if I wanted to store 10 items in a hash table, I would make it 11 cells large. However, I use 10 cells throughout this chapter because it makes the hashing functions easier to explain. I will go more in depth on this topic later on in this chapter.

0	1	2	3	4	5	6	7	8	9

Figure 8.2

This is a basic hash table, which is really just an array.

Now you want to insert Player 1 into the table. Where would you put him? The easiest and most common way of placing a key into a hash table is to `modulo` the key by the size of the table.

For example, Player 1 would be placed into cell 3 because 945253 % 10 = 3. Likewise, Player 2 would be placed in cell 5, and Player 3 would be placed in cell 9, yielding an array that looks like Figure 8.3.

			P1		P2				P3

Figure 8.3

This is a 10-cell hash table with three players in it, stored by key.

Whenever you want to access a player by their key, you just use a simple algorithm like this:

```
player = table[key % 10];
```

This example is a very simple hash table, and it has many problems, which will be addressed later on.

You can see how a hash table can be a powerful tool, though. Because of the way you look up keys, the algorithm to determine whether an item is in the table is essentially instantaneous. An ideal hash table can search for items in O(c) time, which is a tremendous benefit for fast programs.

Collisions

One of the major problems with a hash table is that collisions occur frequently for simple tables. For example, try inserting these two players with these keys into the ten-cell table: 143,674 and 645,394.

You can't. Because both numbers modulo down to 4, they should both be placed into the same cell, but a cell can only hold one item! This is called a *collision*. The only ways to resolve a collision are to use a *hashing function* or modify the table in a way that makes collisions okay.

I'll explore both methods for you.

> **TIP**
> Remember when I said to use prime numbers for your table size? That was because you get fewer collisions when you modulo a key by a prime number. Having fewer collisions makes your tables easier to work with and more efficient. There is a complicated mathematical reasoning behind this, but it is okay to just assume that this is true for us.

Hashing Functions

Most hash tables are more complex than the one I just showed to you. In fact, most of the time, just using a modulo function is a very bad way to store data into a hash table.

One method of solving collisions is to use a *hashing function*. The word *hash*, when applied to food, means to mince or mash. The same definition applies here; you need to hash the data so that it will fit into a table easier.

> **NOTE**
> Note that the modulo function used in the basic hash table is a hash function for integers. There are many ways to hash data, but modulo is the most common. For that reason, all of the hash functions in this book will produce an integer, which will then be hashed with a modulo function to fit within the table. In my experience, this is the best general-purpose hashing method.

Digit Addition

A simple alternative hashing function used on a key from 0 to 1,000,000 would be to add all of the digits together. For example, if you add all of the digits from the two numbers that collided with the modulo method, you would get these results:

1 + 4 + 3 + 6 + 7 + 4 = 25 and 6 + 4 + 5 + 3 + 9 + 4 = 31. Because these numbers are larger than the boundaries of the array, you have two options. You may expand the table so that it has 54 cells (the largest number that can be obtained using this method is 9 + 9 + 9 + 9 + 9 + 9 = 54), or you may use the method I describe in the next section.

> **CAUTION**
> Using digit addition solved the collision in the case that was shown, but it still produces collisions. For example, 123,456 and 654,321 both hash to 21 using digit addition, even though they are different keys.

Double Hashing

The second solution I will show you is called *double hashing*. This method involves using one function to hash a key and then using the same function, or possibly a different function, to hash the result of the first function.

For example, if you used these two numbers again, 143,674 and 645,394, and hashed them both using the digit addition method, you would get 25 and 31. You could then hash these numbers again, using the same method, and you would get 7 and 4, which both fit into the 10-cell table.

Another double hashing method would be to use the same digit addition function for the first hash, but then use `modulo` for the second hash. In that case, you would get 25 and 31 again, but they would modulo down to 5 and 1.

Other Hash Functions

There are literally an infinite number of hash functions you could use on an integer. I'm sure you are already thinking of a few. You could multiply the integers by a constant, divide them, perform binary arithmetic on them, or any combination of those methods.

Unfortunately, no hash function is perfect. No matter what method you use, you will end up with collisions if your dataset is large enough. When choosing a hash function, it is usually best to test it out on data that you are expecting to process. If one function produces no collisions and another does, then it is obvious which function you should choose.

If you are unaware of the exact type of data you will be getting, then it is impossible to create a function that you know will not cause collisions. This issue can only be solved by changing the structure of a hash table.

Hashing Strings

There is one more important hash function I want to show you. Besides integers, the other popular datatype that is frequently hashed is strings. The following algorithm does a really good job at hashing strings into an integer with very few collisions:

```
unsigned long int StringHash( const char* p_string )
{
    unsigned long int hash = 0;
    int i;
    int length = strlen( p_string );
    for( i = 0; i < length; i++ )
    {
        hash += ( (i + 1) * p_string[i] );
    }
    return hash;
}
```

This method is based on the fact that a character in a string is essentially an integer. This way, you can look at a string as a number where each digit is a number from 0–255 (for example, a base-256 number). This method is similar to the digit addition method, but instead of just adding the digits, it multiplies each digit by an integer and then adds them.

You can look at a string like it appears in Figure 8.4. The string "Hello!" is really an array of 6 integers: 72, 101, 108, 108, 111, and 33.

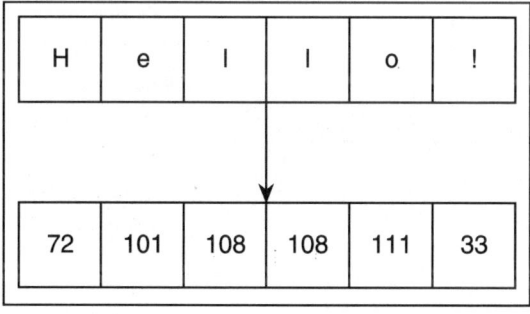

Figure 8.4

This is how you represent a string as a number.

Now, using the algorithm, you would multiply the numbers like this: (72 * 1) + (101 * 2) + (108 * 3) + (108 * 4) + (111 * 5) + (33 * 6). This gives you 1783 as the integer value.

Multiplying each letter of the string by its index makes the hash function useful because you don't have the problems that plain digit addition has. You can reverse the string and it will become a totally different hash value.

Enhancing the Hash Table Structure

There is no perfect hash function. You will probably always end up with collisions. Most people realize this and have created ways to handle these collisions. There are many methods of dealing with collisions without modifying the underlying hash table structure, but I feel that they are usually inferior solutions.

Linear Overflow

For example, one popular method is called *linear overflow*. With this method, you hash a number and then try to insert the number into the index that the hash function created. If there is an item already in the hash table at that index, you increment the index and try to insert it again. If that index is full, then you increment the index again and repeat the method until you find an empty index.

For example, if you hashed a key to 3 and indexes 3 through 6 were already full, you would need to jump all the way over to index 7 before you found an empty cell. Figure 8.5 demonstrates this.

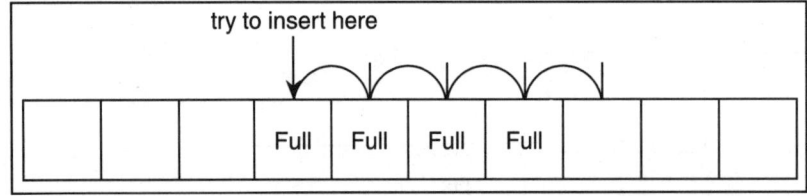

Figure 8.5

This shows a linear overflow collision resolution. The function inserts the item into the first open cell it finds after it hashes the key.

Personally, I think this method is ridiculous and destroys the benefits of a hash table. In order to find out if an item exists within the hash table, you have to search *every* index in the table to find out if it is in there! This turns the fast O(c) hash table search time into a slow O(n) time.

Even worse, if you put data into a cell that it didn't hash to and you later get data that hashes into that same cell, you're making the data even more spread out and inefficient. I wouldn't bother with this kind of collision resolution unless I was absolutely forced to.

Quadratic Overflow

There are many other methods based on the same idea, such as *quadratic overflow* collision resolution, where instead of incrementing the index by 1, you increment the index by 1^2 (1) and then 2^2 (4) and then 3^2 (9) and so on until you find an open index. The end result is the same; you still need to search the entire table to find something. This method is even worse, in my opinion, because there is no easy way to tell if you've searched through the entire table!

Linked Overflow

This leads me to the method that works best in my opinion, *linked overflow*. This method gives each cell in the hash table a linked list.

Inserting into a Linked Overflow Table

To demonstrate how these work, I will go back to the original collision problem. I'm using a 10-cell array for the table and using modulo-10 to insert the keys into the table. Now, I want to insert the following players into the table:

Player 1: 345,752

Player 2: 546,182

Player 3: 798,500

Player 4: 123,430

These keys hash down to 2, 2, 0, and 0 using modulo-10. Previously, this would have caused a problem because there are two collisions. However, because each cell of the table now contains a linked list, I can insert each player into the list in the appropriate cells, giving me a table that looks like Figure 8.6.

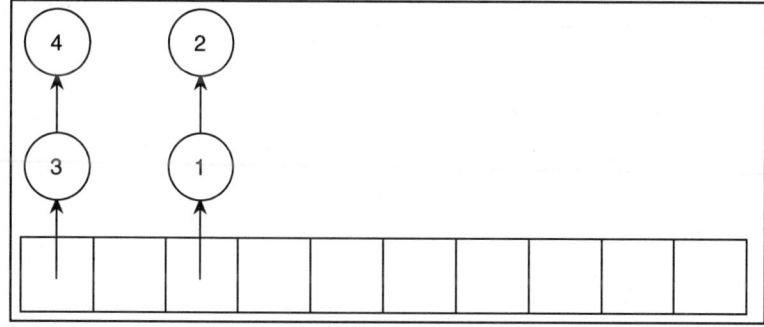

Figure 8.6

This is a linked overflow hash table. Each cell has a linked list in it to hold all keys that hash into that cell.

Using this method, you don't have to worry about collisions at all! Whenever two hashes collide, the data is just appended to the back of the list.

Searching for Keys

If your hash function is efficient and doesn't cause many collisions, then theoretically you achieve an almost instant search time when searching for data in a hash table. In order to search for data within this kind of table, you first hash the key to find the desired index. Once you have found the correct index, you need to search the linked list within that cell and nowhere else. If you find the data, you've searched through only one or two items (depending on how well your hash function works, it could be more). If you don't find the data, you've still only searched through one or two items!

This beats the heck out of the other collision resolution methods I've shown you because you don't waste your time searching for data that isn't in the table.

Of course, because you could theoretically use a bad hash function that stores every item in the same linked list, the search algorithm is considered to be $O(n)$, but with a good hash function, it comes remarkably close to approaching $O(c)$.

Graphical Demonstration: Hash Tables

This is Graphical Demo 8-1, located on the CD in the directory \demonstrations\ch08\Demo01 - Hash Tables\.

Compiling the Demo

This demonstration uses the SDLGUI library that I have developed for the book. For more information about this library, see Appendix B, "The Memory Layout of a Computer Program."

To compile this demo, either open up the workspace file in the directory or create your own project using the settings described in Appendix B. If you create your own project, all of the files you need to include are in the directory.

In the other chapters of this book, I usually put the graphical demonstrations near the front of the chapter. I felt, however, that I needed to build up to the linked overflow hash table before I showed you a graphical demo. I only showed you the primitive hash table types in order to lead up to the linked table so that you would understand the concepts behind them. I would not use anything but a linked hash table in real life, however.

This demonstration will show you how a linked hash table works internally. Figure 8.7 shows a screenshot of the demo in action.

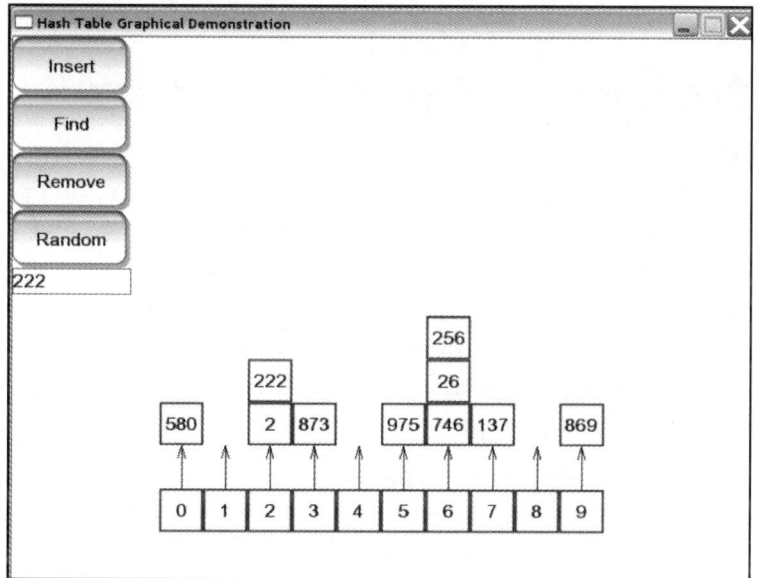

Figure 8.7

This is a screenshot from Graphical Demonstration 8-1.

Table 8.1 shows a listing of the commands and their effects in the demo.

Table 8.1 Commands for Graphical Demo 8-1

Button	Effect
Insert	This button tries to insert the number in the text box into the hash table.
Find	This button finds the given key in the hash table.
Remove	This button removes the given key from the hash table.
Random	This puts a random number into the text box.
Text Box	This is where you can type in numbers to insert, search for, or remove.

The demo shows a 10-cell hash table, the same kind I've been using for the entire chapter so far. The hash table is designed to store three-digit integers where each integer is its own key. In reality, the key and the data stored in the table do not have to be the same, but I go into that later. For simplicity, each number stored in the table is its own key value.

Figure 8.7 shows a hash table where I've inserted 10 random numbers. Note that the most numbers contained within any cell is three (in cell 6). This means that in order to find out if a given key is contained within this particular hash table, you will make *at most* three comparisons!

Implementing a Hash Table

Now it is finally time to create a hash table class. The code from this section is contained in the \structures\HashTable.h file on the CD. As I have stated before, there are two pieces of data associated with a hash table entry: a key and the actual data that will be entered into the table.

The key for the data must be unique for the data that it is associated with. For example, if you live in the United States, every person is issued a *Social Security number (SSN)*. This would be a very good key to use if you were putting people into a hash table, because SSNs are unique; no two people have the same SSN.

When you put data into a hash table, you put in both data and the key associated with the data. The hash table will remember the key and the data. Whenever you want to search for data in the hash table, you tell the table which key you are looking for, and the table will return the data if it exists.

The HashEntry Class

Because the hash table needs to store two pieces of information for every item you insert, it is easiest to create a class that holds both pieces of data. Because both pieces of data can be of different types, the `HashEntry` class will have two template parameters:

```
template< class KeyType, class DataType >
class HashEntry
{
public:
    KeyType m_key;
```

```
    DataType m_data;
};
```

The two template parameters are a `KeyType` and a `DataType`.

The HashTable Class

The `HashTable` class will have the same two template parameters as the `HashEntry` class. Table 8.2 shows a listing of all the functions the `HashTable` class will support.

Table 8.2 HashTable Functions

Function Name	Purpose
Constructor	This creates the hash table with a given size and a fixed hash function.
Insert	This inserts a `KeyType`/`DataType` couple into the hash table.
Find	This finds the given key in the table and returns a pointer to the data.
Remove	This finds the given key in the table and removes the data associated with it.
Count	This returns the number of entries that are in the table.

The Data

The `HashTable` class will need to have several member variables. It needs to keep track of the size of the table, the number of entries within the table, the array of linked lists that makes up the actual table, and a function pointer to the hash function. If you are unfamiliar with function pointers, please read Appendix A, "A C++ Primer," where I explain them.

```
template< class KeyType, class DataType >
class HashTable
{
public:
    typedef HashEntry<KeyType, DataType> Entry;
```

```
        int m_size;
        int m_count;
        Array< DLinkedList< Entry > > m_table;
        unsigned long int (*m_hash)(KeyType);
};
```

The typedef on Line 5 is there to make your life easier. Without this typedef, you need to type HashEntry<KeyType, DataType> whenever you want to use a HashEntry, which makes the code long and ugly. The typedef condenses this down to just Entry, saving us lots of typing and making the code easier to read.

The size and the count are obvious in their function.

The third member variable, m_table, is an array of DLinkedLists. Each linked list in each cell of the array contains Entrys.

The fourth member variable is a function pointer to the hash function. The hash function takes a key as a parameter and returns an unsigned long integer. I have the hash function as a function pointer for several reasons.

First, it is nice to be able to give the hash table a hash function that is independent from the table. This allows you to use all different kinds of data in the table. Some hash table implementations build the hash function right into the table, which makes it extremely limiting. This way, you can have two hash tables that store the same keytypes and datatypes, but both tables can use a different hash function.

Second, it is easy to make the hash table keep track of the hash function, so the hash table automatically hashes keys that are passed into the table. This way, the user of the table doesn't have to remember to hash the keys; he or she can just pass the key directly into the table.

Third, you don't want the hash function to change. If the user is allowed to change the hash function, the hash table becomes worthless. For example, say the user inserts a key/data pair into the table using one hash function. Then the user changes the hash function and tries to search for the same key. If the new hash function hashes the key to a different number, then the table will not find the data, even though it is in the table!

You will see how the hash function pointer works later on.

The Constructor

The constructor for the HashTable will take two parameters: the size of the table and a pointer to the hash function.

```
HashTable( int p_size, unsigned long int (*p_hash)(KeyType) )
    : m_table( p_size )
{
    // set the size, hash function, and count.
    m_size = p_size;
    m_hash = p_hash;
    m_count = 0;
}
```

On the second line of code, I use the standard C++ constructor notation to call the constructor of m_table so that it is initialized with the correct size. If you are unfamiliar with this notation, please read Appendix A, where I explain this.

The Insert Function

As I have stated before, the Insert function will take a key and data couple and insert them into the table.

```
void Insert( KeyType p_key, DataType p_data )
{
    Entry entry;
    entry.m_data = p_data;
    entry.m_key = p_key;
    int index = m_hash( p_key ) % m_size;
    m_table[index].Append( entry );
    m_count++;
}
```

First, an Entry structure is created with the key and the data that are passed in.

Then, the m_hash function pointer is called on the key that was passed in. Because the function is supposed to return an unsigned long int, that result may be out of bounds for the table. Because of this, the result is then modified using the modulo function so that it becomes a valid index for the table.

Finally, the entry is appended to the end of the linked list in the cell that index points to, and the count is incremented.

> **NOTE**
> Note that this hash table essentially uses the *double hashing* method I described earlier. First, the key is hashed into an integer, and then that integer is hashed again using the modulo **function**.

The Find Function

This function is designed to search the hash table to see if a certain key is in the table. If so, it will return a pointer to the entry structure that the key is in. If not, it will return 0.

```
Entry* Find( KeyType p_key )
{
    int index = m_hash( p_key ) % m_size;
    DListIterator<Entry> itr = m_table[index].GetIterator();
    while( itr.Valid() )
    {
        if( itr.Item().m_key == p_key )
            return &(itr.Item());
        itr.Forth();
    }
    return 0;
}
```

The key is hashed into an index using the same exact method that you used when inserting the key into the table. Then an iterator is created, which points to the linked list in the cell that the key hashed to.

The function then iterates through the linked list, checking to see if the keys match. If they do, then a pointer to the entry is returned. If not, it keeps looping. If the key isn't in the table, then 0 is returned.

> **NOTE**
> Please note that the Find function uses the == operator to compare keys. This means that the keys need to support the == operator. Note that this makes things a little more difficult in some cases. For example, if you were to use a char* string as a key, the hash table wouldn't really work the way you wanted it to because the == operator only compares the address of the strings to see if they are equal. If you wanted to see if the letters in the string were equal, you'd need to use the strcmp function instead (in string.h). I demonstrate how to fix this problem later on.

The Remove Function

The Remove function is essentially the same as the search function, but instead of returning a pointer to the entry, it removes the entry from the table.

The function returns a boolean. True means that an entry was found and removed; false means that the entry didn't exist.

```
bool Remove( KeyType p_key )
{
```

```
        int index = m_hash( p_key ) % m_size;
        DListIterator<Entry> itr = m_table[index].GetIterator();
        while( itr.Valid() )
        {
            if( itr.Item().m_key == p_key )
            {
                m_table[index].Remove( itr );
                m_count--;
                return true;
            }
            itr.Forth();
        }
        return false;
    }
```

Example 8-1: Using the Hash Table

I've put together a simple text-based demo for you to run to see how a hash table works. You can find it on the CD in the directory \examples\ch08\01 - Using the Hash Table\.

First of all, this demo uses a hash table where both the keys and the data are integers. The keys don't have to be the same as the data, however. Figure 8.8 shows a screenshot of the program running.

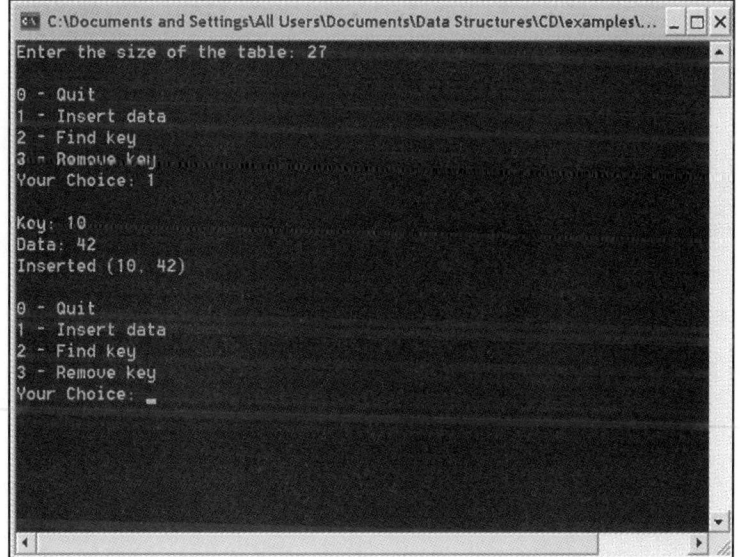

Figure 8.8

This is a screenshot from Example 8-1.

The Hash Function

The first thing you need to do is create a hash function. For this simple demo, I used a very basic hash function that doesn't modify the key at all:

```
unsigned long int Hash( int k )
{
    return k;
}
```

So whatever key is passed into the hash function is returned unmodified.

Creating the Hash Table

Now you need to create the hash table. The program asks you for the size of the table, which is placed into the size variable.

```
HashTable<int, int> table( size, Hash );
HashEntry<int, int>* entry;
```

The table is created with the size that you've entered and the Hash function. Note that a pointer to a HashEntry is also created. This is used for searching the table later on.

Inserting Keys

If you choose the Insert data option from the menu, the program will ask you to enter a key and data pair. Once you have entered those, it inserts them into the hash table:

```
table.Insert( key, data );
```

Finding Keys

The program asks you to enter a key to find. Once you have done so, it searches for the key in the table:

```
entry = table.Find( key );
```

If the key exists, entry will point to the entry that contains the key and the data. If not, entry will be 0.

Removing Keys

Removing a key is just like searching for one; the program asks you for a key and then tries to remove it:

```
table.Remove( key );
```

Application: Using Hash Tables to Store Resources

This is Game Demonstration 8-1, which can be found on the CD in the directory \demonstrations\ch08\Game01 - Resources\.

> ### Compiling the Demo
>
> This demonstration uses the SDLGUI library that I have developed for the book. For more information about this library, see Appendix B.
>
> To compile this demo, either open up the workspace file in the directory or create your own project using the settings described in Appendix B. If you create your own project, all of the files you need to include are in the directory.

It has become more and more common for games to have elaborate scripting systems, but even if they don't, they usually have a mod system implemented where you can make custom maps and characters. In both cases, most of these systems allow you to specify game resources with their names instead of a number.

For example, in a game I might be able to say that a certain wall should use a bitmap named "stone." Without hash tables, the game would need to search through every bitmap it has loaded, checking to see if there is one named "stone." This can take quite a while, and because you want the game to be as fast as possible, this option is out of the question.

The better method to use would be to use a hash table. The hash table would use strings as keys and bitmaps as data. This is what I've done with this game demo.

The String Class

I mentioned before that you cannot easily use strings as the keys with the `HashTable` class. This was because the built-in string type is `char*`, which is a pointer, and whenever you used the == operator on a pointer, it would compare the address of the strings and not the contents.

The easiest way around this would be to use a string wrapper class. In this solution, you create a small class that contains a string and has a few helpful functions.

```cpp
class String
{
public:
    char m_string[64];
    String()
    {
        strcpy( m_string, "" );
    }
    String( char* p_string )
    {
        strcpy( m_string, p_string );
    }
    bool operator== ( String& p_right )
    {
        return !strcmp( m_string, p_right.m_string);
    }
};
```

You'll note first that the string is very primitive; it is limited to 64 characters (63 plus the `NULL` terminator). I did this for simplicity's sake; I'd rather not get into the complex pointer manipulation involved in more complex classes for such a simple demo.

There are two constructors. The first one takes no parameters and sets the string to an empty string.

The second constructor takes a `char*` as a parameter and copies it into the string. This structure allows you to do things like this:

```cpp
String str( "hello!" );
```

The third function is the most important. It is an overloaded comparison operator (if you are not familiar with operator overloading, please read Appendix A). This allows you to compare two strings using the == operator, and it will return true or false. For example:

```
String str1( "hello!" );
String str2( "Hey!" );
if( str1 == str2 )
    // strings are equal
else
    // strings are unequal
```

The demo uses a slightly modified `StringHash` algorithm, which I discussed earlier. The only change is that the function works with the `String` class instead of `char*`s now. There is no need to list the code here.

Using the Table

You will be using the `String` class as the keys for the resources. For this demo, the only resources you will be using are graphics, so the `SDL_Surface*` will be the datatype.

```
HashTable< String, SDL_Surface* > g_table( 7, StringHash );
```

The table is seven cells in size because I've included seven bitmaps with the demo.

Whenever you want to add a bitmap into the table, all you need to do is this:

```
g_resource = SDL_LoadBMP( "sky.bmp" );
g_table.Insert( "sky", g_resource );
```

The first line loads a bitmap from disk into `g_resource`, which is a global `SDL_Surface*`. The second line inserts the bitmap into the hash table with the name "sky". Now, all you need to do to load the sky bitmap again is to do this:

```
HashEntry< String, SDL_Surface* >* entry;
entry = g_table.Find( "sky" );
if( entry != 0 )
    g_resource = entry.m_data;
```

The hash table quickly finds the resource you asked for—almost instantly.

How the Demo Loads Resources

In the demo, there is a text box into which you can type resource names. Whenever you type a name and press Enter, it calls this function:

8. Hash Tables

```
void Find()
{
    String str( g_name );
    HashEntry< String, SDL_Surface* >* entry;
    entry = g_table.Find( str );
    if( entry != 0 )
        g_resource = entry->m_data;
    else
        g_resource = 0;
}
```

The g_name variable is a char* that contains the string that is in the text box. The function creates a String and copies the contents of the text box string into it and then creates a HashEntry. The function then searches the table and sets the g_resource variable if the resource was found.

Playing the Demo

The demo is quite simple. Figure 8.9 is a screenshot from the demo in action.

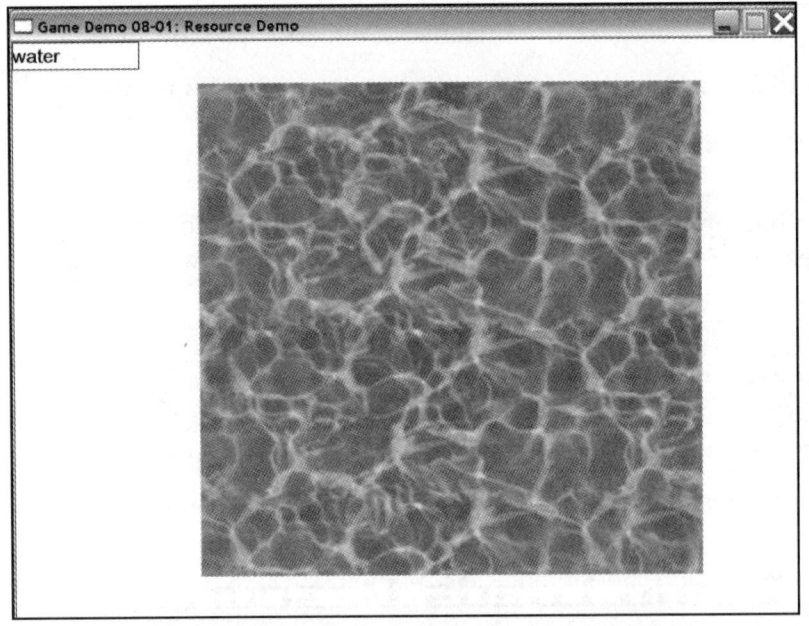

Figure 8.9

This is a screenshot from Game Demonstration 8-1.

When the demo starts out, there is a text box in the upper-left corner of the screen and nothing else. You type the name of a resource into the text box and press Enter, and the requested resource will be drawn on the screen.

The valid resources for this demo are sky, water, water2, fire, snow, vortex, and stone.

Conclusion

I hope that you've gotten a good idea of what hash tables are and what they're good for. Essentially, they have the fastest known search time of all data structures in existence. Most databases use hash tables or variants of them.

Table 8.3 shows a listing of the speeds of the various hash table functions.

Table 8.3 Hash Table Function Speeds

Function	Worst Case	Best Case
Insert	$O(c)$	$O(c)$
Find	$O(n)$	$O(c)$
Remove	$O(n)$	$O(c)$

Keep in mind that these figures are only for the linked hash table. You could technically replace the linked list with an array, but that would either slow everything down or take up more space. That is because you cannot be sure how many cells each array will have when you create the array. I've never seen a hash table implemented this way, so don't worry about it.

Keep in mind that the worst-case figures there rarely happen if you have a good hash function. The best-case figures happen more often than not if your hash function produces few collisions.

If done correctly, hash tables offer potentially instant search times.

CHAPTER 9

TYING IT TOGETHER: THE BASICS

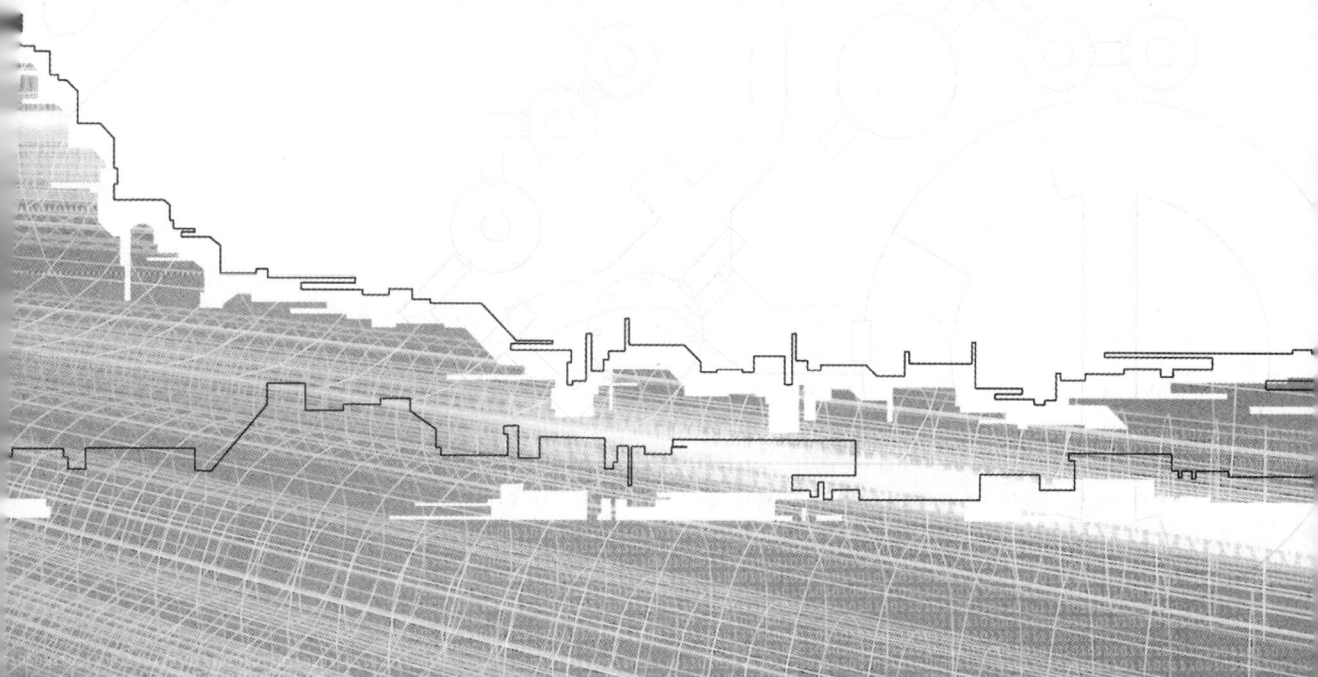

9. Tying It Together: The Basics

Congratulations! You have just finished reading about all of the basic data structures. Each of the previous chapters introduced you to a new data structure, showed you how it worked, and gave you an example of how it works in computer games. Most of the advanced chapters in this book make use of the structures from this part of the book, so it is a good idea to be well acquainted with them.

This chapter, however, goes over a different sort of data structure topic: how to create classes for things in your games.

Learning about data structures isn't just about learning which container classes are good in which circumstances. You should also know a little about how to design the classes in your game so that you can store game data efficiently.

In this chapter, you will learn:

- How to use classes
- How to make your games bug safe by hiding data
- How to make your games flexible by using inheritance
- How to use virtual functions
- What the different types of inheritance are and how they work
- What Real-Time Type Information (RTTI) is
- How to enable RTTI in Visual C++
- How to avoid using RTTI
- How to design a simple adventure game
- How to make a map editor for the adventure game

Why Classes Are Good

What is a game? Most games are *reality simulators*, which try to simulate aspects of the real world. So what is the most logical way to store data in a game, then? It makes sense to store all of your data in classes that represent the *nouns* of your world (a *noun* in English is defined as a person, place, or thing).

Each one of these nouns can perform tasks, called *verbs* (a *verb* in English is defined as a word that describes an action).

In programming, classes are nouns, and their functions are verbs. You can take the English sentence:

```
The hero hits the monster!
```

And turn that into code:

```
Hero.Hit( Monster );
```

This is one aspect of *object-oriented programming (OOP)*. In the past, game developers have typically avoided OOP because early implementations were slow and game developers wanted to squeeze every bit of speed out of their games to push the limits. Games like *DOOM* ran on a 386 with no problem because the programmers at i.d. software used some *assembly language* (ASM) and a lot of low-level C code to program the game. Assembly language is a very basic kind of computer language where you actually control each individual instruction that the computer will execute. When a compiler compiles your C or C++ code, it turns it into assembly.

Even though *DOOM* was mostly C code, the assembly was there in a few parts. See, way back in the bad old days of the early 1990s, it was a good idea to write parts of your code in assembly language, especially the parts that would be executed many times. Compilers back then weren't too smart, and people like John Carmack and Michael Abrash (the people who programmed *DOOM*) found clever ways to make their assembly language faster than the code the compiler would produce.

Back then, games were relatively simple. You could get away with writing in C and ASM because the programs were not large and complex.

Using ASM in games has now died out completely because processors have gotten very complex, and compilers almost always produce faster code than you could produce by hand.

However, C is still used a lot in game programming, but more and more people are learning how C++ can make game programming much easier and flexible.

OOP is a very natural way of representing games because you naturally think in terms of objects and verbs.

Storing Data in a Class

Before classes (and structures—for the purpose of this chapter, whenever I refer to classes, I mean structures as well) were around, all you could use to store your data in was global memory. This method is shown in Figure 9.1.

9. Tying It Together: The Basics

Without Arrays

```
int playerhealth;
int playerx;
int playery;

int monster1health;
int monster1x;
int monster1y;

int monster2health;
int monster2x;
int monster2y;

int monster3health;
int monster3x;
int monster3y;
```

Figure 9.1

This is how programmers used to store data globally.

With this method, you stored each variable globally, and whenever you wanted to add a new monster or player, you would have to add new variables for each one and find a new name that was available. This isn't very flexible.

After global memory came arrays. Arrays made things easier, as you can see in Figure 9.2.

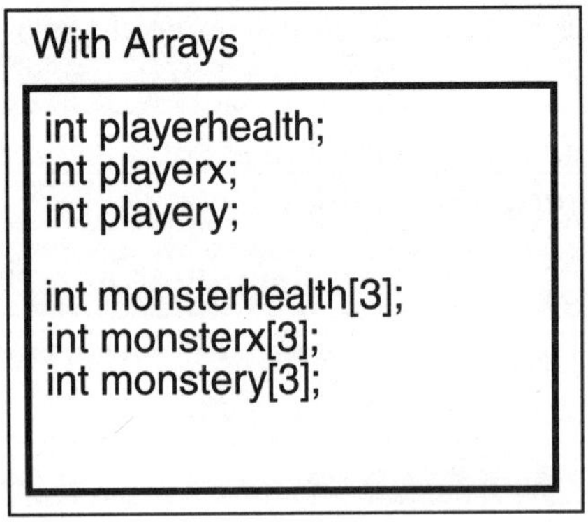

With Arrays

```
int playerhealth;
int playerx;
int playery;

int monsterhealth[3];
int monsterx[3];
int monstery[3];
```

Figure 9.2

Arrays allowed you to keep better control of your variables.

Now you can reference each monster's statistics by its number in the arrays. But this method also has problems; what happens when you want to add a new variable to the monsters and players? Then you have to find the array declarations and add a new array for each.

Enter classes, as seen in Figure 9.3.

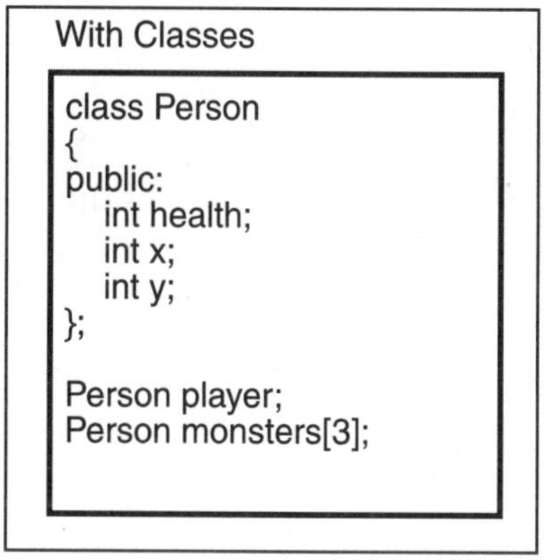

```
With Classes

class Person
{
public:
    int health;
    int x;
    int y;
};

Person player;
Person monsters[3];
```

Figure 9.3

Classes allow you to make your games even more flexible.

Now, both the player and the monster use the same class, and whenever you want to change the class, all of the monsters and players will automatically use the changes.

Hiding Data

I hear this question almost on a daily basis: "Why the hell would I want to hide my data?!" There are many reasons for this.

Implementing a Class with No Data Hiding

Take this simple class, for example:

```
class Person
{
public:
    int m_health;
    int m_score;
};
```

> **NOTE**
>
> The `public` keyword means that anyone can modify and read the data in the class.

Now imagine a simple game where you gain points whenever your health increases and lose points whenever you lose health. While coding the game, you put this sequence of code in all over the place:

```
player.m_health -= damage;
player.m_score -= damage;
```

In other places, you put this segment of code:

```
player.m_health += bonus;
player.m_score += bonus;
```

And for a while, that works. Whenever your player gets health, his score goes up, and whenever your player loses health, his score goes down.

Imagine that you change your mind a few days later (you never change your mind, do you?) and decide that you want to double the amount of points the player gets or loses when his health changes.

This means that you have to manually find every place in your code where you modified the score. If you did it many times, I guarantee that you will miss one, and you will end up with a hard-to-find bug.

Even worse, what happens if you forget to add or subtract the score once when you are modifying the health? That's another hard-to-find bug right there!

Implementing a Class with Data Hiding

In the previous example, anyone was free to go in and mess around with the data in the class. This is generally a bad thing because it can cause many small mistakes to appear in your game.

Now, imagine if you re-implemented that class using data hiding:

```
class Person
{
private:
    int m_health;
    int m_score;
public:
    int GetHealth()    { return m_health; }
    int GetScore()     { return m_score; }
    void ChangeHealth( int p_change )
    {
        m_health += p_change;
```

```
        m_score += p_change;
    }
};
```

The functions that read and write to hidden variables are called *accessor* functions because they access the data.

> **NOTE**
> The `private` keyword makes it so that nothing inside a class can be accessed from outside of the class. Class data is always private by default.

"But that code is so much longer!" says the nay-sayer. Yes, that's correct. But what would you rather do: spend an extra minute typing out accessor functions or spend an extra few hours tracing down a bug? I thought so.

"But that code is also slower!!" Yes, correct again. However, you can easily speed the code up so that it is just as fast by using the `inline` keyword. See Appendix A, "A C++ Primer," if you are unfamiliar with inlining functions.

Now, whenever the player's health is changed, this function is called:

```
player.ChangeHealth( -damage );
```

or

```
player.ChangeHealth( bonus );
```

First of all, using the function is much cleaner in the code because you can tell that the health is being changed by the name of the function. Second of all, you don't care *how* the health is changed, you only care that it is changed. You trust the `Person` class to take care of all the little details for you automatically.

For example, your game has been going along nicely, but you're getting bored and want to add new features, so you decide that you want to add a *speed* variable to your player, which determines how fast the player can move. Naturally, if your player is at full health, he can move fast, but if he's almost dead, then he can barely move.

```
class Person
{
private:
    int m_health;
    int m_score;
    int m_speed;
```

```cpp
public:
    int GetHealth()    { return m_health; }
    int GetScore()     { return m_score; }
    int GetSpeed()     { return m_speed; }
    void ChangeHealth( int p_change )
    {
        m_health += p_change;
        m_score += p_change;
        m_speed = m_health / 10;
    }
};
```

The three lines in bold show the differences in this class from the previous version. The speed will always be the health of the player divided by 10, which is an arbitrary number that doesn't really mean anything in this example.

So, now you can see how much more flexible your games can be if you use data hiding. In fact, there are a few more things you may want to implement in this `ChangeHealth` function, such as a *health cap*, which limits the maximum amount of health you can get, or a *death detector*, which detects if the health goes below 0 and acts upon that.

Every time you make a change to what the class does inside of the class, you are saving yourself lots of pain and bugs.

Inheritance

Inheritance is one of those subjects that no one likes. Unfortunately, it is also a very cool feature to use, but only when used correctly.

So what is so neat about inheritance? If you don't know too much about it already, here is a little primer.

Think about a dog for a moment. A dog *is-a* mammal. A mammal *is-a* vertebrate (something that has a backbone or spine), and a vertebrate *is-a* living thing.

The key to inheritance is the *is-a* relationship. Whenever something *inherits* from something else, it is said to be a more refined version of the base. Figure 9.4 shows an incomplete *inheritance tree* for living things.

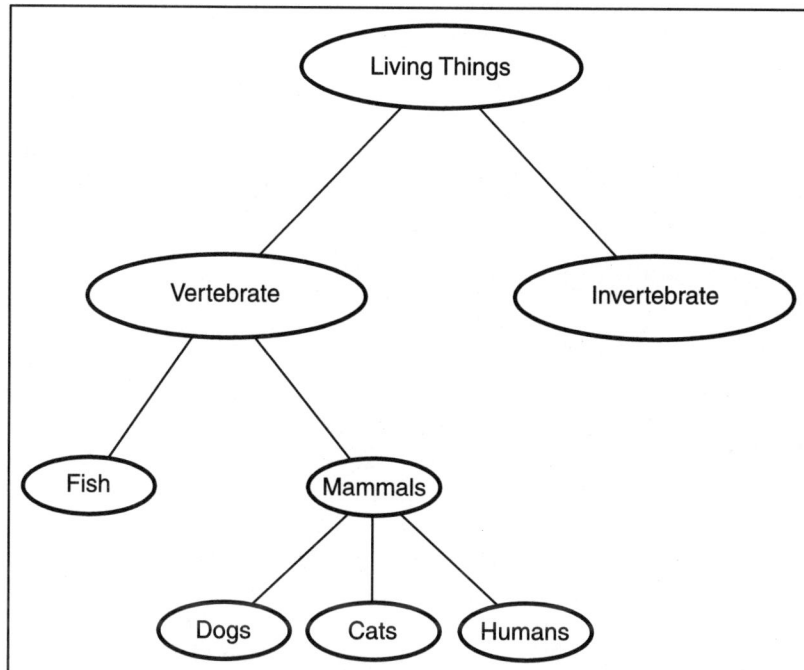

Figure 9.4

This is an incomplete inheritance tree of some common living things.

Both the vertebrates and the invertebrates *inherit* from the living things category; that is, they share some of the same aspects. Fish and mammals *inherit* from the vertebrates category, and all fish and mammals share the vertebrate properties: They have backbones.

It goes even further than that. Cats, dogs, and humans all inherit from the mammal category; we all share similar respiratory systems and have hair.

Things that inherit from other things are said to be *children*. Dogs and cats are children of the Mammals category. Likewise, mammals are called the *parents* of the dogs and cats.

So what does inheritance mean for a game?

Think about the objects in your game and see if you can figure out an inheritance tree. Figure 9.5 shows a simple one I made for this book.

9. Tying It Together: The Basics

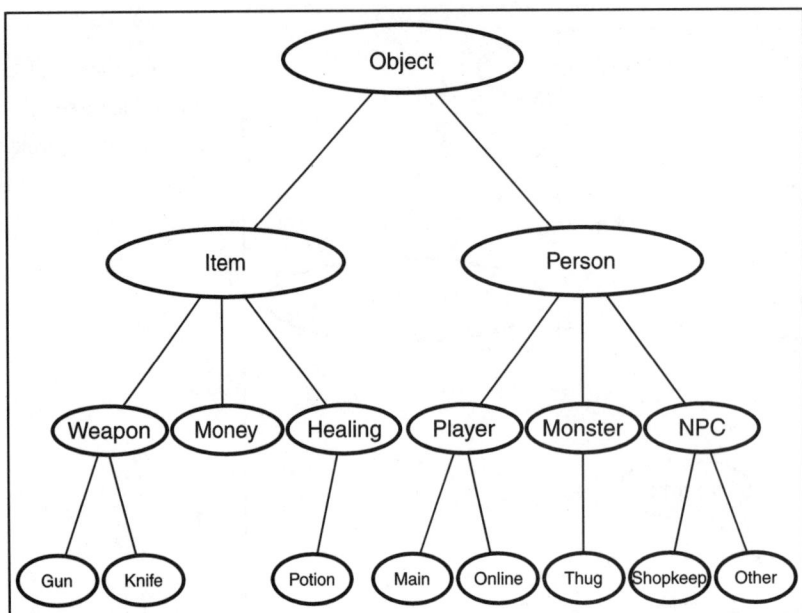

Figure 9.5

This is a game object inheritance tree.

The Object Class

So how does this actually help you program a game? Look at this simple class outline for the Object class:

```
class Object
{
public:
    virtual void Draw()    { Draw( g_screen, blank, m_x, m_y ); };
    int GetX() { return m_x; };
    int GetY() { return m_y; };
    int SetX( int p_x ) { m_x = p_x; };
    int SetY( int p_y ) { m_y = p_y; };
protected:
    int m_x;
    int m_y;
};
```

Ignore the Draw command for a moment; I get into that in a bit. Look at the *x* and *y* variables. Every object in the game will have an *x* and a *y* coordinate representing its position on the game map.

> **NOTE**
>
> The protected keyword is almost the same as the private keyword. The difference is that inherited classes cannot access private members of their parents, but they can access protected members.

For example, within the game, you will declare an array of objects:

`Array<Object*> g_objects( OBJECTS );`

After this, you will fill the array with objects, but don't worry about that for now; I show you how in a bit. For now, just assume that the array is full of object pointers.

> **NOTE**
> For reasons that I explain in a bit, you are required to use pointers in order to take advantage of the benefits of inheritance.

Now, whenever you want to read or change the coordinates of any object, you just do this:

```
g_objects[object].SetX( x );
g_objects[object].SetY( y );
```

And so forth.

Well, now you have an object class that is only capable of storing coordinates. What use could that be?

Virtual Functions

The `Draw` function of the `Object` class has a funny word in front of it: *virtual*. This word essentially means "this function is valid for this class, but inherited classes may change what this function does."

See, the object class has a `Draw` function, and this function draws a blank bitmap onto the main screen, which isn't what you want. Later on, when other classes inherit from the `Object` class, they will re-implement this function so that it works properly.

Pure Virtual Functions

When you look at the implementation of the `Draw` function and you see that it draws absolutely nothing, you should be thinking to yourself, "Why bother?"

That's a good way to think, because you know that the *sub-classes* (classes that inherit from the *parent class*) will just implement their own method of drawing.

So, instead of wasting your time writing a function that does nothing, you can declare the function as *pure virtual*, which means that it will not have an implementation in this class and it will definitely be redefined in later classes.

Here is how you redefine the Draw function to be pure virtual:

```
virtual void Draw() = 0;
```

The = 0 part is what makes it pure. This says, "This function is empty, but subclasses will implement it for me."

However, there is one gotcha, which is either good or bad, depending on how you look at it. None of these lines of code will compile:

```
g_objects[0] = new Object;
Object obj;
Array<Object> objectarray( OBJECTS );
```

The compiler will stop and say: `Cannot instantiate class Object due to the following pure virtual members: void Draw().`

Because these classes have pure virtual functions, they cannot be used directly. These classes are called *abstract* classes because they don't actually exist. Instead, these classes describe what can be done (called the *interface*) and let other classes actually implement these features (the *implementation*).

Why Do You Need to Use Pointers?

When you think about a class in a computer program, it is just a chunk of memory. For instance, you have a class named Item, and you create three of them, as shown in Figure 9.6.

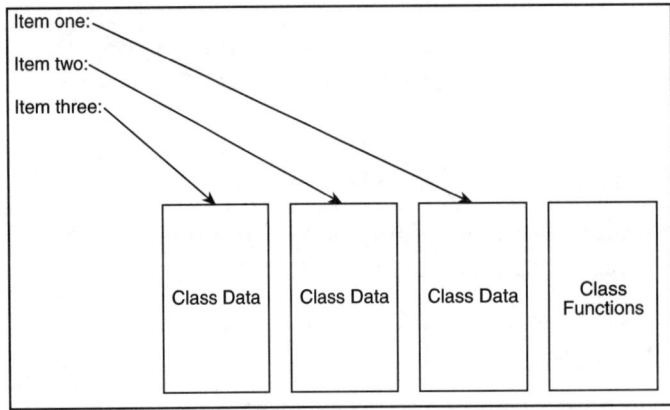

Figure 9.6

Here are three instances of the Item class. Each instance holds its own data, but the functions used on that data are all stored in one place in memory.

Whenever you create a new instance of the Item class, a new chunk of memory containing the data of that class is created. What happens when you add functions to that class? Is the actual function code added to each class so that every instance of the class has its own code representing the functions? (See Appendix B, "The

Memory Layout of a Computer Program," if you are unfamiliar with how instruction code is stored in a computer.)

This is a wasteful approach. The actual code for the functions is never changed, so why should each instance of a class have its own code? Instead, the code is stored in one single place in memory, such as the last box in Figure 9.6.

Now, whenever you make a function call in a program, the compiler actually does something neat. Imagine that the Item class has a function called Draw for a moment:

```
Item one;
one.Draw();
```

Whenever the compiler sees this, it manually translates it into what actually happens in the computer. (This code will not actually work if you type it in, but it is theoretically what happens.)

```
Item one;
Item::Draw( &one );
```

Whenever the compiler creates a class function, it adds an extra parameter: a pointer to the class that the function is a part of. Therefore, an instance of the Item class is actually passed into the function as a pointer. (You can access that pointer by using the this keyword. See Appendix A for more information.)

Now, enter inheritance. When you pass an object into a function, the function needs to know how to access the data and call the functions.

If the Item class inherits from the Object class, Figure 9.7 shows how the Object functions work with this.

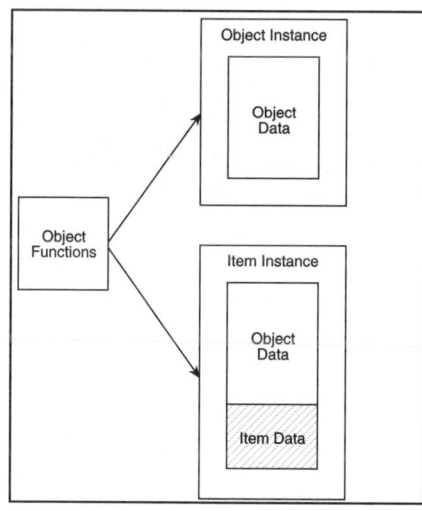

Figure 9.7

This is how the Object *functions view* Objects *and* Items *that are passed into it. The function cannot see the extra* Item *variables.*

If you *pass by value* an Object into a function that wants an Object, there is no problem. This is because the entire Object is placed onto the stack (see Appendix B). However, what happens when you pass an Item into the function, instead of an Object? In that case, the entire Item is copied onto the stack as well, but there is a problem. Items are larger than Objects, so they occupy more room on the stack. This messes up the entire function because it accesses parts of the Item, thinking that they are something different.

Whenever you try to pass by value an Item into a function that expects an Object, the compiler gives you an error. Instead, you must use pointers because they always take up the same amount of room on the stack. Whenever a function accesses an Item or an Object, it gets the address of the object, finds the address of the item it wants to access, and uses that, instead of a value on the stack.

How Virtual Functions Work

Virtual functions are quite complex, and you might wonder how they work. When you use non-virtual inheritance, every inherited class executes the same code whenever a single function is called. Therefore, an Item and an Object both execute the same code for non-virtual functions. However, if you have a virtual function, such as the Draw function, the actual code that is called can be changed depending on what kind of class it is.

In this section, I will explain non-pure virtual functions.

As soon as you add one virtual function to a class, a *virtual function table* is added to each instance of the class. This table is essentially a table of *function pointers* (see Appendix A) that point to a function. Figure 9.8 shows this.

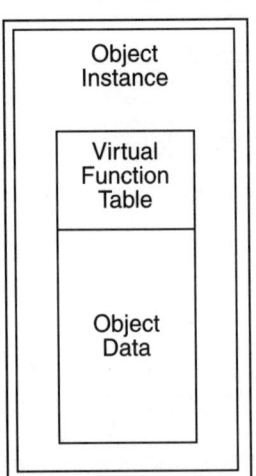

Figure 9.8

A virtual function table is added to each class instance whenever a virtual function exists in the class.

Now, whenever you create an instance of the `Object` class, it has one virtual function entry, for the `Draw` function, and it points to the `Object`'s drawing code.

Whenever you create an `Item`, it fills in the table entry with a pointer to the `Item`'s drawing code, as shown in Figure 9.9.

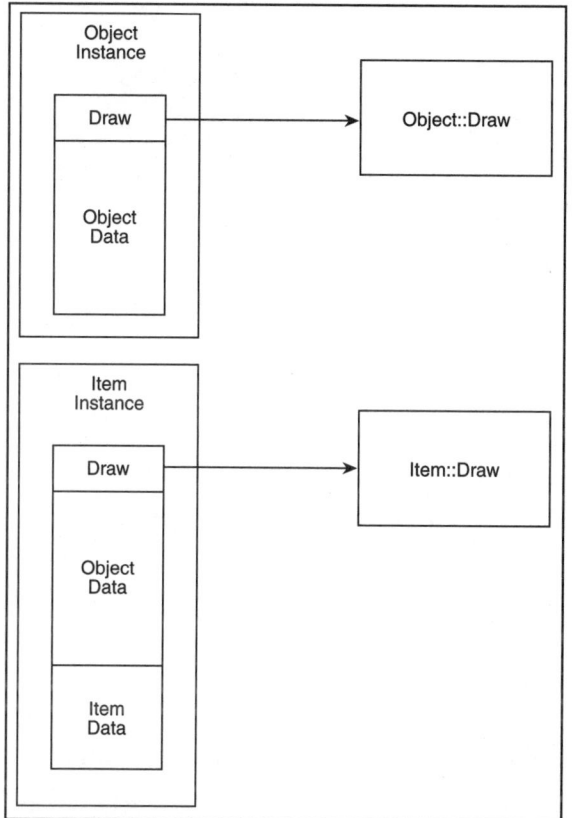

Figure 9.9

Each instance of a class points to the function code it will execute.

Now, whenever you call the `Draw` function of an `Object` or an `Item`, it will dereference the pointer in the virtual function table and call the function at that address. There is a little overhead associated with the function calling because you need to dereference the pointers first, but not much.

Because a class with a pure virtual function cannot be instantiated, the virtual function pointer table will always hold a valid pointer.

The Item Class

Now you should think about what kinds of data you want to store in an item class. For demonstration purposes, the only new thing that the Item class will have is a graphic (using the SDL_Surface class—see Appendix C, "Introduction to SDL").

```
class Item : public Object
{
protected:
    SDL_Surface* m_graphic;
public:
    void Draw()
    {
        SDLBlit( g_screen, m_graphic, m_x, m_y );
    }
    void SetGraphic( SDL_Surface* p_graphic )
    {
        m_graphic = p_graphic;
    }
};
```

On the first line, the class is declared as an Item, and it inherits from the Object class.

Inheritance Types

The public keyword in the first line deals with the type of inheritance you are using. You will almost always use public inheritance when inheriting classes. Table 9.1 shows a listing of the different types of inheritance and who can access which types of variables in the base class.

Table 9.1 Inheritance Types

Inheritance Type	Class Can Use	Others Can Use
Public	public, protected	public
Private	public, protected	none

Figure 9.10 shows the relationship between a base class, a publicly inherited class, and some other class or function accessing the other two classes. The child class can access all of the public and protected members of the base, but private members are hidden. Other classes and functions can access the public members of the child class, and they can access the public members of the base class as well.

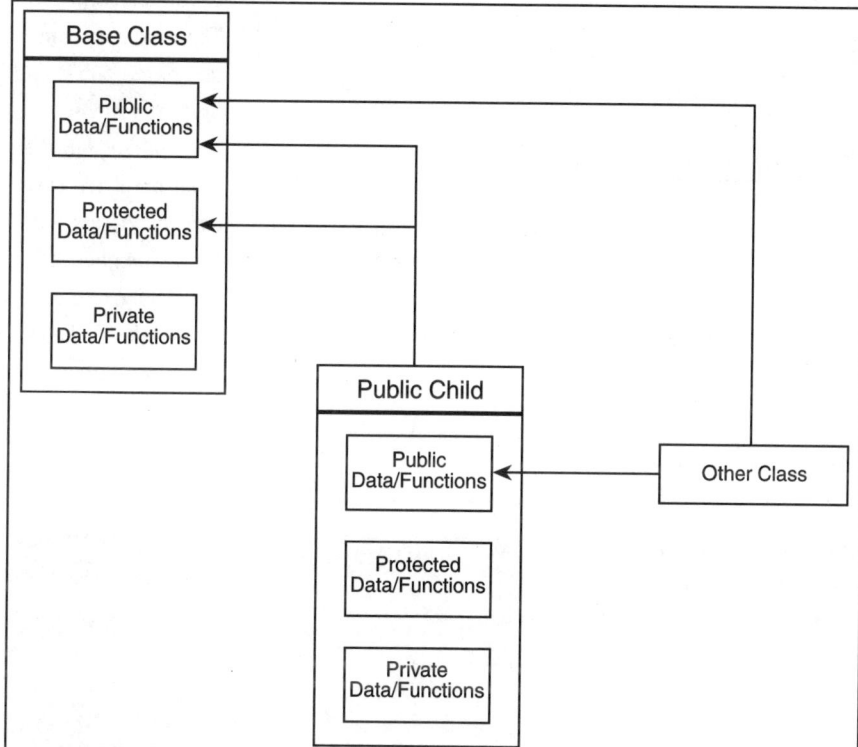

Figure 9.10
This figure shows how classes can access different class members using public inheritance. The child class can access the public and protected members of its parent, and the other unrelated class can access only public members of both the child and the parent.

So what this means is that not only can you use the Draw and SetGraphic functions of the Item class, but you can also use the GetX, GetY, SetX, and SetY functions of the Object class!

If you used private inheritance, though, things would be different. Figure 9.11 shows the relationship between the classes in private inheritance.

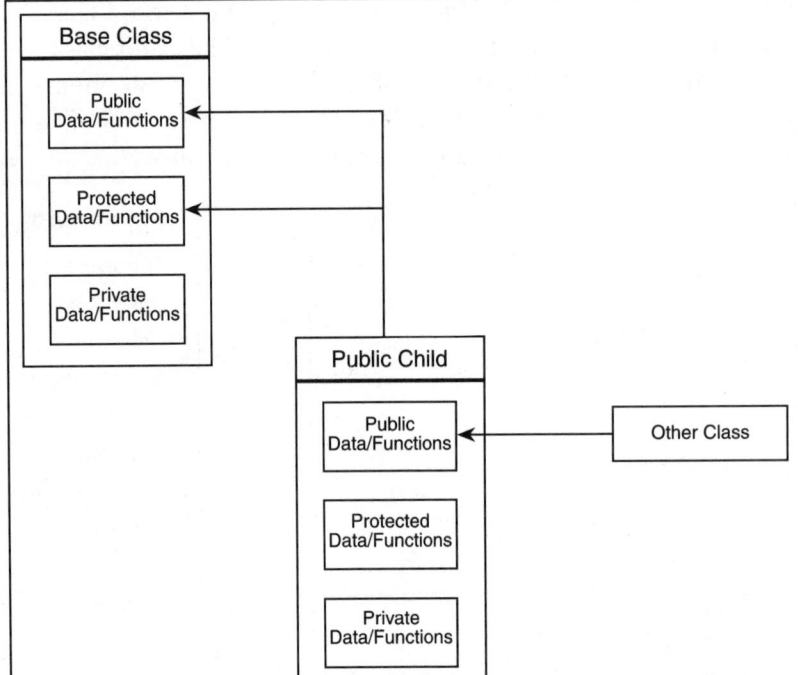

Figure 9.11
This figure shows how classes can access different class members using private inheritance. The child class can access the public and protected members of its parent, but the other unrelated class can only access the public members of the child. External classes do not know about the parent.

In private inheritance, the child class has access to the public and protected members of the base class, but outside classes and functions no longer have any access to any members of the base class.

If you inherited the Item class from the Object class using private inheritance, you would not be able to use the GetX, GetY, SetX, and SetY functions outside of the Item class.

> **NOTE**
> Private inheritance has its uses, but they are very limited, and it's not often used (I've only used private inheritance once before). I included it here for completeness so you won't be confused if you see it used elsewhere. Nothing in this book uses private inheritance.

The Person Class

Now, think of the kinds of things you want in a player class. Every person in the game must have some sort of health indicator, right? How about an inventory of items, too?

```
class Person : public Object
{
```

```cpp
    protected:
        int m_health;
        Item* m_inventory[16];
        SDL_Surface* m_animation[16];
        int m_currentframe;
    public:
        Person()
        {
            int i;
            for( i = 0; i < 16; i++ )
            {
                m_animation[i] = 0;
            }
            m_currentframe = 0;
        }
        int GetHealth()   { return m_health; };
        void SetHealth( int p_health ) { m_health = p_health; };
        Item* GetInventory( int p_index )
        {
            return m_inventory[p_index];
        }
        void SetInventory( int p_index, Item* p_item )
        {
            m_inventory[p_index] = p_item;
        }
        void SetFrame( int p_frame, SDL_Surface* p_graphic )
        {
            m_animation[p_frame] = p_graphic;
        }
        void Draw()
        {
            SDLBlit( g_screen, m_animation[m_currentframe],
                     m_x, m_y );
        }
        void SetFrame( int p_frame ) { m_currentframe = p_frame; };
        int GetFrame() { return m_currentframe; };
};
```

This is getting somewhat complex, isn't it? The Player class adds four new variables: a health, an inventory array, an array of graphics, and a frame counter. The health is easy to set and get, using the two accessor functions near the top, but the inventory array is a little bit more difficult to use.

The inventory array is limited to 16 items and has two functions to retrieve or insert items at the various indexes.

Keep in mind that this class is just a hypothetical class and not something

> **NOTE**
> I chose not to use the `Array` class in this demonstration because it would actually confuse things a little bit, as it is resizable and requires a complex constructor. I just want to focus on the general class structure for now.

that you should use in a real game. The graphic array is limited to 16 different graphics.

> **NOTE**
> In real life you would probably want the graphic array at a variable size, depending on the kind of artwork you use. Or, if you are not even using 2D, you would have the 3D representation of the `Person` class stored there. The point I am trying to make with this class is that `Item`s are usually stationary objects and require only one graphic, and `Person`s are usually animated objects and require a more complex representation in the game world.

Using the Classes in a Game

Now that I have showed you three very basic classes, I want to show you how they are used within a game.

First, let's say you keep one large array of `Object`s:

```
Array<Object*> g_objects( 1024 );
```

This array can store up to 1024 objects. Now, throughout the game, you fill up the array with people and items:

```
g_objects[0] = new Person;
// set up the person here
g_objects[1] = new Item;
// set up the item here
// continue adding persons and items...
```

Now, this is your global array of items. What is so neat about it? What happens if you want to draw every item in your game?

```
int i;
for( i = 0; i < g_objects.Size(); i++ )
{
    if( g_objects[i] != 0 )
        g_objects[i].Draw();
}
```

This little function draws every single object in the game (if it exists), and it doesn't care *how* it is drawn! The `Item` class and the `Person` class theoretically draw in two totally different ways, and your renderer doesn't even care! *This* is the power of inheritance.

The `Object` class says to you: "Every single child of `Object` will know how to draw itself."

Using the Child-Specific Features

Unfortunately, there is a flaw using this method to store data in the game. Say you know that you put a `Person` into index 0 of the `g_objects` array and you wanted to change his health.

You would think that you could do this:

```
g_objects[0].SetHealth( 100 );
```

This line will not compile; the compiler will complain that the `SetHealth` is not a member of the `Object` class! Now, before you call your compiler stupid and kick it to death, you should know that the compiler is right; the `Object` class does not have a `SetHealth` function. See, the compiler looks at everything in that array and sees them all as `Objects` and not their actual classes.

The compiler doesn't know that the `Object` in index 0 is actually a `Person`, so you have to tell it that. Telling the compiler this, however, is an ugly process.

The first thing you need to do is make sure your compiler supports a feature called *Run Time Type Information (RTTI)*. Most newer compilers do. Microsoft Visual C++ supports this feature, but it is not enabled by default. Instead, you need to turn it on manually.

Enabling RTTI in Visual C++

Figures 9.12 and 9.13 show screenshots of the menus you should go to. First, open your project and go the Project menu and select Settings. Next, make sure the Settings For field says All Configurations, and then switch to the C++ tab. In the

Category field, select C++ Language. Finally, click on the box that says Enable Run-Time Type Information (RTTI).

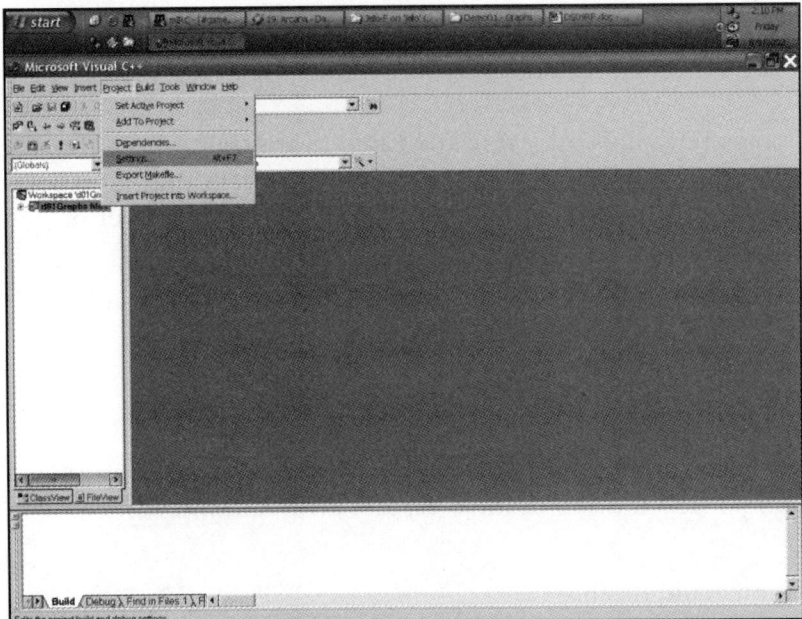

Figure 9.12

Go to the Project menu, and then select the Settings option.

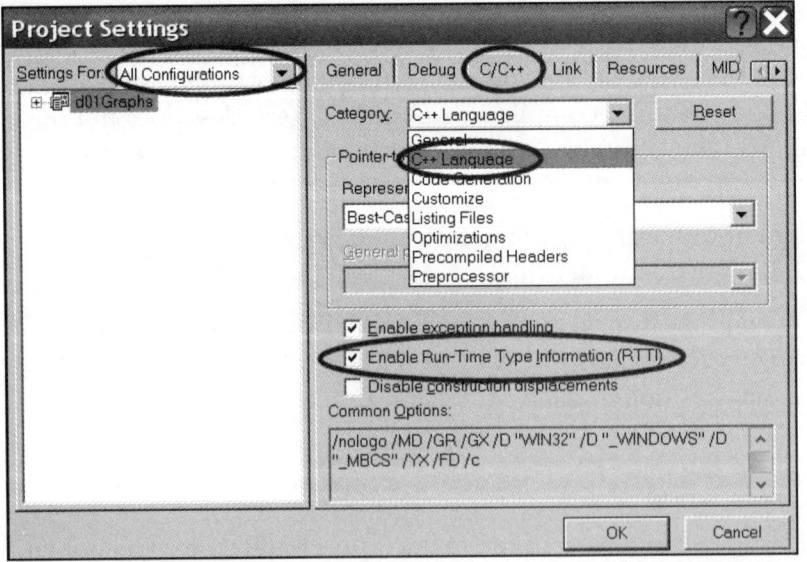

Figure 9.13

These are the settings you need to have enabled to use RTTI.

Now your project is set up to use RTTI, which is what you need to use to tell your compiler that an `Object` is really a `Person`.

Using RTTI

Now, say that you know that the first item in the item array is a `Person`. This is the "correct" way to convert it into a `Person` class:

```
Person* p = 0;
p = dynamic_cast<Person*>( g_objects[0] );
```

This code makes use of a new keyword called the `dynamic_cast` operator, which is the "safe" way to convert a parent class into a child class. If everything was successful, `p` is now a valid `Person`, and you can change his health. This process is called *down-casting*.

What happens if that index wasn't actually a `Person`, but an `Item` instead? Say you did this:

```
g_objects[0] = new Item;
Person* p = 0;
p = dynamic_cast<Person*>( g_objects[0] );
```

> **NOTE**
> Why do you need to specifically enable RTTI in Visual C++? The designers of the compiler feel that RTTI is a very slow feature and should only be used sparingly, and they are correct. I deal with this matter later.

> **NOTE**
> You're not actually converting data at all. What you are doing is copying the pointer over into a new pointer so that the compiler knows what features it has. Both pointers point to the same exact data, except that a pointer to an `Object` doesn't know about all the extra data that is in the class. If you tried just saying `p = g_objects[0]`, the compiler would complain because it doesn't know if `g_objects[0]` is a `Person` or not yet. This is for your safety, which I will show you in a bit.

What does `p` contain? Because you tried converting an `Item` into a `Person`, the `dynamic_cast` operator detects this and just returns 0 instead of a valid pointer. This prevents you from accidentally trying to turn an `Item` into a `Person` or vice versa.

Another Way, Without RTTI

There is another way to convert parent classes into child classes, but you must be absolutely certain that the classes are what you think they are, or you will get some very bad bugs.

This method doesn't use RTTI and is much faster, but much less safe, too:

```
Person* p = (Person*)g_objects[0];
```

This is just the standard C typecasting method; the compiler will treat any object in that array as a `Person` after this line, even if it isn't a person!

Figure 9.14 shows the representation of the `Item` and the `Person` classes in memory.

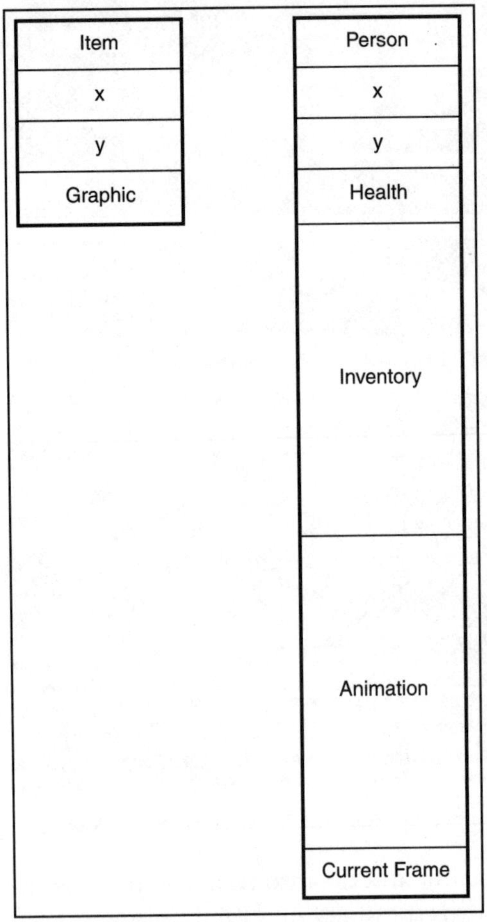

Figure 9.14

This is the memory representation of the two classes. Only the first two variables, the x and the y coordinates, are shared between them.

Item
x
y
Graphic

Person
x
y
Health
Inventory
Animation
Current Frame

Both classes have their coordinates in the same place because they inherit from the `Object` class, but the similarities end there.

When you accidentally treat an `Item` as a `Person` and then try accessing something a `Person` has but an `Item` doesn't, you end up with a big error. Look at where the graphic and the health data members are for each class. Look at this code, for example:

```
g_objects[0] = new Item;
// fill in item information
```

```
Person* p = (Person*)g_objects[0];
p.SetHealth( 100 );
```

This sets up an `Item` in the first index and then treats it as a `Person` and modifies the health of the `Person`. There is one problem: You're trying to modify data that doesn't exist! When you modify the health of this fake player, the function changes the data in the place in memory where the health *should* be if it were a player, which is the same place where the `Item` class stores its graphic pointer!

So when you do this, you're modifying the pointer of an `Item` graphic and not the health of a player.

It gets even worse. What happens when you try to modify the inventory or the animation pointers of this fake player? The `Item` class doesn't even have memory down there, so you have no idea what you are reading or writing over!

Finding bugs caused by this kind of programming is next to impossible.

Tips

So it seems that both methods have catches, and neither one seems to be a clear winner. The unsafe method is much faster, but can lead to disastrous bugs. The safe way is very slow, however, and you really don't want to be doing stuff like that in a game.

I'll leave you off with a few tips. First of all, inheritance is a very complex subject, one that takes many years to master. I have kept inheritance usage in this book to an absolute minimum, and almost none of the chapters use it. If you didn't really understand what this section is about, don't worry about it; almost no one understands it right away.

If you find yourself needing to down-cast your classes a lot, then that is a sign that your design is inefficient. Inheritance is a very neat feature that allows us to reuse code, but you should only use it when it makes sense. I will show you a more proper example of how to use inheritance in the next section.

Making a Game

The rest of this chapter is concerned only with making a simple tile-based game using the data structures from this part of the book and the design techniques discussed in this chapter.

The game demo is pretty complex, and it is the largest game demo in the book so far. All of the source code for this entire section is on the CD in the directory \demonstrations\ch09\Game01 - Adventure v1\.

> ### Compiling the Game
>
> This game uses the SDLHelpers library that I have developed for the book. For more information about this library, see Appendix B.
>
> To compile this game, either open up the workspace file in the directory or create your own project using the settings described in Appendix B. If you create your own project, all of the files you need to include are in the directory.

Adventure: Version One

The game is called *Adventure: Version One*. The name isn't very imaginative, but remember, this is a demonstration. The game will be upgraded and expanded in later chapters of the book after you learn more-complex data structures and algorithms (see Chapters 16, "Tying It Together: Trees," 19, "Tying It Together: Graphs," and 24, "Tying It Together: Algorithms").

Designing the Base

The first thing you are going to do when designing a game (after you've already figured out what genre and what motif you will be using) is to lay out the major classes that will be used in the game.

When designing a game, it always comes down to this: How will you store the data?

To find this out, you need to first think about what kind of objects (things) you will have in the game. In this game, which is relatively simple, there are *Items*, *People*, *Maps*, and *Cells*.

After you decide on objects, you need to figure out the relationships between the Items.

Items represent non-animated things that sit on the ground (armor, weapons). People represent animated creatures that can move around on a map and pick up items on the ground. Maps are a collection of Cells, and Cells hold Items or People.

It usually helps to draw a diagram so you can visualize the relationship between the objects, like Figure 9.15 shows.

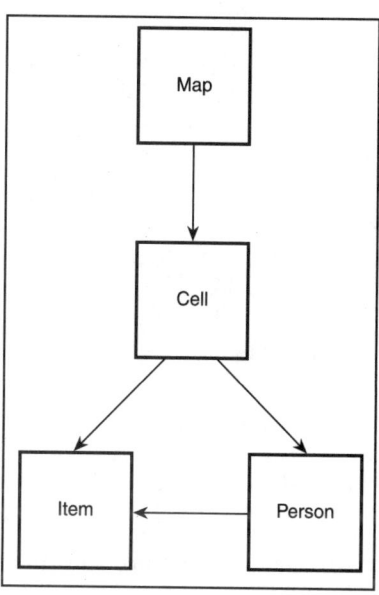

Figure 9.15

This is a simple class relationship diagram. The arrows show which classes contain others.

At the top of the chain is the map class, which will be the basis of the game. The map is made up of a bunch of cells, and each cell can contain an item and a person. Furthermore, the person will know about items and will have items in its inventory.

When you have worked out the general design, you can then focus on one of two design methods: *bottom-up* design or *top-down* design.

When you start at the top, you decide what features the top classes will need and work your way down. I prefer this method over bottom-up design because it gives you a greater sense of the whole game.

At this point in the design, you should be thinking more about *what* your game will do rather than *how* to do it. Therefore, you shouldn't be thinking about code at all at this point.

The Map

Because the first design already contains cell structures, you might have guessed that I am designing a tile-based map structure. Each cell will be a tile, and these tiles will be pieced together to form the entire map.

Until now, the only tile arrangements you have seen in this book are 2D (and 3D) tilemaps (in Chapters 5, "Multi-Dimensional Arrays," and 6, "Linked Lists"), so it would make sense that this is the kind of tilemap that the game will use.

However, I want to show you an example of good data structure design, so when designing the map, you should not assume that the cells are arranged in any specific manner right now. Instead, you want to design the class with these parameters in mind:

- You can access each cell in the map by an index.
- Each cell also has *x* and *y* coordinates.
- Each cell can hold one item and one person.
- You can move in four directions from each cell (north, east, south, west).
- The map can draw itself on the screen.
- The map should know which cells are blocked.
- The map should know the direction any person should move to get closer to another person.
- The map will have a viewer, which is a person that determines where the map is drawn on screen.

The `Map` class will be abstract and virtual, meaning that it will not have a specific implementation defined. This means that the `Map` class for this game demo will define *what* the map can do with the map, but not *how* it is done. This is an important point for expandable structure design, and the reason for this method will become completely obvious in Chapter 19, when a new `Map` class is added and seamlessly weaved into the game project.

The Cells

Although the `Cell` class is integral to the layout of the map, it is still only a conceptual class at this point in time. As a programmer, when accessing the map, you won't be touching the cells directly. Instead, you will tell the map what to store in each cell, and so on. Therefore, you really shouldn't be thinking about the cells too much at this point.

The Items

The items in the game won't be too complex. There are two major types of items: weapons and armor. None of these items are animated, so each item will need to hold only one graphic. Items should also know which cell and what coordinates they are at in the map (this is thinking ahead; maybe someday you will implement a system where you keep track of an item and where it is on the map).

If the item is a weapon, then you need two pieces of data about it: how long it takes between attacks and how much damage it does. Some weapons are lighter than others, so you will be able to attack with them more often than others.

If the item is armor, then it will have a strength to it, which determines how strong the armor is.

The last thing an item can do is block a path. Some items, like trees and walls, can block a cell on the map so that you can't walk through it.

The People

People in the game are like items, only they are a lot more complex. Here is a list of the attributes that a person can have:

- The cell that the person is in
- The x and y coordinates of the person
- Health, 0-100
- Armor, 0-100
- The direction that the person is facing
- A collection of items, representing the inventory of the person
- Something that keeps track of the current item that the person is using
- A bunch of graphics representing the person walking in each direction
- Timers that keep track of when the person can attack or move next
- A handicap, which determines how fast or slow the person is

Designing the Interfaces

After you compile a list of all of the features that your classes will use, you want to create *interfaces* for them. Sometimes interfaces are called *stubs*, and they are basically just a list of all the functions you will be using for the classes.

The Map Interface

Here is a listing of the map interface (which is a condensed version of the class found in the Map.h file; I've removed the comments because all of the functions are pretty much self-explanatory here):

```
class Map
{
protected:
    Person* m_viewer;
public:
    Map()
    Person* GetViewer()
    void SetViewer( Person* p_viewer )

    virtual void Draw( SDL_Surface* p_surface,
                       int p_midx, int p_midy ) = 0;
    virtual bool CanMove( Person* p_person, int p_direction ) = 0;
    virtual void Move( Person* p_object, int p_direction ) = 0;
    virtual int GetCellNumber( int p_cell, int p_direction ) = 0;
    virtual Item* GetItem( int p_cell ) = 0;
    virtual void SetItem( int p_cell, Item* p_item ) = 0;
    virtual Person* GetPerson( int p_cell ) = 0;
    virtual void SetPerson( int p_cell, Person* p_person ) = 0;
    virtual int GetNumberOfCells() = 0;
    virtual int GetClosestDirection( Person* p_one, Person* p_two ) = 0;
};
```

The first three functions are non-virtual. It is assumed that every map will have a person as a viewer, so it is safe to implement the viewer functions in the Map class.

Every other function, however, depends on the implementation of the map and is not actually implemented in the Map class.

The Draw function draws the map on the given surface, treating the p_midx and p_midy variables as the midpoint of the screen.

The CanMove function determines if a person can move in the selected direction. When it has been determined that he can move, you can then call the Move function to actually move the person.

The GetCellNumber function gets the number of an adjacent cell to the given cell number. If the function returns -1, there is no valid cell in that direction.

The GetClosestDirection function, when given two Person pointers, will find the direction that the first person needs to move to get closer to the second person.

The rest of the functions are used to get and set items and people in various cells and get the number of cells in the map.

Now, look at the interface of the map. Does it reveal anything about the actual implementation of the map? Does the setup say that you have to use a 2D array for the tilemap? It doesn't, and that is the beauty of such a system; you can swap out many different kinds of maps and the game engine that uses this map interface will not need to be changed at all. This feature will be demonstrated in far more depth in Chapter 19.

The Object Interface

Look back to the requirements of the `Item` and `Person` classes and see if you can find any similarities between them.

Notice how they both have three variables in common: The *x*, *y*, and cell coordinates. Using this idea, you can see that these two classes are clearly related somehow in that they are both stored on the map using the same coordinate system.

My original design for this game had both the `Item` and `Person` classes being inherited from the same base class, and each cell on the map would contain a pointer to this `Object` class. However, after dissecting the design, I ended up concluding that this wasn't a very good way to run the game. The game needs to frequently tell the difference between items and people so that a person doesn't try picking up another person or an item doesn't pick up a person. It turns out that making the map only store things as generic objects might make your game a little more flexible (yes, it would be cool to treat everything as objects so you can attack items and people at the same time, but in a game interface, it doesn't add much to the gameplay), but it requires a significant amount of work.

So instead of the map being class-agnostic, it specifically knows about items and people. However, because both classes share the same coordinate system, it makes sense to create one base class that implements these features, and the `Item` and `Person` classes will inherit from them:

```
class Object
{
protected:
    int m_x, m_y;
    int m_cell;
public:
    Object()
    {
        m_x = 0;
        m_y = 0;
```

```
        m_cell = 0;
    }
    int  GetCell()              { return m_cell; }
    void SetCell( int p_cell )  { m_cell = p_cell; }
    int  GetX()                 { return m_x; }
    void SetX( int p_x )        { m_x = p_x; }
    int  GetY()                 { return m_y; }
    void SetY( int p_y )        { m_y = p_y; }
};
```

The benefit of having a class such as this is that it is easily expandable. Of course, having six functions to read and write three variables seems kind of stupid, but remember what I told you at the beginning of the chapter: When you need to add features to this class later on, you will be thankful that you did it this way.

Another benefit of this base class is that all items inherited from it get the same implementation. If you decide to go 3D and add a z dimension, then you can easily add that variable and its appropriate accessor functions.

The Item Interface

Now you need to design the functions to access your Item class. Using the requirements that you determined previously, you should come up with something like this:

```
class Item : public Object
{
public:
    Item();
    int  GetType();
    void SetType( int p_type );
    int  GetSpeed();
    void SetSpeed( int p_speed );
    int  GetStrength();
    void SetStrength( int p_strength );
    void SetGraphic( SDL_Surface* p_graphic );
    SDL_Surface* GetGraphic();
    void SetBlock( bool p_block );
    bool CanBlock();
    void SetArmor( bool p_armor );
    bool IsArmor();
};
```

There are functions to determine what type the item is (the game will have hard-coded item types—6 is an axe, for example), the speed and strength of the item (speed is ignored for armor types), the graphic of the item, whether it can block your path, and whether it is armor or not.

The Person Interface

Last, there is the person interface. You need to figure out what a person can do, given the requirements.

At this point, you know that this class isn't abstract, so you should start thinking about the implementation. You know that the `Person` class will have a collection of items, so you need to think about how you are going to store those items. You could simply go for an arrayed approach and limit yourself to a given number of items. This method sort of makes sense because you, as a person, can only hold so many items at any given time. Of course, the problem with this method is that while you can probably only hold one large sword at a time, you can hold thousands of feathers.

For a simple flexible system, why not use linked lists? Although linked lists aren't that great for items that are created and deleted a lot, they are perfect for something like an inventory.

Here's the data listing for the class (which can be found in the Person.h file):

```
class Person : public Object
{
protected:
    int m_health;
    int m_armor;
    int m_type;
    int m_direction;
    DlinkedList<Item*> m_inventory;
    DListIterator<Item*> m_currentweapon;
    SDL_Surface* m_graphics[DIRECTIONS][FRAMES];
    int m_lastattack;
    int m_lastmove;
    int m_attackmodifier;
```

Now that you've seen the data in the class, here are the constructors, destructors, and operators:

9. Tying It Together: The Basics

> **NOTE**
> Note that the class is defined entirely in-line. That means that the function bodies are all in the .h file. For this listing, I have removed the function bodies, so that you can see all the functions of the class listed in one place easily. So the actual header file does not look like the code listing you see here.

```
public:
    Person()
    ~Person()
    Person( Person& p_person )
    void operator= ( Person& p_person )
```

The last two functions allow you to copy a person over into another person, essentially making a clone. However, because the `Person` class is more complex than other classes and stores classes of other data types (the inventory of items, in particular), you need to make sure that the person is copied over correctly (see Appendix A for more information on copy constructors).

> **NOTE**
> The reason for the assignment operator and copy constructor has to do with two copy methods called *shallow cloning* and *deep cloning*. If you don't have a copy constructor or an assignment operator, then C++ performs a shallow clone on the class whenever you do this: `itemA = itemB;`. Whenever there are pointers in that class, the value of the pointer is copied over, so both objects point to the same member object. If either of the objects deletes it, then the other object is in trouble. Because of this, you should create a copy constructor and an assignment operator that copy the class correctly.

```
    void SetDirection( int p_direction );
    int GetDirection();
    void SetPersonType( int p_type );
    int GetPersonType();
    void SetHealth( int p_health );
    int GetHealth();
    void SetArmor( int p_armor );
    int GetArmor();
    DListIterator<Item*> GetItemIterator();
    void AddItem( Item* p_item );
    int GetItemCount();
    void NextWeapon();
    void PreviousWeapon();
    Item* GetCurrentWeapon();
```

```
void SetGraphic( SDL_Surface* p_graphic, int p_direction, int p_frame );
SDL_Surface* GetGraphic();
void SetAttackTime( int p_time );
int GetAttackTime();
void SetMoveTime( int p_time );
int GetMoveTime();
void SetAttackModifier( int p_modifier );
int GetAttackModifier();
```

All of the previous functions are accessor functions. They are all pretty much self-explanatory, with the exception of a few. The `GetItemIterator` function will return a `DListIterator<Item*>`, but the iterator will be pointing to the current item instead of the start of the inventory. This is done this way because it is easier to use. If you need an iterator at the start of the inventory, you can easily just reset the iterator.

The `NextWeapon` and `PreviousWeapon` functions move the current weapon iterator to the next weapon or previous weapon in the inventory.

Whereas the `SetGraphic` function takes two parameters that determine which frame and direction a graphic should appear in, the `GetGraphic` function doesn't have any parameters. This is to make drawing the sprite easier. Whenever the function is called, it returns a pointer to the graphic that should be drawn at that point in time. If the person is facing north, then this function will return the appropriate graphic.

Finally, there are the more complex functions, which accomplish a lot of work:

```
    void Attack( Person* p_person );
    void GetAttacked( int p_damage );
    bool IsDead();
    void PickUp( Item* p_item );
};
```

The `Attack` function makes a person attack another person. The `GetAttacked` function is called whenever the person is attacked. The `IsDead` function determines if the person is dead, and the `PickUp` function makes the player pick up an item. After an item is passed into the `PickUp` function, you don't have to worry about it anymore; the player keeps track of the item from now on.

Creating an Implementation for the Map

Before you go any further, take a look at Figure 9.16. This figure shows an updated class diagram for the game.

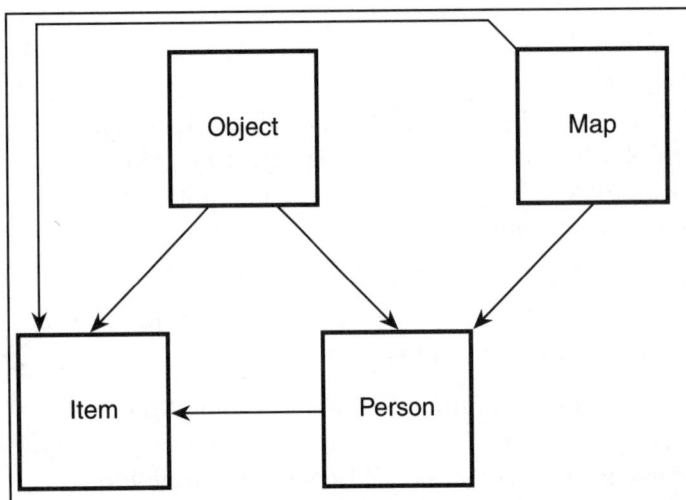

Figure 9.16

Here is the updated class diagram for the game.

This is your *game engine interface*. The *game logic module*, which makes these things actually work, will (theoretically) only know about these classes.

Now you want to actually create an implementation for the map. For this demo, you are going to use a more complex version of the tilemap from Chapter 5. This class is contained in the Tilemap.h file.

The Direction Table

In this game engine, you can move in four directions: north, east, south, and west. Each of these directions is associated with a number from 0 through 3. North is 0, east is 1, south is 2, and west is 3.

To make it easy to move around the map given an *x* and a *y* coordinate, you can easily make a 2D array that contains offsets for each direction:

```
const int DIRECTIONTABLE[4][2] = { { 0, -1 },
                                   { 1, 0 },
                                   { 0, 1 },
                                   { -1, 0 } };
```

This means that if you are moving north (direction 0), you add 0 to the *x* coordinate and -1 to the *y* coordinate. This is usually accomplished like this:

```
x = x + DIRECTIONTABLE[direction][0];
y = y + DIRECTIONTABLE[direction][1];
```

The TileCell Class

Back in Figure 9.15, there was a `Cell` class, but somehow while I was designing the overall design, the `Cell` class kind of disappeared. The reason it disappeared was because the `Cell` class is more of an implementation-specific class rather than an interface class. Besides, there really is no reason to give the user of the system access to the `Cell` class; he should do everything through the `Map` class interface instead.

However, now that you are implementing a tilemap, you need to create a `Cell` class that will store information about each cell. Because each cell will hold a person and an item, it obviously needs to contain pointers to these classes. Also, features of the geometry may block certain cells, so there needs to be some way to tell if the cell is blocked or not. Here is the class:

```
class TileCell
{
public:
    bool m_blocked;
    Item* m_item;
    Person* m_person;

    TileCell()
    {
        m_blocked = false;
        m_item = 0;
        m_person = 0;
    }
};
```

"Wait a minute!" you might be saying. "You broke all of your accessor rules!" True. However, this `Cell` class will be closely related to the `Tilemap` class, and the class is simple, so the accessor functions aren't entirely necessary.

The TileMap Class Interface

Now that you are focusing on an implementation rather than an interface, you need to start thinking about how you are going to store the data in the map.

For the graphics, a 3D array will be used so that you can use some cool layered tilemapping effects. The cells in this array will store the index of the tile graphics, which means that the graphics themselves will be stored in an array.

However, that is not all the information you need. In addition, a 2D array will store instances of the `TileCell` class defined previously.

Granted, the `TileCell` class could have contained a linked list of integers, so you could store the tilemap like the Game Demo 2 from Chapter 6, but this method makes it easier to load levels from disk.

Finally, there is one more piece of data the `Tilemap` class keeps track of: an array of graphics, which the tilemap will use to draw its tiles.

Here is the code listing for the data in the class, which is in the TileMap.h file:

> **NOTE**
> If you wanted to make a linked-layer tilemap like the one from Chapter 6, you can easily make a `LinkedTileMap` class inherited from the `Map` class, and the game logic wouldn't care. As long as the map does what its interface says it does, everything will work perfectly.

> **NOTE**
> Like the Person.h file, the non-virtual functions of this class are implemented in-line, so the header file does not look exactly like this.

```
class TileMap : public Map
{
protected:
    Array3D<int> m_tiles;
    Array2D<TileCell> m_tilemap;
    SDL_Surface** m_tilebmps;
```

The class inherits from the `Map` class and defines the three data members as specified previously. Now, here is a listing of the new functions that the `TileMap` class adds:

```
    TileMap( int p_x, int p_y, int p_z, SDL_Surface** p_tilebmps );
    ~TileMap();
    void SetTile( int p_x, int p_y, int p_z, int p_tile );
```

```
    int GetCell( int p_x, int p_y );
    void LoadFromFile( char* p_filename );
};
```

There is the constructor, which takes three coordinates: the width, height, and depth of the tilemap. It also takes a pointer to an array of `SDL_Surface` pointers so the tilemap knows which tiles to draw.

Then there is a destructor. This is important because the map keeps track of the people and items on the map, and all of these people and items need to be deleted when the map is deleted. The destructor does this.

The next function sets the graphic value of certain cells throughout the map. The `GetCell` function gets the cell number of a pair of *x* and *y* coordinates, and last, the `LoadFromFile` function does just what it says and loads a map from a file on disk.

The TileMap Class Implementation

Because the `TileMap` class *is-a* map, it needs to implement all of the pure virtual functions that the `Map` class had, as well as its own functions. In addition, because there are many plain accessor functions that do nothing more than directly set the value of a member variable or return the value of a member variable, I will not show the source for those functions here.

The Constructor

Here is the code for the `TileMap` constructor:

```
TileMap( int p_x, int p_y, int p_z, SDL_Surface** p_tilebmps )
        : m_tiles( p_x, p_y, p_z ), m_tilemap( p_x, p_y )
{
    m_tilebmps = p_tilebmps;
}
```

This function uses the standard constructor member-initialization to construct the 3D and 2D arrays (if you are unfamiliar with this notation, please see Appendix A). Then the `m_tilebmps` pointer (which points to an array of graphics, which represent the tiles) is set to point to the array that was passed in.

The Destructor

The destructor, as I have said before, is very important to this class. The map contains all of the people and items in the game, and when the map is deleted, these should be as well.

```
~TileMap()
{
    int x, y;
    for( y = 0; y < m_tilemap.Width(); y++ )
    {
        for( x = 0; x < m_tilemap.Height(); x++ )
        {
            if( m_tilemap.Get( x, y ).m_item != 0 )
                delete m_tilemap.Get( x, y ).m_item;
            if( m_tilemap.Get( x, y ).m_person != 0 )
                delete m_tilemap.Get( x, y ).m_person;
            m_tilemap.Get( x, y ).m_item = 0;
            m_tilemap.Get( x, y ).m_person = 0;
        }
    }
}
```

The function goes through every cell in the map, and if an item or person exists in any of the cells, it is deleted and the pointer is set to zero.

The GetCell Function

This function returns the cell number of any given *x* and *y* coordinates in the map. Remember in Chapter 5 when I showed you how to convert those coordinates so that you could store a 2D array as a regular array? This map will use the same encoding. So cell (0,0) will be 0, (1,0) will be 1, and so forth.

```
int GetCell( int p_x, int p_y )
{
    return p_y * m_tiles.Width() + p_x;
}
```

The LoadFromFile Function

This next function is somewhat long and complex, and you won't completely understand it until you go over the map editor in the next game demo from this chapter (Game Demonstration 9-2). I will try to make it as simple as possible, though.

The map format that this game uses can theoretically have many different sizes of maps because the constructor lets you use different sizes as the dimensions. However, the file format that the map editor uses assumes that the map will be 64 × 64 tiles and have two layers.

The file will actually store four layers, like Figure 9.17 shows.

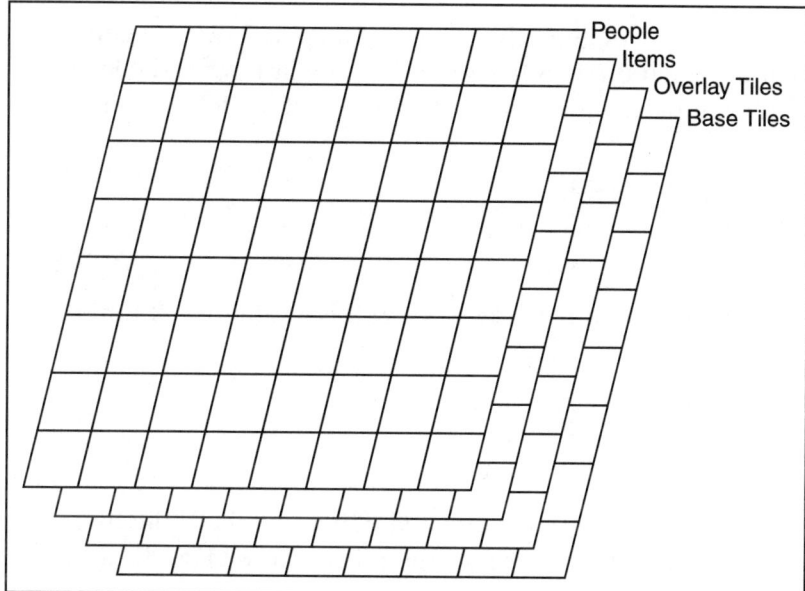

Figure 9.17

The map file format is stored as a four-layered 2D array.

The first two layers should be familiar to you; they both serve the same functions as they did in the game demo from Chapter 5. The base layer stores all valid tiles, and the second layer stores *overlay* tiles, which are usually transparent and let you achieve some nice transition effects.

The third layer is the item layer. Each cell can only store one item, so it is somewhat easy to keep track of items in the map when editing it. It also prevents two or more items from occupying the same cell, which cannot happen in the game. The fourth layer is the same, except that it stores people instead of items.

Each cell in the map file will store one integer. This integer will correspond to a given cell, item, or person. For example, in the game, tiles 0 through 3 are all grass tiles, 4 and 5 are snow tiles, and so on. Items 0 through 5 are walls, 6 is an axe, and so on. There are only three types of people, though, and this is a special case. Person 0 is assumed to be the player, and people 1 and 2 are enemies.

```
void LoadFromFile( char* p_filename )
{
    int x, y;
    int item;
    int person;
```

```
Array2D<int> items( 64, 64 );
Array2D<int> people( 64, 64 );
```

There are two integers to loop through each tile on the map and two integers that are used to load item and person indexes from the file. The last two variables are 2D arrays, which are only temporary for this function and will be deleted when the function ends.

```
FILE* f = fopen( p_filename, "rb" );
if( f == 0 )
    return;
```

This section of code opens the file and checks to see if it is a valid file. If not, then the function just returns without doing anything.

```
fread( m_tiles.m_array, 64 * 64 * 2, sizeof(int), f );
fread( items.m_array, 64 * 64, sizeof(int), f );
fread( people.m_array, 64 * 64, sizeof(int), f );
```

In this part, the whole file is read in three chunks. The first line reads the first two layers of the map, which are the tiles, and it puts them into the `m_tiles` 3D array (which should be of size 64 × 64 × 2).

After that, the third layer (items) is read into the item array. Finally, the fourth layer is read into the people array.

Because the items and people are now stored in separate 2D arrays, you need to go through those arrays and convert the numbers into actual `Items` and `Persons`:

```
for( y = 0; y < 64; y++ )
{
    for( x = 0; x < 64; x++ )
    {
        item = items.Get( x, y );
        if( item != -1 )
        {
            m_tilemap.Get( x, y ).m_item =
                MakeItem( item, x, y, GetCell( x, y ) );
        }
    }
}
```

This segment loads in the item number at each cell. If the number is -1, then that means that there is no `Item` in that cell, and nothing should happen. If there is an `Item`, however, the function then calls a helper function, called `MakeItem`, which takes the item number, its coordinates, and its cell number and converts them into an actual `Item`. I explain this helper function in more detail later on.

```
            person = people.Get( x, y );
            if( person != -1 )
            {
                m_tilemap.Get( x, y ).m_person =
                    MakePerson( person, x, y, GetCell( x, y ) );
```

After it loads the Item, it looks to see if there is a Person in that cell as well. If so, then it calls the MakePerson helper function to create a new Person. However, this doesn't end here—it goes on:

```
                if( person == 0 )
                {
                    SetViewer( m_tilemap.Get( x, y ).m_person );
                }
            }
        }
    }
}
```

If the Person in the current cell has a type of 0, then the Person is the player in the game. So the function then calls the SetViewer function to set the viewer of the map. There is one tiny little flaw in this function, however. If there is more than one type 0 Person on the map, then the last one it finds will become the player, and all other ones will be AI-controlled enemies.

The Draw Function

Now all of the new TileMap functions are implemented, so you must implement the Map functions. The first of these is the Draw function, which draws the tilemap onto the screen, so that the map is centered around the viewer. Here is the code listing:

```
void Draw( SDL_Surface* p_surface, int p_midx, int p_midy )
{
    int x, y, z;            // counting variables
    int px, py;             // pixel coordinates
    int ox, oy;             // offset coordinates
    int current;
    Item* i;
    Person* p;
```

The x, y, and z variables will be used to loop through the 3D tilemap array, px and py are used to store the pixel coordinates of a tile, and ox and oy are used to store the pixel offset coordinates of the viewer. This means that px and py will store the coordinates of the tile in *world space*. World space is the coordinates of things located in the world. The ox and oy coordinates keep track of how many pixels things in the world space need to be moved over to get into *screen space*. Figure 9.18 shows an 800 × 600 screen that is currently viewing a 1024 × 1024 (-pixel) tilemap.

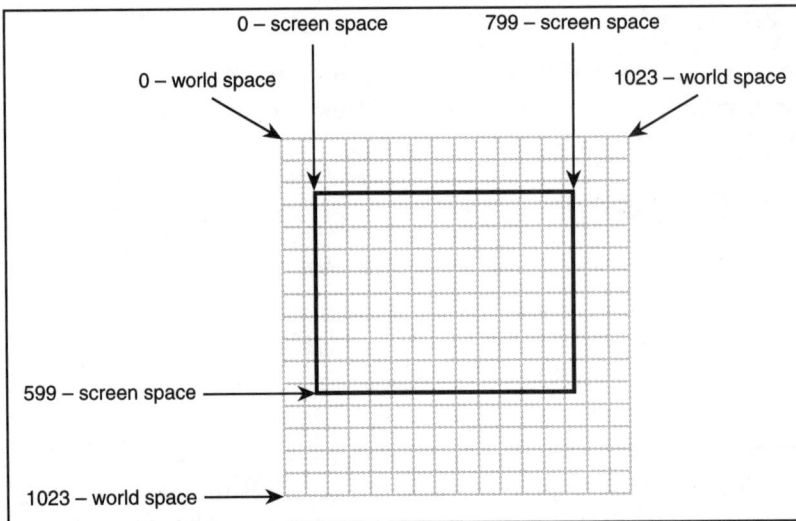

Figure 9.18

This figure depicts the two different coordinate systems: world space and screen space.

The tiles start at (0,0) in world space, but the screen is smaller and at a different part of the map. You can see from the figure that cell (1,2) is drawn at the upper-left corner of the screen. The world space coordinates for that cell are (64,128) because each cell is 64 pixels square, so you need to find a way to convert those coordinates so that they are drawn in the correct place on the screen. Because this is a 2D *linear* conversion, all you need to do is calculate the offset and add it to the drawing coordinates. You'll see how this works in a bit.

```
int minx = m_viewer->GetX() - (p_midx / 64) - 1;
int maxx = m_viewer->GetX() + (p_midx / 64) + 1;
int miny = m_viewer->GetY() - (p_midy / 64) - 1;
int maxy = m_viewer->GetY() + (p_midy / 64) + 1;
```

The previous section of code declares four integers and calculates values for them. These four values are the coordinates of the tiles that are on the edge of the screen. Examine the first line, for example. It retrieves the *x* coordinate of the viewer first. Then it takes the p_midx value, which is the midpoint of the screen in pixels. As the game runs in 800 × 600 mode, this should be 400. (Technically, it's 399.5, but we don't have to be that exact.) Then it divides 400 by 64 (because the tiles are 64 × 64 pixels square) to get the number of tiles that will fit in that part of the screen. It subtracts the number of tiles from the *x* coordinate of the viewer and then subtracts another tile, just to be safe.

These lines determine the bounds of the cells that are actually visible on the screen. For example, if the viewer was at (20,16), it would calculate `minx` to be 20 − (400 / 64) −1, which ends up being 13. This means that any cells with an *x* coordinate less than 13 are not on the screen at all and therefore should not be drawn. The four lines of code do the same thing for each edge of the screen.

```
if( minx < 0 )                     { minx = 0; }
if( maxx >= m_tiles.Width() )      { maxx = m_tiles.Width() - 1; }
if( miny < 0 )                     { miny = 0; }
if( maxy >= m_tiles.Height() )     { maxy = m_tiles.Height() - 1; }
```

Now this section of code makes sure that the calculated coordinates are valid. There are negative cells, but you obviously don't want to try drawing them; so if either of the `min` variables are negative, they are set to zero instead so that it starts drawing at the edge of the map. Likewise, it checks to see if either of the `max` variables have gone past the edge of the array and resets those.

```
ox = (-m_viewer->GetX() * 64) + p_midx - 32;
oy = (-m_viewer->GetY() * 64) + p_midy - 32;
```

This is the last part of the initialization, which calculates the offset coordinates so that the tile that the viewer is on is drawn in the center of the screen. Figure 9.19 shows how this works in the *x* axis.

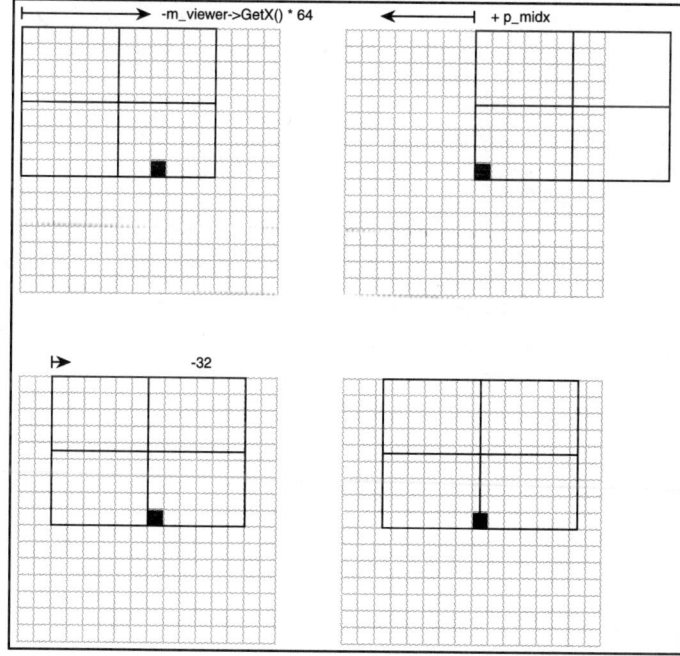

Figure 9.19

This shows how to calculate the screen offset for the black tile, which the viewer is on.

Even though the figures show the screen moving, keep in mind that you are actually moving around the coordinates of the tiles. First, you subtract the number of pixels from the end of the map to the viewer tile, which places the viewer tile at the left side of the screen. Then, to center the viewer on the screen, half of the width of the screen is added to the offset. Even though it is closer to the middle of the screen now, it still isn't exactly in the center. The tile is 64 pixels wide, so just subtract 32 pixels from the offset, and the tile is centered on the screen! The process works the same way for the y axis.

> **NOTE**
> Theoretically, because you are dealing with units of measurement, you should be able to access coordinates on a decimal scale. However, pixels are discreet objects, and you can only access them on integer boundaries. This can bring a few *off-by-one* errors into your code because whenever you use integer division, you usually truncate the remainder. Just be aware that you can never get the *exact* center of a pixel because you can only draw whole pixels on the screen.

```
for( y = miny; y <= maxy; y++ )
{
    for( x = minx; x <= maxx; x++ )
    {
        px = x * 64 + ox;
        py = y * 64 + oy;
```

Remember how the tilemap was rendered in the tilemap demo from Chapter 5? The method used there just drew every tile on the map. This is somewhat wasteful, so this newly updated algorithm is more efficient and starts drawing tiles starting at the boundaries that were calculated before. This way, the algorithm only draws tiles that will be shown on the screen.

At each cell, the algorithm calculates the world coordinates of the tile, adds the screen offset coordinates, and stores that into px and py.

```
        for( z = 0; z < m_tiles.Depth(); z++ )
        {
            current = m_tiles.Get( x, y, z );
            if( current != -1 )
                SDLBlit( m_tilebmps[current], p_surface, px, py );
        }
```

This is the inner loop that goes through all the layers of the current cell and draws them from the bottom up. The current tile number is loaded into the current variable and then compared to −1, which represents the empty tile. If the tile isn't empty, then it is drawn on the screen.

```
            i = m_tilemap.Get( x, y ).m_item;
            p = m_tilemap.Get( x, y ).m_person;
            if( i != 0 )
                SDLBlit( i->GetGraphic(), p_surface, px, py );
            if( p != 0 )
                SDLBlit( p->GetGraphic(), p_surface, px, py );
        }
    }
}
```

Finally, the `Item` and the `Person` of the tile are extracted. If either of them are valid, then they are also drawn. `Items` are drawn first, and then `People` are drawn on top.

The CanMove Function

This function is pretty easy to implement if you use all of the features available to you.

```
bool CanMove( Person* p_person, int p_direction )
{
    int newx = p_person->GetX() + DIRECTIONTABLE[p_direction][0];
    int newy = p_person->GetY() + DIRECTIONTABLE[p_direction][1];
```

First you get the coordinates for the cell that is in the direction that you want to go.

```
    if( newx < 0 || newx >= m_tiles.Width() ||
        newy < 0 || newy >= m_tiles.Height() )
        return false;
```

Then you check to see if those coordinates are in bounds of the map. If not, the function returns `false`.

```
    if( m_tilemap.Get( newx, newy ).m_blocked == true )
        return false;
```

Now check to see if the path is blocked by the geography.

```
    if( m_tilemap.Get( newx, newy ).m_person != 0 )
        return false;
```

Then check to see if there is a `Person` blocking the path.

```
    if( m_tilemap.Get( newx, newy ).m_item != 0 )
    {
```

```
            if( m_tilemap.Get( newx, newy ).m_item->CanBlock() == true )
                return false;
    }
```

Finally, check to see if an `Item` is blocking your way.

```
    return true;
}
```

If the function has reached this point, then you know that nothing is blocking the path into the cell, so it returns `true`.

The Move Function

This function physically moves a `Person` from one cell into another.

```
void Move( Person* p_person, int p_direction )
{
    int newx = p_person->GetX() + DIRECTIONTABLE[p_direction][0];
    int newy = p_person->GetY() + DIRECTIONTABLE[p_direction][1];
    if( CanMove( p_person, p_direction ) == true )
    {
```

First, calculate the coordinates of the cell that you want the `Person` to move into and make sure that the `Person` can move into that cell.

```
        m_tilemap.Get( newx, newy ).m_person = p_person;
        m_tilemap.Get( p_person->GetX(), p_person->GetY() ).m_person = 0;
        p_person->SetX( newx );
        p_person->SetY( newy );
        p_person->SetCell( GetCell( newx, newy ) );
    }
}
```

When you know that the `Person` can move into the new cell, the pointer to that `Person` is placed into the new cell and the pointer to the `Person` is removed from the old cell. Because a `Person` cannot move into a cell that is occupied by another `Person`, you can be sure that this function won't write over any existing `Person`.

After that, the new coordinates are given to the `Person`, as well as the new cell number.

The GetCellNumber Function

This function retrieves the number of a cell in any given direction. It will return the cell number if there is a cell in the given direction, but return -1 if the cell doesn't exist (if it is off the edge of the map, for example).

```
int GetCellNumber( int p_cell, int p_direction )
{
    int x, y;
    y = p_cell / m_tiles.Width();
    x = p_cell - (y * m_tiles.Width());
    x = x + DIRECTIONTABLE[p_direction][0];
    y = y + DIRECTIONTABLE[p_direction][1];
```

The first two lines calculate the *x* and *y* coordinates of the current cell number by reversing the algorithm that turns a 2D array coordinate into a 1D array coordinate. The *y* coordinate is calculated by dividing the cell number by the width of the map (the remainder is truncated), and then the *x* coordinate is calculated by subtracting the total of the *y* coordinate multiplied by the width of the map from the cell number.

After that, the adjacent cell coordinates are calculated.

```
    if( x < 0 || x >= m_tiles.Width() ||
        y < 0 || y >= m_tiles.Height() )
        return -1;
    return GetCell( x, y );
}
```

Finally, the function checks to see if the cell is within the bounds of the map. If not, then it returns -1. If it is within the bounds, then it returns the cell number.

The GetClosestDirection Function

This function calculates which direction will get one Person closer to another. This will be quite useful in calculating the AI of the enemies in the game. For right now, you don't know of anything more complex, so you just want to use a simple little algorithm to do it:

```
int GetClosestDirection( Person* p_one, Person* p_two )
{
    int direction = -1;
    if( p_one->GetY() > p_two->GetY() )
        direction = 0;
    else if( p_one->GetX() < p_two->GetX() )
        direction = 1;
    else if( p_one->GetY() < p_two->GetY() )
        direction = 2;
    else if( p_one->GetX() > p_two->GetX() )
```

```
        direction = 3;
    return direction;
}
```

This checks the relative *x* and *y* coordinates of the two players. If the first player has a greater *y* value than the second, this means that the first player is to the south and therefore must move north to get closer.

The next three blocks follow in the same manner, figuring out which direction will get the first player closer to the second player. Finally, the direction is returned.

The Item Class Implementation

For right now, every function in the `Item` class is just a plain accessor function that either sets or gets the value of each member variable. Because of this, there really isn't any reason to post the implementation of this class.

The Person Class Implementation

The `Person` class is a little bit more complex than the `Item` class, but not by much. Some of the functions are just plain accessor functions that do nothing but return the value of or set a member function. These functions will not be shown.

The Constructor

When a `Person` is constructed, it is always a good idea to set the data inside the `Person` so that it doesn't contain random data. This constructor does that:

```
Person()
{
    m_type = 0;
    m_health = 100;
    m_armor = 100;
    m_direction = 2;
    m_currentweapon = m_inventory.GetIterator();
```

These lines set up the `Person` so that he is type 0, has full health and armor, and is facing south. The last line retrieves an iterator from the inventory linked list. Even though the iterator will be invalid, because the inventory is empty, the iterator will now be pointing to the list. If you didn't call that line, the iterator wouldn't be pointing at any list.

```
    int f, d;
    for( d = 0; d < DIRECTIONS; d++ )
```

```
        {
            for( f = 0; f < FRAMES; f++ )
            {
                m_graphics[d][f] = 0;
            }
        }
```

This loop goes through the graphics array and clears all the graphics.

```
        m_lastmove = 0;
        m_lastattack = 0;
        m_attackmodifier = 0;
}
```

Last, the function clears the timers to 0 and sets the attack modifier to 0 as well.

The Destructor

The destructor of a `Person` is very important in this game. Because every `Item` in the game is an actual object that is created at one point in time using the `new` function to allocate memory, the `Items` must eventually be deleted as well, or else you will get a memory leak.

So when a `Person` dies, everything that the `Person` has in its inventory should be deleted. The destructor handles this:

```
~Person()
{
    DListIterator<Item*> itr = m_inventory.GetIterator();
    for( itr.Start(); itr.Valid(); itr.Forth() )
    {
        if( itr.Item() != 0 )
            delete itr.Item();
    }
}
```

This loop makes sure that every item in the inventory is deleted.

The Copy Constructor and Assignment Operator

I approached this issue previously when I showed you the interface of this class. Here is the actual implementation of these two functions:

```
Person( Person& p_person )
{
```

```
        *this = p_person;
}

void operator=( Person& p_person )
{
    int d, f;
    m_health    = p_person.m_health;
    m_armor     = p_person.m_armor;
    m_type      = p_person.m_type;
    m_direction = p_person.m_direction;
    for( d = 0; d < DIRECTIONS; d++ )
    {
        for( f = 0; f < FRAMES; f++ )
        {
            m_graphics[d][f] = p_person.m_graphics[d][f];
        }
    }
    m_lastattack = p_person.m_lastattack;
    m_lastmove   = p_person.m_lastmove;
    m_attackmodifier = p_person.m_attackmodifier;
    m_x = p_person.m_x;
    m_y = p_person.m_y;
    m_cell = p_person.m_cell;
}
```

The copy constructor basically just calls the assignment operator by dereferencing the `this` pointer (see Appendix A). The statement `*this = p_person` literally says, "The value of this current `Person` should be set to the value of the parameter."

The assignment operator essentially copies everything over, with the exception of two things: the current weapon iterator and the inventory linked list. This is because, as of right now, there is no need to copy the inventory of a `Person` over. Maybe someday you might need that functionality, but you don't right now, so it isn't implemented. The iterator should *never* be copied over from one `Person` to another because the iterator's copy constructor will now make the iterator in the current `Person` point to the inventory of the other `Person`, which is not a good idea.

The SetDirection Function

This function sets the direction of the `Person`, but it also does a little error checking as well.

```
void SetDirection( int p_direction )
{
    m_direction = (p_direction + 4) % 4;
}
```

First, it adds 4 to the new direction, and then it modulos that by 4. The reason this is done is so that you can do easy turns in the game. For example, if you want the `Person` to turn left, you just subtract 1 from the direction. Instead of requiring all the code outside of this class to check to see if the new direction is −1, this handles it for you. This adds 4 to that, which gives you direction 3. It works the same way in the other direction too, which is what the `modulo` function is for. Anything larger than 3 will be wrapped down to the 0–3 range.

The SetHealth Function

A player's health can range from 0–100. It is important that it never goes outside of these ranges if you assume that it will always be in there somewhere.

The function that sets the health of a player manages this for you:

```
void SetHealth( int p_health )
{
    m_health = p_health;
    if( m_health < 0 )
        m_health = 0;
    if( m_health > 100 )
        m_health = 100;
}
```

If the health dips below 0, then it is automatically reset to 0, and if the health goes above 100, then it is reset to 100 again.

The SetArmor Function

The function that sets the armor of the player is exactly the same:

```
void SetArmor( int p_armor )
{
    m_armor = p_armor;
    if( m_armor < 0 )
        m_armor = 0;
    if( m_armor > 100 )
        m_armor = 100;
}
```

The AddItem Function

This function adds an item to the inventory of the player.

```
void AddItem( Item* p_item )
{
    m_inventory.Append( p_item );
    if( m_currentweapon.Valid() == false )
    {
        m_currentweapon.Start();
    }
}
```

The item is first appended to the end of the inventory list. After that, the function checks to see if the current weapon iterator is valid. If the iterator is invalid, then the `Person` didn't have any items in the inventory. Now that it has one, you can set the current weapon to the first item in the list (remember, this is because this simple game only allows weapon items in a `Person`'s inventory).

The NextWeapon and PreviousWeapon Functions

These functions move the weapon to the next or previous weapon in the list.

```
void NextWeapon()
{
    m_currentweapon.Forth();
    if( m_currentweapon.Valid() == false )
        m_currentweapon.End();
}
void PreviousWeapon()
{
    m_currentweapon.Back();
    if( m_currentweapon.Valid() == false )
        m_currentweapon.Start();
}
```

Both functions move the iterator and then check to see if it has been moved past the end of the list. If so, then the iterator is moved back to the end that it passed.

The GetCurrentWeapon Function

This function returns a pointer to the current weapon in the player's inventory.

```
Item* GetCurrentWeapon()
{
```

```
    if( m_currentweapon.Valid() )
        return m_currentweapon.Item();
    return 0;
}
```

The function makes sure that the iterator is valid first, and then it returns the item. If the iterator wasn't valid, then 0 is returned, meaning that the player doesn't have a current weapon.

The GetAttackTime Function

When the game wants to know when the last time the player has attacked, this function is called. However, this function does a little more than just return the last time the player has attacked:

```
int GetAttackTime()
{
    return m_lastattack - m_attackmodifier;
}
```

It takes the time that the player last attacked and subtracts the attack modifier from it. If this value is positive, it has the effect of making the computer think that the player attacked earlier than he did. A positive attack modifier makes the player attack faster.

Likewise, a negative attack modifier would make the player attack slower.

The Attack Function

This is the function that is called whenever you want the player to attack another player:

```
void Attack( Person* p_person )
{
    Item* weapon = GetCurrentWeapon();
    p_person->GetAttacked( weapon->GetStrength() );
}
```

The function gets the current weapon from the `Person` (note that it assumes that the weapon will be valid; you may want to add some error checking here) and tells the target that it was attacked with the strength rating of the weapon. Though this is just a simple system, it does its job. In more complex systems, you may want to add random numbers to the damage (see Chapter 22, "Random Numbers," for more information on random numbers) or modify the damage based on the strength of the player or any other system you can think of.

This is also a good point to add death detection. If you killed the Person, then you might want something to happen to the current Person, such as gaining experience points.

The GetGraphic Function

This function retrieves the current graphic of the player, based on the time and the direction he is facing.

```
SDL_Surface* GetGraphic()
{
    int index = (SDL_GetTicks() % 1000) * FRAMES;
    index /= 1000;
    return m_graphics[m_direction][index];
}
```

This makes the animation loop through once every second. First, the current time (in milliseconds) is retrieved via the SDL_GetTicks function, and then it is moduloed by 1,000. You now have a number from 0–999, which is then multiplied by the number of frames. After that, the number is divided by 1,000, which should give you the current frame number.

For example, if you have four frames and the timer returns 12,430, then this is what it does: 12,430 is moduloed by 1,000, giving you 430, which is then multiplied by 4. This gives you 1,720. Now the number is divided by 1,000, which gives you 1.72. Because the division is an integer division, the decimal is chopped off, which gives you 1 as the frame number.

Finally, the graphic in the 2D array using the current direction and the current frame is returned.

The GetAttacked Function

This is the function that is called whenever a player is attacked by another player. This function takes a damage value as a parameter:

```
void GetAttacked( int p_damage )
{
    int newdamage = (p_damage * (100 - m_armor) ) / 100;
    SetHealth( GetHealth() - newdamage );
    SetArmor( GetArmor() - p_damage );
}
```

I'm not going to spend much time explaining this function because it doesn't really have much to do with the data structures. Basically, if you have 80 armor, then the amount of damage done to you is reduced by 80 percent. Then the armor is degraded by the amount of damage.

The IsDead Function

A person is dead if he has no health:

```
bool IsDead()
{
    return (m_health == 0);
}
```

The PickUp Function

This is the function that is called whenever a person picks up an item from the map.

```
void PickUp( Item* p_item )
{
    if( p_item->IsArmor() )
    {
```

First, it checks to see if the item is armor. If so, then the person shouldn't actually pick it up, but instead should have the strength of the armor added to the person's armor.

```
        SetArmor( m_armor + p_item->GetStrength() );
        delete p_item;
        return;
    }
```

Once that happens, the armor is deleted, and the function exits.

```
    AddItem( p_item );
}
```

If the item isn't armor, then it is just added to your inventory.

Creating People and Items

Earlier, I used two functions in the code, `MakeItem` and `MakePerson`. These functions, when called, will produce an item or a person, copying them from an array of templates (not to be confused with the C++ template feature).

Figure 9.20 shows how this is accomplished.

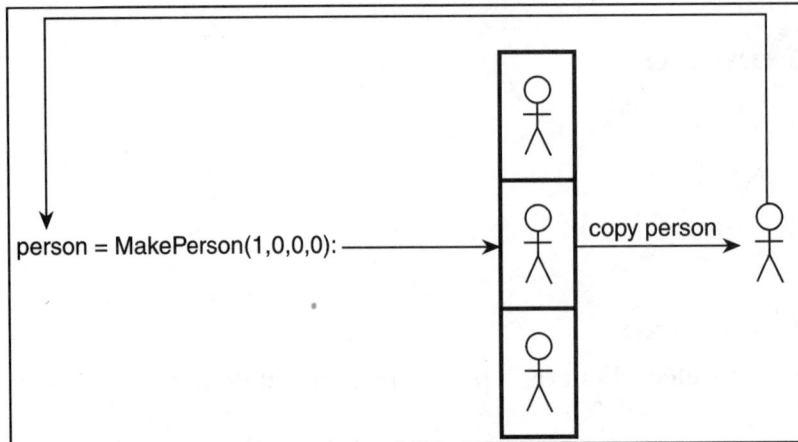

Figure 9.20

This shows how the MakePerson function works. It copies a Person out of the template array and returns the new Person.

There is an array filled with three Persons, and whenever you ask for a Person of type x, it looks up the Person at index x in the array, copies that Person, and returns it. It works the same way with the Items.

Here is the code for the MakeItem function and the global array that is associated with it:

```
Item g_itemtemplates[16];

Item* MakeItem( int p_type, int p_x, int p_y, int p_cell )
{
    Item* i = new Item;

    *i = g_itemtemplates[p_type];
    i->SetX( p_x );
    i->SetY( p_y );
    i->SetCell( p_cell );
    return i;
}
```

This game demo limits the number of item templates to 16; if you want more, you should make the array larger.

This creates a new Item, copies the Item over from the template, and sets the x and y coordinates and then the cell number.

> **NOTE**
>
> Note that the global arrays for both of these functions are meant to be filled out by the actual game so that none of the templates are hardcoded into the engine. This allows you to have more flexibility.

The `MakePerson` function is very similar, with one major difference:

```
Person g_persontemplates[16];

Person* MakePerson( int p_type, int p_x, int p_y, int p_cell )
{
    Person* p = new Person;

    *p = g_persontemplates[p_type];
    p->SetX( p_x );
    p->SetY( p_y );
    p->SetCell( p_cell );

    p->AddItem( MakeItem( 8, 0, 0, 0 ) );
    return p;
}
```

This function creates a `Person`, but it also gives the `Person` a knife (`Item` number 8). Yes, this is a crude hack, but I couldn't think of an easier way to do it that would not have taken another page of code.

Game Logic

Finally, the game engine is complete. However, you don't quite have a game yet. Now you need to create the *game controlling logic*, which controls your engine. All of the code for this part is stored in the file g0901.cpp.

Data and Initialization

The first thing you need to do is declare the data and initialize it. Here are the global constants:

```
const int TILES         = 24;
const int ITEMS         = 14;
const int PEOPLE        = 3;
const int MOVETIME      = 750;
```

There are 24 tiles, 14 items, and 3 people. Likewise, each AI-controlled person can move one square every 750 milliseconds.

After that, there are the global variables. There are a few graphics:

```
SDL_Surface* g_tiles[TILES];
SDL_Surface* g_items[ITEMS];
```

```
SDL_Surface* g_people[PEOPLE][DIRECTIONS][FRAMES];
SDL_Surface* g_statusbar;
SDL_Surface* g_verticalbar;
SDL_Surface* g_youlose;
```

These store the tile graphics, the item graphics, the people graphics, the status bar, another vertical status bar, and the graphic that is displayed when you die. How boring.

```
Map* g_currentmap = 0;
Person* g_currentplayer = 0;
Array<Person*> g_peoplearray( 128 );
int g_peoplecount;
bool g_dead = false;
bool g_cheat = false;
```

Now, here are the game-logic related variables. There is a pointer to the current map and a pointer to the current player, as well as an array of people. This array will be used later on, when AI is computed. It stores pointers to all of the people on the map for easy access. There is also an integer that keeps track of how many people are in the array.

Then there are two booleans, which have to do with the current game state. At the start, the player is neither dead nor cheating, so they are both false.

The Init function that initializes everything is somewhat long, so I will cut out most of the repetitive things:

```
void Init()
{
    int x;
    int d, f;
    g_tiles[0] = SDL_LoadBMP( "grass1.bmp" );
    // ... lots of bitmap loading
```

The function declares three looping variables and then starts loading the tile bitmaps. The item and person bitmaps are also loaded into their appropriate arrays.

In the next part, the item templates are set up:

```
    for( x = 0; x < ITEMS; x++ )
    {
        g_itemtemplates[x].SetType( x );
        g_itemtemplates[x].SetGraphic( g_items[x] );
```

```
    }
    for( x = 0; x < 6; x++ )
    {
        g_itemtemplates[x].SetBlock( true );
    }
    g_itemtemplates[6].SetSpeed( 1500 );
    g_itemtemplates[6].SetStrength( 15 );
    // ... lots of weapon loading ...
    g_itemtemplates[12].SetStrength( 30 );
    g_itemtemplates[12].SetArmor( true );
    // ... more armor loading ...
```

First, the function goes through each item in the template and assigns it a type number. Then it tells each item which graphic it will be using by loading the graphic pointers from the g_items array.

After that, it goes through the first six items and tells them that they can block the path. The first six items in this demo are wall segments.

Finally, it goes through and sets the speed and strength of all the items and the strength of all the armor.

The same thing happens with the people templates:

```
    for( x = 0; x < PEOPLE; x++ )
    {
        g_persontemplates[x].SetPersonType( x );
        for( d = 0; d < DIRECTIONS; d++ )
        {
            for( f = 0; f < FRAMES; f++ )
            {
                g_persontemplates[x].SetGraphic( g_people[x][d][f], d, f );
            }
        }
    }
    g_persontemplates[1].SetArmor( 10 );
    g_persontemplates[1].SetHealth( 20 );
    g_persontemplates[1].SetAttackModifier( -500 );
    g_persontemplates[2].SetArmor( 15 );
    g_persontemplates[2].SetHealth( 30 );
    g_persontemplates[2].SetAttackModifier( -300 );
```

The templates for people 1 and 2 are modified, but not person 0. Persons 1 and 2 are made to be much weaker than you are, and slower as well.

```
SetNewMap( "default.map" );
```

Finally, the map is loaded using the default.map file. This function will be shown later on.

The LoadMap Function

This function will take a filename, load the file, create a new map from that file, and return it.

```
Map* LoadMap( char* p_filename )
{
    TileMap* t = new TileMap( 64, 64, 2, g_tiles );
    t->LoadFromFile( p_filename );
    return t;
}
```

In this game demo, you know that the map file format contains only 64 × 64 × 2 TileMaps, but you don't want to expose the actual game logic to that fact. So this function is created to hide the fact that it is loading a tile map. The reasons for this function become perfectly clear in Chapter 19.

So the function creates a new TileMap, loads the map from file, and finally returns the TileMap.

> **NOTE**
> When the function returns a TileMap, the users of this function don't know it. The users of this function only know that they are getting a Map and don't care *how* it works, as long as it works. This is one of the more useful features of object-oriented programming.

The SetNewMap Function

Whenever you want to switch maps in the program (which doesn't actually happen in this demo, but you should always allow for the possibility) or load the map in the beginning, you should call this function.

This function will load a new map from file, delete the current map (if any), and set the current player and map.

```
void SetNewMap( char* p_filename )
{
    int x;
```

```
Map* newmap;
newmap = LoadMap( p_filename );
```

The new map is loaded using the `LoadMap` function.

```
g_peoplecount = 0;
for( x = 0; x < newmap->GetNumberOfCells(); x++ )
{
    if( newmap->GetPerson( x ) != 0 )
    {
        AddPersonToArray( newmap->GetPerson( x ) );
    }
}
```

Now, the `g_peoplecount` variable is reset to 0, which means that the global people array is now empty. Even if it has people in it already, it is assumed that they are contained in the current map. When the current map is deleted, all of these people will be deleted anyway.

So after the count is reset to 0, the function goes through every cell in the new map and puts all of those people into the people array.

```
    if( g_currentmap != 0 )
    {
        delete g_currentmap;
    }
    g_currentmap = newmap;
    g_currentplayer = newmap->GetViewer();
}
```

Finally, the program checks to see if there is a current map, and if so, it is deleted. Then the current map is set to the new map, and the current player is set to the current viewer of the new map.

Miscellaneous Functions

The game uses a bunch of miscellaneous functions to accomplish things. However, none of them are really important for knowing *how* to store and design your game data, so I am leaving them out of the book. If you are interested in their implementations, they are fully commented and can be found in the g0901.cpp file. These functions are `DrawStatus`, which draws the status bar and the inventory on the screen, `AddPersonToArray`, which adds a person to the global person array (how exciting!), and `Distance`, which calculates the distance between two objects.

Now on to the more interesting functions!

The Artificial Intelligence

Artificial Intelligence (AI) hasn't been discussed at all in this book up until this point. Some of the later chapters (Chapters 15, "Game Trees and Minimax Trees," and 18, "Using Graphs for AI: Finite State Machines," specifically) have a lot to do with AI, so I don't want to show you anything too complex right now. This demo will just use a simple (and somewhat stupid) AI for the computer characters.

Here is the function that performs the AI calculations for all the people in the game:

```
void PerformAI( int p_time )
{
    int i;
    float dist;
    int x = g_currentplayer->GetX();
    int y = g_currentplayer->GetY();
    int direction;
```

> **NOTE**
>
> There is a new book being published by Premier Press with information specifically about advanced AI techniques. It is called *AI Techniques for Game Programming* by Mat Buckland. It is supposed to be very good, going over a great deal of advanced AI techniques, such as neural networks and genetic algorithms. That material is really an extension of the material presented in this book because both of those AI methods directly utilize some of the structures in this book. For example, genetic algorithms use *bitvectors* (see Chapter 4, "Bitvectors"), and neural networks use *graphs* (see Chapter 17, "Graphs"). I'm looking forward to it.

This function needs to know the current time of the game to figure out what the people should be doing, so that is passed in as a parameter.

Then, five local variables are defined.

```
    for( i = 0; i < g_peoplecount; i++ )
    {
        if( g_peoplearray[i] != g_currentplayer )
        {
```

The function loops through every person in the global person array and then checks to see if that person is the current player or not. If it is the current player, then the function does nothing. (You don't want the computer to calculate AI for the player!) If not, then it continues:

```
            direction =
                g_currentmap->GetClosestDirection( g_peoplearray[i],
                                                    g_currentplayer );
```

This code segment determines which direction the AI needs to move to get closer to the player.

```
            dist = Distance( g_peoplearray[i], g_currentplayer );
```

Then the function calculates the distance from the AI to the player.

```
            if( dist > 1.0f && dist <= 6.0f &&
                p_time - g_peoplearray[i]->GetMoveTime() > MOVETIME )
            {
                g_peoplearray[i]->SetMoveTime( p_time );
                g_peoplearray[i]->SetDirection( direction );
                g_currentmap->Move( g_peoplearray[i], direction );
            }
```

If the distance is less than 6 tiles and greater than 1 tile, then the AI needs to move closer to the player. Also, the function checks to see if the right amount of time has passed since the AI has last moved. If so, then the AI is okay to move. The move time of the AI is reset to the current time, the direction the AI is facing is changed to face the direction he is moving, and finally, the AI is actually moved.

```
            if( dist <= 1.0f )
            {
                g_peoplearray[i]->SetDirection( direction );
                Attack( g_peoplearray[i] );
            }
        }
    }
}
```

If the distance is less than or equal to 1, then the AI is in range to attack the player, so the AI turns toward the player and attacks.

The Attack Function

This is the function that is called in the game whenever a person initiates an attack.

```
void Attack( Person* p_person )
{
    int time;
    int difference;
```

```
int cell;
Item* weapon;
Person* person;
```

The person that is passed in is the person that is attacking. The function will determine what he is attacking later.

```
time = SDL_GetTicks();
difference = time - p_person->GetAttackTime();
weapon = p_person->GetCurrentWeapon();
```

The current time and the amount of time since the person last attacked are calculated. Then the weapon of the person is retrieved.

```
if( difference >= weapon->GetSpeed() )
{
    cell = g_currentmap->GetCellNumber( p_person->GetCell(),
                                        p_person->GetDirection() );
    person = g_currentmap->GetPerson( cell );
```

If the time between the last attack and the current time is more than or equal to the speed of the weapon, then the person can attack. So the cell that the person is facing is retrieved, and the function then tries to get a pointer to the person in that cell.

```
    if( person != 0 )
    {
        p_person->Attack( person );
        p_person->SetAttackTime( time );
    }
}
}
```

If there was a person in that cell, then the first person attacks him, and his attack time is reset. If there wasn't, nothing happens.

The Pickup Function

This function is called whenever a person wants to pick up something from the floor.

```
void PickUp( Person* p_person )
{
    Item* i = g_currentmap->GetItem( p_person->GetCell() );
    if( i != 0 )
```

```
        {
            p_person->PickUp( i );
            g_currentmap->SetItem( p_person->GetCell(), 0 );
        }
    }
```

The function gets a pointer to the item in the cell that the person is in, and if an item exists, then the person picks it up, and the pointer in the cell is cleared.

The CheckForDeadPeople Function

Finally, this is the last independent function in the game logic. This function goes through all of the people in the person array and checks to see if any of them are dead. If so, then they are removed from the game.

```
void CheckForDeadPeople()
{
    int i;
    Person* p;
    for( i = 0; i < g_peoplecount; i++ )
    {
        if( g_peoplearray[i]->IsDead() )
        {
```

The function scans through and looks for any people that are dead.

```
            if( g_peoplearray[i] == g_currentplayer )
            {
                g_dead = true;
                return;
            }
```

If the person who died is the current player, then the game is over, so the g_dead flag is set, and the function returns.

```
            p = g_peoplearray[i];
            g_peoplearray[i] = g_peoplearray[g_peoplecount - 1];
            g_peoplecount--;
            i--;
            g_currentmap->SetPerson( p->GetCell(), 0 );
            delete p;
        }
    }
}
```

If the dead person isn't the current player, then an AI was killed. The function saves a pointer to the dead person and then uses the fast remove algorithm from Chapter 3, "Arrays," to move the last person down into the index of the dead person. The function then sets the person pointer in the cell he was in to zero and deletes the person.

The Game Loop

And at long last, here is the game loop. There is a lot more code to this section than I will paste here; however, a lot of it doesn't really have much to do with the overall structure of the game. And it's messy too. Most of the ugly code will be commented out in the next listing:

```
Init();
while( 1 )
{
    // if user presses '[', move to the previous weapon
        g_currentplayer->PreviousWeapon();
    // if the user presses ']', move to the next weapon
        g_currentplayer->NextWeapon();
    // if the user presses 'ENTER', try to pick up an item
        PickUp( g_currentplayer );
    // if the user presses 'SPACE', try to attack a person
        Attack( g_currentplayer );
    // if the user presses 'C', toggle the cheat mode
        g_cheat = !g_cheat;
```

After all of that code, the main loop tries to figure out if you're moving in a direction:

```
    int direction = -1;
    // if the user pressed 'UP'
        direction = 0;
    // if the user pressed 'DOWN'
        direction = 2;
    // if the user pressed 'LEFT'
        direction = 3;
    // if the user pressed 'RIGHT'
        direction = 1;
```

By this point, if the user pressed one of the four direction keys, `direction` will be a value from 0 through 3. If not, then it will be −1.

```
if( direction != -1 )
{
    g_currentplayer->SetDirection( direction );
    g_currentmap->Move( g_currentplayer, direction );
}
```

This checks to see if the user wants to move, so it sets the direction of the player and then moves him in the right direction.

```
if( g_dead == false )
{
    PerformAI( SDL_GetTicks() );
    CheckForDeadPeople();
    if( g_cheat == true )
        g_currentplayer->SetAttackTime( 0 );
    if( g_currentmap != 0 )
        g_currentmap->Draw( g_window, WIDTH/2, HEIGHT/2 );
    DrawStatus();
}
```

At this point in time, the loop checks to see if the user is dead or not. If he's not dead, then it performs the AI calculations at the current time. After the AI is performed, the loop checks for dead people.

The next section checks to see if the player is cheating. The cheat mode in this game lets you attack instantaneously, so it sets the attack time of the player down to 0, which makes the computer think that you've never attacked.

If the current map exists, then it is drawn on the screen, and finally, the status bar is drawn as well.

```
    else
    {
        SDLBlit( g_youlose, g_window, 0, 0 );
    }
}
```

If the player is dead, then nothing happens except that a screen appears that says "You lose." That's all there is to the game!

Playing the Game

It took quite a bit of code to actually get to this point, so now you should enjoy it: Sit back, relax, and play the delightfully simple game.

There are a few commands in this game. First, to move around, you must use the four arrow keys on your keyboard. Whenever you are on top of an item, you can press the Enter key to pick it up.

When you are facing an enemy and want to attack him, press the spacebar. Your attack meter on the right of the screen will reset to zero and slowly go up to full again when you can attack again. If you want to switch what weapon you are currently using, press either the left square bracket ([) or the right square bracket (]) on your keyboard.

Escape exits the game.

Figure 9.21 shows a screenshot of the game in action.

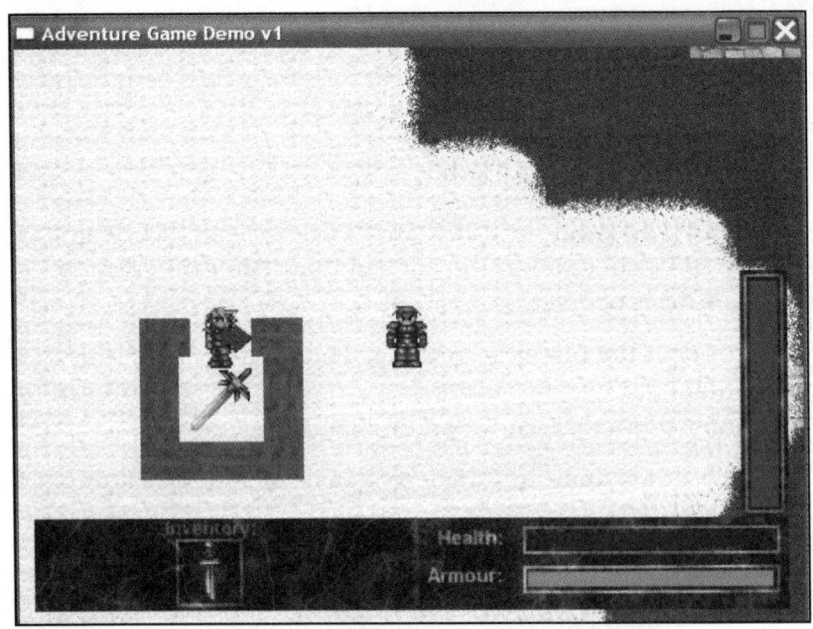

Figure 9.21

Here is a screenshot from the game.

Unfortunately, due to my slim deadlines, I was unable to obtain animated directional sprites for all three characters in the game, so only the main player will have full sprite animations. The other characters will have a large arrow pasted on them to indicate which direction they are facing, as you can see in the figure.

Game 2—The Map Editor

Now, you must be tired after reading that huge section about designing the game. Luckily, the map editor is *much* easier to program (you can take a sigh of relief now).

The map editor is Game Demonstration 9-2, which is on the CD in the directory \demonstrations\ch09\Game02 - Map Editor\. Because the map editor's primary purpose is to load, edit, and store maps, I focus primarily on these areas. The editor has some extra graphics features (such as the mini-map and current-tile highlighting), but those are included only as a bonus. If you are interested in them, you can view the source on the CD, which is all commented, of course.

The Map

Earlier, I showed you how the data is stored on disk. It is stored in a 3D array with dimensions of 64 × 64 × 4, with each layer stored as shown in Figure 9.17.

The bottom two layers are the tiles, the third layer stores the items, and the fourth layer stores the people on the map. Here is the 3D array that stores the map information:

```
Array3D<int> g_map( 64, 64, 4 );
```

The map editor is like a drawing application; you select a tile to draw, and wherever your mouse is, if the button is down, a tile is drawn. So that you can do this, the entire map will be displayed on the screen all the time.

The Drawing Information

There are a few variables needed to store information about which tile is being drawn:

```
int g_currenttile = -1;
int g_currentlayer = 1;
```

These two variables determine which tile should be drawn and which layer it should be drawn on. The variables are set to start off by clearing tiles on layer 1 because -1 is the clear tile value. Layer 0 is the bottom tile layer, 1 is the overlay tile layer, 2 is the item layer, and 3 is the person layer.

There is one other important variable:

```
bool g_mousedown = false;
```

This remembers whether the mouse button is down or not. Whenever it is down and the mouse moves, you want to draw a tile on the map.

The Tile Drawing

As I have said before, whenever the mouse is moved around, a tile is drawn on the map:

```
SDL_GetMouseState( &x, &y );
x = x / 8;
y = y / 8;
if( x < g_map.Width() && y < g_map.Height()
    && g_mousedown == true )
{
    g_map.Get( x, y, g_currentlayer ) = g_currenttile;
}
```

The mouse coordinates are retrieved into x and y. Because the entire map is drawn on the screen at once, the tiles have been shrunken down to 8 × 8 tiles, so you just divide the coordinates by 8 to get the coordinates of the tile in the map.

After that, it checks to see if the tile coordinates are valid and if the mouse button is down. If so, then the tile at those coordinates and the current layer is set to the tile that is being drawn. It's as simple as that.

Saving the Map

Saving the map is an amazingly simple process using the C-standard library file IO functions (see Chapter 3 and Appendix A):

```
void Save()
{
    FILE* f = fopen( g_filename, "wb" );
    if( f == 0 )
        return;
    fwrite( g_map.m_array,
            g_map.Depth() * g_map.Height() * g_map.Width(),
            sizeof(int),
            f );
    fclose( f );
}
```

The function opens up a file using the global g_filename string and returns if the file could not be opened. Then, the contents of the file are read into the array of g_map. The data stored on disk is in integer form (4 bytes), and there are 64 × 64 × 4 cells. This means that the file will take up 65,336 bytes on disk, or exactly 64 kilobytes.

Loading the Map

Loading the map is just as easy as saving the map.

```
void Load()
{
    FILE* f = fopen( g_filename, "rb" );
    if( f == 0 )
        return;
    fread( g_map.m_array,
           g_map.Depth() * g_map.Height() * g_map.Width(),
           sizeof(int),
           f );
    fclose( f );
}
```

The file is opened and then read into the array so that you can edit it.

Using the Editor

The editor is pretty simple to use. I've included a small tileset to be used with the editor, and it includes grass, snow, and stone base tiles, as well as two sets of snow overlay tiles and walls, items, and players. Figure 9.22 shows a screenshot of the editor

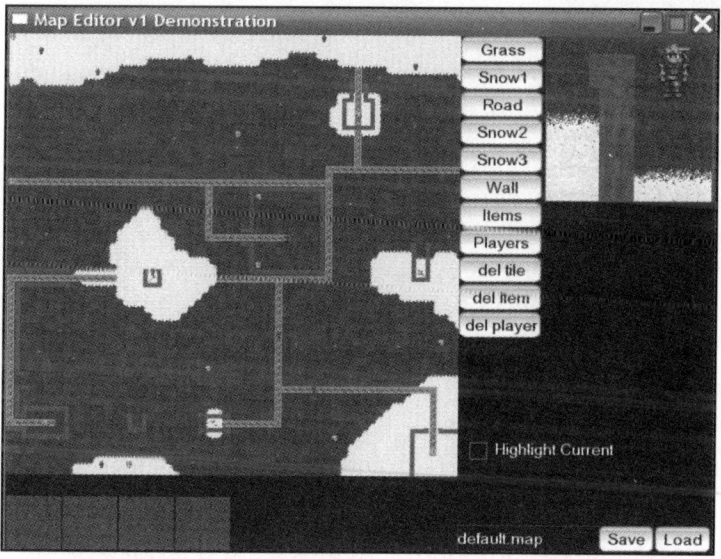

Figure 9.22

Here is a screenshot from the map editor.

On the upper-left side of the screen is the entire map. Each tile is represented as an 8 × 8 square, so the entire thing can fit.

Below the map is the palette of tiles. Only eight tiles can be displayed at a time, so the tiles you can draw are arranged in *groups*. You can select which group of tiles you want to draw from by using the buttons on the right-hand side of the map.

After you select the group you want to draw from, a new palette appears on the bottom. Click on one of the tiles in that palette to choose it as the current tile. A red outline will appear around the tile, and now you can move the mouse over the map and start drawing!

You can type the name of a file to load in the box on the bottom of the screen and then either load that file into the current map or save the current map to that filename.

The final feature is the check box on the right side of the screen. If you click that, then every tile that is the same as your selected tile is drawn in blue on the map. This allows you to easily see where items are on the map.

Play around with it; I've included a map file called default.map.

Conclusion

This was one huge chapter, wasn't it? That is because games are a huge topic. Just that simple little game demo took 80 percent of this chapter to explain, and it is nowhere near as complex as some games in the stores!

Hopefully, this chapter has taught you how to design your classes better so that you can make your games much more flexible than you could before.

You need to keep your eyes open for places where you should use classes and inheritance. These can be the most important tools you have. Don't worry if you don't get the hang of them right now; using inheritance is quite complex, and it took me a while to understand it, too. If you feel that you need to know more about inheritance and other complex object-oriented subjects, tons of books out there cover these subjects.

One more thing you should notice is the lack of any RTTI in the game demos in this chapter. There wasn't any need for them, which usually tells you that your design is pretty good. Remember: Don't use RTTI unless it is absolutely necessary.

This chapter was large because it covered material about how to design classes to store your game. The chapters that expand upon the demos from this chapter (Chapters 16, 19, and 24) will be shorter because the base is now complete, and these chapters will be adding features relating to the structures in the sections of the book they were in.

PART THREE

Recursion and Trees

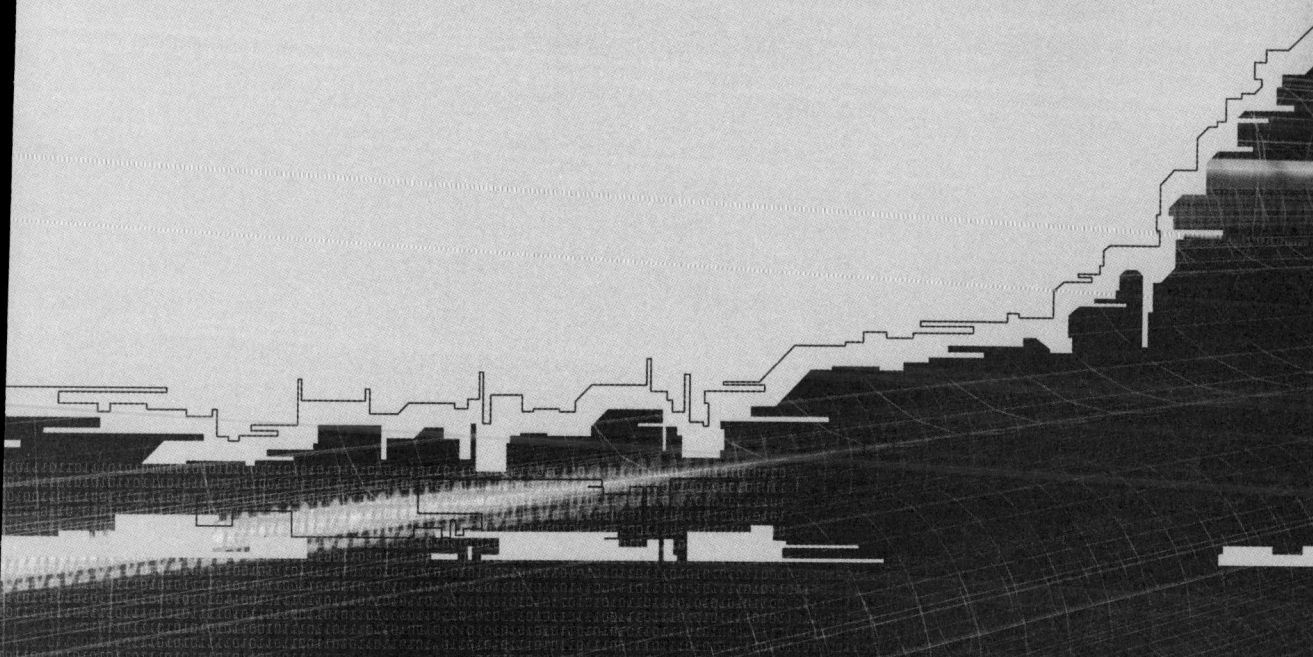

10 Recursion

11 Trees

12 Binary Trees

13 Binary Search Trees

14 Priority Queues and Heaps

15 Game Trees and Minimax Trees

16 Tying It Together: Trees

CHAPTER 10

RECURSION

Up until now, you've only learned about the simple linear data structures. While they are the most common structures out there, they can be limiting sometimes. With this part of the book, I introduce you to some new concepts in data structures: *recursive* data structures. I have no doubt that the mention of that word has caused some of you to cringe in fear; recursion is a difficult concept to learn for some people.

Recursion is not some evil thing invented by CS professors to punish you; it's a really powerful tool that you can use to solve some problems.

In this chapter, you will learn

- What recursion is
- What the Towers of Hanoi Puzzle is
- How to solve the Towers of Hanoi Puzzle using recursion
- How to think recursively

What Is Recursion?

Recursion is a very difficult concept for some people to understand. I'll just throw the basic definition of recursion out to you right now: *Recursion* is the ability of a function to call itself.

Now, that doesn't seem so difficult, does it? Years ago, in the bad old days, computer languages didn't support recursion. See the section called "The Stack" in Appendix B, "The Memory Layout of a Computer Program," to find out why.

The reason most people don't understand recursion is not because it is difficult to *understand*, but that it is difficult to *apply*. To properly understand recursion, you have to understand *why* you should use it, not *how* it is used.

The problem is that there really aren't any simple problems that demonstrate how recursion can be used. I see a lot of books that use recursion to calculate things like the *Fibbionacci series* (it's basically a sequence that looks like this: 1, 1, 2, 3, 5, 8, 13,... you add the previous two numbers to arrive at the next in the sequence) or to calculate a power, x^y. The truth of the matter is that both of these common examples can be solved easier, faster, and more cleanly using *iteration*. Iteration is just a fancy way of describing a `for`-loop.

So what kinds of problems are better solved using recursion? As you'll see in Chapter 20, "Sorting Data," the fastest sorting algorithm known to us is recursive. You'll also see countless examples throughout Part III of the book, because every structure used in this part is recursive. You'll even see recursion in action in Chapter 17, "Graphs."

You cannot escape recursion. Sure, you can ignore it and pretend that you don't need to know it, but you're missing out on a huge tool in game programming. Most *Artificial Intelligence (AI)* algorithms are recursive, and AI is one of the most popular fields in game programming these days.

A Simple Example: Powers

As I stated previously, you can use recursion to calculate the answer to the mathematical formula: x^y. The very first thing you need to do is try to find out *how* the function can be represented in terms of itself. Here is a simple example: the first few powers of 2, 3, and 4. They are listed in Table 10.1.

10.1 The Powers of 2, 3, and 4

Power (y)	2^y	3^y	4^y
0	1	1	1
1	2	3	4
2	4	9	16
3	8	27	64

Look at the row where y is 0. Note how every entry is 1. This will be the *base case* of the recursive function. Whenever the function detects that y is 0, it will return 1.

This is the function so far:

```
int Power( int x, int y )
{
    if( y == 0 )
```

```
        return 1;
}
```

This version of the function isn't really functional at this point; it only works with a power of 0.

Now you want to look at the function and see how it can be represented in terms of itself. Look at the second row in Table 10.1, and see if you can come up with a relation with the first row.

If you think about the function in terms of itself, you can see that the power of 1 is the same as x * Power(x, 0), which is $x * 1$. So, 2^1 is 2 * 1, and 3^1 is 3 * 1, and so forth.

For further proof, go down one more level, and look at the third row. You can just as easily represent the value of x^2 like this: x * Power(x, 1), which expands to x * (x * Power(x, 0)). Because you know that Power(x, 0) is equal to 1, you can see that the entire thing compresses down to x * x * 1, or just x * x, which is the same thing as x^2.

So, when y is not equal to 0, then the value of the function is x * Power(x, y - 1). Here is a listing of the final function:

```
int Power( int x, int y )
{
    if( y == 0 )
        return 1;
    else
        return x * Power( x, y - 1 );
}
```

> **NOTE**
> At this point in time, you might be wondering, "Why use recursion to calculate the power of a number?" The answer is this: You shouldn't. You can calculate the power of a number much easier by using a simple for-loop. This was intended as a simple example, just to show you how recursion works.

The Towers of Hanoi

I will demonstrate more advanced recursion to you by using the most classic example. If there is a book that discusses recursion without showing you the *Towers of Hanoi* problem, then it is incomplete in my opinion.

The Towers of Hanoi was a popular children's puzzle, invented over 100 years ago by a mathematician by the name of Edouard Lucas. In the game, there are three pillars, and any number of discs is placed on the leftmost pillar. Figure 10.1 shows an arrangement with three discs. Note that all the discs are a different size. The pillars are assigned the numbers 1, 2, and 3, and the discs are assigned the letters *a*, *b*, and *c*.

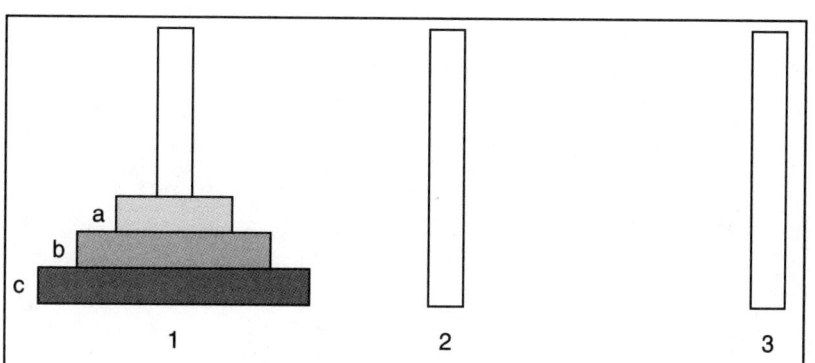

Figure 10.1

This is a simple Towers of Hanoi setup with three discs on the first pole.

The Rules

The goal is to move the discs around so that the tower on Pillar 1 is moved to Pillar 3. There are two rules:

- A larger disc can *never* be placed on top of a smaller disc.
- You can only move one disc at a time.

Solving the Puzzle

So how would you go about solving the game in Figure 10.1? It turns out that this particular game needs seven moves to be solved. Here they are:

1. Move *a* to 3.
2. Move *b* to 2.
3. Move *a* to 2.
4. Move *c* to 3.
5. Move *a* to 1.
6. Move *b* to 3.
7. Move *a* to 3.

Figure 10.2 shows the first three steps of the process. Essentially, they move the top two discs onto Pillar 2.

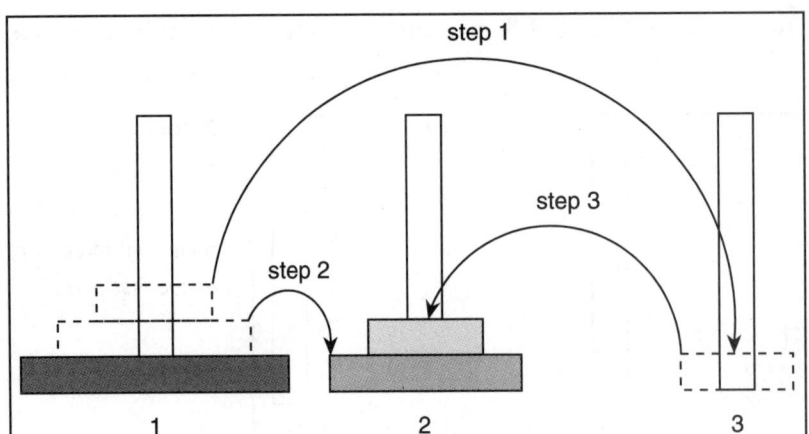

Figure 10.2

This figure shows steps 1, 2, and 3.

Now take a look at Figure 10.3, which shows Step 4.

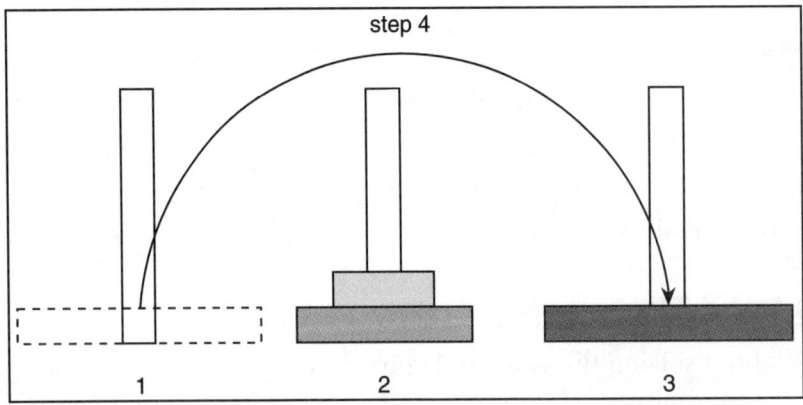

Figure 10.3

This figure shows step 4.

Finally, take a look at Figure 10.4, which shows the last three steps: 5, 6, and 7.

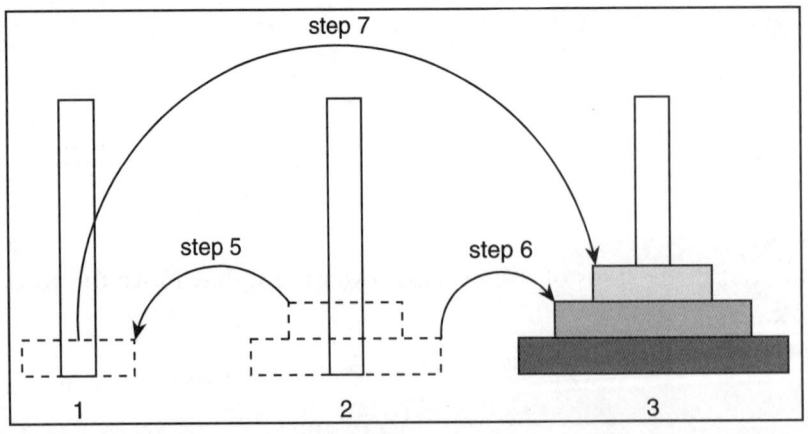

Figure 10.4

This figure shows steps 5, 6, and 7.

The Towers of Hanoi

Well, that wasn't so difficult, was it? What happens when you add a fourth disc to the puzzle, though? Four discs require 15 moves to solve, and it's more difficult if you don't know the trick to solving it.

Now that you know how the basic puzzle works, though, you can move on to trying to solve it with an algorithm.

Solving the Puzzle with a Computer

I want you to sit down (if you're not already doing so...) and think about this problem for a few minutes. I want you to think about how you would create an algorithm to solve The Towers of Hanoi. If you already know the answer, you can skip the rest of the chapter.

Keep thinking; I'll wait right here until you come back.

Okay, time's up! Have you got an answer for me? Probably not. That's because making an iterative solution to this puzzle is a very difficult thing to do.

Instead of iteration, you need to use recursion to solve the puzzle. Take a look back at Figures 10.2, 10.3, and 10.4. I split the figures up that way for a reason. What happens if, instead of looking at the movements as seven commands, you look at them as if they were three commands?

1. Move Discs *a* and *b* onto Pillar 2 (Figure 10.2).
2. Move Disc *c* onto Pillar 3 (Figure 10.3).
3. Move Discs *a* and *b* onto Pillar 3 (Figure 10.4).

An iterative solution to the problem involves itself at the lowest level; it will look at the positions of every disc and figure out which disc to move and where to move it. That is very difficult to do.

What I've done is split the three-disc problem into three different parts instead of seven. This is a recursive problem, where you condense the problem into this one small algorithm:

If you want to move *n* discs:

1. Move the top *n-1* discs to Pillar 2.
2. Move the nth disc to Pillar 3.
3. Move the *n-1* discs from Pillar 2 to 3.

Well, that's easy to say, but the rules say you can only move one disc at a time, right? You can think of moving the top *n-1* discs to Pillar 2 as the *same problem,* just with one less disc!

1. Move the top *n-2* discs to Pillar 3.
2. Move the *n-1* disk to Pillar 2.
3. Move the *n-2* discs from Pillar 3 to 2.

Wait a moment for that to sink in...

Remember in *The Matrix* when Neo said, "Whoa..."? That was my exact reaction when I first understood this. This is a very cool solution.

Let me expand this to four discs now. How would I solve four discs? I would move the top three discs to Pillar 2, move the bottom disc to Pillar 3, and then move the top three discs to Pillar 3. Figure 10.5 shows this process.

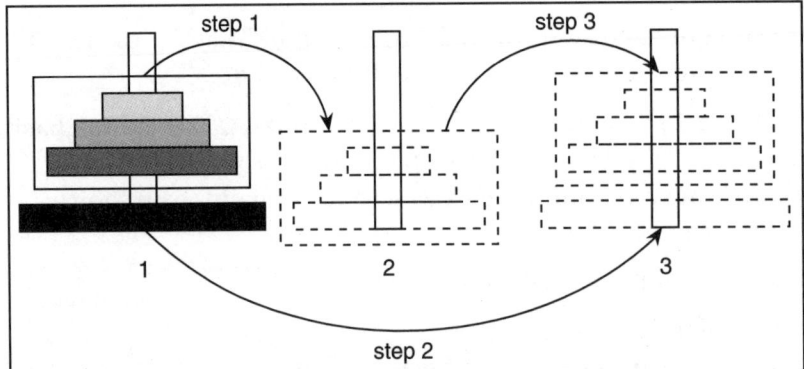

Figure 10.5

Solving for four discs involves moving the top three discs to Pillar 2, the bottom disc to Pillar 3, and the top three discs to Pillar 3.

In Figure 10.5, the top three discs are in a box. The algorithm doesn't care how many discs are in the box, it just moves them all to Pillar 2. The algorithm then moves the bottom disc to Pillar 3 and then moves the contents of the box onto Pillar 3.

Take a look at the psuedocode algorithm:

```
Hanoi( int n, int start, int destination, int open )
    Hanoi( n - 1, start, open, destination )
    Move( n, start, destination )
    Hanoi( n - 1, open, destination, start )
```

The algorithm takes four parameters: the number of discs to move, the number of the starting pillar, the number of the destination pillar, and the number of the open pillar.

The algorithm *recursively* moves the top *n-1* discs from the starting pillar onto the open pillar, moves the bottom disc from the starting pillar onto the destination pillar, and then moves the top *n-1* discs from the open pillar onto the destination pillar.

Terminating Conditions

The algorithm is missing one thing, though: It doesn't end. This algorithm, as it is now, will keep calling itself over and over again. This is a very bad thing because every time the function is called, it pushes more data onto the stack. (See Appendix B.) Eventually, the stack will run out of room, and the program will crash. This is called a *stack overflow*.

So you need to add a *terminating condition*, which tells the function that it is done and shouldn't call itself anymore. The easiest way you can do this is to check to see if *n* is 0. Obviously, if *n* is 0, then the function isn't supposed to move any discs and should exit out. The improved function looks like this:

```
Hanoi( int n, int start, int destination, int open )
   if( n != 0 ) then
      Hanoi( n - 1, start, open, destination )
      Move( n, start, destination )
      Hanoi( n - 1, open, destination, start )
```

Example 10-1: Coding the Algorithm for Real

This is Example 10-1, and can be found on the CD in the directory \examples\ch10\01 - Towers of Hanoi\.

Now, you've reached the point where you should (hopefully) understand the solution. That huge complicated puzzle is reduced to only nine lines of code! Isn't that neat?

```cpp
void Hanoi( int n, int s, int d, int o )
{
    if( n > 0 )
    {
        Hanoi( n-1, s, o, d );
        cout << "Moving " << n << " from " << s << " to " << d << endl;
        Hanoi( n-1, o, d, s );
    }
}
```

Instead of actually storing the discs in a data structure somewhere and moving them around, this algorithm just prints out the moves that are made.

Here is how you would call the function:

`Hanoi( 3, 1, 3, 2 );`

This says: Move four discs from Pillar 1 onto Pillar 3, where Pillar 2 is empty.

Example 10-1 asks you to enter the number of discs you want to solve for and then runs the Hanoi function until it is solved.

CAUTION

Do not run this example with more than 16 discs unless you want to wait a very long time for it to complete. This is because the number of moves made in the Towers of Hanoi problem is $2^n - 1$. If n is 16, it will move the discs 65,535 times. It needs twice as many, 131,071 moves, to solve the problem for 17 discs!

Figure 10.6 shows a screenshot from the example. The screenshot shows the moves needed to solve for four discs. If you're up to it, you can draw it on paper to verify it.

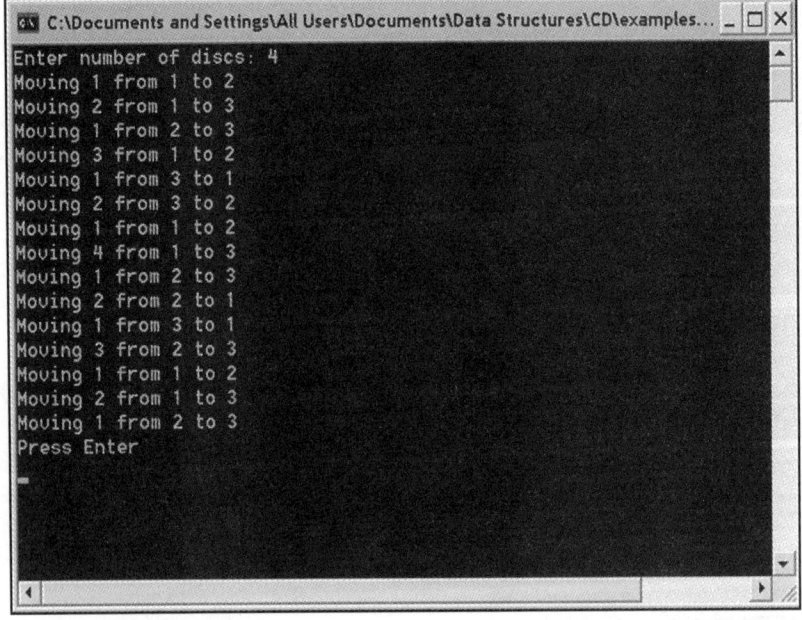

Figure 10.6

Here is a screenshot from the Towers of Hanoi example.

Graphical Demonstration: Towers of Hanoi

Just for fun, I've included a little graphical demonstration of the Towers of Hanoi. If you're interested, it can be found on the CD in the directory \demonstrations\ch10\demo01 - towers of hanoi\.

> ## Compiling the Demo
>
> This demonstration uses the SDLGUI library that I have developed for the book. For more information about this library, see Appendix B.
>
> To compile this demo, either open up the workspace file in the directory or create your own project using the settings described in Appendix B. If you create your own project, all of the files you need to include are in the directory.

If you browse the source, notice how I use *queues* to store the moves of the discs and *stacks* to store the discs on the pillars. That is a nice application of some of the structures you've learned about already.

Figure 10.7 shows a screenshot from the demo.

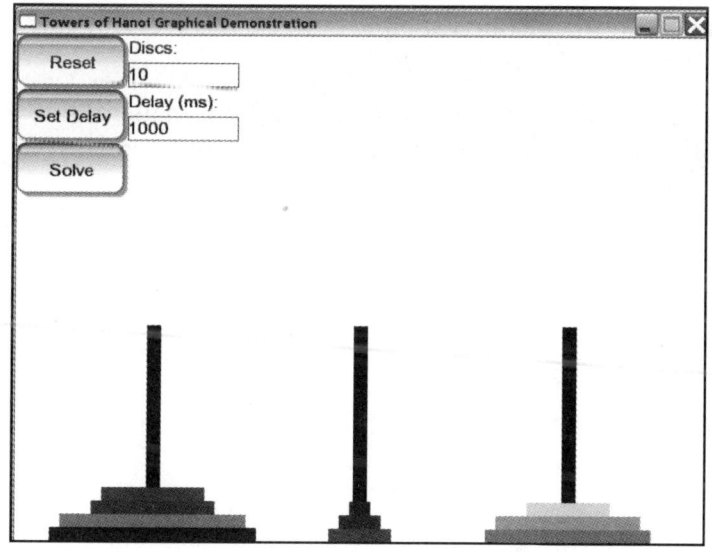

Figure 10.7

Here is a screenshot from the Towers of Hanoi demo.

Table 10.2 shows the commands in the demo.

Table 10.2 Towers of Hanoi Commands

Button	Function
Reset	This resets the game and moves all the discs back to Pillar 1.
Set Delay	This sets the number of milliseconds that will pass between disc movements.
Solve	This causes the demo to solve the puzzle for you.

The demo can solve any number of discs from 1–10.

Conclusion

I hope this was a useful introduction to recursion for you. I have by no means covered every detail about recursion, but I've given you a first glimpse, which should serve for now. As I progress through the book, I will show you more recursion examples, and you should begin to get a grasp of why it is important.

The main thing I want you to get from this chapter is how to think recursively. Essentially, you should try to see different problems in computer science in different ways. The Towers of Hanoi is an interesting example because it is very difficult to solve iteratively, but very simple to solve recursively.

Recursion is a simple concept. It tries to break down a problem into smaller parts, essentially defining the problem as a larger problem that can be solved in terms of itself.

CHAPTER 11

TREES

By now, you should have a solid understanding of the basic data structures, especially linked lists. You should also be fairly comfortable with the concept of recursion. If you're not entirely confident of these two areas, go back and read Chapter 6, "Linked Lists," and Chapter 10, "Recursion," because much of what I show you in this chapter builds upon the concepts in those chapters.

You will probably not find any of the structures discussed from this point on in a professional container library, such as STL. The reason is that these structures are now becoming very specific; they are meant for a special purpose and cannot easily be applied to general problems.

This chapter is about *trees* in the most general sense. Sometimes they are called *general trees*, but I just refer to them as trees.

In this chapter, you will learn

- What a tree is
- How trees are recursive
- How to build a tree
- How to move around a tree
- How to build a tree class
- How to build a tree iterator class
- How to traverse a tree using a recursive function
- How to use trees to store plotline information in games

What Is a Tree?

Go outside and look at a tree. In case that is not possible, I provide you with a nice diagram of a tree in Figure 11.1.

Figure 11.1

This is a tree.

The tree has several major components. The largest is the trunk, or *root*, at the bottom. *Branches* come off of the trunk, and they spread out into *twigs*, which have *leaves*. The general structure of the tree spreads out from the root.

If you think about it, a branch is really nothing but a smaller root, right? So a twig is nothing but a smaller branch as well. By looking at a tree in this manner, it is easy to see how it is considered a recursive structure. Essentially, each level is a smaller version of the level before it (except for the leaves).

Figure 11.2 shows how a tree container class looks. Instead of being drawn with the root at the bottom, though, it is drawn with the root on top. It usually makes more sense to draw them this way. Before I go any further, I'll introduce some terminology. Table 11.1 shows the common names for nodes in a tree; it refers to Figure 11.2.

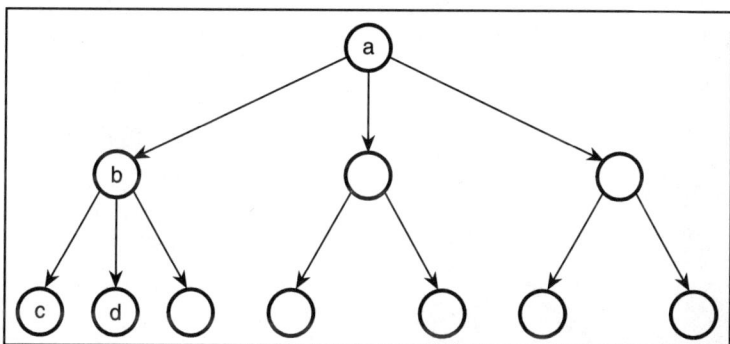

Figure 11.2

This is a tree when it's represented inside a computer.

Table 11.1 Tree Terminology

Term	Description	Example (Figure 11.2)
Root	Topmost node in a tree	Node *a* is the root.
Child	A node below another in a branch	*b* is a child of *a*.
Parent	A node above another in a branch	*b* is the parent of *c*.
Sibling	A node on the same level as another	*c* is a sibling of *d*.
Leaf	A node with no children	*c* and *d* are leaves.
Level	Describes the height of a node	*a* is at level 0, *b* is at level 1, and *c* and *d* are at level 2.
Subtree	A tree contained within another tree	*b* is the root of a subtree of *a*.

Now that you know the terminology of a tree, I can go into a little more detail. A tree, like a linked list, is a *node-based structure*. The nodes point to the next node in the structure. However, a linked list points to only one node, whereas a tree node can point to any number of children.

> **NOTE**
> You can think of a linked list as a very basic tree. A linked list is simply a tree in which each node has only one child.

The Recursive Nature of Trees

Trees are considered a recursive data structure because trees are said to contain themselves. The last entry in Table 11.1 gives you a brief glimpse into this nature: Every child of a tree is a tree on its own. Figure 11.3 shows an example.

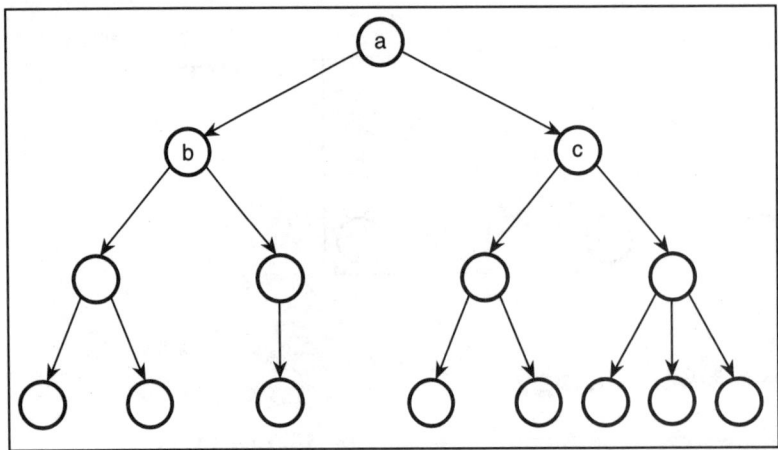

Figure 11.3

Here is a tree that demonstrates the recursiveness of trees; nodes b and c are trees themselves.

There are 3 nodes labeled in this tree: *a*, *b*, and *c*. Node *a* is the root of the entire tree. However, if you look a little lower, you can see that node *b* is the root of a smaller tree, and so is node *c*.

So you can easily say that a tree is a structure that holds trees!

Common Structure of Trees

The tree structure is very similar to a linked list, as I've said before. A tree is node-based, so each node needs a way to point to its children. In a general tree, each node can have any number of children.

So what data structure that you know of can easily be expanded to hold any number of items? That's right, linked lists!

So each node will have a linked list where each node in the list points to another tree node. Whew, what a mouthful! Figure 11.4 can better illustrate what is going on in a tree node.

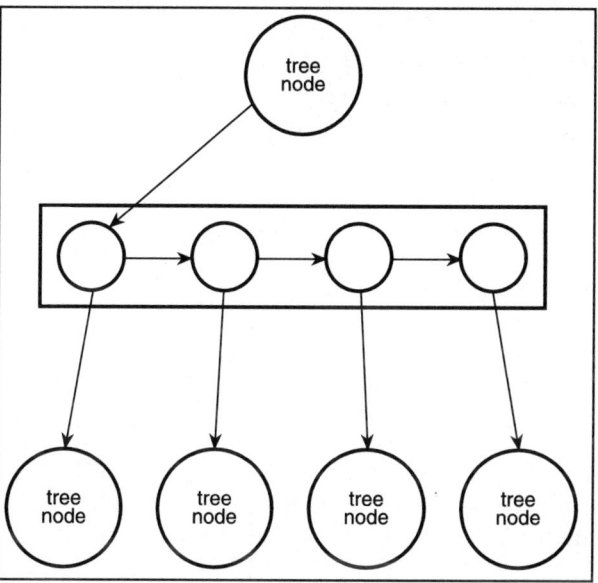

Figure 11.4

This is the internal representation of a tree node. The structure in the box is a linked list, where each node points to a tree node.

The figure shows a tree node that has four children. The top node has a linked list, which is shown inside the box. The linked list has four nodes, each of which holds a tree node pointer.

> **TIP**
>
> As you can see, the tree structure is built using linked list concepts, and it actually uses a linked list inside. The rest of the data structures in this book are primarily built upon the data structures that I cover in Part I. Therefore, it is very important that you understand everything in Part I before you continue.

Graphical Demonstration: Trees

This is Graphical Demonstration 11-1, which you can find on the CD in the directory \demonstrations\ch11\Demo01 - Trees\.

Compiling the Demo

This demonstration uses the SDLGUI library that I have developed for the book. For more information about this library, see Appendix B, "The Memory Layout of a Computer Program."

To compile this demo, either open up the workspace file in the directory or create your own project using the settings described in Appendix B. If you create your own project, all of the files you need to include are in the directory.

This is the most complex demonstration in the book so far, so I need to do a lot of explaining before you can just jump into the demo and start playing around. Figure 11.5 shows a screenshot of the demo.

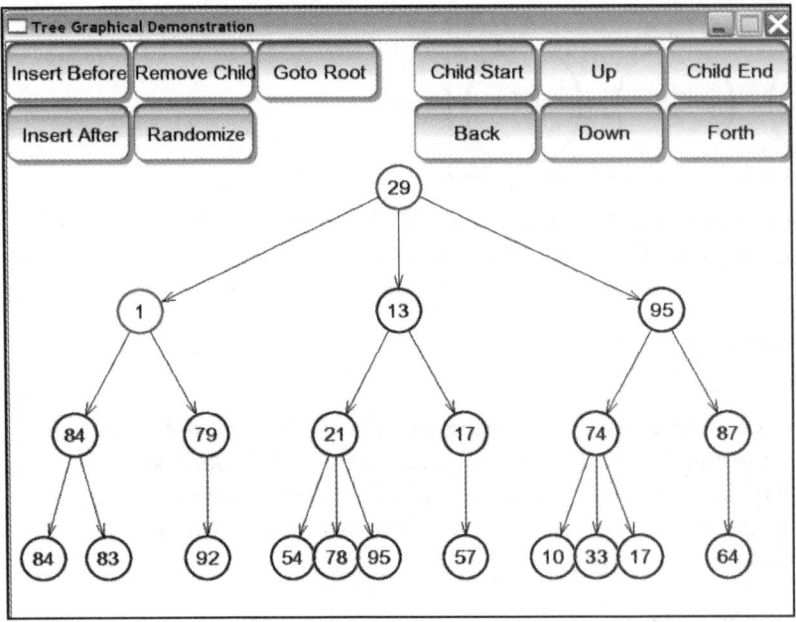

Figure 11.5

Here is a screenshot from Graphical Demonstration 11-1.

The first thing you should notice is that there are more buttons than there were in previous demos. This is because trees are the most complex structures in the book so far.

One thing that you won't see in the screenshot is that two of the nodes are colored differently. If you start up the demo, the root node will be colored red (node 29 in Figure 11.5), and the root's first child will be colored blue (node 1 in Figure 11.5).

When you iterate through a tree, you really need two iterators. If you are unfamiliar with what an iterator is, please read Chapter 6.

The first iterator, which is represented in red in the demo, keeps track of the current tree node. The second iterator, which is blue in the demo, keeps track of the current child of the current node.

Because the children in a tree are stored in a linked list, the blue iterator is just a normal `DListIterator`. Table 11.2 shows a listing of the commands in the demo and their functions.

Table 11.2 Graphical Demonstration 11-1 Commands

Command	Function
Insert Before	Inserts a new node to the left of the blue node
Insert After	Inserts a new node to the right of the blue node
Remove Child	Removes the blue node from the tree
Randomize	Creates a new random tree
Goto Root	Moves the red iterator to the root of the tree
Child Start	Moves the blue iterator to the first child of the red node
Back	Moves the blue iterator to the previous child of the red node
Up	Moves the red iterator to the parent of the current red iterator
Down	Moves the red iterator to the current child node (blue)
Child End	Moves the blue iterator to the last child of the red node
Forth	Moves the blue iterator to the next child of the red node

There are a lot of commands, and it's okay if you don't understand how they work just yet. I'm going to take you through a little tutorial with the demo.

> **TIP**
>
> If you want to see a cool application of recursion when dealing with trees, take a look at the source code for this demo. The `DrawSubTree` algorithm is recursive, and it is very simple, too. Essentially, the function draws a node and then calls itself to draw every child node.

Tutorial

First, run the program. You should end up with a random tree like the one in Figure 11.5. Now, click the Remove Child button. This should remove the blue node from the tree. Click that button until there is only one node left in the tree. You should only need to click it two or three times.

Now that you have an empty tree, here's how to build one.

Step 1: Build a Basic Tree

In this step, I want you to add three children to the root node. To do so, you must complete these commands:

1. Goto Root.
2. Click Insert After three times.

After you do this, you should have a tree that looks like Figure 11.6. The numbers in your nodes will be different, but just pay attention to the structure for now.

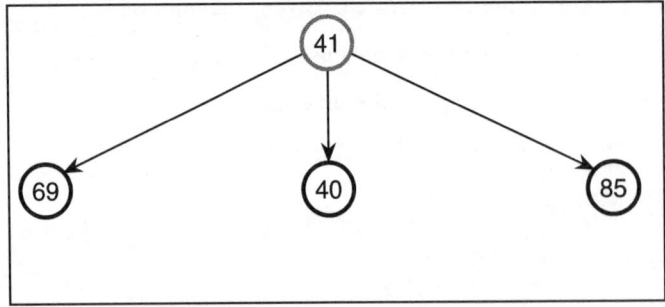

Figure 11.6

Here is the tree after Step 1.

Step 2: Traverse the Tree

Now that you have built a basic tree, I want you to traverse the tree by using the buttons on the right side of the screen.

1. Click Child Start.
2. Click Forth.
3. Click Back.
4. Click Child End.
5. Click Back.
6. Click Down.

Your red node should now be the middle node on the second level of the tree. During Steps 1–5, you should have seen the blue node moving back and forth, as if you were traversing a doubly linked list.

Step 3: Build a More Complex Tree

Now I want you to build a more complex tree. Your red node should still be on the middle node in the second level.

1. Click Insert After twice.
2. Click Child Start.
3. Click Down.
4. Click Insert After twice.
5. Click Up.
6. Click Forth.
7. Repeat Steps 3, 4, and 5.

After Step 7, you should have a tree that looks similar to Figure 11.7.

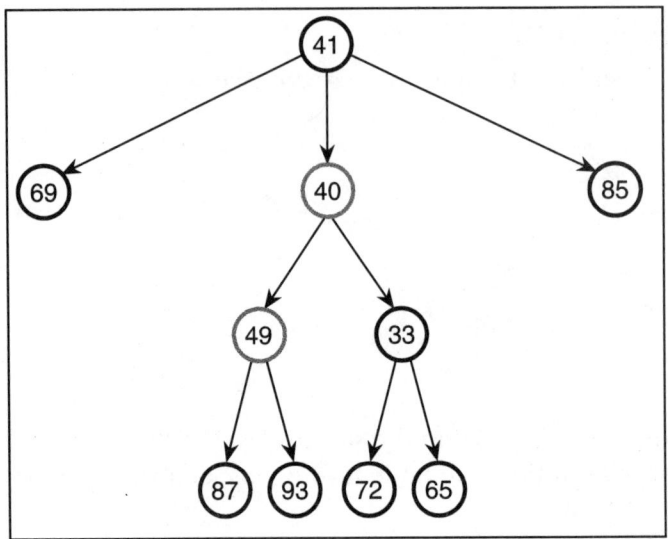

Figure 11.7

This is the tree after Step 3.

Step 4: Play Around

Now that you've created a neat-looking tree, I want you to play around with the commands—see what you can come up with. The program doesn't have any limits on the number of nodes you can add, but adding too many might make the program run slowly.

I want you to get acquainted with the manner in which you build and manipulate trees.

> **NOTE**
> The method that you just used to build your tree is called *top-down tree construction*. There is another method to build trees, called *bottom-down*, but the demo doesn't support this method of tree building. I show you how this is done later on.

Building the Tree Class

The file containing all the tree classes can be found on the CD in the \structures\ directory. It's named Tree.h.

Now you should have some idea of how trees are structured. Although the actual structures themselves are not very complicated, working with the trees can get difficult.

I'll be perfectly honest with you: The classes that you are about to see are on their third major revision. When I first started working on the source code, I wanted to build the tree so that it was nicely contained within a single class and easy to work with, like all of the classes I've used previously in the book. This method ended up being more work than it was worth, and it was more complicated to use!

So I decided to use an ultra-simplistic approach and create just the node class with very few functions. This approach didn't work, either. When I was writing Graphical Demonstration 11-1, I realized that I would end up re-writing *all* of the iterator functions if I ever wanted to use the tree class in another program.

My third and final revision of the class uses a mixture of these two approaches, as you'll see in this section. I ended up creating an iterator class so that you don't have to constantly rewrite the most-used functions.

The Structure

I already explained how general trees are structured, so I'll just post the code to show you how it looks.

```
1: template<class DataType>
2: class Tree
3: {
4: public:
5:     typedef Tree<DataType> Node;
6:     DataType m_data;
7:     Node* m_parent;
8:     DLinkedList<Node*> m_children;
9: };
```

As usual, I'm using a templated class so that you can store any type of data you want into the tree.

The first thing to note is on line 5. On that line, I used a `typedef` so that using the tree class is easier to do. Now, instead of saying `Tree<DataType>` whenever you want to use a node, you can just type `Node` instead. `Typedefs` make life so much easier.

On line 6, I define the holder for the data, just like the linked list classes.

On line 7, I put a pointer to the parent node. I like having a parent pointer in my trees because it allows me to easily backtrack, but having a pointer to the parent node is not necessary.

On line 8, I define the linked list of nodes that will store the pointers to the node's children.

All in all, this is not a difficult structure to visualize on a node-per-node basis.

The Constructor

Here is the code for the constructor:

```
Tree()
{
    m_parent = 0;
}
```

I want you to pay attention to the fact that the parent is cleared to 0. Whenever I deal with tree nodes, the node is considered a root node if the parent pointer is 0.

Also, note the other cool thing: Because the DLinkedList class already has a constructor, the m_children list is automatically initialized and holds 0 nodes.

The Destructor

Whenever a tree node is deleted, you need to make sure that it is properly cleared from memory. However, this process is not like deleting a linked list node. For example, take a look at Figure 11.8.

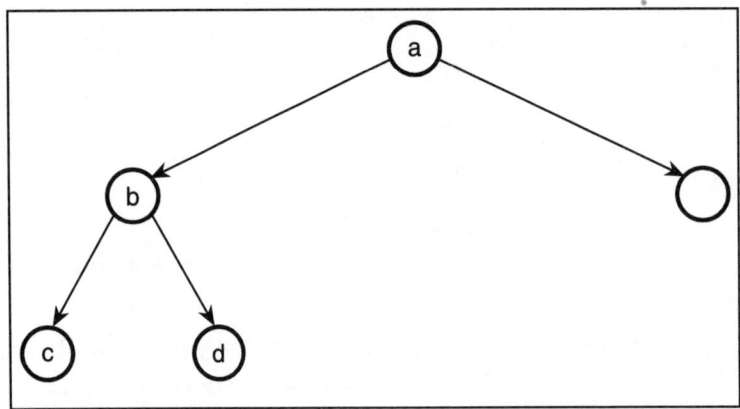

Figure 11.8

This is a tree that is used in the destruction example.

You determine that you no longer want node *b* in the tree in Figure 11.8. How do you go about removing the node from the tree?

Perhaps the easiest thing to do would be to take nodes *c* and *d* and add them as children to node *a*. Or maybe you want to make some other arrangement, and you can move *c* and *d* around to different places in the tree.

But how do you determine where those nodes go? You really can't do that with a general-purpose tree. The previous method is usually only used in specific tree types, such as the *binary search tree* (see Chapter 13, "Binary Search Trees") and *heaps* (see Chapter 14, "Priority Queues and Heaps").

However, most of the time, you will find that the children of any given node are *directly* related to its parent. If you remove the parent node, you should also remove the children nodes as well as all of their children, and so on. So if you want to remove node *b*, you need to remove node *c* and *d* as well. If *c* or *d* had any children, you should remove them, continuing this way down to the bottom of the tree. To do this, you call the trees' Destroy function:

```
// destructor
~Tree()
{
    Destroy();
}
```

The Destroy Function

The Destroy function is called whenever a node is destructed or whenever you want to delete all of a tree's children. Note that it uses recursion; if you aren't familiar with recursion yet, please go back and read Chapter 10. The function is very simple if you think about it recursively:

```
 1: void Destroy()
 2: {
 3:     DListIterator<Node*> itr = m_children.GetIterator();
 4:     Node* node = 0;
 5:     itr.Start();
 6:     while( itr.Valid() )
 7:     {
 8:         node = itr.Item();
 9:         m_children.Remove( itr );
10:         delete node;
11:     }
12: }
```

The function starts off by creating an iterator to the list of children. Then, for each child in the list, the function removes the pointer from the child list (line 9) and then deletes the node (line 10).

So how is this function recursive? Well, the destructor of each child node is called whenever a node is deleted, and the destructor calls the Destroy function. So, in effect, the function is recursive.

Look back to Figure 11.8. If you were to delete node *b* from that tree, this function would first loop through and remove *c* and *d* from its child list and then delete *c* and *d*. But the act of deleting *c* and *d* calls their destructors, which in turn calls Destroy again! If those nodes had any children, they would be deleted, too! This function is one large chain reaction that deletes every single node in a subtree. Isn't recursion neat?

The Count Function

The Tree class has one more function: Count. This function counts the number of nodes in a subtree and returns the result.

```
int Count()
{
    int c = 1;
    DListIterator<Node*> itr = m_children.GetIterator();
    for( itr.Start(); itr.Valid(); itr.Forth() )
        c += itr.Item()->Count();
    return c;
}
```

Note that this function is also recursive. (Are you noticing a trend?) The function creates an integer variable, c, and sets it to 1. That 1 represents the current node.

Then, an iterator to the child list is retrieved, and the function loops through every child and adds the count of the child to c. Finally, c is returned.

In effect, this algorithm says: The count of any subtree is equal to 1 plus the count of each child.

The Tree Iterator

I mentioned before that this class has undergone several variations. The first method I tried used an iterator, and the second didn't use any at all. This is the third version, in which I made the iterator into one class that is easily managed. This way, you won't have to rewrite every iterator function on your own when working with trees.

The Structure

The `TreeIterator` structure is simple; it only has two variables:

```
template<class DataType>
class TreeIterator
{
public:
    Node* m_node;
    DListIterator<Node*> m_childitr;
};
```

The first variable is a pointer to the current node, and the second is a `DListIterator`, which points to the current child in the current node. If you don't understand why there are two iterators, please go back and play around with Graphical Demonstration 11-1. That demo gives you a good idea of why two iterators are needed.

This iterator class neatly encapsulates both iterators into one class so that they are easier to use.

The Basic Iterator Functions

These are the basic iterator functions, which allow you to create an iterator and set it up to point to a node.

The Constructor

The tree iterator is different from the linked list iterators you've used before. Instead of getting an iterator from a general list object, you pass a tree node into the iterator's constructor.

```
// constructor
TreeIterator( Node* p_node = 0 )
{
    *this = p_node;
}
```

This function calls the assignment operator, which I go over next. Before that, however, I want to clarify how an iterator is used.

> **NOTE**
> If you do not pass a node into the constructor, this function still works. The = 0 in the parameter list says, "If the user didn't pass anything in as a parameter, then use the value 0 instead."

Say you have a tree node that you want to get an iterator for, like this:

```
Tree<int>* node = new Tree<int>;
```

This node is just a plain integer tree node with no children and no parents. It doesn't really matter, though; this same method works with any tree node pointer. Now you want to get an iterator to that node, which you can do in one of two ways:

```
TreeIterator<int> itr( node );
itr = node;
```

The first line of code uses the constructor to make the iterator point to the node. The second method uses the assignment operator to do the same thing.

The Assignment Operator

The assignment operator for the iterator class is somewhat confusing at first, but you'll understand it after you work with trees a little more.

```
void operator= ( Node* p_node )
{
    m_node = p_node;
    ResetIterator();
}
```

The first strange thing is that the operator takes a tree node pointer as a parameter, which is something you don't usually see when dealing with assignment operators. However, when you're working with nodes, you usually are dealing with node pointers, right? The function takes pointers as a parameter so it is easier to work with.

So the function takes a node pointer as a parameter. It then sets the m_node pointer to point to the tree node. After that, the function calls the ResetIterator helper function, which makes the m_childitr iterator point to the first child of p_node. That particular sequence of code is called often in the iterator, and rather than copying the code 20 times, I placed it into a function of its own.

The ResetIterator Function

This resets the child iterator, and it is meant to be called whenever the m_node pointer is changed. It is really just a helper function and is not meant to be called outside of the iterator class.

```
void ResetIterator()
{
    if( m_node != 0 )
    {
        m_childitr = m_node->m_children.GetIterator();
    }
    else
    {
        m_childitr.m_list = 0;
        m_childitr.m_node = 0;
    }
}
```

The first part checks to see whether the node is 0. If not, then it resets `m_childitr` to point to the child list of `m_node`. If the node is 0, then it is invalid, so you need to make the child iterator invalid, too. If not, then the child iterator might be pointing to the child list of a different node.

The Vertical Iterator Functions

The following functions are the so-called *vertical* iterator functions because they deal with moving the iterator up and down through the tree.

The Root Function

This simple function moves the iterator to the root of the tree. Notice how this function would not be possible if the tree node class didn't point to its parent.

The code is pretty simple, so I'm not going to bother pasting it here. The basic premise is this: While the current node's parent is not 0, move the iterator up one level.

> **NOTE**
> Note that if you invalidate the iterator somehow, you can't call this function to move back to the root because the iterator has no idea of where the root node actually is. You need to manually reset the iterator using the assignment operator.

The Up Function

The Up function is very similar to the Root function, except that it moves the iterator up only one level, and it might actually go past the root node. Because of that, this function could possibly invalidate the iterator if you make it go past the root.

```
void Up()
{
    if( m_node != 0 )
    {
        m_node = m_node->m_parent;
    }
    ResetIterator();
}
```

This function makes sure that the node is valid before it does anything. If so, then it moves the iterator up to the previous node.

The Down Function

This function is the opposite of Up; it moves the iterator downward to the current child iterator. However, if the child iterator isn't valid, this function doesn't do anything.

```
void Down()
{
    if( m_childitr.Valid() )
    {
        m_node = m_childitr.Item();
        ResetIterator();
    }
}
```

The Horizontal Iterator Functions

The *horizontal* functions of a tree iterator are called so because they allow you to move the current child iterator back and forth, like a linked list iterator. They are ChildForth, ChildBack, ChildStart, and ChildEnd.

However, there really is no point in pasting the code here; these functions are all one line long and directly call the DListIterator version of the same function.

The Other Functions

The iterator class has several other functions that make it easier to add and remove nodes to the tree and to access their contents.

The functions are `AppendChild`, `PrependChild`, `InsertChildBefore`, `InsertChildAfter`, `RemoveChild`, `ChildValid`, and `ChildItem`. Notice something about all of these? These functions all correspond to functions within the linked list classes!

Because all of these functions directly call linked list iterator functions, there is no need for me to paste them here, either.

Building a Tree

There are two common methods of building trees: top-down and bottom-up. They are used in different situations, depending on what you want a tree to do.

Top Down

I've already shown you how to build a tree one way, which is called *top-down* construction. I used this method in Graphical Demonstration 11-1. In this method you create the root node of the tree first, and then add children from there.

Bottom Up

There is another way to build trees, however, and it is very different from top-down. This method is called *bottom-up* construction, mainly because the tree is built with the bottom nodes first (the leaves) and then expanded upward. This method of tree construction is not used as often as top-down, but there are several uses for it. For example, when building *Huffman trees*, bottom-up construction is used. You'll see what Huffman trees are in Chapter 21, "Data Compression," when I show you different methods of compressing data.

Traversing a Tree

You can traverse the nodes in a tree in many ways. Using the tree iterator is one of them, but that method is sometimes too difficult to use if you just want to perform a function on every single node in the tree.

You can use two different simple methods when you want to traverse a tree, and they are both recursive.

The Preorder Traversal

The first method I show you is the *preorder* traversal. You'll see why it is called so when you look at the pseudo-code:

```
Preorder( node )
    Process( node )
    For each child
        Preorder( child )
    end For
end Preorder
```

This algorithm accepts a node as a parameter and uses a function named `Process`. You shouldn't care what `Process` does; it is just a function that does something to the node.

The function first processes the node that is passed into the function. It then loops through each child and calls `Preorder` on each child node.

Let me show you how this is run through on a simple tree. Figure 11.9 shows the tree.

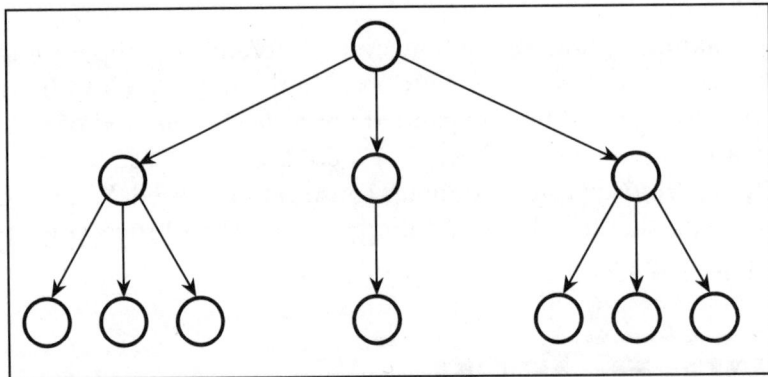

Figure 11.9

This is the sample tree that is used in the traversal examples.

Now, you call `Preorder` on the root node, so that gets processed first. The root has three children, so the function calls `Preorder` on each child. The function calls `Preorder` on the leftmost child first, which means that the leftmost child gets processed second. Now the function loops through all of the children of the leftmost child of the root, so the three children are processed third, fourth, and fifth. Now the function jumps back up to the second child of the root and repeats the process.

The order in which the nodes are processed is shown in Figure 11.10.

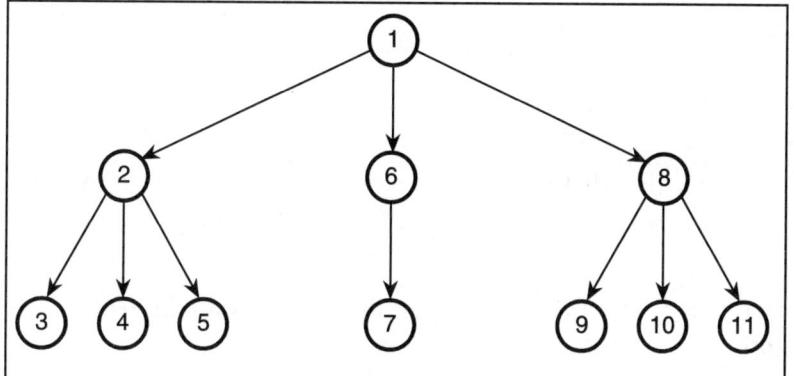

Figure 11.10

This is the order in which nodes are processed with Preorder.

In a preorder traversal, each subtree is processed before the next subtree is processed. You can see why it is called a preorder search from the algorithm; the current node is processed *before* the children.

Coding the Preorder Function

Now you need to actually put the algorithm into code. The method I used for the Preorder function is very flexible, and the code looks very ugly because of it.

The Preorder function takes a function pointer as a parameter. You've seen function pointers before in Chapter 8, "Hash Tables," but in case you aren't familiar with them, you can read more about them in Appendix A, "A C++ Primer."

```
1: template <class DataType>
2: void Preorder( Tree<DataType>* p_node, void (*p_process)(Tree<DataType>*) )
3: {
4:     p_process( p_node );
5:     DListIterator<Tree<DataType>*> itr = p_node->m_children.GetIterator();
6:     for( itr.Start(); itr.Valid(); itr.Forth() )
7:         Preorder( itr.Item(), p_process );
8: }
```

First off, the function is a template function. This allows Preorder to work on any type of tree easily.

On line 2, the function takes a node pointer and a function pointer as parameters. The function that is passed into Preorder is a simple function, which takes a Tree pointer as a parameter and doesn't return anything. I show you how to use this shortly.

On line 4, the `p_process` function pointer is called on the node.

On line 5, an iterator to the child list of the node is retrieved, and the function uses this iterator to loop through each child node and call `Preorder` on them in lines 6 and 7.

Using the Function Pointer

Say you have a tree of integers already built, and its name is `g_tree`. Now, you want to add together every number in the tree, but you don't want to bother using an iterator to do this.

So, you create a function called `sum`, which sums together the contents of tree nodes and puts them into a global integer named `g_sum`:

```
void sum( Tree<int>* p_node )
{
    g_sum += p_node->m_data;
}
```

Now, all you need to do to `sum` together the values of all the nodes in `g_tree` is to call these two lines of code:

```
g_sum = 0;
Preorder( g_tree, sum );
```

The first line clears the sum, and the second line traverses the tree, calling `sum` on each node.

The Postorder Traversal

The other major traversal type for trees is called the *postorder* traversal. If the preorder traversal was called *pre* order because it processed the current node *before* the child nodes, what do you think the *post* order traversal does?

That's right—it processes the current node *after* the child nodes.

```
Postorder( node )
    For each child
        Postorder( child )
    end For
    Process( node )
end Postorder
```

If you were to postorder traverse the tree from Figure 11.9, the nodes would be processed in the order shown in Figure 11.11.

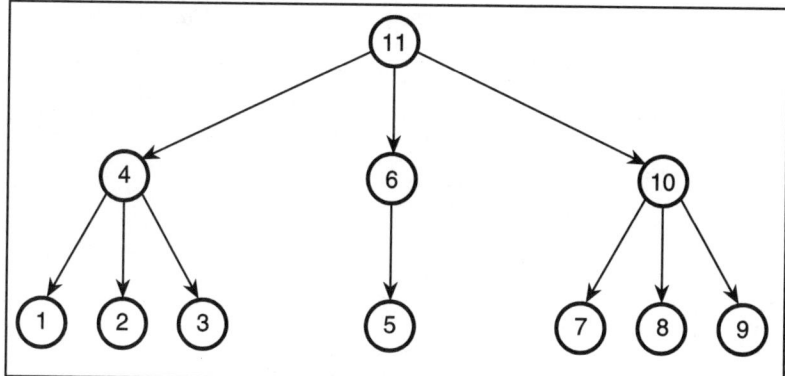

Figure 11.11

This is the order in which the nodes are processed using the postorder traversal.

This time, `Postorder` is called on the first child of the root, then the first child of that node, so that the first node to be processed is a leaf node. You can see from the figure that every child node is processed before its parent node.

I won't bother to paste the code for the actual `Postorder` function because it is so similar to the `Preorder` function. If you want to see it, it is in the tree.h file in the \structures\ directory on the CD.

Graphical Demonstration: Tree Traversals

This is Graphical Demonstration 11-2, which can be found on the CD in the directory \demonstrations\ch11\Demo02 - Tree Traversal\.

Compiling the Demo

This demonstration uses the SDLGUI library that I have developed for the book. For more information about this library, see Appendix B.

To compile this demo, either open up the workspace file in the directory or create your own project using the settings described in Appendix B. If you create your own project, all of the files you need to include are in the directory.

This demonstration is very simple; it only has three buttons, as shown in Figure 11.12.

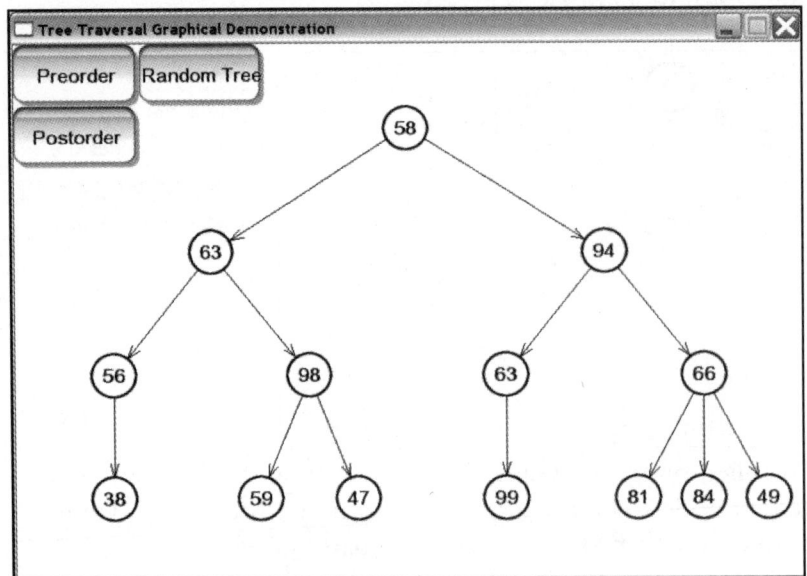

Figure 11.12

Here is a screenshot from Graphical Demonstration 11-2.

The Random Tree button generates a new random tree, as in the previous demo.

The other two buttons, Preorder and Postorder, make the demo go into an animation. The demo highlights the nodes using the preorder or postorder algorithms at 750 millisecond intervals. If you clicked Preorder, for example, Node 58 would be highlighted first, and then 63, and then 38, and then 98, and so on.

Game Demo 11-1: Plotlines

This is Game Demonstration 11-1. It is on the CD in the directory \demonstrations\ch11\Game01 - Plotlines\.

Compiling the Demo

This demonstration uses the SDLHelpers library that I have developed for the book. For more information about this library, see Appendix B.

To compile this demo, either open up the workspace file in the directory or create your own project using the settings described in Appendix B. If you create your own project, all of the files you need to include are in the directory.

For years and years, games have been *linear* with their stories and plots. What does this mean? You start the game and you play around, progressing from level to level, until you beat the game. Figure 11.13 shows how the levels progress throughout the game. Notice that it is a straight line, which is where the term *linear* comes from.

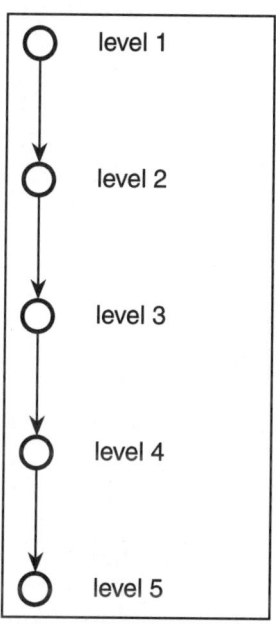

Figure 11.13

This is a linear level progression. Each level leads to the next.

Well, these types of games can be fun the first time through, but they tend to get boring. If you play the same levels over and over again, the game could get boring really quickly.

Now, imagine a game where the actions you take in the game directly affect the plot of the game. Say that at one point in the game, you are required to make a choice that will cause the game to branch out, and everything that happens during the rest of the game happens as a result from your choice.

For example, at level 2, you're required to make a choice; from that point, the game is different, depending on the choice you made. Figure 11.14 shows this.

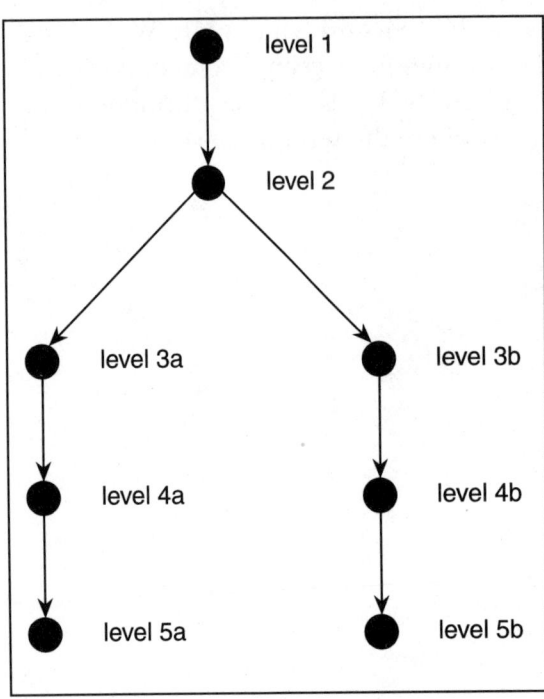

Figure 11.14

This is a branching level progression. You can choose which path to take at level 2.

Now, whenever you play through the game, you can go with branch *a* the first time and branch *b* the second time!

It turns out that trees are the ideal structure to store game data like this. You can see how the level progression from Figure 11.14 looks like a tree, albeit a basic one.

Using Trees to Store Plotlines

Obviously, creating a branching plotline takes a lot of work, and because the purpose of the demo is to show you how the data structure works, this demo doesn't really have a plot. Instead, I'll call the different story branches *a, b, c,* and so on. If you want, you can make up a plotline for yourself in your head—just don't make it too bad; I hate games with bad plots!

The first thing you need to do is create a storyline. In this little demo, the storyline will look like Figure 11.15.

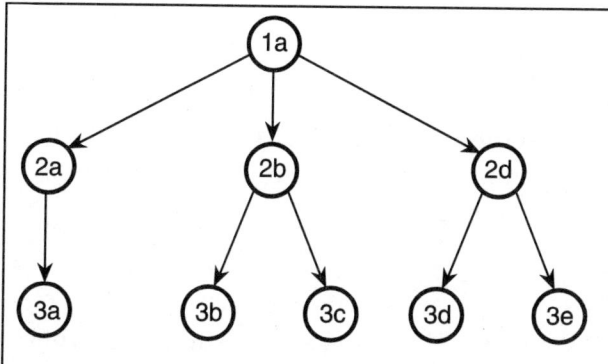

Figure 11.15

Here is the branching plotline for the demo.

Declaring the Tree

The premise of the demo is simple; when a level is completed, the player has a choice of which level to go to next. This information is stored in a tree:

```
Tree<int>* g_tree;
TreeIterator<int> g_itr;
```

The g_tree pointer will always point to the root of the tree, and the g_itr pointer will point to the current level in the tree.

The tree only stores integers, which represent which tile the level is made up of. Each level in the game demo has a different tile.

Initializing the Tree

The root of the tree is then initialized:

```
g_tree = new Tree<int>;
g_tree->m_data = 0;
g_itr = g_tree;
```

The root node is created with the value 0, which means that the player starts out on level 0. On line 3, the global iterator is assigned to point to the root node, which means that the player starts out on the root level.

After the root is initialized, a temporary iterator named itr is created so that I can build the tree with it. Using this iterator, I build the tree using the iterator functions:

```
TreeIterator<int> itr;
Tree<int>* node;
itr = g_tree;
// add the '2a' branch
```

```
node = new Tree<int>;
node->m_data = 1;
itr.AppendChild( node );
```

This code shows the addition of level 2a to the tree. The other seven levels of the tree are added in the same fashion; the iterator is moved around and child nodes are appended to the tree to give you the tree in Figure 11.15.

Changing Levels

Whenever the player "wins" a level in the demo, the demo switches to a state where it selects the next level.

The screen that draws the levels that are available for choosing uses the child iterator of g_itr to loop through each child and draw it.

```
for( g_itr.ChildStart(); g_itr.ChildValid(); g_itr.ChildForth() )
{
    // draw the level that the current child contains
}
```

When the user selects a level, the child iterator is moved to the correct level. The integer x will contain the number of the child which the player selected.

```
g_itr.ChildStart();
while( x > 0 )
{
    g_itr.ChildForth();
    x--;
}
g_itr.Down();
```

When the child iterator is in the correct place, the Down function is called, moving the iterator to the next level.

Playing the Game

The game starts off with a little dude standing on some weird alien world at the top left corner of the screen. Your mission? You are to use the arrow keys on the keyboard to successfully walk him off the edge of the screen to the right. It might be difficult and you might not succeed, but you'll make me proud by trying!

Okay, you really can't lose. There are no enemies or obstacles. Figure 11.16 shows the opening screen.

Figure 11.16

This is a screenshot of Level 0.

After you have successfully moved your little dude across the screen to the right, the level selection screen appears, as shown in Figure 11.17.

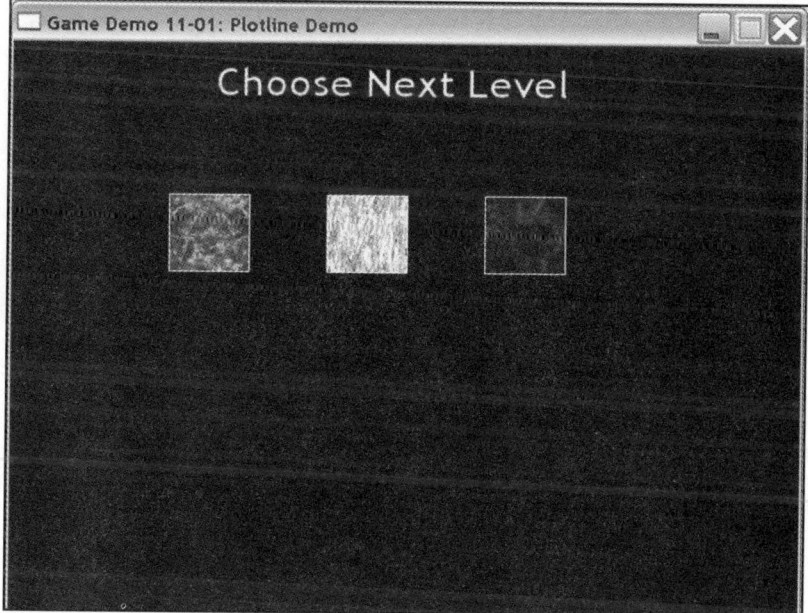

Figure 11.17

This is the level selection screen.

You use the mouse to click on one of the tiles to select the next level. That's pretty much all there is to the demo.

Conclusion

One thing you should realize about trees is that they are complex structures. They are obviously not suitable for storing any types of data, like arrays and linked lists are, so that makes trees a more specialized structure.

Only certain types of data can be stored in trees, but which kind? It turns out that hierarchical data fits nicely into trees, but that's not all. I only went into one use of trees; there are many.

For example, you could store AI decision paths into a tree. Imagine the AI process of a character within a shoot-'em-up game, as shown in Figure 11.18.

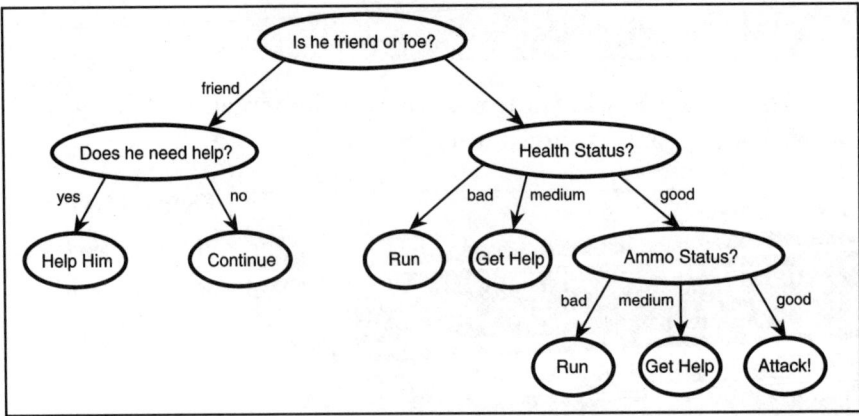

Figure 11.18

This is an AI decision tree showing the thought process of a character when he sees another character in the game.

So, as you can see, there are tons of uses for trees. The main purpose of this chapter was to introduce you to the concepts of trees and practice your recursion skills.

The next few chapters go over some more specialized trees and their uses.

CHAPTER 12

BINARY TREES

12. Binary Trees

In the previous chapter, you learned about general trees, which are trees that can have any number of branches per node. Now I'm going to show you the most popular variant of the tree structure: the *binary tree*.

In this chapter, you will learn

- What a binary tree is
- Some common traits of binary trees
- Two common implementations of binary trees
- How to program a linked binary tree
- How to perform the two tree traversals on a binary tree
- How to perform a new traversal specific to the binary tree structure
- How to build a simple arithmetic expression parser using binary trees

What Is a Binary Tree?

A binary tree is a very simple variant of the general tree structure, and it is often used in game programming. In fact, almost every tree-based structure in this book uses a binary tree as its base.

Simply put, a binary tree is a tree that can have up to two children. These two children are usually called the *left* and the *right* children of the tree. Figure 12.1 shows a binary tree node.

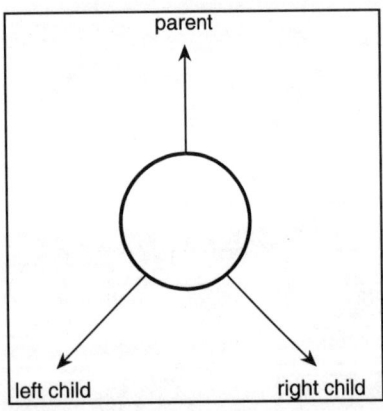

Figure 12.1

This is a binary tree node.

As you can see, there really isn't much to learn about plain binary trees because they are the simplest of all tree structures. A binary tree can have several traits that general trees cannot have, though.

Fullness

A binary tree can be *full*. Because each node can have a maximum of two child nodes, you can fill up a tree so that you cannot insert any more nodes without making the tree go down a level.

Figure 12.2 shows a full four-level binary tree.

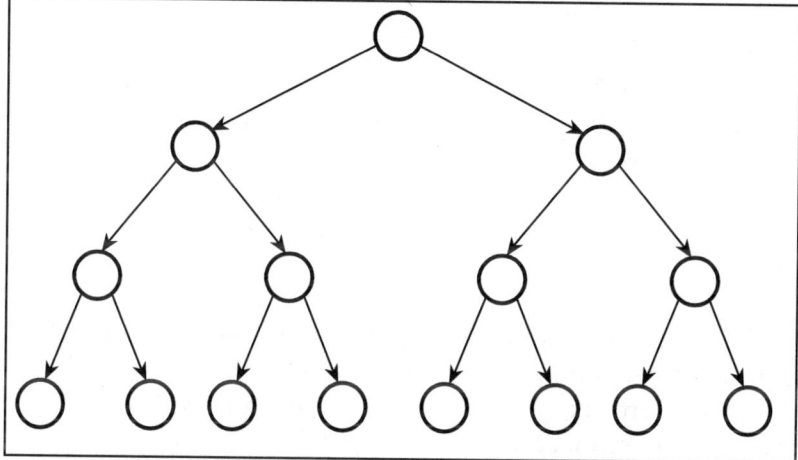

Figure 12.2

Here is a full binary tree. You cannot add more nodes to this tree without making it increase in size by another level.

In a full binary tree, every leaf node must be on the same level, and every non-leaf node must have two children.

Denseness

Another property of binary trees is called *denseness*. Sometimes this is also called *completeness* or *leftness*. A dense binary tree is similar to a full tree, except that in the bottom level of a tree, every node is packed to the left side of the tree.

Figure 12.3 shows a dense binary tree.

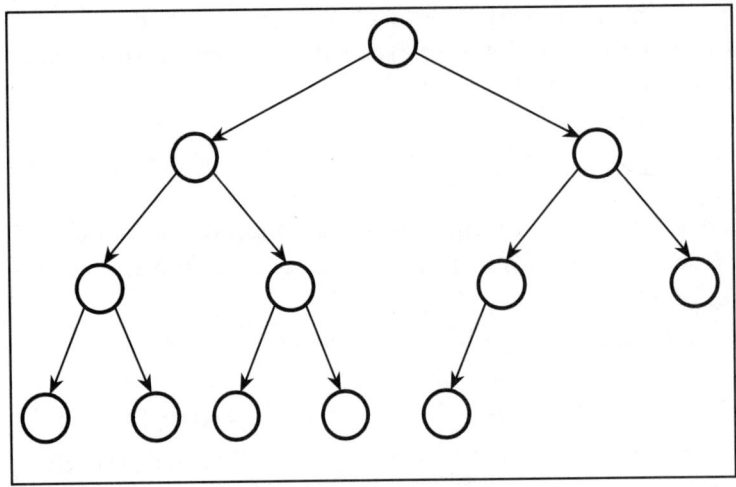

Figure 12.3

Here is a dense binary tree. Every level is full, except the last level, where the nodes are all packed to the left of the tree.

Denseness is an important trait with some variants of binary trees, as you'll see later on in this chapter and when I teach you about heaps in Chapter 14, "Priority Queues and Heaps."

Balance

Even though I don't really use this trait in this book, I feel it is important enough to mention. A *balanced* tree is a tree in which every node in the tree has approximately as many children in the left side as the right side. This property becomes important when using some of the binary search tree (*BST*) variants, such as *AVL trees* and *red-black trees (RBT)*. I discuss BSTs in Chapter 13, "Binary Search Trees," but not AVL trees or RBTs. They are fairly complex and used to solve specific problems that don't occur in most game programming situations; we will skip them because this is a game programming book.

Structure of Binary Trees

You can store a binary tree in two ways. The first method is the most common, and it's very similar to the `Tree` class. The second method is not as common, but it has its uses.

Linked Binary Trees

A *linked* binary tree is just like the regular tree structure and therefore is node-based. Instead of using a linked list of child pointers, though, the linked binary tree node has two *fixed* pointers. The fixed pointers either point to the left or right child nodes or contain 0 if the node doesn't have a child. The structure for these kinds of nodes is shown in Figure 12.4.

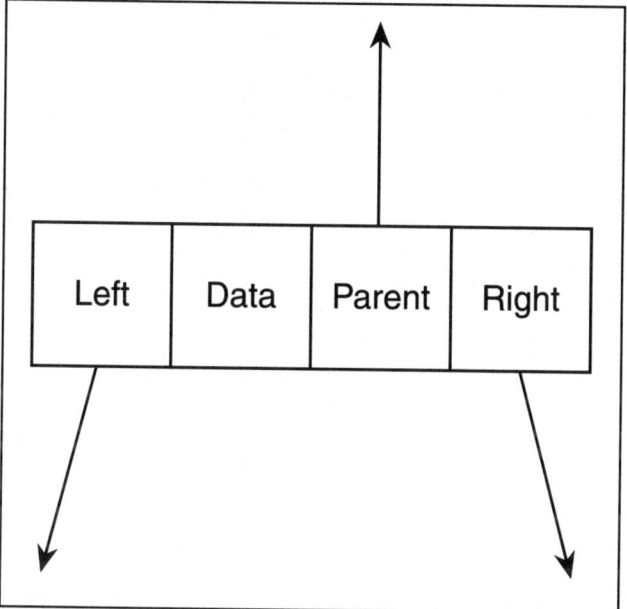

Figure 12.4
This is a linked binary tree node.

The three boxes with arrows coming out of them are all pointers that point to another node structure. Note that I included a parent pointer in the node; even though it is not necessary, I feel that it saves a lot of trouble when working with binary trees.

This method of structuring nodes is great because it allows for an effectively limitless tree size due to the linked nature of the tree.

Arrayed Binary Trees

There is another method of storing binary trees, however. You've seen how a binary tree can be full because the number of children in a binary tree is fixed at two.

Because you know that a binary tree can only have a certain number of nodes depending on the height of the tree, you can make certain assumptions. For example, imagine what would happen if you turned every node from the full binary tree in Figure 12.2 into an array cell. Figure 12.5 shows what I mean by this.

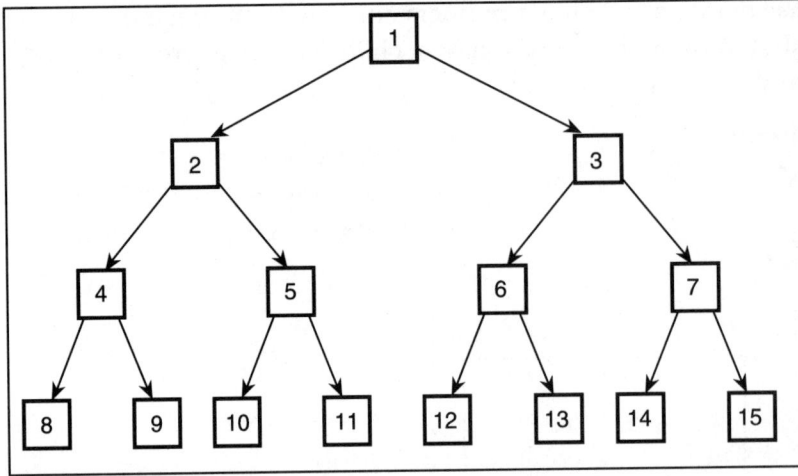

Figure 12.5

This is a full binary tree where the nodes have been turned into array cells.

Pay particular attention to the order in which I numbered the cells. The root starts at index 1 and the numbering goes from left to right all the way down to the last node on the right, 15. Now, imagine if you concatenated all of the cells into an array of cells, like Figure 12.6 shows.

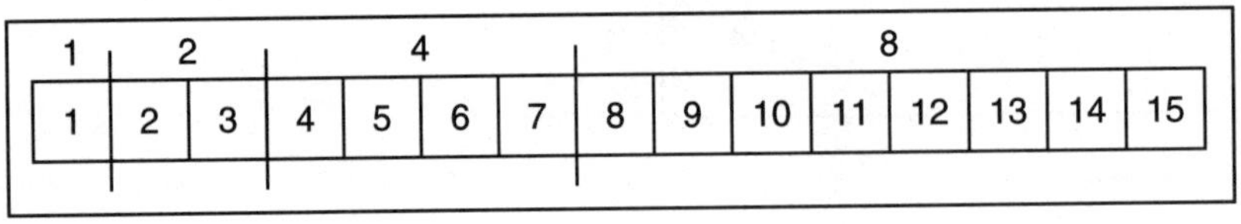

Figure 12.6

This is how you would represent a binary tree as an array.

The array is separated into four different segments, each with a number on top. The segments represent the levels of the tree. The first segment is only one cell in size because there is only one root node. The second segment contains two cells because there are two nodes on the second level of a binary tree. Likewise, the third segment has four cells, and the fourth segment has eight cells.

Size of Arrayed Binary Trees

The number of nodes on a level of a full binary tree doubles with each new level, and follows this formula: nodes for level $n = 2^{n-1}$. Therefore, the number of nodes required for level 5 would be 2^4, or 16.

The total number of cells in a binary tree of a particular depth follows this formula: cells for depth $n = 2^n-1$. For example, in the four-level tree in Figure 12.5, there are $2^4 - 1$ nodes, or 15. A binary tree with five levels requires 31 nodes.

Traversing Arrayed Binary Trees

You don't need iterators to traverse arrayed binary trees. A few easy algorithms allow you to determine the index of the left, right, and parent nodes of a binary tree cell.

Take a look back at Figure 12.5 and see if you can find a relationship between the index of any node and its left child. It is easy to see that the index of the left child of any node is twice the index of its parent. By using this knowledge, you can create a function that determines the left child of any cell in the tree:

left = index * 2;

That was easy enough, wasn't it? Now, see if you can figure out how to calculate the index of the right child of any cell. Because the right child of any node is only one index higher than the left child, you can use that formula to create the formula for finding the right child:

right = index * 2 + 1;

The last thing you need to figure out is how to get to the parent node from any node in the tree. If you look at the formula for finding the left node and reverse it, you get this:

parent = index / 2;

That works for left children, because the left children are all even numbers and are divisible by 2, but what about right children? What happens when you divide 3 in half? Although 3/2 is 1.5, the extra 0.5 is cut off because these algorithms are using integers, giving 1 as the result. So the parent algorithm works on any node.

Size Efficiency

I've said before that arrayed binary trees are not as common as linked trees. This is due to several reasons, but first, look at Figure 12.7.

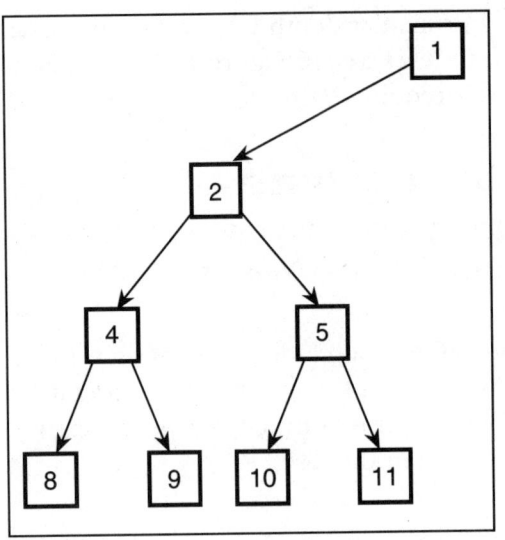

Figure 12.7

Here is another binary tree, where a lot of space is wasted.

The tree in Figure 12.7 is the same as the tree in Figure 12.5, but the entire subtree starting with index 3 has been removed. Imagine how this tree looks when stored into an array, though. Figure 12.8 shows this.

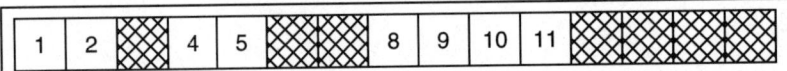

Figure 12.8

This is the tree from Figure 12.7 stored in an array.

The tree from Figure 12.7 has 8 nodes, but the array has 15 cells, which means that 7 cells are empty! That's almost half of the array!

Granted, the last 4 cells are unused, so you could chop them off the array, but what happens if you insert a left child onto node 8? Then the child would need to be stored into cell 16, requiring you to resize the array.

This example shows that using arrays to store binary trees is very inefficient if your trees aren't full or dense.

Graphical Demonstration: Binary Trees

This is Graphical Demonstration 12-1, which you can find on the CD in the directory \demonstrations\ch12\Demo01 – Binary Trees\.

Compiling the Demo

This demonstration uses the SDLGUI library that I have developed for the book. For more information about this library, see Appendix B, "The Memory Layout of a Computer Program."

To compile this demo, either open up the workspace file in the directory or create your own project using the settings described in Appendix B. If you create your own project, all of the files you need to include are in the directory.

Figure 12.9 shows a screenshot from this demonstration. The demo has eight different buttons, and Table 12.1 has a listing of what they do.

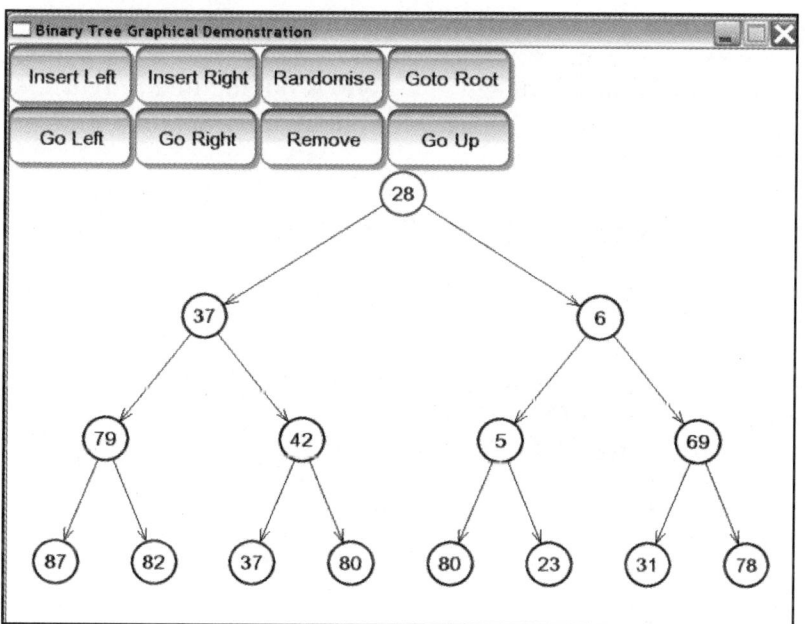

Figure 12.9

Here is a screenshot from the binary tree demonstration.

Table 12.1 Binary Tree Demonstration Commands

Command	Action
Insert Left	Inserts a new node to the left of the current node if there is none
Insert Right	Inserts a new node to the right of the current node if there is none
Go Left	Moves the current node to the left child node
Go Right	Moves the current node to the right child node
Randomize	Randomizes the tree
Remove	Removes the current node, unless it is the root
Goto Root	Moves the current node iterator to the root of the tree
Go Up	Moves the current node iterator up one level

As in the Tree graphical demonstration, the current node is highlighted in red. Play around with the demo to familiarize yourself with binary trees a bit more.

Coding a Binary Tree

All of the code for the Binary Tree structure and algorithms is located on the CD in the file \structures\BinaryTree.h.

Lucky for you, coding a binary tree isn't nearly as difficult as coding a general tree. In fact, you don't even need an iterator class with a binary tree; you can just as easily use a pointer to a node as the iterator.

Note that I'm not including an `Arrayed Binary Tree` class. Because an arrayed binary tree is essentially an array, there is no need to include one.

The Structure

As I stated before, the binary tree class has four variables:

```
template<class DataType>
class BinaryTree
{
```

```
public:
    DataType m_data;
    Node* m_parent;
    Node* m_left;
    Node* m_right;
};
```

They are the data, a pointer to the parent, and a pointer to the left and right children.

The Constructor

The constructor exists to clear the pointers so that they aren't filled with garbage data when a node is created.

```
BinaryTree()
{
    m_parent = 0;
    m_left = 0;
    m_right = 0;
}
```

The Destructor and the Destroy Function

The destructor of the BinaryTree class just calls the Destroy function, like the Tree class did, so there is no need to paste the code here.

However, the Destroy function is slightly different than before:

```
void Destroy()
{
    if( m_left )
        delete m_left;
    m_left = 0;
    if( m_right )
        delete m_right;
    m_right = 0;
}
```

This function determines if the node has a left child and deletes it if it does, and then it determines if it has a right child and deletes it if it does. As before, the function is recursive because the destructor of each child node calls Destroy.

The Count Function

The Count function is only slightly modified from the Tree version; instead of looping through the child list, it calls the Count function on each child of the node.

```
int Count()
{
    int c = 1;
    if( m_left )
        c += m_left->Count();
    if( m_right )
        c += m_right->Count();
    return c;
}
```

Note that it checks to see if each child node exists before calling the Count function on it.

Using the BinaryTree Class

This is Example 12-1, which can be found on the CD in the directory \examples\ch12\01 – Binary Tree\.

This example takes you through the process of building a simple three-level full binary tree.

The first step is to declare the tree root and an iterator:

```
BinaryTree<int>* root = 0;
BinaryTree<int>* itr = 0;
```

After that, you need to initialize the root of the tree:

```
root = new BinaryTree<int>;
root->m_data = 1;
```

Then you create the left and right child nodes of the root node:

```
root->m_left = new BinaryTree<int>;
root->m_left->m_data = 2;
root->m_left->m_parent = root;

root->m_right = new BinaryTree<int>;
root->m_right->m_data = 3;
root->m_right->m_parent = root;
```

Now, the iterator is put to work to create the nodes lower down in the tree:

```
itr = root;
itr = itr->m_left;
itr->m_left = new BinaryTree<int>;
itr->m_left->m_data = 4;
itr->m_left->m_parent = itr;

itr->m_right = new BinaryTree<int>;
itr->m_right->m_data = 5;
itr->m_right->m_parent = itr;
```

The iterator is first pointed at the root node and then is moved down to the left node of the root. After that, node 4 is inserted at the left of node 2, and node 5 is inserted at the right.

Now you want to go back up one level:

```
itr = itr->m_parent;
```

And now go back down to the right and do the same thing:

```
itr = itr->m_right;
itr->m_left = new BinaryTree<int>;
itr->m_left->m_data = 6;
itr->m_left->m_parent = itr;

itr->m_right = new BinaryTree<int>;
itr->m_right->m_data = 7;
itr->m_right->m_parent = itr;
```

As you can see, iterating through a binary tree is simple because you know there are only two children per node.

Traversing the Binary Tree

If you remember, the general tree structure had two simple traversal methods: the preorder and the postorder. The binary tree structure allows for another type of traversal, called the *inorder* traversal, as well.

I'll show you how to accomplish all three. The actual C++ code for these functions is in the BinaryTree.h file and is almost identical to the code for the general tree traversal functions, so I won't include it here. If you need clarification, the "Traversing a Tree" section in Chapter 11, "Trees," describes how the traversal functions work.

The Preorder Traversal

The preorder traversal for a binary tree is simple, and it is almost identical to the algorithm used for general trees:

```
Preorder( node )
    process( node )
    Preorder( node.left )
    Preorder( node.right )
End Preorder
```

It is important to note that the left node is processed before the right node; that is the general convention used by all binary trees.

The Postorder Traversal

Just like last time, the postorder traversal processes the current node after the child nodes:

```
Postorder( node )
    Postorder( node.left )
    Postorder( node.right )
    process( node )
End Postorder
```

The Inorder Traversal

So, if the *pre*order traversal processes the current node *before* the children, and the *post*order traversal processes the current node *after* the children, what do you think the *in*order traversal does?

That's right, it processes the current node in between the children nodes:

```
Inorder( node )
    Inorder( node.left )
    process( node )
    Inorder( node.right )
End Inorder
```

This traversal assures that the entire left subtree of every node is processed before the current node and the right subtree. Remember this traversal; you'll be using it for a neat trick in Chapter 20, "Sorting Data."

Figure 12.10 shows the order in which nodes are processed in a binary tree using the inorder traversal. Note the general trend of processing the nodes from left to right.

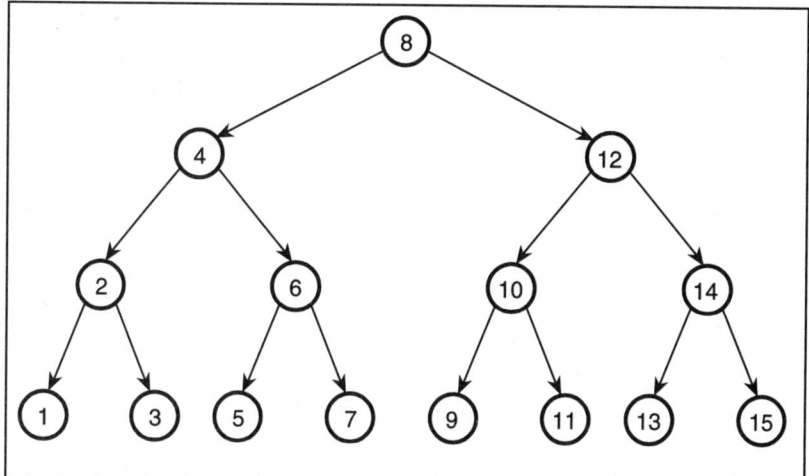

Figure 12.10

This is the order of nodes processed using the inorder traversal.

Graphical Demonstration: Binary Tree Traversals

This is Graphical Demonstration 12-2, which is located on the CD in the directory \demonstrations\ch12\Demo02 - Binary Tree Traversals\.

> ### Compiling the Demo
>
> This demonstration uses the SDLGUI library that I have developed for the book. For more information about this library, see Appendix B.
>
> To compile this demo, either open up the workspace file in the directory or create your own project using the settings described in Appendix B. If you create your own project, all of the files you need to include are in the directory.

This demonstration is almost the same as Graphical Demonstration 11-2, except that it has an extra button to execute the inorder traversal. Figure 12.11 shows a screenshot of the demo in action.

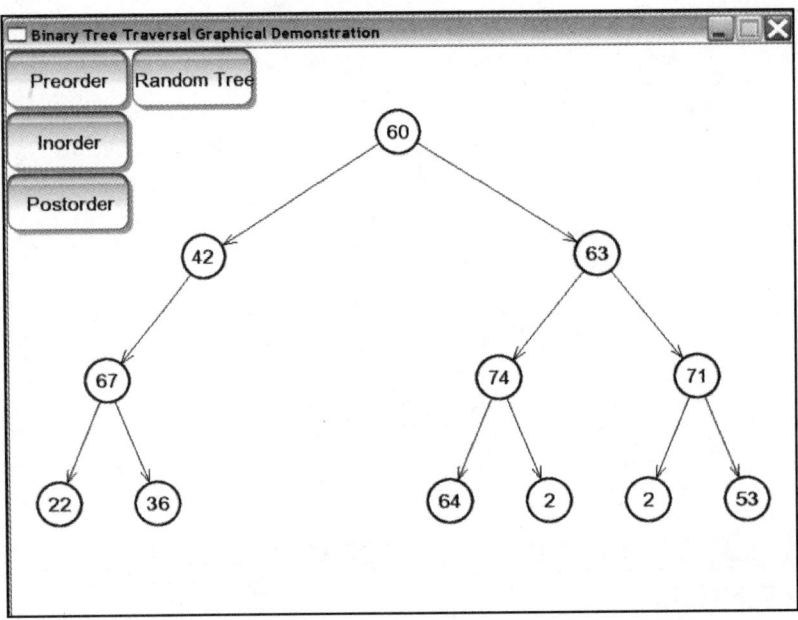

Figure 12.11

Here is a screenshot from the traversal demo.

As before, the nodes will be highlighted for 700 milliseconds while they are being processed to show you the order in which they are visited by the algorithms.

Application: Parsing

This next topic, although it's a little advanced, is a really neat application of binary trees. The code for this section is on the CD in the directory \demonstrations\ch12\Game01 - Parsing\.

> ### Compiling the Demo
>
> This demonstration uses the SDLGUI library that I have developed for the book. For more information about this library, see Appendix B.
>
> To compile this demo, either open up the workspace file in the directory or create your own project using the settings described in Appendix B. If you create your own project, all of the files you need to include are in the directory.

Parsing is the act of breaking up a sentence into easy-to-understand segments. For example, when you read a sentence, your mind mentally parses it into a form that makes sense to you.

Take the following sentence, for example: "Bob runs up the hill." Your mind recognizes that sentence, and it has parsed it into several segments. I don't want to turn this into an English lecture, but a lot of computer language theory is based in concepts that English linguists invented.

The sentence can be broken up into these fragments: verb phrase, preposition, noun phrase. Bob runs, up, the hill. The two phrases can then be broken down further; the verb phrase is a combination of a noun and a verb, and the noun phrase is a combination of an article and a noun. Figure 12.12 shows the tree that is created when your mind parses the sentence.

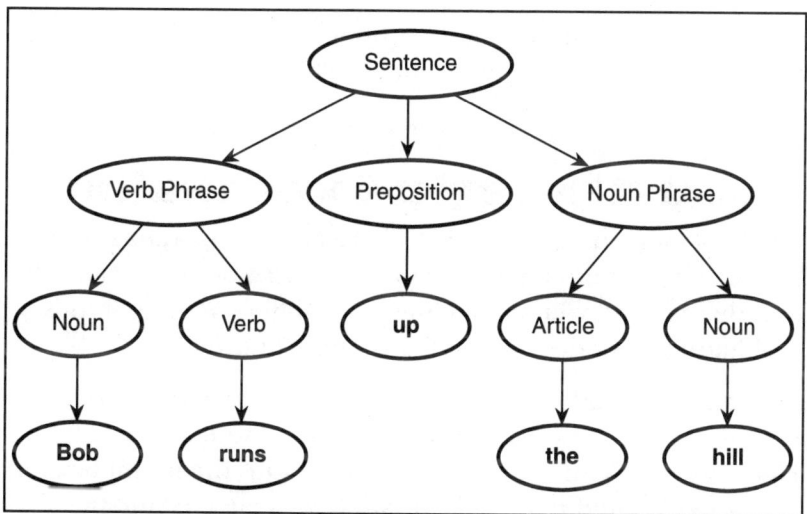

Figure 12.12

This is a parse tree for an English sentence.

Now, don't be put off if you didn't understand that; this is a complex topic in English, after all. I showed that to you so that you can begin to understand how computers parse the code that you send into your C++ compiler.

"Okay," you say, "parsing is important when you're making compilers, but what the heck does it have to do with game programming?"

I'm sure you've played *Quake* before. If you have made custom maps for *Quake*, you know that *Quake* has a *scripting system* known as *QuakeC*. This system allows you to add little bits of C code to *Quake* maps so that code is executed when the player or monsters do something on the map.

A scripting system essentially allows you to make *very* customizable maps for a game. I'm sure you've played some of the *Quake modules* (*mods*) before. One of my favorites is *Team Fortress Classic* (*TFC*). These mods allow you to drastically change the way the game operates, expanding upon the original game's capabilities.

One of the reasons games like *Quake* are so popular is because they are so modifiable.

This section introduces you to basic arithmetic parsing, which is the first step toward creating your very own scripting system.

Arithmetic Expressions

Don't be confused by that big name; arithmetic expressions are really just mathematical formulas involving numbers and variables. $x = 24 + y$ is an arithmetic expression.

The standard four operators in math are addition, subtraction, multiplication, and division. All four of these operators are *binary* operators, which means that they operate on two numbers.

Parsing an Arithmetic Expression

Look at this expression for a moment: $2 * (y / z)$. There are two operators in this expression: multiplication and division. Each operator has a *term* on the *left* and the *right* sides of itself. Does that remind you of anything—possibly something in this chapter? That's right—binary tree nodes have left and right children!

So you can treat the operator as a node and put the terms into the left and right nodes of a binary tree. For example, the term inside the parentheses can be viewed like the first tree in Figure 12.13. Then, if you create a node with the multiplication symbol in it and put 2 as the left child node and the subtree created inside the parentheses as the right child node, you get the second tree in Figure 12.13.

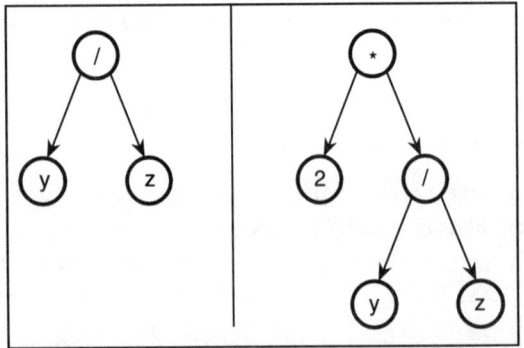

Figure 12.13

This is the parse tree for the arithmetic expression $2 * (y / z)$.

Well, now you've got a tree; what do you do with it? You can perform a postorder traversal on the tree to calculate its value!

For example, you start at the root node and tell it to return the value of the left node first. The left node just returns 2. Then, you tell the right node to return its value. Because the right node is another operator, the postorder algorithm is called again. The division node asks its left node for its value, which is *y*, and then asks the right node for its value, which is *z*. Now that both child nodes have returned their values, the division node can divide *y* by *z* and return the result back up to the multiplication node. Now that the multiplication node has the values of both of its children, it multiplies both of them together and returns that result! Whoa, that's cool.

Recursive Descent Parsing

I'm going to show you an amazingly simple demonstration of what is called *recursive descent* parsing, which you can use to parse a simple arithmetic expression and turn it into a tree that your program can then use as a simple script.

Tokens

The first thing you need to do is turn the actual arithmetic expression into a list of *tokens*. A token is basically a structure that says, "This is a number," "This is an operator," or "This is a variable."

I'll first create an enumerated type, which will help you determine the type of a token:

```
enum TOKEN
{
    NUMBER,
    VARIABLE,
    OPERATOR,
    LPAREN,
    RPAREN
};
```

After that, I create the actual Token class:

```
class Token
{
    TOKEN m_type;
    float m_number;
```

```
    int m_variable;
    int m_operator;
};
```

This class has a type variable that determines which of the following three variables is valid.

If the type of the token is NUMBER, then m_number will hold the number. If the type of the token is VARIABLE, then m_variable will hold the number of the

> **NOTE**
> More-complex implementations of a token class would use the C++ union directive and have a different class structure for each kind of token type. If you don't know what a union is, don't worry; I'm not using them in this demo because this demo is simple.

variable (you'll see how this works in a bit). If the token is OPERATOR, then m_operator has a number from 0–3, where 0 is addition, 1 is subtraction, 2 is multiplication, and 3 is division.

Variables

This very simple demo only has four variables for now, so the only valid values of m_value are 0–3. More-complex systems might have more variables than this. The most complex systems don't use this method at all; instead, they store information about whether the variable is global or local and the memory offset and datatype of the variable. It gets very complex.

For this system, the only valid variables are c, s, t, and l, which stand for cosine, sine, time, and life. The cosine and the sine variables keep track of the cosine and sine of the current game time. The time variable keeps track of the current time of the system, and the life variable keeps track of the amount of life that the player has left.

Scanning

The process of converting the text string into a stream of tokens is called *scanning*, or *tokenizing*. The scanner will read each part of an expression into a string and then determine if it is an operator, variable, number, or parenthesis.

The code for this process isn't very complex, but it is long, bulky, and boring.

The scanning process for a simple system works like this:

1. Read in a character.
2. If the character is one of the four variables, create a variable token.
3. If the character is one of the four operators, create an operator token.

4. If the character is a number, read in the rest of the number and create a number token.
5. Place the token into a queue.
6. Repeat.

You can find the code in the g12-01.cpp file on the CD if you're really interested (the Scan function); I have decided not to include it here because it doesn't have anything to do with trees. The scanner just provides an easy way of turning a string of characters into a queue of items that the parser recognizes.

Parsing

There are basically two different forms for an arithmetic expression term:

1. It can be a single constant or variable.
2. It can be two constants or variables with an operator in between.

I established previously that the operators in this demo are all binary; they operate on two numbers. In languages like C++, you can chain operators together, like this:

c + s + t

For simplicity, the parser doesn't support statements like that. Instead, parentheses must surround two of the variables. Either of these corrections is acceptable:

c + (s + t)
(c + s) + t

So the parser's job is to view the queue of tokens and turn it into a binary tree. The parser is a recursive function, which makes your life much easier.

I'm going to show you the pseudocode algorithm in a few sections so you can understand what is going on.

The parse algorithm takes a queue of tokens and returns a tree. The algorithm also creates three tree nodes as local variables:

```
Tree Parse( Queue )
    Tree left, center, right
```

Now, the first thing to do is to check the first token.

```
if Queue.First == LPAREN
    Queue.Dequeue
    left = Parse( Queue )
```

```
        Queue.Dequeue
else if Queue.First == VARIABLE or NUMBER
    left = VARIABLE or NUMBER
Queue.Dequeue
```

There are three valid token types for the first token of the queue. If the first token is a left parenthesis, then the parenthesis is taken off the queue and the rest of the queue is passed into the parse algorithm again. The result of the recursively called parse algorithm is placed into the left tree node. Theoretically, the parse algorithm should have removed everything after the first left parenthesis up to a matching right parenthesis, so there should be a right parenthesis at the front of the queue. That is also removed from the queue.

> **CAUTION**
> Real parsers would check to see if the queue actually contained a right parenthesis after the parse algorithm returns. If it isn't a right parenthesis, the string that is being parsed is illegal. For the purposes of the demo, I left error checking out, but you should be aware that a clean system would use error checking. I recommend using exceptions if you know how to use them.

If the first token was a variable or a constant number instead, then the left tree node is made into a leaf node that contains information about the variable or constant.

Finally, the token is removed from the queue. After the first token is processed, the algorithm decides if the term is just a single variable or number or if it is two variables or numbers separated by an operator.

If the current term is just a single variable or number, then that token has already been processed and the queue will either be empty or have a right parenthesis at the front.

```
if  Queue.Empty or Queue.Front == RPAREN
    return left
```

The function returns the left node at this point because it contains the single term.

If it isn't a single term, then the queue must contain an operator:

```
if Queue.Front == OPERATOR
    center = OPERATOR
Queue.Dequeue
```

If the queue doesn't contain an operator at the front, then the string is invalid, and the parser should handle the error by informing the user. For simplicity, this demo doesn't have that kind of error checking.

Now that you've gotten to this point, there is only one more token to process for the term. Like the first token, the only valid types it can be are variables, numbers, or left parentheses:

```
if Queue.First == LPAREN
    Queue.Dequeue
    right  = Parse( Queue )
    Queue.Dequeue
else if Queue.First == VARIABLE or NUMBER
    right = VARIABLE or NUMBER
Queue.Dequeue
```

And finally, attach the left and right children to the center and return it:

```
center.left = left
center.right = right
return center
```

If you can think recursively, this algorithm will appear amazingly simple for the task it does. If you don't quite understand recursion yet, I'll show you a few examples on how this algorithm works.

Using the Algorithm

First, I'll start off with the simplest example:

t

This is a single-variable term. Naturally, you should expect the parser to return a tree with one node: t at the root. The algorithm looks at the token, sees that it is a variable, and then sets the left node so that it is a variable node.

Now the function checks the queue and sees that it is empty, so it returns the left node, giving us a simple one-node tree with t in it.

Now I'll move on to a more complicated example:

t + (5 * c)

The first step is the same; the left node is turned into a variable node. The second step is different, however. Last time, the queue was empty; this time, an operator token is in it.

So now the algorithm creates the center node and turns it into a +.

Now it looks at the next token, which is a left parenthesis. So it strips off the parenthesis and passes the queue (which contains 5 * c) now) into the parse algorithm again.

This time, the second parse algorithm strips off the 5 and makes the left node a constant number node. It strips off the star and turns the center node into a multiplication operator node. Finally, it strips off the c and turns the right node into a constant node. The second parse algorithm then returns the center node up to the first parse algorithm.

Now the result of the second parse algorithm is placed in the right node and the first center node is returned, resulting in the tree in Figure 12.14.

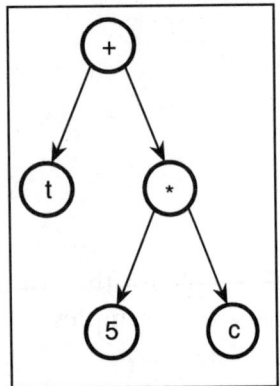

Figure 12.14

The parse tree for a simple expression.

Now you can see how recursion is your friend here: It takes care of those nasty nested parentheses automatically so you don't have to mess around with them much.

Source Listing

Here is the source code listing for the `ParseArithmetic` function used in the demo. Pay attention to where the comments are; they alert you as to where proper error checking should be inserted.

```
BinaryTree<Token>* ParseArithmetic( LQueue<Token>& p_queue )
{
    BinaryTree<Token>* left = 0;
    BinaryTree<Token>* center = 0;
    BinaryTree<Token>* right = 0;
    // make sure the queue has something in it.
    if( p_queue.Count() == 0 )
        return 0;
    // take off the first token and determine what it is
    switch( p_queue.Front().m_type )
    {
    case LPAREN:
```

```
        p_queue.Dequeue();
        left = ParseArithmetic( p_queue );
        // if( p_queue.Front().m_type != RPAREN )
            // this is where you would throw an error;
            // the string is unparsable with our language.
        p_queue.Dequeue();
        break;
    case VARIABLE:
    case NUMBER:
        left = new BinaryTree<Token>;
        left->m_data = p_queue.Front();
        p_queue.Dequeue();
        break;
    // case OPERATOR:
        // this is where you would throw an error;
        // the string is unparsable with our language.
    }
    if( p_queue.Count() == 0 )
        return left;
    if( p_queue.Front().m_type == RPAREN )
        return left;
    // if( p_queue.Front().m_type != OPERATOR )
        // this is where you would throw an error;
        // the string is unparsable with our language.
    center = new BinaryTree<Token>;
    center->m_data = p_queue.Front();
    p_queue.Dequeue();
    // make sure the queue has something in it.
    if( p_queue.Count() == 0 )
        return 0;
    // take off the third token and determine what it is
    switch( p_queue.Front().m_type )
    {
    case LPAREN:
        p_queue.Dequeue();
        right = ParseArithmetic( p_queue );
        // if( p_queue.Front().m_type != RPAREN )
            // this is where you would throw an error;
            // the string is unparsable with our language.
        p_queue.Dequeue();
        break;
```

```
        case VARIABLE:
        case NUMBER:
            right = new BinaryTree<Token>;
            right->m_data = p_queue.Front();
            p_queue.Dequeue();
            break;
    //  case OPERATOR:
    //      // this is where you would throw an error;
    //      // the string is unparsable with our language.
        }
        center->m_left = left;
        center->m_right = right;
        return center;
    }
```

You can probably see why I didn't just paste the code right away; pseudo-code is almost always easier to understand.

Executing the Tree

Now that the parser has built the parse tree, you need to be able to evaluate it somehow. I mentioned before that you can use a simple postorder traversal to evaluate the tree, which is what I will show you now.

The Evaluate function is also (take a guess!) recursive! Gee, that was surprising, wasn't it? I hope you're beginning to see a trend when using trees. Recursion really makes some things easy.

The function will evaluate a tree node, returning a float value. There are three types of nodes, so I'll split the code up into five parts: the beginning, the three node types, and the end.

Here is the beginning:

```
float Evaluate( BinaryTree<Token>* p_tree )
{
    if( p_tree == 0 )
        return 0.0f;

    float left = 0.0f;
    float right = 0.0f;
```

This sets everything up first. If the node passed into the algorithm is 0, then 0 is returned. If not, then the left and right variables are set to 0.

Now, the algorithm uses a switch statement to determine which of the three node types it is:

```
switch( p_tree->m_data.m_type )
{
case VARIABLE:
    return g_vars[p_tree->m_data.m_variable];
    break;
```

The first node type is a variable. Because the demo has four valid variables, all four variables are stored in an array, g_vars. The m_variable member of the Token class will contain a number from 0 to 3, so the function gets that number and returns the correct value from the variable table.

```
case NUMBER:
    return p_tree->m_data.m_number;
    break;
```

The second node type is a constant number. This case is easy; it just returns the number stored within the token.

```
case OPERATOR:
    left = Evaluate( p_tree->m_left );
    right = Evaluate( p_tree->m_right );
    switch( p_tree->m_data.m_operator )
    {
    case 0:
        return left + right;
        break;
    case 1:
        return left - right;
        break;
    case 2:
        return left * right;
        break;
    case 3:
        return left / right;
        break;
    }
}
```

The third node type is the most interesting: the operator. If the node is an operator, then it recursively calls the Evaluate function on its left and right children, determines which operation to execute on the two values, and returns the result.

```
        return 0.0f;
}
```

Last, in case something messed up, 0 is returned at the end. Hopefully nothing did, but it is always safe to do so anyway.

Playing the Demo

This is the most complex demo in the book so far, so it needs a fair amount of explanation. Figure 12.15 shows a screenshot from the demo in action.

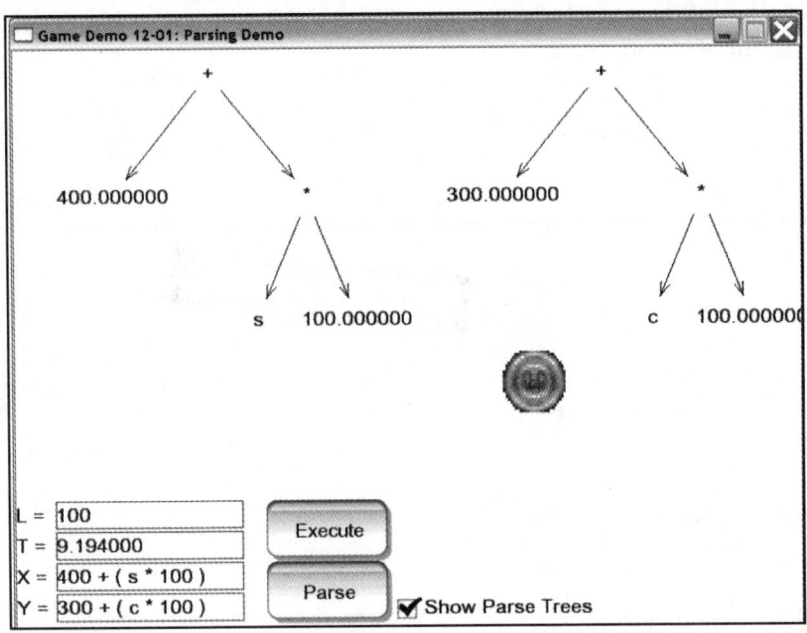

Figure 12.15

Here is a screenshot from the demo.

At the bottom are four text boxes. They represent the life of the player, the current time, and the *x* and *y* formulas for the player. You'll be using the bottom boxes to control the position of the player on-screen.

To start off, try entering these two lines into the *x* and *y* boxes:

```
t * 100
0
```

Now check the check box on the right of the screen so that it will display the parse trees. After that, click the Parse button; you should see two trees drawn on the screen now. The *x* tree is on the left and the *y* tree is on the right. This way, you can visually see how your expression was parsed by the system.

Next, you want to set up your life variable. You can click on the *L* box and enter a life value.

You cannot modify the *T* value, though. The Execute button is a toggle that resets the time to 0 when you click it and then starts the demonstration.

Now that you've entered your formula, click the Execute button. A UFO should appear on the screen at the upper left, and it should move to the right at 100 pixels per second. It will take 8 seconds to travel off the screen, and you need to reset it when it's done. Clicking the Execute button again will stop the demo from running.

I urge you to play around with different formulas to see what you can accomplish. Table 12.2 holds some of the cool ones that I've discovered.

> **NOTE**
> A lot of the formulas in Table 12.2 use the c and s variables, which are the sine and cosine of the time. If you know *trigonometry*, then the effect of these variables should be obvious to you. This book doesn't teach trigonometry, but trig isn't a requirement for the book, so the best I can do is tell you to sit back and enjoy the pretty effects that they produce. If you don't know trigonometry, though, you're missing out on a lot. Trig is one of the most important math subjects you can use when programming games.

Table 12.2 Cool Formulas

x	y	Effect
400 + (c * 100)	300 + (s * 100)	Makes the ship fly around in circles
t * 100	300 + (s * 100)	Makes the ship fly in a sine wave pattern
400 + (c * 200)	300	Makes the ship fly back and forth rapidly
(t * t) * 10	300	Makes the ship slowly accelerate off the screen
400 + (c * (t * 10))	300 + (s * (t * 10))	Makes the ship slowly circle out of control

I made these formulas after playing around for a minute; I'm sure you can come up with some even neater ones. For example, you could make the speed of the spaceship depend on the amount of health you have left. The possibilities are endless.

Conclusion

This chapter turned out to be a lot longer than I expected, mainly due to the extensive parsing section I included. I hope you understood it, because parsing is a very neat area of game developing. Nothing beats a game that is 100 percent extendible and modifiable.

If anything, this chapter should have reinforced the idea that recursion is a very important area of programming. Some people may say that recursion is too slow for game programming, and they are sometimes right. The key is knowing when recursion is used *best*.

Binary trees aren't very exciting on their own, but I included them here to lead up to the next few chapters. BSTs (see Chapter 13), heaps (see Chapter 14), and Huffman trees (see Chapter 21, "Data Compression") all use binary trees as their base. In addition, a lot of trees that aren't covered in this book are based on binary trees, such as AVL trees and red-black trees, as I mentioned before.

CHAPTER 13

Binary Search Trees

13. Binary Search Trees

Previously, you learned about recursion, general trees, and binary trees. This chapter deals with a variant of the binary tree called a *Binary Search Tree (BST)*. The BST is a structure where recursion is more important in determining how the data is stored rather than how the data is accessed. You'll see what I mean by this later in the chapter.

In this chapter, you will learn

- What a BST is
- How to insert data into a BST
- How to find data in a BST
- How to code a BST class
- How to use a BST to search for resources in a game

What Is a BST?

Imagine that you have to sort a group of people by height so that you can easily search for someone by their height later on. How would you go about doing this?

Figure 13.1 shows six people that you need to sort.

Figure 13.1

Don't hate them because they're beautiful.

The easiest way to sort them is to find the shortest person and put him/her first, and then find and place the next shortest, and so on. This method of sorting on a computer is slow, though. You can stand back and immediately see the shorter people in the line of people waiting to be sorted; the computer can't do that. The computer would need to look at every person in line to find out who is the shortest.

Instead, why don't you do something clever? Pick a midpoint (say, 5 feet, 6 inches) and look at the first person in line. If he/she is below that height, you move him/her to the left. If he/she is above that height, you move him/her to the right. Now, whenever you want to search for someone of a particular height, all you need to do is determine which half of the line that height would be in and search only that half of the line!

For example, if you wanted to find someone with a height of 6 feet, you would look in the right half of the line because no one who is 6 feet tall would be in the left half.

Figure 13.2 shows the group of people *partitioned* in half.

Figure 13.2

The perfume models are now partitioned into two groups, the tallest on one side, and the shortest on the other.

This sorting method is employed by the Binary Search Tree data structure. It attempts to split data in half to make searching easier.

Inserting Data into a BST

Say you have a queue of data that you want to search through. You take the first item off the queue and put it as the root of the tree. Then, you take the next item off the queue and compare it with the root. If it is less than the root, then you make it the left child of the root. If it is more than the root, then you make it the right child of the root.

Now, repeat the process. Take another item off the queue and do the same thing. If a node already exists on the left or the right children, then you go down another level and compare the items again.

For example, say you have a queue containing this data: 4, 2, 6, 5, 1, 3, 7. The first step is to take off the 4 and insert it as the root node in a BST. Then you take off the 2 and compare it with the 4. Because 2 is less than 4, you insert 2 as the left child of the root. Then you take off 6, which is placed as the right child of the root because it is more than 4. Figure 13.3 shows the first three steps.

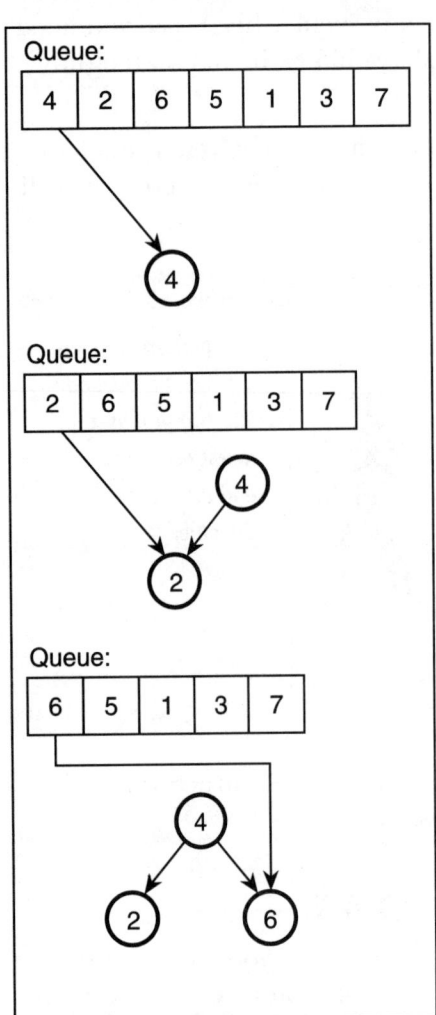

Figure 13.3

This is how you insert the first three nodes into the BST.

After you have completed that step, you want to insert 5 into the tree. First, you compare it with 4 at the root, and because it is larger than 4, you try to insert it to the right. However, there is already a node to the right! So you compare the 5 with the 6 in the right node; because 5 is less than 6, you insert the 5 as the left child of the 6. Likewise, the 1 is compared to the 4 and then the 2 and then inserted as the left child of the 2. Figure 13.4 shows these two steps.

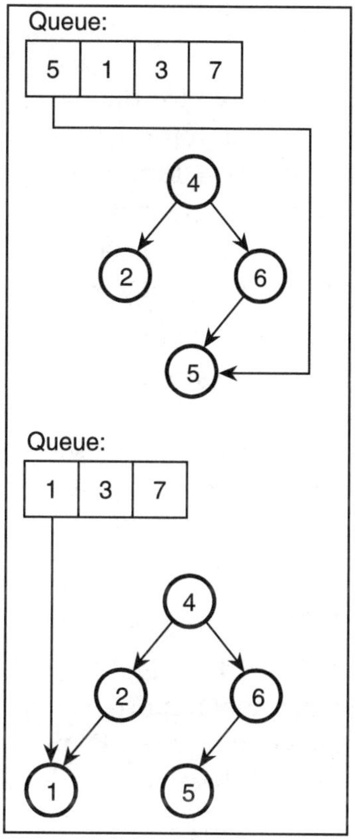

Figure 13.4

This is how you insert the next two nodes.

See if you can figure out where the 3 and the 7 go. Figure 13.5 shows where they are inserted if you're stumped.

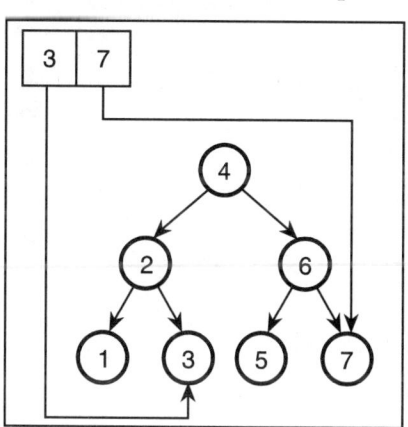

Figure 13.5

Finally, this is how you insert the last two nodes.

So, now that you have the final BST in Figure 13.5, see if you can figure out why I've partitioned the data like this.

Finding Data in a BST

Now that the data has been inserted into the tree, how do you search for the data quickly? By using the same algorithm, of course! If you want to search for 3, you compare it with 4, go left, compare it with 2, and go right, and you've found it! That was nice and easy, wasn't it? In fact, the most comparisons you can make when searching for something within this tree is 3, and there are 7 items within the tree. If the tree was one level larger, it could hold 15 items, but the most comparisons you could make would be 4!

In Chapter 1, "Basic Algorithm Analysis," I introduced you to the logarithm function. The base-2 logarithm of 8 is 3 (because $2^3 = 8$ and the logarithm is the inverse of the power function), and the base-2 logarithm of 16 is 4 ($2^4 = 16$). You can see that the BST search algorithm is roughly $O(\log_2 n)$. However, this is the best-case scenario; you will see why in a bit.

Removing Data from a BST

There is a BST node removal algorithm, but I don't cover it here. The algorithm is long and messy, and because I consider BSTs to be of only marginal importance to general game programming, I refer you to an article I've included on the CD in the \goodies\articles\ directory entitled *Trees Part II: Binary Trees*. It has the complete algorithm for removing nodes from a BST.

The BST Rules

You must always follow two rules for every node in a BST:

1. Every node in the left subtree must be less than the current node.
2. Every node in the right subtree must be greater than the current node.

You can see that this is a recursive definition; it applies to *every* node in the tree. You can also see that these rules effectively (in an optimal tree) split the amount of data you need to search through by half for every level you search in the tree.

Sub-Optimal Trees

I admit it: The first BST example I gave you was doctored. I fixed the data so that the tree ends up being full. However, data is usually not organized like that, and it usually produces BSTs that are not optimal.

First, let me show you the absolute worst case for inserting data into a BST. Say you have a queue of this data: 1, 2, 3, 4, 5. Inserting this data into a BST creates the tree shown in Figure 13.6.

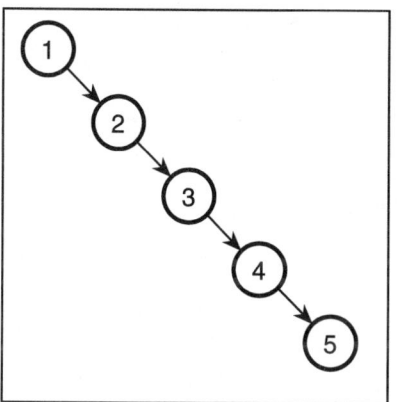

Figure 13.6

This is a worst-case BST; it looks just like a linked list.

The 1 is inserted as the root, the 2 as the right child of 1, the 3 as the right child of 2, and so on. What does this resulting tree look like? A linked list, of course. There is no branching done at all in this tree, and if you want to search for data within it, you're stuck doing a linear search, $O(n)$, which is considerably slower than $O(\log_2 n)$. This is rather unfortunate, and there are ways around this, but they are beyond the scope of the book. *AVL trees*, *splay trees*, and *red-black trees* are all special forms of BSTs that perform *rotations* on the nodes when they are inserted so that the tree ends up more balanced.

As long as the data you are inserting is somewhat random, you will end up with decent trees. However, if data is sorted already or has some statistical correlation, you might end up with less than optimal trees.

Graphical Demonstration: BSTs

This is Graphical Demonstration 13-1, which you can find on the CD in the directory \demonstrations\ch13\Demo01 - BSTs\.

> ### Compiling the Demo
>
> This demonstration uses the SDLGUI library that I have developed for the book. For more information about this library, see Appendix B, "The Memory Layout of a Computer Program."
>
> To compile this demo, either open up the workspace file in the directory or create your own project using the settings described in Appendix B. If you create your own project, all of the files you need to include are in the directory.

This demonstration is fairly simple because the BST structure is fairly simple to use. Figure 13.7 shows a screenshot from the demo in action.

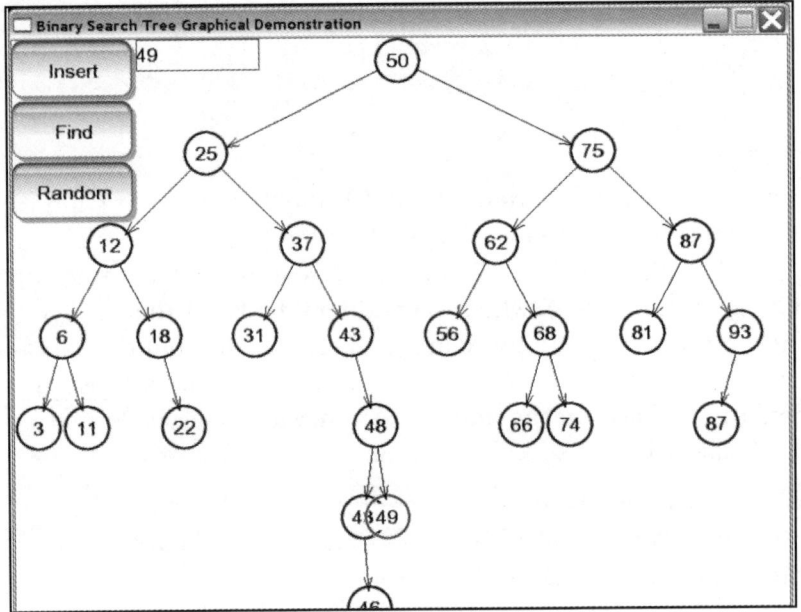

Figure 13.7

Here is a screenshot from the BST demo.

As you can see from the screenshot, the demo has three buttons and a text box. You can type any number from 0–99 in the text box, or you can click the Random button to insert a random number into the text box.

After you have a number in the text box, you can do two things with it: You can either insert that number into the BST or search for that number in the BST.

Clicking either button makes the demo follow a path down the tree, either trying to insert a node or just finding a node.

Play around with it and get to know how BSTs work a little better.

Coding a BST

The code for the Binary Search Tree is located on the CD in the file \structures\BinarySearchTree.h.

The Structure

The binary search tree uses a binary tree as its underlying structure, but the actual class is just a container; it has a pointer to the root node and a comparison function.

```
template <class DataType>
class BinarySearchTree
{
public:
    typedef BinaryTree<DataType> Node;
    Node* m_root;
    int (*m_compare)(DataType, DataType);
};
```

Comparison Functions

You've seen function pointers a few times already in this book; the hash functions for hash tables (see Chapter 8, "Hash Tables") and the process functions for the tree traversals (see Chapters 11, "Trees," and 12, "Binary Trees") come to mind. This time, I introduce you to the idea of comparison functions.

The idea here is that you are probably going to be storing complex structures in the BST, right? So how, exactly, does one determine if one class is "larger" or "smaller" than another? Sure, it's easy with integers, but what about other classes, say, a complex game player class?

Using a custom comparison function allows you to customize how data is stored in the BST. For example, you may want to store characters in a BST based on how much life they have left and search based on that. Then, sometime down the road, you might want to make a different BST that stores characters, but this time you want to search based on another attribute—perhaps how strong the character is. By using a comparison function, this change is easy; you can make a new function that compares the strength of two characters instead of the health.

The definition of the comparison function is simple: It takes two parameters of type DataType and returns an integer. The integer return value can have three meanings. If the number is negative, then the left parameter is less than the right. If the number is 0, then the two parameters are equal. If the number is positive, then the left parameter is more than the right.

For example, you can create a simple comparison function for integers, like this:

```
int CompareInts( int left, int right )
{
    return left - right;
}
```

If the left is less than the right, then the result is negative. If they are equal, then the result is 0. If left is larger than right, then the result is positive.

The Constructor

The constructor function basically takes a comparison function as a parameter and sets the root to null.

```
BinarySearchTree( int (*p_compare)(DataType, DataType) )
{
    m_root = 0;
    m_compare = p_compare;
};
```

> **NOTE**
> Note that the comparison function is set in the constructor because you don't want it to change after you've already inserted items into the tree. If you could change the comparison function, you'd end up invalidating the tree because it would search differently.

The Destructor

The destructor should simply delete the root node. Remember from Chapter 12 that the BinaryTree destructor recursively destroys every node in the tree. That makes this function really simple:

```
~BinarySearchTree()
{
    if( m_root != 0 )
        delete m_root;
}
```

The Insert Function

Now comes the Insert function. There are two ways you can insert the node into the binary tree; one is recursive, and the other is iterative. The recursive function in this case is pointless because this isn't really a recursive algorithm. So instead of recursion, I use the iterative algorithm. I split this up into a few segments so that it is easier to understand.

```
void Insert( DataType p_data )
{
    Node* current = m_root;
    if( m_root == 0 )
        m_root = new Node( p_data );
```

This first segment takes a piece of data as a parameter and creates an iterator named current, which points to the root of the tree. If the root is empty, the function creates a new root node.

If not, the function continues:

```
    else
    {
        while( current != 0 )
        {
```

This segment starts the while loop. The function travels down the tree while the iterator is valid, and as soon as the function inserts a node into the tree, it sets the iterator to 0 so that the loop will exit.

```
            if( m_compare( p_data, current->m_data ) < 0 )
            {
                if( current->m_left == 0 )
                {
                    current->m_left = new Node( p_data );
                    current->m_left->m_parent = current;
                    current = 0;
                }
                else
                    current = current->m_left;
            }
```

The previous segment of code does a few things. It first compares the data in the current node with the data that you want to insert into the tree. If the result of the m_compare function is less than 0, you want to insert it into the left child. The next step is to check if the left child exists. If not, create a new left child and set `current` to 0. If it does, then move the current pointer to the left.

This next code segment does the same thing, but to the right this time:

```
            else
            {
                if( current->m_right == 0 )
                {
                    current->m_right = new Node( p_data );
                    current->m_right->m_parent = current;
                    current = 0;
                }
                else
                    current = current->m_right;
            }
        }
    }
}
```

And that's the function.

The Find Function

This function is almost the same as the Insert function except that it just returns a pointer to the node if it finds the data in the tree.

> **CAUTION**
>
> This function does *not* check for duplicated data. Typically, BSTs do not allow for duplicated data to be entered into the tree, but sometimes they do. Because this BST class doesn't support node removal, you're just wasting space if you insert duplicated data into the tree—the `Find` function will never find it.

```
Node* Find( DataType p_data )
{
    Node* current = m_root;
    int temp;
    while( current != 0 )
    {
        temp = m_compare( p_data, current->m_data );
        if( temp == 0 )
            return current;
        if( temp < 0 )
            current = current->m_left;
        else
```

```
            current = current->m_right;
        }
        return 0;
}
```

If the data isn't found in the tree, this function returns 0.

Example 13-1: Using the BST Class

This is Example 13-1, which demonstrates how to use the `BinarySearchTree` class with integers. The source code for this example is on the CD in the directory \examples\ch13\01 - Binary Search Trees\.

The example uses the `CompareInts` function I showed you earlier to store integers in a BST:

```
void main()
{
    BinarySearchTree<int> tree( CompareInts );
    BinaryTree<int>* node;
    // insert data
    tree.Insert( 8 );
    tree.Insert( 4 );
    tree.Insert( 12 );
    tree.Insert( 2 );
    tree.Insert( 6 );
    tree.Insert( 10 );
    tree.Insert( 14 );
    // these searches are successful
    node = tree.Find( 8 );
    node = tree.Find( 2 );
    node = tree.Find( 14 );
    node = tree.Find( 10 );
    // these searches return 0
    node = tree.Find( 1 );
    node = tree.Find( 3 );
    node = tree.Find( 5 );
    node = tree.Find( 7 );
}
```

Application: Storing Resources, Revisited

This is Game Demonstration 13-1, and you can locate it on the CD in the directory \demonstrations\ch13\Game01 - Resources Revisited\.

> ### Compiling the Demo
>
> This demonstration uses the SDLGUI library that I have developed for the book. For more information about this library, see Appendix B.
>
> To compile this demo, either open up the workspace file in the directory or create your own project using the settings described in Appendix B. If you create your own project, all of the files you need to include are in the directory.

When you think about them, binary search trees are nothing more than a different version of the hash tables from Chapter 8. They are designed for storing data so that you can retrieve it again quickly by using a key.

Because of this, I want to go back to Game Demonstration 8-1 and rewrite it so that it uses Binary Search Trees instead.

The Resource Class

You may have noticed that using a BST is slightly different than using a hash table; whereas a hash table used a key/value pair to store and retrieve data, my BST class doesn't do that. Instead, it just stores the data right in the tree. This particular quirk of my implementation causes me to code the demo a little differently.

First of all, I create a `Resource` class, which will have two things, a string and an `SDL_Surface` pointer:

```
class Resource
{
public:
    char m_string[64];
    SDL_Surface* m_surface;
};
```

The Comparison Function

The next thing that I need to do is to create the comparison function. Because you want to search the tree for string matches, you'll use the standard C `strcmp` function to compare the strings.

```
int ResourceCompare( Resource p_left, Resource p_right )
{
    return strcmp( p_left.m_string, p_right.m_string );
}
```

Luckily, the `strcmp` function returns a negative number if the left string is less than the right string, 0 if they are equal, and a positive number if the left is greater than the right!

So this function compares resources based on name only, not based on the actual bitmap that the `Resource` class contains. This is important when you search for something in the tree.

Inserting Resources

Inserting resources into the tree is similar to inserting them into a hash table except that instead of inserting a string/surface pair into the tree, you create a resource structure first.

```
Resource res;
res.m_surface = SDL_LoadBMP( "sky.bmp" );
strcpy( res.m_string, "sky" );
g_tree.Insert( res );
```

The `strcpy` function copies the string into the resource's name. This step is repeated for every resource in the demo.

Finding Resources

To search for a resource, you need to set up a *dummy* resource, which doesn't contain a surface, but only a string:

```
Resource res;
strcpy( res.m_string, g_name );
```

The `g_name` variable is a string that contains the name of the resource you are searching for. The `m_surface` variable of `res` is left blank.

After that, you declare a binary tree node pointer, which will hold the node that is returned from the BST's Find function:

```
BinaryTree<Resource>* node = 0;
node = g_tree.Find( res );
```

Now the BST will compare the dummy resource's name with the name of the resources in the BST, and if it finds a match, it will return the node that contains the resource. When the node is returned, all you need to do is determine whether it is valid and then use it:

```
if( node != 0 )
    g_resource = node->m_data.m_surface;
else
    g_resource = 0;
```

Playing the Demo

The demo plays exactly like Game Demo 8-1. Figure 13.8 shows a screenshot of the program in action.

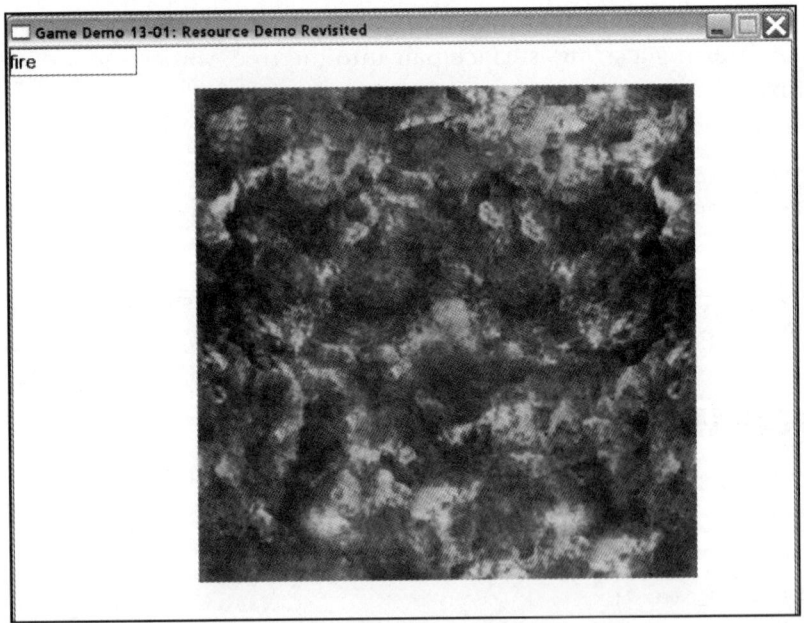

Figure 13.8

Here is a screenshot from the demo.

As before, you enter the name of the resource you want to load into the text box, and it loads the resource for you automatically. The valid resource names are sky, water, water2, snow, fire, vortex, and stone.

Conclusion

I'm going to be honest with you: Binary Search Trees don't really do much that a hash table doesn't do better. Whereas a hash table's search time runs close to $O(c)$, the best-case search time for a BST is still higher than that, at $O(\log_2 n)$. So why did I even bother to teach you BSTs?

Well, BSTs introduce you to the concept of recursively storing data. This concept becomes very important when you get into the more advanced trees used in game programming, such as *Binary Space Partition* (*BSP*) trees. BSPs are a really neat form of tree that splits polygons in a 3D (or even 2D—John Carmack used them in *DOOM*) world so that you can easily determine which polygons in a scene are visible. The concepts used in BSP trees are remarkably similar to the concepts of BSTs.

All in all, I hope you're getting a feel of how recursive tricks are used to split up large amounts of work into smaller problems.

CHAPTER 14

PRIORITY QUEUES AND HEAPS

14. Priority Queues and Heaps

The subjects I introduce you to in this chapter build off of two previous subjects in this book: queues from Chapter 7, "Stacks and Queues," and binary trees from Chapter 12, "Binary Trees." The structures in this chapter are used quite often in game programming, but not directly. More often, *priority queues* and *heaps* are *helper* structures, which help you solve a problem. You'll see them used again several times in this book, so this is an important chapter to read.

In this chapter, you will learn

- What a priority queue is
- What a heap is
- How a heap is structured
- How to use a heap as a priority queue
- How to create a heap using an array
- How to use a heap in a game to implement a simple AI

What Is a Priority Queue?

You should already know what a queue is by now: The line down at your local supermarket is one example. The first person who gets in line gets checked out first, and the last person gets checked out last. Pretty much everything in life where you stand in line is a queue: the tollbooth to go over a bridge, the line at the Department of Motor Vehicles (yuck), and even the line at a nightclub.

If you've ever seen nightclub lines at the movies, you can see that they are different kinds of queues than a normal queue. Very Important People (VIPs) always seem to go right up to the bouncer and get let into the club without waiting in line! That's not a queue—it's a *priority queue*.

In a priority queue, data is associated with a *priority value*, and that value determines how it is placed in the queue. For example, if you placed this data into a normal queue in this order—4, 2, 5, 3, 1—you would end up with the queue in Figure 14.1.

What Is a Priority Queue?

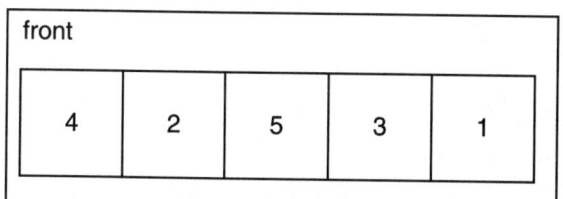

Figure 14.1

This is a normal queue.

The data would be processed in the order that it was inserted into the queue: first 4, then 2, then 5, and so on.

Now, pretend that the number that is being inserted into the queue is its priority value: the higher the number, the higher the priority. Insert the five numbers into a priority queue in the same order, and you get the queue in Figure 14.2.

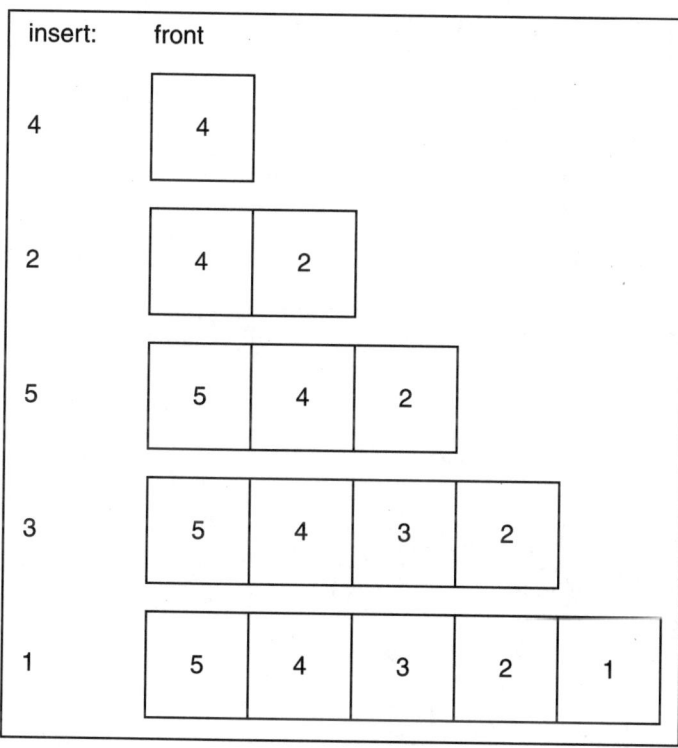

Figure 14.2

This is a priority queue, having five items inserted into it.

You can see that as items are inserted into the priority queue, they aren't just added to the back of the queue. Instead, they are placed in order into the queue. For example, because the queue is empty when 4 is inserted, it is the only item in the queue. Then, 2 is inserted. Because 2 is less than 4, it goes behind 4. Then 5 is inserted, which is larger than 4, so it is placed at the front of the queue. 3 is placed between 4 and 2, and 1 is placed at the end of the queue.

The more important items are placed closer to the front. That's pretty much all there is to the priority queue concept. Removing items from the priority queue is the same as before; the front item is removed first.

There are several ways to implement priority queues. The easiest way is to have a linked list for the queue. Whenever you insert an item, search through the list until you find the right place to insert the item. Although this method is straightforward and easy to understand, it is slow. In fact, almost no one really makes a priority queue like that.

Instead, there is a much faster and more efficient method of making a priority queue using special binary trees called *heaps*.

What Is a Heap?

A *heap* is a special kind of binary tree in which every node is greater than all of its children. This definition is somewhat similar to the BST definition from Chapter 13, "Binary Search Trees," which says that for a tree to be a heap, every node in the tree must have the heap property.

For example, Figure 14.3 shows a sample heap.

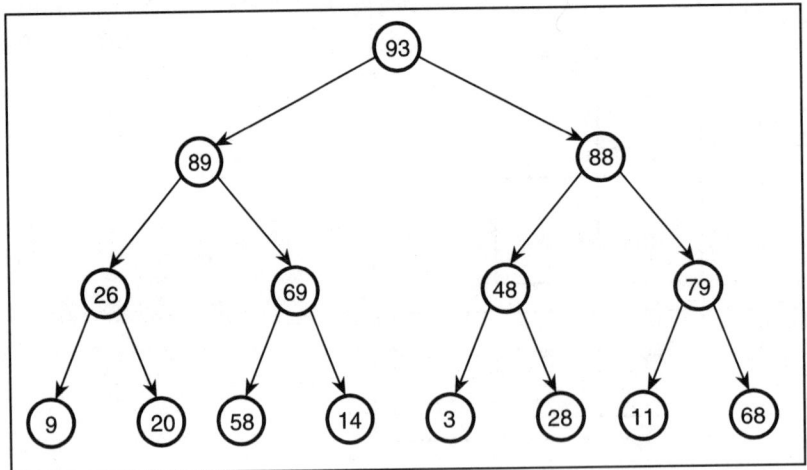

Figure 14.3

A heap is a binary tree where every node is greater than all of the nodes in its subtrees.

The root node in this tree holds the highest value, 93. Every single child node of the root holds a smaller value. Because every node in the tree is larger than all of its children, you know that the second highest value in the tree is one of the root's children. You can't immediately determine where the third highest value in the tree is, though, because it might be the other child of the root or it might be somewhere on the third level of the tree.

Why Can a Heap Be a Priority Queue?

Because the highest value in a heap is always at the root node, the heap can easily be used as a priority queue. To access the *front* value in the priority queue, all you need to do is look at the root.

Adding and removing the items from the heap is a little bit difficult to understand at first, so let me show you what kind of heaps are used for making a priority queue.

Needed Heap Attributes

In Chapter 12, I introduced to you the binary tree property called *denseness*. To build a quick priority queue, the heap needs to be dense. I show you why when I go over the algorithm used to insert items into the heap.

Also, heaps are usually implemented as *arrayed binary trees* instead of *linked*. This is due to the need for the heap to be dense; determining if a linked tree is dense is a much more complicated task than determining if an arrayed tree is dense.

Inserting an Item into a Heap

Inserting an item into a heap is an interesting problem. How would you maintain the heap property for every node in the tree?

You could try to start at the root and swap nodes around until every node is in the right place, but that is a complex and time-consuming algorithm. You also end up with the problem of having a non-dense and unbalanced tree, which is bad because you want to keep the tree as balanced as possible (this will become clear in a bit).

The easiest way to insert a node into a heap is to use an algorithm called the *walk up* algorithm. The basic theory is this: Insert the new item at the bottom of the tree and then make it *walk up* the tree until it is above every node that is less than it and below a node that is larger than it.

For example, take the heap in Figure 14.4. There are four levels in the tree; the first three are totally full. Because the only node on the fourth level is all the way to the left, this heap is also dense.

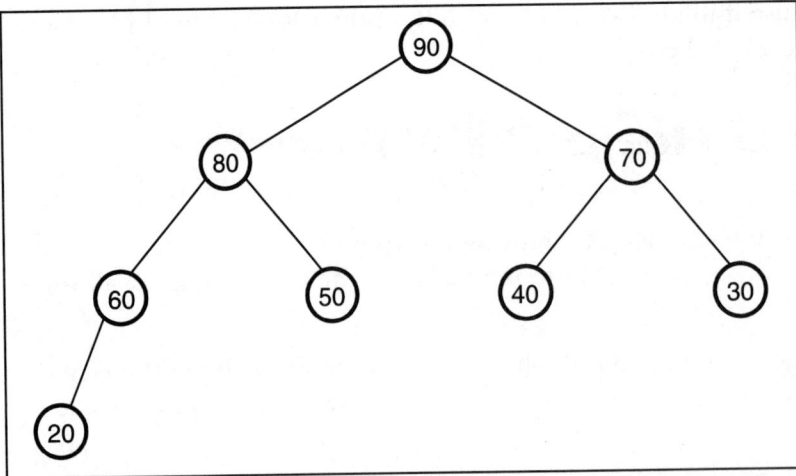

Figure 14.4

This is a four-level heap.

The algorithm for inserting an item into the heap is actually quite easy when you understand how it works. Say you want to insert the number 85 into the heap from Figure 14.4. To keep the heap dense, you are going to place it in the first open node on the lowest level, which is the right child of 60. This produces the tree shown in Figure 14.5.

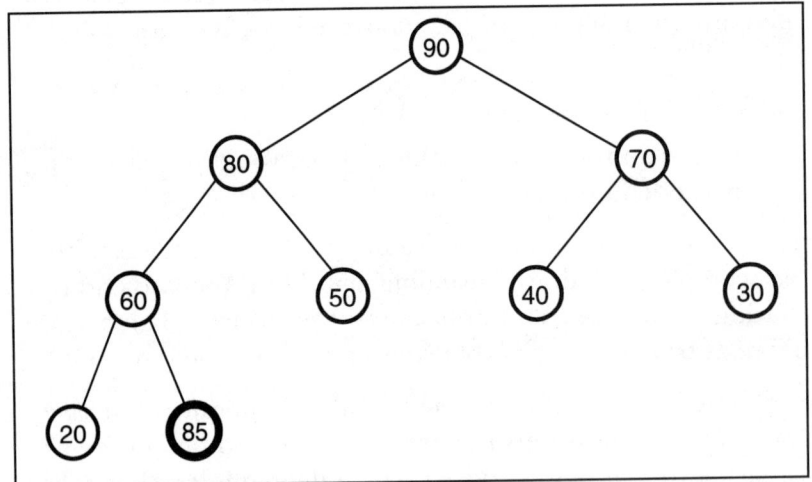

Figure 14.5

Step 1 is to insert a new item at the bottom.

Now the tree is still dense, but it is no longer a heap. Node 60 and node 80 are both invalid, because 85 is larger than them both, but below them in the tree. Now you need to *walk* 85 up the tree into the correct place. The first step is to compare 85 with its parent, 60. Since 85 is more than 60, they need to be swapped. Figure 14.6 shows the resulting tree from the first swap.

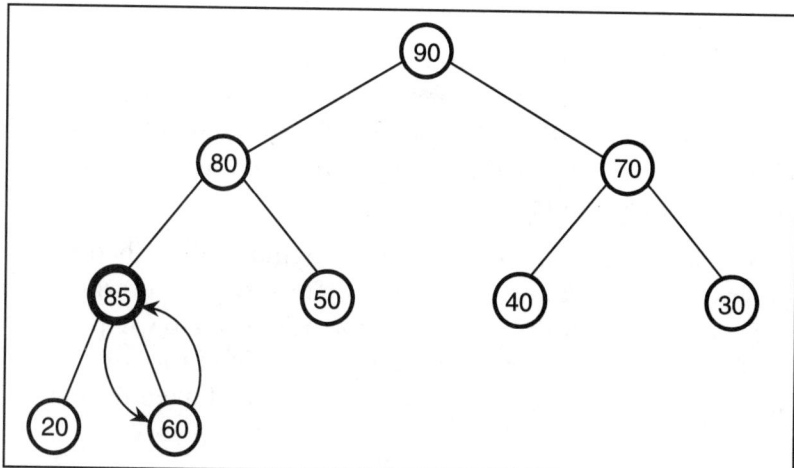

Figure 14.6

Then you swap 60 and 85 to make it more like a heap.

After the swap, one node is still invalid in the tree: node 80. You need to compare 85 with its parent again and swap them if it is larger. Figure 14.7 shows the tree after the second swap.

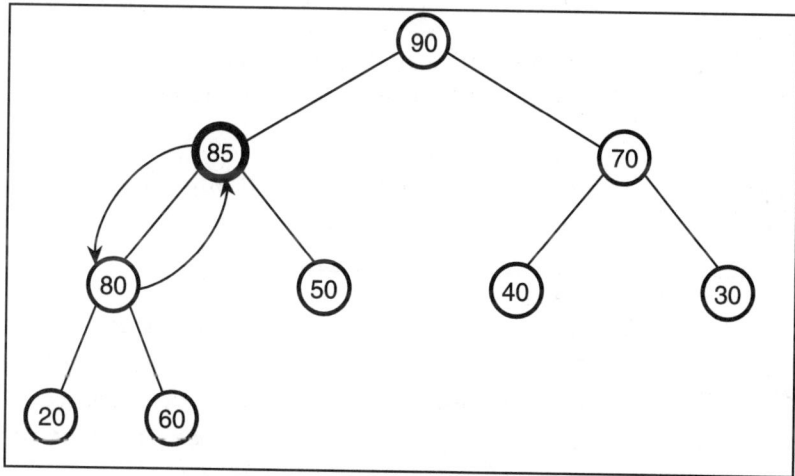

Figure 14.7

Then swap 85 and 80 to turn the tree into a heap.

After the second swap is made, one more comparison is done: 85 is compared with the root node, 90. Because 90 is larger than 85, the algorithm is complete, and the tree is a heap again. If you were inserting 95 into the heap, it would have been swapped into the root node.

Using this method, the next item to be inserted into the heap would be placed as the left child of node 50; that keeps the tree dense. Then the same walk-up algorithm would be executed on the new item until the tree is a heap again.

Because a heap is always dense, it is easy to figure out how long inserting an item takes. On a four-level tree, you make at most three comparisons on an insertion. On a five-level tree, you make at most four comparisons, and so on. Because the number of items in the tree doubles with each new level, yet the number of comparisons required to insert an item only increases by one for each new level, you can see that this is an $O(\log_2 n)$ algorithm.

If you implemented a priority queue using the linked list method I described earlier, you would potentially have to look at every item in the list to find out where to insert the item, making it an $O(n)$ algorithm. If you remember back to Chapter 1, "Basic Algorithm Analysis," $O(\log_2 n)$ is significantly faster than $O(n)$ for large datasets, so you can see how the heap is considerably faster than a linked list for priority queue insertion.

Removing an Item from a Heap

Because you're using the heap as a priority queue, the only item you are interested in removing is the root of the tree, but this algorithm works for any item in the heap anyway.

So you want to remove the root node from Figure 14.4. Great, you removed the root node, but what happens next? How do you move data up the tree so that it remains a heap?

The easiest way is to take the lowest node in the tree and move it into the root node, which will give you Figure 14.8.

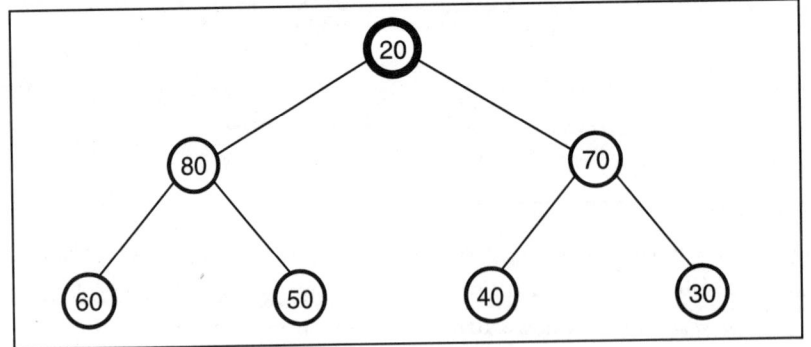

Figure 14.8

The first step of removing the root is to replace the root with the bottommost item.

Now the tree is no longer a heap because the root node is less than its children, so you need to do something to the tree to make it a heap again. This time, instead of walking the node *up* the tree, you'll walk the node *down* the tree. However, walking a node down the tree is a little more difficult because you have two choices of where to move the node now instead of just one. The choice is an easy one, however. To keep the tree a heap, just move the larger of the two children up. In the example, the 20 at the root is swapped with 80 because 80 is the largest child. The result is shown in Figure 14.9.

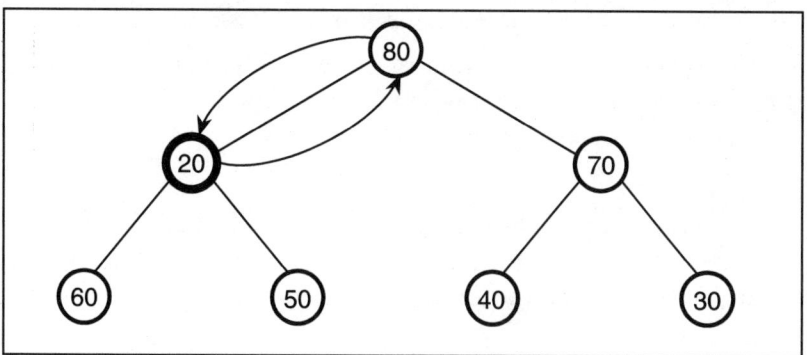

Figure 14.9

This is the first swap.

After you do that swap, you need to check to see if you need to swap the node again. If either one of the children is larger than the current node, then swap them. In the example, you would swap 20 with 60 because 60 is the largest child node. The resulting tree is shown in Figure 14.10.

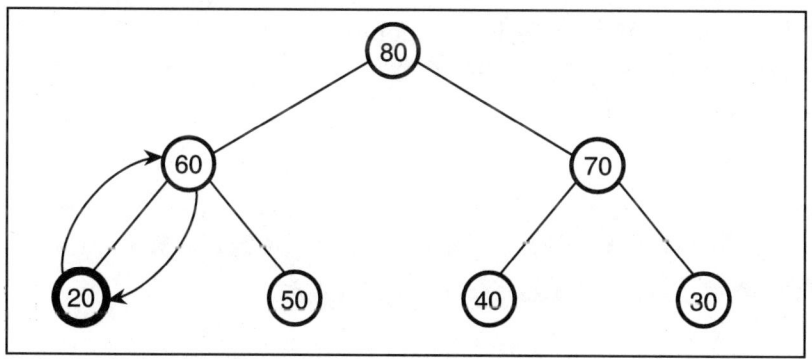

Figure 14.10

This is the second swap.

After this swap, you've reached the bottom of the tree, and it is now a heap again! For reference, if you were to remove 80 from this tree, 30 would be moved up into the root and walked down because 30 is the bottom-most and right-most node. Remember, the idea is to keep the tree dense because dense trees are the most efficient.

> **NOTE**
> Note that the walk-down algorithm works for any node you want to remove in the heap. You can remove any node, move the last node into its place, and use the walk-down algorithm on it, and it will create a valid heap for you.

Because this algorithm always moves the bottommost node, the tree always remains dense, so this algorithm is $O(\log_2 n)$ as well. However, because the walk-down algorithm performs two comparisons at every level, it takes about twice as long as the walk-up algorithm.

You might note one disadvantage of this algorithm, though. The linked-list priority queue can remove items instantly, using an $O(c)$ algorithm, because all it needs to do is remove the front node (remember, the Linked List RemoveHead algorithm is $O(c)$).

So this means that the heap removal algorithm is much slower than the process of removing the top node of a linked-list priority queue.

Heap Efficiency

Even though heap removal is slower than list removal, it is proven that heaps are still the most efficient implementation of priority queues. Tables 14.1 and 14.2 show an example of the number of comparisons needed for the two different priority queue implementations.

Table 14.1 Comparisons Made When Inserting and Removing from a Linked-List Priority Queue

Data Size	List-Insertion	List-Removal	List-Total
7	7	0	7
15	15	0	15
31	31	0	31
63	63	0	63
127	127	0	127

Table 14.2 Comparisons Made When Inserting and Removing from a Heap

Data Size	Heap-Insertion	Heap-Removal*	Heap-Total
7	3	6	9
15	4	8	12
31	5	10	15
63	6	12	18
127	7	14	21

*Remember: The walk-down algorithm performs two comparisons at every level.

In a seven-item priority queue, the linked queue clearly wins out because inserting another item and then removing the front takes at most seven comparisons, but the heap requires at most nine. When you get past seven nodes, though, the heap clearly shows its superiority, especially at larger datasets, such as 127 items. Inserting another item into a linked priority queue with 127 items in it requires at most 127 comparisons, but the heap requires at most 21!

Graphical Demonstration: Heaps

This is Graphical Demonstration 14-1, which you can find on the CD in the directory \demonstrations\ch14\Demo01 – Heaps\.

Compiling the Demo

This demonstration uses the SDLGUI library that I have developed for the book. For more information about this library, see Appendix B, "The Memory Layout of a Computer Program."

To compile this demo, either open up the workspace file in the directory or create your own project using the settings described in Appendix B. If you create your own project, all of the files you need to include are in the directory.

This demonstration is fairly simple; there are only three commands. You can enqueue a number into the heap, dequeue the top of the heap, and place a random number into the text box. Figure 14.11 shows a screenshot from the demo.

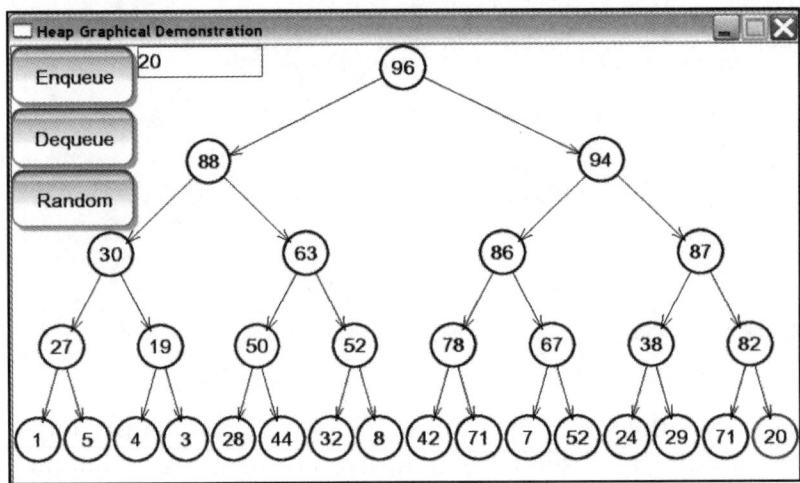

Figure 14.11

Here is a screenshot from the heap demo.

When you insert a node into the heap, it is placed at the bottom of the heap and colored red. The demo then moves the node up in the tree using the walk-up algorithm, following the progress with the red node.

The same thing occurs when removing a node from the heap; the bottom node is moved into the root, and the new root is walked down the tree, highlighted in red.

Play around with the demo so that you understand how a heap works before going on to the next section.

Coding a Heap Class

All of the code for heaps can be found on the CD in the file \structures\heap.h.

I mentioned earlier that heaps are best coded using an arrayed binary tree. I also said in Chapter 12 that there really is no point in creating a specific arrayed binary tree class because using an arrayed binary tree is just as simple as using an array.

Because of this, the Heap class will inherit directly from the Array class so that you can use all of the nifty features of an array within the Heap.

The Structure

The only two things needed in addition to the array variables that are inherited are a variable to keep track of how many items are actually within the heap and a function pointer that points to a comparison function.

I introduced you to comparison functions in Chapter 13 when I showed you binary search trees. The concept is exactly the same in this chapter; you pass in a comparison function to the heap so that it knows if an object is larger than another or not.

```
template <class DataType>
class Heap : public Array<DataType>
{
public:
    int m_count;
    int (*m_compare)(DataType, DataType);
};
```

The Constructor

Because the Array constructor requires a size parameter and the Heap is an array, the Heap constructor also takes a size parameter. It also takes a function pointer to the comparison function.

```
Heap( int p_size, int (*p_compare)(DataType, DataType) )
: Array<DataType>( p_size + 1 )
{
    m_count = 0;
    m_compare = p_compare;
}
```

The second line of code calls the Array constructor and creates an array one cell larger than the requested heap size. Remember back to Chapter 12: Arrayed binary trees need to have the root at index 1 to work correctly, so the array is created one cell larger because index 0 is going to be unused.

> **NOTE**
> You can modify this so that you don't waste space and subtract 1 from every index you access in the Heap class, but I chose not to use this method because the code looks ugly and I want to show you how the class works more than how to optimize it.

The Enqueue Function

This is the function that is called whenever an item is inserted into the heap:

```
void Enqueue( DataType p_data )
{
    m_count++;
    if( m_count >= m_size )
        Resize( m_size * 2 );
    m_array[m_count] = p_data;
    WalkUp( m_count );
}
```

The function takes the data you want to insert as a parameter and increases the count of the heap.

Because you're using an array for the implementation, you need to check to see if you're overflowing the array. The function checks to see if the array is full, and if so, doubles its size.

After that, it places the new item into the last open index in the array and calls the WalkUp function on the new data.

The WalkUp Function

This function does most of the work when inserting a new node into the heap. It is designed to move a piece of data through the tree until the tree has become a valid heap again.

```
 1: void WalkUp( int p_index )
 2: {
 3:     int parent = p_index / 2;
 4:     int child = p_index;
 5:     DataType temp = m_array[child];
 6:     while( parent > 0 )
 7:     {
 8:         if( m_compare( temp, m_array[parent] ) > 0 )
 9:         {
10:             m_array[child] = m_array[parent];
11:             child = parent;
12:             parent /= 2;
13:         }
14:         else
15:             break;
```

```
16:     }
17:     m_array[child] = temp;
18: }
```

The `WalkUp` function takes an index as a parameter, allowing you to call the function on any cell within the tree.

The function then creates two index variables on lines 3 and 4. These variables represent the current child and parent indexes as it walks up the tree.

On line 5, the function creates a temporary local variable, `temp`, which stores the data that is being walked up the tree. This is just a little optimization, which is demonstrated by Figure 14.12.

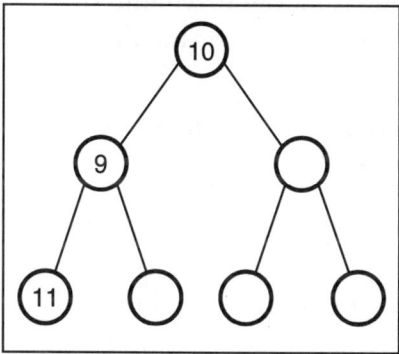

Figure 14.12

This is an invalid heap.

Now, it is obvious that node 11 is in the wrong place in this tree and should be moved up to the root node. The walk-up algorithm I demonstrated before would swap 9 and 11 and then swap 10 and 11. This process is a waste, however, because you know that 11 will eventually be placed at the root.

Instead, this optimized function places 11 in a temporary variable, moves 9 to replace 11, moves 10 to replace 9, and moves 11 into the root. Figure 14.13 shows this sequence of events.

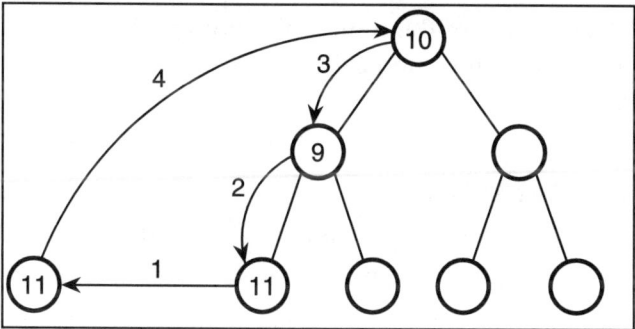

Figure 14.13

This shows the optimized `WalkUp` function.

Instead of moving 11 into where node 9 was, you skip that step and move it directly to the root. Although this example had only trivial savings, much larger trees will be faster.

Now, back to the function! On line 6, the function starts a loop that will continue until the parent index is 0, which means that the child index will point to 1, the root of the tree.

On line 8, the function determines if the node you are walking up is in the correct place or not by checking the value of the parent node. If the parent node is greater than the node that is being walked up, the function uses the `break` keyword on line 15 to break out of the while-loop because the node can't be moved up anymore.

If the parent node is less than the node, then the node is moved down into the child node on line 10 and both the parent and child pointers are divided by 2, moving them up one level.

Finally, on line 17, the data that was to be moved up is moved into the cell that `child` points to, which is the same as step 4 in Figure 14.13.

The Dequeue Function

The `Dequeue` function performs the setup for removing the root node of the heap.

```
void Dequeue()
{
    if( m_count >= 1 )
    {
        m_array[1] = m_array[m_count];
        WalkDown( 1 );
        m_count--;
    }
}
```

If the heap isn't empty, then the function moves the item at the bottom of the heap to the root (overwriting the top node) and then calls the `WalkDown` function on the root.

The WalkDown Function

This function is very similar to the `WalkUp` function, except that it is a little more difficult to detect the bottom of the heap than the top and you need to choose which indexes to swap.

This function will use the same optimization used with the WalkUp function; it stores the data that it is walking down in a temporary variable while nodes are moved up the tree.

```
1: void WalkDown( int p_index )
2: {
3:      int parent = p_index;
4:      int child = p_index * 2;
5:      DataType temp = m_array[parent];
6:      while( child < m_count )
7:      {
8:          if( child < m_count - 1 )
9:          {
10:             if( m_compare( m_array[child], m_array[child + 1] ) < 0 )
11:             {
12:                 child++;
13:             }
14:         }
15:         if( m_compare( temp, m_array[child] ) < 0 )
16:         {
17:             m_array[parent] = m_array[child];
18:             parent = child;
19:             child *= 2;
20:         }
21:         else
22:             break;
23:     }
24:     m_array[parent] = temp;
25:}
```

The function starts out with the same variables that the WalkUp function did: a parent and child index and a temporary variable. The item that is being walked down the tree is placed in temp.

Then, on line 6, a while-loop is started, which loops through the tree until the child index is larger than the size of the tree.

Line 8 is important because it starts the block of code that detects which child node of the current parent is larger. For example, look at the tree in Figure 14.14.

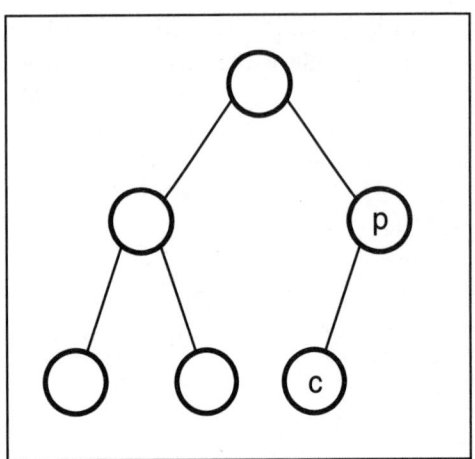

Figure 14.14

The function must check whether p has only one child.

The parent index is pointing to node *p*, and the child index is pointing to node *c*. The code on line 8 determines if the right child of *p* exists. In this example, it doesn't, so *c* is automatically assumed to be the larger child of *p*. If *p* had two children, then the code on lines 10–13 detects this and finds out which child is larger. If the right child is larger than the left, then the `child` index is incremented because the index of the right child of any node is one larger than the index of the left child.

Now that the function knows which child node it wants to move upward, it determines whether the child node needs to be moved upward by comparing it to the temp node on line 15. If no swap needs to be made, the function exits out of the while-loop on line 22. If a swap needs to be made, the function moves the parent node into the correct child node and then moves both the `parent` and `child` indexes down a level on lines 18 and 19.

Finally, the value in `temp` is placed into the correct index on line 24 when the loop is finished executing.

Application: Building Queues

This is Game Demo 14-01, which you can find on the CD in the directory \demonstrations\ch14\Game01 - Building Queues\.

Compiling the Demo

This demonstration uses the SDLGUI library that I have developed for the book. For more information about this library, see Appendix B.

To compile this demo, either open up the workspace file in the directory or create your own project using the settings described in Appendix B. If you create your own project, all of the files you need to include are in the directory.

I'm sure you've played a *Real-Time Strategy (RTS)* game before—there are many famous ones, including *Warcraft*, *Starcraft*, and *Command & Conquer*. In these games, you usually have some sort of building or factory that allows you to produce your units in the game.

For example, in *Starcraft*, you can build a factory that lets you make tanks and mechs.

These systems use simple queues for building units; when you tell a factory to build a unit, it places the unit in the queue. Although priority queues aren't used much in these situations, you can use them for a very simple *Artificial Intelligence (AI)*.

For example, say you have an RTS game that has three units: a worker, an attacker, and a defender. A very simple AI would assign an importance to each of the units:

- Defenders are the most important; you need them to defend your base.
- Workers are moderately important; you need them to build and repair your base.
- Attackers are the least important; you only need to consider attacking after your base is well defended.

Now, whenever the AI wants to create a new unit, it places the units into a priority queue. Using this system, defenders will always end up at the front of the queue, workers after them, and attackers at the end of the queue.

The little system I've created works like this: You have four factories, each of which can be turned on or off. You also have a priority queue of units that you want to build. Whenever a factory is available to manufacture a unit, the factory starts making the item at the front of the priority queue.

The Units

As I stated before, the game has three unit types, which are stored in an enumerated type:

```
enum UNIT
{
    ATTACKER,
    WORKER,
    DEFENDER
};
```

Creating a Factory

The Factory class is simple—it has only four variables:

```
class Factory
{
public:
    UNIT m_currentUnit;
    int  m_startTime;
    bool m_working;
    bool m_functioning;
};
```

The factory knows what kind of unit it is currently producing, so it has a UNIT variable, called m_currentUnit.

After that, the factory keeps track of when it started making the unit. Each unit takes 10 seconds to complete, so when the current time is 10 seconds more than this value, the factory outputs the new unit into the game world.

The next two variables are Booleans. The first Boolean, m_working, keeps track of whether or not the factory is working on a unit or not. Sometimes the factory can be idle, and if so, this Boolean would be false.

The other Boolean determines if the factory is functioning. This has many meanings in a game. For example, the factory could be damaged badly or have no power, and so on. Whenever this Boolean is false, the factory cannot start working on a new unit.

There are four factories in this game, and they are placed in a global static array:

```
Factory g_factories[4];
```

The Heap

Because the Heap class is the only (and most efficient) implementation of a priority queue that I've shown you, you have to use a heap in the game as a priority queue.

```
Heap<UNIT> g_heap( 64, CompareUnits );
```

The heap holds UNITs, and it starts off being able to hold 64 of them. Because the Heap class automatically resizes itself when needed, you can enqueue as many units as you want. Flexibility is a really neat feature.

The heap also uses a function called CompareUnits as its comparison function. Here is what the function looks like:

```
int CompareUnits( UNIT p_left, UNIT p_right )
{
    return p_left - p_right;
}
```

The p_left and p_right variables are both UNITs and not integers, so how will you determine which one is greater than the other? If you remember how C++'s enumerations work, each enumeration is really just an integer. In the UNIT enumeration, ATTACKER has a value of 0, WORKER has a value of 1, and DEFENDER has a value of 2. So the function subtracts the right from the left, just like you did with the integer comparison function I showed you earlier.

> **CAUTION**
>
> Treating enumerations like integers works on most compilers, but some compilers don't like it. Truly picky compilers might say, "You cannot subtract enums—they aren't real numbers!" But you can fool them by performing an *explicit cast* on the enums. To cast an enum to an integer, all you need to do is this: (int)(p_left). Then, p_left is converted into its integer equivalent.

Enqueuing a Unit

Enqueuing a unit onto the heap is a very simple task; all you need to do is type this:

```
g_heap.Enqueue( ATTACKER );
g_heap.Enqueue( WORKER );
g_heap.Enqueue( DEFENDER );
```

These three lines enqueue an Attacker, a Worker, and a Defender on the queue. Of course, given their priorities, the Defender will be moved up to the front of the queue because it has the highest priority of them all.

Starting Construction

In the demo, you need to loop through the factories to see if any of them are able to start construction of a new unit.

```
1: for( x = 0; x < 4; x++ )
2: {
3:     if( g_factories[x].m_working == false &&
4:         g_factories[x].m_functioning == true &&
5:         g_heap.m_count > 0 )
6:     {
7:         g_factories[x].m_currentUnit = g_heap.Item();
8:         g_factories[x].m_working = true;
9:         g_factories[x].m_startTime = SDL_GetTicks();
10:        g_heap.Dequeue();
11:    }
12:}
```

The loop goes through each factory and checks three things. First, it makes sure that the factory isn't already making something (line 3). If it is, then m_working would be true. Second, it makes sure that the factory is functioning (line 4). Finally, it makes sure that a new unit is waiting to be produced on the queue. If there is, then the count of the heap will be more than 0 (line 5).

If all three of these conditions are met, then the current factory will start construction. First, the current unit of the factory is set to whatever unit is at the front of the queue (line 7). Then, the factory is told to start working (line 8), and the time that construction started is recorded using the SDL_GetTicks function (line 9). After the factory has been set up to construct a new unit, the new unit is removed from the heap (line 10).

Completing Construction

Now you need a way to determine when construction is completed. This is also done with a loop:

```
1: for( x = 0; x < 4; x++ )
2: {
3:     if( g_factories[x].m_working == true )
4:     {
5:         if( SDL_GetTicks() - g_factories[x].m_startTime > 10000 )
6:         {
7:             g_factories[x].m_working = 0;
```

```
8:         }
9:     }
10:}
```

The loop goes through all four factories again, this time just checking to see if they are currently producing a unit (line 3). If they are, then it checks to see how long they have been working on the current unit (line 5). This line of code subtracts the time that the factory started working from the current time. `SDL_GetTicks` returns a number in milliseconds. There are 1,000 numbers per second and, therefore, 10,000 in 10 seconds. The `if` statement on line 5 checks to see if more than 10,000 milliseconds have passed, and if so, then the unit has been completed.

On line 7, the factory is stopped. Because this simple demo doesn't actually do anything with the units that are created, this is where you would add code to physically place the unit into the game so that the player can actually use it.

Playing the Demo

Figure 14.15 shows the game demo in action.

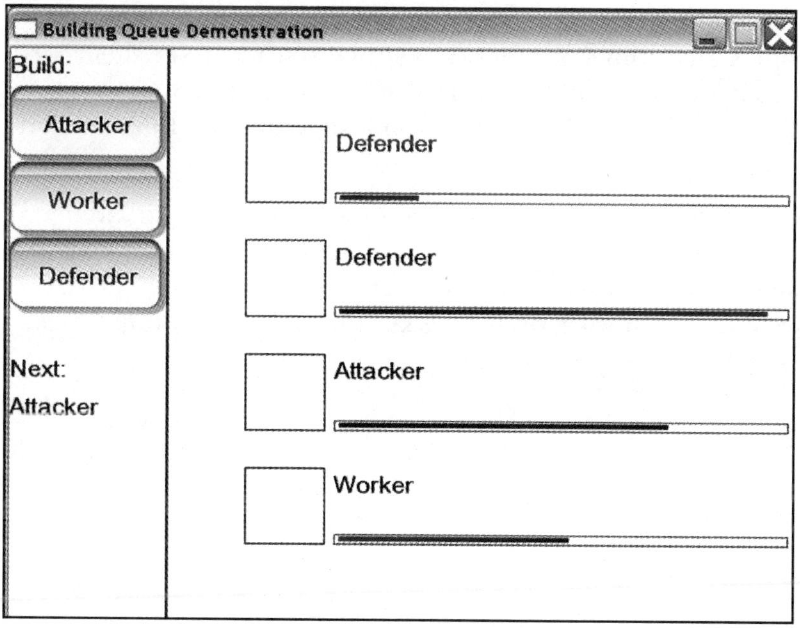

Figure 14.15

Here is a screenshot from the demo.

On the left side of the screen, there are three buttons. Clicking any one of these buttons adds a new unit onto the queue. Below the buttons, the next unit in the queue is displayed.

On the right are four factories, each with a progress bar and a text field saying which unit they are currently building. By clicking on the factory boxes to the left of the progress bars, you can turn the factories on or off. When a factory is turned off, the box will turn red, signifying that it is not functioning.

You'll notice the priority queue at work as soon as all the factories are busy. For example, start building four Attackers, and when they are building, add a few more Attackers to the queue. After you have done that, quickly add a Worker or Defender to the queue; it will immediately be placed above the Attackers that are already on the queue.

So the AI ends up creating the more important units before the least important units unless they have already started construction. This is a very simple way of implementing an AI for an RTS game.

Conclusion

The priority queue isn't something you will use as much as a linked list or an array in a game; nevertheless, it's a useful data structure. Instead of being used directly in applications, though, you'll find that priority queues are used far more often in conjunction with complex algorithms or other data structures. You'll see them used a few more times in this book, in Chapters 21, "Data Compression," 23, "Pathfinding," 24, "Tying It Together: Algorithms," and Appendix D, "Introduction to the Standard Template Library."

The main thing I wanted to emphasize, however, was how much time you save by storing data recursively in a tree. You've seen two examples now, the binary search tree and the heap, each of which stores data in a different way, but stores the data so that you don't have to do much work on it. The key to making fast programs is to find ways to do less work.

CHAPTER 15

Game Trees and Minimax Trees

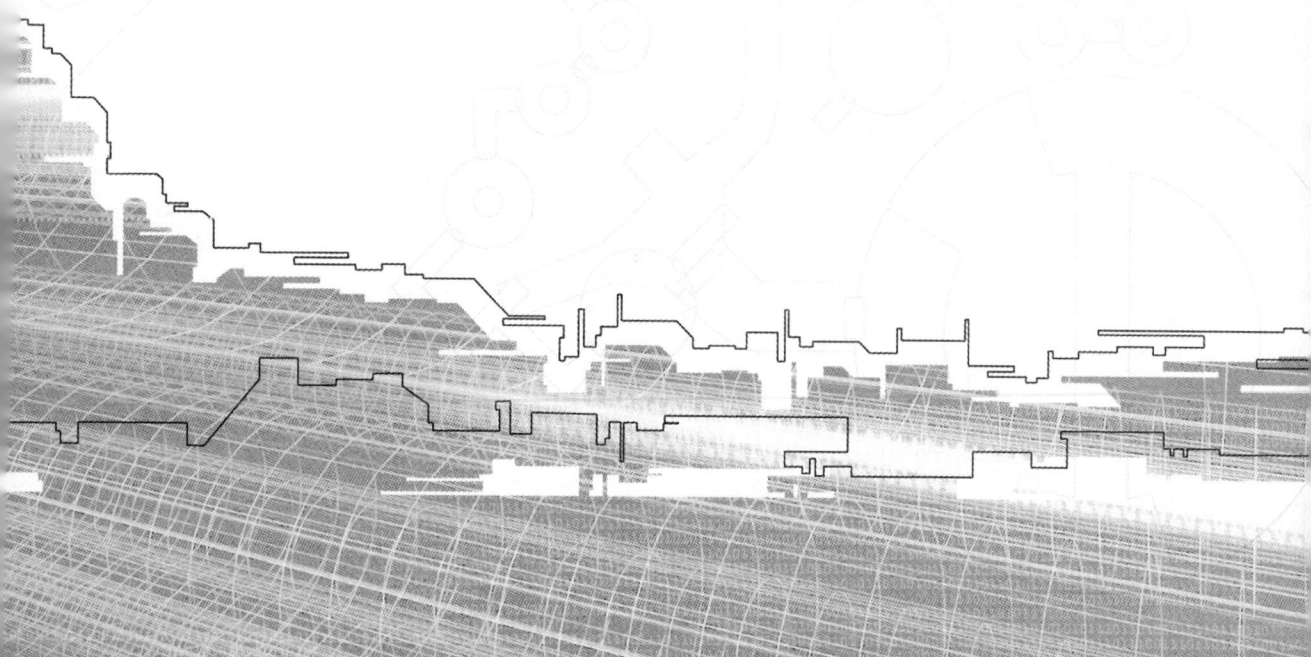

15. Game Trees and Minimax Trees

Until this point in the book, I have shown you data structures that can be used for any type of game. None of the structures was specific to a certain genre. This chapter introduces you to a data structure that departs from this non-specific nature.

Almost all of the game demos and examples in the book so far mimic *real-time* games, or games which run continuously in time. I have overlooked *discrete* games—games where the players take turns playing. Some of the oldest discrete games, such as checkers, chess, and tic-tac-toe, were around long before computers were. The structures introduced in this chapter are designed to map out the progress of these types of games and aid the computer in figuring out how to beat you in them.

In this chapter, you will learn

- What a game tree is
- What a minimax tree is
- How to generate game trees and minimax trees for a simple game
- How to store game states
- How to program a simple game using minimax trees
- How to prevent infinite recursion in more complex games
- How to limit the minimax algorithm by using limited depth searching

What Is a Game Tree?

A *game tree* isn't a special new data structure—it's a name for any regular tree that maps how a discrete game is played.

I'll start with a simple example, Rocks. In this game, you have different piles of rocks, with one or more rocks in each pile. The game has two players, who take turns taking one or more rocks from a single pile until one pile is left. When one pile is left, your goal is to force your opponent to remove the last rock. The person who removes the last rock loses.

Figure 15.1 shows a simple setup for a game of Rocks.

Figure 15.1

This is a simple game of Rocks with two piles. The first pile has two rocks, and the second pile has one.

In the figure, there are two piles. The first pile has two rocks, and the second pile has only one rock. If you are the first player, you have three choices:

- Remove one rock from pile 1.
- Remove two rocks from pile 1.
- Remove one rock from pile 2.

You can start the game off with one of those three moves. You can create a simple game tree to represent these moves, as shown in Figure 15.2.

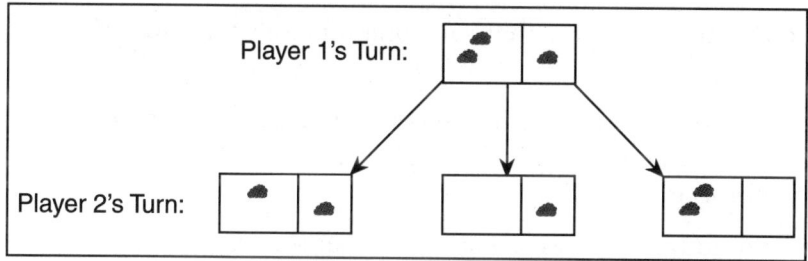

Figure 15.2

Here are the first two levels of a game tree, demonstrating the three possible moves.

After Player 1 has moved, it is now Player 2's turn. His choice of a move is limited to the current state of the game, however. In the leftmost state of Figure 15.2, Player 2 has two choices: He can remove one rock from pile 1 or one rock from pile 2.

His choice for the middle state is even less useful He can only remove one rock from pile 2. Of course, because this is the last rock, Player 2 has lost the game.

On the right state, Player 2 has two options again: He can remove one or two rocks from pile 2.

Figure 15.3 shows the game tree for all five of these moves and goes down one more level to show you the complete game tree.

15. Game Trees and Minimax Trees

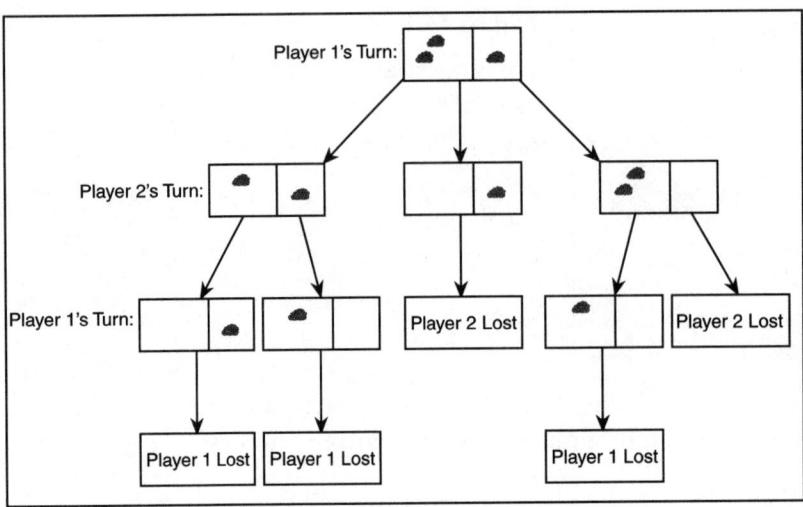

Figure 15.3

This is the complete game tree, demonstrating every possible move in the game.

The game is entirely complete by the time the fourth level is reached—the game can have up to three moves because there were only three rocks. You can also tell from the tree that there are five total outcomes from the game because there are five leaf nodes. The game always ends on a leaf node because there are no more moves that can be made.

So what can you tell about the game tree that you couldn't easily tell about the initial game setup?

If you are Player 1, the obvious first move is the second one, removing the two stones from pile 1. By doing that, you are forcing Player 2 to lose, because he has no other option and cannot possibly win.

Another thing you would notice if you were Player 1 is that the leftmost move, removing one rock from pile 1, is a death sentence. If you make that move, then you have given Player 2 a free win, because no matter what move he makes, there is no chance for you to win in that branch.

If you take the third route on the opening move, then Player 2 decides the outcome of the game. If Player 2 removes both rocks in pile 1 (a very stupid move), he loses. If he only removes one rock, then he forces you to remove the last one, and you lose.

What Is a Minimax Tree?

A *minimax* tree is the same as a game tree. In fact, it's not even a tree; it's actually an algorithm that is used on a game tree. Everyone calls it a minimax tree, though, so I will, too.

What Is a Minimax Tree?

The minimax algorithm is a really neat way of transforming a game tree into data that a computer can analyze so it can make an intelligent choice about which move is the best at the moment.

The minimax algorithm is designed for two players: Min and Max. The algorithm works like this: Max starts, so he has the dominant position and he will be the aggressor in the game. Every time he moves, he chooses the best move for himself. Min is on the defensive, and every time she moves, she will try to put Max in the worst position possible.

> **NOTE**
> Max moves first, so why don't they call them maxmin trees? I have no idea. I guess minimax sounds better.

To make a minimax tree, you need to use an algorithm called a *heuristic* algorithm. A heuristic is really just a fancy word that means *general rule of thumb*. Different AIs for different games have different heuristic functions for different purposes. The job of a heuristic function is to look at a move in a game and evaluate if it is a good move or a bad move.

The minimax algorithm works like this: It goes down to every leaf node and analyzes the state of the game at that point. It then uses the heuristic algorithm to produce a number. A high number means that the state is good for Max and bad for Min, and a low number means that the state is bad for Max and good for Min.

For example, look at the game in Figure 15.3 again. I'm going to use a very simple heuristic algorithm that returns 1 if Max wins and 0 if Max loses.

The first step of this process is shown in Figure 15.4.

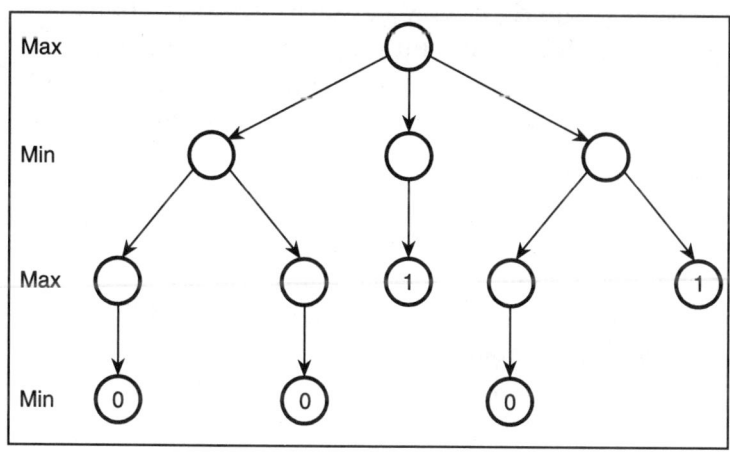

Figure 15.4

The first step of the minimax algorithm is to give an initial value to the end states of the game. When Max wins, a 1 is placed in the node. When Min wins, a 0 is placed in the node.

The algorithm analyzes all five leaf nodes of the game tree from Figure 15.3. The states where Player 1 (Max) lost are made into a 0, and the states where Player 2 (Min) lost are made into a 1.

After that has been completed, the minimax algorithm backtracks through the tree. Whenever it is Min's turn, she selects the move that has the lowest score. Whenever is it Max's turn, he selects the move that has the highest score.

Figure 15.5 shows the backtracking.

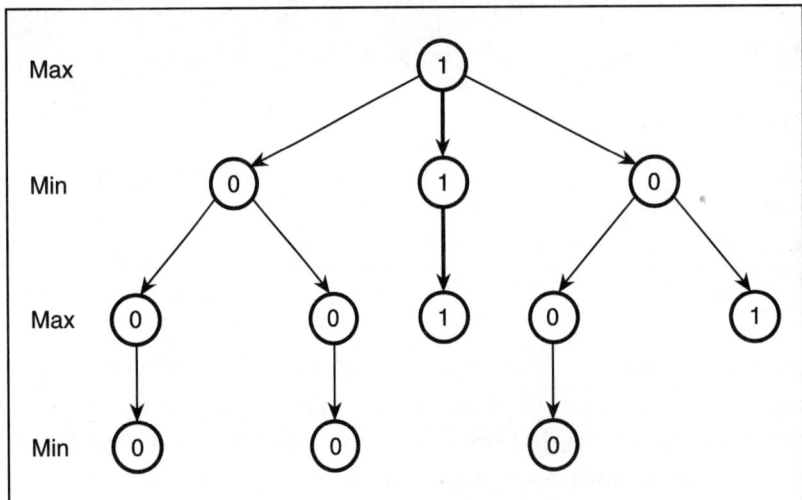

Figure 15.5

This is a full minimax tree that has been backtracked through. The path that is taken by the minimax algorithm is in bold.

Look at the lowest node on the left side and its parent node. The parent node is on Max's turn, so Max takes the highest child node. Unfortunately for Max, there is only one child node, and it contains 0, so a 0 is placed in the parent node. The same goes with the next node over to the right on Max's turn—the only choice is a loss for Max. There is one other branch on Max's turn if you traverse the tree going right and then left from the root. This node also becomes a 0 because it only has one child.

Now take a look at all the nodes on Min's first move. Min has two choices on the leftmost move, both of which end in 0. Because Min is looking for the lowest score possible, this situation is good, because two 0s mean that Max can't win. The next node over is bad for Min; it only has one child, and it contains 1. Min has no choice, however, so Min must take that value. The third child of the root finally offers a choice for Min; its two children contain a 0 and a 1. Because it is Min's turn, she selects the 0. If it were Max's turn, he would have selected the 1.

Finally, the root node is evaluated. It has three children, and Max needs to choose the node with the largest value. Because two of the nodes are 0 and only one is 1, Max chooses the node with the 1 in it.

What does all this mean? How do you use this information to determine which move Max will make? Because Max chose the node with the 1 in it, his next move will be to take the middle path and remove the two rocks from pile 1. After that move, Min has no choice and will lose.

Say, for example, Max was an inferior player, perhaps a human, who took the third path instead of the second path and removed the one rock from pile 2. Now it is Min's turn, and she has two choices. The minimax algorithm has decided that she will follow the left path, because it is 0, and this eventually leads to Max losing.

One more thing needs explanation, however. What if there are two options with the same Min or Max value? What path should the AI take? You can see that this situation occurs in the left child of the root node in the example tree. It is Min's turn, and both moves are 0, so which one should she take? The heuristic algorithm you used to generate the score values treats both paths of the tree equally because they have the same value, so you can take either path. A random number can be used to make the computer AI seem more lifelike, or you could just take the first lowest path you find. The choice is up to you.

Graphical Demonstration: Minimax Trees

This is Graphical Demonstration 15-1, which can be found on the CD in the directory \demonstrations\ch15\Demo01 - Minimax trees\.

Compiling the Demo

This demonstration uses the SDLGUI library that I have developed for the book. For more information about this library, see Appendix B, "The Memory Layout of a Computer Program."

To compile this demo, either open up the workspace file in the directory or create your own project using the settings described in Appendix B. If you create your own project, all of the files you need to include are in the directory.

This is just a simple graphical demonstration that shows you how a few different minimax trees are generated. The demo uses the same game that I showed you previously—the rock pile game. Figure 15.6 shows a screenshot from the demo.

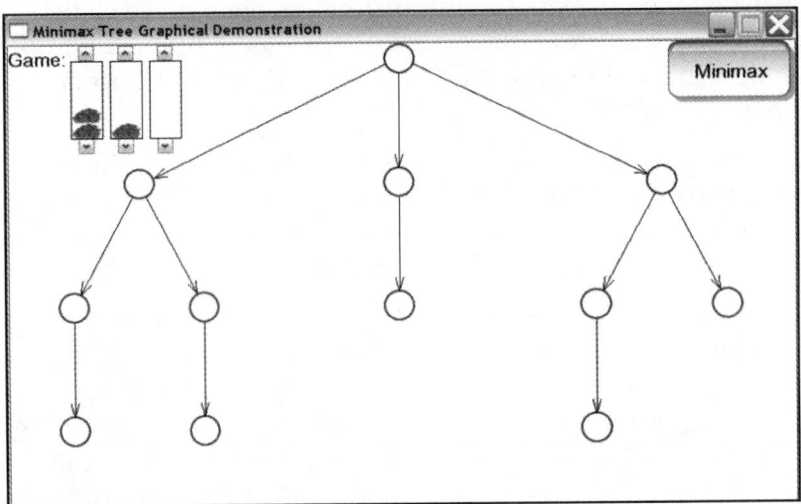

Figure 15.6

Here is a screenshot from the demo.

Notice the three little boxes at the top. Those boxes represent your rock piles. The demo allows up to three piles. You can use the arrows above and below the piles to increase or decrease the number of rocks in a given pile. I decided to limit the number of total rocks in the demo to 4, though, because any more than that will cause everything to look very messy.

The screenshot shows a configuration you should be familiar with; it is the same rock pile configuration I showed you earlier.

Every time you add or remove a rock from a pile, the game tree is automatically updated on the screen. Even though the game tree doesn't show you which states each nodes represent, it is fairly easy to figure out. The algorithm I used to figure out the next gamestate from each node works like this: Try to subtract one rock from pile 1, two rocks from pile 1, three rocks from pile 1, and four rocks from pile 1, and then switch to pile 2 and repeat.

So in the figure, the leftmost subtree from the root represents the game if you removed one rock from the first pile, the middle subtree represents the game if you removed two rocks from the first pile, and the right subtree represents the game if you removed one rock from the second pile.

After you have set up the desired rockpile configuration, all you need to do is click the Minimax button and the program will generate the minimax values for each node.

> **NOTE**
>
> Note the order in which the program generates the minimax values. Recognize it? It is our old friend, the postorder traversal! You first saw the postorder traversal in Chapter 11, "Trees." The postorder traversal works like this: For each node, it figures out the minimax values for all of its children, picks the min or max value depending on whose turn it is, and then returns up the tree.

Figure 15.7 shows a screenshot from a different game setup after it has been calculated.

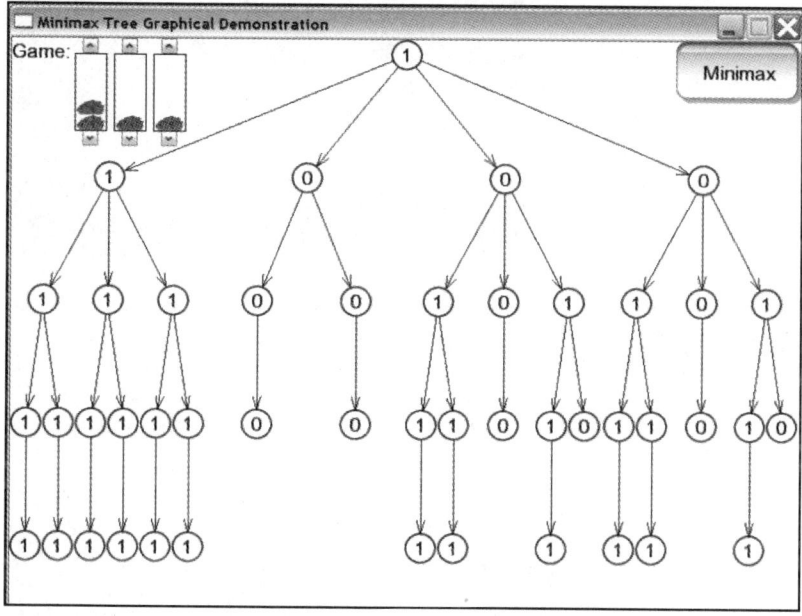

Figure 15.7

This is a screenshot of a more complex game, solved by the minimax algorithm.

If Max is smart, he can win the game on the first move by removing one rock from pile 1. Every path after that move leads to a win on his part. If not, he removes both rocks from pile 1 and forces himself to lose.

Game States

Normally, this is where I would jump into the code for the data structure described in this chapter. However, the code for the minimax tree already exists; it's just a plain tree. Instead of coding a minimax tree, I want to instead go over more concepts involved with minimax trees. The first concept is a *game state*.

A discrete game will have a certain state at any given time. The state of a rock pile game stores how many rocks are in each pile. The state of a tic-tac-toe game stores which boxes are empty, have Xs, or have Os. The state of a chess or checkers game stores the locations of each of the markers on the game board.

To use a minimax tree, you need to be able to store this state somehow. Not only that, but you must also do so efficiently.

So now you need to figure out a good way to store a game state. In Graphical Demonstration 15-1, I used a three-cell array to store the number of rocks in each pile. This example was easy to figure out, though.

How about a game like tic-tac-toe? In tic-tac-toe, you have a 3x3 grid in which each cell can have one of three different values: it can be empty, it can have an X, or it can have an O. Figure 15.8 shows a sample tic-tac-toe board.

NOTE
I initially wanted to show you minimax trees for tic-tac-toe. I decided that it was simple enough to show you. I was wrong; the complete game tree for tic-tac-toe has 10 nodes after the first move, 82 nodes after the second move, and 586 nodes after the third move. There are around 900,000 total nodes for a complete expansion of tic-tac-toe, which is kind of hard to draw on paper or show on a computer screen. Because I wanted to show you a complete minimax tree first, I skipped over tic-tac-toe and made a much simpler game example.

TIP
Because games like tic-tac-toe can have up to 900,000 total nodes in their game trees, storing game trees can take huge amounts of memory. Making your game states take as little memory as possible is important.

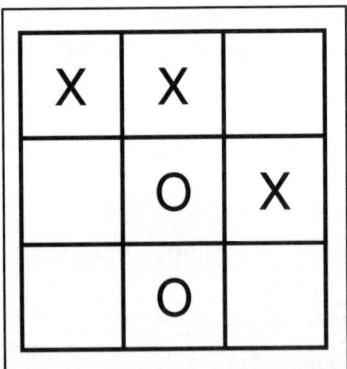

Figure 15.8

This is a sample tic-tac-toe game board.

If you don't already know, the object of the game is to get three of your symbols in a row, either horizontally, vertically, or diagonally.

The game has nine squares, each of which can contain one of three different things. If you had two squares, there would be a total of nine different states, as shown in Figure 15.9.

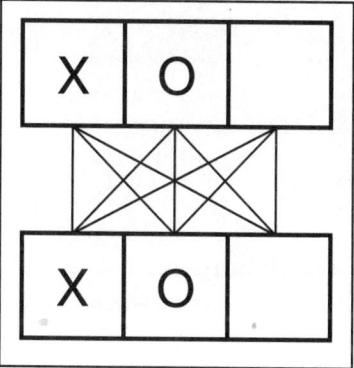

Figure 15.9

These are the possible two-celled combinations; each line represents a pair of cells. There are nine lines.

If you count all the lines, you'll see that there are nine of them. Likewise, if you add another cell, you'll need to multiply 9 by 3, to get 27 different combinations. One cell is 3^1, two cells is 3^2, and three cells is 3^3, so 9 cells is 3^9, or 19,683 different gamestate combinations.

The easiest way to store a tic-tac-toe game state would be to use a nine-celled array of chars where each cell contains 0, 1, or 2 (empty, X, or O).

> **NOTE**
>
> If you know how to represent numbers in different bases, such as base 2 (binary), base 3 (trinary), base 8 (octal), or base 16 (hexadecimal), just to name a few, you might have seen that you can store the game state as a single nine-digit base-3 number. Because each digit in a base-3 number can be 0, 1, or 2, this fits nicely. For example, the base-10 number 19,682 (one less than the maximum number of states) expands to the base 3 number 222,222,222. Because the maximum number of states is 19,683, you can store the state of a tic-tac-toe game in a 16-bit integer (2 bytes), which has a maximum value of 65,535 (or a total of 65,536 values, including 0). Compare this with the 9 bytes required for a char array and you can see how much better this method is. The only downside, of course, is the extra processing power required to convert a base-10 number into a base-3 game state. As always, the memory versus speed tradeoff exists.

> **NOTE**
> Note that not every game state is valid for a game of tic-tac-toe. For example, the base 3 number 19,682 converts to 222,222,222, which is a board filled completely with Os. Obviously, this state can never be reached in a real game of tic-tac-toe because X and O alternate turns. So there are actually about half as many valid game states for tic-tac-toe, or around 10,000.

More Complex Games

How about a game like checkers or chess? How would you go about storing the gamestate of those games?

Both of them operate on an 8 × 8 grid, so you have 64 cells right there. A full game of checkers only uses half of those squares, though, because your pieces stay on the black squares, so you can cut that down to 32 cells.

Checkers also only uses two units, a normal piece and a king, so each cell can have up to 5 different values: empty, red piece, black piece, red king, black king. You could use a large 32-cell array of chars (32 bytes). There are at most 24 pieces on the field at one time, so you could also have a 24-cell array of bytes keeping track of the location and the type of each unit (24 bytes). It only takes three bits to keep track of each coordinate ($2^3 = 8$), and you'll have an extra two bits to keep track of what kind of unit each piece is ($2^2 = 4$, which is how many different units there are).

Chess uses all 64 cells, though, and has many more units than checkers does. There are six units per team (king, queen, bishop, knight, rook, pawn), so each cell can have 13 different values. Using an array of 64 cells would take 64 bytes for each game state, but with chess it's probably a better idea to keep track of each player individually. There is a maximum of 32 pieces on the board at any time in a chess game, so that splits the game state size in half. Again, you'd use three bits per coordinate, using just six bits of a char. However, this time, each index in the array defines what a unit is. For example, index 0 would mean "white's king", and 16 would mean "black's king", and so on.

Application: Rock Piles

This is Game Demonstration 15-1, which is located on the CD in the directory \demonstrations\ch15\Game01 - Rock Piles\.

Application: Rock Piles

> **Compiling the Demo**
>
> This demonstration uses the SDLGUI library that I have developed for the book. For more information about this library, see Appendix B.
>
> To compile this demo, either open up the workspace file in the directory or create your own project using the settings described in Appendix B. If you create your own project, all of the files you need to include are in the directory.

Now the time has come to implement a game using a minimax tree. This section shows you how to actually code the rock pile game.

The Game State

First of all, you need to be able to store a rock pile game state. I call this class the `RockState` class. I separate the data in the class into two areas.

First, there is the actual game state data:

```
int m_rocks[PILES];
```

This is just a simple array. The `PILES` constant is defined at the top of the program; in this particular program, `PILES` is 5. The array contains simple integers; each pile has a certain number of rocks in it. Obviously, the number is positive, because there shouldn't ever be a negative number of rocks in a pile.

Second, to make things simpler, I have included more data in the `RockState` class:

```
int m_minimaxValue;
Tree<RockState>* m_nextState;
```

The first variable, `m_minimaxValue`, holds the minimax value of the game state. Because the game states will be stored in a game tree and a minimax tree will have the same structure, why not combine them into one structure? So the program, when it creates the minimax tree, will go through the game tree (in which every node will hold a `RockState`) and automatically fill in the minimax value for each state.

The next variable is a tree node pointer. The same algorithm that fills in the minimax values also fills in the pointer in each game state. Each game state will point to the next node in the game tree, or the choice that the computer would make at any point in the game. Look at Figure 15.10 for an example.

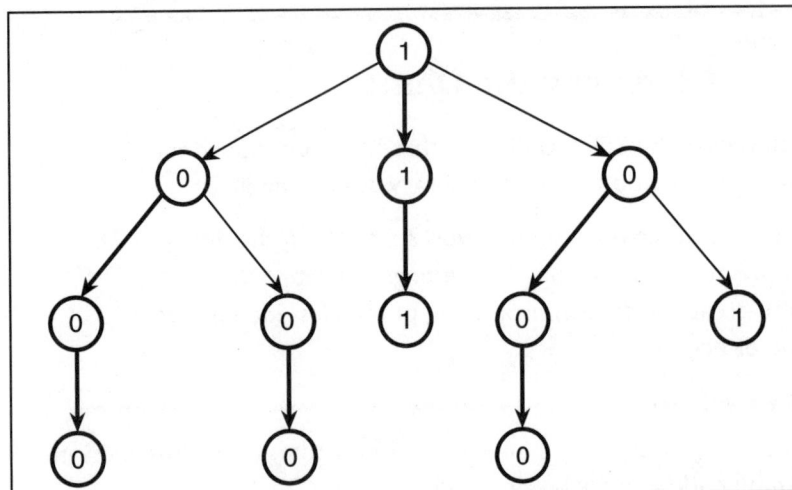

Figure 15.10

The node pointers point to the game state that the AI should move to next. They are represented by the bold lines.

When the minimax algorithm for this game demo goes through the tree and calculates the minimum and maximum values for each node, it also keeps track of the child node that has the min or max value. For example, in the root node from Figure 15.10, the minimax algorithm detects that the middle child has the max value of all of its children. Therefore, the algorithm sets the m_minimaxValue variable to 1 and sets the m_nextState pointer to point to the middle child node. In Figure 15.10, every node's m_nextState pointer is shown in bold.

The Constructor

The constructor of the RockState is meant to clear all the variables so that you can tell whether a state has been initialized.

```
RockState()
{
    int x;
    for( x = 0; x < PILES; x++ )
        m_rocks[x] = 0;
    m_minimaxValue = -1;
    m_nextState = 0;
}
```

The function goes through each pile and sets the rocks to 0. Then it sets the minimax value to –1. Because the only valid minimax values are 0 and 1, you can tell right away if the minimax algorithm has processed this state.

Finally, it sets the next state pointer to 0 so that it doesn't point to something random in memory.

The Equivalence Operator

The next function is used to determine if two states are equal to each other.

```
bool operator== ( RockState& p_rock )
{
    int x;
    for( x = 0; x < PILES; x++ )
    {
        if( m_rocks[x] != p_rock.m_rocks[x] )
            return false;
    }
    return true;
}
```

This function compares the number of rocks in all of the piles in each state, and if any pile is different from another, it immediately returns false. If the loop ends and it hasn't exited the function yet, then all of the piles are the same, and the function should return true.

The Empty Function

This function checks to see if a rock pile is empty; this is important because the game ends when all piles are empty.

```
bool Empty()
{
    int x;
    for( x = 0; x < PILES; x++ )
    {
        if( m_rocks[x] != 0 )
            return false;
    }
    return true;
}
```

This function loops through each pile and checks if any of them are not empty. If any aren't empty, then the function immediately returns false. If they are all empty, then it returns true.

The Global Variables

There are many global variables used in this game, and each one is used for a different purpose.

```
Tree<RockState>* g_tree;
RockState g_startingState;
Tree<RockState>* g_current = 0;
bool g_playing = false;
bool g_hint = false;
bool g_yourturn = true;
bool g_gameOver = false;
```

The variables for the most part should be self-explanatory by their names, but let me go over them just in case.

The g_tree variable is a pointer to the game tree. Each node holds RockStates.

The g_startingState variable holds the initial state of the game. The game demo will allow you to customize this when you first start the program.

The g_current pointer points to the node in the game tree that contains the current game state. For example, when the game just starts out, it will point to the root of the game tree.

The g_playing boolean determines if the game is being played yet. There are basically two states in the game: creating the rock piles and actually playing the game. If this is false, then you're still setting up the rock piles.

The g_hint boolean determines if the game should show you a hint on what move you should make next. This feature works by analyzing the minimax tree and seeing what move the computer would make if it were playing. Isn't that cool?

The g_yourturn boolean determines whose turn it is. If true, then it's your turn, if false, then it is the computer's turn.

Last, there is the g_gameOver variable, which determines if the game is over or not. Basically all this does is tell the game that nothing can be done but exit.

Generating the Game Tree

Now that you have the game state class and the tree variable defined, you need to make a function that will generate a game tree for you.

Luckily for you, this can be done very simply by using *recursion* (there's that word again!). All you need to do is pass in a game state to the function, and it will figure out every possible state that can be reached from the current state. It will then recursively call the function on all of those new states. The function then returns a game tree, starting at the state that it was given.

Application: Rock Piles 447

```
1: Tree<RockState>* CalculateTree( RockState p_state )
2: {
3:      int i;
4:      int rocks;
5:      Tree<RockState>* tree = new Tree<RockState>;
6:      Tree<RockState>* child = 0;
7:      RockState state;
8:      TreeIterator<RockState> itr = tree;
9:      tree->m_data = p_state;
10:     for( i = 0; i < PILES; i++ )
11:     {
12:         for( rocks = 1; rocks <= p_state.m_rocks[i]; rocks++ )
13:         {
14:             state = p_state;
15:             state.m_rocks[i] -= rocks;
16:             child = CalculateTree( state );
17:             itr.AppendChild( child );
18:         }
19:     }
20:     return tree;
21: }
```

The function is meant to take a `RockState` as a parameter and return a game tree starting at that state.

It starts out by creating two integers: `i` and `rocks`. These two integers will be used to loop through the current state and generate a new state. I show you how this is done in a little bit.

On lines 5 and 6, two tree node pointers are created. The first one is called `tree`, and it is initialized to point to a new tree node, which will be the tree node that this function generates. The second pointer, `child`, will be used to hold temporary tree pointers and is initialized to 0.

On line 7, a temporary `RockState` variable is declared. This variable will hold the modified states that can be reached from the current state.

On line 8, a `TreeIterator` is declared and made to point to the tree. This iterator will be used to insert child nodes into the tree.

On line 9, the game state that was passed into the function is placed inside the tree node.

Now, the function starts generating all the possible states that can be reached from the current state. This is accomplished by using a simple algorithm. Figure 15.11 shows the four states that are generated on a sample state.

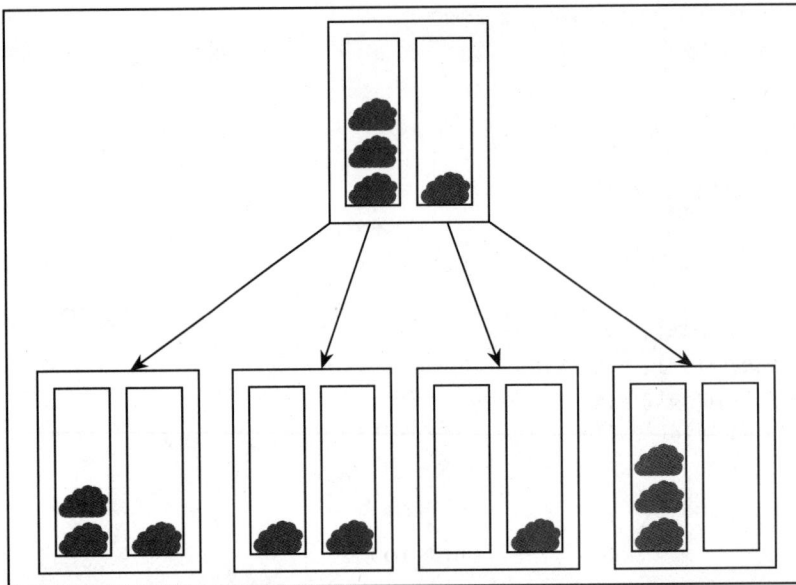

Figure 15.11

These are the four states that can be reached from the current state.

First, the algorithm tries to subtract one rock from the first pile, producing the child state on the left of Figure 15.11. Then it tries to subtract two rocks from the first pile, and then three, and it continues until there are no more rocks to subtract from that pile. Then it moves to the next pile and repeats the process.

For each newly generated state, the function recursively calls itself to generate a new game tree based on that new state. This happens on line 16, and the result is placed in the `child` node pointer.

Using the `tree` iterator, the child is then added as a child to the tree node.

> **NOTE**
> Note that this algorithm is essentially the same as a *preorder* tree traversal. The current node is created, and then all of the children are created, and so on.

When the loop is complete, the function returns the tree node that was generated. I hope you can see how recursion made your job really easy in this function by splitting the problem up into little pieces.

Generating the MiniMax Tree

Now you need a function that will traverse the game tree and fill in the minimax values. I start by showing you the recursive postorder function that calls the minimax calculation algorithm.

```
void MiniMax( Tree<RockState>* p_tree, bool p_max )
{
    TreeIterator<RockState> itr = p_tree;
    for( itr.ChildStart(); itr.ChildValid(); itr.ChildForth() )
    {
        MiniMax( itr.m_childitr.Item(), !p_max );
    }
    CalculateMiniMaxValue( p_tree, p_max );
}
```

This function is very simple. You send it a tree node to calculate the minimax value of, as well as a boolean named p_max. This boolean is meant to determine whose turn it is. If it is true, then it is currently Max's turn. If it is false, then it is currently Min's turn.

The function first creates a tree iterator that points to the tree node passed into the function. Then it loops through each child and recursively calls the MiniMax function on each child. Note that the p_max boolean is flipped using the ! operator. This is because on the current level, if it is Max's turn, the next level down will be Min's turn, and vice versa.

Finally, the CalculateMiniMaxValue function is called on the current node. This function does exactly what its name implies—it calculates the minimax value of the node.

> **NOTE**
>
> Note that this algorithm is essentially the same as a *postorder* traversal because it processes all the children first and then processes the current node.

The Heuristic Function

Next, you need to create a heuristic function, a function that generates a value that determines how "good" a given state is for a player. In the minimax algorithm, it is assumed that the heuristic function will generate high numbers if the state is good for Max and low numbers if the state is good for Min.

In this simple game, the only states that are evaluated are the ending states of the game, and there can only be two outcomes for those states: Max won or Min won. Therefore, the heuristic function you will be using only generates two different values: 0 or 1. A 0 means that Min has won the game, and a 1 means that Max has won the game.

```
int Heuristic( RockState p_state, bool p_max )
{
    return p_max;
}
```

The function takes in a state and a boolean. The boolean is used to determine whose turn it is when this state is reached. The only time this function is called on a state is when the rock piles in the state are totally empty, so in this demo, the p_state parameter is ignored.

> **NOTE**
> Even though the state parameter is ignored, it is still included here to demonstrate a point. Later on, you'll see heuristic functions that actually do use the state to calculate a value.

So the only thing this function does is evaluate whose turn it is when the game ends. If it is Max's turn when there are no more rocks, that means that it was Min who removed the last rock. Therefore, this state should return a 1, because Max has won this game. Because p_max is 1 if it is Max's turn, the function simply returns the value of the boolean. Likewise, if it is Min's turn when the game ends, it just returns 0.

The MiniMax Calculation Function

This is the function that the MiniMax function shown previously calls to generate the minimax value of each node in the tree. It is quite long and complex, so allow me to separate it into different sections so you can better understand how it works.

First of all, the function takes a game state node and a boolean as parameters. These function exactly as they did with the MiniMax function.

```
void CalculateMiniMaxValue( Tree<RockState>* p_tree, bool p_max )
```

After that, the first thing the function does is check to see if the node has any children. If it has no children, that means that the node is an ending state of the game, so the heuristic function should be called on that state to determine its value.

```
{
    if( p_tree->m_children.m_count == 0 )
    {
```

```
        p_tree->m_data.m_minimaxValue = Heuristic( p_tree->m_data, p_max );
        return;
    }
```

After the node has been set with its heuristic value, the function just returns. There is no need to do anything else.

If the node has children, you need to apply the minimax algorithm to the node. This involves a few things. You need an integer that will keep track of the current lowest or highest value that has been found so far. You must also use a `tree` iterator to loop through each child.

```
    int minmax;
    TreeIterator<RockState> itr = p_tree;
    itr.ChildStart();
    minmax = itr.ChildItem().m_minimaxValue;
    p_tree->m_data.m_nextState = itr.m_childitr.m_node->m_data;
    itr.ChildForth();
```

After the two variables are declared, they are initialized. The iterator is told to point to the very first child in the tree node, and the `minimax` variable is set to the minimax value of the first child node. The line directly below that makes the `m_nextState` pointer of the current node point to the first child node. Finally, the iterator is moved forward to the next child.

After the iterator is moved to the next node, the loop to find the minimum or maximum value begins. Here is the loop if it is Max's turn:

```
    if( p_max == true )
    {
        while( itr.ChildValid() )
        {
            if( itr.ChildItem().m_minimaxValue > minmax )
            {
                minmax = itr.ChildItem().m_minimaxValue;
                p_tree->m_data.m_nextState = itr.m_childitr.m_node->m_data;
            }
            itr.ChildForth();
        }
    }
```

And here is the loop to find the minimum value when it is Min's turn:

```
    else
    {
```

```
        while( itr.ChildValid() )
        {
            if( itr.ChildItem().m_minimaxValue < minmax )
            {
                minmax = itr.ChildItem().m_minimaxValue;
                p_tree->m_data.m_nextState = itr.m_childitr.m_node->m_data;
            }
            itr.ChildForth();
        }
    }
```

Both loops are almost identical; one looks for larger values, and the other looks for smaller values. If either loop detects a smaller/larger value than the previous smallest/largest value, then the function resets the `minimax` variable to the newer min/max value and sets the current node's `m_nextState` pointer to point to the child node that has the new min/max value.

Last, the current node's `minimax` value is updated to the min/max that was found, and the function ends:

```
    p_tree->m_data.m_minimaxValue = minmax;
}
```

That's all there is to calculate the minimax tree.

Simulating Play

Two functions are used in this demo to simulate gameplay. The first one calculates what happens when the player moves, and the second one calculates what happens when the computer moves.

The Player's Turn

Whenever the player of the game makes a move, the program calls a function called `ClickRock`. Here is the function:

```
1: void ClickRock( int p_pile, int p_rock )
2: {
3:     RockState newstate = g_current->m_data;
4:     TreeIterator<RockState> itr = g_current;
5:     if( p_rock > newstate.m_rocks[p_pile] )
6:         p_rock = newstate.m_rocks[p_pile];
7:     newstate.m_rocks[p_pile] -= p_rock;
```

```
8:        for( itr.ChildStart(); itr.ChildValid(); itr.ChildForth() )
9:        {
10:           if( itr.ChildItem() == newstate )
11:           {
12:               g_current = itr.m_childitr.Item();
13:               return;
14:           }
15:        }
16:}
```

The function takes two parameters: which pile the player is removing rocks from and how many rocks to remove.

On line 3, the function creates a new temporary state variable, which is initialized to the same state as the current state. On line 4, a tree iterator is created, and it is pointed toward the current tree node.

The code on lines 5 and 6 determines if the user is trying to remove more rocks than are currently in the pile. If so, then the function decreases the number of rocks to remove so that every rock from that pile is removed. For example, if the player tries to remove 6 rocks from a pile with only 3 rocks, the function will only remove 3 rocks. This is just to ensure that there is never a negative number of rocks in a given pile.

On line 7, the function creates the new game state by subtracting the correct number of rocks from the requested pile. Now that the new game state has been created, you need to search every child node to find which node contains the same state as the new state. This loop takes place on lines 8–15. When the node is found, the g_current pointer is set to point to the new current node, and the function exits.

The Computer's Turn

The function for the computer's turn is much simpler because of the minimax tree. The tree has already been generated, so the computer knows which move it should make at every game state in the game.

```
void OpponentMove()
{
    g_current = g_current->m_data.m_nextState;
}
```

> **NOTE**
> This function has had all the unimportant GUI code stripped from it in the book; don't be afraid if you notice that there is extra code in the version on the CD.

This function was remarkably simple, wasn't it? Because the minimax tree generation already did all of the work, each node has an `m_nextState` pointer to the state that the computer would make. The `g_current` pointer is simply moved to the next state.

Playing the Game

There are two phases to the game. In the first phase, you set up a game to play. In the second phase, you actually play the game.

Setting Up the Game

Figure 15.12 shows a screenshot from the first phase of the demo.

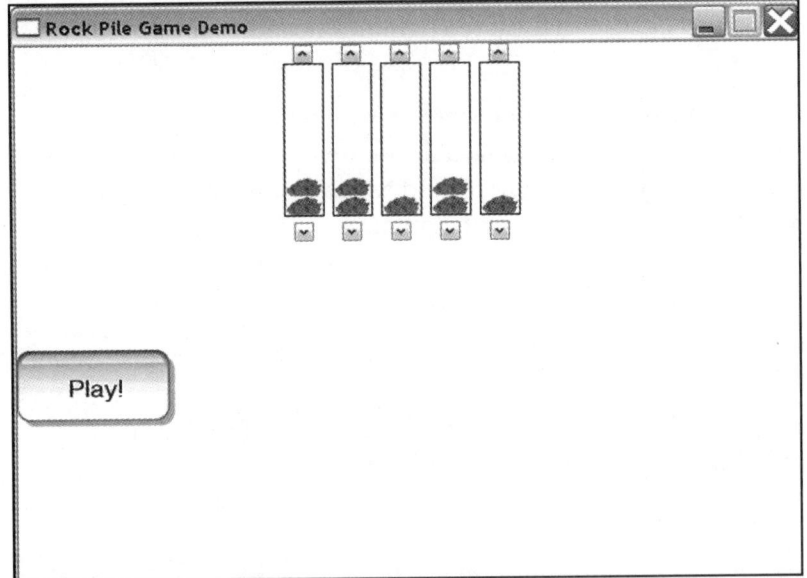

Figure 15.12

This is a screenshot of the phase of the demo when you set up the game board.

This setup is very similar to the one you saw in Graphical Demonstration 15-1, earlier in this chapter. You use the buttons on the top of each pile to add a rock to the pile and the buttons on the bottom to subtract a rock. For speed reasons, the demo is limited to a total number of 8 rocks. I tried 16, but the minimax tree took a few minutes to generate on my old K6-2 300MHz system, which was too long.

After you are done setting up the piles, you click Play!

Playing

Figure 15.13 shows a screenshot from the playing section of the demo.

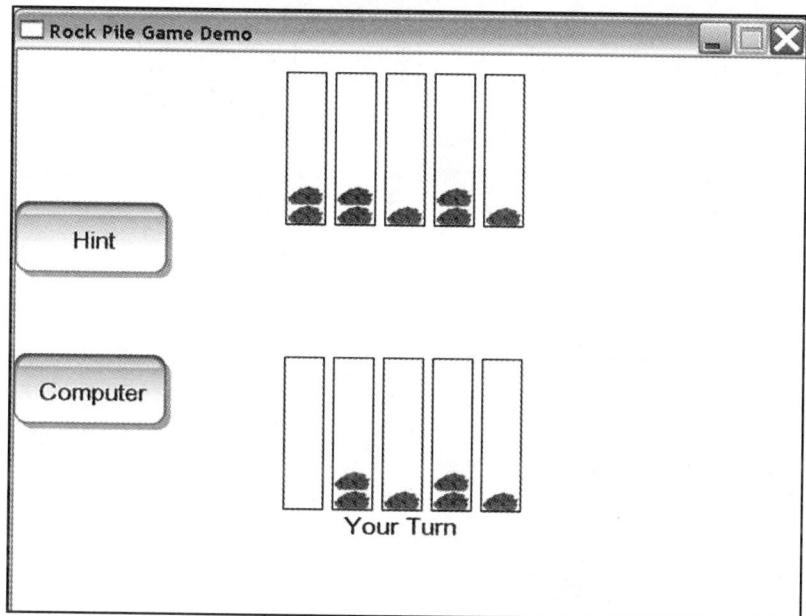

Figure 15.13

Here is a screenshot while playing the game.

This time, there are two buttons. The first button, Hint, toggles the hint display. This is the game state shown in the middle of the screen. Figure 15.13 shows a game in which the hints are on. The hint state drawn shows the next state the computer would move to if it were playing. For example, if it were the computer's turn in Figure 15.13, it would want to remove the two rocks from the first pile on the left.

The current game state is shown at the top of the screen, and the game will tell you whose turn it is by displaying Your Turn or My Turn. Whenever it is your turn, you have to click on the rocks that you want to remove.

For example, if you wanted to remove only one rock from the first pile, you would click on the bottom rock. To remove two rocks from that pile, click on the second rock, and so on. The same goes with every pile.

You always move first in this game. After you have made your move, it becomes the computer's turn. Rather than moving immediately, however, the computer waits until you click the Computer button. When you click that button, the computer moves, and it is your turn again.

You'll find that you can win most games by following the hints, but there are some games that you just cannot win.

More Complex Games

Up to this point, I've only really shown you one game using the minimax tree algorithm. Unfortunately, this one game is very simple. I mentioned earlier that with 16 rocks, it took my old computer two minutes to calculate a game tree. That is quite a long time; imagine how long it would take to calculate the full tree for tic-tac-toe.

Or worse yet, imagine how you would calculate the complete minimax tree for a game of checkers... you can't!

Never-Ending Games

Checkers is a game played on an 8 × 8 grid, and there are two players. The squares of the board alternate color, as shown in Figure 15.14. Each piece in the game can only move on the black squares of the board.

Figure 15.14

This is a checkerboard.

The pieces of the game can only capture pieces of the other team by jumping over them. This is really all that you need to know about the game for now.

Now, consider the game in Figure 15.15. There are two pieces on the board, and they make the four moves shown in the figure.

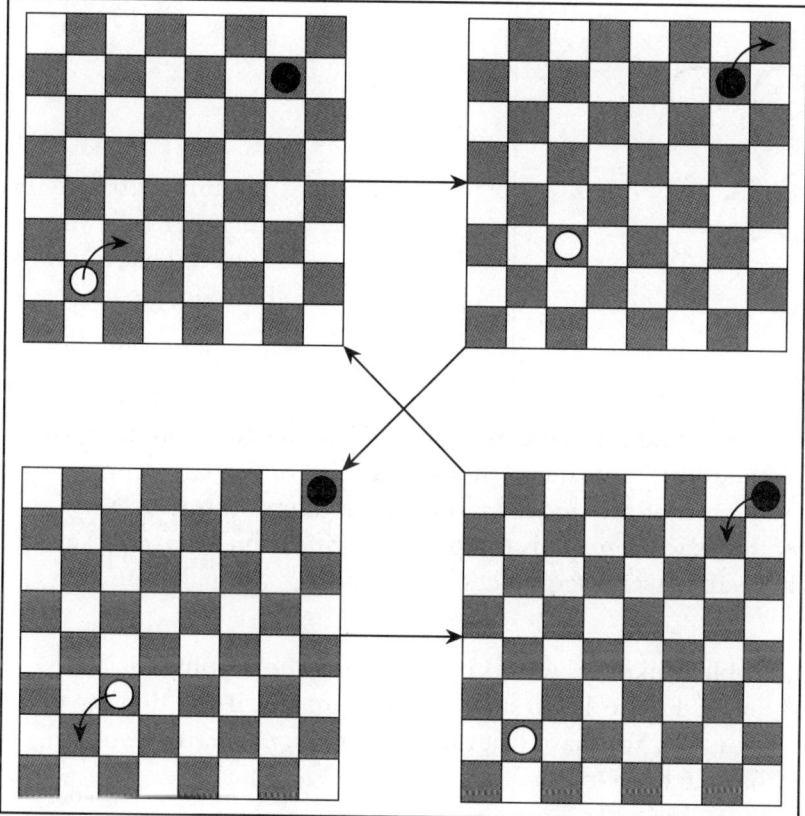

Figure 15.15

Here are four consecutive moves in a checkers game that will result in the same game state at the end.

After the four moves are made, the game is in the same exact state that it was in before. In the rock pile game, this could never happen; no matter what moves you made, the game could never end up in a state that it was in previously.

These particular moves lead to a problem; if they are repeated over and over again, the recursive game tree generator will never complete; you'll run out of memory and the computer will crash.

Imagine that the states in Figure 15.15 are named 1, 2, 3, and 4. The game tree for State 1 may lead to many different states, but the only one you are concerned with is State 2. State 2 leads to State 3, State 3 leads to State 4, and finally, State 4 leads back to State 1. Figure 15.16 shows a sample game tree.

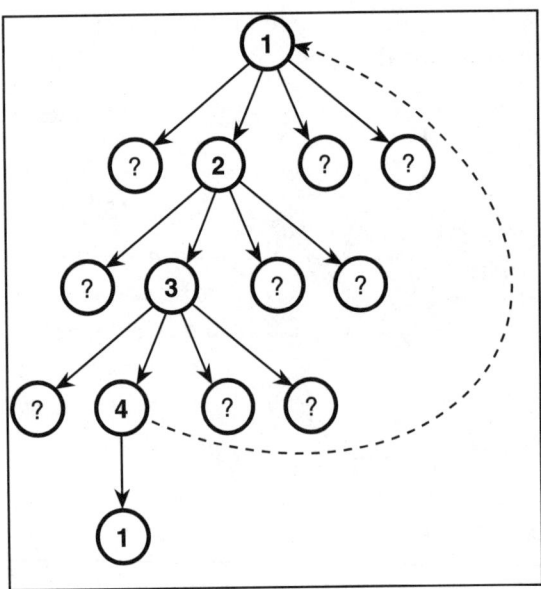

Figure 15.16

Here is a partial game tree for the four checkers moves from Figure 15.15.

The states marked with the question marks represent the states that you don't care about at this point, so they aren't expanded at all. Note that a regular recursive algorithm will think that both of the nodes marked 1 are different states, even though they are the same exact state. This is a problem with games like checkers and chess, because there are certain sequences of moves that will make the game play on forever.

The only way to fix a problem like this would be to make node 4 point back to node 1, as the dotted line in Figure 15.16 shows. Unfortunately, if you do this, the game "tree" is no longer a tree. You have just made it into a *graph*, which you will learn more about in Chapter 17, "Graphs."

To do something like this, you need to be able to find out if a given state has been processed before. Although this seems like an impossibly difficult task, you previously learned about a data structure that can help you out immensely: the hash table.

You need to create a hash function that hashes a game state into an integer. Whenever you process a new state, you check to see if the state is already in the hash table. If not, then process the state as usual and add the new state into the hash table. If the state already exists in the hash table, then just link the current node with the node in the hash table. Here is some pseudo-code showing how this would work:

```
Tree CalculateGameTree( Gamestate )
    Tree node
```

```
    for each next gamestate
        if HashTable.has( next gamestate )
            node.AddChild( HashTable.find( next gamestate ) )
        else
            node.AddChild( CalculateGameTree( next gamestate ) )
            HashTable.add( next gamestate )
        end if
    end for
    return node
end function
```

Obviously, this pseudo-code is a lot less complex than any real C++ function you would make. For instance, the part where each next state is generated is left out.

You can see how this can be really fast if you remember the speed of hash tables from Chapter 8, "Hash Tables." You get an almost instant search and retrieval time by using them, so even if you have millions of states, it takes almost no effort to search to see if you've already processed a state before.

The great thing about this algorithm is that you don't waste your time re-processing game states that you have already processed. This method very neatly solves the never-ending game problem.

Huge Games

In the opening move of chess, there are 20 different possible moves. The second move also has another 20 possibilities. No matter what piece you move and where you move it, there are more than 20 moves on the third move of the game, and the same goes for the fourth. By the time you get to the fifth move of the game, you have more than 160,000 possible states! Chess is a huge game.

If you play a medium game with only 50 turns and assume only 20 possible moves per turn, you end up with 112×10^{63} different moves, which is called 112 vigintillion. (I didn't even know that word existed until I decided to just look it up right now.) Assuming that each node in your gametree used a modest 64 bytes, that many nodes would take up 6 quattuordecillion yottabytes (I'm really not making this up), 6×10^{57} gigabytes, or 7×10^{63} kilobytes. If you could store the information about a single atom in one kilobyte, you'd be well on your way to being able to store the entire galaxy in that much memory, because it is estimated that there are around 10^{66} atoms in the Milky Way galaxy.

Needless to say, the number of possible moves in chess is simply staggering, and we'll never (I'm 99 percent sure of this, at least) be able to generate a complete game tree for chess. So kids, please don't try that at home.

Limited Depth Games

So how in the world would someone implement a minimax algorithm on a chess game? Well, you would use a *limited-depth* algorithm. These algorithms, instead of generating every possible end state of the game, only look ahead a certain number of moves. The depth that the algorithm looks to is called the *ply* of the game. Looking ahead two moves is called *2-ply*, four moves is *4-ply*, and so on.

When you're using a limited depth, the heuristic function becomes much more important because the computer must now use more "thought". Instead of analyzing which game paths lead directly down to a winning state, it must now look down a few moves and determine the strength of every state at that level.

It may sound difficult at first, but when you think about it, this method is really simple. For example, you could just count the number of pieces left on the board, add one for every piece that Max has left, and subtract one for every piece that Min has left.

In a simple checkers heuristic, if Max has 10 pieces and Min has 7 pieces, the value of that state is 3. If the roles were reversed, the value of that state would be –3.

In games like chess, this method is somewhat stupid because the computer will view losing the most important piece in the game the same as losing the least important piece. Because of this, you may want to assign values to each of the pieces. Luckily, chess scoring rules already assign each piece in the game a value ranging from 1 point for the weakest piece (the pawn) to 9 points for the strongest piece (the queen). Of course, the most important piece, the king, has no value; to have your king captured would be to end the game. Using this system, the computer would sacrifice nine pawns before it would give up its queen, making it look pretty smart.

So what ply should you use for a game? That depends entirely on the circumstances of the game, and what system you play it on. You should experiment with a low ply at first and then slowly increase the ply until the game takes too long to play. For example, the most powerful chess computer in the world, Deep Blue, only has a ply of 12.

Conclusion

I would have liked to have shown you a more complex game, something similar to checkers that would demonstrate looping trees and limited depth searches, but alas, I just don't have the room. This chapter is already much larger than I planned, and judging from the feedback I got from my fellow game programmers, minimax trees aren't a subject that appeals to the majority of game programmers.

I've covered the most important aspects of minimax trees, and I've shown you enough to finally conclude with a point to this chapter. There are a few complex topics that I have left out, such as *alpha-beta* pruning, which is a method that tries to determine which branches of the tree it doesn't need to evaluate.

In 1989, Gary Kasperov, one of the world's best chess players, stated, "Human creativity and imagination will truly triumph over silicon and wires," when asked if he ever thought a computer could beat a human in chess. In 1996, Deep Blue defeated him once in a six-game match, but he ultimately won the match. In 1997, he fought an improved Deep Blue and lost two games, only winning one game.

Why did Kasperov lose the match? Was it because the computer was smarter than he was? Hardly. The computer is a dumb machine; it does nothing but what it is told, and it only gives the illusion of thought. Kasperov lost because playing chess against a human is very different than playing chess against a computer. Deep Blue in 1997 was capable of looking at 200 million game states per second. How many different game states can a human analyze per second? Two? Three?

Minimax trees show an interesting method of playing games, which is called *brute force*. The minimax algorithm looks at *every* state it can and makes a decision based on that. The computer will even look at the most stupid moves, moves that a human mind will discard immediately. Naturally, because of this, minimax trees are very limited in their usefulness and most of the time end up being used for very simple turn-based games. This chapter has led up to the idea of trying to make the computer work *smarter*, not harder. Obviously, it is impossible for a computer to analyze every single outcome of its moves in a real-time game, so the minimax algorithm is entirely inappropriate for those types of games. I show you more about trying to make the computer work smarter in Chapter 24, "Tying It Together: Algorithms," when I go over pathfinding.

CHAPTER 16

Tying It Together: Trees

16. Tying It Together: Trees

By now, I hope you've gotten more of an idea of what trees are and how they are used in game programming. In this chapter, I show you how to use tree-like branching concepts in your game that are similar to the ones used in Game Demonstration 11-1.

In this chapter, you will learn

- How to alter the map format to store more information
- How to alter the game to handle the new exit information
- How to alter the map editor to handle the new exit information

Expanding the Game

This chapter is primarily concerned with expanding the game base from Chapter 9, "Tying It Together: The Basics," to add map branching capabilities. For this simple game, there can be a total of three exits leading to different maps.

You can think of each map as a tree node in itself, like Figure 16.1 shows.

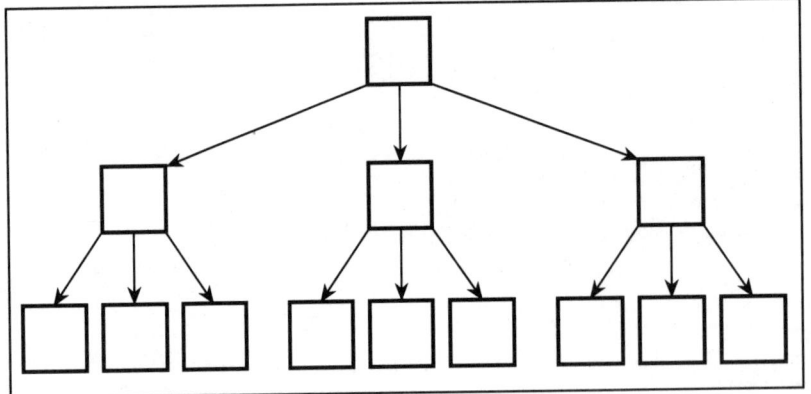

Figure 16.1

Here is a hierarchy of maps. Each map can potentially lead to three other maps, creating a tree structure.

You saw this functionality before in Chapter 11, "Trees," in Game Demonstration 11-1.

Altering the Map Format

The first thing you need to figure out is how you're going to modify the map format so that it stores information on which map it should load next when one of the exits is entered. For demonstration purposes, I chose to limit the number of exits to three. The map format will stay the same as before, but this time, three strings representing the filenames of the next maps will be added to the end of the file. Figure 16.2 shows the differences between the two map formats. The one on the left is the format used in Chapter 9, and the one on the right is the format used in this chapter.

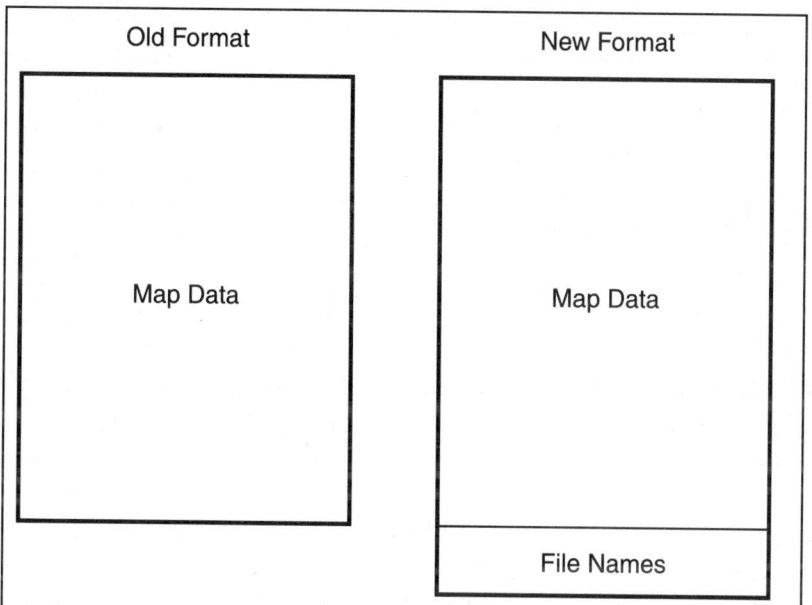

Figure 16.2

This figure shows the differences in the map file formats. The format on the left is from Chapter 9, and the one on the right is the modified version for this chapter.

When you think of a string, it is usually just an array of characters. Every cell in the array may have a letter in it, but more often, it won't. A string that can hold up to 64 characters may have only 10 characters in it.

So how do you save this to a disk? You could store the size of the string to disk and then save the actual string after that. The benefit of this method is that you save space and you can store strings with different lengths. The problem with this method, however, is that it makes searching for things within the file very difficult.

For example, if you are trying to find some data after the text strings, you need to go to where the strings are, find out how long they are, and skip over them. This makes it very difficult to jump around the file.

An easier way is to assume that the string will have a maximum length and set aside that much space in the file for it. Then, if you ever need to skip around the file, you know exactly how long the data is. The down side is that space is wasted using this method. However, the amount of space the text takes up compared to other data is negligible, so this really isn't a large problem.

Figure 16.3 shows these two methods compared.

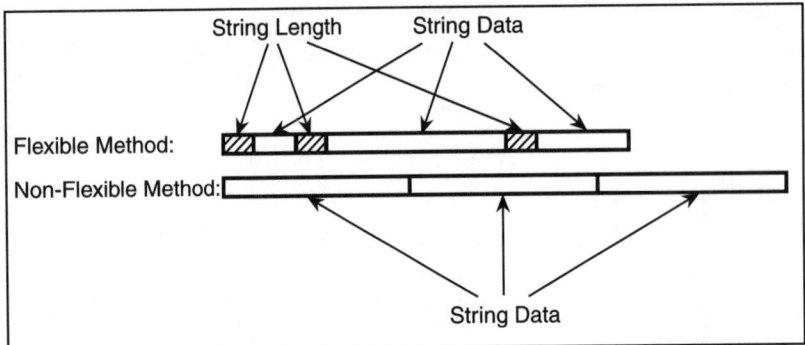

Figure 16.3

Here is a comparison of the way strings can be stored. The top method stores an integer first, which is the size of the string, and then stores the actual string; in contrast, the bottom method stores the entire string buffer.

Even though the first method is smaller, the second method is faster to move around in. I decided to use the second method in the demo and limit the string buffers to 64 characters. Because standard C strings require a null character at the end of the string, the filenames of the levels can have up to 63 characters in them. This should be enough for any game of reasonable length.

Game Demo 16-1: Altering the Game

This is Game Demonstration 16-1, which you can find on the CD in the directory \demonstrations\ch16\Game01 - Adventure v2\. Most of the source was copied over from Game Demonstration 9-1 and then modified to add the new features. Because of this, I will only show you what functions were modified and how.

> **Compiling the Demo**
>
> This demonstration uses the SDLHelpers library that I have developed for the book. For more information about this library, see Appendix B, "The Memory Layout of a Computer Program."
>
> To compile this demo, either open up the workspace file in the directory or create your own project using the settings described in Appendix B. If you create your own project, all of the files you need to include are in the directory.

Luckily, not too many things have changed. Three new types of items were added to the map: numbers 14, 15, and 16. These items represent the red, green, and blue vortexes, which will be used to transport you from one map to another.

There may be more than one vortex of the same color on the map, but they all lead to the same map.

The vortexes are Items, so that will be the first class to modify.

The New Item Class

In the previous demo, it was assumed that someone could pick up all items. However, you don't want the exits being picked up, do you? Now you need a function that checks to see if the item can be picked up or not.

Also, while planning for the future, you might want to add more items that are not exits, but can't be picked up, either (like a tree). Therefore, you need a way to find out whether the item is an exit.

Finally, if the item is an exit, you need to be able to find out what kind of exit it is. Because there are a total of three different exits allowed per map, you should be able to tell which of the three exits this current item is.

Determining Whether the Item Is Gettable

To determine whether an item is gettable, you need to add one variable and two accessor functions:

```
bool m_canGet;
void SetGet( bool p_get )   { m_canGet = p_get; }
bool CanGet() {   return m_canGet;  }
```

Pretty simple, isn't it? Then, when items are initialized in the game, if they can be picked up, they have their `m_canGet` boolean set with the `SetGet` function.

Determining Whether the Item Is an Exit

Adding this ability is similar to adding the previous ability:

```
bool m_isExit;
void SetExit( bool p_exit )    { m_isExit = p_exit; }
bool IsExit() { return m_isExit; }
```

These are also just plain accessor functions.

Determining the Exit Number

Finally, if the item is an exit, you need a way to determine what kind of exit it is:

```
int m_whichExit;
void SetExitNumber( int p_exit )    { m_whichExit = p_exit; }
int GetExitNumber() { return m_whichExit; }
```

This variable is an integer. In this particular demo, the only valid numbers are 0 through 2, but you can change that. There is no need to build that limitation into the code.

The Constructor

Finally, a few lines need to be added to the constructor:

```
m_canGet = true;
m_isExit = false;
m_whichExit = -1;
```

These say that by default an item that can be gotten is not an exit, and the exit number is invalid. These are the most popular values for normal items, so whenever you create an exit item, you need to be sure to reset these values.

The Modified Map Class

Now that the `Item` class has been modified, you need to modify the `Map` class so that you can retrieve exit names.

First, you need a way to store the names of the exits in the map. This is accomplished by using a 2D array of characters:

```
char m_exits[3][64];
```

This array defines three strings that are 64 characters long. Whenever you want to access a certain string, all you need to do is this:

```
char* string = m_exits[0];
```

Then you will have a pointer to the first string in the array. This function handles this for you because the string array is hidden:

```
char* GetExitName( int p_exit )
{
    return m_exits[p_exit];
}
```

Modifying the TileMap Class

Now that you've modified the `Map` class, you need to modify the map-loading algorithm in the `TileMap` class so that it loads the exit names for you. These lines of code are added right after the map is loaded in the `LoadFromFile` function:

```
fread( m_exits[0], 64, sizeof(char), f );
fread( m_exits[1], 64, sizeof(char), f );
fread( m_exits[2], 64, sizeof(char), f );
```

That's it! All three strings are read into the string array.

Modifying the Player Class

In the game engine from Chapter 9, there was never any need to copy the inventory of a person over into the inventory of another person, so that functionality wasn't programmed in.

However, now the maps are going to be switched in the game. When a new map is created, so is a new current player. This means that the inventory from the old current player needs to be copied into the new current player.

> **NOTE**
>
> As a game-logic decision, I have decided to copy *only* the inventory over. The health and armor of the player can remain at full. This is because in the game, the vortexes *recharge* the player and give him full health and armor.

This function copies the inventory of the parameter person into the current person:

```
void CopyInventory( Person* p_person )
{
```

```
Item* item;
DListIterator<Item*> itr = p_person->GetItemIterator();
while( m_inventory.Size() > 0 )
{
    delete m_inventory.m_head->m_data;
    m_inventory.RemoveHead();
}
```

The above loop goes through the inventory of the current person and deletes all the items in the inventory.

```
m_currentweapon.Start();
for( itr.Start(); itr.Valid(); itr.Forth() )
{
    item = new Item;
    *item = *itr.Item();
    AddItem( item );
}
}
```

Then this loop copies everything over from the other person's inventory. After this function is complete, the inventories of both people will be the same.

Modifying the Game Logic

Now that the game engine has been modified to handle exits, you need to modify the game logic to handle them as well.

Loading the Exit Templates

The following code sets up the item templates so that when a map is loaded, the items are created correctly:

```
g_itemtemplates[14].SetGet( false );
g_itemtemplates[14].SetExit( true );
g_itemtemplates[14].SetExitNumber( 0 );

g_itemtemplates[15].SetGet( false );
g_itemtemplates[15].SetExit( true );
g_itemtemplates[15].SetExitNumber( 1 );

g_itemtemplates[16].SetGet( false );
g_itemtemplates[16].SetExit( true );
g_itemtemplates[16].SetExitNumber( 2 );
```

Earlier, I said that the three new items were numbered 14, 15, and 16. These represent the first, second, and third exits. You can't pick up any of them, so the `SetGet` function is called and `false` is passed in. They are all exits, so the `SetExit` function is called, and `true` is passed in. Finally, their corresponding exit numbers are set.

The PickUp Function

Now, whenever a person tries to pick up an item, you need to check if he is actually picking up an item. The item might be an exit, so you want the player to go through the exit instead of picking it up. Here is the new function:

```
void PickUp( Person* p_person )
{
    Item* i = g_currentmap->GetItem( p_person->GetCell() );
    if( i != 0 )
    {
        if( i->CanGet() == true )
        {
            p_person->PickUp( i );
            g_currentmap->SetItem( p_person->GetCell(), 0 );
        }
        else if( i->IsExit() == true )
        {
            char* filename = g_currentmap->GetExitName( i->GetExitNumber() );
            SetNewMap( filename );
        }
    }
}
```

The new code is listed in bold; everything else is the same from the previous project. If the item can be gotten, then the function makes the player pick up the item. If not, then the function checks to see if the item is an exit. If it is, then the name of the exit is retrieved, and the `SetNewMap` function is called to load the new map.

The SetNewMap Function

Finally, you need to modify the `SetNewMap` function so that it loads a new map correctly.

The changed portions are highlighted in bold:

```
void SetNewMap( char* p_filename )
{
    int x;
    Map* newmap;
    Person* newperson;
    newmap = LoadMap( p_filename );
    newperson = newmap->GetViewer();
    g_peoplecount = 0;
    for( x = 0; x < newmap->GetNumberOfCells(); x++ )
    {
        if( newmap->GetPerson( x ) != 0 )
        {
            AddPersonToArray( newmap->GetPerson( x ) );
        }
    }
    if( g_currentplayer != 0 )
    {
        newperson->CopyInventory( g_currentplayer );
    }
    if( g_currentmap != 0 )
    {
        delete g_currentmap;
    }
    g_currentmap = newmap;
    g_currentplayer = newmap->GetViewer();
}
```

The only thing this function adds is a call to the `CopyInventory`, which copies the inventory of the current player into the new player if the current player exists.

Playing the Game

The gameplay for this version of the game is the same, with the addition of the map-switching functions. As you saw before, all you have to do is press Enter when you're over a vortex.

Figure 16.4 shows a screenshot of the game when the player is approaching a vortex.

Expanding the Game 473

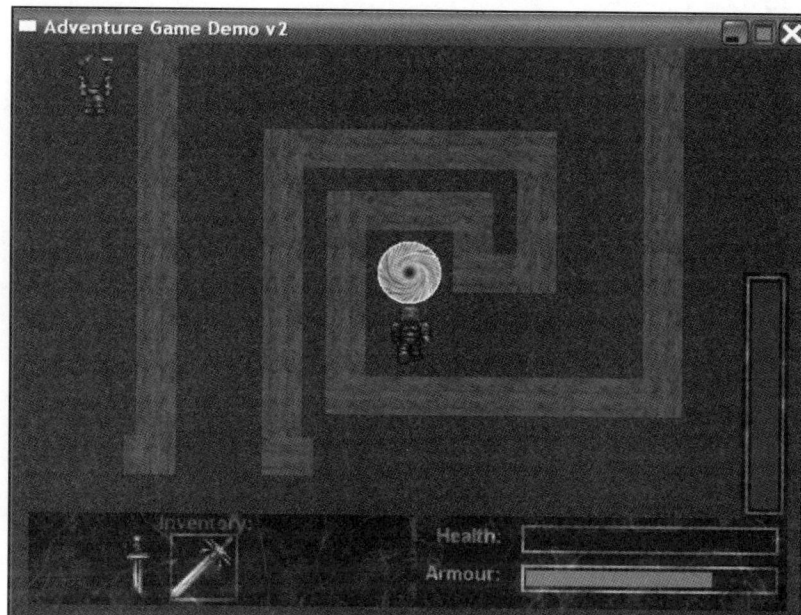

Figure 16.4

Here is a screenshot from the demo.

The Map Editor

The new version of the map editor is on the CD in the directory \demonstrations\ch16\Game02 - Map Editor\.

The map editor required very few changes to support the vortex tiles. The most complicated part of the code was adding the part that would load and save the names of the next levels to disk.

> ### Compiling the Demo
>
> This demonstration uses the SDLGUI library that I have developed for the book. For more information about this library, see Appendix B.
>
> To compile this demo, either open up the workspace file in the directory or create your own project using the settings described in Appendix B. If you create your own project, all of the files you need to include are in the directory.

Saving the Exits to Disk

The `Save` function is modified so that the following lines of code are added after the map data is stored:

```
fwrite( g_exits[0], 64, sizeof(char), f );
fwrite( g_exits[1], 64, sizeof(char), f );
fwrite( g_exits[2], 64, sizeof(char), f );
```

These lines of code essentially write the three strings to disk.

Reading the Exits from Disk

The `Load` function is modified to look almost the same as the `LoadFromFile` function in the `TileMap` class from the previous demo, and these three lines are added:

```
fread( g_exits[0], 64, sizeof(char), f );
fread( g_exits[1], 64, sizeof(char), f );
fread( g_exits[2], 64, sizeof(char), f );
```

Playing the Demo

The rest of the demo was modified to add the three vortex graphics to the editor, using the same methods as the demo from Chapter 9.

Figure 16.5 shows a screenshot from the demo.

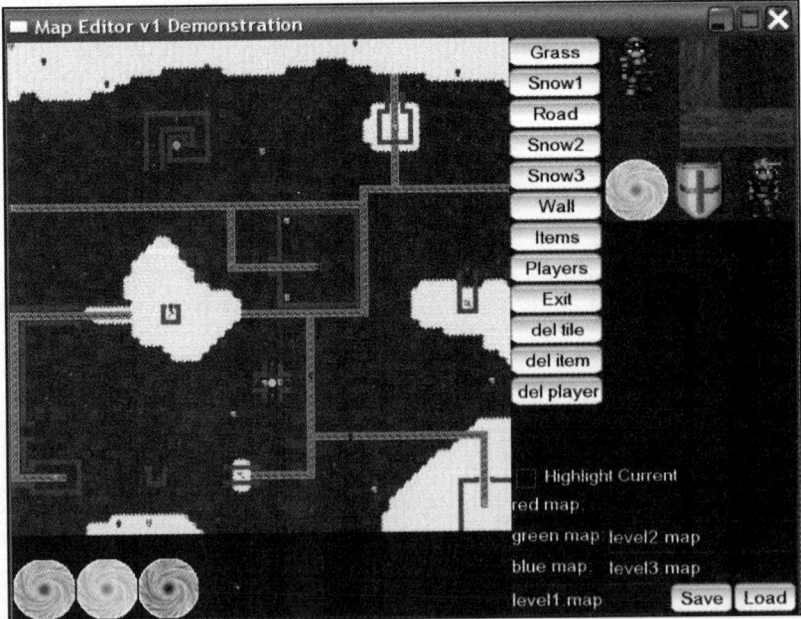

Figure 16.5

Here is a screenshot from the map editor demo.

You'll notice that there are only four new things on the map: three text boxes and one new button. The new button opens up the Exit palette, which allows you to draw one of the three vortexes. Each one has a different color: red, green, or blue. Whenever the player enters a red vortex, the map name in the red map text box will be loaded. The same goes for the green and blue vortexes. For example, on this map, if the player enters a green vortex, he will be taken to level2.map, and if he enters a blue vortex, he will be taken to level3.map. That is all there is to it.

Further Enhancements

This was just one simple enhancement to the game involving trees. In reality, there are many more that you can implement if you have the time to.

For example, the game could use the arithmetic script system from Chapter 12, "Binary Trees," to load functions for the different characters. These functions could then be used to determine how much damage a person does based on certain factors in the game or any number of things.

If your game also had a skill system, you could use trees to represent skill trees, like RPGs such as *Diablo 2* do. For example, in those kinds of games, you have a tree representing all of the skills you have. When you start off, you can choose one general area of skills you want to be able to use, such as fighting skills or healing skills.

Later on in the game, you will be faced with sub-sets of the skill categories, and you need to choose which of these sub-sets you want to be able to use, such as armed weapons, unarmed combat, magical healing, or standard real-world medical techniques, such as stitching and finding medicines. A tree is perfect for storing this kind of information.

Conclusion

This chapter is fairly short, but that is a good thing. The design for the game engine developed in Chapter 9 is flexible, and you can see how easy it is to add features to a game when you have a good solid foundation underneath.

In Chapters 19, "Tying It Together: Graphs," and 24, "Tying It Together: Algorithms," I go over even more enhancements to the game engine, mostly dealing with the topics from the sections that those chapters are in.

PART FOUR

Graphs

17 Graphs

18 Using Graphs for AI: Finite State Machines

19 Tying It Together: Graphs

CHAPTER 17

GRAPHS

Now that you've learned about all of the basic data structures and all of the tree data structures, it's time to learn about the most complex and flexible data structure in the book, the *graph* data structure. Graphs are used for all sorts of things, and believe it or not, you used a form of a graph previously in this book. I won't tell you where right now, so see if you can figure out where you've used them before.

In this chapter, you will learn

- What a graph is
- How graphs relate to linked lists and trees
- The basic parts of a graph
- The difference between weighted and unweighted graphs
- The difference between bi-directional and uni-directional graphs
- How a tilemap is a graph
- What an adjacency table graph is
- What a direction table graph is
- What a linked graph is
- Two ways to traverse graphs
- How to code a linked graph class
- How to make a direction table graph dungeon
- How to make a portal engine using linked graphs

What Is a Graph?

To understand what graphs are and where they stand in relation to everything else, you need to first look back on what you already have learned about node-based data structures.

Linked Lists and Trees

In Chapter 6, "Linked Lists," you learned about linked lists. A linked list is a node-based structure in which every node in the list points to one node (ignore doubly linked lists for the moment). Figure 17.1 shows a linked list.

What Is a Graph?

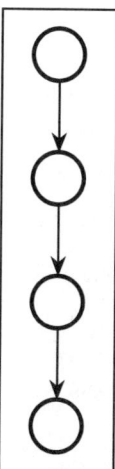

Figure 17.1

This is a linked list.

> **NOTE**
>
> Figure 17.1 is drawn vertically, unlike the linked lists you have seen before in the book. Don't worry about it; I did it to illustrate a point.

After you learned about linked lists, you moved onto trees in Chapter 11, "Trees." You learned that a tree is a node-based data structure where each node in the tree can point to any number of *children* nodes. Figure 17.2 depicts a tree.

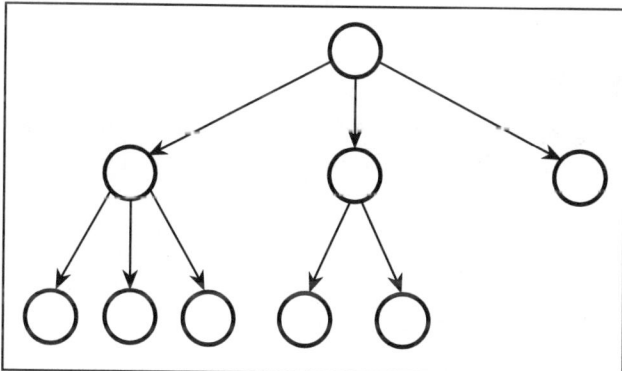

Figure 17.2

This is a tree.

There is an important relationship between a linked list and a tree that you should be able to see: A linked list is really a tree. If you look at Figure 17.1, you can see how a linked list is really just a tree where each node points to only one node.

Graphs

If you can make a linked list more flexible so that it becomes a tree, you can also do the same thing with a tree.

If you take a tree and make it possible for each node in the tree to point to any other node in the tree, you end up with a graph. Figure 17.3 shows a sample graph.

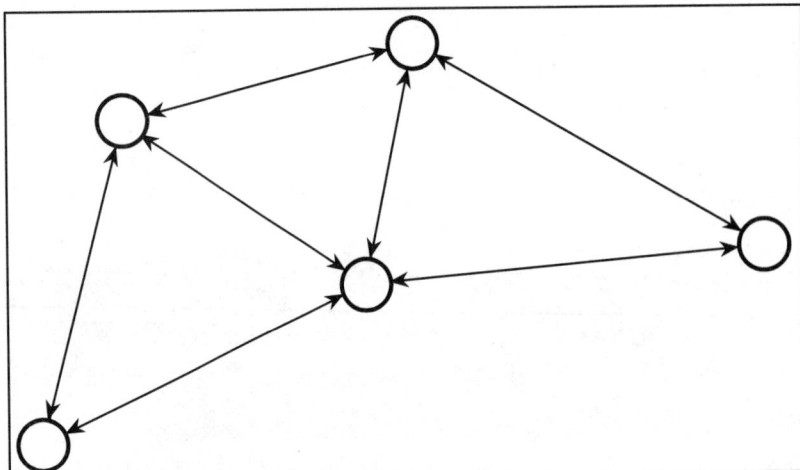

Figure 17.3

This is a graph, where any node can point to another.

Quite simply, a graph is a node-based data structure where any node can point to any other node. You can see that a tree is a graph where the nodes branch out, and a linked list is a graph where the nodes are lined up in a chain.

Parts of a Graph

There are two things that make up a graph. You already know about the *nodes*, represented by the circles in all of the figures. The nodes contain the actual data in the data structure.

The other part of a graph is the *arcs*. An arc is basically a line connecting one node to another. The linked list and tree data structures didn't need the concept of an arc, but they are important to graphs, as you'll see later on.

Types of Graphs

There are many different types and implementations of graphs. I'll show you the most important variations.

Bi-Directional Graphs

The simplest kind of graph is a *bi-directional* graph. This is a graph in which each arc in the graph points to *two* nodes. For example, take a look at Figure 17.4. In this graph, node A points to node B, and node B points to node A. You can think of every arc in the graph as a two-way street; you can get from A to B and you can get from B to A.

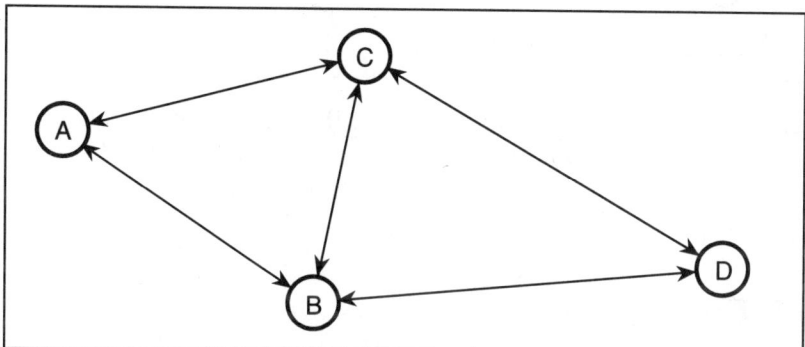

Figure 17.4

This is a bi-directional graph. Each arc points to two nodes.

Uni-Directional Graphs

A *uni-directional* graph is a little bit more limited than a bi-directional graph. In a uni-directional graph, each arc can only point to one node, so you end up with a graph like the one in Figure 17.5.

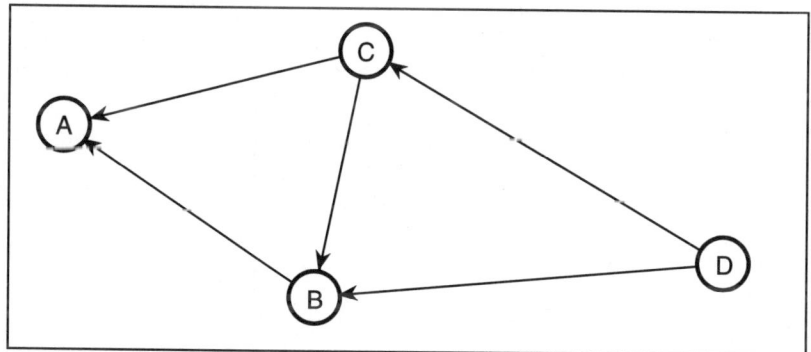

Figure 17.5

This is a uni-directional graph. Each arc points only to a single node.

Note how the arrowhead on the arc between nodes A and B in the figure points to node A, but not B. You can think of this as a one-way street; you can get from B to A, but you can't go back the other way.

To simulate a bi-directional graph using a uni-directional graph, you'd need to add another arc going from A to B, like Figure 17.6 shows.

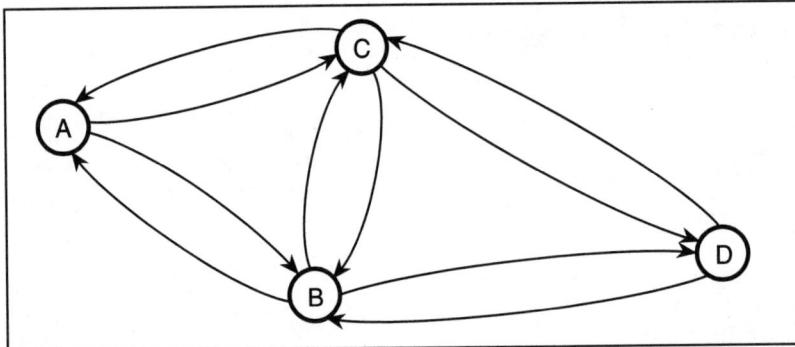

Figure 17.6

This figure shows you how to simulate a bi-directional graph using a uni-directional graph.

This approach to a graph seems a little wasteful because the number of arcs is potentially doubled, but uni-directional graphs give you a little bit more control over the structure than bi-directional graphs. I touch on this more later when I explain how to use graphs in games.

Weighted Graphs

Weighted graphs (sometimes called *networks*) introduce a new level of complexity for graphs. Imagine you have a map of the available flights on a particular airline in the United States, like Figure 17.7 shows.

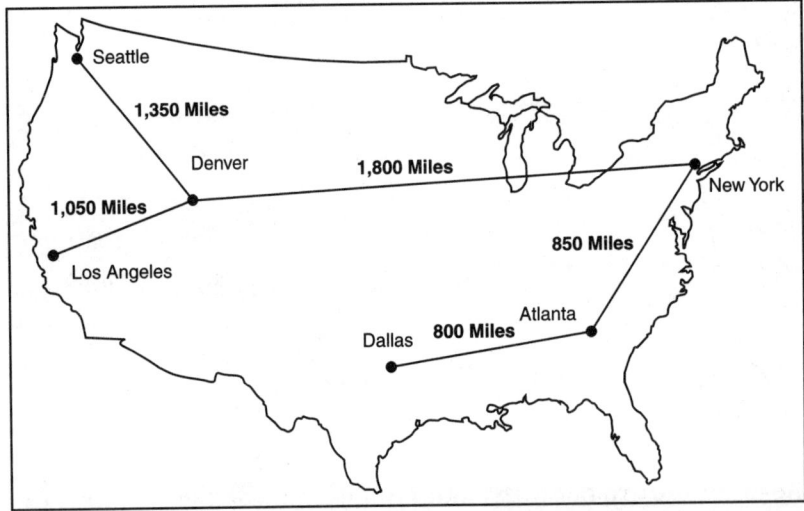

Figure 17.7

This is a weighted graph, where the distance to go from one city to another is stored in the arc.

You can view the map as a graph easily enough. The six cities are the nodes of the graph, and the lines between the cities are the arcs. Each arc in the map has a *weight* (sometimes known as the *cost*) associated with it. In the case of this map, the weight is the number of miles between the cities connected by the arcs.

Tilemaps

You should be thinking, "Hey! Didn't I already learn about tilemaps?" The answer is yes. If you think about it for a moment, you can see that a tilemap is really just a different form of a graph. Figure 17.8 shows a figure of a 4 × 4 2D tilemap, like you've seen before.

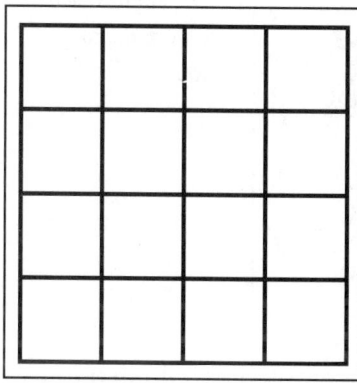

Figure 17.8

This is a 2D tilemap.

Now, take the map apart and turn each square in the tilemap into a node. Each of the new nodes will have an arc connecting it to the tiles that were next to it in the tilemap. Figure 17.9 shows how a 4 × 4 tilemap can be viewed as a graph.

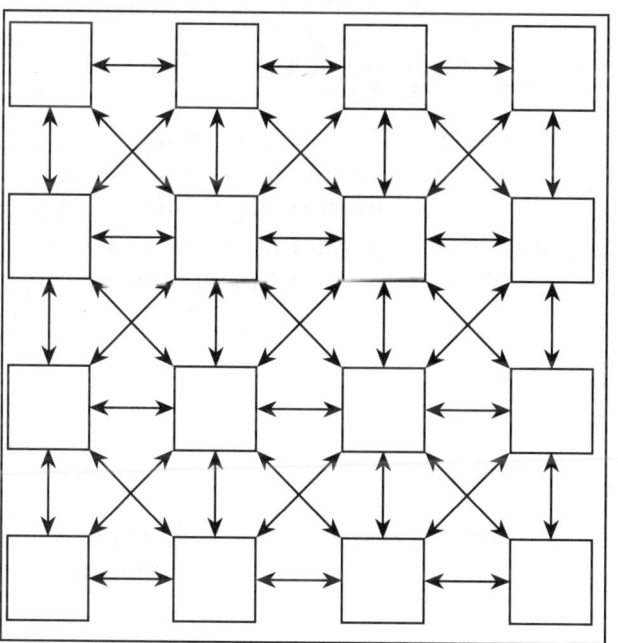

Figure 17.9

This is a 2D tilemap when viewed as a graph. There are bi-directional arcs connecting every adjacent square.

As you can see, it is assumed in a tilemap that there is a pathway open from one tile to another. The arcs serve to visualize the paths that are available in a tilemap.

If you're into hex-tile games (many strategy games use hex-tiles), Figure 17.10 shows an example of how to visualize a hex map as a graph.

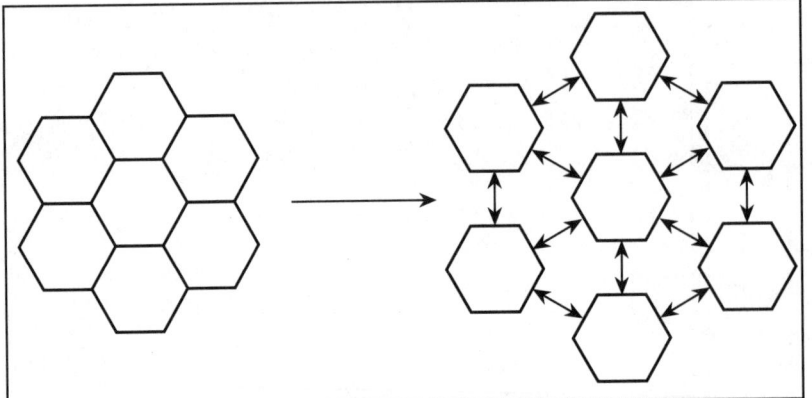

Figure 17.10

This is a hex-tilemap converted into a graph.

It is worthwhile to note that while a tilemap is essentially a graph, it is a limited form of a graph. For example, in a plain tilemap, each tile can only have up to eight arcs because each tile is adjacent to eight other tiles. The same goes with the hex-tilemap, only this time each tile can have up to six arcs and no more. A "pure" graph data structure doesn't have a limit on the number of arcs each node can have.

Implementing a Graph

Let me first start out by saying that there are many different ways to implement a graph. You have already seen one way to implement a graph: by using 2D Arrays for tilemaps. The arcs in tilemaps are only a theoretical structure; they don't actually exist. Instead, it is assumed that at each tile, you can go right (add 1 to x), go left (subtract 1 from x), go up (subtract 1 from y), go down (add 1 to y), or go in any of the four diagonal directions.

There are many more ways to represent a graph in a computer. I'll introduce you to some of the more common methods.

Adjacency Tables

The first method of storing a graph is called the *adjacency table* method. Like the tilemapping method, this method also uses 2D arrays. However, it uses them in a different manner.

Adjacency tables are always square. For example, look back at Figure 17.7, the map of the United States. There are a total of six nodes, so the adjacency table would be a 6 × 6 array. Figure 17.11 shows the adjacency table for the graph from Figure 17.7

	New York	Atlanta	Denver	Seattle	Dallas	Los Angeles
New York		850	1800			
Atlanta	850				800	
Denver	1800			1350		1050
Seattle			1350			
Dallas		800				
Los Angeles			1050			

Figure 17.11

Here is the adjacency table for Figure 17.7.

So how does the table work? It's really simple: If you want to know the cost to get from city A to city B, you look up city A on the *x* axis of the array and city B on the *y* axis, and the cost is in the cell (A,B). New York to Atlanta is 850 miles, and vice-versa.

If you're using a non-weighted graph, you could just use booleans in the cells, where 1 means that the two nodes are connected and 0 means that they aren't connected.

NOTE

Whenever I use the word *cost*, it is referring to the weight of an arc. Usually, when dealing with graphs, the cost of an arc has to do with how much "work" it takes for you to go from one place to another. In the distance-table graph, the cost is measured in miles.

The first thing you should notice about this method is the wasted space. In a graph with n nodes, you will need n^2 cells to store the arc information. There are a total of 5 Bi-directional arcs in the graph, yet you are required to use 36 cells for this information.

Another thing you may notice is that this method is really only suited toward uni-directional graphs. Because Figure 17.7 is bi-directional, you are required to put the weight information into the adjacency table twice to simulate each arc in the graph.

On the positive side, looking to see if an arc exists is really quick with this method.

Direction Tables

I'm making this name up because I've never seen this method actually named. This method also uses a 2D array to store adjacency information, but it is usually more compact than the adjacency table method. This method is certainly related to the adjacency table method, however.

This method assumes that there are a limited number of *directions* you can take from any given node, which makes it well suited for limited tilemap-like graphs. For example, if you assume that any given node can have four exits—north, south, east, and west—your 2D array would be of the size $N \times 4$, where N is the number of nodes in the graph.

For example, Figure 17.12 shows a graph and the direction table that is associated with the graph.

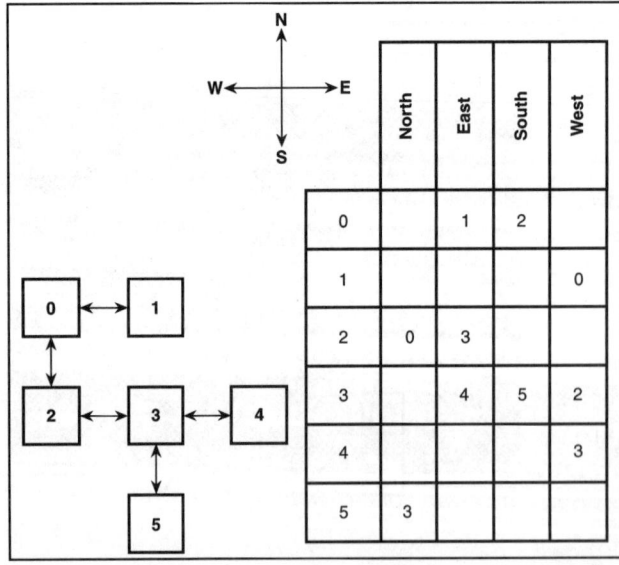

Figure 17.12

Here is a graph and its direction table. Each entry in the table denotes an exit.

	North	East	South	West
0		1	2	
1				0
2	0		3	
3		4	5	2
4				3
5	3			

The way that this method works may not be completely obvious at the first glance, but this is the same exact method I used to store the maps of my very first computer game, which was a dungeon text-adventure game. The way it works is this: To see what exits room R has, go down the *y* axis to that room, and then look at the exits. For example, in Figure 17.12, you can see that room 3 has three exits. Room 4 lies to the east, room 5 is to the south, and room 2 lies to the west. Because there is no entry for the north exit, room 3 has no exit to the north.

This is a very elegant way of storing dungeon-like maps—maps with long and twisty passages and hallways.

You may notice that this method is also suited for uni-directional maps. This use can work in your favor. For example, what if you want the player to be able to walk from room 3 to room 5 but not be able to walk back (because the door slams shut and gets locked)? All you need to do is remove the north entry for room 5, and voila, the player can no longer get from room 5 back into room 3.

I show you how to implement these kinds of maps later on, in a game demo.

General-Purpose Linked Graphs

Most graphs you will encounter will probably be of the *linked* variety, similar to the way linked trees are implemented.

Bi-Directional Graphs

The simplest way to implement a bi-directional graph would be to have two different structures, a graph node and a graph arc. The graph would hold an array (or a linked list—the choice is up to you, depending on how you're going to use the graph) of graph nodes and have an array (or a linked list) of arcs. The graph nodes would only be responsible for storing the data for that particular node; the arcs would have two pointers and possibly a weight variable, depending on whether or not the graph is weighted. Figure 17.13 shows this setup.

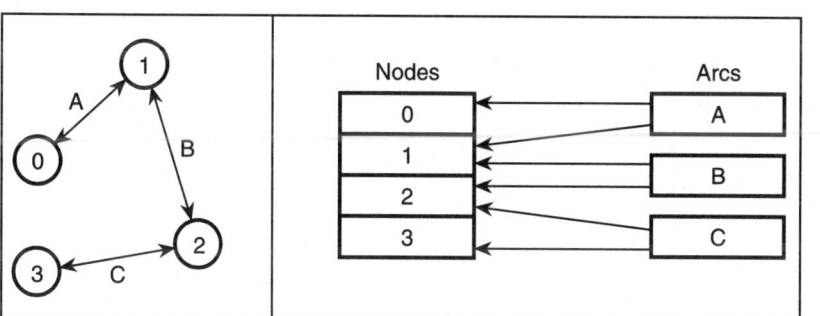

Figure 17.13

This is a bi-directional linked graph. Each arc points to two nodes.

There are four nodes and three arcs in the graph on the left of the figure, and the right side of the figure shows the internal representation of this graph. There is an array of four nodes, containing the data of the graph, and an array of three arcs. Arc A points to nodes 0 and 1, B points to 1 and 2, and C points to 2 and 3.

This method of storing graphs is somewhat awkward because the nodes don't point to the arcs. To find out if any node connects to another, you need to search through all of the arcs, which can be a long process on large graphs.

To fix the lookup problem, you can add a linked list of arc pointers to each node so that each node knows which arcs it connects to. This method gets very messy, though, as you can see in Figure 17.14.

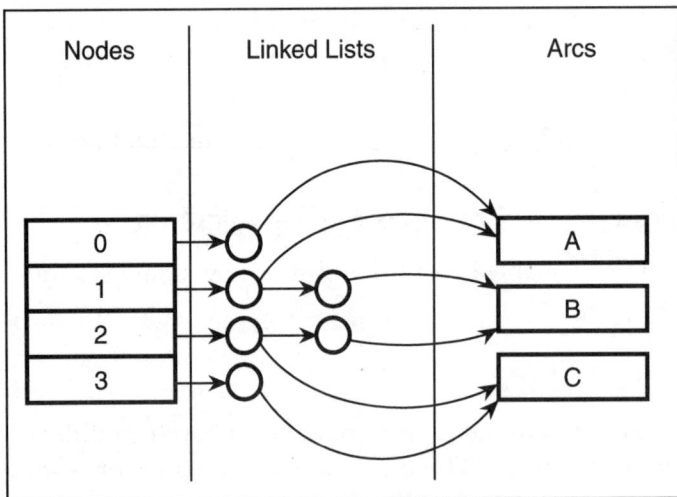

Figure 17.14

Making the nodes point back to the arcs not only takes up more room, but also involves a lot of housekeeping work.

You should notice that the lines pointing from the arcs back to the nodes are missing in the figure; they still exist, but I couldn't add them in without making the figure look totally incomprehensible, which should say something about this method. It is a pain in the butt to implement, is even more difficult to manage and modify, and takes up a lot of memory. (Look at all the pointers all over the place!)

Needless to say, this method is stupid because it takes up more room with all of the pointers, and will make your graph much slower because of all the links between the nodes and the arcs that it needs to keep track of. It is often far easier to implement a bi-directional graph using a uni-directional graph structure.

Implementing a Graph 491

> **NOTE**
> My suggestion is this: Don't store your graphs using the structure I just described in this section. I wanted to show you one bad approach to storing graphs so that you can see how much more efficient other methods are.

Uni-Directional Graphs

This is the most common form of a linked graph that you will see, as it is very flexible and speedier than the bi-directional method.

The basic premise is somewhat similar; you have a node class and an arc class, but the graph data structure will have an array (or linked list) of nodes, but not arcs. The arc class is essentially just a pointer to one node (and possibly a weight as well), so each node in the graph will have a linked list of these arcs, like Figure 17.15 shows.

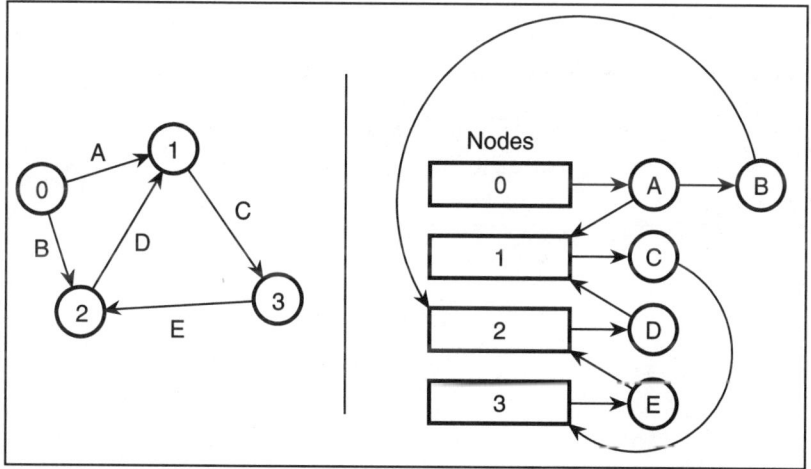

Figure 17.15

Here is a uni-directional graph, where each node (the boxes) has a linked list of arcs (the circles), and each arc points to one node.

The left side of the figure shows the graph, and the right shows the internal representation of the graph. Each node has a linked list of arcs that point back to a node. This method is simple and easy to develop, and to see if any node connects to another, all you need to do is search through the linked list of the starting node (rather than every arc in the entire graph for the bi-directional graphs). This is the linked graph implementation that I show you later on in the chapter.

Graphical Demonstration: Graphs

This is Graphical Demonstration 17-1, which you can find on the CD in the directory \demonstrations\ch17\Demo01 - Graphs\.

> ## Compiling the Demo
>
> This demonstration uses the SDLGUI library that I have developed for the book. For more information about this library, see Appendix B, "The Memory Layout of a Computer Program."
>
> To compile this demo, either open up the workspace file in the directory or create your own project using the settings described in Appendix B. If you create your own project, all of the files you need to include are in the directory.

This demo will show you how a uni-directional graph is created and linked graphically. Figure 17.16 shows a screenshot from the demo.

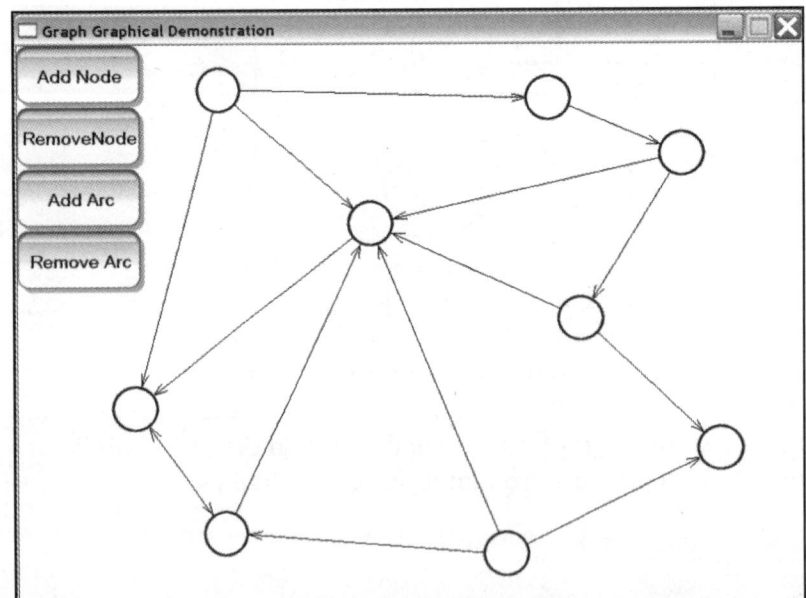

Figure 17.16

This is the screenshot from the demonstration.

The demonstration has four buttons, which you use for adding or removing nodes or arcs from the graph.

When you click on the Add Node button, a gray circle appears on your cursor. When you have moved the circle to where you want to put it, click your mouse button. A new node will now be in your graph.

When you click on the Remove Node button, all you have to do is highlight the node you want to remove with your mouse and click it; the node will be removed.

To add an arc to the graph, click on Add Arc first. After you have done that, click on the node where the arc starts. It should turn red and stay that way no matter where your cursor moves. Now move the cursor to the destination node and click that. A new arc should appear that connects the two nodes.

The process for removing an arc is identical to adding an arc: Click the button and click the starting node and the destination node.

> **NOTE**
> The demo uses a uni-directional graph as its basis. Therefore, you can add arcs from one node to another, but if you try removing arcs in the opposite order, nothing will happen because no arc is connecting the two nodes in the other direction.

Graph Traversals

There are two different ways to traverse a graph. The first method, called the *depth-first search*, is almost the same as one of the tree traversal algorithms. The second method, the *breadth-first search*, is a lot more useful to game programming.

One of the ways that these traversals differ from regular tree traversals is that they can be started on any node in the graph, whereas tree traversals always start at the root. This is because a graph traversal/search is meant to process every node that is reachable from a certain node or stop when a given node is found.

The Depth-First Search

Let me start off by saying that the depth-first search is almost the same as the tree's preorder traversal. Previously, I said that a tree is really just a limited form of a graph, so let me start off by showing you a tree again. Figure 17.17 shows a plain two-level tree with each node numbered by its order in a preorder traversal (see Chapter 11 if you are unfamiliar with this traversal method).

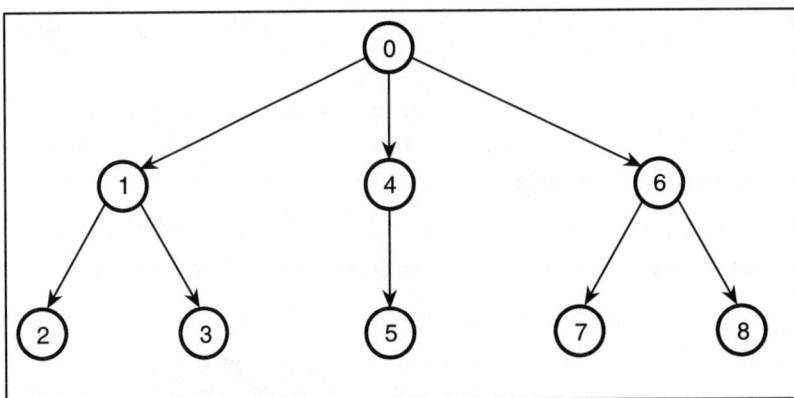

Figure 17.17

A preorder traversal on a tree is the same as a depth-first search on a graph. Each complete path is followed before a new branch is started.

First, the root node is processed, and then the algorithm follows one branch from the root node all the way down to the leaf. After that, it backtracks up to the last node with another branch (node 1 in the figure) and processes the next branch all the way to the bottom.

Now I want to show you how to perform a depth-first search on a real graph. Figure 17.18 shows a simple eight-node graph, which looks very similar to a tree.

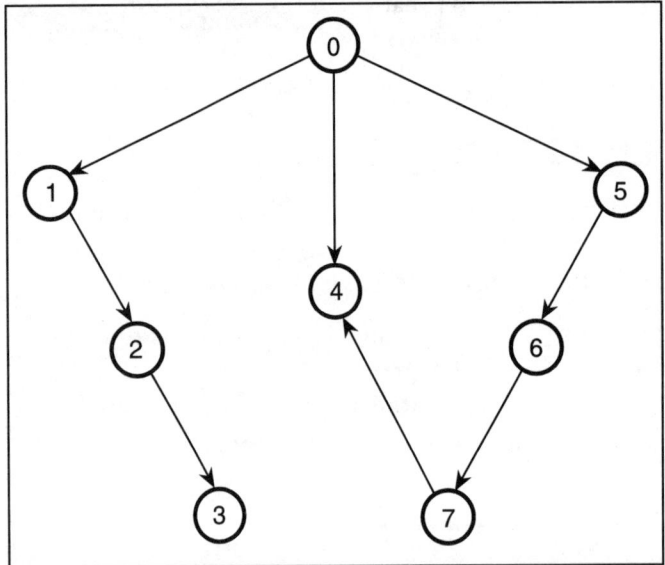

Figure 17.18

This is the order in which the nodes are processed during a depth-first search on a simple graph.

The only thing preventing this graph from looking entirely like a tree is the link from node 7 pointing to node 4. The depth first traversal is started on node 0, which promptly travels down the path 1, 2, 3. After this path has been explored, the algorithm backtracks and looks for the next open path to travel down, which starts on node 4. Because node 4 doesn't lead anywhere, the algorithm backtracks to 0 again and takes the path starting with node 5.

Eventually, the algorithm ends up at node 7, which is where the algorithm becomes different from the preorder traversal algorithm. In a tree, it is not possible for two nodes to point to the same node, but it happens all the time in a graph. When the algorithm reaches node 7, it sees that this node points to node 4, but node 4 was already processed. Most of the time, you don't want nodes to be processed more than once in one traversal, so you need to have some way to determine whether a node has already been processed or not. I call this process *marking* the nodes.

You can use many methods to mark the nodes. For example, you can create a bitvector (see Chapter 4, "Bitvectors") that determines which nodes have been marked already. Or, if you are using a linked node class, you could put a boolean in the node class that determines if a node has been visited before or not.

If you mark each node as it is processed, when the algorithm reaches node 4 for the second time, it will ignore it.

Let me show you the pseudo-code for the depth-first search:

```
DepthFirst( Node )
    Process( Node )
    Mark( Node )
    For Every Child of Node
        If NotMarked( Child )
            DepthFirst( Child )
        End If
    End For
End Function
```

The two lines in bold are the only things that are different from a preorder tree traversal.

> **TIP**
>
> In the real world, depth-first searches are always implemented using a stack. Each node, as it is processed, is placed on the stack. When a node that has no children is processed, it is popped off the stack, and the previous node is checked to see if it has any un-processed nodes. I used recursion here because it is easier to understand. Even though the recursive method for this is usually slower, it doesn't really matter since it is rarely used in game programming anyway. I just wanted you to know that this search exists.

The Breadth-First Search

Whereas the depth-first search went to the bottom of each search path first (hence the name *depth*), the *breadth-first search* is broader. (*Breadth* is a synonym for *broadness*.) This search method works by processing each node that is one step away from the starting node, and then every node that is two steps away, and then three steps, and so on.

Figure 17.19 shows a graph that has been traversed using the breadth-first search.

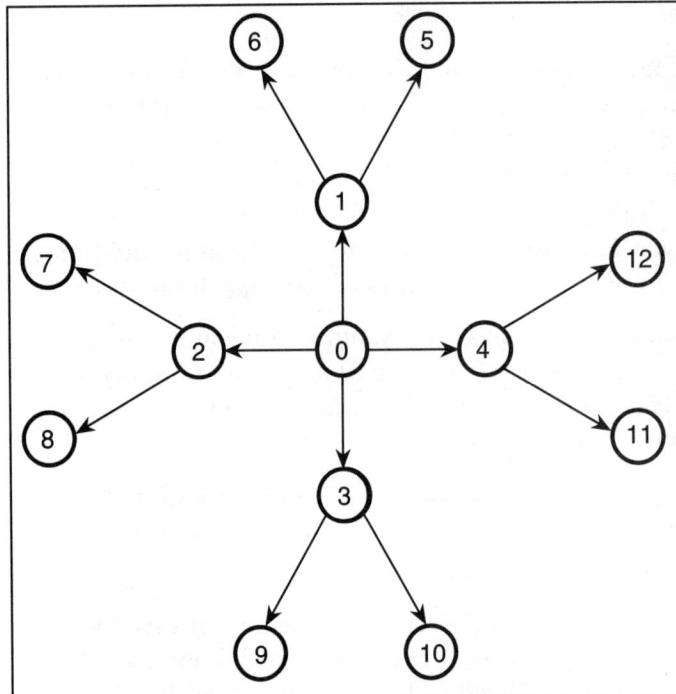

Figure 17.19

The breadth-first search processes all the nodes that are closest to the starting node first.

Notice how the four nodes connecting to node 0 are processed first, and then the nodes connecting to each of those nodes are processed after that. The breadth-first search is an outward search, where the nodes closest to the starting node are processed first and the farthest nodes are processed last.

Although this search is very simple to visualize, it is a little more difficult to put into code than the depth-first search is. To implement the algorithm, you need to enlist the help of our old pal the queue. (See Chapter 7, "Stacks and Queues," if you need a refresher.)

> **NOTE**
> The breadth-first search is very important in game programming—so important, in fact, that I dedicate an entire chapter to algorithms based on the breadth-first search: Chapter 24, "Tying It Together: Algorithms."

Here is the pseudo-code for the breadth-first search algorithm:

```
BreadthFirst( Node )
    Queue.Enqueue( Node )
```

```
    Mark( Node )
    While( Queue.IsNotEmpty )
        Process( Queue.Front )
        For Each Child of Queue.Front
            if NotMarked( Child )
                Queue.Enqueue( Child )
                Mark( Child )
            end if
        end For
        Queue.Dequeue()
    End While
End Function
```

As you can see, this function is a little more complex, and it isn't recursive, either. I'll have to illustrate this example a little bit more for you. Figure 17.20 shows a ten-node graph, which I will use to illustrate the algorithm.

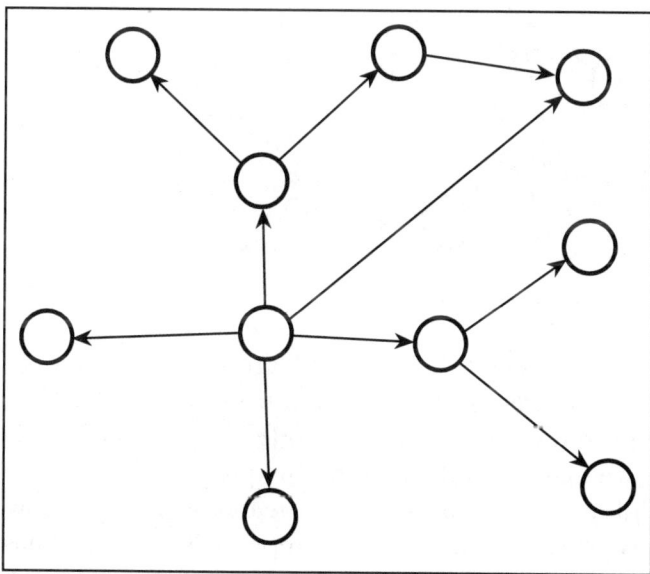

Figure 17.20

This is the graph that I demonstrate the breadth-first search on.

The node that this algorithm will start with is the center node in the graph—the one with five arcs coming out of it and no arcs leading into it.

The algorithm starts off by enqueing the middle node into the queue and marking it. When that step is completed, the while-loop starts, and it doesn't end until the queue is empty. Remember, the breadth-first search algorithm marks nodes as they are put into the queue instead of when they are processed. This is a small optimization that prevents nodes from being placed into the queue more than once. This becomes much more important later on, when I discuss finding paths through huge graphs in Chapter 24.

After the `while`-loop starts, it processes the node in front of the queue. After that, it looks at all the children of the node, and it adds them to the queue if they aren't marked. This ends up giving you the graph in Figure 17.21.

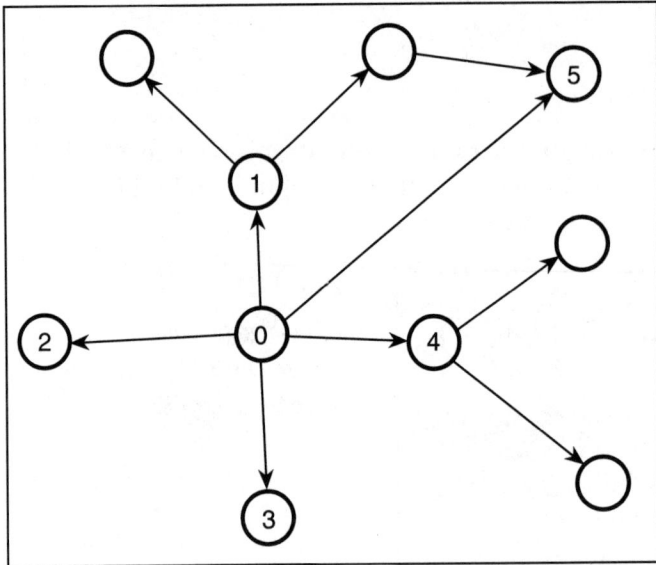

Figure 17.21

After the first iteration of the BFS, all nodes one arc away from the center are now processed, marked, and in the queue.

At this point, node 0 is processed, and nodes 1, 2, 3, 4, and 5 are all marked and on the queue. Node 0 has no more children, so it is removed from the queue. Now, node 1 is at the front of the queue, and the loop repeats. Node 1 is processed, and then the two children of node 1 are marked and added to the queue as nodes 6 and 7. Because it has no more children, 1 is removed from the queue, and 2 is now at the front of the queue, which is processed, and the loop repeats. This time, 2 has no children, so nothing is added to the queue. The same situation occurs with node 3: It has no children, so it is processed and removed from the queue, with nothing new added.

Node 4 is just like node 2; it is processed, and its two children are added to the queue as 8 and 9, and then 4 is removed. Node 5 has no children, so it is processed and removed from the queue, and finally, something interesting happens. Node 6 has one child, node 5. However, node 5 has already been marked, so it is not added into the queue. Finally, all of the rest of the nodes have no children, so they are processed and removed from the queue. Figure 17.22 shows the final order of processing.

> **NOTE**
> Make a special note of this: When node 5 was added to the queue, it was marked but not processed. When node 6 was processed, it only needed to check to see if node 5 was marked and not if it was processed already. It is possible for a node to be marked but not processed, so you don't want to add it to the queue again. This is why nodes are marked as they are put into the queue and not as they are processed.

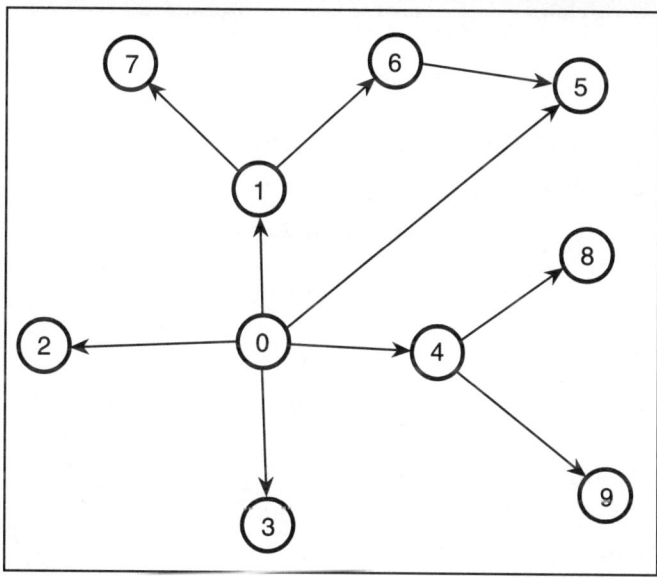

Figure 17.22

Here is the final processing order of the BFS.

A Final Word on Graph Traversals

In this section, I only showed you the pseudo-code for the traversals and not any actual code. I get to the code later on when I show you how to code a linked graph class. In Chapter 24, I even show you many different ways to code different BFS variations on different types of graphs, so you haven't seen the end of them yet.

The DFS isn't an important algorithm in game programming, but the BFS definitely is, for reasons that will become very clear in Chapter 24. The one thing that these algorithms have in common is that they process every node that is reachable from a given starting point. In uni-directional graphs, this is important because of the many different one-way routes that can exist in a graph.

Using this method, you can easily check to see which nodes are reachable by processing them or check which nodes are unreachable by checking to see if they aren't marked.

Graphical Demonstration: Graph Traversals

This is Graphical Demonstrations 17-2, which you can find on the CD in the directory \demonstrations\ch17\Demo02 - Traversals\.

Compiling the Demo

This demonstration uses the SDLGUI library that I have developed for the book. For more information about this library, see Appendix B.

To compile this demo, either open up the workspace file in the directory or create your own project using the settings described in Appendix B. If you create your own project, all of the files you need to include are in the directory.

This demo is almost the same as Graphical Demonstration 17-1, with the addition of two buttons that animate the two traversal algorithms for you. You build a graph the same way that you did for the previous demo, and when you are done, you click on one of the traversal buttons.

After you do that, you should move your mouse cursor over the node you want to start the traversal on and click it. The animation will start and the order in which the numbers are processed will appear in the nodes as they are processed.

Figure 17.23 shows a screenshot from the demo.

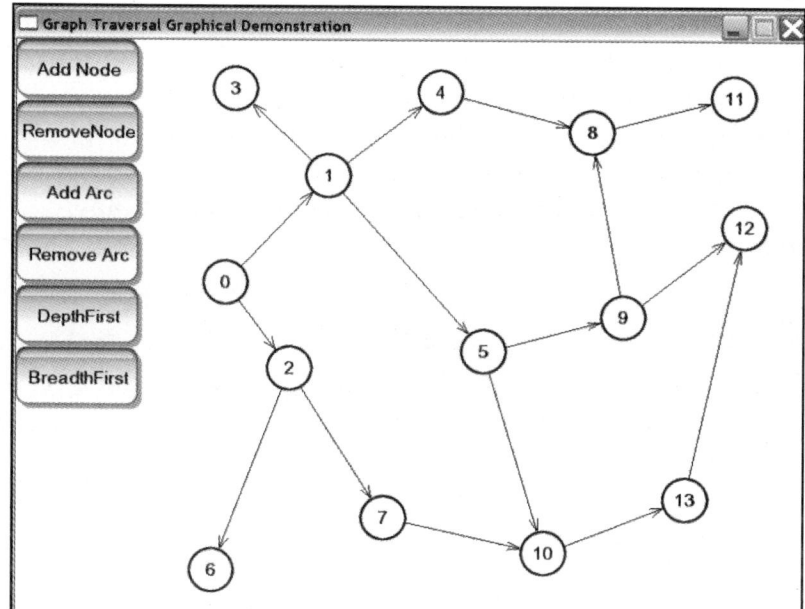

Figure 17.23

Here is a screenshot from the demo.

The Graph Class

Now I will show you how to program a linked-node uni-directional weighted graph class. The other graph types (direction tables, adjacency tables, and tilemaps) are simple and need nothing more than a 2D array to implement.

However, a flexible linked graph class is a little more difficult to program. The code in this section can be found on the CD in the file \structures\graph.h.

All of the graph classes use two template parameters, a `NodeType` and an `ArcType`. The `NodeType` datatype determines the kind of data that is stored in each node, and the `ArcType` datatype determines the kind of data that is stored in each arc (the *weight* or *cost* of the arc).

The GraphArc Class

This is just a simple class that is meant to store a pointer to a node and associate a weight with the arc:

```
template<class NodeType, class ArcType>
class GraphArc
{
public:
```

```
    GraphNode<NodeType, ArcType>* m_node;
    ArcType m_weight;
};
```

There isn't much to explain about this class except that it is flexible enough that you can use any kind of datatype for the weight of the arc. For example, you can use integers or floats or even create a custom weight class to use with this. Most of the time, you'll probably just use numbers.

The GraphNode Classes

After you have the arc class, you need to create a node class. This class will be a little bit more complex than the tree node class, but not much.

The Structure

This simple node class only needs three variables:

```
template<class NodeType, class ArcType>
class GraphNode
{
public:
    typedef GraphArc<NodeType, ArcType> Arc;
    typedef GraphNode<NodeType, ArcType> Node;

    NodeType m_data;
    DLinkedList<Arc> m_arcList;
    bool m_marked;
};
```

The two `typedefs` at the top are there to make your life easier; instead of typing `GraphArc<NodeType, ArcType>` every time you want to use an arc, all you need to type is `Arc`. The same goes with the `GraphNode` class.

After that, the three variables are declared. The graph holds its data in `m_data`, just like every other node class in this book.

Like the tree node class, this class has a linked list. Instead of holding pointers to other nodes, though, the linked list holds `Arcs`.

Finally, the last variable is a boolean, and it determines if the node has been marked or not. This is important when you are performing searches and traversals on the graph. You remember them from earlier.

The Functions

Like the linked list and tree node classes you've seen before, this class needs a few helper functions to make it easier to use. The functions of the graph node class are primarily concerned with adding, finding, and removing arcs from the node, the most common operations.

All of these functions are relatively simple.

Adding an Arc

This function adds an arc to the current node, leading to a different node with a given weight.

```
void AddArc( Node* p_node, ArcType p_weight )
{
    Arc a;
    a.m_node = p_node;
    a.m_weight = p_weight;
    m_arcList.Append( a );
}
```

The function takes a pointer to the destination node and a weight for the arc. After that, it creates a temporary arc and sets the arc's node pointer and weight variables. Then, it uses the linked list's `Append` function to add the new arc to the end of the node's arc list. Like I said, it is pretty simple.

Finding an Arc

The algorithm for this is fairly simple; all you need to do is use a linked list iterator to search through every arc until you find the one that points to the node you want.

```
Arc* GetArc( Node* p_node )
{
    DListIterator<Arc> itr = m_arcList.GetIterator();
    for( itr.Start(); itr.Valid(); itr.Forth() )
    {
        if( itr.Item().m_node == p_node )
            return &(itr.Item());
    }
    return 0;
}
```

The function returns a pointer to the arc, so you can modify it if you want. Also, because it returns a pointer, it can return 0 if the arc you want to find doesn't exist in the node.

The function simply makes a linked list iterator and loops through, checking to see if the arc you want to find is located within the arc list. If so, then the function uses the & operator to get the address of the arc and returns it. If the loop terminates before the function ends, then the arc doesn't exist in the node, so 0 is returned.

Removing an Arc

Removing an arc is the same as finding an arc, except the line where the address of the arc is returned is changed into this:

```
m_arcList.Remove( itr );
```

The arc is removed from the arclist, and the function returns. Of course, if the arc isn't found in the arclist, then the function does nothing.

The Graph Class

The last class that is used is the actual Graph class. This class manages all of the nodes and has functions to add nodes, remove nodes, add arcs, remove arcs, clear the marks on the nodes, and traverse the nodes.

The Structure

You can choose to implement your Graph class in a few different ways, as I've mentioned a few times before. You've already seen the node class, so you know that I prefer to use linked lists for arcs. Because arcs in a graph are usually likely to change often, I wanted to use a simple class that is easy to insert and remove items from.

The node situation is a little different, though. In most graph applications, nodes are inserted and removed far less often, so I prefer to have an array of nodes in the graph rather than a linked list. The choice is really up to you, but this implementation will use an array of graph nodes.

```
template<class NodeType, class ArcType>
class Graph
{
public:
    typedef GraphArc<NodeType, ArcType> Arc;
    typedef GraphNode<NodeType, ArcType> Node;
```

```
        Array<Node*> m_nodes;
        int m_count;
};
```

Again, the arc and the node `typedefs` are present to make life easy on you, so your code doesn't end up looking ugly.

The graph class only has two variables in it: an array of `Node` pointers and a `count` variable. As you can guess, the array holds the nodes in the graph. Because I'm using an array, the graph will not always have a full array of nodes, so the count variable keeps track of the number of nodes that are actually in the graph at the moment.

The Constructor

Because the graph has an `Array` in it and the `Array` class requires a parameter to determine what size it should be, the `Graph` class also needs a constructor to do the same thing.

Also, because the node array holds pointers and the array will probably contain junk data when it is initialized, you need to loop through the array and clear every index to 0.

```
Graph( int p_size ) : m_nodes( p_size )
{
    int i;
    for( i = 0; i < p_size; i++ )
        m_nodes[i] = 0;
    m_count = 0;
}
```

The `Graph` constructor takes an integer, which will determine the size of the node array. On the first line, the standard "member constructor" notation is used to initialize `m_nodes` to the proper size.

After that, the function loops through each index in the array and clears it to 0. You don't want the node pointers pointing to nodes that don't actually exist.

Finally, the count variable is set to 0.

The Destructor

The destructor is fairly simple, and it is needed to delete all of the nodes in the graph.

```
~Graph()
{
    int index;
    for( index = 0; index < m_nodes.m_size; index++ )
    {
        if( m_nodes[index] != 0 )
            delete m_nodes[index];
    }
}
```

It is just a simple loop that deletes any nodes that are valid. Remember, some nodes in the array may not be valid, so you need to check if they are 0 or not.

Adding a Node to the Graph

One of the benefits of using an array for storing nodes is that you can easily access the nodes by using an index number. This method of storing the nodes makes it easy to add and remove nodes to the graph.

```
bool AddNode( NodeType p_data, int p_index )
{
    if( m_nodes[p_index] != 0 )
        return false;
    m_nodes[p_index] = new Node;
    m_nodes[p_index]->m_data = p_data;
    m_nodes[p_index]->m_marked = false;
    m_count++;
    return true;
}
```

The function takes two parameters: the data that you want to store in the node and the index where you want the node to be placed. If a node already exists, the function doesn't add the new node and returns `false`, signifying that the operation failed.

If the index is empty, then a new node is created at the index, and its data is set to the data from the parameter `p_data`. Its `m_marked` flag is also cleared, and the count of the graph is increased by one. Finally, the function returns `true`, which means that it was successful.

Removing a Node from the Graph

Removing a node from a graph isn't as simple as you may think it is. Sure, you could just delete the node from the graph, but what happens then? Figure 17.24

shows a graph before and after you delete a node if you just delete the node and do nothing else.

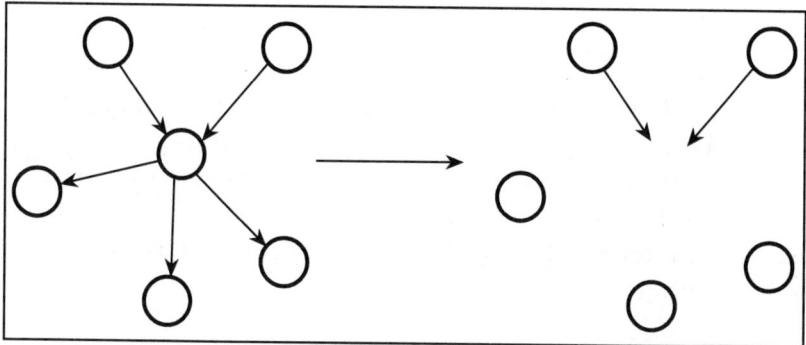

Figure 17.24

Deleting a node without deleting the arcs that point to it can cause large bugs.

You can see that all arcs coming out of that node are deleted, but all arcs pointing to the deleted node still exist! The two nodes are now pointing to a node that doesn't exist anymore, which is a very bad thing.

So, to delete a node in a graph, you need to search through every node in the graph to see if it points to the node you want to delete. This makes the node removal algorithm very slow, but it is a necessity to keep the graph valid.

To make the function more readable, I separate it into sections.

```
void RemoveNode( int p_index )
{
    if( m_nodes[p_index] == 0 )
        return;
```

First, the function takes the index of the node you want to remove. If the node doesn't exist, the function returns and doesn't do anything.

```
    int node;
    Arc* arc;
```

These two variables are declared next; they will be used to loop through all the nodes in the graph and store the results of searching for arcs.

Now the loop starts:

```
    for( node = 0; node < m_nodes.Size(); node++ )
    {
        if( m_nodes[node] != 0 )
        {
```

```
        arc = m_nodes[node]->GetArc( m_nodes[p_index] );
        if( arc != 0 )
            RemoveArc( node, p_index );
    }
}
```

This goes through every node in the graph. For each node, if it is valid, it checks to see if there is an arc from the current node pointing to the node you want to remove. If there is, then `arc` will have a pointer to the arc that exists between the two nodes. If there isn't, `arc` will be zero. If an arc exists from `node` to `p_index` (the index of the node that is being removed), then the `RemoveArc` function is called to remove the arc from the graph.

Finally:

```
    delete m_nodes[p_index];
    m_nodes[p_index] = 0;
    m_count--;
}
```

The node is deleted, the index that it was in is cleared to 0, and the count is decreased by 1.

As you can see, deleting a node from a graph is a slow algorithm. Its worst case performance is $O(n^2)$ because you have to search through every node, and every arc in every node, which is essentially a doubly nested `for`-loop (remember that in a graph, each node can point to every other node in the graph, which means that in the worst case, every node has a pointer to every other node).

Adding an Arc to the Graph

The function to add an arc to the graph is made simple by the helper functions that I showed you earlier in the node class.

```
bool AddArc( int p_from, int p_to, ArcType p_weight )
{
    if( m_nodes[p_from] == 0 || m_nodes[p_to] == 0 )
        return false;
    if( m_nodes[p_from]->GetArc( m_nodes[p_to] ) != 0 )
        return false;
    m_nodes[p_from]->AddArc( m_nodes[p_to], p_weight );
    return true;
}
```

The function adds an arc from index `p_from` to index `p_to` with a weight of `p_weight`. The first thing the function does is make sure that both nodes exist, and if either of them doesn't exist, the function returns `false`, for failure.

After that, the function checks to see if an arc already exists from the first node to the second. If so, the function exits with `false` again because you don't want to be adding two arcs from one node to another in a graph.

Finally, the function calls the `AddArc` function on the first node, adding the second node and the weight to its arc list, and then returns `true`, signifying that the function completed successfully.

Removing an Arc from the Graph

The arc removal algorithm is similar to the `AddArc` function:

```
void RemoveArc( int p_from, int p_to )
{
    if( m_nodes[p_from] == 0 || m_nodes[p_to] == 0 )
        return;
    m_nodes[p_from]->RemoveArc( m_nodes[p_to] );
}
```

First, the function verifies that both nodes exist in the graph. If either of them doesn't exist, the function exits without doing anything.

Then, the function calls the `RemoveArc` function of the first node, telling it to remove the second node.

Finding an Arc in the Graph

This function is almost the same as the arc removal function, but instead of removing the arc, it returns a pointer to the arc:

```
Arc* GetArc( int p_from, int p_to )
{
    if( m_nodes[p_from] == 0 || m_nodes[p_to] == 0 )
        return 0;
    return m_nodes[p_from]->GetArc( m_nodes[p_to] );
}
```

That's all there is to it.

Clearing All the Marks

This function is here to clear all the marks on every node, which you should do before calling the traversal algorithms.

```
void ClearMarks()
{
    int index;
    for( index = 0; index < m_nodes.m_size; index++ )
    {
        if( m_nodes[index] != 0 )
            m_nodes[index]->m_marked = false;
    }
}
```

The function clears the mark on every valid node. Very simple.

The Depth-First Search

Earlier, I showed you the pseudo-code for this algorithm, and here I show you how it is actually coded.

```
void DepthFirst( Node* p_node, void (*p_process)(Node*) )
{
    if( p_node == 0 )
        return;
```

The function takes a node pointer, which is the starting node, and a function pointer. (You've seen them before in Chapter 11 and Chapter 15, "Game Trees and Minimax Trees," and I also explain them in Appendix A, "A C++ Primer.") The function pointer is a function that takes a node pointer as a parameter and processes the node, allowing you to use the same algorithm with different processing functions.

If the node that is being processed is null, then the function just exits.

```
        p_process( p_node );
        p_node->m_marked = true;
```

Now the node that is passed into the function is processed and marked.

```
        DListIterator<GraphArc<Coordinates, int> > itr =
            p_node->m_arcList.GetIterator();
        for( itr.Start(); itr.Valid(); itr.Forth() )
        {
```

```
            if( itr.Item().m_node->m_marked == false )
            {
                DepthFirst( itr.Item().m_node, p_process );
            }
        }
    }
```

This last section creates an iterator and iterates through all the arcs in the current node. If any of the arcs point to a node that isn't marked, the function recursively calls the `DepthFirst` function on that node, which is almost the same as the tree preorder traversal function.

The Breadth-First Search

As with the depth-first search, the breadth-first search algorithm has already been given to you, so here is the code:

```
void BreadthFirst( Node* p_node, void (*p_process)(Node*) )
{
    if( p_node == 0 )
        return;
```

The parameters are the same with this function and the `DepthFirst` function, and so are the first two lines of the function. If the starting node is null, then the function just exits.

```
    LQueue<Node*> queue;
    DListIterator<Arc> itr;
```

Now the queue and the arc iterator are created.

```
    queue.Enqueue( p_node );
    p_node->m_marked = true;
```

This is the first step of the actual algorithm; the starting node is placed in the queue and marked.

Here is the main loop:

```
    while( queue.Count() != 0 )
    {
        p_process( queue.Front() );
        itr = queue.Front()->m_arcList.GetIterator();
        for( itr.Start(); itr.Valid(); itr.Forth() )
        {
```

```
            if( itr.Item().m_node->m_marked == false )
            {
                itr.Item().m_node->m_marked = true;
                queue.Enqueue( itr.Item().m_node );
            }
        }
        queue.Dequeue();
    }
}
```

While the queue is not empty, the loop processes the first node on the queue and then adds all non-marked child nodes from the first node onto the queue and marks them. Finally, the first node is dequeued, and the loop repeats.

Application: Making a Direction-Table Dungeon

This is Game Demo 17-1, which can be found on the CD in the directory \demonstrations\ch17\Game01 - DTDungeon\.

> ### Compiling the Demo
>
> This demonstration uses the SDLHelpers library that I have developed for the book. For more information about this library, see Appendix B.
>
> To compile this demo, either open up the workspace file in the directory or create your own project using the settings described in Appendix B. If you create your own project, all of the files you need to include are in the directory.

Earlier, I showed you how a *direction table* graph works, and I said that all it needs is a 2D array. In this demo, I show you how to implement one.

The Map

The first thing you need is an array that stores the map:

```
Array2D<int> g_map( ROOMS, DIRECTIONS );
```

Application: Making a Direction-Table Dungeon

The array simply stores integers. If you access the array with a certain room and direction, the contents of the array at that index should be the number of the room that the exit leads to, as I showed you previously.

The demo has two constant variables, ROOMS and DIRECTIONS, which specify the number of rooms there are in the dungeon and how many directions there are. (This demo only supports four directions.)

Creating the Map

The map that is used in the demo is fairly simple and only has 16 rooms. Figure 17.25 shows the map that is used in the demo and its direction table.

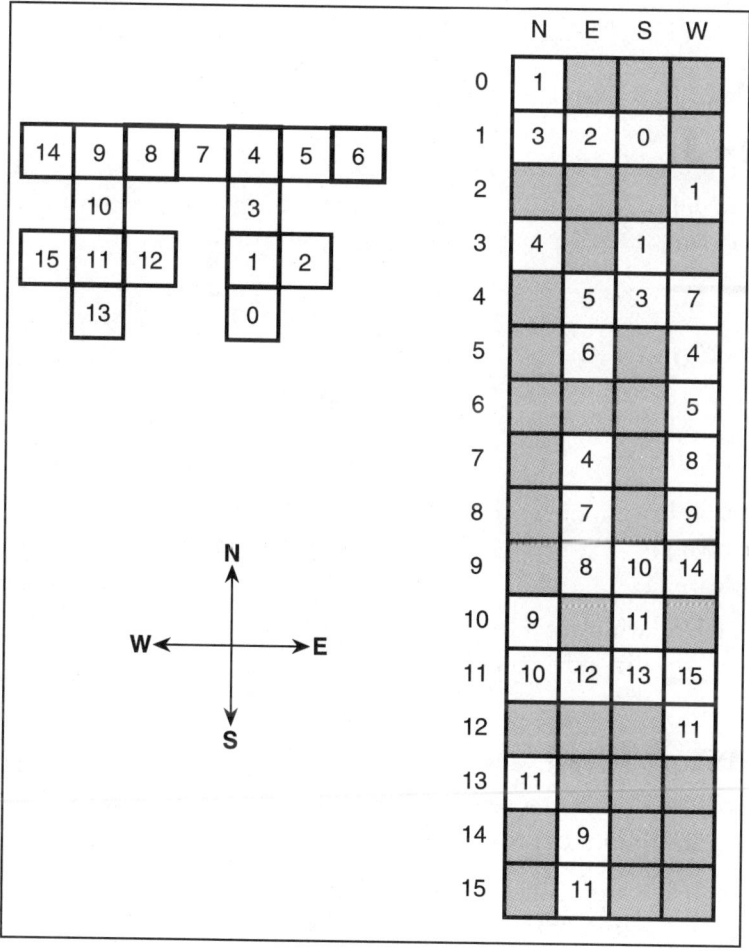

Figure 17.25

Here is the map in the demo and its direction table.

You should already know how to read this table; if not, please go back and re-read the section in this chapter where I introduce them to you.

If you look at the direction table, I've shaded all the invalid entries. All of this data needs to be stored in a 2D array somehow, so I've picked an arbitrary value that means, "This exit is invalid." That number is −1.

Because most of the entries in the table are invalid, it makes sense to fill the entire table with −1 first and then overwrite the valid entries with their correct values. The function that creates the map will first fill in every cell with −1, like this:

```
int room, direction;
for( room = 0; room < ROOMS; room++ )
{
    for( direction = 0; direction < DIRECTIONS; direction++ )
    {
        g_map.Get( room, direction ) = -1;
    }
}
```

After that, the function will fill in the valid entries:

```
g_map.Get( 0, 0 ) = 1;

g_map.Get( 1, 0 ) = 3;
g_map.Get( 1, 1 ) = 2;
g_map.Get( 1, 2 ) = 0;

g_map.Get( 2, 3 ) = 1;

g_map.Get( 3, 0 ) = 4;
g_map.Get( 3, 2 ) = 1;
```

There are 30 entries altogether, which is a lot to show, so I just showed you the entries for the first four rooms. I'm sure you get the idea.

Drawing the Map

I admit it; I found a use for the depth-first search. I used it to draw the map simply because it is easier to program than a breadth-first search.

The `DrawMap` function is recursive and is just a modified depth-first search. It takes the current room number and *x* and *y* drawing coordinates as its parameters.

The Helper Structures

I've used a few "helper" structures to make this function easier to program, however.

The first is a bitvector (see Chapter 4 if you are unfamiliar with bitvectors):

```
Bitvector g_marked( ROOMS );
```

This bitvector keeps track of which rooms have been marked during the drawing process because there isn't a specific node class that can be used to contain a marked boolean. The array is the same size as the number of rooms in the map, so each node corresponds to an index within the bitvector.

The next helper structure is a 2D array:

```
int directionarray[4][2] = { { 0, -64 },
                             { 64, 0 },
                             { 0, 64 },
                             { -64, 0 } };
```

This is simply an array that tells the algorithm how many pixels to move horizontally or vertically in each direction. For example, direction 0 corresponds with north, which is up on the computer screen. If you are drawing the tile directly north of the current tile, the *x* coordinate doesn't change at all, which is the meaning of the 0 in the first index. Of course, a computer screen's coordinates increase when going from the top to the bottom, so you need to subtract 64 pixels (the tile is 64 pixels high) to draw the tile on top of the current one.

The same goes for the other three directions; direction 1 (east) is 64 pixels to the right, direction 2 (south) is 64 pixels downward, and direction 3 (west) is 64 pixels to the left.

The DrawMap Function

Now you finally get to draw the map!

```
void DrawMap( int p_room, int p_x, int p_y )
{
    SDLBlit( g_tile, g_window, p_x, p_y );
    g_marked.Set( p_room, true );
```

Remember, the first part of the DFS algorithm is to process the current node, and this does so by drawing the current node. Then it marks the current node.

After that, it loops through all four directions of the current node:

```
int room;
int direction;
for( direction = 0; direction < DIRECTIONS; direction++ )
{
    room = g_map.Get( p_room, direction );
    if( room != -1 )
    {
        if( g_marked[room] == false )
        {
            DrawMap( room,
                     p_x + directionarray[direction][0],
                     p_y + directionarray[direction][1] );
        }
    }
}
```

For each direction, the function retrieves the value of the 2D array and stores it in room. If the room number isn't –1, then it is a valid exit, so the function then checks to see if that room has been marked. If it hasn't been marked, the function recursively calls itself and tells itself to draw the new room at the appropriate coordinates.

Simple enough, right?

Moving Around the Map

Finally, you need some method of moving around the map. Luckily for you, this process is simple and painless.

First of all, the program has a global integer that stores the index of the room that the player is currently in:

```
int g_room = 0;
```

From that line, you can see that the player starts off in room 0 in this demo.

Now, whenever a key is pressed, this segment of code is executed:

```
x = -1;
switch( event.key.keysym.sym )
{
```

```
case SDLK_UP:
    x = 0;
    break;
case SDLK_RIGHT:
    x = 1;
    break;
case SDLK_DOWN:
    x = 2;
    break;
case SDLK_LEFT:
    x = 3;
    break;
}
```

The four keys that change x are the up, right, down, and left arrow keys on the keyboard. Each key corresponds to a direction; the up arrow key is direction 0 (north), and so on. Whenever an arrow key is pressed, x is changed to the correct direction.

Now that you know that the user wants to move somewhere, you need to check to see if she can move in that direction:

```
if( x != -1 )
{
    if( g_map.Get( g_room, x ) != -1 )
        g_room = g_map.Get( g_room, x );
}
```

First, make sure *x* is a valid direction by making sure it isn't –1. If so, then check to see that the entry in the direction table isn't –1, either. If not, then the player is moving to a valid room, and the function makes the current room index point to the new room. This is a very simple and elegant way to store and move around simple maps.

Playing the Demo

The demo is very simple to play; all you do is move the little dude around the map using the arrow keys. Figure 17.26 shows a screenshot from the demo in action.

518 17. Graphs

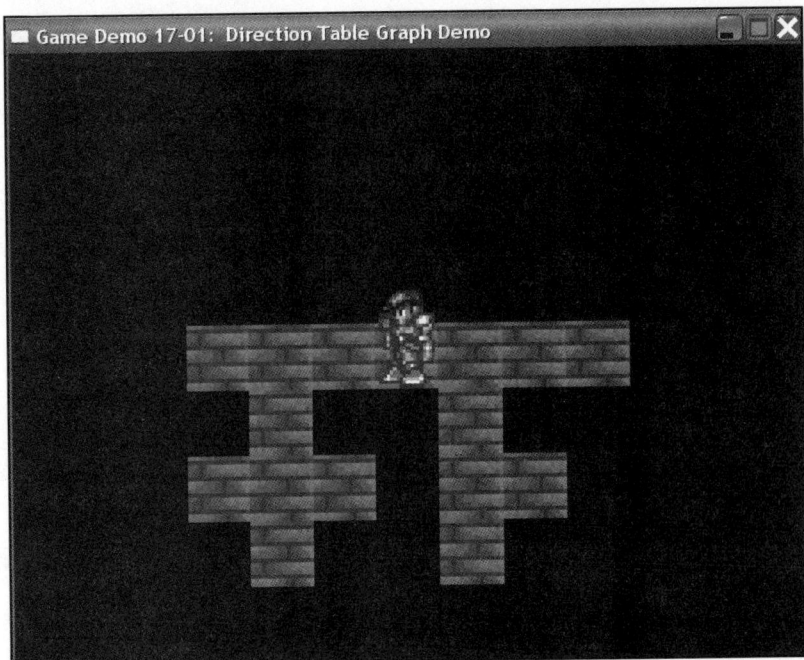

Figure 17.26

Here is a screenshot from the game demo.

Application: Portal Engines

This is Game Demo 17-2, which can be found on the CD in the directory \demonstrations\ch17\Game02 – Portals\.

> ### Compiling the Demo
>
> This demonstration uses the SDLHelpers library that I have developed for the book. For more information about this library, see Appendix B.
>
> To compile this demo, either open up the workspace file in the directory or create your own project using the settings described in Appendix B. If you create your own project, all of the files you need to include are in the directory.

Portal engine was a huge buzzword a few years ago, right after the *BSP* phase of the game industry. Games like *Descent*, *Quake2*, and the ill-fated *Prey* used portal engines to gain a huge boost in performance.

Application: Portal Engines

First I want to start off by telling you an optimization hint. Most people, when they start programming in 3D (or even 2D), think that they can just throw the entire game's graphics at the video card and let the clipping and culling algorithms sort everything out.

This is an inefficient method of rendering things, however. It is far more efficient to figure out what the user can see and then tell the video card to only draw that.

> **NOTE**
> *Clipping* and *culling* are two words that mean similar things. When you draw things on the screen, sometimes you send a bunch of pixels, and some of them might be off the screen. When the computer figures out which ones aren't on the screen, this is called *clipping*. Earlier in the drawing cycle, you should figure out which whole items cannot be seen and prevent them from even being sent to the video card to be drawn. This process is called *culling*.

> **TIP**
> It is more efficient to send less information to the video card because any information you send to the card must travel down the slow system *bus*. This bus is many times slower than the video card or the processor, and most of the time, if you send too much graphics data that won't even be drawn in the end, your performance is going to go down the tubes.

So the portal method of drawing game levels is very efficient because it segments a level into many different parts and then determines which segments should be drawn.

> **NOTE**
> Because I do not have the space or time to teach you 3D graphics, I can only show you this process working in a 2D environment. I hope you don't mind, but the focus is on the data structures involved, not the graphics.

Sectors

The very first thing that happens is that the level is broken up into sectors. If you've made custom levels for any first-person shooter game since *Doom*, you probably know what a *sector* is. A sector is simply a room in a level, like Figure 17.27 shows.

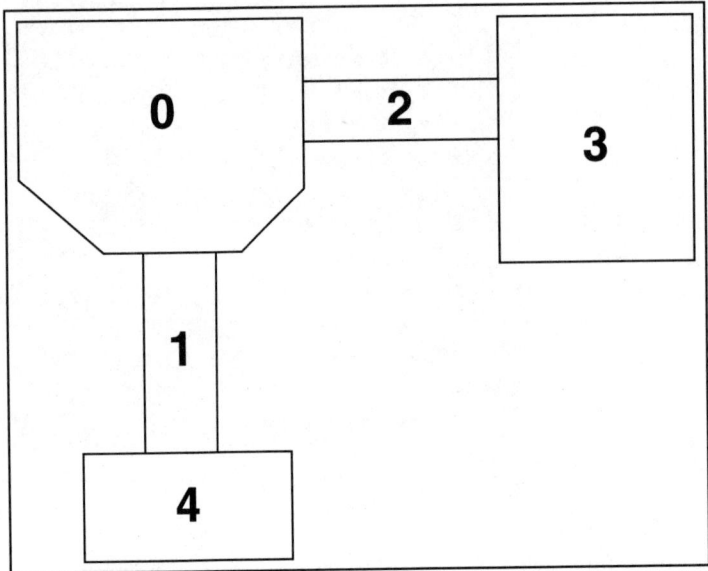

Figure 17.27

This is a five-sector level.

This is a simple overhead view of a level in a game that is separated into five sectors. This can very easily be broken down into a graph, as you might guess (this is a chapter about graphs, after all!), which you can see in Figure 17.28.

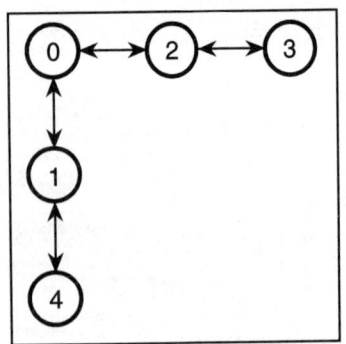

Figure 17.28

This is the level represented as a graph.

See, a portal engine keeps track of the number of exits in any given room so that you know which portals are visible and which sectors can be seen through a portal. Thus, you can send only a few sectors out of any given level to be drawn instead of the whole level.

Determining Sector Visibility

A true portal engine uses a *visibility* algorithm, which determines which sectors are visible from any given sector and viewpoint. This is a complex algorithm that takes a long time to perfect, and it is somewhat outside of the scope of this book, so I want to show you instead a quick little hack that allows you to quickly draw adjacent sectors while still keeping most of the benefits of a portal engine.

The Depth-Limited Depth-First Search

The method I'm going to show you is called the *depth-limited depth-first search* (DLDFS). Using this method, you can control how many levels of a depth-first search are traversed. For example, look at the graph in Figure 17.29.

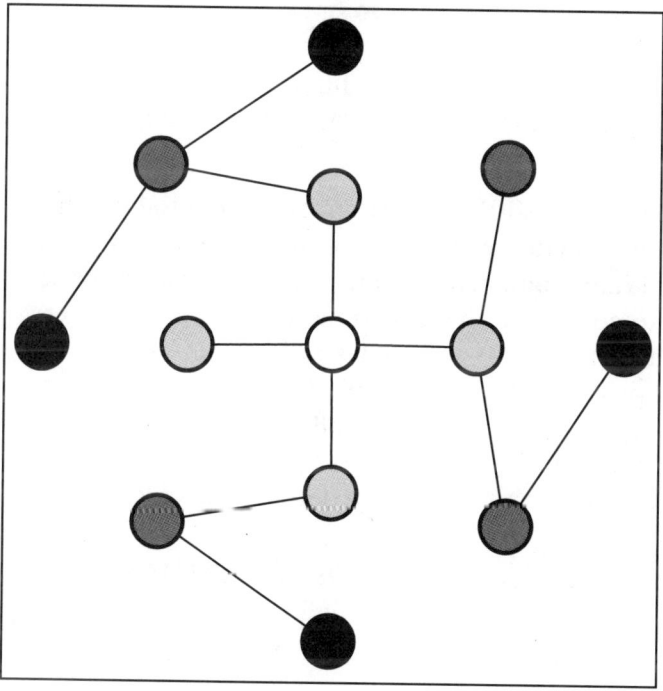

Figure 17.29

Here is another graph, color-coded from lightest to darkest by the number of arcs each node is from the center.

The graph in the figure is color-coded by depth from the center node, which is white. All nodes that are one arc away from the center node are light gray, all nodes that are two arcs away from the center node are dark gray, and all nodes that are three arcs away from the center node are black. Using a DLDFS algorithm, you can specify how deep the search goes. For example, if you want the algorithm to only visit nodes within two arcs from the starting node, the black nodes in the figure would not be processed. If you tell the algorithm to only visit one arc from the center, then it will not process the black nodes or the dark gray nodes.

The DLDFS search works exactly like the regular DFS, except that it has one more parameter:

```
DepthFirst( Node, depth )
    if depth — 0, then return
    Process( Node )
    Mark( Node )
    For Every Child of Node
        If NotMarked( Child )
            DepthFirst( Child, depth - 1 )
        End If
    End For
End Function
```

The bold lines of code show you the only lines that are different in a DLDFS. The algorithm checks to see if the depth is 0, and if so, it returns and doesn't process any further.

Later on, when the function recursively calls itself, it subtracts 1 from the depth parameter and passes that into the function call. This is another great example of recursion. If you look at Figure 17.29 again, you can say, "I want to process every node within two arcs of the white node," but that gets translated into, "I want to process every node within one arc of the light-gray nodes", which can then be translated again into, "I want to process every node within 0 arcs of the dark-gray nodes." So that is essentially what you are doing. If you call this function on the center node with a depth value of 3, then the function will process the white node and then call the function on each of its children with a depth value of 2.

Using the DLDFS in a Portal Engine

Using this method, you can limit the number of sectors that are drawn at any given time. In the demo, I've picked an arbitrary limit of three levels, but this number really depends on how the sectors are arranged.

Using the DLDFS, you can be assured that only sectors within a certain range are drawn, which can be quite a cool effect, as you'll see in the demo.

Coding the Demo

Now that I've got most of the theory out of the way, I can get onto the good stuff: code! When I first started making this demo, I thought it would be very difficult to do and wouldn't demonstrate much. To my surprise, the demo turned out to be very easy to code, and the result was great!

The Sector Class

The very first thing you need is a sector class. For this demo, I'm using a very primitive rectangle-based sector class. Even games like *DOOM* had much more complex sector formats than this.

The sector class has four integers: *x* and *y* coordinates and a height and a width:

```
class Sector
{
public:
    int x;
    int y;
    int w;
    int h;
};
```

> **NOTE**
>
> More complex sector classes will probably use an array of vertexes, which define walls. If you're using a 3D engine, the vertexes will probably be grouped into triplets of triangles, and if you're using a "2.5D" engine like *DOOM*, the vertexes will be grouped into pairs to form the vertical line segments that turn into walls. The idea behind an engine like this is to minimize the amount of things that are drawn, so the sector class might know which items or characters are within the sector at any given time. That way, you can quickly draw only those characters and items that are within the sector.

The Map

I created a 16-sector map for use in the demo, which is shown in Figure 17.30.

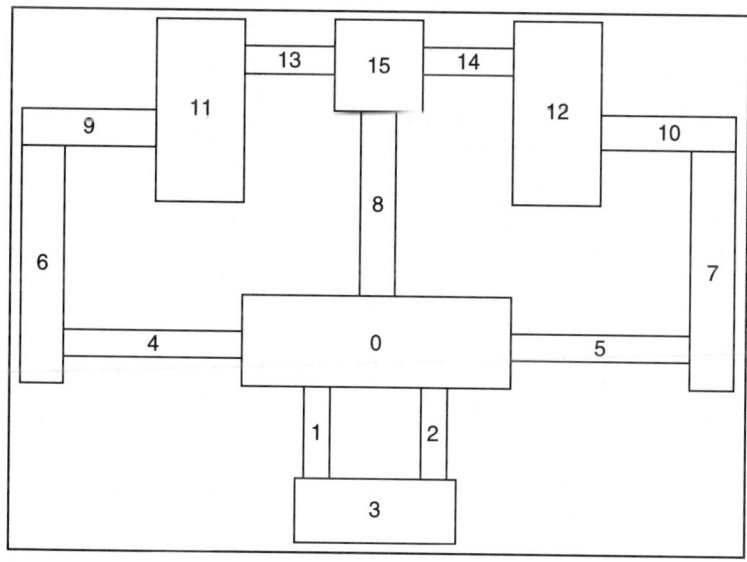

Figure 17.30

Here is the map used in this demo.

Each sector is labeled with its sector number. I used graph paper to draw the map and figure out the coordinates of each sector, which I did not include in the figure, because it would be too crowded.

In the demo, the graph is declared like this:

```
Graph<Sector, int> g_map( ROOMS );
```

The ROOMS variable is actually a constant declared at the beginning of the program that allows you to easily change how many rooms are used in the demo. The graph nodes hold Sectors, which I showed you previously, and the arcs hold ints, though they really don't mean anything in this demo.

> **TIP**
>
> In a real-world game, you'd use an unweighted graph for this demo. However, because I'm limited on space, I can only show you one graph class without weight, so I'm stuck with using it. In essence, it is far easier for me to ignore the weight on the arcs and sacrifice a little memory in the demo rather than code a whole new unweighted graph class.

Initializing the Map

The map is initialized in a special function called InitialiseMap. Because the map initialization is a long and tedious function, I only show you the sections that are important.

First, you need to create each sector in the map and add it to the graph. This is how the first sector is created:

```
Sector s;
s.x = 300;
s.y = 400;
s.w = 300;
s.h = 100;
g_map.AddNode( s, 0 );
```

The sector has a position of (300,400) and a size of 300 × 100. On the final line, the sector is added to the graph into index 0. This function then continues to repeat the process for all 16 sectors in the map.

> **TIP**
>
> It would be far easier to store the map data on disk somewhere so that you can easily create an automated function that reads the file and creates a map based on the information in the file. The file format would probably store the number of sectors in the map, the coordinates and size of each sector, and finally, which sectors are linked to other sectors.

After all of the sectors are added to the map, you need to connect the sectors with their portals (which is really just another name for an arc).

From Figure 17.30, you can see that Sector 0 connects to Sectors 1, 2, 4, 5, and 8. Therefore, the code to attach those sectors looks like this:

```
g_map.AddArc( 0, 1, 0 );
g_map.AddArc( 0, 2, 0 );
g_map.AddArc( 0, 4, 0 );
g_map.AddArc( 0, 5, 0 );
g_map.AddArc( 0, 8, 0 );
```

Each line adds an arc from Sector 0 to one of the other sectors with a weight of 0 (remember, the weights aren't used in this demo).

Now, because this is a uni-directional graph class, you need to add arcs from all five of those sectors back to sector 0. This code shows the arcs that Sector 1 has:

```
g_map.AddArc( 1, 0, 0 );
g_map.AddArc( 1, 3, 0 );
```

Sector 1 leads back to Sector 0 and has an arc leading to Sector 3.

NOTE
You don't *need* to add two arcs to every pair of sectors that are connected, of course. You can achieve some neat "hidden room" effects by using only one arc. For example, if you didn't add an arc from Sector 1 or Sector 2 to Sector 3, then you can't see Sector 3 from either of those hallways, but the sector still exists.

Drawing the Map

Like I said before, the engine will use a depth-limited depth-first search to draw the map. I gave you the pseudo-code for that, and now here is the full code:

```
void DrawMap( GraphNode<Sector, int>* p_node, int p_x, int p_y, int p_depth,
SDL_Color p_col )
{
    if( p_depth == 0 || p_node == 0 )
        return;
    SDLBox( g_window,
            p_node->m_data.x - p_x, p_node->m_data.y - p_y,
            p_node->m_data.w, p_node->m_data.h,
            p_col );
    p_node->m_marked = true;
    DListIterator< GraphArc<Sector,int> > itr;
```

```
    itr = p_node->m_arcList.GetIterator();
    for( itr.Start(); itr.Valid(); itr.Forth() )
    {
        if( itr.Item().m_node->m_marked == false )
        {
            DrawMap( itr.Item().m_node, p_x, p_y, p_depth - 1, p_col );
        }
    }
}
```

The function is a little bit more complex than the pseudo-code I showed you earlier, but it isn't difficult to comprehend. The *x* and *y* coordinates passed into the function serve as the *global offset* of the map, which means that each sector will be drawn relative to those coordinates. This allows you to easily scroll the map around by changing the coordinates.

The function basically draws a rectangle to represent the sector. I know it's boring, but it does the job. The rest of the function should make plenty of sense because this is the third variation of the DFS you've seen in this chapter.

Calling the DrawMap Function

Finally, the game demo calls the `DrawMap` function twice:

```
g_map.ClearMarks();
DrawMap( g_map.m_nodes[g_current], g_x - WIDTH/2, g_y - HEIGHT/2,
         100, GREY );
g_map.ClearMarks();
DrawMap( g_map.m_nodes[g_current], g_x - WIDTH/2, g_y - HEIGHT/2,
         DEPTH, WHITE );
```

Now, what is the point of calling `DrawMap` twice? It's for demonstration purposes. The demo first clears all the map marks and then calls `DrawMap` with a depth value of 100. This means that on the small map I'm using, the entire map will be drawn in gray. After that, the map is drawn again with a depth value of DEPTH instead, and in white. DEPTH is a constant that has a value of 3 in this demo, but you can change it and recompile it if you want. 3 seems to work best for the demo, though.

So what does this accomplish? The entire map is always drawn on the screen all the time in gray so you can see what it looks like, but the sectors that are actually drawn using a proper depth are highlighted in white, which is a very neat effect.

Playing the Demo

Figure 17.31 shows a screenshot from the demo in action. You are the little red dot in the center of the screen, and you're supposed to move around the map. I didn't implement bounds checking, so you can walk off the map into the black void, but please don't do that. Instead, try to focus on moving around the hallways and paying attention to which sectors are drawn (white) and which aren't (gray).

You use the arrow keys to move around.

Figure 17.31

Here is a screenshot from the demo.

You can see that most of the time, the only sectors that are white are the ones that are visible from the current sector, which is pretty cool. You did that by using a very simple algorithm. There was no need to go ahead and make a perfect *line-of-sight* algorithm that detects which sectors are visible at any given time.

Remember, the key to game programming is to work smarter, not harder.

Conclusion

This is a pretty big chapter, but it's also a pretty big subject. As you can see from all the examples I've given you in this chapter, graphs in game programming are almost always used to store map or level information. This isn't a trivial matter, because maps are a huge part of most games out there; you optimize maps for drawing or find paths through them.

There are many uses for graphs besides maps, but not too many of them apply to game development directly. I go a little more in-depth into graphs in Chapters 18, "Using Graphs for AI: Finite State Machines," 19, "Tying It Together: Graphs," and 23, "Pathfinding."

Chapter 18

Using Graphs for AI Finite State Machines

So far, you've only used graphs for one purpose: storing map data in a game. I said that graphs aren't used for much more in game programming, but there are a few ways to use graphs to simulate artificial intelligence (AI) in a computer. I show you one of the simpler methods, using *finite state machines*.

In this chapter, you will learn

- What a finite state machine is
- How to use FSMs to simulate artificial intelligence
- How to create FSMs
- How to add additional states
- How to add conditional states
- How to create two different AI machines and use them in a game

What Is a Finite State Machine?

Imagine that you're making a shooter game and you start working on the AI for the computer-controlled characters. How would you control what they are doing?

One of the oldest ways of determining their actions is to use something called *states*. Each computer-controlled character in the game will be in a specific state at any given time. For a shooter, the character might be guarding a checkpoint, looking for ammo, looking for health, or fighting. Those are four examples of states.

Using state-based AI is one form of a *high-level* AI. It is called high-level because the methods used in this chapter don't care how the character is currently following his state (if he's looking for ammo, the methods you use don't care how he finds it). Instead, the methods in this chapter are more concerned with how the player knows what state he is in.

I start off with a very simple example, using the four states I mentioned before. First, start off by drawing four boxes on paper, like Figure 18.1 shows.

What Is a Finite State Machine?

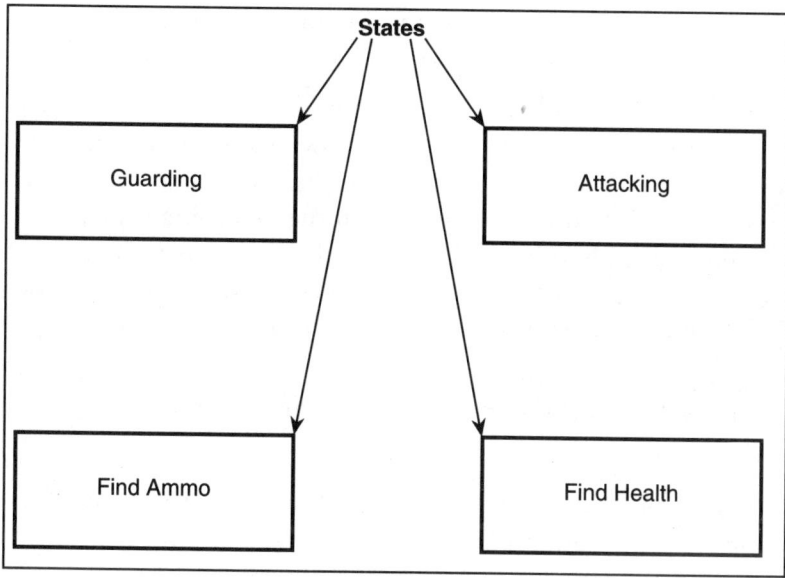

Figure 18.1

Here are the four AI states.

This should already look suspiciously like a graph to you—a graph with no arcs. Okay, so now what? The AI, when the game starts off, should be in a default state. In this example, you probably want to put your character at a checkpoint and make him guard it by default, so the AI is in the Guarding state. Now, what happens if the AI sees an enemy? He should immediately start attacking, right? Okay, then, what happens when you kill the enemy? He should start looking for health to fix himself.

Figure 18.2 shows the arcs that connect the different states when different events occur.

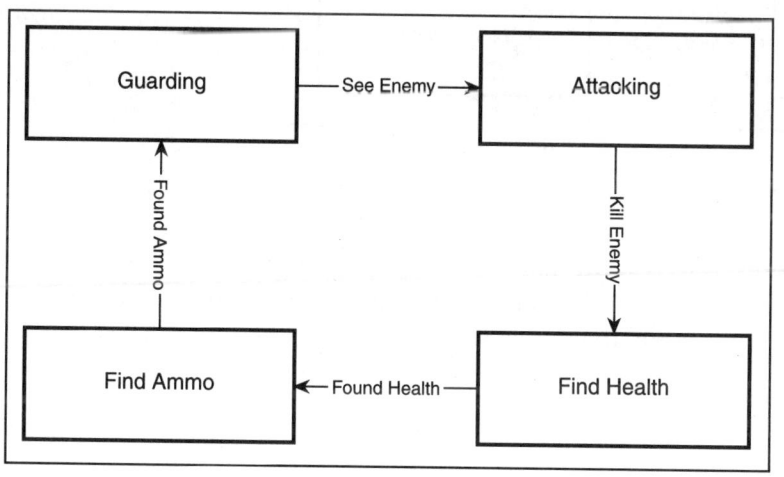

Figure 18.2

Now the states are connected with event-arcs.

Congratulations—you've just created your very first finite state machine. In this simple example, there are four states and four events. Combining these states (nodes) and events (arcs) into a graph produces a finite state machine.

Here's how it works: At any given state, whenever an event occurs, if there is an arc leading from the current state and that arc corresponds to the event that occurred, the arc points to the new state. For example, if the AI is in the Guarding state and the event See Enemy occurs, then the AI immediately switches to the Attacking state. Likewise, if the AI is Attacking and the Killed Enemy event occurs, the AI then switches to the Find Health state so he can replenish himself for the next attack.

One additional note: If an event occurs, but has no arc from the current node, then it is assumed that the AI stays in the same state. If the AI finds health while he is guarding, he just keeps guarding.

Admittedly, this example is simplistic, and you can probably see a flaw in it right away: What happens if the AI sees another player while he is searching for health or ammo? That can be fixed easily enough, as Figure 18.3 shows.

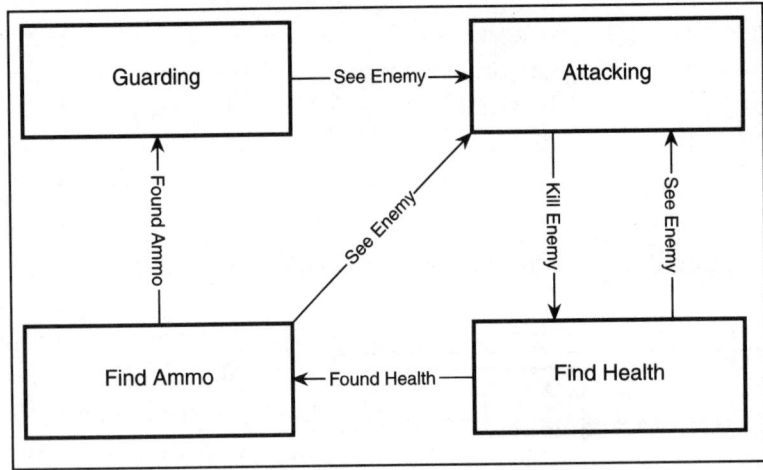

Figure 18.3

This AI is a little smarter because it acts on more events.

Now, no matter what state the AI is in, he will immediately stop what he's doing and attack an enemy if he sees one. Of course, this is also somewhat limited; the AI will suicidally attack any enemy that he sees, even if he has no ammo or is close to dead.

Complex Finite State Machines

If you want your AIs to be smarter, you can create even more complex state machines with more states and more events. Sometimes drawing these complex machines can get a little cumbersome, though.

Imagine that you are making a new machine that is more complex and can handle team-based behavior and let the AI know when to run away from a battle.

In this little example, the AI will have the following states:

- Guarding – AI is guarding base.
- Attacking/Full Health – AI is attacking and has full health.
- Attacking/Injured – AI is attacking, but is injured.
- Finding Health – AI is looking for health.
- Finding Ammo – AI is looking for ammo.
- Finding Base – AI is looking for its base so the AI can guard it.
- Running for Help – AI is running away from an enemy, looking for help.
- Finding Enemy/With Help – AI has help following and is looking for an enemy.
- Finding Enemy/Full Health – AI has full health and is searching for an enemy.
- Following Ally – AI is following an ally.

So there are 10 states in this particular machine, which is a lot more complex than the last machine. Here are the events:

- See Enemy – AI sees an enemy.
- Get Injured – AI gets hit by something.
- Seriously Injured – AI gets hit badly and is about to die.
- Kill Enemy – AI just killed an enemy.
- Found Health – AI just found some health.
- Found Ammo – AI just found some ammo.
- Found Base – AI just found the base.
- Found Help – AI found an ally who will follow.
- Ally Needs Help – An ally asks AI for help.

That's nine different events, much more than the four events from the first example. Now, put them together and you will probably get something like Figure 18.4.

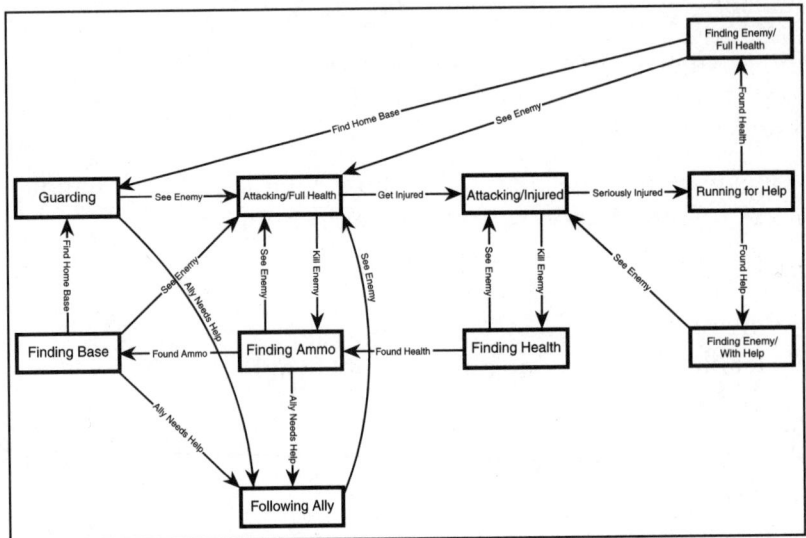

Figure 18.4

Here is a large finite state machine AI.

At a first glance, that machine looks incredibly complex, and you're correct—it is. However, you may notice some things missing that you think should be there. For example, what happens if the AI runs out of ammo? Shouldn't there be an Out of Ammo event? Well, for this example, I elected to leave that out. Granted, the AI would become a magnitude "smarter" if I had included that possibility, but the figure is already complex enough. In this example, I assume that the AI will have some sort of ammo-less weapon (fists? knife? chainsaw?), so it can always attack.

Another thing you may think is missing is an Ally Needs Help arc from the Finding Health state to the Following Ally state. Well, I decided not to include that, because if you're looking for health, you're in no condition to help friends yourself, so you turn them down.

There are many possibilities in this machine, and that's the beauty of using this method for AI: You can customize it any way you want.

The machine in Figure 18.4 is reasonably complex. The AI knows if it needs to get health after a battle or not, and it knows to run away and find help if it is about to die. After a battle, the AI tries to replenish its ammo and then finds its way home. You can see that this is a pretty cool method of implementing a high-level AI.

Implementing a Finite State Machine

The best thing about finite state machines is that they are *fast*. When I say "fast," I mean "incredibly super-duper fast." I'll show you what I mean.

To implement a finite state machine, you use a 2D array. Down one side of the array, the states are listed. Down the other side, the events are listed. This table is called a *state transition table*. Figure 18.5 shows the state transition table for the machine from Figure 18.3.

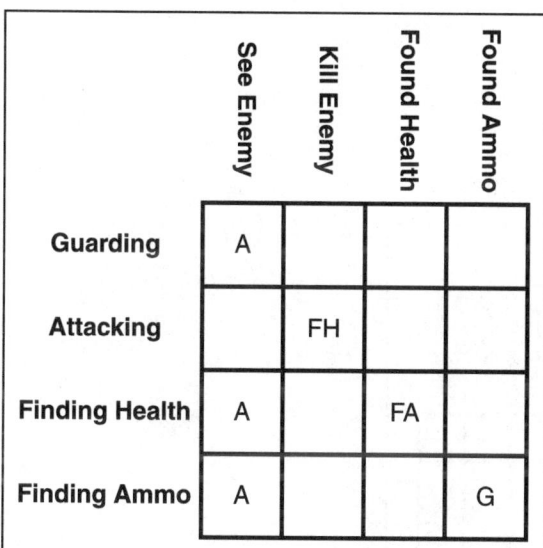

Figure 18.5

Here is the state transition table for the machine in Figure 18.3.

Now, whenever an event occurs, the program will look up the current state on the vertical axis and then look up what event occurred on the horizontal axis. Whichever value is in the cell is the new state. For example, in the figure, if the AI is in state Guarding and the event See Enemy occurs, then the AI switches to the Attacking state because it is in the cell. Determining which state the AI should be in on any event is almost instant.

In the table, whenever a cell is blank, it is assumed that the state will stay the same, so the real transition table would look like Figure 18.6 instead.

	See Enemy	Kill Enemy	Found Health	Found Ammo
Guarding	A	G	G	G
Attacking	A	FH	A	A
Finding Health	A	FH	FA	FH
Finding Ammo	A	FA	FA	G

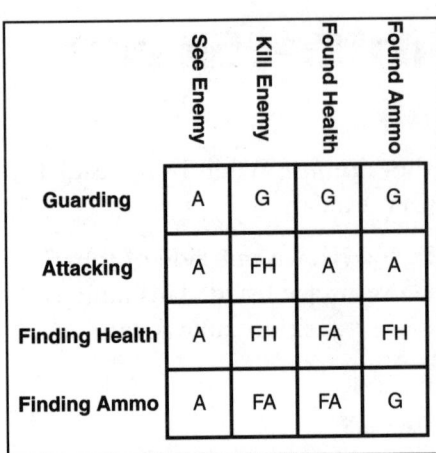

Figure 18.6

Here is the full state transition table.

I usually find it easier to leave the cells blank when I'm drawing the tables because it makes them easier to read.

Figure 18.7 shows you the state transition table for the machine in Figure 18.4.

	See Enemy	Get Injured	Seriously Injured	Kill Enemy	Found Health	Found Ammo	Found Base	Found Help	Ally Needs Help
1: Guarding	2								10
2: Attacking/FH		3		5					
3: Attacking/I			7	4					
4: Finding Health	3				5				
5: Finding Ammo	2					6			10
6: Finding Base	2						1		10
7: Running for Help					9			8	
8: Finding Enemy/WH	3						1		
9: Finding Enemy/FH	2						1		
10: Following Ally	2								

Figure 18.7

This is the state transition table for the machine in Figure 18.4.

Graphical Demonstration: Finite State Machines

This is Graphical Demonstration 18-01, which can be found on the CD in the directory \demonstrations\ch18\Demo01 – Simple FSM\.

> **Compiling the Demo**
>
> This demonstration uses the SDLGUI library that I have developed for the book. For more information about this library, see Appendix B, "The Memory Layout of a Computer Program."
>
> To compile this demo, either open up the workspace file in the directory or create your own project using the settings described in Appendix B. If you create your own project, all of the files you need to include are in the directory.

This demonstration will let you manually step through the machine from Figure 18.3 to show you how it works.

On the left side of the screen there are four buttons, which correspond to the four events that can occur in this machine. Clicking on any of the buttons will cause that event to occur.

In the center of the screen is the machine, and the current state will always be highlighted in red.

Figure 18.8 shows a screenshot from the demo.

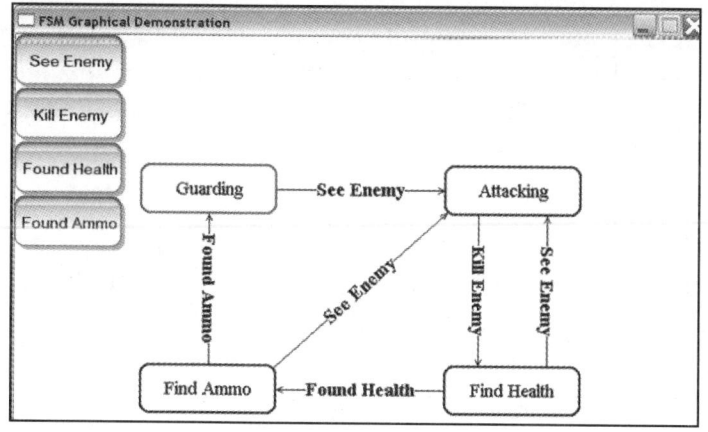

Figure 18.8

Here is a screenshot from the demo.

Even More Complex Finite State Machines

The finite state machines I showed you previously are called *pure* finite state machines. An entire area of computer science is dedicated to studying finite state machines. I only showed you a very limited form of a finite state machine called a *deterministic finite automaton*, or a *DFA* for short. I have a textbook on the subject that dedicates a lot of space to proving various things about DFAs, and let me assure you, it is very nasty stuff. Chances are, you'll never even use 90 percent of the theory behind DFAs unless you become a *discrete mathematician*, someone who does nothing but study computer-related mathematics.

> **NOTE**
> You really don't have to understand what a DFA is or even what the name means. If you already know, well, congratulations!

Using the DFA model, you can see from the machine from Figure 18.4 that I had to do a lot of messing around to make the AI detect if he should get health or not. What if there was a better and easier way to do this without needing 50 different states to detect the current health status of the AI?

There is a way to do this, and it breaks the standard DFA model, but I don't care; I just use whatever works.

Multiplying States

First, let me show you how to create a "pure" DFA model of a finite state machine, just so you can see how cumbersome it is.

If you look back to the machine in Figure 18.4, you can see that several states are duplicated to implement a "smart" AI who can tell if he's wounded or not—for example, the Attacking state and the Finding Enemy state. This can get to be a big pain in the butt later on with more complex AIs.

You are essentially storing the current *physical* state of the player into the state machine, as well as his *action* state.

Now, imagine if there were two physical states for the player: good health and bad health. I'm going to use the machine from Figure 18.3 as an example.

Now, because there are four different action states and two different physical states, then you need eight states to create this machine. Why eight states? Well, for each different action state, the player can be in two different physical states, and 4 × 2 = 8. Figure 18.9 shows the resulting machine (plus an extra event, Injured).

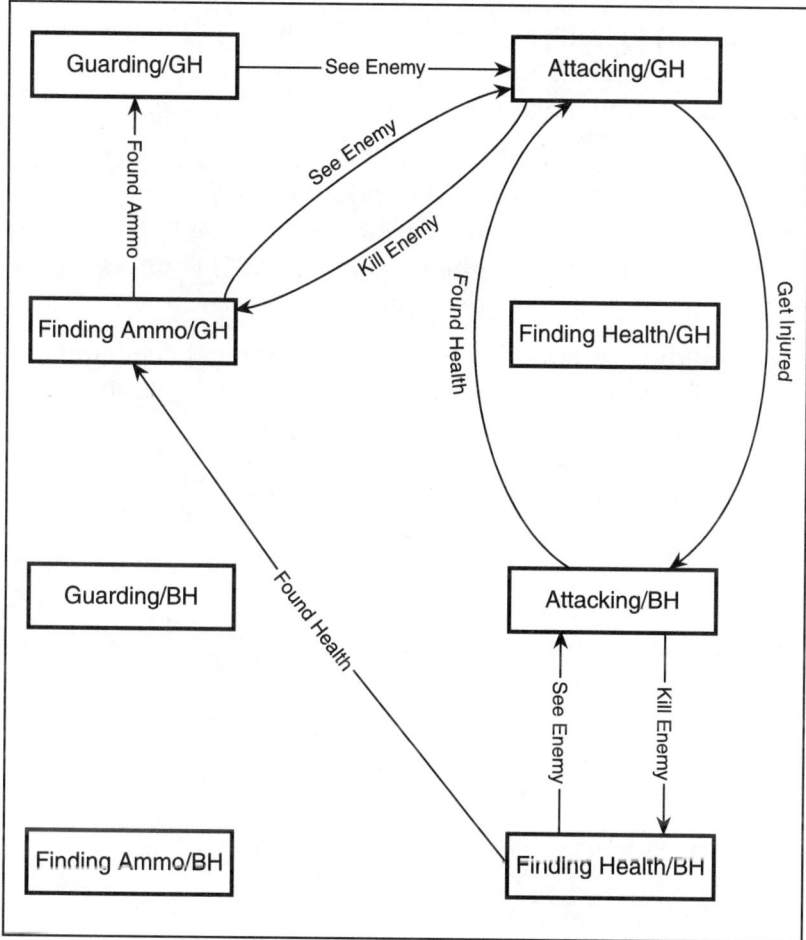

Figure 18.9

Here is the machine from Figure 18.3 with two different physical states.

The four states in the top half of the figure represent the player when he has good health, and the four states on the bottom represent the player when he has bad health. Follow the arcs for a while to become familiar with how the machine works.

You can see that this machine is smarter than the machine from Figure 18.3 in a few ways. First of all, if the AI kills an enemy while he still has good health, he just goes and looks for ammo instead of searching for health that he doesn't need.

If the player is attacking and he has bad health and he picks up some ammo during the battle, then he goes immediately back to the Attacking/Good Health state.

Now, you should notice something: Three of the states aren't used. The Finding Health with Good Health state is worthless; why would the AI look for health when he doesn't need it?

Also, the Finding Ammo with Bad Health state is worthless; why would the AI try searching for ammo before he is healed? Same thing with the Guarding with Bad Health state; the AI won't guard until he knows that he can guard properly.

These three states aren't used in this AI, but you may find a use for them with different AIs. You could make a very vigilant guard who stays at his post even when he's about to die, or you could make a gung-ho guard who values ammo more than health; the choices are up to you. The main point is that there will be unused states in this type of AI, which can make it somewhat complicated to design.

To illustrate, let me show you the addition of another physical state: the amount of ammo that the player has left. For simplicity, I'll have two values: high ammo and low ammo.

Unfortunately, that means that the number of possible states in this machine is 16, twice as many as before! There are four action states, two health states, and two ammo states, so $4 \times 2 \times 2 = 16$.

Figure 18.10 shows the new machine.

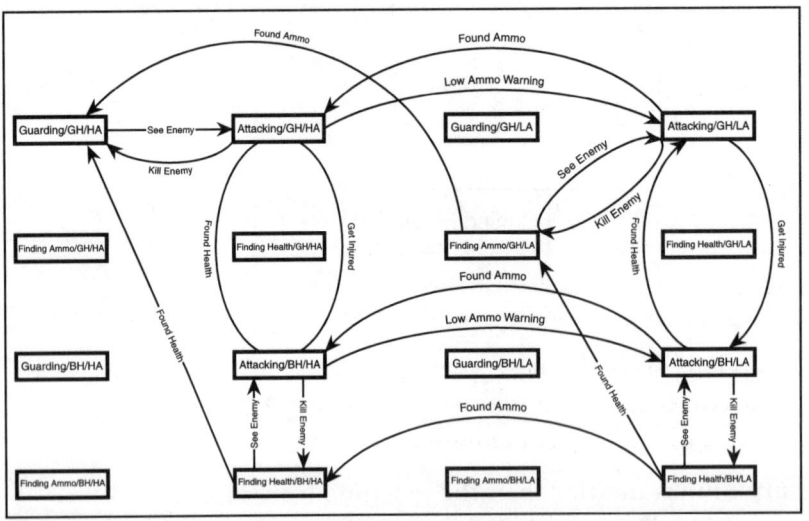

Figure 18.10

Here is the machine with two ammo states.

This time, you can see that eight states aren't used at all for this AI, which is fully half of them. In this machine, it is assumed that if you're guarding, then you have good health and high ammo; if you're finding health, then you have low health; if you're finding ammo, then you have good health and low ammo; and so on. Again, as before, you can customize the machine any way you want to make it work with a specific goal in mind.

Conditional Events

Now, take one look at the machine from Figure 18.10, and you can see that it is complex. Furthermore, if you're in any one of the four attacking states, the actual attacking algorithm won't care what your health or ammo status is, so why have four states that do the same thing?

There is a way to change the DFA model so that your machines not only look simpler, but also become easier to understand.

Instead of using extra states to store the player information, you can instead store that information in the event arcs. For example, in the Finding Health state, when a Found Health event occurs, it checks the ammo status. If the AI has low ammo, it switches to the Finding Ammo state; if not, it switches to the Guarding state. Figure 18.11 shows the machine from Figure 18.10 converted into a smaller machine using this method.

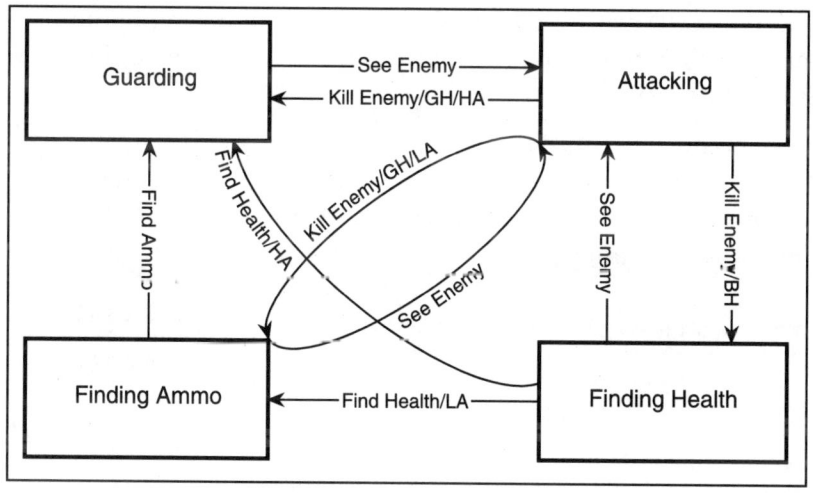

Figure 18.11

This is Figure 18.10 converted into a smaller machine by using conditional event arcs.

Now you're back down to 4 states and 9 arcs. For reference, Figure 18.10 had 16 states and 20 arcs. This new machine is easier to understand as well. For example, if the AI is in the Attacking state and he kills someone, there are a total of three choices: If his health is low, then he finds health; if his ammo is low and his health is high, then he finds ammo; and if his ammo is high and his health is high, then he goes back to guarding.

> **NOTE**
>
> Please note that by using this system, there is no need for the Low Ammo or Injured events. In the previous system, those events served only to update the current state so that it could "remember" if you were injured or had low ammo. Now, these conditions are evaluated when a major state change occurs, so there is no need for them. However, in a more complex system, you may plan on keeping those events so that you can make your AI do something smart if it has low health or ammo.

Representing Conditional Event Machines

Unfortunately, there really isn't a single easy way to represent a Conditional Event Finite State Machine. I'll show you the easiest method to do so, using a data structure you should be familiar with already.

Multi-Dimensional Arrays

First, you should recall that a 2D array is almost always used to store simple finite state machines without conditional events. One axis is the current state, and the other axis is the event that occurred.

Now, think of a simple system where the only physical player attribute is health and, as you used it before, it has two values: good health and bad health. Start off by drawing a grid that shows every possible combination of the events and the player's health, like Figure 18.12 shows.

	See Enemy	Kill Enemy	Found Health	Found Ammo
Good Health				
Bad Health				

Figure 18.12

There are eight combinations of events.

You can see how the events combined with a single physical state create a 2D array of possible event occurrences. Now, bear with me here for a moment. Remember when I said that the easiest way to represent a plain finite state machine was to use a 2D array with the states on one axis and the events on the other axis? Well, what if the events are a 2D array, like in Figure 18.12? Then we'd have a 2D array of arrays, or an array of 2D arrays. If you remember back to Chapter 5, "Multi-Dimensional Arrays," this is the same thing as a 3D array! Figure 18.13 shows this.

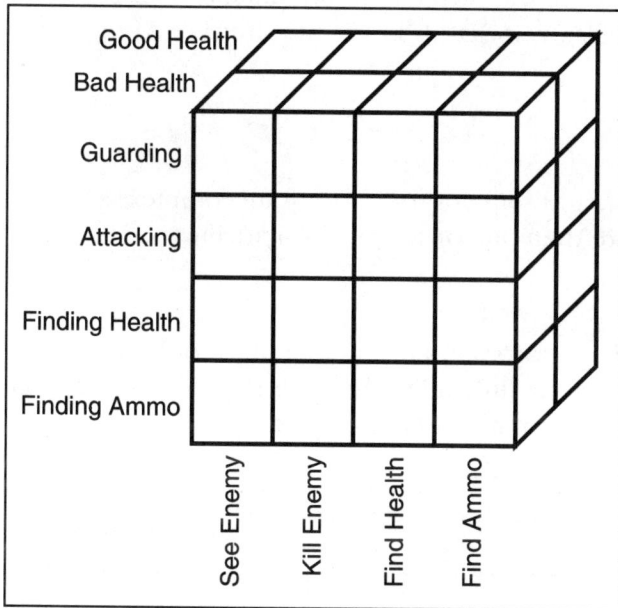

Figure 18.13

This is the finite state machine represented as a 3D array, with 16 combinations.

To access which state comes next, you go to the index of the current state, the event that occurred, and the current health state, and the new state should be in that cell.

This method is extremely fast because looking up an array index is practically instantaneous. There is a downside, though; this method takes up a lot of memory. In the previous example, if the transition from any state doesn't need any conditionals (for example, no matter what health the AI has, he will always attack an enemy when he sees it), then there is repeated data in the array, and space will be wasted.

It gets even worse when you add more conditional attributes, though. If you add the ammo state into the equation, that adds a whole new variable. You will then require a 4D array, which increases the entire size of the array by a magnitude. For example, if there were two ammo states, the 4D array would need 64 cells (4 states × 4 events × 2 health states × 2 ammo states)! With more action states and more physical states, however, this number will grow much larger. Adding another value to the health state, for example (good health, medium health, bad health), will increase the size of the array to 96 cells (4 states × 4 events × 3 health states × 2 ammo states)!

There is some good news at the end of the tunnel, though. Typically, in a very large game, you'll have many players following the same AI pattern, so there is no need to have a different machine for every AI; they can all use the same machine. Because the lookup method is very fast, you can also have hundreds of AI players running all at the same time!

Other Methods

There are other methods, of course, and some of them are quite complex, especially when you get past having more than one or two physical attributes.

Linked Ranges

Some methods keep a linked list of *ranges* for certain values in each of the 2D array cells, so they go through each node in the linked list checking to see if a variable is in a certain range. Figure 18.14 shows a simple linked list of ranges.

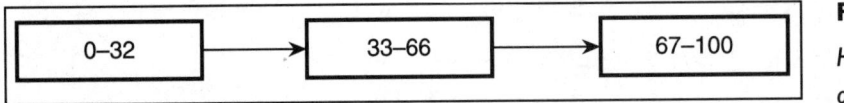

Figure 18.14

Here is a linked list of ranges.

The linked list nodes contain a range, and it will know what state is next. On any given state/event combo, the algorithm iterates through the linked list, checking to see if a physical state value fell within one of those ranges, and if so, the node with the range that matches the given attribute will have the next state in it.

Of course, you can easily see that this method requires more work than the array method, but it is generally more flexible because you can define custom ranges for each state, depending on the event. For example, say you have two events, See Enemy and Ally Needs Help. Now, the AI would need to make a choice based on his health when seeing an enemy, so say the AI attacks if his health is above 66 percent and runs if his health is below 66 percent. Now, with the other event, your AI will follow the ally and help him if the AI has more than 50 percent health, but not help him if the AI has less than 50 percent health because he needs to find health quickly. Using the array method, you need to create at least three different health states: Less than 50 percent, Between 50 and 66 percent, and More than 66 percent.

Using the linked list method, each event only needs two ranges, though. The See Enemy event will have 0–65 and 66–100, and the Ally Needs Help event will have 0–49 and 50–100. You can see the space savings right away.

It gets even better for events that aren't conditional at all. For example, if you created a suicidal AI bot that would attack any enemy, no matter his health, then you would only need one range for the See Enemy event, 0–100.

This method gets very difficult to use with more than one variable, however, which leads us to the next method...

> **CAUTION**
> Be careful when you're comparing ranges because this is a common place to make off-by-one errors. You might think that the bottom half of a 50-50 split is 0–50, but it is actually 0–49. Remember: Counting on a computer usually starts with 0.

Trees

Trees! And you thought you saw the last of them a few chapters ago...

Trees can be used to store complex range combinations. For example, look back to Figure 18.11 again, and look at the Attacking state. There are three different arcs from that state with the Kill Enemy event, but in reality, there are four different outcomes. If the AI kills an enemy with good health and high ammo, he goes back to guarding again. If the AI has good health but low ammo, he starts looking for ammo. If the AI has bad health and high ammo, he goes off looking for health, and he does the same thing if he has bad health and low ammo.

Now, imagine if you set up a tree like Figure 18.15.

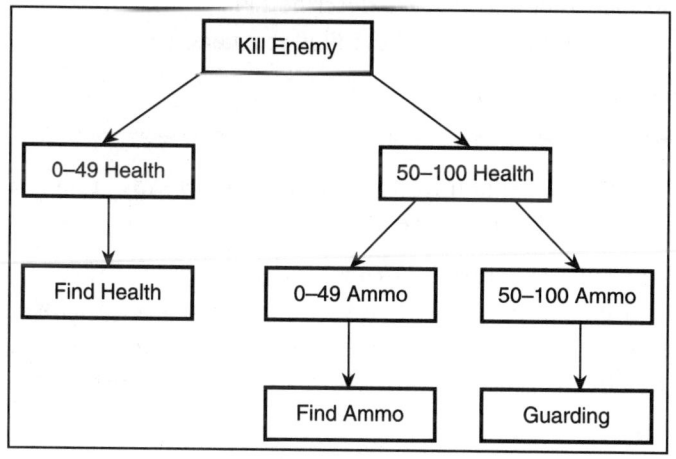

Figure 18.15

This is a tree representing the various physical state ranges.

Wow, isn't that cool? This method should remind you of something that you saw earlier. Near the end of Chapter 11, "Trees," I showed you decision trees, which are remarkably similar to this method.

This is essentially using a decision tree for each state and event combination, so you would end up with a 2D array of trees. This method can get pretty complex quickly, though, and every time an event occurs, you need to search through the tree for the right set of ranges.

Because of this, this method can be slow when you have many AIs running at the same time. However, in complex AIs that check the status of many physical states, this method may be the only way to go to keep your memory sizes down to a reasonable level.

Graphical Demonstration: Conditional Events

This is Graphical Demonstration 18-2, which you can find on the CD in the directory \demonstrations\ch18\Demo02 – Conditional Events\.

> ### Compiling the Demo
>
> This demonstration uses the SDLGUI library that I have developed for the book. For more information about this library, see Appendix B.
>
> To compile this demo, either open up the workspace file in the directory or create your own project using the settings described in Appendix B. If you create your own project, all of the files you need to include are in the directory.

This demo, like the first one, is based on a machine I've shown you already. This time, the demo is based on the machine from Figure 18.11.

In addition to the four event buttons from Graphical Demonstration 18-1, there are now two text boxes that hold the AI's health and ammo status. For the purpose of this demo, health and ammo below 50 are Bad Health or Low Ammo and anything above 50 is Good Health or High Ammo. Figure 18.16 shows a screenshot from the demo in action.

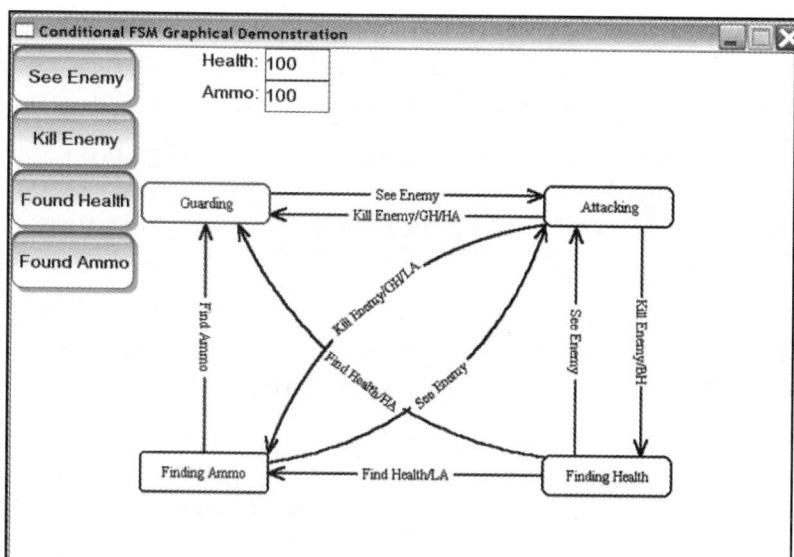

Figure 18.16

This is a screenshot from the demo.

Game Demo 18-1: Intruder

This is Game Demonstration 18-1. It is located on the CD in the directory \demonstrations\ch18\Game01 - Intruder\.

Compiling the Demo

This demonstration uses the SDLHelpers library that I have developed for the book. For more information about this library, see Appendix B.

To compile this demo, either open up the workspace file in the directory or create your own project using the settings described in Appendix B. If you create your own project, all of the files you need to include are in the directory.

Now I want to take you through the construction of a very simple game demo that uses the FSM AI model that I've shown you throughout the chapter. In this game, you will play the part of an intruder who is trying to get into a building. However, there are guards in front of the building (oh, no!), and they will stop at nothing trying to prevent you from entering the building.

So, naturally, you want to create an AI that has more of an emphasis on guarding the entrance of a base. Just to spice things up a little, though, I'm going to have *two* different types of guard AIs instead of just one! Yeah, how's that for a deal?

The first AI type is called the *defender* AI, which, as you can imagine, defends the base vigilantly. He will stand by the base and defend it; it is much more important to defend the base to him than to go off hunting for health or running after the intruder.

The second AI type is called the *attacker* AI. This AI will hunt you down and follow you until either you or he dies. If he doesn't die, then he hunts down health and eventually meanders over to the base again. He isn't as concerned with defense as a defender is.

The AIs will have four different states, and the great thing about each machine is that they both use the same states! You'll see why this is important later on.

The states that the AI can be in in this demo are Guarding, Attacking, Finding Health, and Finding the Base. I removed ammunition from the equation to make the game easier to program.

The events that can happen are these: See Intruder, Kill Intruder, Found Health, Found Base, and Out of Range. Most of these are easily understandable, except the last one. The last event, Out of Range, occurs when the AI moves out of the *defense zone*, which is an arbitrary range around the base. This event is designed so that the defender AI can determine if it has gone too far away from the base and should return.

Finally, there is one physical state in this game, health. The two possible health states are Good Health and Bad Health, like you used before.

Figure 18.17 shows the machines for the two different AIs.

Game Demo 18-1: Intruder

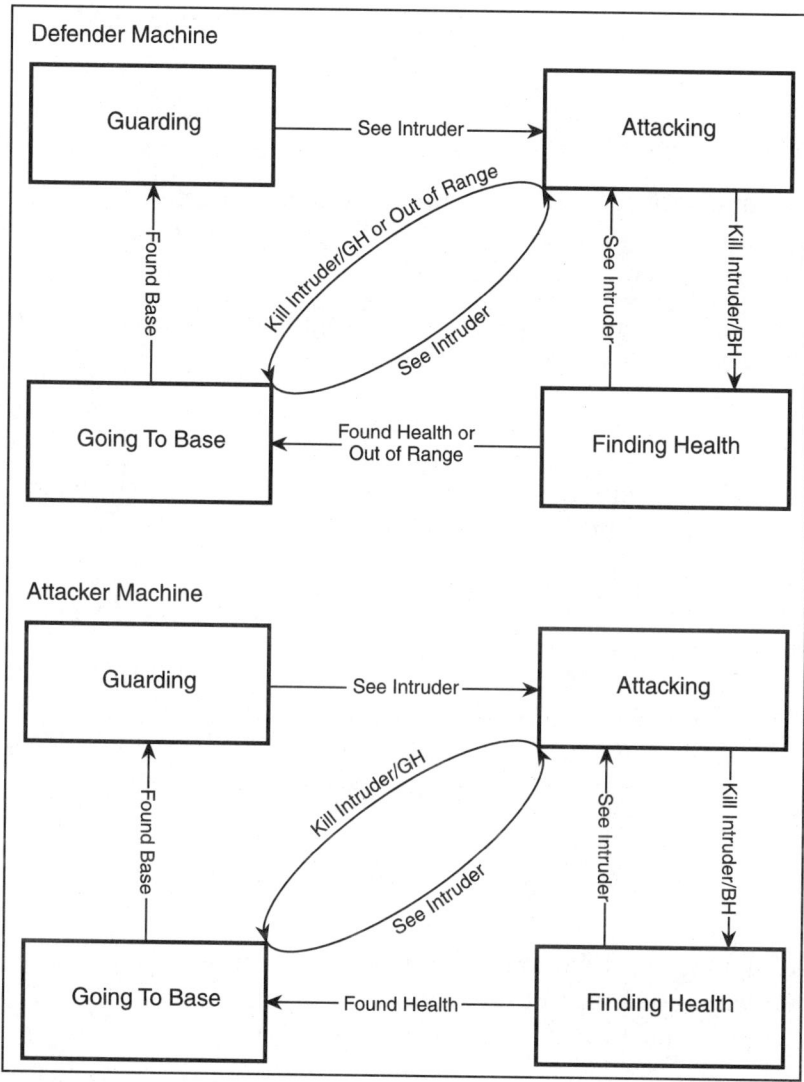

Figure 18.17

Here are the machines for the defender and attacker AIs.

Study them for a little bit and try to figure out what they do on your own.

You can see that the attacker AI looks similar to many of the AIs that I've shown you before. When it is guarding the base and it sees an intruder, it immediately starts attacking. If it kills the intruder and gets hurt in the process, then it tries to find health. If not, then it finds its way back to base. Finally, when it finds the base, it goes back into the Guarding state.

The defender AI is almost the same, with a few additions. Now, at the Attacking and Finding Health states, if the AI moves out of the defense zone, it will get an

Out of Range event and will switch into the Finding Base state. This prevents the defender AI from walking outside of the defense zone.

The Code

Code-wise, this is the most complicated demo in the book so far. The parts dealing with the finite-state-machine logic were the easy parts; the difficult parts were actually implementing what the AI does at certain states.

There is simply no way to get the entire code from the program into this book, as it is very large, but I'll show you the most important things.

The Constants

I used a few constant variables within the program. To make things more customizable, you can change these values and re-compile them if you want.

```
const float DEFENSEZONE    = 256.0f;
const float VISUALZONE     = 64.0f;
const float ATTACKZONE     = 16.0f;
const float GETZONE        = 8.0f;
const float PLAYERSPEED    = 64.0f;
const float AISPEED        = 48.0f;
```

The first four constants are the zones of the game. The defense zone, as I've mentioned before, is the zone that the defenders cannot leave. In the demo, the default radius for this value is 256 pixels, so the defenders never go more than 256 pixels away from their base.

The second zone, the visual zone, is the zone in which the AIs can see things. When the player enters within 64 pixels of the AI, the See Intruder event is set off. Likewise, this is the range at which the AIs also see their home base.

The attack zone describes how close you must be to attack someone. I go into the attack system more in depth later on.

And finally, there is the get zone, which determines how close you have to be to an object (a health pack, for instance) to pick it up.

After that is the player speed. Players can move up to 64 pixels per second in horizontal and vertical directions.

> **NOTE**
> Because of the simple system I've implemented, the player can actually move up to 90 pixels per second when moving diagonally. Because this demo isn't really concerned with movement consistency, I didn't want to take the extra time to make this algorithm perfect. In other words, don't worry about it.

The AI is a little slower and can only move at 48 pixels per second. This allows you to maneuver around them and outrun them to test how their AI works.

The Enumerations

These are all fairly obvious:

```
enum AIType
{
    ATTACKER,
    DEFENDER
};
enum AIState
{
    GUARDING,
    ATTACKING,
    FINDINGHEALTH,
    FINDINGBASE
};
enum AIEvent
{
    SEEINTRUDER,
    KILLINTRUDER,
    FOUNDHEALTH,
    FOUNDBASE,
    OUTOFBOUNDS
};
enum HealthState
{
    GOODHEALTH,
    BADHEALTH
};
```

There are two AI types, four states, five events, and two health states.

The AI Class

Now I'll show you the class used to store all of the AIs in the game.

```
class AI
{
public:
    AIState m_state;
    AIType m_type;
    float m_x, m_y;
    int m_health;
    void Init( AIType p_type, float p_x, float p_y, int p_health )
    {
        m_type = p_type;
        m_x = p_x;
        m_y = p_y;
        m_health = p_health;
        m_state = GUARDING;
    }
};
```

Each AI has a current state (guarding, attacking, and so on), a current type (attacker/defender), a position in the world, and a health variable. There is also a function called Init that will initialize the AI with the given parameters and set the AI to the GUARDING state.

The game will have an array of these AIs so that you can have a bunch of them at the same time.

The Globals

There are a number of global variables in the game demo to make it easier to use.

The Machines

First of all, there are the two finite state machines:

```
AIState g_defender[4][5][2];
AIState g_attacker[4][5][2];
```

They are both 3D arrays and hold AIStates. Remember that a finite state machine with one physical state requires a 3D array, so the dimensions match up to the number of states (4) times the number of events (5) times the number of health states (2).

I'll show you how they are initialized later.

The AIs

After that, there are the AIs:

```
AI g_AIs[8];
int g_numAIs = 0;
```

The array of AIs is limited to 8, so there can be at most 8 AIs in the game at any time. The g_numAIs variable keeps track of how many AI's are actually in the game at any given time.

The Player

Because this is a simple game demo, it is assumed that there is only one player, and the player's variables are all stored as globals:

```
float g_x = 700.0f;
float g_y = 500.0f;
int g_dx = 0;
int g_dy = 0;
int g_health = 75;
```

> **TIP**
> In real games, players are not implemented like this, especially if you want the game to be expandable. See Chapter 9, "Tying It Together: The Basics," for more details.

The player starts off at position (700,500), which is on the lower right side of the screen. The g_dx and g_dy variables store whether or not the player is holding down any arrow keys.

Other Globals

Finally, there are other miscellaneous globals that are used throughout the demo.

First, there are the coordinates of the base that the AIs are defending:

```
float g_basex = 0;
float g_basey = 0;
```

This puts the base at the top-left corner of the screen in the demo.

Then there is the array of health packs:

```
int g_healthPacks[8][2];
```

This is a 2D array that holds the locations of all eight health packs in the demo. For example, if you wanted the *x* coordinate of the third health pack, you would access it like this: g_healthPacks[3][0], and the *y* coordinate would be this: g_healthPacks[3][1].

Finally, there are the timer variables:

```
int g_timer;
int g_combattimer;
int g_timedelta;
```

The first variable, g_timer, holds the time of the game when the last frame was started. The combat timer keeps track of when the last combat round occurred, and the time delta variable keeps track of how much time has passed since the last frame updated.

Initializing the Machines

Now you get to initialize the machines so that they look like the machines from Figure 18.17. This isn't too difficult.

The First Step

First of all, I mentioned before that all of the empty cells in a finite state machine are assumed to point to the same state (see Figures 18.5, 18.6, and 18.7). Most of the cells in a finite state machine transition table are empty, so it makes sense to create an automated loop that fills in all of the empty cells first and then write over the cells that lead to different states later.

For this, you need a loop:

```
int state;
int event;
for( state = 0; state < 4; state++ )
{
    for( event = 0; event < 5; event ++ )
    {
        g_attacker[state][event][0] = (AIState)state;
        g_attacker[state][event][1] = (AIState)state;
        g_defender[state][event][0] = (AIState)state;
        g_defender[state][event][1] = (AIState)state;
    }
}
```

This loops through all four states and all five events. Inside the loops, the good health/bad health cells for both machines are filled in with the current state value.

Initializing the Arcs

The act of initializing each of the machines is simple, but it requires many lines of code. Therefore, I'm going to show you a few examples and not the entire piece of code.

```
g_attacker[GUARDING][SEEINTRUDER][GOODHEALTH] = ATTACKING;
g_attacker[GUARDING][SEEINTRUDER][BADHEALTH] = ATTACKING;
```

Using the enumerated values that you defined earlier, this looks very readable, doesn't it? These lines basically say this: When the attacker machine is in the guarding state, sees an intruder, and has good health, move into attack mode.

The second line says the same thing, except that the attacker machine has bad health.

Let me show you one more example:

```
g_defender[ATTACKING][KILLINTRUDER][GOODHEALTH] = FINDINGBASE;
g_defender[ATTACKING][KILLINTRUDER][BADHEALTH]  = FINDINGHEALTH;
g_defender[ATTACKING][OUTOFBOUNDS][GOODHEALTH]  = FINDINGBASE;
g_defender[ATTACKING][OUTOFBOUNDS][BADHEALTH]   = FINDINGBASE;
```

These four lines handle two events for the defender machine. When the defender is attacking and he kills the intruder and he still has good health, then he goes to find the base. If he has bad health, he starts to look for health.

The second event occurs when the defender leaves the defense zone. No matter what health he has, he turns around and starts heading back to the base, because a defender cannot leave the defense zone.

Pretty easy, isn't it?

Handling Events

Handling an event in the demo is pretty simple. It involves calculating the current health state and then doing a lookup in the machine to see what state is next.

```
void Event( int p_AI, AIEvent p_event )
{
    HealthState health = BADHEALTH;
    if( g_AIs[p_AI].m_health > 50 )
    {
        health = GOODHEALTH;
    }
    if( g_AIs[p_AI].m_type == ATTACKER )
    {
        g_AIs[p_AI].m_state =
            g_attacker[g_AIs[p_AI].m_state][p_event][health];
    }
    else
    {
```

```
        g_AIs[p_AI].m_state =
            g_defender[g_AIs[p_AI].m_state][p_event][health];
    }
}
```

The function takes the index of the AI that is processing the event and which event has occurred. In the first part of the function, it determines whether the health of the AI is good or bad.

After that, the computer determines which machine the AI is using, the defender or the attacker machine. Then it looks up the state of the current AI using the correct machine: `g_attacker` if he is an attacker, and `g_defender` if he is a defender. The new state is looked up using the current state, the event, and the health state of the current AI.

The Auxiliary Functions

This is a very complex demo. In fact, it demonstrates far more than just finite state machine AI. However, because this is a FSM chapter and I am limited on space and time, I cannot possibly go into depth about every function used in this demo.

I have tried my best to separate everything not related to the AI into neat little functions that act separately from the AI. These functions are listed in Table 18.1.

Table 18.1 The Auxiliary Functions

Function	Purpose
AddHealthPack	Adds a random health pack into the game
MatchHealthPacks	Determines if an AI or the player is within range of picking up a health pack and returns its index
FindClosestAI	Returns the index of the closest AI
FindClosestHealthPack	Returns the index of the closest health pack
MoveAI	Moves the AI toward the given coordinates at the correct speed
AIAttack	Makes the AI attack the player if he is in range and the right amount of time has passed
AddAIs	Adds all 8 AIs to the game
Distance	Calculates the distance between two sets of coordinates

Some of these functions are complex, like the `MoveAI` function. That function requires some basic knowledge of trigonometry to understand, but unfortunately I have no room to teach trigonometry in this book. Each of these functions is commented in detail, so if you are interested in them, you may look at their source on the CD. But for the purpose of this book, all you need to know is that these functions do as they are told; you don't need to know how they actually work.

The ProcessAI Function

This is the big function that processes all of the AI events in the game. It makes heavy use of the auxiliary functions I just mentioned, and because it does, it should be fairly easy to comprehend.

As with most large functions in the book, I separate this into segments so I can explain it better:

```
void ProcessAI( int p_AI )
{
    int i;
```

First of all, the function takes the index of the AI that is being processed. After that, it creates a generic variable, `i`, which will be used for various things in the function.

```
    i = MatchHealthPacks( g_AIs[p_AI].m_x, g_AIs[p_AI].m_y );
    if( i != -1 )
    {
        Event( p_AI, FOUNDHEALTH );
        g_AIs[p_AI].m_health = 100;
        AddHealthPack( i );
    }
```

The first thing the function does when it gets to work is check if the AI has picked up a health pack. This section of code makes use of the `MatchHealthPacks` auxiliary function to find out if the current AI is in range to pick up a health pack. If it returns −1, then the AI isn't in range, and nothing happens. If the AI is in range, then a `FOUNDHEALTH` event is passed into the AI, and his health is set to its full value again. Finally, a new health pack is added into the game, as the game always keeps 8 health packs in the world.

```
    if( Distance( g_AIs[p_AI].m_x,
                  g_AIs[p_AI].m_y,
                  g_basex,
```

```
            g_basey ) <= VISUALZONE )
    Event( p_AI, FOUNDBASE );
```

After that, the AI checks to see if it can see the base. It does this by checking to see if the distance between the AI and the base is less than the VISUALZONE constant. If so, then a FOUNDBASE event is sent to the AI.

```
    if( Distance( g_AIs[p_AI].m_x,
                  g_AIs[p_AI].m_y,
                  g_x,
                  g_y ) <= VISUALZONE )
        Event( p_AI, SEEINTRUDER );
```

Then it checks to see if the AI can see the player. If so, then a SEEINTRUDER event is sent to the AI.

```
    if( Distance( g_AIs[p_AI].m_x,
                  g_AIs[p_AI].m_y,
                  g_basex,
                  g_basey ) >= DEFENSEZONE )
        Event( p_AI, OUTOFBOUNDS );
```

Then it checks to see if the AI has left the defense zone, and if so, it sends an OUT-OFBOUNDS event to the AI.

Now that all of the event checking has been processed, the function continues on and performs all the actions of the AI:

```
    if( g_AIs[p_AI].m_state == ATTACKING )
    {
        if( Distance( g_AIs[p_AI].m_x,
                      g_AIs[p_AI].m_y,
                      g_x, g_y ) <= ATTACKZONE )
        {
            AIAttack();
        }
        else
        {
            // move the AI closer to the player
            MoveAI( p_AI, g_x, g_y );
        }
    }
```

If the AI is in attack mode and he is within attacking distance of the player, then the AI attacks him.

If the AI is not within attacking distance, then the AI moves closer to the player, chasing after him.

```
if( g_AIs[p_AI].m_state == FINDINGBASE )
{
    MoveAI( p_AI, g_basex, g_basey );
}
```

If the AI is trying to find the base, he moves closer to the base.

```
if( g_AIs[p_AI].m_state == FINDINGHEALTH )
{
    i = FindClosestHealthPack( g_AIs[p_AI].m_x, g_AIs[p_AI].m_y );
    MoveAI( p_AI, g_healthPacks[i][0], g_healthPacks[i][1] );
}
}
```

And finally, if the AI is finding health, the function finds out which health pack is closest to the AI and moves the AI toward the health pack.

See, that was a long function, but when you think about it, it really is quite simple to use.

Playing the Demo

The demo is quite simple to play. You're the little black square, the blue squares are health packs, the green squares are defenders, and the red squares are attackers. Your health bar is on the left side of the screen, and the AIs' health bars are on the top right of the screen.

Figure 18.18 shows a screenshot of the demo in action.

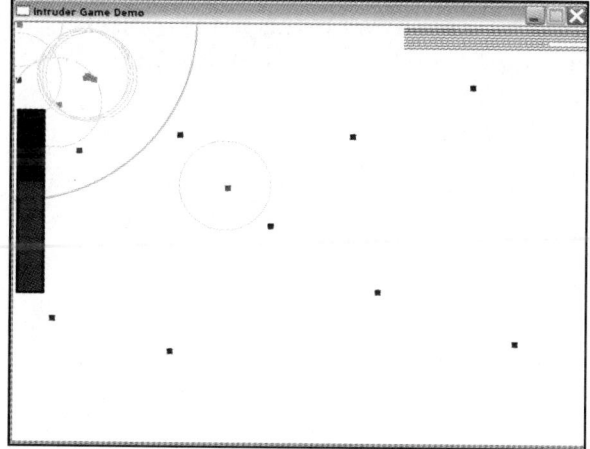

Figure 18.18

Here is a screenshot from the demo.

It looks kind of simple for a game demo, but I decided to use simplicity for this one because I wanted you to see the whole game screen at all times. This way, you can mess around and then watch what the AI does in response even if you're on the other side of the map. Of course, this meant that I needed to use very small graphics, and they looked bad, so I used squares instead.

The dark gray circle at the top left of Figure 18.18 represents the defense zone of the AIs, and the light gray circles represent the AIs' visual zones. If you walk within those circles, they can see you.

You move your guy around using the arrow keys on your keyboard, and whenever you get within attacking range of one of the AIs, you automatically attack them once every second. Each time you die, you are respawned where you first started, so don't worry about dying. In fact, I recommend that you die a few times so you can see what the AIs do when you die.

Conclusion

The material covered in this chapter is usually taught to senior-level college students. In fact, over half of my class failed this topic in college. Granted, there is a lot more to this topic that I showed you, but this is the first 6 weeks of a 15-week course, or over one-third of the information.

I guess my point is that this is a difficult subject to learn, depending on how you learn it. When I first learned about finite state machines, it was in relation to game AI, and I was naturally interested. I did well in my class because I already knew a lot of the material and because I was able to apply it to a real-world solution.

When I was playing around and testing the Graphical Demonstrations for this chapter, my brother was watching me, and he said, "Wow, that is really cool." He doesn't know anything about computer programming and he understood the basic principles easily. So I hope you had no problem with this subject.

If there is one thing I want you to get out of this chapter, it is how easy it is to make a finite state machine AI. I want you to understand how fast they are in real life and how easy it is to change the entire behavior of one machine by changing the arcs around.

You saw from the game demo that I had two machines that operated very differently, but they used the same code for every AI! The only difference was the addition of a few arcs to the defender machine to make it head back to the base if it wandered too far away.

The topic of real-time AI in computer games is a vast one, and I've by no means covered even a fraction of it. I feel that this is a good enough start for now, though. You might want to look into algorithms to minimize redundant machines.

CHAPTER 19

TYING IT TOGETHER: GRAPHS

19. Tying It Together: Graphs

You've just finished the part of the book dealing with graphs, so now you want to do something with them.

This chapter continues to expand the game demo that I developed in Chapters 9, "Tying It Together: The Basics," and 16, "Tying It Together: Trees." As you might guess, this chapter is concerned with adding graph features to the game engine.

In this chapter, you will learn

- How to design a new map format that uses directionmaps
- How to extend the Map interface of the Adventure game to accommodate the new maps
- How to create an editor that loads and saves directionmaps
- How to convert a directionmap into a grid and back for easy editing
- How to convert older tilemap files into the new tilemap file format

The New Map Format

The feature that will be added to the game is an entirely new map format. This is the same type of map that I used in Game Demonstration 17-1. Remember, instead of having a giant square tilemap like the game has been using up until this point, the map will now be a collection of rooms in which each room knows which rooms are connected to it. If you don't remember how these work, Figure 19.1 should refresh your memory.

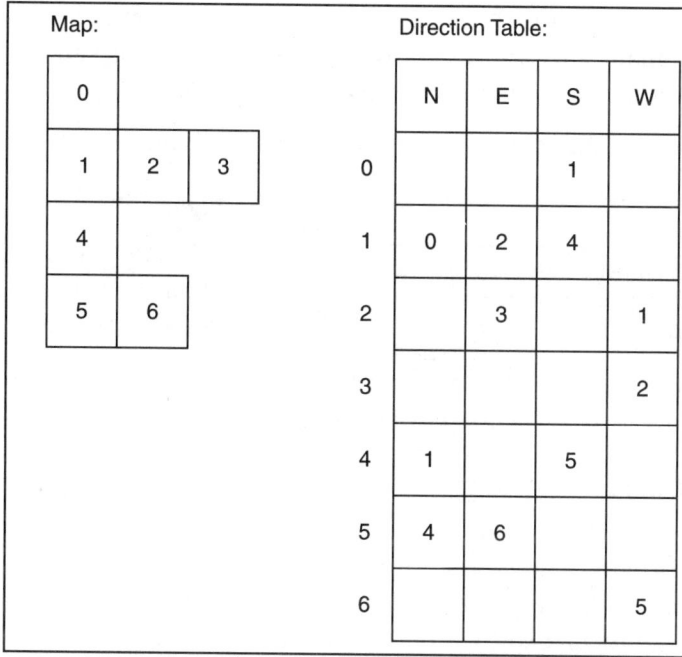

Figure 19.1
Here is a direction-table map.

The graphical representation of the map is on the left, but the computer representation of the map is in the table on the right. The table has two variables; the index on the vertical axis represents the room numbers. Each room can have four exits; there are four entries per room, representing the exits. The value in these entries represents the number of the room that exit leads to.

For example, if you look at the entry for room number 1, you can see that going north leads you to room 0, east to room 2, and south to room 4. The entry for west is blank because there is no exit to the west. Basically, the table encodes an adjacency graph.

The New Room Entry Structure

Now, that was just a simple format that defines map information only. To make a new map format for the game, you need more information.

Because you want every room in the map to have two tile layers (the base tile and the overlay tile) and an item and a person, you need to add those into the format.

Also, you will want each room in the map to know its relative x and y coordinates when compared to other rooms in the map. This is useful for moving around the map so you can see where a room lies in relation to another room. If you read

Chapter 9 where the `Map` class interface and `Object` class were designed, you should remember that the `Object` class maintains *x* and *y* coordinates so that objects can find out which direction they should move to get closer to another object.

Figure 19.2 shows the structure of a single room entry for this map format.

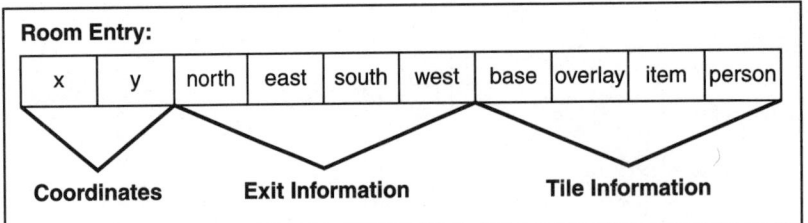

Figure 19.2

This is the structure of a map entry for a direction-table map.

The File Format

Now that you are going to have two different map formats in the game, you need some way to differentiate the formats. The easiest way to do something like this is to add an *identification number* at the front of the map format. Using this method, you assign a number to each map format so that a map loader can tell what kind of map you are trying to load.

For example, I am going to assign the number 0 to the tilemap format from Chapters 9 and 16 and the number 1 to the directionmap format from this chapter.

Therefore, when the map is loaded, the function that loads it reads in the first number in the file and checks to see what it is. If it is 0, then it knows that you are loading a tilemap, and if it is 1, then it knows that you are loading a directionmap.

> **NOTE**
>
> Unfortunately, the tilemap file format doesn't have a 0 at the beginning of the file. This is going to cause some problems, but I deal with this matter later on, in Example 19-1 and Game Demonstration 19-3.

Unlike a tilemap, a directionmap will not have a set number of rooms in it. Instead, the number of rooms can vary, so you need to store the number of rooms in the map after the map identification.

Then you store the array of map entries. Finally, the three exit strings are stored at the end of the file, just like they are in the tilemap format. What you end up with is a file looking like the one in Figure 19.3.

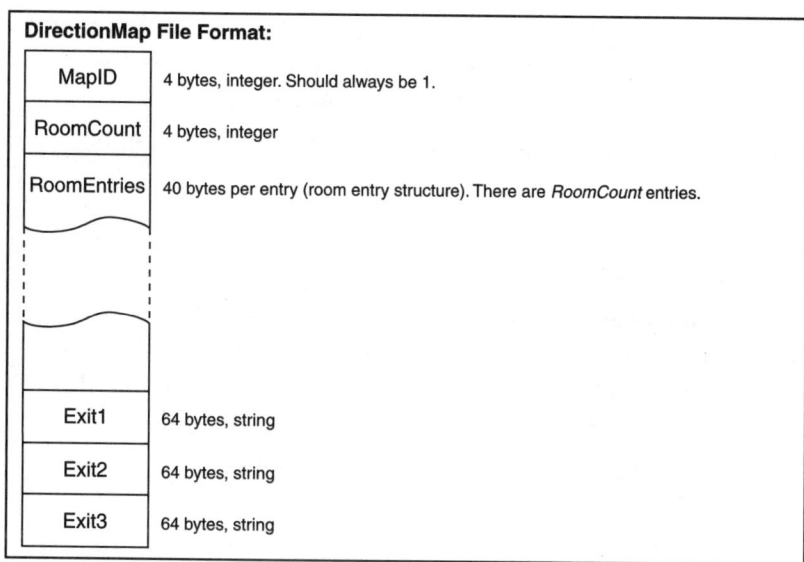

Figure 19.3
This is the directionmap file format.

Game Demonstration 19-1: Adding the New Map Format

This section deals with Game Demonstration 19-1. The source code for this chapter is on the CD in the directory \demonstrations\ch19\Game01 - Adventure v3\, and this is the third version of the adventure game that I have developed for the book in Chapters 9 and 16 so far.

Compiling the Demo

This demonstration uses the SDLHelpers library that I have developed for the book. For more information about this library, see Appendix B, "The Memory Layout of a Computer Program."

To compile this demo, either open up the workspace file in the directory or create your own project using the settings described in Appendix B. If you create your own project, all of the files you need to include are in the directory.

When designing the Map class in Chapter 9, I made some design choices that might not have made sense to you at the time, such as making the map be accessible by cell number *and* 2D coordinates and making every function virtual.

This chapter will show you why I made those choices and why they make the game so flexible.

The DirectionMap

You want to add an entirely new map format to the game. Years ago, before object-oriented programming was invented, you probably would have just designed the game with one format in mind, and when you wanted to add something like this to the game, you had a few options. Unfortunately, almost all of those options involved recoding the entire map system to work with the new maps. This always took a lot of work and frequently caused lots of new bugs.

Instead of doing that, you're going to create a new class that inherits from the Map class: the DirectionMap. This class and all accompanying classes are in the DirectionMap.h file.

The DirectionCell Class

This class is almost equivalent to the TileCell class in the tilemap implementation of the map. It will store data about a single cell/room in the map. Like the TileCell class, this class will also know if the cell is blocked and which item and person is stored in the cell.

However, it adds a few new items as well.

The class needs to know about the exits from the cell, the *x* and *y* coordinates of the cell, and the number of the base and overlay tiles. Here is a listing of the data from the class:

```
class DirectionCell
{
public:
    bool m_blocked;
    Item* m_item;
    Person* m_person;
    int m_exits[4];
    int m_tiles[2];
    int m_x;
    int m_y;
};
```

Also, the class has a constructor, which constructs each cell so that it doesn't contain junk data:

```
DirectionCell()
{
    m_blocked = false;
    m_item = 0;
    m_person = 0;
    m_exits[0] = -1;
    m_exits[1] = -1;
    m_exits[2] = -1;
    m_exits[3] = -1;
    m_tiles[0] = -1;
    m_tiles[1] = -1;
    m_x = -1;
    m_y = -1;
}
```

Note that the exits are all initialized to −1. Because room 0 is a valid room, the value −1 is used to denote that there is no exit in that direction, just like −1 is used to say that the tile number is invalid as well.

The MapEntry Class

This is a simple class that will be used to load data from disk. Because the map files store an actual number representing the item and the person, and the `DirectionCell` class will store pointers to the `Item` and `Person` classes, you can't directly load each room into its `DirectionCell` class, so this class is needed as an intermediate step.

Here is the class listing:

```
class MapEntry
{
public:
    int x;
    int y;
    int directions[4];
    int layers[4];
};
```

This data corresponds exactly with the data shown in Figure 9.2.

The DirectionMap Class

As I've said before, the `DirectionMap` class will inherit from the `Map` class. This means that it needs to implement all of the functions from that class on its own. The great thing about this method is that the game cannot tell the difference between a tilemap and a directionmap. Think about that statement for a moment.

This means that the game and the `Map` class have made an agreement. The `Map` class has promised to perform certain functions, and the game will utilize those functions. The game does not care about *how* those functions are implemented, it only cares that the `Map` class does what it has promised to do.

The `TileMap` class implemented all of the `Map` functions using a 64 × 64 grid implementation, but the game doesn't actually care how the map is represented. Likewise, the `DirectionMap` class will support all of the same functions, yet it accomplishes these functions in a different way.

Why is this a good way to program? Because you can essentially create an infinite number of map implementations, and as long as they all implement the `Map` interface, the game does not need to ever change the way it works. This is the same method that I use in this chapter. The actual game logic will not need to be changed *at all*, yet it still uses the new map seamlessly.

The Data

Whereas the `TileMap` class needed two arrays (a 2D array for cell info and a 3D array for tile info), the `DirectionMap` class only needs a single 1D array to store the cells in the map:

```
class DirectionMap : public Map
{
protected:
    Array<DirectionCell> m_rooms;
    SDL_Surface** m_tilebmps;
};
```

The `m_rooms` array holds a bunch of `DirectionCells`, which represent each cell in the map. Also, like the `TileMap` class, this has a pointer to an array of `SDL_Surfaces`, which represents the tileset that will be used with this map.

> **NOTE**
>
> If you know a little bit more about object-oriented design than I have taught you, then you may be asking, "Why did you duplicate the `m_tilebmps` data in these two classes? Wouldn't it be better to have this in the `Map` class?" You have a valid point here; however, there is a reasoning to this method. The `Map` class does not explicitly say that it will be using bitmaps to draw the rooms. Instead, you might make a variant that will actually draw a 3D map using textures and all sorts of cool geometry.

The DirectionMap Functions

The `DirectionMap` class only has three functions on top of the `Map` functions: a constructor, a destructor, and the `LoadFromFile` function.

The Constructor

The constructor will set the tileset pointer according to its parameter:

> **NOTE**
> The `LoadFromFile` function is not part of the `Map` class because you may create some sort of `RandomMap` class someday that randomly creates maps using an algorithm. Therefore, saying that all maps can be loaded from disk doesn't really make sense.

```
DirectionMap( SDL_Surface** p_tilebmps )
        : m_rooms( 0 )
{
    m_tilebmps = p_tilebmps;
}
```

Note also that the `m_rooms` array is initialized to size 0 so that it takes up no room. This is because you don't know how many rooms the map will hold, and guessing at this point doesn't make much sense.

The Destructor

The destructor is vital in this class because the map keeps track of all of the items and people on it, and when the map is deleted, all the items and people must be, too.

```
~DirectionMap()
{
    int x;
    for( x = 0; x < m_rooms.Size(); x++ )
    {
        if( m_rooms[x].m_item != 0 )
            delete m_rooms[x].m_item;
        if( m_rooms[x].m_person != 0 )
            delete m_rooms[x].m_person;
        m_rooms[x].m_item = 0;
        m_rooms[x].m_person = 0;
    }
}
```

This basically loops through every room in the map, and if a room has an `Item` or a `Person` in it, they are deleted and set to zero. This will assure that you get no memory leaks.

The LoadFromFile Function

This function will load a directionmap from disk using the same file format you saw in Figure 9.3.

```
void LoadFromFile( char* p_filename )
{
    int x;
    int maptype;
    int cells;
    MapEntry entry;
```

The function takes a string as the parameter; this is the name of the file that the function will load. The x variable is used to count through each room in the map, and the maptype variable stores the ID of the map (the first value in Figure 9.3). The cells variable keeps track of the total number of cells in the map, and the entry variable is used to store the raw cell data as it is loaded from disk.

```
    FILE* f = fopen( p_filename, "rb" );
    if( f == 0 )
        return;
```

As with almost all of the file loading/saving functions in this book, the file is opened and checked to see if it was actually opened. If not, the function returns and does nothing.

```
    fread( &maptype, 1, sizeof(int), f );
    if( maptype != 1 )
    {
        fclose( f );
        return;
    }
```

Then the type of the map is read in from the file. If the type is not 1, then the map is of a format that this class doesn't know about. Remember from before that the ID 1 means that the file is a directionmap. So if the type isn't 1, then the function closes the file and returns without doing anything else.

```
    fread( &cells, 1, sizeof(int), f );
    m_rooms.Resize( cells );
```

Then the number of cells is read in from the file and the m_rooms array is resized to hold the current amount of rooms.

> **NOTE**
> Please note that this function will cause a memory leak if a map is already loaded. The array is resized, and if the new map is smaller than the old map, the cells at the end of the map are destroyed, but the cells don't destroy their contents when they are destroyed. Also, when the rooms are loaded in, they overwrite all the data that is already in the cells, causing the items and people to be lost. This function is only meant to be called once, right after the map is constructed. If you need to load another map from file, destruct the map and create a totally new one.

```
for( x = 0; x < cells; x++ )
    {
        fread( &entry, 1, sizeof(MapEntry), f );
```

Next, a single `for`-loop goes through each room in the map and loads in the map entry for the current room.

```
        m_rooms[x].m_tiles[0] = entry.layers[0];
        m_rooms[x].m_tiles[1] = entry.layers[1];
        m_rooms[x].m_x = entry.x;
        m_rooms[x].m_y = entry.y;
```

The tile data and the coordinate data are just copied over from the `MapEntry` structure into the `DirectionCell` structure.

```
        if( entry.layers[2] != -1 )
        {
            m_rooms[x].m_item = MakeItem( entry.layers[2],
                                          entry.x,
                                          entry.y,
                                          x );
        }
```

However, the items and people cannot be loaded the same way. Instead, the function checks to see if the item in the cell is not –1 (–1 means that an item doesn't exist in that cell). If so, then the `MakeItem` function is called to create a new `Item` using the global person template. If you don't remember how this function works, please go back to Chapter 9 and review it.

```
        if( entry.layers[3] != -1 )
        {
```

```
            m_rooms[x].m_person = MakePerson( entry.layers[3],
                                              entry.x,
                                              entry.y,
                                              x );
        if( entry.layers[3] == 0 )
        {
            SetViewer( m_rooms[x].m_person );
        }
    }
```

The same thing happens with the person in each cell, with one addition. Remember person number 0 is considered the player of the map, so whenever person 0 is detected, the function sets the viewer of the map to that person.

```
        m_rooms[x].m_exits[0] = entry.directions[0];
        m_rooms[x].m_exits[1] = entry.directions[1];
        m_rooms[x].m_exits[2] = entry.directions[2];
        m_rooms[x].m_exits[3] = entry.directions[3];
    }
```

Last, the exits of each room are loaded from the `MapEntry` class into the current `DirectionCell`.

```
    fread( m_exits[0], 64, sizeof(char), f );
    fread( m_exits[1], 64, sizeof(char), f );
    fread( m_exits[2], 64, sizeof(char), f );
    fclose( f );
}
```

After all of the rooms are loaded in, the names of the exits are loaded from the file, and the file is finally closed.

The Map Functions

Now that you've created the data and the `DirectionMap`-specific functions, you want to go ahead and implement all of the regular `Map` functions.

The Draw Function

First up is the `Draw` function, which draws the map on the screen. There are several ways to accomplish the drawing of this map. You could do a *breadth-first* traversal on the map and draw every cell, or you could do a *limited-depth-first* traversal and only draw cells that are a certain depth from the cell that the viewer is in. However, neither of these methods is a very good choice.

Game Demonstration 19-1: Adding the New Map Format

If you use the breadth-first drawing algorithm, then you need a queue to help you draw everything. If you use the depth-first method, then you need a stack or a recursive function, which uses a stack anyway.

Because the drawing function will be called often, you want this function to be as fast as possible. Unfortunately, both of the previous methods are somewhat slow because they need extra structures to process the cells in the map.

There is a simpler method right under your nose, though. Each cell keeps track of its *x* and *y* coordinates in relation to the other cells, so you can use this information to determine where each cell is drawn. You can just go through every cell in the map and draw it using its coordinates. There is no need to perform a complicated traversal algorithm.

```
void Draw( SDL_Surface* p_surface, int p_midx, int p_midy )
{
    int i, z;                // counting variables
    int px, py;              // pixel coordinates
    int ox, oy;              // offset coordinates
    int current;
    Item* item;
    Person* person;
```

The variables used are similar to those used in the `TileMap`'s `Draw` function (from Chapter 9), but instead of *x* and *y* coordinates to loop through a tilemap, there is just one index variable, `i`, which will loop through every cell in the map.

```
    ox = (-m_viewer->GetX() * 64) + p_midx - 32;
    oy = (-m_viewer->GetY() * 64) + p_midy - 32;
```

As before, the function calculates the offset of the viewer and the coordinates of the cell that the viewer is on. Then it can calculate how to move the cells so that the cell that the viewer is on is centered on the screen. See Chapter 9 for more information about this.

```
    for( i = 0; i < m_rooms.Size(); i++ )
    {
        px = m_rooms[i].m_x * 64 + ox;
        py = m_rooms[i].m_y * 64 + oy;
```

Now the function loops through every cell in the map and calculates the pixel coordinates for each room.

```
            for( z = 0; z < 2; z++ )
            {
                current = m_rooms[i].m_tiles[z];
```

Now it loops through both layers of the cell and gets the tile number for each layer.

```
                if( current != -1 )
                {
                    SDLBlit( m_tilebmps[current], p_surface, px, py );
                }
            }
```

If the tile number isn't –1, then it is a valid tile, and it should be drawn.

```
            item = m_rooms[i].m_item;
            person = m_rooms[i].m_person;
            if( item != 0 )
                SDLBlit( item->GetGraphic(), p_surface, px, py );
            if( person != 0 )
                SDLBlit( person->GetGraphic(), p_surface, px, py );
        }
    }
```

Finally, it checks to see if the item and person in the cell are valid. If either of them is, then it is drawn on the map, too.

The CanMove Function

Determining if a person can move in a certain direction is even easier with a directionmap than it is with a tilemap because you don't have to find the *x* and *y* coordinates of the adjacent cell; the directionmap actually points directly to the next room, so you can tell what it is immediately.

```
bool CanMove( Person* p_person, int p_direction )
{
    int cell = GetCellNumber( p_person->GetCell(), p_direction );
    if( cell == -1 )
        return false;
```

This function utilizes the `GetCellNumber` function to get the number of the cell in the given direction. If it returns –1, then this function returns false because a player cannot walk into a wall.

```
    if( m_rooms[cell].m_blocked == true )
        return false;
```

```
if( m_rooms[cell].m_person != 0 )
    return false;
```

Then the function checks to see if the cell in that direction is blocked and if a person is in that cell. You cannot move into either of those kinds of rooms, so if either of them is true, false is returned.

```
if( m_rooms[cell].m_item != 0 )
{
    if( m_rooms[cell].m_item->CanBlock() == true )
        return false;
}
```

Finally, it checks to see if there is an item blocking the path into the new cell. If there is, then it returns false.

```
    return true;
}
```

If it has passed all of those tests, then the cell is not blocked, and a player can move into it, so true is returned.

The Move Function

This function also works in a similar way to the TileMap version.

```
void Move( Person* p_person, int p_direction )
{
    int newcell;
    if( CanMove( p_person, p_direction ) == true )
    {
```

First, it makes sure that the person can move in the given direction.

```
        newcell = GetCellNumber( p_person->GetCell(), p_direction );
        m_rooms[newcell].m_person = p_person;
        m_rooms[p_person->GetCell()].m_person = 0;
        p_person->SetX( m_rooms[newcell].m_x );
        p_person->SetY( m_rooms[newcell].m_y );
        p_person->SetCell( newcell );
    }
}
```

After that, it retrieves the number of the new cell and moves the person into the new cell. After that, it removes the pointer to the person from the old cell and updates the *x* and *y* coordinates and the cell number of the person.

The GetItem and SetItem Functions

These functions just get and set an item at a certain cell number.

```
Item* GetItem( int p_cell )
{
    if( p_cell >= GetNumberOfCells() || p_cell < 0 )
        return 0;
    return m_rooms[p_cell].m_item;
}
void SetItem( int p_cell, Item* p_item )
{
    if( p_cell >= GetNumberOfCells() || p_cell < 0 )
        return;
    m_rooms[p_cell].m_item = p_item;
}
```

Both functions check to make sure that the cell is in-bounds first and then get or set the item pointer in the correct cell.

The GetPerson and SetPerson Functions

These functions are almost the same as the `GetItem` and `SetItem` functions listed previously:

```
Person* GetPerson( int p_cell )
{
    if( p_cell >= GetNumberOfCells() || p_cell < 0 )
        return 0;
    return m_rooms[p_cell].m_person;
}
void SetPerson( int p_cell, Person* p_person )
{
    if( p_cell >= GetNumberOfCells() || p_cell < 0 )
        return;
    m_rooms[p_cell].m_person = p_person;
}
```

The GetCellNumber Function

This is the function that gets the number of a cell, given a cell and a direction. This function is much easier with a directionmap than it was with a tilemap because each cell in a directionmap points to the adjacent cell instead of needing an algorithm to calculate the number of an adjacent cell.

```
int GetCellNumber( int p_cell, int p_direction )
{
    return m_rooms[p_cell].m_exits[p_direction];
}
```

The function first accesses the `m_rooms` array to get the starting room and then accesses its `m_exits` array to find out the number of the room in the given direction.

The GetNumberOfCells Function

This is a pretty simple function; it just returns the size of the room array:

```
int GetNumberOfCells()
{
    return m_rooms.Size();
}
```

The GetClosestDirection Function

Finally, here is the function that will determine which direction a person has to go to get closer to another person.

For now, this function is the same as the `GetClosestDirection` function in the `TileMap` class. This will change in Chapter 24, "Tying It Together: Algorithms," however.

```
int GetClosestDirection( Person* p_one, Person* p_two )
{
    int direction = -1;
    if( p_one->GetY() > p_two->GetY() )
        direction = 0;
    else if( p_one->GetX() < p_two->GetX() )
        direction = 1;
    else if( p_one->GetY() < p_two->GetY() )
        direction = 2;
    else if( p_one->GetX() > p_two->GetX() )
        direction = 3;
    return direction;
}
```

Changes to the Game Logic

If you look at the kinds of maps that are best represented by a tilemap, you can see that they are usually outdoor maps. That's because the outdoors is a wide-open area, and a tilemap represents that kind of environment.

Indoor environments are a different story, however. Indoor areas are usually small and separated by many walls and hallways. Coincidentally, directionmaps represent these kinds of environments much better than tilemaps do.

Now look at the image sets for both types of environments. For the first two iterations of the game, the tilemap class has used a standard grass/snow image set, which you usually see outdoors. If you're going to be using the directionmap to represent indoor maps, though, you probably don't want to see grass and snow on the map. Instead, you'll need another type of image set.

The New Image Set

For the games' medieval motif, I have decided to go with a dark-stone and dirt feel so that it seems like the player is in a dungeon or cavern. Now the game will have two different image sets (also known as a *tileset*). In the earlier versions of the game, the single tileset and its size were stored in the game like this:

```
const int TILES = 24;
SDL_Surface* g_tiles[TILES];
```

Because there isn't a single tileset anymore, I needed to add another tileset and a way to differentiate between the two. So I renamed the original tileset like this:

```
const int OUTDOORTILES = 24;
SDL_Surface* g_outdoortiles[OUTDOORTILES];
```

And the new tileset like this:

```
const int DUNGEONTILES = 14;
SDL_Surface* g_dungeontiles[DUNGEONTILES];
```

As with the original tileset, the new tileset is loaded within the Init function:

```
g_dungeontiles[0] = SDL_LoadBMP( "stone.bmp" );
// lots more bitmap loading ...
```

Now, only one more change needs to be made to the game logic to get this working.

Game Demonstration 19-1: Adding the New Map Format

The New LoadMap Function

In Chapter 9, I showed you that the game demo will separate the map-loading logic into a function called `LoadMap`, but I told you that the explanation would have to wait until Chapter 19, "Tying It Together: Graphs." Well this *is* Chapter 19, so I suppose I should explain it to you.

In the first two versions of the game, the only map type was a tilemap, so it was easy to assume that this was the kind of map that the game would always use. I showed you how to avoid this thinking, however, and showed you how to abstract the tilemap into an interface called the `Map` class. However, there is still a problem with that method: Someone somewhere needs to know when to create a tilemap. You can't just take a file and say, "Load this map," without knowing what kind of map it is.

So this functionality was separated from the rest of the game and placed into a function called `LoadMap`. This function takes the name of a map file, creates a new map, and then returns a pointer to that map. Outside of this function, *nothing* in the actual game logic knows *anything* about tilemaps or directionmaps; they all use the generic `Map` class.

So now that you've added a new map type to the game, you need to modify the `LoadMap` function so that it can create `DirectionMaps`, too. The function is essentially a heavily extended version of the old version.

```
Map* LoadMap( char* p_filename )
{
    int maptype;
    FILE* f = fopen( p_filename, "rb" );
```

In the old version, you assumed that you would be loading a tilemap. Now, you don't know what kind of map you will be loading. Remember the ID number tacked onto the front of each file that denotes what kind of map it is? The function must now check that, so the file is opened in this function.

```
    TileMap* tmap;
    DirectionMap* dmap;
```

Then a `TileMap` and `DirectionMap` pointer are declared.

```
    if( f == 0 )
        return 0;
```

If the file could not be opened, it returns an empty pointer.

```
    fread( &maptype, 1, sizeof(int), f );
    fclose( f );
    if( maptype == 0 )
    {
        tmap = new TileMap( 64, 64, 2, g_outdoortiles );
        tmap->LoadFromFile( p_filename );
        return tmap;
    }
    else if( maptype == 1 )
    {
        dmap = new DirectionMap( g_dungeontiles );
        dmap->LoadFromFile( p_filename );
        return dmap;
    }
    return 0;
}
```

After that, the type of the map is loaded into `maptype`, and the file is closed. At this point, `maptype` should be either 0 or 1, so those are the two conditions that are tested. If the map type is 0, then you know that the file contains a tilemap, so a new `TileMap` is created with the outdoor tileset, loaded from the file, and then returned.

If the type is 1, then a new `DirectionMap` is created with the dungeon tileset, loaded from the file, and then returned. If the number isn't 0 or 1, then you have no idea what kind of file is being loaded, so the function just returns 0.

Playing the Game

Now that the game has been modified to take advantage of the new map format, you can actually play the game. The gameplay is the same as before, and there is one directionmap level included for you to play around with: `level4.map`.

You can get to that level by entering the red vortex on level 1, the green vortex on level 2, or the blue vortex on level 3. Figure 19.4 shows a figure of that level.

Figure 19.4

Here's a screenshot of the directionmap level. Note the black blanks in an irregular pattern. This is not possible with a tilemap, but it's easy to do with a directionmap.

Converting Old Maps

When I introduced the idea of an ID number in each map file, I said you needed a way to convert an old map produced from the level editors from Chapters 9 and 16 so that it has an ID number in it as well.

Example 19-1 shows you how to accomplish this. You can find this on the CD in the directory \examples\ch19\01 - Map Converter\.

Basically, all you want to do is load in the entire tilemap file, write out the ID, and then write the entire map out again.

```
void main()
{
    char filename[64];
    Array3D<int> mapdata( 64, 64, 4 );
    char exits[3][64];
    int maptype = 0;
    FILE* f = 0;
```

Here is all the data used in the conversion. The filename comes first; it is a string limited to 64 characters. Then there are the four-layer tilemap and the three exit strings. Both of those structures represent the entire tilemap.

After that is the map type variable, which is set to 0 to denote that this is a tilemap. Finally, the file is declared.

```
cout << "Enter a filename: ";
cin >> filename;
cout << "converting file...";
```

After that, the filename is requested from the user of the program.

```
f = fopen( filename, "rb" );
fread( mapdata.m_array, 64*64*4, sizeof(int), f );
fread( exits[0], 64, sizeof(char), f );
fread( exits[1], 64, sizeof(char), f );
fread( exits[2], 64, sizeof(char), f );
fclose( f );
```

This sequence of code opens up the file for reading and then reads in all of the map data and exit data, and closes the file again. At this point, all of the valid data is now in the memory of the computer.

```
f = fopen( filename, "wb" );
fwrite( &maptype, 1, sizeof(int), f );
fwrite( mapdata.m_array, 64*64*4, sizeof(int), f );
fwrite( exits[0], 64, sizeof(char), f );
fwrite( exits[1], 64, sizeof(char), f );
fwrite( exits[2], 64, sizeof(char), f );
fclose( f );
}
```

In the second part of the program, the file is opened again, this time in `wb` mode. This mode destroys all the contents of the file, so you're writing over the old file.

Then the map type is written out, and the map data, the exit data, and the file are closed. That was pretty simple, wasn't it?

Now, if you've created a really cool map using the map editors from Chapter 9 or 16, you can easily convert them to use with the new version of the game.

The Directionmap Map Editor

This is Game Demonstration 19-2, which you can find on the CD in the directory \demonstrations\ch19\Game02 - DirectionMap Editor\.

> ### Compiling the Demo
>
> This demonstration uses the SDLGUI library that I have developed for the book. For more information about this library, see Appendix B.
>
> To compile this demo, either open up the workspace file in the directory or create your own project using the settings described in Appendix B. If you create your own project, all of the files you need to include are in the directory.

Now that you have a game and a new map format created, you need a way to make maps with the new map format. This map editor will be used to create directionmaps.

The actual editor is essentially the same as the editor from Chapter 16. A few buttons have been moved around and renamed to use the dungeon tileset, but those are just cosmetic differences.

If you read on, I list the most important differences in the game demo.

The Initial Map

Previously, when the program started out it would loop through every tile on the map and set the base layer to a random value from 0 through 3. In the outdoor tileset, these four values represent one of the four grass tiles, so the entire map started out covered in grass. This was essential for a tilemap because the base layer of a tilemap can never be empty.

However, with a directionmap, things are different. To make editing the map easier, the map is still going to be stored in a 64 × 64 × 4 3D array, but when it is loaded or saved to disk, the editor will run it through a conversion function.

Because a directionmap is supposed to represent sparse indoor environments, the initial map will be completely empty. This also means that in the editor, the base tile of any cell in the 3D array can be empty.

Here is the code that initializes the map:

```
for( y = 0; y < g_map.Height(); y++ )
{
```

```
    for( x = 0; x < g_map.Width(); x++ )
    {
        g_map.Get( x, y, 0 ) = -1;
        g_map.Get( x, y, 1 ) = -1;
        g_map.Get( x, y, 2 ) = -1;
        g_map.Get( x, y, 3 ) = -1;
    }
}
```

All four layers of the map are cleared to nothing so that when you start the map editor, the map is completely empty.

Setting and Clearing Tiles

In a tilemap, you had a full 64 × 64 grid to work with, and it was assumed that every single tile existed. When using a directionmap, you can have weird map shapes that don't conform to a rectangle. See Figure 19.5 for an example.

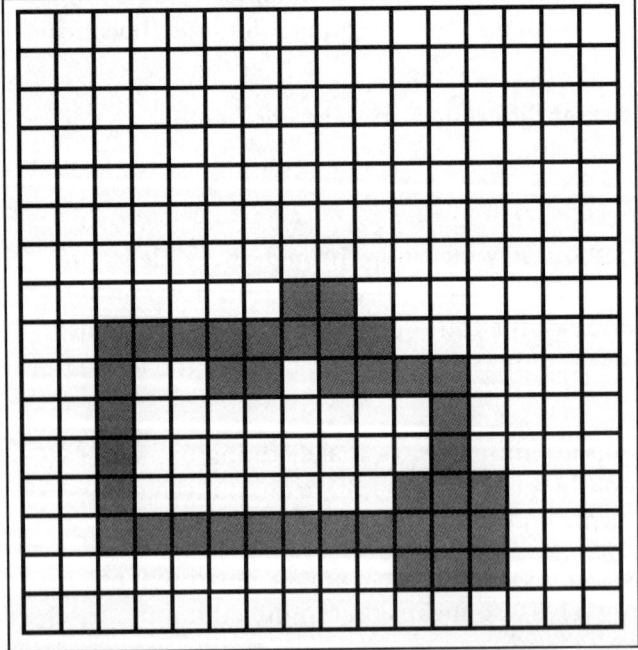

Figure 19.5

This is a grid containing a directionmap. Only the cells that have gray in them are actually rooms in the map.

In the figure is a grid, and some of the cells in the grid are gray. These gray cells represent the actual map—all the white cells are empty, cells that don't exist in the map.

When creating a directionmap, all of the cells in the 64 × 64 grid will be part of the void, and they will be blank. How does the program tell if a cell is part of the map or part of the void, then? This editor uses a simple assumption: If a cell has a base tile (on layer 0), then it is part of the map. If the base tile is –1, then the cell is part of the void.

When converting a map from the grid form into the directionmap form, it goes through and picks out all of the cells that have a base tile value of 0 or more and ignores everything else.

Now, because a room doesn't exist if it doesn't have a base tile, you don't want the map editor to be able to draw items, people, and overlay tiles on cells that aren't part of the map, so the part of the program that actually draws the current tile onto the map is modified a little bit. To make the program cleaner, the function has now been moved into its own separate function:

```
void DrawTile( int p_x, int p_y )
{
    int z;
```

This function takes the coordinates of the cell on the grid that the user wants to draw on. The rest of the drawing information is stored in global variables, which are easy to access in this function.

```
    if( p_x < g_map.Width() && p_y < g_map.Height() )
    {
        if( (g_currentlayer > 0 && g_map.Get( p_x, p_y, 0 ) == -1) )
            return;
```

First, the function makes sure that the coordinates are valid coordinates on the map. If so, then it continues. The second if statement in the previous code segment implements a check on the base tile. If you are drawing a non-base tile (current layer is more than 0) and the current base tile doesn't exist (the value is –1), you are trying to draw an item, a person, or an overlay on a room that doesn't exist in the map. The function knows this, so it exits out and doesn't actually draw the tile.

```
        if( g_currentlayer == 0 && g_currenttile == -1 )
        {
            for( z = 0; z < 4; z++ )
            {
                g_map.Get( p_x, p_y, z ) = -1;
            }
        }
```

The preceding code segment is somewhat important. Previously, whenever you wanted to clear the tile on a given layer, the g_currentlayer variable was set to the layer that you wanted to clear, and the g_currenttile variable was set to –1. Then, whenever you draw on the map, a –1 is placed into the current layer, and any item that was there is now cleared. Unfortunately, there is a problem with this method. If you clear the base tile in a directionmap, you are actually deleting the entire room. Using the old method of clearing a layer would not work because the base tile would be cleared, but the overlay, item, and person layers would not be. Then your map would look weird in the editor and not even work right in the game because all of these tiles would just be ignored.

So, whenever the function detects that you are trying to clear the base layer, it loops through all four layers on that cell and clears them all, essentially deleting the entire cell from the map.

```
        else
        {
            g_map.Get( p_x, p_y, g_currentlayer ) = g_currenttile;
        }
    }
}
```

If you're not clearing the base layer, then the current tile is written to the map.

Loading a Map

You should know what the file format for the directionmaps look like by now. If not, please go back and take a look at Figures 19.2 and 19.3.

The `MapEntry` class from Game Demonstration 19-1 is also used in this game demo. If you remember, this class follows the structure shown in Figure 19.2 and stores information about a single room in the map.

Here is the function listing:

```
void Load()
{
    MapEntry entry;
    int x, y, z;
    int cells;
```

The `entry` variable loads in each map entry, the `x`, `y`, and `z` variables loop through the grid, and the `cells` variable holds the number of rooms in the map.

```
for( z = 0; z < 4; z++ )
{
    for( y = 0; y < g_map.Height(); y++ )
    {
        for( x = 0; x < g_map.Width(); x++ )
        {
            g_map.Get( x, y, z ) = -1;
        }
    }
}
```

This code segment goes through every cell in the entire map and clears it out to −1. When a new map is loaded, each room is read in from disk and then placed into the grid. When this happens, you may end up getting cells from a previous map enmeshed into the cells of the map that you are loading, so this clears out the map and prevents this from happening.

```
FILE* f = fopen( g_filename, "rb" );
if( f == 0 )
    return;
fread( &x, 1, sizeof(int), f );
if( x != 1 )
{
    fclose( f );
    return;
}
```

The previous code segment tries to open the map for reading. If it can't be opened, then the function just returns. Then the function reads in the ID of the map and returns if the ID isn't 1 (which is the ID for all directionmaps).

```
fread( &cells, 1, sizeof(int), f );
for( x = 0; x < cells; x++ )
{
```

After that, the number of rooms in the map is read in and a `for`-loop is started that will loop through every room in the file.

```
fread( &entry, 1, sizeof(MapEntry), f );
for( z = 0; z < 4; z++ )
{
    g_map.Get( entry.x, entry.y, z ) = entry.layers[z];
}
```

The entry of each room in the file is read into the *entry* variable. The *x* and *y* variables of each entry tell the editor at which grid position each room should be placed. Then the function loops through each layer of the entry and copies the tile value of the entry into the map grid at the coordinates of the entry. Note that all exit information for each room is discarded; the editor assumes that two rooms next to each other will automatically be connected, so this information is automatically generated when the map is saved back to disk.

```
    }
    fread( g_exits[0], 64, sizeof(char), f );
    fread( g_exits[1], 64, sizeof(char), f );
    fread( g_exits[2], 64, sizeof(char), f );
    fclose( f );
}
```

Finally, the level exit information is read from the file into the three exit strings, and the file is closed.

Saving a Map

Saving a directionmap to disk is a slightly more complicated process than loading one in because it requires more processing.

When saving a directionmap to disk from a grid form, several things need to happen. First, the function needs to go through each cell in the grid and pick out which cells are valid rooms and which ones aren't. Every time it finds a new valid room, it is assigned a new cell number, which will be the room's number in the directionmap.

After every valid cell has a number, the function then needs to go through each cell again and calculate its exit information. After that has happened, the rooms can be saved to disk. Here is the function:

```
void Save()
{
    MapEntry entry;
    Array2D<int> cellnumbers( g_map.Width(), g_map.Height() );
    int tilecount = 0;
    int x, y, z;
    int ax, ay;
    int d;
```

Again, there is a `MapEntry` variable, but this time it will be used to save each room to disk instead of loading it. After that is a 2D array called `cellnumbers`. This array will store the room number of each cell in the grid if it is a valid room.

The `tilecount` variable will be used to keep track of the number of rooms in the map, as well as assign room numbers to each one during the first pass. The rest of the variables are used for storing temporary results and looping.

```
FILE* f = fopen( g_filename, "wb" );
if( f == 0 )
    return;
```

As usual, the function tries to open the file to write to and returns if it could not do so.

```
for( y = 0; y < g_map.Height(); y++ )
{
    for( x = 0; x < g_map.Width(); x++ )
    {
        if( g_map.Get( x, y, 0 ) != -1 )
        {
            cellnumbers.Get( x, y ) = tilecount;
            tilecount++;
        }
    }
}
```

Now the loop goes through each base tile in the grid. If it finds a base tile that isn't empty, then the number of that cell is set to the current tile count, and the tile count is incremented. This means that the very first room the function finds will be room number 0, and the next one will be 1, and so on.

```
x = 1;
fwrite( &x, 1, sizeof(int), f );
fwrite( &tilecount, 1, sizeof(int), f );
```

At this point, the first pass has completed, so you are ready to write the map to disk. The ID number, 1, is stored into x, which is then written to the file. The number of rooms in the map is written next.

```
for( y = 0; y < g_map.Height(); y++ )
{
    for( x = 0; x < g_map.Width(); x++ )
    {
```

```
            if( g_map.Get( x, y, 0 ) != -1 )
            {
```

Now the second and final pass is started. It goes through every cell once again and picks out the cells that have a base tile.

```
                entry.x = x;
                entry.y = y;
```

The x and y coordinates of the current room entry are set to be the same as the coordinates of the room on the 64 × 64 grid. This is an easy way to tell where the rooms are in relation to each other.

```
                for( d = 0; d < 4; d++ )
                {
                    ax = DIRECTIONTABLE[d][0] + x;
                    ay = DIRECTIONTABLE[d][1] + y;
```

Now the function loops through all four directions from the current cell, computes the coordinates of the current adjacent cell, and stores them into ax and ay. After those coordinates have been calculated, the function needs to find out if those coordinates are valid on the grid:

```
                    if( ax >= 0 && ax < g_map.Width() &&
                        ay >= 0 && ay < g_map.Height() )
                    {
                        if( g_map.Get( ax, ay, 0 ) != -1 )
                        {
                            entry.directions[d] =
                                cellnumbers.Get( ax, ay );
                        }
                        else
                        {
                            entry.directions[d] = -1;
                        }
                    }
                }
            }
```

After it has verified that the coordinates are on the map, it needs to check to see if the cell in those coordinates is a real room or part of the void. If it's real, then the entry of the current room is updated so that the direction pointer points to the room that is in the adjacent cell. The room number is retrieved from the cellnumbers array that was calculated in the first pass.

If there is no cell there, then the direction entry is set to –1, which means that there is no exit in that direction.

```
            for( z = 0; z < 4; z++ )
            {
                entry.layers[z] = g_map.Get( x, y, z );
            }
            fwrite( &entry, 1, sizeof(MapEntry), f );
        }
    }
}
```

The tile numbers of each layer of the entry are set to the same values as the cell in the grid, and then the entry is written to disk. When every room has been written, that is the end of the second pass.

```
    fwrite( g_exits[0], 64, sizeof(char), f );
    fwrite( g_exits[1], 64, sizeof(char), f );
    fwrite( g_exits[2], 64, sizeof(char), f );
    fclose( f );
}
```

Finally, the three exit strings are written to disk, and the file is closed. You now have a directionmap on disk!

Using the Editor

The editor, with the exception of the new tileset and the del base button, is virtually identical to the editor from Chapter 16. This editor will only read and write directionmap files, so don't try editing tilemap files in this editor—it won't work.

Figure 19.6 shows a screenshot of the editor in action, editing the level I provided for the demo.

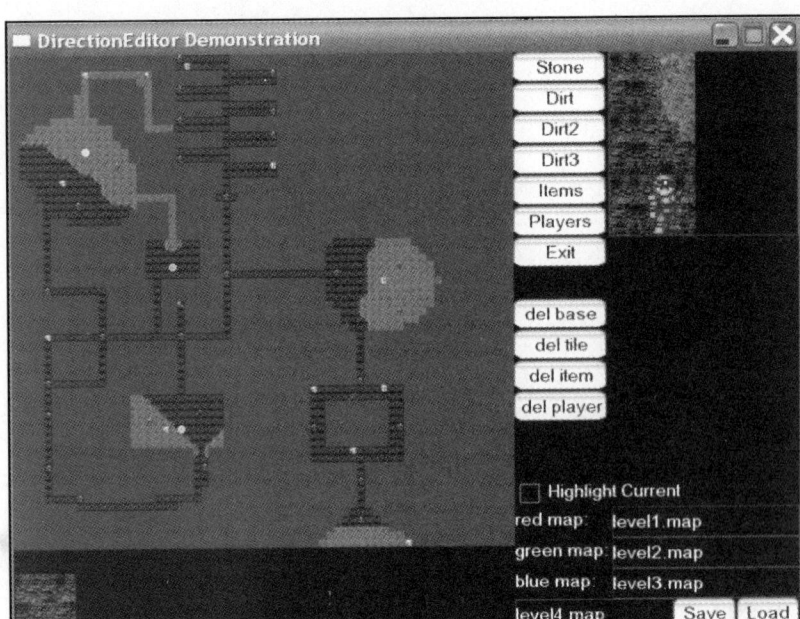

Figure 19.6

Here is a screenshot from the directionmap dungeon editor.

Play around with it, and see what you can do.

Upgrading the Tilemap Editor

There is one more thing that needs to be done—a very quick edit to the old tilemap editor from Chapter 16 so that it supports the new ID number on tilemaps. This update is so simple that I probably don't need to mention it, but it is here for completeness nonetheless.

The updated map editor is on the CD in the directory \demonstrations\ch19\Game03 - TileMap Editor\.

The *only* two things that are changed are the Load and Save functions.

The Save Function

The code in bold has been added to the function:

```
void Save()
{
    int maptype = 0;
```

```
    FILE* f = fopen( g_filename, "wb" );
    if( f == 0 )
        return;
    fwrite( &maptype, 1, sizeof(int), f );
    fwrite( g_map.m_array,
            g_map.Depth() * g_map.Height() * g_map.Width(),
            sizeof(int),
            f );
    fwrite( g_exits[0], 64, sizeof(char), f );
    fwrite( g_exits[1], 64, sizeof(char), f );
    fwrite( g_exits[2], 64, sizeof(char), f );
    fclose( f );
}
```

The code just saves the map ID before all the rest of the data.

The Load Function

The code in bold has been added to this function from the previous version:

```
void Load()
{
    int maptype = 0;
    FILE* f = fopen( g_filename, "rb" );
    if( f == 0 )
        return;
    fread( &maptype, 1, sizeof(int), f );
    if( maptype != 0 )
        return;
    fread( g_map.m_array,
           g_map.Depth() * g_map.Height() * g_map.Width(),
           sizeof(int),
           f );
    fread( g_exits[0], 64, sizeof(char), f );
    fread( g_exits[1], 64, sizeof(char), f );
    fread( g_exits[2], 64, sizeof(char), f );
    fclose( f );
}
```

The code reads in the map type and quits if it is not the type that is expected.

Conclusion

Hopefully, now you can see how designing your game structures to be flexible at the very beginning can really save you a lot of work later on when you want to add features to the game.

Although I could have used tons of other examples to integrate graphs into this chapter, this chapter had two major points I wanted to get across. First and foremost, I wanted to show you how easy it is to extend your game if you design it correctly. A computer program is nothing more than data and functions that operate on that data, so it is *essential* that you design your data correctly from the start. Second, I wanted to reinforce some graph-like concepts in this chapter and show you how to use directionmaps.

I hope you understand everything in this chapter. You have now completed the data structure segment of the book. From now on, you will be learning about popular algorithms used in game programming, a subject that goes hand-in-hand with data structures.

PART FIVE

Algorithms

- **20** Sorting Data
- **21** Data Compression
- **22** Random Numbers
- **23** Pathfinding
- **24** Tying It Together: Algorithms

CHAPTER 20

SORTING DATA

20. Sorting Data

When people teach you how to sort data in a book, they usually either put the information up near the front of the book or spread the information haphazardly throughout the book. I've decided to use a different method. Now that you've learned about every structure in the book, I feel it is safe to introduce you to some of the more famous algorithms.

Sorting data is an important subject because just about every program out there sorts data in one way or another. In this chapter, you will learn

- What the bubble sort is
- How to code the bubble sort
- What the heap sort is
- How to code the heap sort
- What the quicksort is
- How to code the quicksort
- How the bubble, heap, and quicksorts compare to each other
- What the radix sort is
- How to code the radix sort

The Simplest Sort: Bubble Sort

Every sorting tutorial or book in the world shows you, or at least mentions, the *bubble sort*. This is because the bubble sort is the easiest sort in the world to code. Unfortunately, it is also one of the slowest sorts in existence.

The bubble sort is a *brute force* sort; it uses a very simple algorithm to actually move data around so that it ends up sorted.

Look at Figure 20.1 for a moment. You want to sort the data in the array on the left so that the highest number is at the top. Using the bubble sort, you would first compare the bottom two indexes, which hold 7 and 2. Because 7 is larger than 2, they are swapped. The process continues, and the indexes containing 7 and 1 are compared. Again, because 7 is larger than 1, they are swapped. This process continues until the 7 is *bubbled* up to the top of the array.

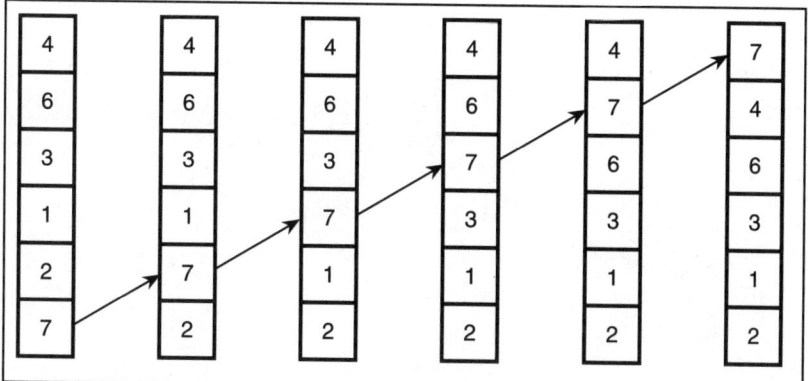

Figure 20.1
This is one pass of the bubble sort.

Now that the highest number in the array has been bubbled up to the top of the array, this process is repeated, as shown in Figure 20.2.

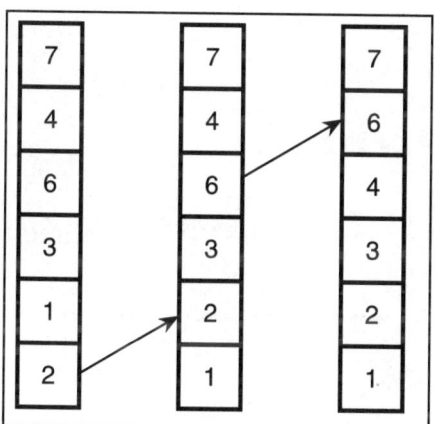

Figure 20.2
This is the second pass of the bubble sort.

Notice that this time fewer swaps occur. This time, the 1 and the 2 are swapped, and then the 6 and the 4 are swapped. Amazingly, after just two passes of the bubble sort, this array was sorted.

Worst-Case Bubble Sort

Unfortunately, it isn't always like this. Most of the time, the bubble sort takes much longer to complete. Take the array in Figure 20.3, for example. On the first pass, 6 is bubbled up to the top. On the second pass, 5 is bubbled up to the top, and this continues with each iteration until it is sorted. This array requires 5 iterations of the bubble sort to become sorted.

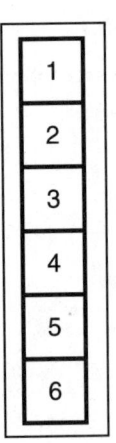

Figure 20.3

Here is the worst-case scenario for a bubble sort.

Because a bubble sort is essentially a doubly-nested for-loop, the algorithm is classified as an $O(n^2)$ algorithm.

All in all, the bubble sort is pretty "dumb."

Graphical Demonstration: Bubble Sort

This is Graphical Demonstration 20-1, which can be found on the CD in the directory \demonstrations\ch20\Demo01 – Bubble Sort\.

Compiling the Demo

This demonstration uses the SDLGUI library that I have developed for the book. For more information about this library, see Appendix B, "The Memory Layout of a Computer Program."

To compile this demo, either open up the workspace file in the directory or create your own project using the settings described in Appendix B. If you create your own project, all of the files you need to include are in the directory.

This demo graphically shows you how the bubble sort actually works. When the demo starts off, the screen is full of a huge mess of colored bars and two buttons, as shown in Figure 20.4.

The Simplest Sort: Bubble Sort

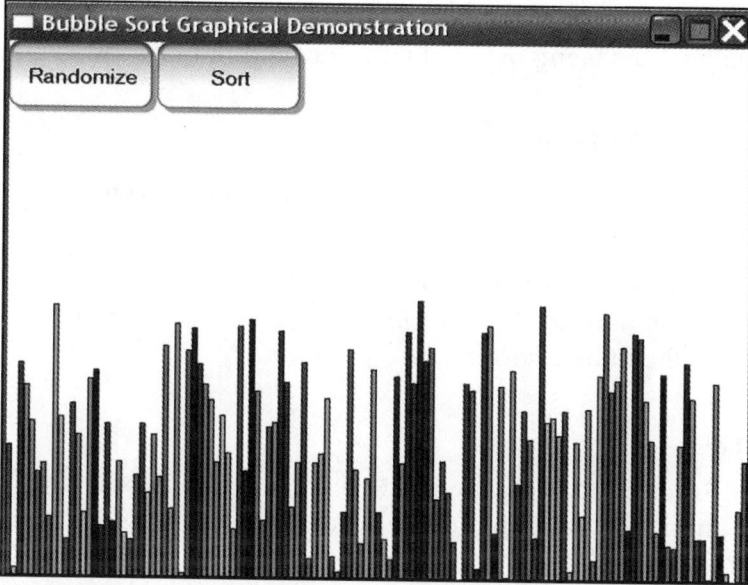

Figure 20.4

Here is a screenshot from the demo.

Clicking the Randomize button will randomize the bars, and clicking the Sort button will start the sorting animation. This will graphically show you how the bubble sort works.

Figure 20.5 shows a screenshot of the same array, sorted.

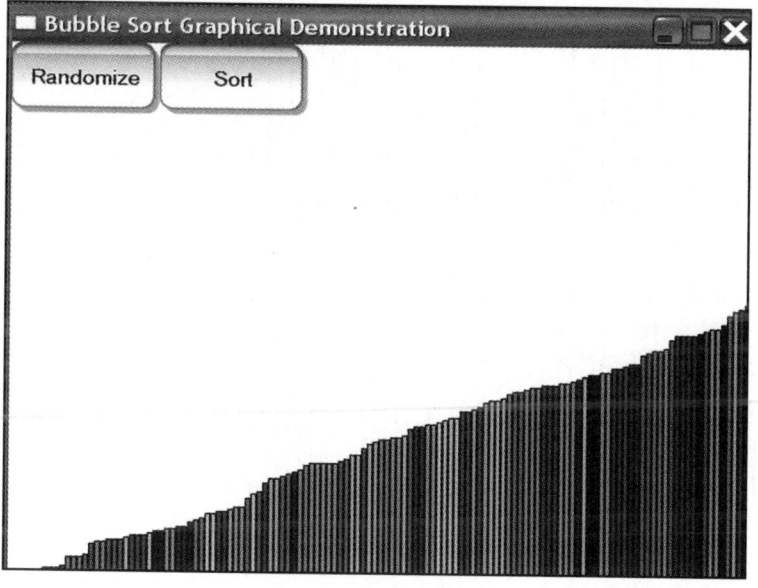

Figure 20.5

Here is the sorted array.

When you're watching the demo, it is very easy to see how the bubble sort works, because you can see the tallest bars being bubbled up to the end of the array.

Coding the Bubble Sort

All of the sorting functions found in this chapter can be found on the CD in the file \structures\sorts.h.

Even though I don't expect you to ever use the bubble sort in real life, the code is available to you to test out if you want to. But trust me when I say that you don't ever want to be caught using the bubble sort in a real program.

Optimizations

There are two things that you need to keep in mind when coding the bubble sort. The first thing you should notice is that if the function doesn't swap any indexes on a single pass, then the array is sorted and the function is complete.

The second thing you should notice is that because the bubble sort moves the highest value into the top index on every pass, you know that the upper x indexes in a bubble sort are sorted after x passes of the algorithm. Figure 20.6 illustrates this point.

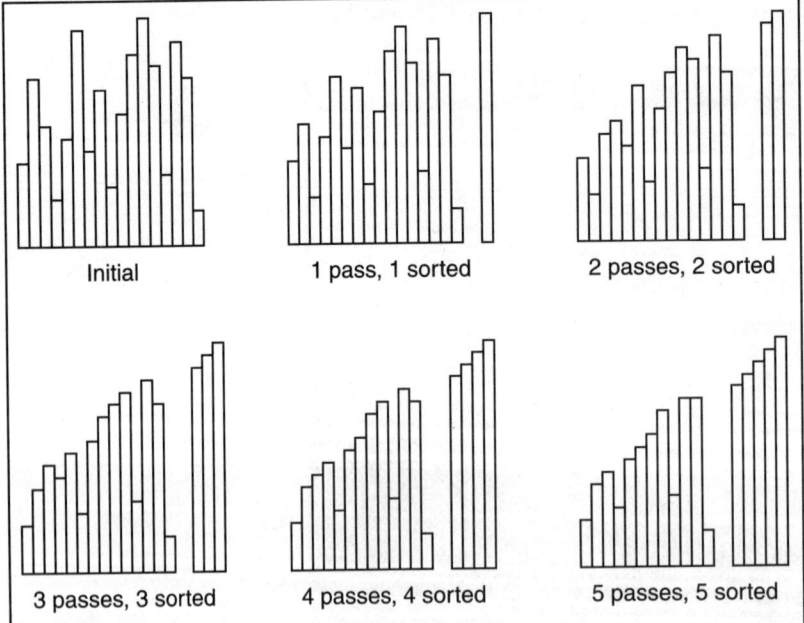

Figure 20.6

The upper x indexes are guaranteed to be sorted after x passes.

So this means that you don't have to do any calculations in the upper part of the array during each pass because you know that the upper part of the array is already sorted.

Psuedo-Code

To start with, let me show you the algorithm in psuedo-code:

```
Bubblesort( Array )
    int swaps = 1
    int top = Array.size - 1
    int index
    while( top != 0 AND swaps != 0 )
        swaps = 0
        for( index = 0; index < top; index++ )
            if Array[index] > Array[index + 1]
                Swap( Array[index], Array[index + 1] )
                swaps++
            end if
        end for
        top--
    end while
end function
```

The function keeps track of how many swaps are made in each iteration. If there weren't any swaps made in the last iteration, then the array is sorted, and the loop will end.

The inner loop goes through the array until it hits the `top` index, which represents the highest unsorted index in the array. This takes advantage of the fact I demonstrated in Figure 20.6 by not bothering to compare indexes in the sorted portion of the array.

The C++ Code

The reason I showed you the pseudo-code for the bubble sort first is because I decided to make the C++ `Bubblesort` function a little more complex, and you might not have understood what the code meant if I just threw it at you.

Templates are a really wonderful thing, you know. They allow you to use the same code over and over again, but I'm sure you already knew that because you've already read Chapter 2, "Templates."

20. Sorting Data

I'll be using templates and function pointers to make the sorting functions in this book as flexible as possible so that you will never need to program another sorting algorithm after you have programmed these.

I've used the notion of comparison functions before in Chapters 13, "Binary Search Trees," and 14, "Priority Queues and Heaps," and I'll be using them here again. To recap, the comparison functions I use in this book take two objects of the same type and compare them. If the left one is less than the right one, then the function returns a number less than 0; if they are equal, the function returns 0; and if the left is greater than the right, the function returns a number greater than 0.

> **TIP**
>
> Comparison functions allow for a great deal of flexibility. For example, if you had an array of pointers to objects, obviously you would not want to compare the pointers using the less-than or greater-than operators, because it would return whether or not the pointer is less than or greater than the other pointer, but it would not compare the actual objects. A comparison function can fix this and even allow you to reverse the sorting order if you want to.

```
template<class DataType>
void BubbleSort( Array<DataType>& p_array,
                 int (*p_compare)(DataType, DataType) )
{
    int top = p_array.Size() - 1;
    int index;
    int swaps = 1;
    while( top != 0 && swaps != 0 )
    {
        swaps = 0;
        for( index = 0; index < top; index++ )
        {
            if( p_compare( p_array[index], p_array[index + 1] ) > 0 )
            {
                Swap( p_array[index], p_array[index + 1] );
                swaps++;
            }
        }
        top--;
    }
}
```

The `p_array` variable is a reference to the array that you want to sort, and `p_compare` is a pointer to the comparison function. The only things that are different from the pseudo-code version is the call to `p_compare`, instead of a less-than comparison, and the C++ template syntax.

Example 20-1

Using the bubblesort algorithm is somewhat easy, which is demonstrated by Example 20-1. You can find this example on the CD in the directory \examples\ch20\01 - Bubble Sort\.

The example will use two arrays, one with integers and one with floats, and it will sort them both using the `BubbleSort` function. To do this, you must first create the comparison functions:

```
int compareint( int l, int r )
{
    return l - r;
}

int compareintreverse( int l, int r )
{
    return r - l;
}

int comparefloat( float l, float r )
{
    if( l < r )
        return -1;
    if( l > r )
        return 1;
    return 0;
}
```

The first function compares integers normally by subtracting the right from the left. If the left is less than the right, then it will return a negative number. If they are equal, it will return 0, and if the left is greater than the right, it will return a positive number.

The second function utilizes the flexible nature of using a comparison function and reverses the order of subtraction so that lower numbers are actually seen as being higher when using that comparison function.

The final function compares floats and returns a number based on how they compare.

> **NOTE**
>
> Most floating point comparison functions are a little more complex than mine here. For example, look at the numbers 1.00001 and 1.00002, which are practically equal for all intents and purposes (except for intensely accurate scientific programs... but this is for games!). This comparison algorithm will see them as different, which may or may not be what you intended. If you wanted to treat really close floats as equal, you would do this by subtracting them and comparing that value with a *threshold* value. This value is arbitrary and can be whatever you want it to be. If you wanted numbers that are less than 0.0001 apart to be considered equal, then that is your threshold value. For the purposes of sorting an array, a threshold is not really needed, which is why I did not include that feature. The code would look somewhat like this: `if( fabs(1-r) < threshold )`. The fabs function finds the absolute value of a float, so this line of code will determine if the two numbers differ by the threshold.

After you create the comparison functions, you move on to creating the arrays:

```
Array<int> iarray( 16 );
Array<float> farray( 16 );
for( index = 0; index < 16; index++ )
{
    iarray[index] = rand() % 256;
    farray[index] = (float)(rand() % 256) / 256.0f;
}
```

This code creates two arrays and fills them with random values. The integer array is filled with integers from 0 to 255, and the float array is filled with floats from 0.0 to 1.0.

Finally, you get to the easy part, sorting the arrays (hooray!):

```
BubbleSort( iarray, compareint );
BubbleSort( farray, comparefloat );
BubbleSort( iarray, compareintreverse );
```

Wasn't that easy? You pass in the array you want to sort and the comparison function. The first two sorts sort the arrays in *ascending* order so that the lowest values are first in the array. The third sort re-sorts the integer array in *descending* order because the comparison function is reversed.

Isn't that neat?

The Hacked Sort: Heap Sort

The heap (see Chapter 14) is one of my favorite data structures. Not only is it very efficient for priority queues, but it can also be used as an efficient sorting algorithm. I call it a *hacked* sort because heaps were never meant to sort data; this is just a neat side effect of the heap data structure.

Just think about it for a moment: The heap is really efficient at inserting items ($O(\log_2 n)$), and really efficient at removing the highest item (also $O(\log_2 n)$). So what would happen if you were able to take the contents of an array, stick them all into a heap, and then remove the highest item one at a time? You'd get a (less efficient) version of the heap sort!

The downside of the algorithm I just described is that it requires twice the space of the array, and if you're sorting large amounts of items, this can be a problem.

So you need to think of a way to keep the data all in one place.

What if there was a way to convert an array of random data into a heap? That would solve half the problem right there.

Luckily, there is a simple algorithm to turn an array into a heap, and it doesn't use any new algorithms to implement it! It's very simple:

1. Find the last index on the second-lowest level of the heap.
2. Call the `WalkDown` function on that index.
3. Decrease the index by one.
4. Repeat steps 2 and 3 until the index is 0.

Amazingly, this simple process converts an array of items into a heap. Figure 20.7 shows you how to treat the array as a binary tree.

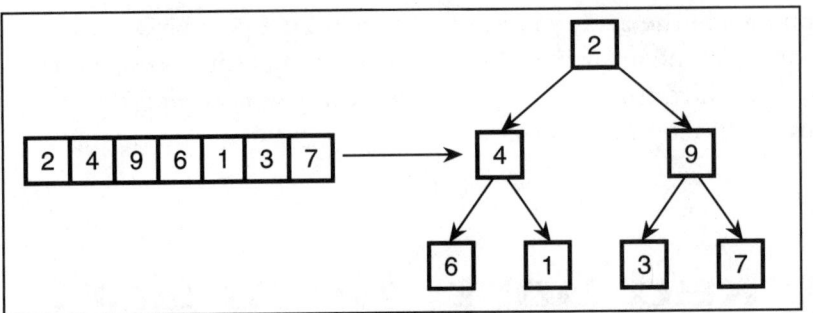

Figure 20.7

This is how you treat an array as a binary tree.

Note that this is just a conceptual conversion; you really haven't done anything to the array except look at it differently so you can understand how the algorithm works better.

Now you can begin the process of converting the array into a valid heap, which is shown in Figure 20.8.

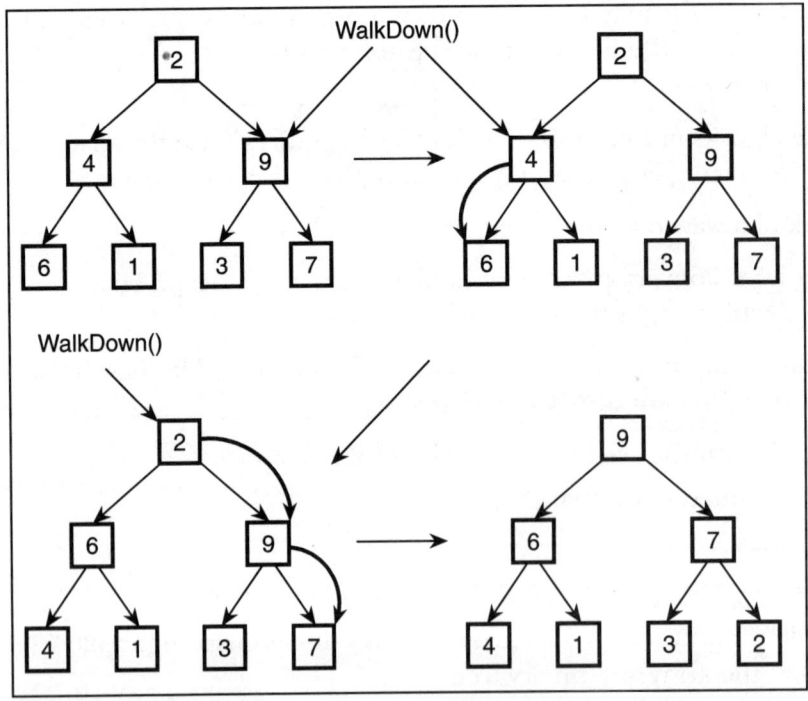

Figure 20.8

This is how you turn the array into a heap.

First you call the WalkDown function on the 9 because it is the rightmost node on the second-lowest level. Nothing happens in this case, though, because the 9 is higher than both the 3 and the 7. Next, you call WalkDown on the 4, and it can be walked down, so it is swapped with the 6. Finally, you call `WalkDown` on the 2, and it is walked down to the bottom of the heap. Congratulations, you now have a heap.

How do you turn the heap into a sorted array, though? Think about two things. One, you always remove the highest item in the heap, and two, when you remove the top of the heap, the size of the heap goes down by one.

In a normal heap, you discard the top of the heap and throw it away because you don't need it anymore, and then you move the last item to the top and walk it down. For a heap sort, instead of discarding the top item, you just swap it with the last item in the array and then perform the walkdown algorithm as usual. Figure 20.9 shows the first two passes of this process.

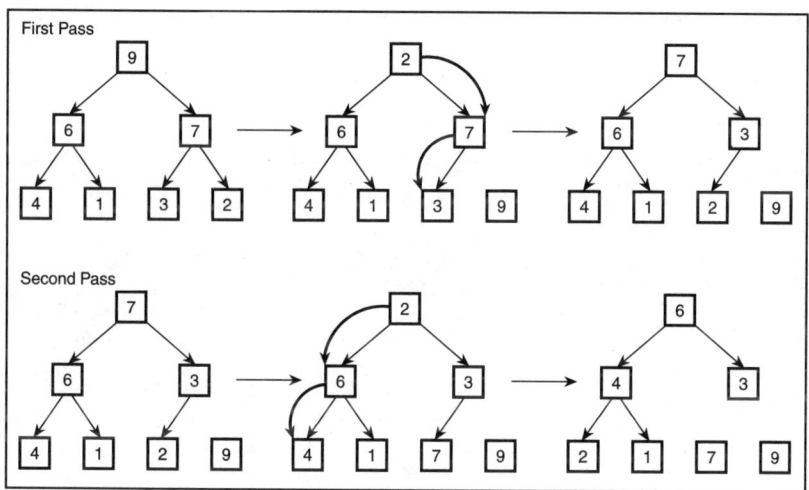

Figure 20.9

Here are the first two passes of the heap sort algorithm on a heap.

The 9 and 2 are swapped first, and the 2 is walked down the tree, which puts 7 in the root. In the second pass, the 7 and the 2 are swapped, and the 2 is again walked down the tree. After these two passes, the last index of the array contains 9, and the second-to-last index contains 7. If you continue using this process, you will eventually end up with a sorted array.

Graphical Demonstration: Heap Sort

This is Graphical Demonstration 20-2, which you can find on the CD in the directory \demonstrations\ch20\Demo02 - Heap Sort\.

20. Sorting Data

> ## Compiling the Demo
>
> This demonstration uses the SDLGUI library that I have developed for the book. For more information about this library, see Appendix B.
>
> To compile this demo, either open up the workspace file in the directory or create your own project using the settings described in Appendix B. If you create your own project, all of the files you need to include are in the directory.

This demo's interface is the same as the previous demo, and the only difference is that it uses the heapsort algorithm to sort the data.

Figure 20.10 shows a screenshot of the demo right after the heap-conversion phase, where the array is now turned completely into a heap.

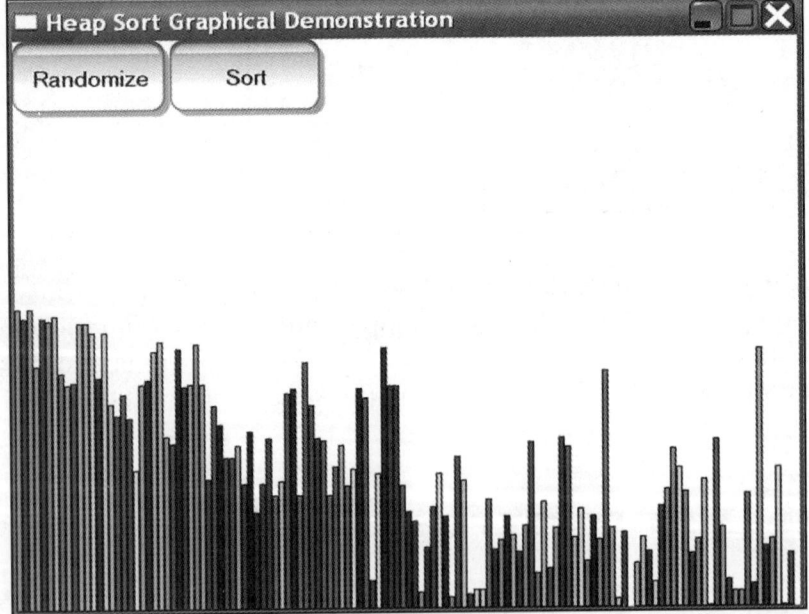

Figure 20.10

Here is a screenshot of the array after it has been turned into a heap.

Figure 20.11 shows a screenshot of the demo in the middle of the sorting phase. You can see that the left part of the array is a heap while the right half is sorted.

The Hacked Sort: Heap Sort

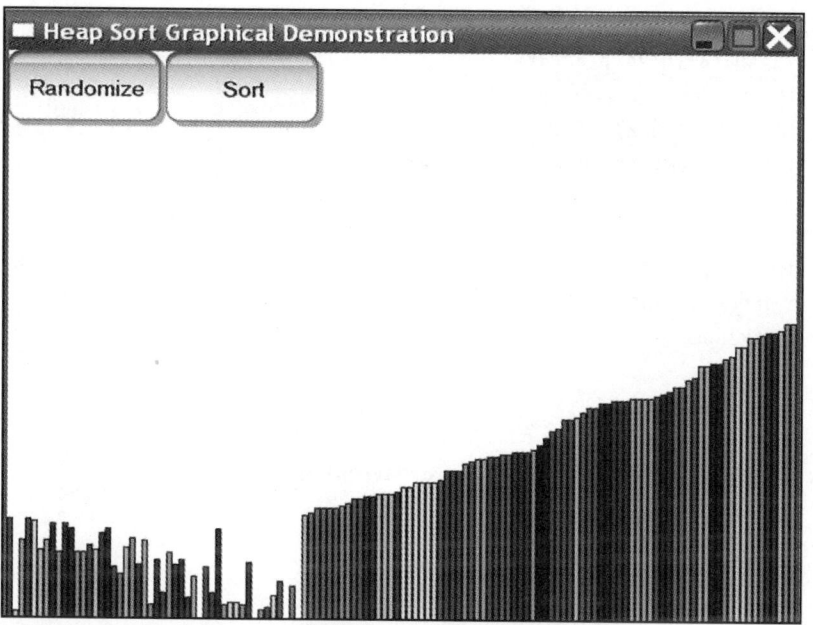

Figure 20.11

Here is a screenshot of the half-sorted array.

The first thing you should notice about this demo is that it is significantly faster than the bubble sort demo (I demonstrate its speed later). The heap sort is a smarter algorithm than the bubble sort; it focuses its efforts into finding the highest item in the array and quickly getting it to the correct position. This is different from the bubble sort, which focuses its efforts in moving the highest item throughout the entire array before it finds the correct place.

The heap sort is an $O(n \log_2 n)$ function. Remember, the `WalkDown` function is $O(\log_2 n)$, and you call it n times. If you remember back to Chapter 1, "Basic Algorithm Analysis," you can see that a $O(n \log_2 n)$ function is much more efficient than an $O(n^2)$ function like the bubble sort.

Coding the Heap Sort

There really isn't much to coding the heap sort because you rely on functions that you've already made.

The WalkDown Function

However, because you want to be able to pass the array into the heap sort function, you won't actually be using the heap class that you used in Chapter 14. Instead, a new stand-alone `WalkDown` function is created so that it works on regular arrays:

```cpp
template<class DataType>
void HeapWalkDown( Array<DataType>& p_array,
                  int p_index,
                  int p_maxIndex,
                  int (*p_compare)(DataType, DataType) )
{
    int parent = p_index;
    int child = p_index * 2;
    DataType temp = p_array[parent - 1];
    while( child <= p_maxIndex )
    {
        if( child < p_maxIndex )
        {
            if( p_compare( p_array[child - 1], p_array[child] ) < 0 )
            {
                child++;
            }
        }
        if( p_compare( temp, p_array[child - 1] ) < 0 )
        {
            p_array[parent - 1] = p_array[child - 1];
            parent = child;
            child *= 2;
        }
        else
            break;
    }
    p_array[parent - 1] = temp;
}
```

The main changes from the heap's `WalkDown` function are highlighted in bold. The function is a template function, so it works on any data type, and it takes a comparison function pointer so you can customize the way the sorting works.

Another change is the way the indexes are accessed. Each index has been decreased by one in this version of the function. If you'll remember, heaps need to be accessed starting at index 1, and arrays start at index 0. For the heap, it is okay to waste one index, but that index is not wasted here, so you need to treat each index properly. For example, if you want to call `WalkDown` on the root, you pass the function index 1 (the root index of a binary tree array), and it will automatically figure out the real index, 0.

The HeapSort Function

Finally, here is the `HeapSort` function, split into sections so you can understand it better.

```
template<class DataType>
void HeapSort( Array<DataType>& p_array, int (*p_compare)(DataType, DataType) )
{
    int index;
    int maxIndex = p_array.Size();
    int rightindex = maxIndex / 2;
```

The three variables that are used are the index, which will loop through the array, the max index, which keeps track of the size of the heap at all times, and the right index, which holds the index of the parent of the lowest node—the first node in the tree that could possibly be walked down.

```
    for( index = rightindex; index > 0; index-- )
    {
        HeapWalkDown( p_array, index, maxIndex, p_compare );
    }
```

The previous code segment starts at the lowest node that can be walked down and walks everything down, turning the array into a heap.

```
    while( maxIndex > 0 )
    {
        Swap( p_array[0], p_array[maxIndex - 1] );
        maxIndex--;
        HeapWalkDown( p_array, 1, maxIndex, p_compare );
    }
}
```

Finally, the algorithm swaps the first and last indexes, decreases the size of the heap, and walks the top index down. This is repeated until the entire array is sorted.

Example 20-2

Example 20-2 can be found on the CD in the directory \examples\ch20\02 - Heap Sort\. This example is the same as Example 20-1, except the calls to `BubbleSort` are replaced with calls to `HeapSort`:

```
HeapSort( iarray, compareint );
HeapSort( farray, comparefloat );
HeapSort( iarray, compareintreverse );
```

That's all there is to it.

The Fastest Sort: Quicksort

This is the last general-purpose sort that I will go into in depth in this book for a very simple reason: The quicksort is the fastest sort (so it isn't just a clever name).

The quicksort is probably the sort that you will use the most in the real world because it is so fast. The quicksort is a recursive algorithm that uses a *divide and conquer* approach to sorting the array.

The basic operation of the quicksort works like this:

1. Pick a pivot index.
2. Move everything that is less than the pivot to the left side of the array.
3. Move everything that is greater than the pivot to the right side of the array.
4. Recursively quicksort the array segment below the pivot.
5. Recursively quicksort the array segment above the pivot.

Sounds simple, doesn't it? It really is simple when you think about it.

Picking the Pivot

The first thing you need to do is pick a pivot. Simple quicksort algorithms usually pick the first or last index in the array and use that as a pivot, but that method has a problem.

For the quicksort algorithm to work efficiently, you need to make sure that the subarrays that are recursively sorted are about equal in size. Figure 20.12 shows a diagram of the different outcomes of a quicksort.

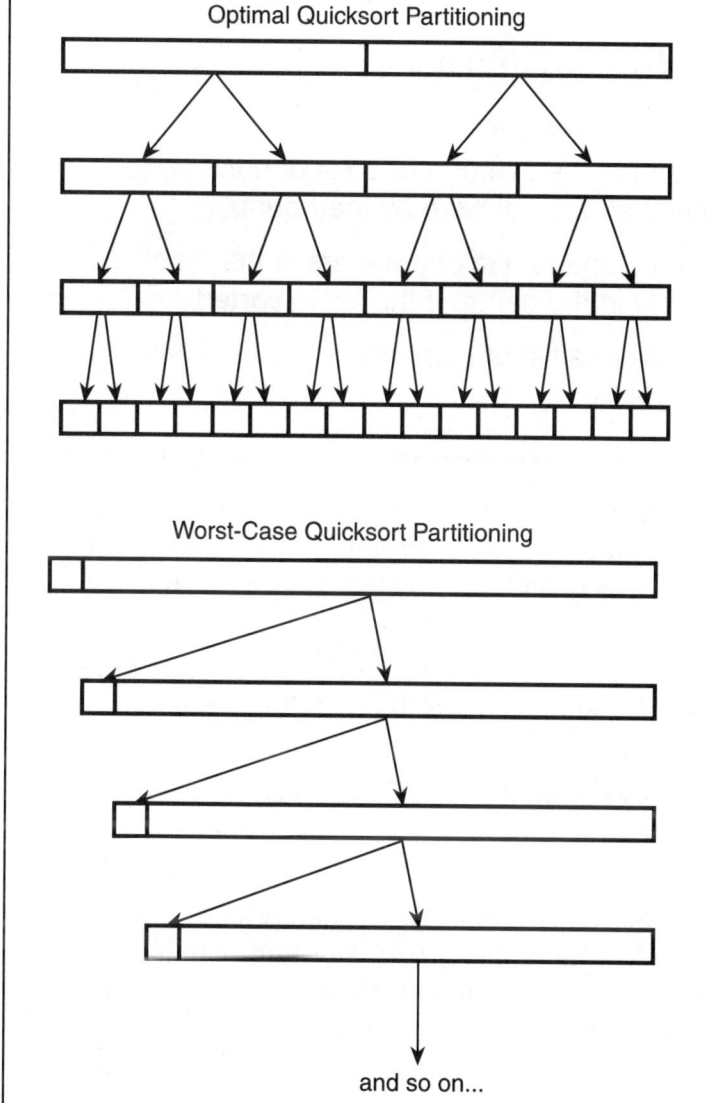

Figure 20.12

These are the best-case and worst-case quicksorts.

On the top, the pivot that is chosen is the *median* value in the array. The median value in a bunch of numbers is the number that will fall in the middle of the array when they are sorted.

> ### Statistics Terms
>
> Here are a few common terms used in statistics:
>
> - mean - The mean is the average of a list of numbers, which is simply their sum divided by their quantity.
> - median - The median of a list of numbers is the number that is exactly in the center if the list is sorted.
> - mode - The mode of a list of numbers is the most frequent value in the list.

So if the median value of the array is picked as the pivot at each level in the function, everything below the pivot is moved to the left, and everything above is moved to the right. The array is split exactly in half, and the quicksort is called on each half. This is the optimal way for the quicksort to operate.

If, on the other hand, you choose a pivot close to the beginning or end of the array, you get the picture on the bottom of Figure 20.12, the worst case. The quicksort has to do lots of work if it looks like that.

Unfortunately, there is no easy way to find the median of the array. In fact, the only way that I know of to find the median of the array is to actually sort it, which is what you're trying to do anyway!

Instead, you must resort to a simple algorithm to find a good pivot; the most famous of these algorithms is called the *median-of-three* algorithm. This algorithm looks at three indexes: the first, the middle, and the last. It then chooses the median of those three indexes and uses that as the pivot.

It turns out that this little optimization usually makes the quicksort an amazingly fast sorting algorithm.

Performing the Quicksort

Now that you've chosen the pivot, you need to do something with the array. The quicksort usually works by scanning downward and then upward, swapping numbers if they are on the wrong side of the array.

To show you how this works, I have to take you through an example. Figure 20.13 shows the array you want to sort and how the pivot is chosen. In this example, you examine 11, 1, and 5 and choose 5 as the pivot because it is the median value of those three.

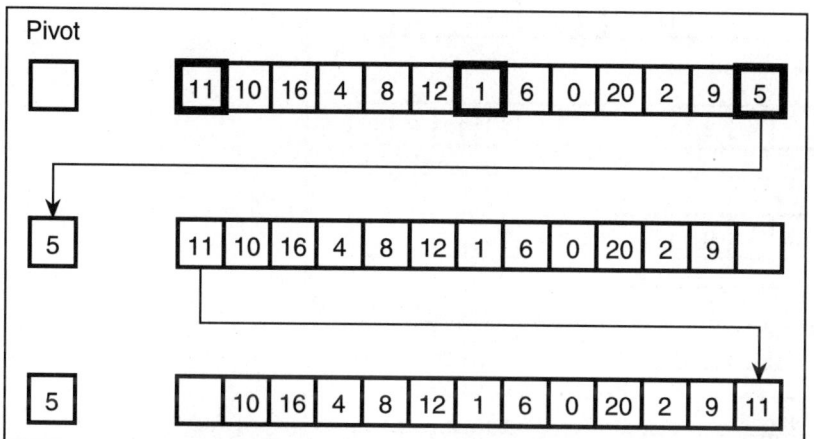

Figure 20.13

This is how you set up an array for the quicksort, by picking a pivot.

Now that you have chosen the pivot, you have an empty cell. In order for the algorithm to work correctly, you need to move that empty cell to the beginning of the array. This isn't a big problem because you can just swap 11 into the empty cell.

You are now ready to begin quicksorting.

After the array is set up, you perform a bunch of *scans* through the array. The first thing to do is to scan downward, starting at the last index in the array. You continue scanning downward until you find a value that is lower than the pivot. At this point you stop scanning and swap that value into the empty cell.

Now, you start at the bottom of the array and scan upward looking for values larger than the pivot. Whenever you find one, it should be swapped into the empty cell.

This process continues until you have found the correct place for the pivot in the array. Figure 20.14 illustrates this process.

20. Sorting Data

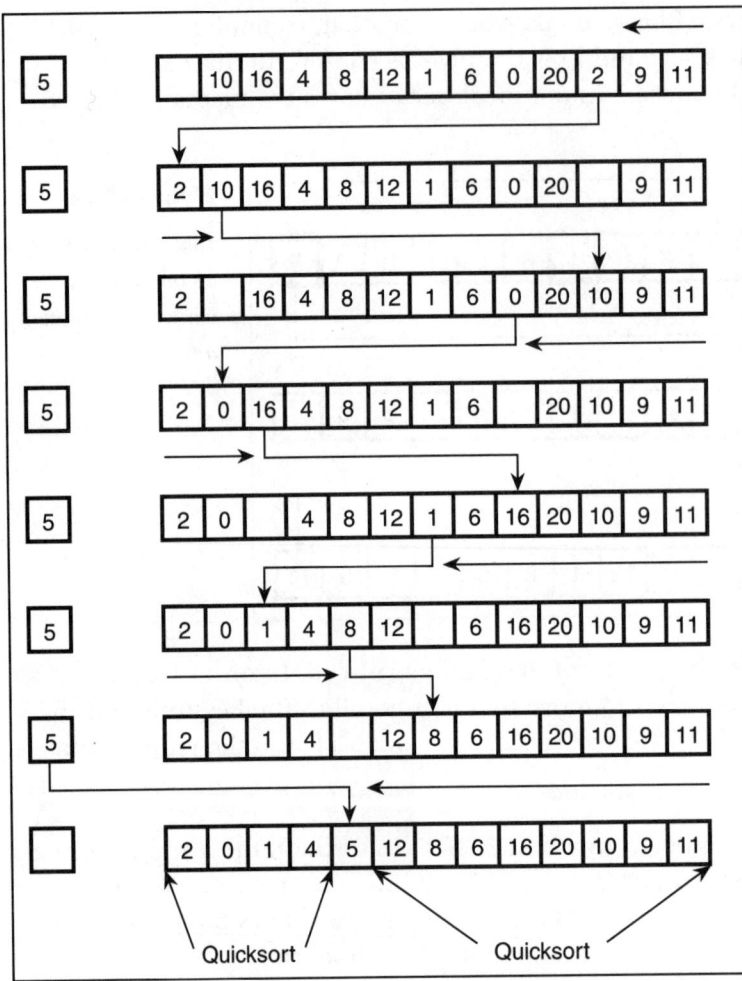

Figure 20.14

Here is the first level of the quicksort algorithm.

You can see that the function starts scanning downward, and when it finds the 2, it moves that into the empty cell because it is less than the pivot, 5.

Next, it scans upward and moves the 10 into the empty cell because it is greater than the pivot. This process repeats, back and forth, until the scanning reaches the empty cell. If you're scanning and you've reached the empty cell going both ways, then you know that you've found the correct position in the array for the pivot, so you place the pivot back into the array and call quicksort on each of the two halves of the array separated by the pivot.

Figure 20.15 shows the recursively called quicksort on the left half of the array.

The Fastest Sort: Quicksort

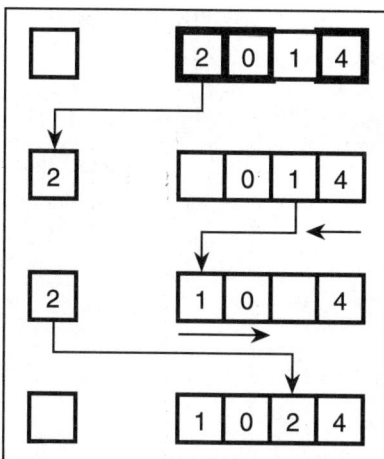

Figure 20.15

This is the quicksort called on the left half of the first partition.

You can see that this little segment is almost sorted now. Just one more call to the Quicksort function should get that little section sorted.

> **NOTE**
> One of the more famous computer scientists, Donald Knuth, recommends that instead of using a quicksort on really small array segments (somewhere around 5 cells), you should instead switch to a faster sort for small segments, such as the bubble sort. Of course, this optimization really only matters when you are sorting trillions of pieces of data, so it is unlikely you will notice much of a difference in any of your games.

Graphical Demonstration: Quicksort

This is Graphical Demonstration 20-3, which can be found on the CD in the directory \demonstrations\ch20\Demo03 - Quick Sort\.

Compiling the Demo

This demonstration uses the SDLGUI library that I have developed for the book. For more information about this library, see Appendix B.

To compile this demo, either open up the workspace file in the directory or create your own project using the settings described in Appendix B. If you create your own project, all of the files you need to include are in the directory.

Again, this demo is just like the previous two, so I'll just leave you with a pretty screenshot demonstrating the partitioning of the array in Figure 20.16.

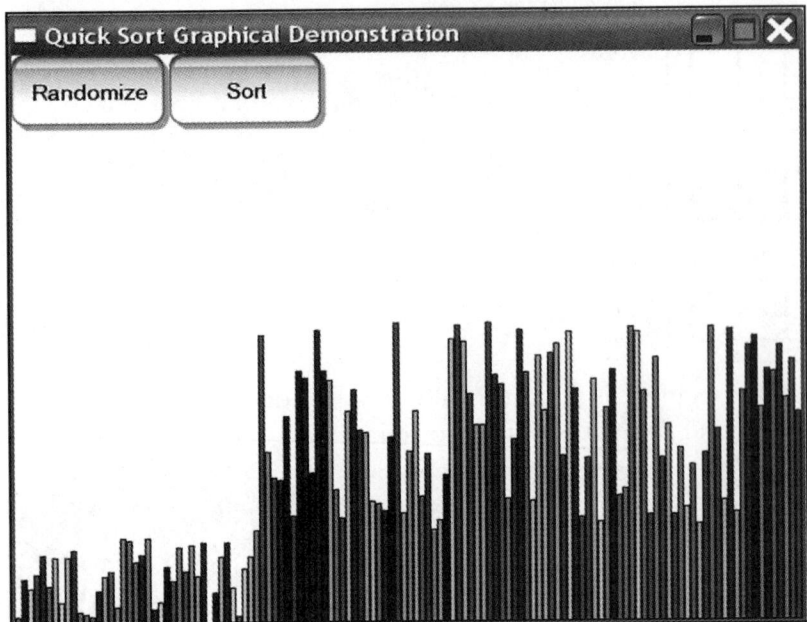

Figure 20.16

Here is a screenshot from the quicksort demo.

As you can see, the first pass of the quicksort has separated the items so that the small items are on the left and the large items on the right.

See, the quicksort is a very fast sorting algorithm because it works smarter than all the rest. Instead of wasting time moving items all over the place, the function focuses on breaking the array in half and splitting up the amount of work done. Even though the quicksort technically has a worst-case performance of $O(n^2)$, which is in the range of the bubble sort, in reality, you will never see that. The quicksort almost always runs in $O(n \log_2 n)$ time, which is the fastest a sort can get.

> **NOTE**
> Even though the heap sort and the quicksort both share the same best-case running time classes, the quicksort will always win. The heap sort involves much more jumping around in memory, which screws up the cache, if you remember from Chapter 3, "Arrays." The quicksort is much more cache-friendly because you do a lot of continuous scanning. Also, the heap sort is slower because it actually does more work—you're calling two $O(n \log_2 n)$ functions, and the quicksort only uses one.

Coding the Quicksort

The `QuickSort` function is very similar to the previous sorting functions because it is templated and makes use of a comparison function.

The MedianOfThree Function

The first thing you need to do is create a function that will find the median of three values in the array and return the index of the median value. As before, I split the function up to make it more understandable:

```
template<class DataType>
int FindMedianOfThree( Array<DataType>& p_array,
                       int p_first,
                       int p_size,
                       int (*p_compare)(DataType, DataType) )
{
    int last = p_first + p_size - 1;
    int mid = p_first + (p_size / 2);
```

The function takes an array as the first parameter, which is where the function will find the median values. The next two parameters, p_first and p_size, tell the function the starting index and the size of the array segment that it is operating on. Remember, because the quicksort is recursive, it operates on many array segments during the process of sorting.

The last parameter is the comparison function.

After that, the function calculates the last index and the middle index of the array.

```
    if( p_compare( p_array[p_first], p_array[mid] ) < 0 &&
        p_compare( p_array[p_first], p_array[last] ) < 0 )
    {
        if( p_compare( p_array[mid], p_array[last] ) < 0 )
            return mid;
        else
            return last;
    }
```

After the indexes have been calculated, you can begin to find the median value. The first step is to find out if the first index has the smallest value. If it does, then both the middle index and the last index are larger, so logically you can figure out that the median value is the lesser of the middle and last indexes.

```
    if( p_compare( p_array[mid], p_array[p_first] ) < 0 &&
        p_compare( p_array[mid], p_array[last] ) < 0 )
    {
        if( p_compare( p_array[p_first], p_array[last] ) < 0 )
            return p_first;
        else
            return last;
    }
```

By the same logic, the function then tests to see if the middle index is the smallest. If so, then the smaller value of the first and last indexes is the median.

```
    if( p_compare( p_array[mid], p_array[p_first] ) < 0 )
        return mid;
    else
        return p_first;
```

Finally, if the function has not ended by this point, you know that the last index is the smallest index in the array, so you compare the middle and first indexes to see which one is lower.

> **NOTE**
> I'm sure there are more efficient implementations of this function. However, they also are convoluted, look ugly, and are very difficult to understand.

The QuickSort Function

Finally, here is the actual `QuickSort` function. I've made a few optimizations to the algorithm to make it more efficient, and I will explain them as I reach them.

```
template<class DataType>
void QuickSort( Array<DataType>& p_array,
                int p_first,
                int p_size,
                int (*p_compare)(DataType, DataType) )
{
```

As with the `MedianOfThree` function, this also has the same four parameters because it can be called on any array segment in the array.

```
int pivot;
int last = p_first + p_size - 1;
int mid;
int lower = p_first;
int higher = last;
```

The first variable is the `pivot`, which you should already be familiar with. The `last` index holds the index of the last cell in the current array segment, and the `mid` index holds the index of the median value of the array.

The `lower` and `higher` variables are used to implement the optimization I mentioned a moment ago. Right now they contain the indexes of the lowest part of the array segment and the highest part of the array segment.

```
if( p_size > 1 )
{
```

At this point, the function checks to make sure that it is sorting an array segment that is larger than one cell. Obviously, an array segment with one cell is already sorted, so there is no need to waste time processing it.

> **NOTE**
>
> I mentioned earlier that it is sometimes more efficient to switch to a different sorting algorithm when the array segment gets smaller. Instead of checking to see if the array size is less than 1 right here, you could check to see if the array size is less than 5 or 6 (or anything you want) and have the function call a different sorting algorithm on the array segment.

```
    mid = FindMedianOfThree( p_array, p_first, p_size, p_compare );
    pivot = p_array[mid];
    p_array[mid] = p_array[p_first];
```

Now the function finds the index of the median value and places that into the pivot. The function then moves the first index of the array into the index where the median value was located so that the first cell in the array is empty.

```
    while( lower < higher )
    {
```

Now the loop begins, and it will continue looping while the lower index is lower than the higher index.

```
        while( p_compare( pivot, p_array[higher] ) < 0 && lower < higher )
            higher--;
```

This code segment starts at the higher index and scans downward until it finds a value lower than the pivot or the higher index becomes equal to the lower index. This is important because it deviates from the algorithm I explained in Figure 20.14. If you could just take a moment to look back at that figure, I will show you what is happening.

The function first looks at 11 and sees that it is larger than the pivot, 5, so it continues downward. It also looks at 9 and ignores that as well. The scan-down loop stops when it reaches the 2 because it is lower than the pivot. At this point in time, `higher` points to the index where 2 is, and `lower` points to the empty index at the start of the array. The next step is to move the 2 into the lower index, which you shall see in a moment, but the interesting part is on the third array in Figure 20.14. The figure shows that it started scanning down from the end of the array again, but why should you waste your time doing that? You know that the 11 and the 9 are already higher than the pivot, so instead of scanning down from the end of the array again, you start scanning down from the `higher` index. It's a neat optimization.

```
if( higher != lower )
{
    p_array[lower] = p_array[higher];
    lower++;
}
```

After the scanning is complete, the function checks to see if the higher and lower indexes are equal or not. If they aren't equal, then the scanning stopped because it found a value less than the pivot, so it moves the value from the higher index to the lower index and increases the lower index by one. This completes the scan-down section.

```
while( p_compare( pivot, p_array[lower] ) > 0 && lower < higher )
    lower++;
```

After the scanning down is completed, the function now scans upward, trying to find a value greater than the pivot.

```
if( higher != lower )
{
    p_array[higher] = p_array[lower];
    higher--;
}
}
```

When a value greater than the pivot has been found, it is moved into the higher index, and the lower index is now considered empty.

```
        p_array[lower] = pivot;
        QuickSort( p_array, p_first, lower - p_first, p_compare );
        QuickSort( p_array, lower + 1, last - lower, p_compare );
    }
}
```

Finally, the pivot is placed back into the array at the correct position, and the two halves of the array (not including the pivot) are recursively quicksorted.

Example 20-3

This is Example 20-3, which you can find on the CD in the directory \examples\ch20\03 - Quicksort\.

This example is very similar to Examples 20-1 and 20-2, except for three lines of code:

```
QuickSort( iarray, 0, 16, compareint );
QuickSort( farray, 0, 16, comparefloat );
QuickSort( iarray, 0, 16, compareintreverse );
```

Note that you must include the starting index and the size parameters in the `QuickSort` call, whereas you didn't with the `BubbleSort` and `HeapSort` functions. This actually allows you to have a little bit more customizability with the functions because you can choose to sort only specific parts of the array instead of the whole thing.

Graphical Demonstration: Race

This is Graphical Demonstration 20-4, which you can find on the CD in the directory \demonstrations\ch20\Demo04 - Race\.

> ### Compiling the Demo
>
> This demonstration uses the SDLGUI library that I have developed for the book. For more information about this library, see Appendix B.
>
> To compile this demo, either open up the workspace file in the directory or create your own project using the settings described in Appendix B. If you create your own project, all of the files you need to include are in the directory.

What would a chapter on sorting be without a hands-on comparison of the speed of the different sorts? Ladies and gentlemen, start your engines!

This demonstration has the same interface as all the other demonstrations in this chapter so far, except that there are now three arrays shown on the screen, like Figure 20.17 shows.

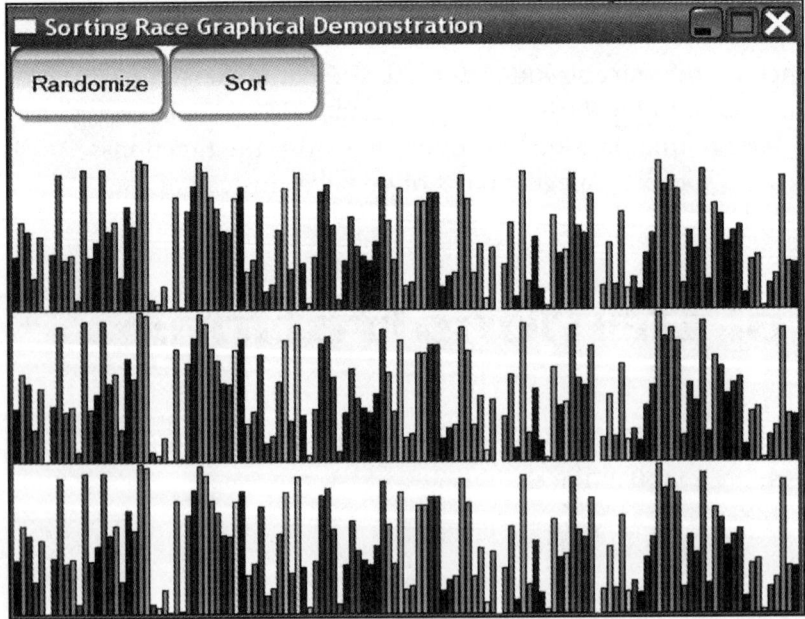

Figure 20.17

This is the initial screen from the demo.

The array on top will be bubble sorted, the array in the middle will be heap sorted, and the array on the bottom will be quicksorted. Care to place any wagers on who will win this race?

And they're off! Figure 20.18 shows a screenshot of the demo when the quicksort completes.

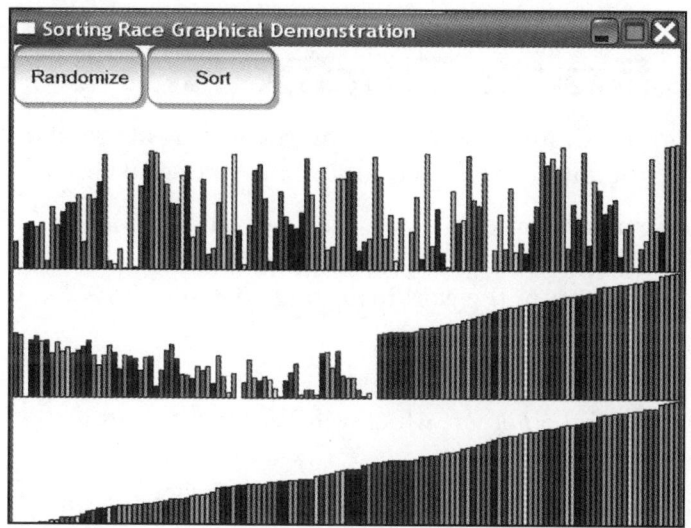

Figure 20.18

Here is a screenshot when the quicksort completes.

The quicksort is clearly the champion here, because it is already sorted when the heap sort is only half done and the bubble sort has barely even started the race!

Figure 20.19 shows a screenshot of the demo when the heap sort completes.

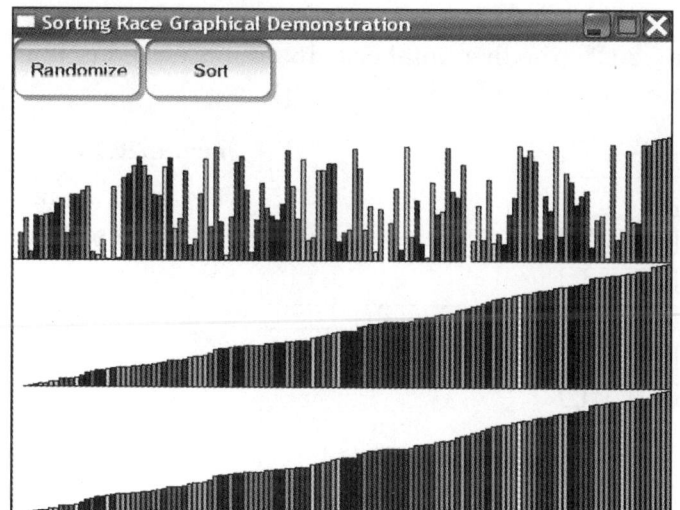

Figure 20.19

Here is a screenshot when the heap sort completes.

Can you believe that? The heap sort, while still being twice as slow as the quicksort, still manages to kick the crap out of the bubble sort! The bubble sort array is still almost entirely unsorted!

Play with the demo, and you will see that the quicksort is clearly superior to all the other sorts and that the bubble sort is to be avoided at any cost!

The Clever Sort: Radix Sort

The three sorts I showed you previously are called *general-purpose* sorting algorithms. They are called that because they can be used to sort any types of data.

There is one more special sorting algorithm that I want to show you, but it is not a general-purpose sort. This sorting algorithm is really only useful for sorting numbers, but it is pretty much the fastest sort in the world (for huge datasets, it is even faster than the quicksort).

The word *radix* means *root* or *base*, and you will see why this sort is called a radix sort soon. (Sometimes it is also called the *bin sort*, which will become obvious in a moment.)

Say you have an array of numbers and you want to sort them using a base-10 radix sort. To do this, you need to set up a collection of ten bins. The bins can be arrays or linked lists; the implementation is up to you. Remember, arrays are faster but take up more memory, and linked lists are more memory efficient but a little slower.

So you set up ten bins and label them from 0 to 9. Now, when you start the radix sort, you look at the last digit of each of the items in the array and then put them in the appropriate bin. In Figure 20.20, the first number is 18, so it is placed in bin 8. The second number is 45, so it is placed in bin 5, and so on.

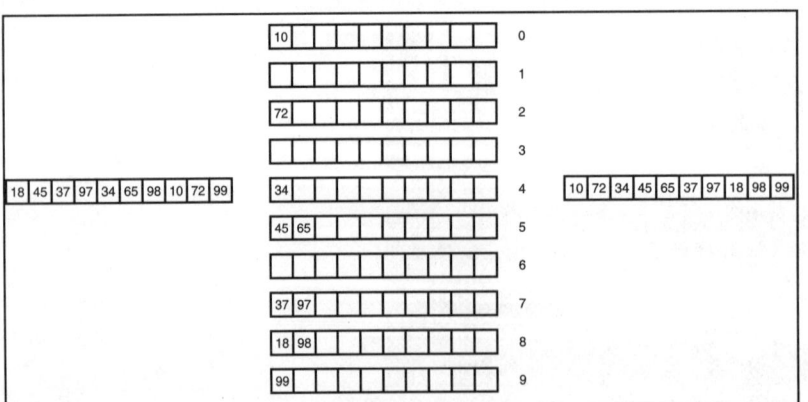

Figure 20.20

This is the first pass of the radix sort.

After the entire array is in the bins, the bins are then emptied into the array again, starting at the first bin, so that 10 is put in first, then 72, and so on.

After the first step has been completed, you repeat the process, this time using the second digit in the numbers. Figure 20.21 shows the second pass.

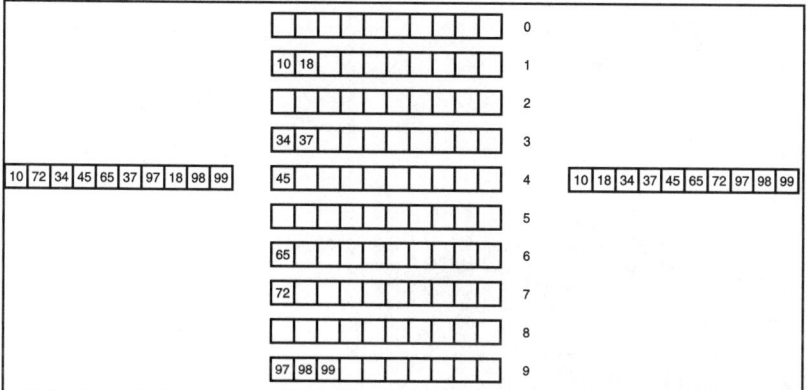

Figure 20.21

This is the second pass of the radix sort.

After that second pass, the entire array is sorted. Note that if you were using three-digit numbers, sorting the array would require three passes.

Graphical Demonstration: Radix Sorts

This is Graphical Demonstration 20-5, which you can find on the CD in the directory \demonstrations\ch20\Demo05 - Radix Sort\.

Compiling the Demo

This demonstration uses the SDLGUI library that I have developed for the book. For more information about this library, see Appendix B.

To compile this demo, either open up the workspace file in the directory or create your own project using the settings described in Appendix B. If you create your own project, all of the files you need to include are in the directory.

Again, the interface is almost identical to the previous sorting demos, except that there are three sorting buttons this time. Figure 20.22 shows a screenshot.

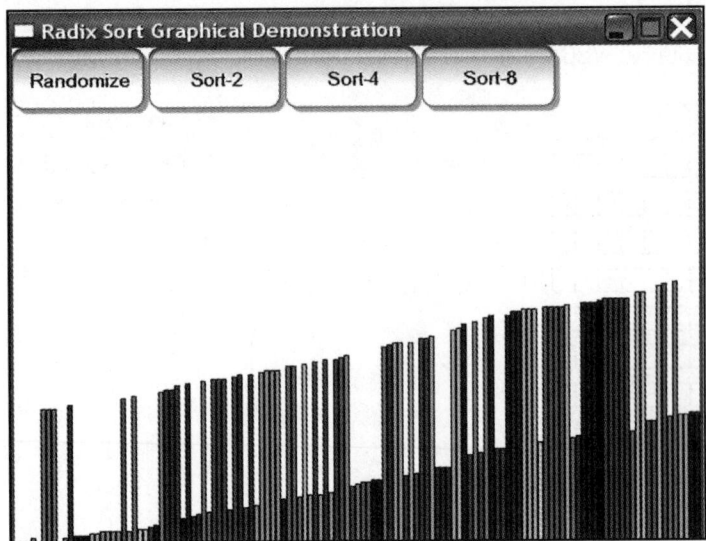

Figure 20.22

Here is a screenshot from the Radix Sort demo.

The three different buttons perform the radix sort using three different bases: base 2, base 4, and base 8.

In base 2, you only need two bins, but it takes seven passes to sort the array because the values go up to 128 ($2^7 = 128$). Base 4 needs four bins, but it only takes four passes to complete. ($4^4 = 256$, which is the smallest power of four above 128. Three passes can only sort numbers up to 64, as $4^3 = 64$.) Finally, base 8 needs only three passes to complete, because $8^3 = 512$, the smallest power of 8 above 128. Two passes can only sort numbers up to 64, because $8^2 = 64$.

So what does this mean? Table 20.1 shows the maximum size of the numbers that the radix sorts can sort with different amounts of passes.

Table 20.1 Radix Sort Passes

Base	1 Pass	2 Passes	3 Passes	4 Passes
2	0–1	0–3	0–7	0–15
4	0–3	0–15	0–63	0–255
8	0–7	0–63	0–511	0–4095
10	0–9	0–99	0–999	0–9999
16	0–15	0–255	0–4095	0–65535

So, you can see from the table that the radix sort becomes more efficient with larger bases, but the tradeoff is that the bins require more space with larger bases.

The upside is that this algorithm is *very* fast for large data sets because the algorithm essentially runs in $O(n)$ time; much better than the quicksort. The downside is that there is a lot of overhead when using this sort, which means that the quicksort usually wins for small amounts of data. For example, the quicksort demo on 128 items runs faster than the base-8 radix sort on 128 items. It isn't until you get into the hundred thousand number range that the radix sort starts to become faster than the quicksort.

Coding the Radix Sort

The radix sort is sometimes difficult to code. You need to first figure out how you want the radix sort to actually work and which structures you're going to use. I mentioned before that you could use either arrays or linked lists for the bins, and that is the major decision.

For the radix sorts in this book, I am assuming that speed is much more important than conserving memory (have you seen the RAM prices lately? You're nuts if you don't have at least 128MB now!), so I will use an array to store the bins.

The Bin Size

To optimize the way the memory is used in the process of the radix sort, I have decided to make all of the bins `static` so that they are not allocated and deallocated when the functions start and end.

To make a static array, though, I needed to use a global constant to determine the maximum size of each bin:

```
const int RADIXBINSIZE        = 1024;
```

The bins have a maximum bin size of 1024, but you can easily change that to a larger number.

Base 2

Base-2 radix sorts take many more passes than other radix sorts because 2 is the smallest base out there.

```
void RadixSort2( Array<int>& p_array, int p_passes )
{
    if( p_array.Size() > RADIXBINSIZE )
        return;
```

The radix sort takes the array you want to sort and the number of passes you want to do on it as parameters.

The first thing the radix sort does is check to see if the array is larger than the bin size. If it is, then the function exits out without sorting the array. Why does it do this? Think about it for a minute; if the array has all even numbers in it (every item has 0 for the last bit), then the first pass of the radix sort will throw them all in the first bin. If the bin isn't as large as the size of the array, you will get an overflow and probably crash the program.

```
    static int bins[2][RADIXBINSIZE];
    int bincount[2];
    int radix = 1;
    int shift = 0;
    int index;
    int binindex;
    int currentbin;
```

Next, the bins and the local variables are declared. The bins are static, so they always stay in global memory, and they aren't allocated and deallocated every time the function is executed.

The `bincount` array keeps track of how many items are in each bin. The `radix` and `shift` variables keep track of the current digit that is being examined and how many places down it needs to be shifted to get a valid bin index. For example, the radix in this starts off at 1 (binary 1) and goes to 2 (binary 10), and then 4 (binary 100), and so on. The `shift` variable keeps track of how many places the radix needs to be shifted to the right to make the binary digit at the lowest position (0 when `radix` is 1, 1 when `radix` is 2, 3 when `radix` is 4, 4 when `radix` is 8, and so on).

The other three variables are used to count through the array.

```
    while( p_passes != 0 )
    {
        p_passes--;
```

Now the loop starts, and it loops through with the number of passes you told it to. This feature is added because you may want to only perform a few passes on an array if you know that it contains small numbers so that you don't waste your time sorting an already-sorted array.

```
bincount[0] = bincount[1] = 0;
for( index = 0; index < p_array.Size(); index++ )
{
    binindex = (p_array[index] & radix) >> shift;
    bins[binindex][bincount[binindex]] = p_array[index];
    bincount[binindex]++;
}
```

This segment first clears the bin counts and then loops through the array. This is the process where the array is sorted into the bins. First, the correct bin index is calculated by extracting the current binary digit (you saw how to extract binary digits in Chapter 4, "Bitvectors") and then shifting it downward.

After that, the item is moved into the correct bin, and the bin count is incremented.

```
index = 0;
for( currentbin = 0; currentbin < 2; currentbin++ )
{
    binindex = 0;
    while( bincount[currentbin] > 0 )
    {
        p_array[index] = bins[currentbin][binindex];
        binindex++;
        bincount[currentbin]--;
        index++;
    }
}
```

The preceding code segment puts the items in each bin back into the array. First, the index of the array is reset to 0, and then the outer loop loops through all of the bins (only two in this case).

Then the inner loop loops through all of the items in each bin and copies them back over into the array.

```
        radix <<= 1;
        shift += 1;
    }
}
```

Finally, the current digit is shifted left by one digit, and the shift variable is incremented.

Base 4

The base-4 radix sort is only slightly different than the base-2 radix sort. Instead of inspecting *individual* bits, you will now be inspecting *pairs* of bits.

First, the initialization is a little different:

```
static int bins[4][RADIXBINSIZE];
int bincount[4];
int radix = 3;
```

Notice that `radix` is now 3, which in binary is 11. You want to extract a pair of bits, so this works nicely. Of course, now that you are inspecting two bits at a time, you need to shift the digit up by two bits now and not just one:

```
radix <<= 2;
shift += 2;
```

That's really all there is to it; the rest of the function is pretty much identical.

Base 16

The base-16 radix sort looks at four bit-digits (also known as *nibbles*) instead of two or one.

```
static int bins[16][RADIXBINSIZE];
int bincount[16];
int radix = 15;
```

Now the radix is 15, which in binary is 1111, because you want to inspect four digits at once.

And finally:

```
radix <<= 4;
shift += 4;
```

You shift the radix up by four bits every pass.

Example 20-4

This is Example 20-4, which you can find on the CD in the directory \examples\ch20\04 - Radix Sort\.

Because the radix sort algorithm in this book only works on integers (you can make one for floats if you want to, although it takes a lot of effort), this example is simpler than the previous examples. In fact, there is no longer any need for a comparison function at all. Unfortunately, due to the lack of a comparison function, the radix sort is very limited in what it can do.

```
Array<int> array( 16 );
int index;
for( index = 0; index < 16; index++ )
{
    array[index] = rand() % 256;
}
```

First fill up an array with 16 values from 0-255 (eight bit values).

```
RadixSort2( array, 8 );
cout << "Integer Array: ";
PrintArray( array );
cout << endl;
```

Then sort the array using the base-2 radix sort, using eight passes. Remember, because the array contains eight bit values, and the base-2 sort only looks at one bit at a time, you need eight passes.

```
RadixSort4( array, 4 );
cout << "Integer Array: ";
PrintArray( array );
cout << endl;
```

The base-4 radix sort looks at two bits at a time, so it only needs four passes.

```
RadixSort16( array, 2 );
cout << "Integer Array: ";
PrintArray( array );
cout << endl;
```

Finally, the base-16 radix sort looks at four bits at a time, so it only needs two passes.

Other Sorts

There are literally tons of sorts out there. I showed you three of the most important sorts (and the bubble sort to show you how *not* to do things).

Some of the other sorts you may hear about are the *insertion sort*, which is an algorithm that basically searches through a sorted array for the right place to put something and inserts it; the *shell sort*, which I don't understand—and the quicksort is faster, anyway; and the *merge sort*, which is another recursive $O(n \log_2 n)$ sort.

However, I chose not to show you that sort here because the quicksort is almost always faster and the merge sort requires an extra array in memory to work. It's really not worth it to learn that sort.

There is one more trick I want you to know about, the *binary search tree* sort. You last encountered BSTs in Chapter 13. Figure 20.23 shows a diagram of a BST to refresh your memory.

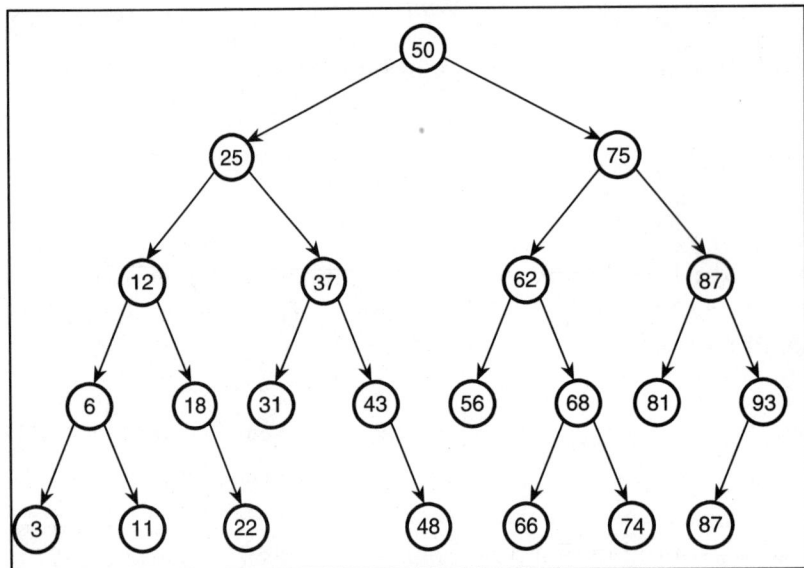

Figure 20.23

This is a binary search tree.

Now, think back to Chapter 12, "Binary Trees," and the *in-order* binary tree traversal. Remember how that worked? If not, please go back and read up on it and then come back here.

I want you to perform an in-order traversal on Figure 20.23 and write down the numbers as you process them. Notice anything? The order is 3, 6, 11, 12, 18, 22, and so on.

The order in which those numbers are listed is sorted. Isn't that cool?

Application: Depth-Based Games

This is Game Demo 20-1, which is on the CD in the directory \demonstrations\ch20\Game01 - Depth\.

Compiling the Demo

This demonstration uses the SDLHelpers library that I have developed for the book. For more information about this library, see Appendix B.

To compile this demo, either open up the workspace file in the directory or create your own project using the settings described in Appendix B. If you create your own project, all of the files you need to include are in the directory.

You often have an array of something in a game that you want to sort, which makes choosing a good sorting algorithm very important in game programming because sorting algorithms typically take a long time.

Perhaps the most popular use of sorting algorithms is depth-sorting. In 2D games like *The Legend of Zelda*, it was common to have sprites appear to be 3D and have the screen look slanted to give some sense of depth.

To accomplish something like this, you need to be able to sort the sprites on the screen by their *y*-coordinates so that players who are lower on the screen appear closer.

> **NOTE**
> Depth sorting is probably even more important today in 3D games. Most video cards these days can support all kinds of neat transparency effects, and in order for them to work correctly, you need to be able to sort your polygons and draw them in the correct order. Although technologies like the z-buffer make sorting less important, you can also get some nice speed increases by sorting your polygons so that the closest polygons are drawn first and therefore avoid *overdraw* by marking pixels that have already been drawn. If you don't know much about 3D programming yet, don't worry about this.

The Player Class

This simple demo will use a simple player class to store players in the game:

```
class Player
{
public:
    int type;
```

```
    float x;
    float y;
};
```

There are four types of players: the hero, the two monsters, and the tree. Okay, technically a tree isn't a player, but it really doesn't matter for now.

The player also has two coordinates, which determine where it will be drawn on the screen.

The Globals

The only global variables in the demo related to drawing the players are these two arrays:

```
Array<Player> g_players( PLAYERS );
Array<Player*> g_sortedplayers( PLAYERS );
```

There are two arrays for a reason: The first array contains all of the players. The second array holds pointers to all of the players in the player array. Every time a frame is drawn, the program sorts the pointers by their *y*-coordinates and then draws them in that order.

The Player Comparison Function

The player comparison function compares the *y*-coordinates of the players. This function is almost exactly like the comparefloats functions from Examples 20-1, 20-2, and 20-3.

```
int CompareY( Player* l, Player* r )
{
    if( l->y < r->y )
        return -1;
    if( l->y > r->y )
        return 1;
    return 0;
}
```

Initializing the Players

This function randomizes the players and copies the pointers to all of them over into the sorted array:

```
void InitPlayers()
{
    int index;
    for( index = 1; index < PLAYERS; index++ )
    {
        g_players[index].type = rand() % 3 + 1;
        g_players[index].x = rand() % WIDTH - 64;
        g_players[index].y = rand() % HEIGHT + 64;
    }
    for( index = 0; index < PLAYERS; index++ )
    {
        g_sortedplayers[index] = &(g_players[index]);
    }
}
```

It is very important that you copy the pointers over to the array before you sort it. If you don't, you will be sorting dead pointers, and you will probably end up crashing your program.

Sorting the Players

Sorting the players is simple.

```
DrawMap();
QuickSort( g_sortedplayers, 0, PLAYERS, CompareY );
DrawPlayers();
```

First the map is drawn, and then the players are sorted by using the `QuickSort` function from earlier, and then the players are drawn.

Drawing the Players

Drawing the players is as simple as looping through the sorted player array and drawing each player in that order:

```
void DrawPlayers()
{
    int index;
    Player* p;
    for( index = 0; index < PLAYERS; index++ )
    {
        p = g_sortedplayers[index];
```

```
            SDLBlit( g_bmps[p->type], g_window, p->x, p->y - g_bmps[p->type]->h );
    }
}
```

The *y*-coordinate manipulation in the call to `SDLBlit` makes sure that the bitmap is drawn with the *y*-coordinate referring to the bottom of the bitmap (as opposed to the top of the bitmap, which is how all blitting algorithms work). Don't worry, all it does is subtract the height of the bitmap from the coordinate and then draw it. If you have sprites with different heights, then this step is absolutely necessary to get a convincing depth effect.

Playing the Game

The game is simple. All you do is use your arrow keys on the keyboard to move the player around the map. Pay attention to how things are drawn, and walk up and down through the trees and monsters. This simple little sorting algorithm makes the game seem a lot more realistic.

Figure 20.24 shows a screenshot from the game. The player is hiding behind a tree.

Figure 20.24

Here is a screenshot from the sorting demo.

Conclusion

There really isn't much more to say about sorting except this: Use the quicksort. Even if you're afraid of recursion and you actually believe those people who say that recursion slows things down (they are wrong, by the way), the quicksort does far less work than any other sort in existence.

There is one final note that needs to be made. Most of the time, the data you will be sorting in a computer game isn't completely random. In fact, many times you can somewhat predict how the data is ordered because you know how your game creates and removes things from arrays. Using this knowledge, you are usually able to optimize your games further, by knowing what areas of your arrays aren't sorted, and then only sorting those portions. So keep an eye out for places that you know contain mostly sorted data.

CHAPTER 21

DATA COMPRESSION

21. Data Compression

You may not think that data compression is a very important topic in game programming today. After all, we have computers now with up to and sometimes more than 1GB of RAM and hard drives with up to 200GB of storage. With DVD-ROMs becoming more common, soon many games will start shipping on them instead of CD-ROMs, giving game developers up to 4.7GB of storage on one disc instead of just 650MB, like on a CD.

So, with all this storage space available, why bother trying to fit as much data into as small of a place as possible?

It wasn't very long ago when people were saying, "I can't imagine an entire game needing 650MB of space." Now there are games that take two or three or even more CD-ROMs. Face it: Game programmers *always* push the edge of available technology. How long do you think it is going to be before DVD-ROMs seem too small to hold a single game? The DVD Consortium is already designing a *new* format, called the *blue ray DVD*, which will hold up to 25GB of data!

In this chapter, you will learn

- Why data is compressed
- How to compress data using RLE compression
- How to code an RLE compression class
- How to use the RLE class to compress and decompress files
- How to compress data using Huffman compression
- How to code a Huffman compression class
- How to use the Huffman class to compress and decompress files

Why Compress Data?

It is not just storage space that drives the need for data compression. There are a few areas of game programming that still require efficient data compression

Data Busses

The most pressing concern today is the rapidly widening gap between the speed of the processors in a system and the data bus. Figure 21.1 shows a diagram of the bus between the *Graphics Processing Unit (GPU)* and the *Central Processing Unit (CPU)*. The GPU is the chip on your video card, and the CPU is the main processor on your motherboard.

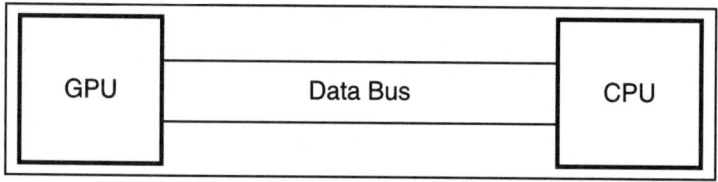

Figure 21.1

This is the bus between the GPU and the CPU.

When your processor wants things drawn, it sends data down the bus to the GPU, which then takes that data and draws it.

Unfortunately, GPUs are getting so fast that they can draw more data than the CPU can actually send to it. This problem is caused by the fact that computer busses are very slow in comparison to the CPU and GPU speeds.

For example, in the early 1990s, you could get a 66MHz 486 processor that ran on a 33MHz bus, which was half as fast. This meant that if the processor wanted information that wasn't in its cache (remember from Chapter 3, "Arrays," that the cache is memory directly on the processor itself), it would have to wait two cycles to get it. Considering that most instructions take longer than two cycles to complete, that wasn't a big deal.

Fast forward a few years to the Pentiums, which ran on a 66MHz bus. The processors ran at up to 233MHz. The processor was running 3.5 times faster than the bus! The processor had to wait even longer to transfer memory around.

I once put together a computer that ran on a 200MHz bus. The AMD Athlon processor runs at 1.5GHz. This means that the processor is now running 7.5 times faster than the bus!

As you can see, the faster processors get, the more waiting they have to do. This is a huge problem for game developers because we want to be able to throw tons of huge textures at the video card to make our worlds look nice and pretty, but the bus just doesn't want to transfer as much as we would like!

Early on, this problem was fixed by putting ultra-fast memory on video cards, like Figure 21.2 shows. This way, whenever the video card needs to draw a big texture, it doesn't need to get the texture from the CPU; it already has the texture in its own memory, and it draws it immediately.

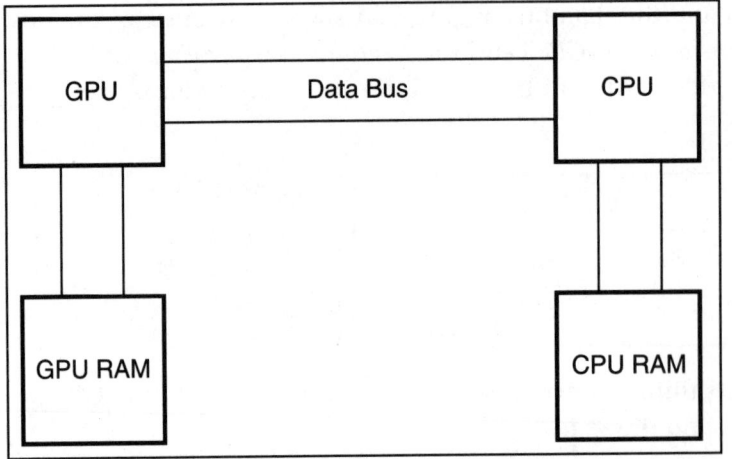

Figure 21.2

This shows localized memory sub-systems for each of the processors.

Another solution to the problem is what the Microsoft XBox did. They used a unified memory system, which looks like Figure 21.3.

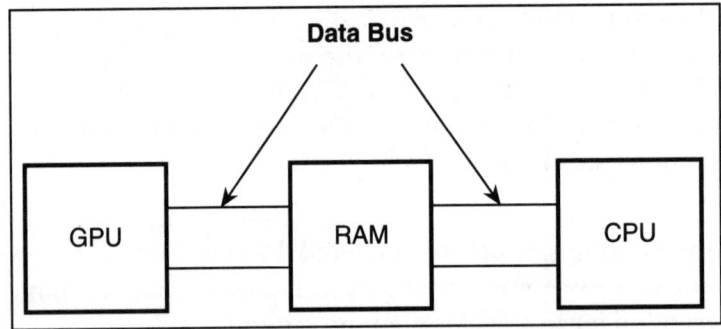

Figure 21.3

This is the bus system for the XBox.

The XBox solved the problem of fast memory access by keeping the memory all in one place instead of duplicating the memory and sending it over the bus to the video card.

Unfortunately, the amount of very fast memory that can be put on video cards or in the XBox is usually not enough for most game programmers, so another solution is needed.

Texture compression was invented, and nowadays most video cards support it. By using texture compression features, you can compress textures to a much smaller size than they were before and toss them all into video card memory, saving lots of space and using less transfer time.

The Internet

As a game programmer, you've been acquainted with the Internet for a while now, I'm sure. The vast majority of the rest of the world is just learning about it, however, and multi-player gaming is the wave of the future. We saw the releases of the blockbusters *Quake 3* and *Unreal Tournament* a few years ago, and now *Massively Multi-player Online Role Playing Games (MMORPG)* are becoming very popular. Some of these games are absolutely huge and have hundreds of people playing at the same time.

Unfortunately, the Internet is still young, and the more people who use it, the slower it will get for everyone. Because of this, you need to make your multi-player games as efficient as possible when sending information over the Internet. It is usually safer to spend a little more effort in making your game memory efficient than to make it wait for lots of data while the players are playing the game.

Run Length Encoding

Perhaps the simplest way to compress data is by using *Run Length Encoding (RLE)*.

To understand how RLE works, you first must think about how data is stored. Whether it is an image, a document, or any other piece of data, the data inside is always broken down into *discrete* elements, which have a definite value. Documents have *characters*, images have *pixels*, and so on.

Sometimes the individual data elements in a piece of data repeat themselves. For example, Figure 21.4 shows the contents of a simple text file that has repeating characters.

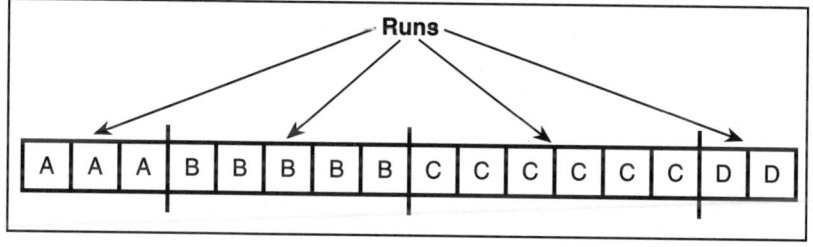

Figure 21.4

Here is a simple text file with repeating characters.

Now, instead of representing each character in that file, wouldn't it be easier to say, "There are 3 As, 5 Bs, 6 Cs, and 2 Ds"? Figure 21.5 shows this.

21. Data Compression

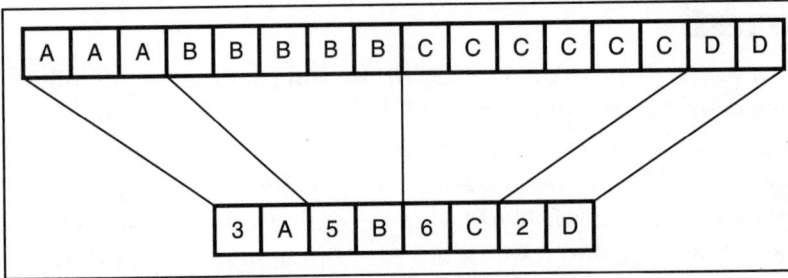

Figure 21.5

This is how you convert text into RLE.

That's all there is to the basic theory of RLE. The idea is that some types of data have *runs* of data that are repeated, and keeping track of the runs is cheaper than keeping track of the actual data. It converts a run of a piece of data into a length and one instance of that data.

What Kinds of Data Can Be Used for RLE?

Because this is a very simple compression scheme, it also has lots of drawbacks. For example, look at the text in Figure 21.6.

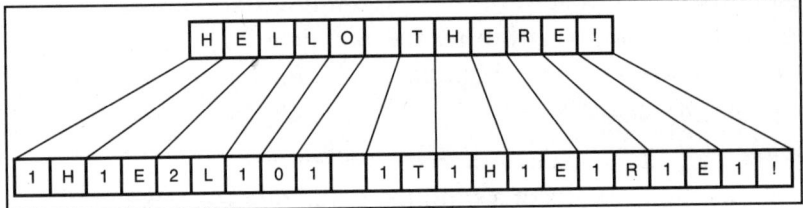

Figure 21.6

This is a bad example of using RLE. The text has almost no repeating characters.

As you can see from the figure, using RLE on the text actually makes it bigger because there are almost no runs in the text at all!

Letters rarely repeat themselves in text files, so text is a very bad kind of data to compress using RLE.

On the other hand, bitmaps with transparency are a really nice kind of data to compress using RLE compression—especially fonts. Look at Figure 21.7 for an example.

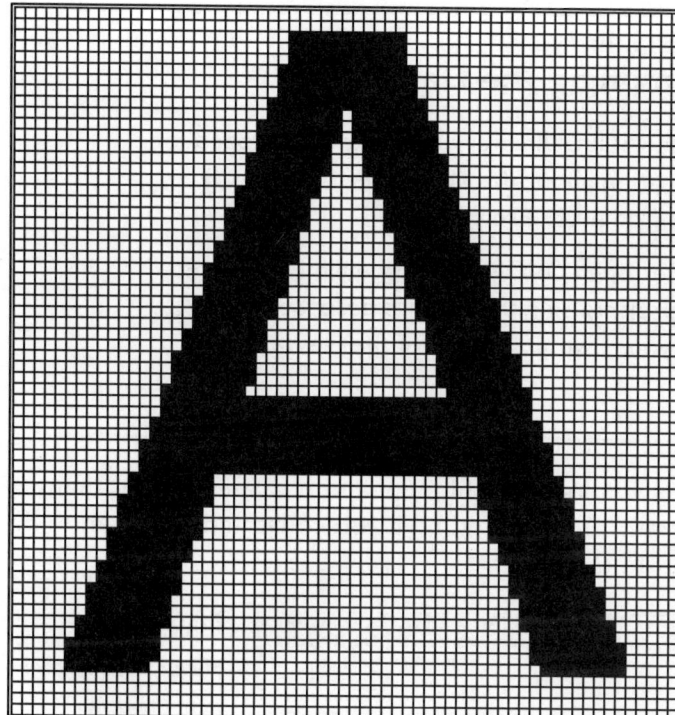

Figure 21.7

This is a 64 × 64 pixel bitmap of the letter A.

In this bitmap, all of the transparent pixels (the pixels that aren't drawn) are white, and all the visible pixels are black. Think of the bitmap as a 2D array for a moment. You can see that a lot of the pixels in the bitmap repeat each other, which makes it ideal for RLE compression.

Look at the first row on the top; you can see that every pixel is white. The same goes with the next row, and the third row has 27 white pixels before a black pixel is seen. If you treat the bitmap like an array, there are 155 white pixels in a row.

After the 155 white pixels, there are 11 black pixels, and then it switches to white again. If you used one byte to store the length of the run and one byte to store the color, then you can condense the first 166 pixels (166 uncompressed bytes, assuming you use 1 byte per pixel) into just 4 bytes!

Isn't that amazing? I'd say so.

Graphical Demonstration: RLEs

This is Graphical Demonstration 21-1, which is on the CD in the directory \demonstrations\ch21\Demo01 - RLE Compression\.

Compiling the Demo

This demonstration uses the SDLGUI library that I have developed for the book. For more information about this library, see Appendix B, "The Memory Layout of a Computer Program."

To compile this demo, either open up the workspace file in the directory or create your own project using the settings described in Appendix B. If you create your own project, all of the files you need to include are in the directory.

This demo is fairly simple. It lets you load in a bitmap, and it calculates how many pixels there are and how many runs there would be if you converted it into an RLE. Figure 21.8 shows a screenshot.

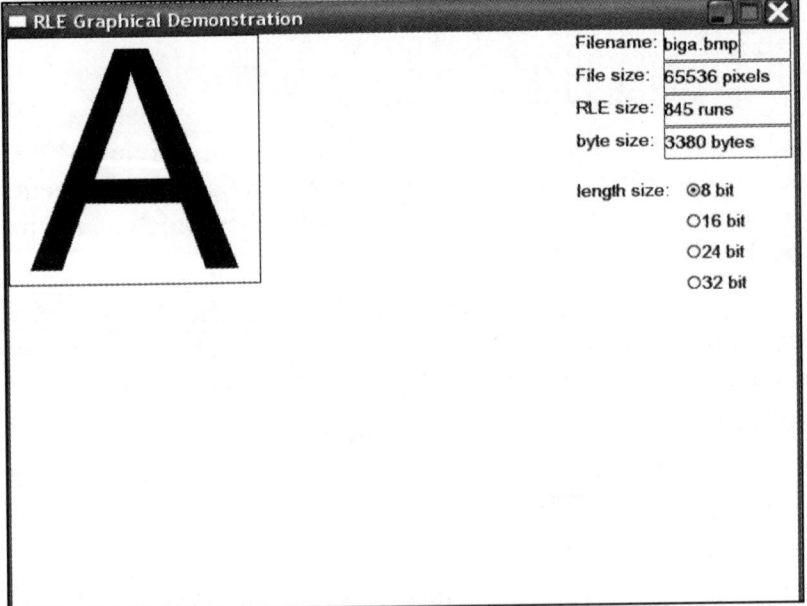

Figure 21.8

Here is a screenshot from the demo.

In the figure, there are four text boxes that contain information about the bitmap file and the RLE it would be converted into. The first box is where you type the name of the BMP file. After you type in the name of the file you want to load, press Enter, and the next three boxes will be loaded with information about the file.

The box labeled File size holds the size of the bmp file, in bytes. This information is not compressed in any way. The next box, RLE size, holds the number of runs that will be needed to store the image, using the current length of a run. The final box, byte size, shows the size of the actual RLE when it is compressed.

Keep in mind that each run takes about twice as much memory as a single pixel, depending on how you store the data.

For example, your length size is up to you. You can use a single byte (8 bits) to store the length of a run, but then you're limited to runs of 255 pixels in length (the highest number an 8-bit number can store is $2^n - 1$, which is 255 when n is 8). You can also use 2 bytes, 3 bytes, or even 4 bytes per run, and the program will calculate those for you.

If you're not quite sure about what I mean by this, look at Figure 21.9, which shows you the four different run combinations that this program uses.

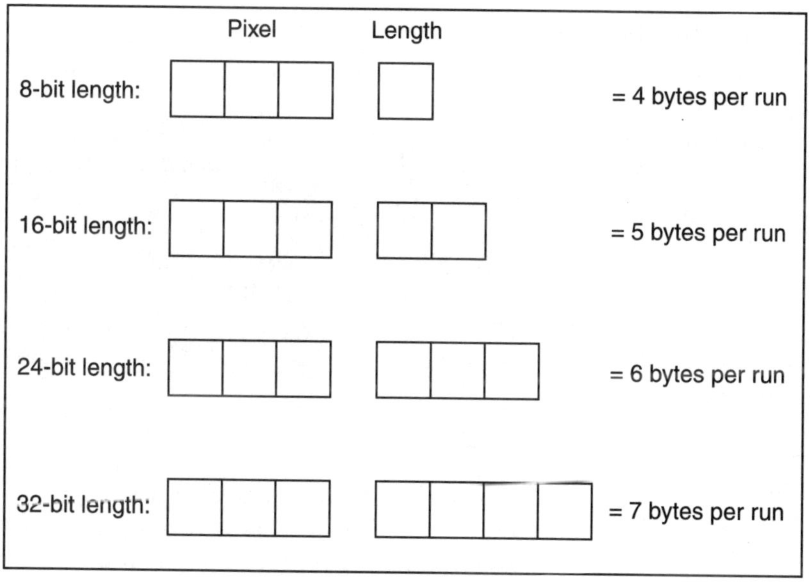

Figure 21.9
These are the available run configurations.

This demo assumes that you will be using 24-bit color for the bitmaps, which is standard for most *true color* bitmap file formats. Each pixel will take 3 bytes. The first run option, 8-bit, uses 4 bytes total for each run. Likewise, the second uses 5 bytes, the third 6 bytes, and the fourth 7 bytes per run if you use 32 bits for the run length.

I have provided several bitmaps for you to test the demo out with. For example, load up the demo and type in a.bmp into the Filename text box and press Enter.

The program should tell you that the bitmap is 4096 pixels. It should also tell you that it will take 206 runs to store the bitmap using an 8-bit length. Because an 8-bit length takes up 4 bytes per run, this bitmap will take up 824 bytes total to store in RLE form. That's a nice compression right there because the actual a.bmp file takes up 5,174 bytes on disk, so you've achieved a 6:1 compression ratio.

Now I want you to switch to 16-bit mode. Note that the number of runs has gone down by one, from 206 to 205. This is because there is one run in the bitmap that is longer than 256 pixels, so it had to be split up into two runs when using an 8-bit length. But even though you've decreased the number of runs, the overall file size has gone up to 1,025 bytes because each run now takes up five bytes instead of just four.

You can switch to 24- and 32-bit modes, too, but you can clearly see that this is a waste of memory because no runs go longer than 65,336 pixels, which is how many pixels a 16-bit run can hold.

Now load the file biga.bmp. In 8-bit mode, there are 846 runs, which takes the RLE size to 3,384 bytes. That bitmap file is 196,662 bytes in size, so you've achieved a 58:1 compression ratio with this bitmap! That's impressive, but you also need to consider that you're using what is essentially a monochrome (black-and-white) bitmap, so there is a lot less change in the image. To compare this compression ratio to a more realistic image, load the bigaa.bmp file, which is the same image with the edges *anti-aliased*.

> **NOTE**
> *Anti-aliasing* is the process of blending sharp edges in a picture so that you don't see the individual pixels.

The anti-aliased image requires 1,820 runs in 8-bit mode, which takes up 7,280 bytes. This is "only" a 27:1 compression ratio, much less than the non-anti-aliased version.

Go back to the biga.bmp file now and switch to 16-bit mode. Notice that this time the runs went down to 819 from 845. In this bitmap, 27 runs were longer than 255 and had to be split up. Unfortunately, even though there were more runs that needed to be split up, it still makes the file bigger in 16-bit mode.

> **TIP**
> I personally recommend always using 1 byte for the run size. In RLE images, you're pretty lucky if you get a lot of runs that are over 256 pixels in size, so it is usually a waste of space to pick a larger length size, like 16 bits, and it is *definitely* not worth it to use 24- and 32-bit lengths.

I only provided one bitmap that is smaller when you go up to the 16-bit length mode, and that is blank.bmp. This bitmap is a blank white 256 × 256 image. In 8-bit mode, there are 258 runs in the image, which take up 1,032 bytes. Switch to 16-bit mode, and the runs drop down to 2! In 16-bit mode, this takes up 10 bytes. Now take it down one more level to 24-bit and you get 1 run, for a total file size of 6 bytes!

The original bitmap file takes up 196,662 bytes, so this is a compression ratio of 32,777:1! Now, hold on a moment, and don't get too excited.

Think about it, RLE is most efficient when storing large amounts of repeating data. But repeating data is boring! Bitmaps that are compressed well using RLE compression aren't very exciting at all!

To demonstrate, load up the marble.bmp and the stone.bmp bitmaps, to see what kind of file sizes you would get with RLE compression.

With the marble bitmap, you get 64,253 runs in 8-bit mode, but there are 65,336 pixels total! That means that there are only around 1,000 runs in the image that have more than 1 pixel in them, which is clearly a waste. Using 8-bit mode, the RLE takes up 257,012 bytes, whereas the actual bitmap takes up only 196,662 bytes—RLE compression actually made the file *bigger*!

The situation is the same with the stone bitmap, which takes up 941,104 bytes as an RLE but 263,222 bytes as a bitmap.

So, you can see that the RLE compression only works on certain kinds of bitmaps.

> **TIP**
> This may not be very relevant with today's games, but a few years ago I was able to receive a really nice speed boost by using RLE sprites. You see, when a sprite is drawn, the video card checks to see which pixels are drawn and which pixels are transparent. By using RLEs, I was able to reduce the number of checks dramatically. So if I had a run of 128 transparent pixels, I could just skip over all 128 pixels and didn't need to check each one like a standard blitter. Of course, most video cards these days are faster using the standard blitter anyway because they store the entire image in video memory, whereas the RLE blitting method requires you to manually send every pixel to draw over the video bus during run time, which makes this method somewhat worthless on modern hardware.

Coding an RLE Compressor and Decompressor

The file that contains all the RLE source code in this section is on the CD in the directory \structures\RLE.h.

In this section, I take you through creating a generic RLE compressor and decompressor.

The Structure

The structure of the RLE class is simple; it will hold an array of runs. A run is really just a pair of data: the actual data and the length.

```
template<class DataType>
class RLEPair
{
public:
    DataType m_data;
    unsigned char m_length;
};
```

This is a templated class, so you can use any type of data you want with the RLE compressor and decompressor. Notice how the length is an unsigned char; this is because this implementation of the RLE algorithm uses an 8-bit length. Remember the analysis from the last section, where I showed that an 8-bit length is almost always a better idea than any other length?

> **NOTE**
> If you're really into flexible programming, you could modify this class so that you can use a variable length type, but I don't think it's worth it because using higher length is only suitable for the rare case when your data has *huge* amounts of repeating data.

So this RLE class is somewhat flexible, but not 100 percent flexible. Some computer science professor out there is calling me an idiot for this, but I don't care (hah!).

After declaring the pair class, the actual RLE container class is declared. Here is the declaration and the data inside the class.

```
template<class DataType>
class RLE
{
```

```
public:
    typedef RLEPair<DataType> Pair;
    Array<Pair> m_RLE;
    int m_runs;
    int m_size;
}
```

The RLE class is templated, so you can store any type of data in it. The only limitation is that the data type you use should support the comparison operator (==).

The class has an array of pairs and keeps track of how many runs are in the array and the number of items that the runs represent.

For example, if you compress an array of 1,000 items into 20 runs, then `m_runs` will hold 20 and `m_size` will hold 1,000. The array itself is automatically resized by the compression function, so you never have to worry about running out of room for the runs.

The Constructor

The constructor just initializes the RLE array to one index and clears the other variables.

```
RLE( )
    : m_RLE( 1 )
{
    m_runs = 0;
    m_size = 0;
}
```

Later on you'll see that the compression algorithm doubles the size of the RLE array every time it runs out of space, so making it one cell in size makes the algorithm easy to use.

The Compression Algorithm

The compression algorithm takes an array of items and turns them into an RLE. This is accomplished using the `CreateRLE` function.

Here is the source code, which is pretty simple when you think about it. I will split it up into sections to explain it better.

```
void CreateRLE( Array<DataType>& p_array )
{
```

```
int currentrun = 0;
int index;
```

The function is very simple and takes an array reference as a parameter. There are two local counting variables, one that keeps track of the current run and one that keeps track of the index in the uncompressed array.

```
m_RLE[0].m_data = p_array[0];
m_RLE[0].m_length = 1;
```

Because the RLE array is always at least one cell in size, it is safe to assume that index 0 is valid. Therefore, the first index in the array is placed into the first run in the RLE array, and the size of the run is set to 1. Note that this function overwrites any RLE information that already exists.

```
m_size = p_array.Size();
```

To complete the function initialization, the size of the uncompressed array is recorded to make decompression easier later on.

```
for( index = 1; index < p_array.m_size; index++ )
{
```

Now the function loops through each item in the uncompressed array.

```
    if( p_array[index] != m_RLE[currentrun].m_data )
    {
        currentrun++;
        if( m_RLE.m_size == currentrun )
            m_RLE.Resize( currentrun * 2 );
        m_RLE[currentrun].m_data = p_array[index];
        m_RLE[currentrun].m_length = 1;
    }
```

If the current item in the uncompressed array doesn't match the item in the current run, you need to start a new run. So the current run index is incremented. After that, the function checks to see if the current RLE array has been filled up, and if so, it doubles the size of the RLE array.

Then the current item in the array is placed into the new run and the length is set to 1.

```
    else
    {
        if( m_RLE[currentrun].m_length == 255 )
        {
```

```
            currentrun++;
            if( m_RLE.m_size == currentrun )
                m_RLE.Resize( currentrun * 2 );
            m_RLE[currentrun].m_data = p_array[index];
            m_RLE[currentrun].m_length = 1;
    }
```

If the next item in the uncompressed array is the same as the item in the current run, the function increases the length of the current run. However, it is not that simple. First, the function needs to check to see if the length of the current run is 255. Remember, because the RLE class uses 8-bit lengths, 255 is the highest run length you can have. If your run is longer than 255 items, you need to split it up into another run. So if the run is too long, the function creates a new run, like before, and sets it up accordingly (resizing the RLE array if necessary).

```
            else
            {
                m_RLE[currentrun].m_length++;
            }
        }
    }
```

If the run didn't overflow, then the length of the current run is just incremented. This ends the loop through the uncompressed array.

```
    // set up the number of runs
    m_runs = currentrun + 1;
}
```

And finally, the number of runs is recorded in the m_runs variable.

> **TIP**
>
> To expand this function to different length sizes, you only need to change the part where it compares the length to 255 (and the pair data structure so that it holds a larger size, of course). If you're using a larger length size, compare the current length with the maximum number of your new length size.

The Decompression Algorithm

Decompressing a RLE is even easier than compressing one. It is accomplished by using the FillArray function:

```
void FillArray( Array<DataType>& p_array )
{
    if( p_array.Size() < m_size )
        p_array.Resize( m_size );
```

This function also takes an array reference. The array will be overwritten with the RLE data, so don't pass in an array of data that you want to keep.

If the array is too small, then it is resized so it is large enough to hold the uncompressed RLE.

```
int currentrun;
int index;
int offset = 0;
```

The first variable serves the same purpose as it did in the CreateRLE function; it keeps track of the run it is currently expanding.

The index and the offset variables keep track of the current position in the uncompressed array.

```
for( currentrun = 0; currentrun < m_runs; currentrun++ )
{
```

The loop to expand the RLE is a doubly nested for-loop. The preceding line of code is the outer loop, which loops through each run in the RLE.

```
    for( index = 0; index < m_RLE[currentrun].m_length; index++ )
    {
```

This is the inner loop, which loops through each item in the current run. If the run's length is 16, this inner loop goes through 16 times. The offset variable keeps track of the index in the uncompressed array where the run begins, and the index variable keeps track of the current item in the run.

```
        p_array[offset + index] = m_RLE[currentrun].m_data;
    }
```

The offset and the index are added to get the correct index in the uncompressed array, and the item in the current run is placed into the uncompressed array.

```
    offset += m_RLE[currentrun].m_length;
}
}
```

Finally, the offset is incremented by the number of items that were in the current run, which gives you the index of the starting place for the next run in the uncompressed array.

The SaveData Function

Most of the time, you want to compress your data and then store it onto disk somewhere, so you want to have a function that can save the data easily.

This function will use the standard C++ file I/O functions. If you are unfamiliar with them, please see Chapter 3, "Arrays," or Appendix A, "A C++ Primer."

```
void SaveData( char* p_name )
{
    FILE* file = fopen( p_name, "wb" );
```

The function takes a string as a parameter and opens it for writing in binary mode (almost every file you will deal with is binary data anyway).

```
    fwrite( &m_size, sizeof(int), 1, file );
    fwrite( &m_runs, sizeof(int), 1, file );
```

The first two things it writes are the size of the uncompressed data and the number of runs that the data takes up when compressed.

```
    fwrite( m_RLE.m_array, sizeof(Pair), m_runs, file );
    fclose( file );
}
```

After that, the actual array of `Pair`s is written out to disk, and the file is closed.

The LoadData Function

There is a function to save data to disk, so there should also be one to load the data back into memory, right? This is that function.

```
void LoadData( char* p_name )
{
    FILE* file = fopen( p_name, "rb" );
```

This time, instead of opening the file in *writing* mode, it is in *reading* mode. (I bet you didn't see that one coming!)

```
    fread( &m_size, sizeof(int), 1, file );
    fread( &m_runs, sizeof(int), 1, file );
```

The function then reads in the size of the uncompressed data and the number of runs in the compressed data.

```
    if( m_RLE.Size() < m_runs )
        m_RLE.Resize( m_runs );
```

If the RLE array is too small to hold the compressed RLE data, it is resized to hold the data.

```
    fread( m_RLE.m_array, sizeof(Pair), m_runs, file );
    fclose( file );
}
```

Finally, the compressed RLE data is read into the RLE array, and the file is closed.

Example 21-1

This is Example 21-1, which you can find on the CD in the directory \examples\ch21\01 - RLE\.

This demo program loads a file and then tries to compress it using RLE compression and saves it back to disk. Because of that, you should copy the files onto your hard drive to run it, or it will fail to work (because it can't write onto the CD-ROM).

The program does a few things: it loads a file, compresses it, writes it out to disk, uncompresses the file into a new array, and compares the contents with the original array.

```
void main()
{
    Array<char> original( 1 );
    Array<char> uncompressed( 1 );
    RLE<char> compressed;
```

The `original` array holds the data that is read from the file. The `uncompressed` array holds the data as it is decompressed out of the RLE again, and the `compressed` variable holds the compressed RLE data.

```
    char filename[80];
    int index;
    cout << "Enter file name: ";
    cin >> filename;
```

The function uses a string to load in the name of the file you want to compress.

```
    original.Resize( GetFileSize( filename ) );
```

Then the function resizes the original array to the size of the file due to a limitation in the array's `ReadFile` function, which only reads in as much memory as the array can store. This way, the entire file can be read in. The `GetFileSize` function is a simple little helper function I included in the file.

```
original.ReadFile( filename );
compressed.Compress( original );
```

The file is then read in and compressed.

```
strcat( filename, ".rle" );
compressed.SaveData( filename );
```

Using the `strcat` function, `.rle` is added to the end of the file name, and the RLE data is then saved to disk using that file name.

```
cout << "Original File Size: " << compressed.m_size << endl;
cout << "Compressed File Size: " << compressed.m_runs * 2 << endl;
cout << "Compression Ratio: ";
cout << (float)(compressed.m_size) / (float)(compressed.m_runs * 2);
cout << endl;
```

Statistics about the RLE are printed out to the screen, including the original file size in bytes and the size of the RLE in bytes (the number of runs times 2, because the data and the length of each run are both 1 byte).

It also prints out the compression ratio; anything larger than 1.0 is good, and anything less than 1.0 means that you actually made the file bigger.

```
compressed.FillArray( uncompressed );
```

The compressed RLE is then decompressed into the `uncompressed` array so it can verify that the data was preserved.

```
cout << "Checking Array Integrity..." << endl;
for( index = 0; index < compressed.m_size; index++ )
{
    if( original[index] != uncompressed[index] )
    {
        cout << "ERROR, DECOMPRESSION UNSUCCESSFUL!!" << endl;
        return;
    }
}
cout << "Arrays match!" << endl;
}
```

This loops through both arrays and compares the items; if any two items don't match, then it prints out an error and quits. If the loop ends, then both arrays matched.

I've provided four test files to use, test1.txt, test2.txt, test3.txt, and test4.txt. Each of these files demonstrates something, so I urge you to open them and see what they look like.

The first file contains 26 different letters repeated a random number of times in a row. This file compressed nicely with about a 38:1 compression ratio.

Test2.txt contains the same pattern as test1.txt, repeated many more times. You should note that this file gets the same compression ratio.

The third test file contains one letter repeated around 600,000 times. From what you know, you should be able to tell that this file will compress wonderfully, and it does! You get around a 127:1 compression ratio.

The final file holds around 200,000 characters, and not a single character is repeated twice. You should be able to tell that this file will not compress at all, but rather expand. In fact, the actual RLE "compression" on this file results in a file that is exactly twice as large.

Example 21-2

This is Example 21-2, which does the opposite of Example 21-1; it loads in a compressed RLE, decompresses it into an array, and then saves the uncompressed data into a new file.

Basically, you're supposed to use Example 21-1 to compress data and then use this example to decompress data back into its original form.

```
void main()
{
    typedef unsigned char uchar;
    Array<uchar> uncompressed( 1 );
    RLE<uchar> compressed;
```

Two structures are declared: the array of uncompressed bytes and the RLE that contains the compressed bytes.

```
    char dataname[80];
    cout << "Enter data file name: ";
    cin >> dataname;
```

The filename string is declared and then read in.

```
    compressed.LoadData( dataname );
    compressed.Decompress( uncompressed );
```

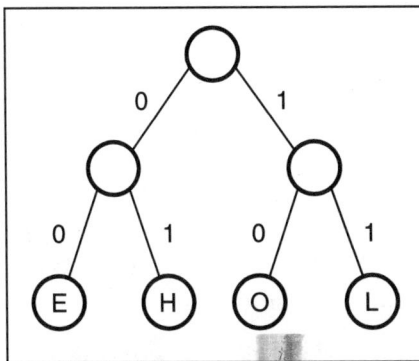

Figure 21.10

Here is a simple Huffman tree.

So what the heck do you do with this?

Imagine you have a binary message: 0100111110. Place your finger on the root node of the tree. You read the binary message in, one bit at a time. Whenever you read in a 0, you move your finger to the left child of the current node, and whenever you read in a 1, you move your finger to the right child of the current node. Whenever you reach a child node, write down that letter and move your finger up to the root node again. Repeat this process until the entire message has been decoded.

Get the message? Hello! If you're not saying "hello" to me right now, then try it again to see if you can correctly decode the message.

Figure 21.11 shows the decoding of the first two letters.

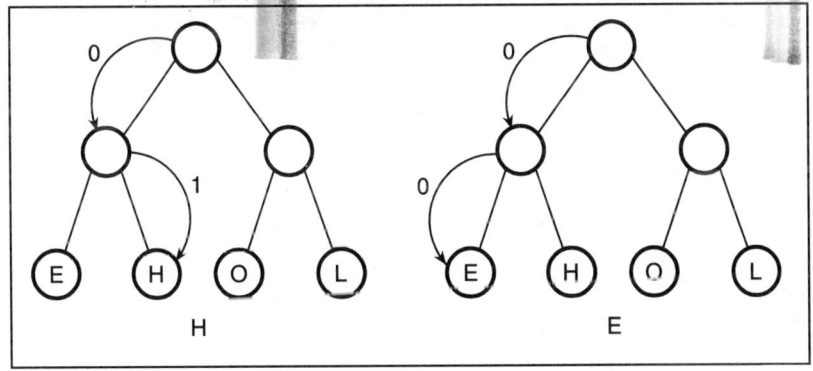

Figure 21.11

This is how you decode the first two letters of the message.

Of course, in that simple example, every character was two bits in length. You'll find that more-complex Huffman trees give varying lengths to different characters.

Let me show you one more example of decoding, this time using a much larger tree. Figure 21.12 shows the tree.

Then the RLE data is loaded from the file and then decompressed into the array.

```
    dataname[ strlen(dataname) - 4 ] = 0;
    uncompressed.WriteFile( dataname );
    cout << "Decompressed to " << dataname << endl;
}
```

The last four characters are chopped off of the filename (it is assumed that the filename will end with the four characters .rle, which is what Example 21-1 adds to the end of each file), and the uncompressed file is then written out to disk.

You can try decompressing all of the RLE files that were provided with the previous example; you will see that they all work flawlessly.

Huffman Trees

Trees again? Oh, no!

Oh, yes. There is no avoiding trees in the wonderful world of game programming, and it turns out that they can be used very efficiently for data compression.

Huffman encoding (invented by David Huffman in 1952 at MIT) works by trying to make the most frequently occurring items in a chunk of data take up the least amount of space.

Think about this for a moment: You have a text file full of characters. Each character takes up one whole byte, or 8 bits. So each byte can represent up to 256 different letters or numbers or symbols. What is the likelihood that every text file out there has at least one instance of every symbol? Not very likely. In fact, most text files rarely use more than 50–60 different characters, so the extra bits needed to provide you with all 256 characters are wasted!

So Huffman encoding attempts to make the most frequent characters take up a small amount of space and the least frequent characters take up the most amount of space.

Huffman Decoding

In order for you to understand how Huffman compression works, it is easiest for me to show you an example of how to decode a binary string first. Figure 21.10 shows a simple Huffman tree.

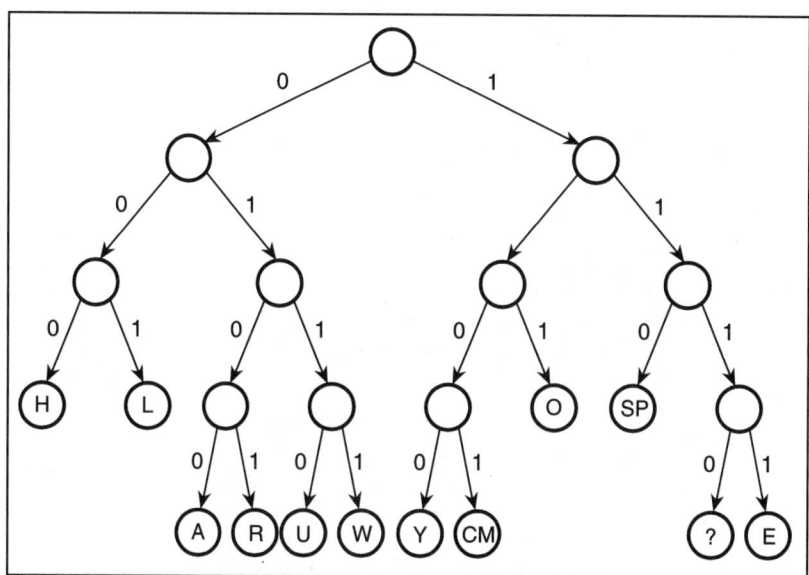

Figure 21.12

Here is a larger Huffman tree.

This time, the message is: 000 1111 001 001 111 1001 110 000 101 0111 110 0100 0101 1111 110 1000 101 0110 1110. See if you can decode it accurately. SP means "space" and CM means "comma," by the way.

The answer is "hello, how are you?"

Pretty simple, isn't it?

Creating a Huffman Tree

The tree in Figure 21.12 didn't just appear, I had to create it. I didn't just throw it together, though, I had to use a special process to create the tree so that the most used characters are higher up and the lesser used characters are down at the bottom of the tree. Notice which characters in the phrase "hello, how are you?" are seen the most. The letter o and the space character are each repeated three times, and they are higher in the tree than most characters—on the third level. This means that they each take three bits.

Characters that only appear once are on the lowest level of the tree, such as w and y, and they take four bits each.

The Frequency Table

The first step you must take when generating a Huffman tree is to create a *frequency table*. This table will hold the frequencies of each character in a sample set of data.

You see, just like RLEs, certain Huffman trees may actually end up making your files bigger. Each Huffman tree is optimized for a certain set of data. The tree in Figure 21.12 was optimized for the phrase "hello, how are you?"

Table 21.1 shows the frequency table for that phrase.

Table 21.1 Frequency Table

Character	Frequency
A	1
E	2
H	2
L	2
O	3
R	1
U	1
W	1
Y	1
Space	3
Comma	1
?	1

Now that you have the frequency, you can move on to generating the tree.

Generating the Tree

This process requires some help from our old pal, the *priority queue* (see Chapter 14, "Priority Queues and Heaps"). The first thing you need to do is put every character into a plain binary tree node and put them into the priority queue, but instead of the characters with the highest frequency going first, the characters with the lowest frequency are first. Figure 21.13 shows the priority queue for this table. Please note that I am using the standard priority queue representation for the drawing, not the heap representation. Heaps make things look complicated in the figures.

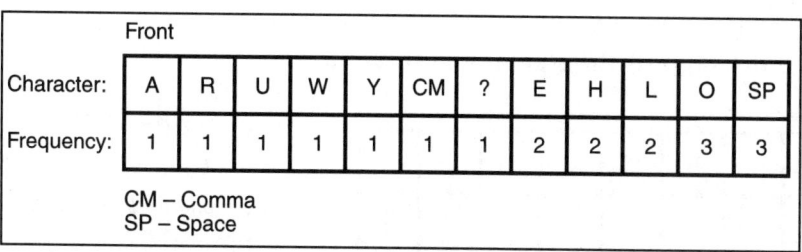

Figure 21.13

This is the initial priority queue.

I will be referring to the frequency of the nodes as the *weight* of the nodes from now on. Now comes the actual tree generation algorithm, which is really quite simple:

1. Take the first node off of the priority queue.
2. Take the second node off of the priority queue.
3. Create a new binary tree node that has the first node as its left child and the second node as its right child.
4. Make the weight of the new node equal to the weight of its child nodes added together.
5. Place the new node into the priority queue.
6. Go to step 1 and repeat until only one node is left in the priority queue.

Let's see this in action! Figure 21.14 shows the first iteration of these steps on the queue.

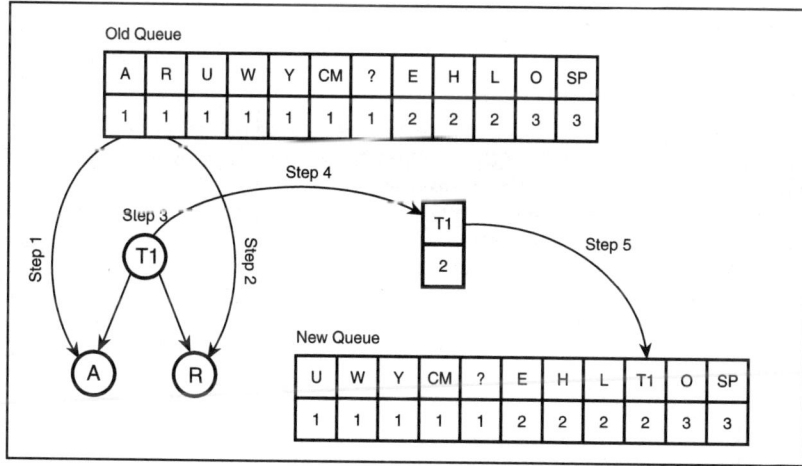

Figure 21.14

Here is the first iteration on the queue.

The queue is also sometimes called a *forest* (because you're building trees in it, get it?). So now you have a bunch of single nodes and one two-level tree in your forest, and you repeat the process. The new node is called T1, which stands for Tree 1.

Figures 21.15, 21.16, 21.17, 21.18, and 21.19 show the complete algorithm. The last tree in Figure 21.19 is the same as the tree in Figure 21.12.

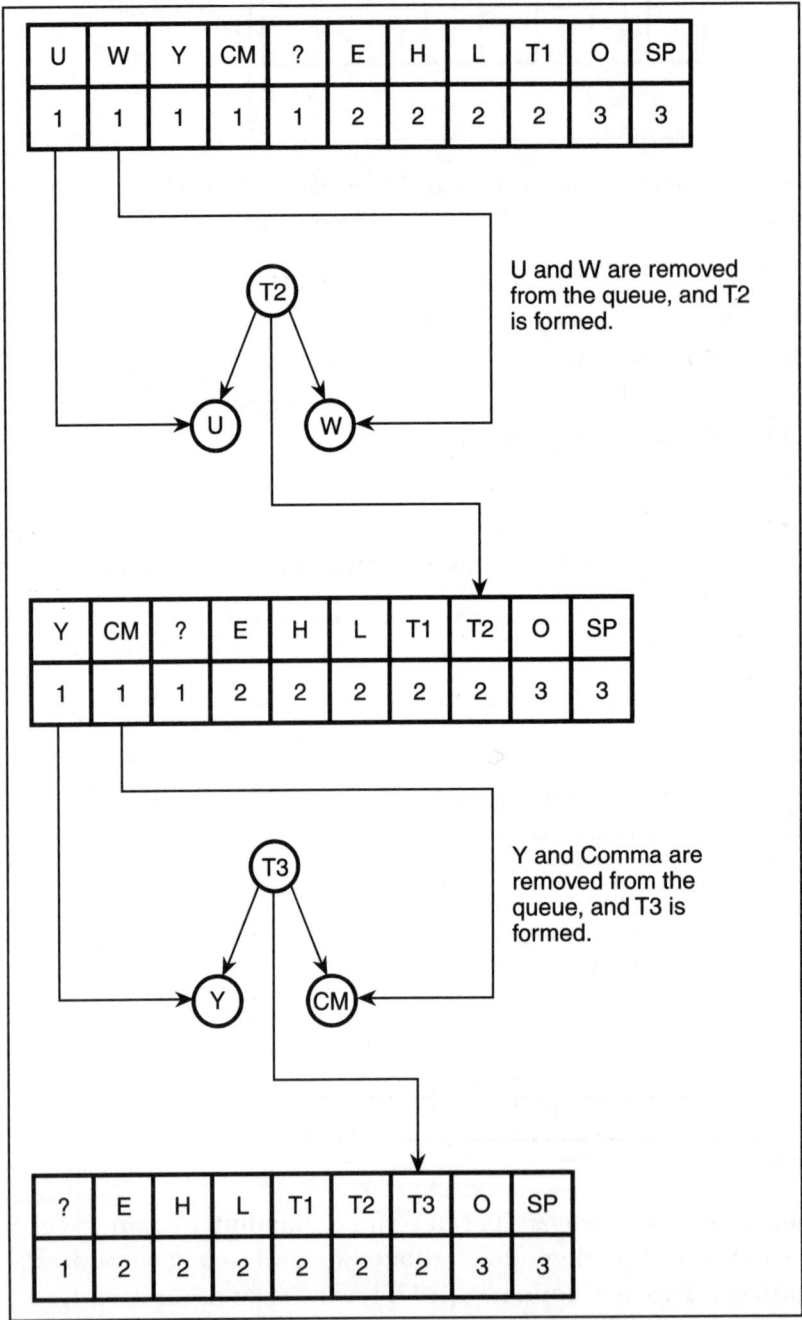

Figure 21.15

These are the second and third iterations.

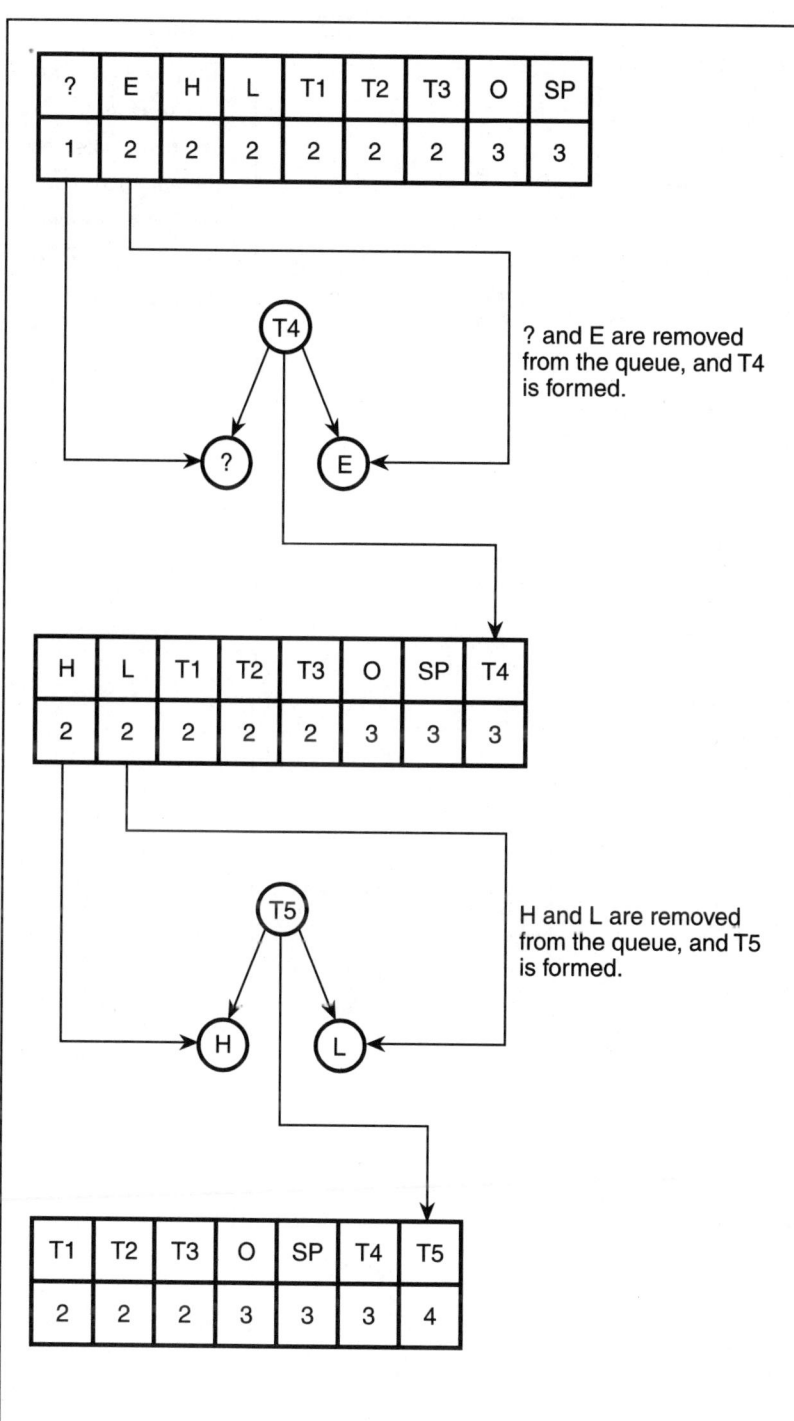

Figure 21.16

These are the fourth and fifth iterations.

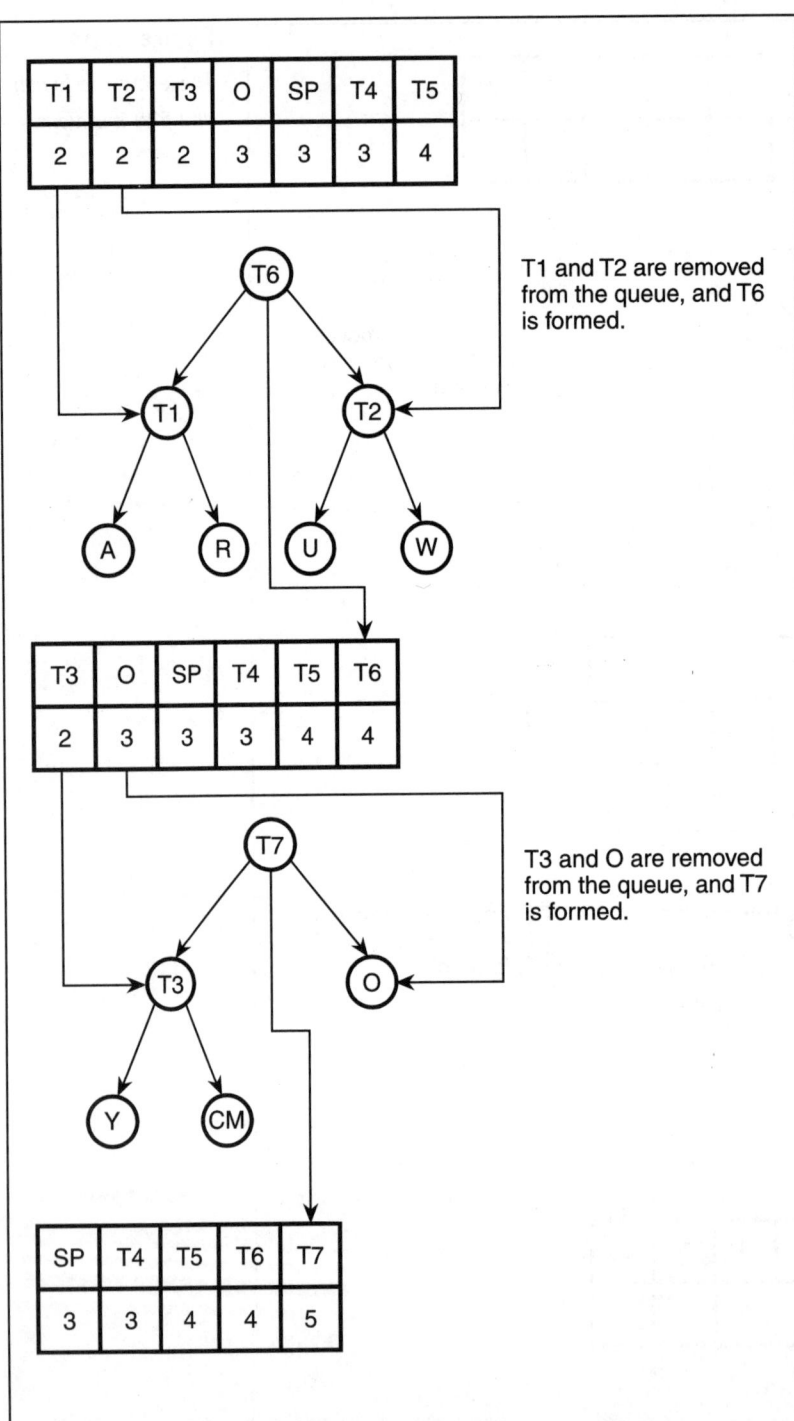

Figure 21.17
These are the sixth and seventh iterations. Note how these iterations are the first to combine trees instead of just the single nodes.

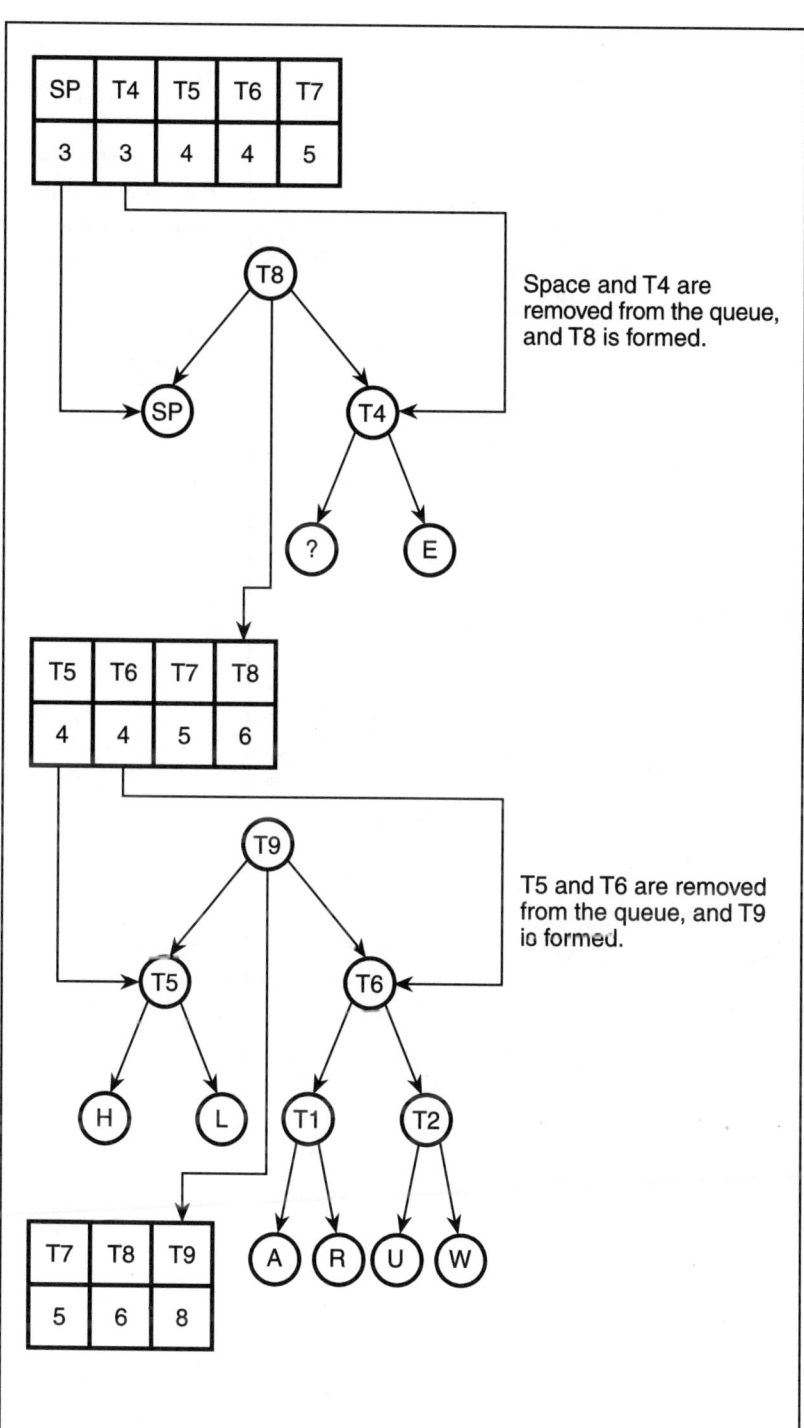

Figure 21.18

These are the eighth and ninth iterations.

674   21. Data Compression

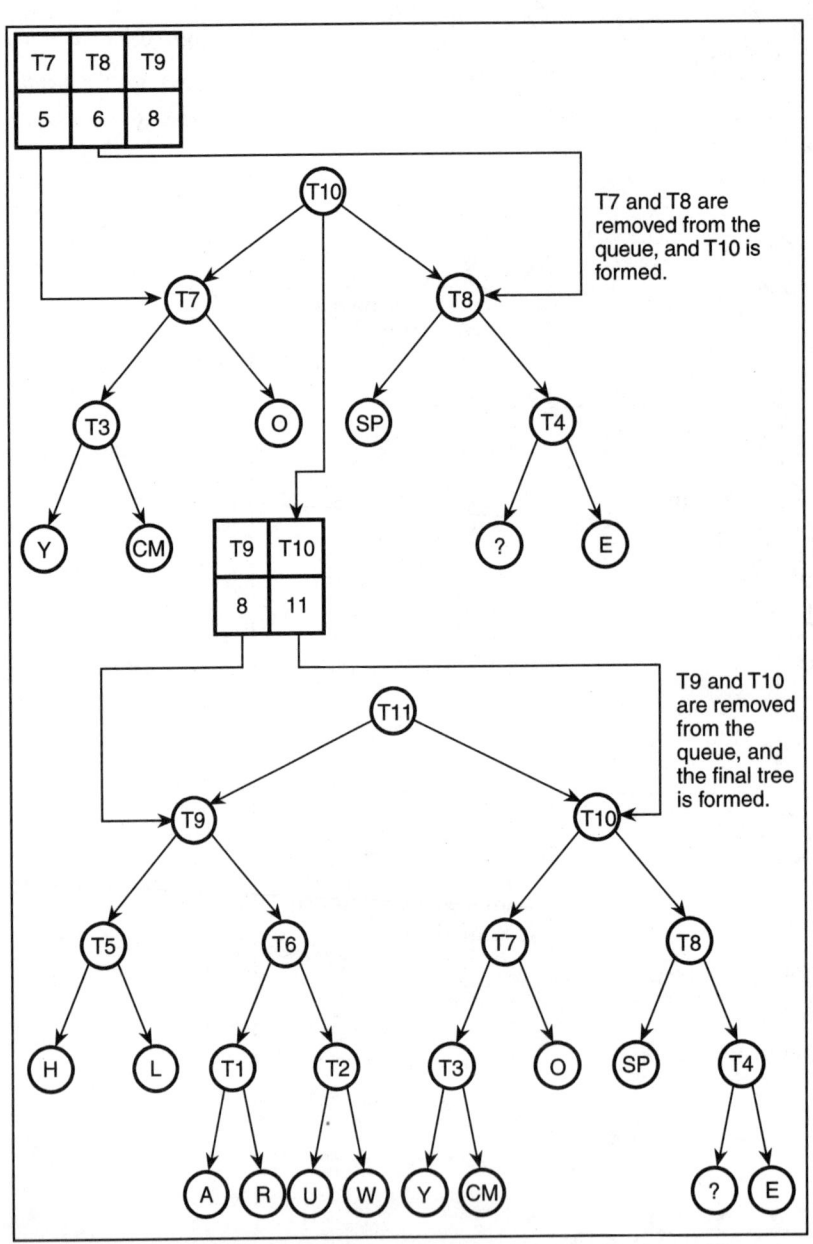

Figure 21.19

These are the tenth and eleventh iterations. These are the last two iterations of the algorithm.

Graphical Demonstration: Creating a Huffman Tree

This is Graphical Demonstration 21-2, which is on the CD in the directory \demonstrations\ch21\Demo02 - Huffman Tree Creation\.

Compiling the Demo

This demonstration uses the SDLGUI library that I have developed for the book. For more information about this library, see Appendix B.

To compile this demo, either open up the workspace file in the directory or create your own project using the settings described in Appendix B. If you create your own project, all of the files you need to include are in the directory.

The demo has one text box and two buttons, only one of which is visible when the demo starts. You start off by typing a string of text into the text box. Then, click the Calculate button. Immediately, the Calculate button disappears, and a bunch of nodes appear at the bottom of the screen. This is the priority queue of nodes.

A new button has appeared—the Iterate button. Pressing it once pulls the first node off of the queue and puts it in the middle of the screen. Pressing it again pulls another node off the queue and also puts that in the middle of the screen.

Pressing the button a third time creates a new node connecting the two nodes in the middle of the screen, and pressing it once more places the new node into the priority queue.

You should continue pressing the Iterate button, watching how the tree is created, until the entire tree is complete.

When the tree is complete, the Calculate button reappears.

NOTE
If you type in the phrase "hello, how are you?" you will get a different tree from the one in Figure 21.12 because this demo puts the items in the priority queue based on their ASCII value, so the comma and question mark and the space are in the queue first instead of the letters.

CAUTION
Trees are big structures, and the demo only runs at 800 × 600 resolution. With larger phrases, the demo may end up drawing trees on top of each other. Don't worry too much about it—there is really nothing that can be done about it.

Figure 21.20 shows a screenshot from the demo.

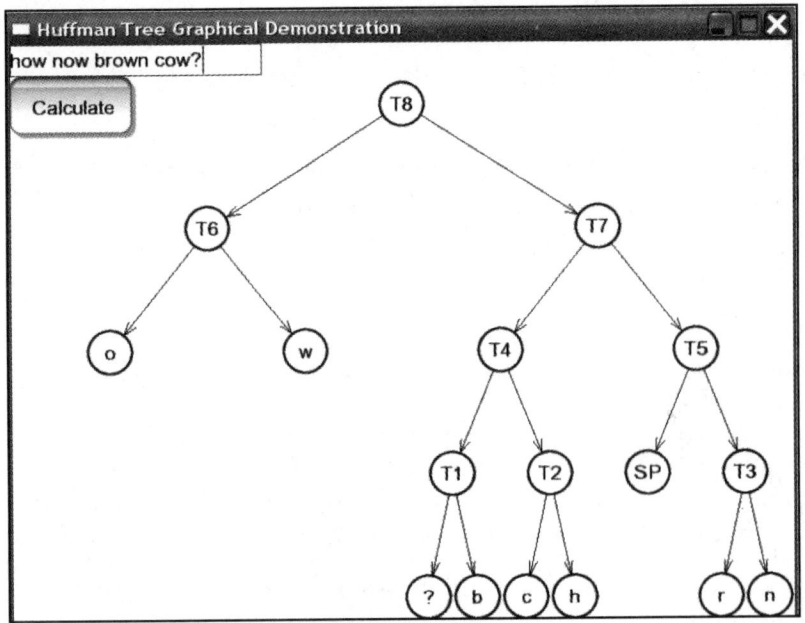

Figure 21.20

Here is a screenshot from the demo.

Coding a Huffman Tree Class

This section takes you through the coding of a Huffman compressor and decompressor class. All of the code is located in the file \structures\huffman.h on the CD.

You'll note that this class builds upon and uses many of the classes you've learned about previously in this book, such as the Array, Bitvector, BinaryTree, and Heap classes.

> **CAUTION**
>
> You must be aware of one thing before you use these classes: They only work on integral (integer) numeric types, and 32-bit numeric types don't work with them (due to a limitation that I explain when you get to it). The demos I show you use 8-bit integers to compress the data, and that seems to work fairly well.

The Huffman Node Class

This is the class that will store all of the relevant information for the nodes in the Huffman tree.

```
template<class DataType>
class HuffmanNode
{
public:
    DataType m_data;
    unsigned long int m_code;
    int m_codeLength;
};
```

Each node has an instance of data in it, m_data, so you know which item the node represents when encoding and decoding.

After that, the node has an `unsigned long int` that stores the actual Huffman code to get to the node. I used this data type because it is 32 bits long and it is unlikely that you will be using any set of data that will end up having a code longer than 32 bits.

> **NOTE**
> If you do end up using data that needs more than 32 bits per code, you could probably use a bitvector here instead of an integer. My reason for using an integer was to save on disk space when this tree structure is written out to disk.

Finally, there is a code length variable, which keeps track of how many bits long the code is. Because a 32-bit integer is being used, this is the only way to keep track of how long the actual code is.

The Frequency Class

The frequency class is used to store (logically enough) the frequency information of a certain instance of data.

```
template<class DataType>
class HuffmanFrequency
{
public:
    DataType m_data;
    int m_frequency;
};
```

The Frequency Comparison Function

Because you're using a heap to store the data, you need a comparison function to get the heap to work. If you remember back to an earlier section, the priority queue needs to put the items with the lowest frequency first:

```
template<class DataType>
int CompareNodes( BinaryTree< HuffmanFrequency<DataType> >* left,
                  BinaryTree< HuffmanFrequency<DataType> >* right )
{
    return right->m_data.m_frequency - left->m_data.m_frequency;
}
```

This function takes binary tree pointers, which contain the actual frequency class. This is because the priority queue actually contains trees, remember?

The function is templated, so it will work with any data type. Because you know that the frequency is an integer, you don't need to mess around with anything but that, so the left is subtracted from the right and returned.

The Huffman Class

This is the class that will actually accomplish everything, such as compressing, decompressing, calculating the tree, and saving and loading the files to disk.

The Declaration, Typedefs, and Data

```
template<class DataType, unsigned long int MaxValue>
class Huffman
{
```

First is the declaration of the class. As usual, the class is templated, so it will work with different datatypes, but only if they are integral datatypes valid for this class (`unsigned char, char, unsigned short int, short int`). I discuss this limitation later on. The main thing to notice from the declaration is the additional template value, `MaxValue`. This tells the `Huffman` class what the maximum value of the data is. For example, if you were using `unsigned char`s, this value should be 255. This is so the class can efficiently store the tables for compression.

```
public:
    typedef HuffmanNode<DataType> Node;
    typedef HuffmanFrequency<DataType> Frequency;
    typedef BinaryTree<Frequency> TreeNode;
```

There are three `typedefs`, which exist to make your life easier. Instead of referencing a node in the Huffman tree as `BinaryTree< HuffmanFrequency< DataType > >`, you can just type `TreeNode` instead. Typedefs, if you haven't noticed yet, make code easier to write and understand.

```
Bitvector m_compressedData;
int m_dataLength;
int m_compressedLength;
```

First, there is the bitvector that stores the compressed data. It is easy to use a bitvector, because Huffman-compressed data is variable in length and doesn't fall on standard bitwise boundaries. Therefore, you need to be able to access individual bits easily, and the bitvector allows you to do just that.

The next two variables store the size of the uncompressed data in units (if the data is chars, then this stores how many bytes the data takes up) and the size of the compressed data in bits.

```
Array<Node> m_huffmanTree;
int m_maxEntry;
```

Next, the actual Huffman tree is declared... but wait! It's an array! No, I didn't lie to you, it really is a tree, I promise. Remember in Chapter 12, "Binary Trees," when you first learned about binary trees and how they can be stored as an array? This is exactly what is happening here—the Huffman tree will be stored in an array. This is mainly because you need to be able to eventually store the tree onto disk somehow, and linked structures don't really transfer to disk well. So the program converts the Huffman tree into an array and uses that.

> **NOTE**
> Of course there are more efficient ways to actually store the tree to disk. Unfortunately, I don't have the time or the room to describe them. A lot of the nodes in the tree array are unused, so there is some amount of wasted space, but it's usually not enough to matter much.

The max entry variable keeps track of the index of the last entry in the tree.

```
    Array<Node> m_lookupTable;
}
```

Finally, there is the lookup table. This table is used to speed up the compression because it stores the code data for each possible data item. This way, if you want to know the code for byte 142, just look up that index, and it will have the right node structure. This way, you don't need to search the tree for each item you want to compress.

The Constructor

The constructor sets up the data in the Huffman structure.

```
Huffman()
        :   m_compressedData( 1 ),
            m_huffmanTree( 1 ),
            m_lookupTable( MaxValue + 1 )
{
    m_dataLength = 0;
    m_compressedLength = 0;
    m_maxEntry = 0;
}
```

It initializes the compressed data and the tree arrays to 1 so they don't take up much room before they are initialized. The lookup table, because it will always remain the same size for a single Huffman structure, is initialized to hold as many indexes as there are valid items. For example, if you are using unsigned chars, then the max value is 255, so the array should hold 256 indexes (0–255). This is one of the reasons you shouldn't use 32-bit data; this would try to create an array with four billion entries (yikes!).

The three counting variables are cleared to 0 because there is no data yet.

Calculating the Tree

This function will calculate the frequency table and Huffman tree for a specific set of data. It is much easier to generate a Huffman tree using a linked binary tree, so that is what the algorithm uses to actually generate the tree. After the tree is generated, the function converts that tree into an array.

```
void CalculateTree( Array<DataType>& p_array )
{
    Array<int> frequencyTable( MaxValue + 1 );
    int index;
```

The function takes an array as its parameter, which it will use to calculate the Huffman tree. First, it declares an array that holds an integer for each possible data item and an index that will be used for looping.

```
    for( index = 0; index <= MaxValue; index++ )
    {
```

```
        frequencyTable[index] = 0;
    }
    for( index = 0; index < p_array.Size(); index++ )
    {
        frequencyTable[ p_array[index] ]++;
    }
```

The first step is to clear the frequency table directly to all 0s and then calculate the frequency of each item in the array. Whenever an instance of a particular data item is found, its entry in the frequency table is incremented by one.

```
Heap<TreeNode*> heap( frequencyTable.Size(), CompareNodes );
TreeNode* parent;
TreeNode* left;
TreeNode* right;
```

After that, a heap is created which will have enough room for every possible item, and it uses the CompareNodes function that was defined earlier.

After that, three tree node pointers are defined, and they will be used in constructing the Huffman tree.

```
    for( index = 0; index <= MaxValue; index++ )
    {
        if( frequencyTable[index] != 0 )
        {
            parent = new TreeNode;
            parent->m_data.m_data = index;
            parent->m_data.m_frequency = frequencyTable[index];
            heap.Enqueue( parent );
        }
    }
```

This loop goes through the frequency table, and whenever it finds an item with a frequency greater than zero (items with no frequency are not added to the tree because they don't exist in the file), a new node is created and added to the heap.

```
    while( heap.m_count > 1 )
    {
        left = heap.Item();
        heap.Dequeue();
        right = heap.Item();
        heap.Dequeue();
        parent = new TreeNode;
```

```
            parent->m_left = left;
            parent->m_right = right;
            parent->m_data.m_frequency = left->m_data.m_frequency +
                                         right->m_data.m_frequency;
            heap.Enqueue( parent );
        }
```

This is the function that actually calculates the Huffman tree. It takes off the first and second items from the heap and puts them into the left and right node pointers. It then creates a new parent node and makes it point to the two nodes that were pulled off the heap. After that, the frequency of the parent node is updated to be the sum of both of its child nodes. Finally, the parent node is added back into the heap.

```
        ConvertTreeToArray( heap.m_array[1] );
        CreateLookupTable();
        delete heap.m_array[1];
    }
```

Now the function converts the tree to an array and stores it into the `m_huffmanTree` array. Then the lookup table is calculated, and the binary tree is deleted.

> **NOTE**
>
> Calculating a tree where only one item exists in the data is not a good idea. Huffman compression doesn't work on data that has only one repeated value because the tree will end up with one node at the root and nothing else. If this happens, then the code for that data doesn't exist, because the length of the code is 0. The tree calculation algorithm will work for such data, but trying to compress it will crash the program. When testing out Examples 21-3 and 21-4, try using `test3.txt` from Example 21-1. You'll see that because the file contains only the letter a, it will not compress and decompress correctly.

Compressing Data

Just like the `RLE` class, the `Huffman` class has a `Compress` function that works the same way. You pass an array into the function and it will compress the data for you.

```
void Compress( Array<DataType>& p_array )
{
    int index;
    int vectorindex = 0;
```

```
int codeindex;
int codelength;
unsigned long int code;
bool value;
```

There are three looping index values. The `index` keeps track of the current index in the uncompressed array, the `vectorindex` keeps track of the current index in the bitvector while it is compressing the data, and the `codeindex` keeps track of the current bit in the code for the current value in the uncompressed array.

The `codelength`, `code`, and `value` variables are used to make the code look better; they are used to retrieve values that will be used later.

```
for( index = 0; index < p_array.Size(); index++ )
{
```

This starts the compression routine. The uncompressed array is scanned through at each index.

```
    code = m_lookupTable[ p_array[index] ].m_code;
    codelength = m_lookupTable[ p_array[index] ].m_codeLength;
```

The code for the current item and its length are both looked up in the lookup table. Remember, the lookup table holds information about every possible item in the array that is being compressed, so if you want to find the code and length for the value 142, that information can be found in the lookup table at that index.

```
    if( m_compressedData.Size() < vectorindex + codelength )
        m_compressedData.Resize( m_compressedData.Size() * 2 );
```

Now that you know the length of the current code, you can check to see if the bitvector is large enough to store the code. If it isn't, then the algorithm just doubles the size of the vector.

```
    for( codeindex = 0; codeindex < codelength; codeindex++ )
    {
        value = (1 << codeindex) & code;
        m_compressedData.Set( vectorindex, value );
        vectorindex++;
    }
}
```

This section of code loops through each bit in the current code and copies each bit over into the bitvector. It shifts a 1 into the place of the bit that you want to extract and performs a *binary-and* on the code to extract the digit into `value`. (See Chapter

4, "Bitvectors," or Appendix A if you are unfamiliar with bit-extraction.) After that bit is extracted, it is then set in the bitvector, and the vector index is incremented.

```
    m_compressedLength = vectorindex;
    m_dataLength = p_array.Size();
}
```

Finally, the length in bits of the bitvector and the length in items of the uncompressed array are both recorded for future use.

The compressed Huffman codes are now stored in the bitvector.

Decompressing Data

Obviously, there needs to be a data decompression function, too, because there is a compression function, so here it is:

```
void Decompress( Array<DataType>& p_array )
{
    int vectorindex;
    int arrayindex = 0;
    int treeindex = 1;
    int value;
```

There are three indexes again, but they aren't all the same as in the compression function. The vector index keeps track of the current bit in the bitvector, and the array index keeps track of the current item in the uncompressed array, but the `treeindex` is new. This variable keeps track of the current node in the Huffman tree as you travel down it, decoding the bits. Note how the `treeindex` is initialized to 1, which is the theoretical root of a binary tree when represented as an array (see Chapter 12).

```
    if( p_array.Size() < m_dataLength )
        p_array.Resize( m_dataLength );
```

If the array isn't large enough to store the compressed data, it is resized so that the data will fit.

```
    for( vectorindex = 0; vectorindex < m_compressedLength; vectorindex++ )
    {
```

This begins the decompression loop. This time, instead of looping through each uncompressed array index, it loops through each bit in the bitvector.

```
        value = m_compressedData[vectorindex];
        treeindex = treeindex * 2 + value;
```

The value of the current bit is extracted from the bitvector, and then the tree index is moved down to the correct child node, depending on the value of the bit. Remember back to Chapter 12, when I showed you how to traverse a binary tree when it is an array? To go to the left child, you multiply the index by 2, and to go to the right child, you multiply the index by 2 and add 1. Well, if the bit is 0, then you want to go to the left child in a Huffman tree, and if the bit is 1, you want to go to the right child. So if value is 0, then the algorithm goes to the left, and if value is 1, it goes to the right. Neat, isn't it?

```
        if( m_huffmanTree[treeindex-1].m_codeLength != 0 )
        {
```

Next, the code length of the current node is retrieved and compared to 0. One is subtracted from the index, though. This is because a binary tree represented as an array starts off at index 1, but to save space and prevent index 0 from being unused, 1 is subtracted from the current tree index. So index 1 is really stored in index 0, and 2 is stored in 1, and so on.

If the code length is 0, then the current node in not a valid node (that is, it is one of the temporary tree nodes that were created to join other nodes together), and the function skips over the next part and looks at the next bit.

```
            p_array[arrayindex] = m_huffmanTree[treeindex-1].m_data;
            arrayindex++;
            treeindex = 1;
        }
    }
}
```

If the code length of the current node wasn't 0, then you've reached a valid node that contains data. That data is retrieved from the current node and placed into the uncompressed array, the array index is incremented, and the tree index is moved back to the root.

At the end of the function, the array will contain the uncompressed data.

Saving the Tree to Disk

Unlike the RLE class, a Huffman compressed chunk of data has two distinct parts. The first part is the tree that is used to compress and decompress data, and the second part is the actual data. So to actually decode the data someday, you need the tree.

This function will save the tree to disk for you.

```
void SaveTree( char* p_name )
{
    FILE* file = fopen( p_name, "wb" );
```

First the file is opened in binary writing mode

```
    fwrite( &m_maxEntry, sizeof(int), 1, file );
```

The size of the tree is stored to disk first.

```
    fwrite( m_huffmanTree.m_array, sizeof(Node), m_maxEntry, file );
    fclose( file );
}
```

And finally, the actual tree is stored on disk.

Loading the Tree from Disk

This function loads a tree from disk.

```
void LoadTree( char* p_name )
{
    FILE* file = fopen( p_name, "rb" );
    fread( &m_maxEntry, sizeof(int), 1, file );
```

The file is opened and the size of the tree is read in.

```
    m_huffmanTree.Resize( m_maxEntry );
```

The Huffman tree is then resized so it has enough room to store the tree.

```
    fread( m_huffmanTree.m_array, sizeof(Node), m_maxEntry, file );
    fclose( file );
    CreateLookupTable();
}
```

Finally, the tree is read in, the file is closed, and the lookup table is re-generated. The table needs to be generated because you loaded in a new tree. If you try to compress data that needs the lookup table and the lookup table doesn't exist, it won't work.

Saving the Data to Disk

This function is used to save the compressed data to disk.

```
void SaveData( char* p_name )
{
```

```
FILE* file = fopen( p_name, "wb" );
fwrite( &m_dataLength, sizeof(int), 1, file );
fwrite( &m_compressedLength, sizeof(int), 1, file );
```

The file is again opened for binary writing, and the size of the uncompressed data and the compressed data are both saved into the file.

```
fwrite( m_compressedData.m_array,
        sizeof(unsigned long int),
        (m_compressedLength / 32) + 1,
        file );
```

After that, the actual compressed data is stored into the disk. Because you are saving a bitvector and the bitvector class uses `unsigned long ints` for its data, you are saving each cell of the bitvector to disk. Each cell contains 32 bits, so divide the number of bits by 32 and that should give you the number of cells that the bits take up. Unfortunately, due to the fact that integer division discards the remainder of the division, the number of cells will be off by one, so you should add one cell to the final total.

```
    fclose( file );
}
```

Finally the file is closed.

Loading the Data from Disk

This function will load the data from disk back into the class.

```
void LoadData( char* p_name )
{
    FILE* file = fopen( p_name, "rb" );
    fread( &m_dataLength, sizeof(int), 1, file );
    fread( &m_compressedLength, sizeof(int), 1, file );
```

The size of the uncompressed data and the compressed bitvector are loaded from the file first.

```
    m_compressedData.Resize( m_compressedLength );
```

Then the bitvector is resized so that it has enough room for the compressed data.

```
    fread( m_compressedData.m_array,
           sizeof(unsigned long int),
           m_compressedData.m_size,
           file );
```

```
            fclose( file );
}
```

Finally, the compressed data is loaded into the bitvector.

Converting the Binary Tree to an Array

Earlier, I told you that you would be converting the binary tree to an array so you can store it to disk easily. This function and the next one after it are the two functions that actually convert the tree into an array.

```
void ConvertTreeToArray( TreeNode* p_tree )
{
    int index;
```

The function takes a binary tree node pointer as its parameter, and this will be the root of the tree that is being converted into an array. An index looping variable is also declared.

```
    index = ( 2 << GetDepth( p_tree ) ) - 1;
```

This part takes a little explaining to understand. There is a function in the binarytree.h file that retrieves the maximum depth of a binary tree. If there is only one node in the tree, then the depth is 0, and so on. Now, if the depth of the tree is 1, there are two levels and a maximum of three nodes. This function calculates the depth, which should end up being 1. It then takes the value 2 and shifts it up by the depth of the tree. Remember, the expression x << n is equivalent to the mathematical formula $x * 2^n$. So you're multiplying 2 by 2 to the 1st power, giving you the value 4. Finally, you subtract 1 from that number, giving you 3, the maximum index of a two-level tree.

This works on any tree of any depth.

```
    if( m_huffmanTree.Size() < index )
        m_huffmanTree.Resize( index );
```

Now that you know the largest possible size of the tree array, the tree array is resized so that the tree will fit into it.

```
    m_maxEntry = 0;
    for( index = 0; index < m_huffmanTree.Size(); index++ )
    {
        m_huffmanTree[index].m_code = 0;
        m_huffmanTree[index].m_codeLength = 0;
    }
```

The maximum entry index is cleared to 0, and then the entire tree has its codes and code lengths set to 0, which means that those nodes are all invalid.

```
    Convert( p_tree, 1, 0, 0 );
}
```

Finally, the recursive `Convert` function is called on the root node. I explain the `Convert` function in the next section.

The Convert Function

The previous function, `ConvertTreeToArray`, doesn't actually convert the tree to an array. Instead, it just sets up the tree array so that the recursive `Convert` function can actually do the conversion.

When you stop to think about it, converting a binary tree to an array is somewhat simple. If a node knows its own index, then it can easily tell its children what indexes they are, right? And after you tell the children nodes what indexes they are, they can tell their children, and so on. You can see how this function works nicely as a recursive function.

Another thing this function does is figure out the length of the code for each node—and the actual code, too.

Here is the function definition:

```
void Convert( TreeNode* p_tree,
              int p_index,
              int p_length,
              unsigned long int p_code )
{
```

The function is called with a node pointer, the index of that node, the length of the code to reach that node, and the actual code to reach that node.

When the function is first called, it is called on the root node. The root has an index of 1, and because there is no code to get to the root node, the length and the code are both 0.

```
    if( p_tree->m_left == 0 && p_tree->m_right == 0 )
    {
        if( p_index > m_maxEntry )
            m_maxEntry = p_index;
        m_huffmanTree[p_index-1].m_data = p_tree->m_data.m_data;
        m_huffmanTree[p_index-1].m_code = p_code;
```

```
            m_huffmanTree[p_index-1].m_codeLength = p_length;
    }
```

The first thing the function does is check to see if the current node is a leaf node (it has no children). If so, then it needs to set the max entry variable to the current index, as it is now the maximum entry in the tree array. Remember, the tree might not actually fill up, so this allows you to see where the last valid entry resides.

Then the data, the code, and the code length are all copied into the tree array at the appropriate index (remember, one is subtracted from the index to offset the tree into index 0, so no extra space is wasted).

This is a leaf node, so there are no other nodes below it, and the recursive function terminates here.

```
    else
    {
        if( p_tree->m_left != 0 )
        {
            Convert( p_tree->m_left,
                     p_index * 2,
                     p_length + 1,
                     p_code );
        }
```

If the current node isn't a leaf node, then it is one of the temporary nodes that were created to join nodes during the tree creation process. It doesn't contain any code or data information because only leaf nodes contain data information.

First, the function checks to see if the left child exists. If it does, then the Convert function is recursively called on the left child. The index is twice that of the current index, and the length is incremented by one. Because going left only adds a 0 to the code, the code doesn't change at all and is passed into the function with no changes.

```
        if( p_tree->m_right != 0 )
        {
            Convert( p_tree->m_right,
                     p_index * 2 + 1,
                     p_length + 1,
                     p_code | (1 << p_length) );
        }
    }
}
```

If there is a right child, the `Convert` function is called on that child. This time, the index is two times the current index plus one, and the length is incremented again. Because a 1 is added to the end of the current code, the bit setting algorithm is used to add a new bit at the current length of the code (see Chapter 4 or Appendix A for more information on bit setting).

So this function not only converts the binary tree into an array, but it also calculates the code and the code length for each piece of data in the tree and sets them, too.

Creating the Lookup Table

This is the helper function that will calculate the lookup table so that compressing data is nice and fast.

```
void CreateLookupTable()
{
    int index;
    for( index = 0; index < m_maxEntry; index++ )
    {
        if( m_huffmanTree[index].m_codeLength != 0 )
        {
            m_lookupTable[ m_huffmanTree[index].m_data ] =
                m_huffmanTree[index];
        }
    }
}
```

This function essentially loops through the entire tree array. Whenever it finds a node that has a non-zero length (meaning that the node is a leaf and has a valid code in it), it copies that node into the lookup table. For example, if a node is found that has the data 12 in it, it looks up the index 12 in the lookup table and copies the node into the table at that index.

Example 21-3

This is Example 21-3, which you can find on the CD in the directory \examples\ch21\03 - Huffman Compression\. Because this example creates files, it will not run correctly on the CD, and you should copy it onto your hard drive to run it properly.

This example is very similar to Example 21-1, except that it will encode a file using Huffman compression instead of RLE compression.

In fact, the entire example is exactly the same, save for these lines:

```
compressed.CalculateTree( original );
compressed.Compress( original );
strcat( filename, ".tree" );
compressed.SaveTree( filename );
filename[ strlen(filename) - 5 ] = 0;
strcat( filename, ".huff" );
compressed.SaveData( filename );
```

The lines in bold are new in this demo; the lines that are not bold are similar to those in Example 21-1.

First, the original array is passed into the `Huffman` class so that it can generate a proper tree for the data. Then the original array is compressed.

Then `.tree` is added to the end of the filename, and the tree is saved to disk using that filename. So if you were compressing `test.bmp`, the tree would be named `test.bmp.tree`.

After that, the last five characters are chopped off of the filename (the `.tree` part), and `.huff` is added to the end. Now the actual compressed data is saved to disk using the new filename (`test.bmp.huff`, using the same example as before).

You can use this example to compress any file you want using Huffman compression.

Test Files

I have included several test files for you to test out. They are biga.bmp, plasma.bmp, plasma2.bmp, and test.bmp. Every file except plasma2.bmp compresses well.

So why doesn't it compress well? The data file ends up only being 96 kilobytes, down from 193K, but the tree file is 286K, which is bigger than the original file!

I have to admit, this is my fault. When I decided to use an array to store the tree, I thought the extra memory usage would be negligible, but it turns out that it makes a big difference. Not only that, but I've discovered a new problem as well: Using a heap for a priority queue in combination with arrayed binary trees gives you huge trees. You see, when you're using a heap, it usually produces trees that are taller than those you get when using a regular priority queue. This doesn't matter much for the actual data compression (both methods compress data at approximately the same ratio), but it does matter when you're storing the tree to disk using an array.

If you've got a hex editor handy, you can open the plasma2.bmp.tree file that was produced and take a look at it; it is almost entirely composed of 0s. This is clearly a waste of space.

However, I don't have the time to show you a better way of storing the trees right now, so I will leave you with this suggestion: RLE compress the tree files. Sure, it's a little more work, but it will compress those huge trees down to a better size.

If you're really ambitious, you might even find a better way to store the tree to disk.

Example 21-4

This is Example 21-4, which you can find on the CD in the directory \examples\ch21\04 - Huffman Decompression\. Because this example creates files, it will not run correctly on the CD, and you should copy it onto your hard drive to run it properly.

This example is almost exactly like Example 21-2, except that it decompresses Huffman files instead of RLE files.

Here are the main differences:

```
compressed.LoadTree( treename );
compressed.LoadData( dataname );
compressed.Decompress( uncompressed );
```

The tree is loaded, the data is loaded, and then the tree is decompressed. Pretty simple, isn't it? Try decompressing the files produced by Example 21-3.

Data Encryption

Data compression is a form of data *encryption*, which is the act of taking a piece of data and making it unreadable to people who don't know how to decode it.

Data encryption is a vast subject, and it is of some importance here. If you were to compress a text file using Huffman compression and then look at the resulting data, would you be able to tell that it was text at one time? Probably not.

One of the most frequent questions I hear from programmers is, "How do I make my graphics and sound so that no one can read it or modify it?" You would normally use a form of data encryption, but you could also use compression. The average person will not know how to decode your Huffman-encoded graphics. This is one easy way to prevent people from ripping your graphics and sound from your game and using them all over the place.

Further Topics in Compression

This chapter only gives you a very brief glimpse into the world of compression. There are tons of methods out there to compress data.

One of the most exciting areas of compression is called *fractal compression*. A fractal is a geometrical object that exhibits repeating and recurring features. For example, if you look at a mountain and then zoom in to a small piece of it, it will look like a smaller mountain. You can zoom in many times, and still see repeating patterns. This type of thing happens all over the place in nature, such as coastlines, forests, flowers, and so on. This type of compression tries to find repeating areas of graphics or data and stores information on that.

Other forms of compression also exist. Another famous method is called *wavelet* compression, which is used a great deal in signal processing because it is a good method of compressing waveform data. I haven't done much research in the field, so I can't say more about it.

Just be aware that the field of data compression is absolutely huge.

Conclusion

This was a big chapter, wasn't it? Well, that's because compression is a huge and complex topic. Compression is important to game programming in many ways, some of which I outlined at the beginning of the chapter.

Now that you know two methods of compression, you can begin to see how data compression in general works.

The two methods that I showed you are called *lossless* compression. When you compress something using lossless compression, it will decompress to the same exact data that it was before the compression. You didn't *lose* any data.

There is another form of data compression that I didn't cover here called *lossy* compression. This is the kind of compression where some of the data is sacrificed to make the compression ratio higher. The JPEG image file format is lossy: It doesn't actually store information about every pixel; instead, it stores information in little 8 x 8 chunks (interestingly enough, JPEGs use RLE *and* Huffman compression in combination with other algorithms).

To give you a better example of lossy compression, look at mp3 audio files. On the first level of mp3 compression, the higher frequencies of sound are removed from the sound file. Standard wave files can store very high frequency sounds that most people cannot hear, so the mp3 format removes this information, among other things. Don't get the impression that this is all mp3 compression does, though, because mp3 compression is a huge and complex task.

I regret not being able to put a game demonstration into this chapter, but I couldn't find a suitable use for data compression in a real-time game. Instead, you can use the four examples in this chapter as tools to compress and decompress your data.

CHAPTER 22

Random Numbers

22. Random Numbers

Almost every game out there uses random numbers to simulate things, whether they are attributes, damage, shooting angles, or other elements. Therefore, random number generation is an important topic in game programming. If you already know a little about random numbers, you might want to skip the first few sections of this chapter. The last part of this chapter is a somewhat complex but interesting subject that I think everyone getting into game programming should read.

In this chapter, you will learn

- How to generate random integers
- How to generate random percents
- How to generate random floating-point numbers
- How to generate non-linear random numbers

Generating Random Integers

I'm sure you are familiar with a die. If not, look at Figure 22.1, which shows a die.

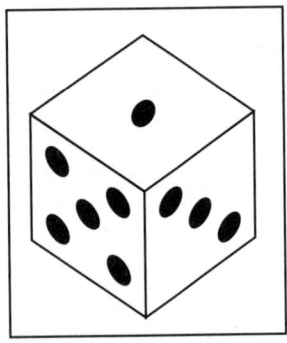

Figure 22.1

A six-sided die can produce a random number from 1–6.

A *die* is typically a 6-sided cube, which has dots on each side of the cube. On a standard die, the sides have 1, 2, 3, 4, 5, and 6 dots, respectively. The die is meant to be dropped onto a flat surface (commonly called *rolling* the die), and the number on top of the die is recorded. There are other kinds of dice as well, with different numbers of sides: 4, 6, 8, 10, 12, 20, and even 100 sides!

In real life, a die is a *random number generator*. You throw it, and it gives you a number from 1 to 6.

The great thing about a die is that every side has an equal chance of coming up on top. The chance that you will get a 1 is 1/6, and the chance that you will get a 5 is also 1/6. This feature is known as an *even distribution*, and it is essential to a pure random number generator. If the die has a tendency to land on 6 more often than any of the other numbers, then it is not a pure random number generator, and it is flawed.

> **NOTE**
> In fact, because the geometry of each face is slightly different in real life due to flaws in manufacturing, no die will give truly random numbers. Try it. Roll a dice 100 times, and calculate the probability of each throw and see if they are equally likely. Each outcome will be around the same probability, but you will find that one number will usually come up more often than the others.

Generating Random Numbers in a Program

There are many ways to generate random numbers in a program. However, almost none of the methods used are truly random. In order for a number to truly be random, it must have the following qualities:

- It must have an even distribution.
- It must *not* be deterministic.
- It must *not* have repeating patterns.

You already know about the first property because I discussed it in the previous section.

If something is *deterministic*, that means that it can be calculated. Take the numerical constant *pi*, for example. The digits of *pi* are deterministic; they can always be determined and will never change. The first digit is always 3, the next is 1, and then 4, and so on.

Unfortunately, most computer-based random number generation algorithms are deterministic, and thus are not truly random. Because random number generators use an algorithm to generate a number, it is almost always possible to pre-calculate what number will be generated. I discuss this property a little more later on.

The third property is a trait of the C++ rand function. The MSVC6 version of rand repeats itself every 2 billion numbers. This number is called the *period* of the random number generator. For example, if you ask it for three random numbers and you get 3, 7, and 2, and then you ask it for 2 billion more numbers, and finally you ask for 3 more, those 3 will be 3, 7, and 2 again.

Two billion is a lot of numbers, so this really doesn't pose a large problem.

Using rand and srand

There are many random number generators out there, some of them better than others. The most popular method is called *linear congruency* random number generating. I would explain to you what the name means, except that it requires a fair amount of mathematical jargon. All you need to know is that this is the method that the C++ rand function uses to generate random numbers. Because I mentioned before that it doesn't generate truly random numbers, it is called a *pseudo random number generator*.

Seeding the Generator

Try this simple example (Example 22-1 on the CD) on your own:

```cpp
#include <iostream.h>
#include <stdlib.h>
#include <stdio.h>

void main()
{
    cout << "Random number: " << rand() << endl;
    cout << "Press enter to continue..." << endl;
    getchar();
}
```

Run it, and watch the output. Figure 22.2 shows a screenshot from when I run it. On my computer, it prints the number 41. It might print something different on your computer.

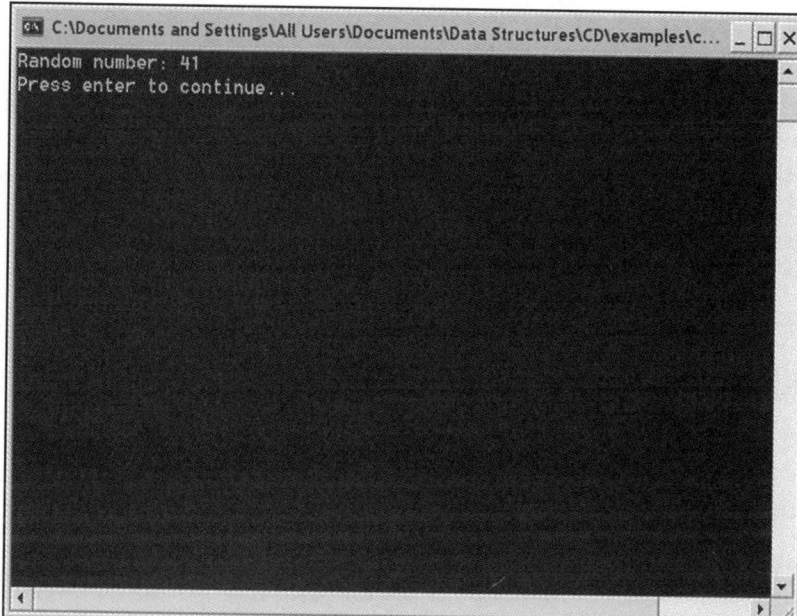

Figure 22.2

Here is a screenshot from Example 22-1.

Now run it again. Why does it return the same value? Isn't it supposed to be random? Well, not quite. The algorithm that rand uses needs a *seed value*.

A seed value is a special number that is used with linear congruency random number generators that determines where the generator should start generating values.

If you don't seed the random number generator, it will generate the same exact sequence of numbers every time you run it.

The seed value acts as the first random number in the sequence. Once you tell the random number generator a seed value, it then calculates a sequence of random numbers based on the seed.

In Example 22-2, I added one line to Example 22-1:

```
srand( 100 );
```

The srand function allows you to set the seed of the random number generator. The seed of a random number generator is usually only set once, at the very beginning of a program. In Example 22-2, I set the seed to 100 and then test the output of rand. On my system, the example returns the number 365. When I run the program again, I still get 365 because the seed value is the same.

> **TIP**
> If you use a constant seed value every time you run the random generator, you will always get the same sequence of random numbers. Although this might seem like an undesirable effect at first, I prefer this behavior over a true random number generator. This method allows me to debug things very easily because I can use the same seed over and over again to simulate the same circumstances if my program crashes.

Using a Non-Constant Seed Value

When I made my very first video game, I used a random number generator to place monsters into random rooms. I played through it once and was pleased with the outcome; it certainly seemed random enough.

I then decided to play it through again, but to my dismay, the monsters were in the same rooms! This frustrated me very much, and it took a long time for me to figure out why this was happening.

Now, a game in which the random numbers never change is going to be very boring, so you need to find a way to seed the random number generator with a different seed every time the program is run.

The most common method is to use the current system time. C++ has a `time` function that returns the current time of the system in seconds. If you use this as the seed value, then the system appears to generate different sequences of random numbers because the system will have a different time every time the `srand` function is called.

Example 22-3 replaces the `srand` line with the following:

`srand( time(0) );`

And now the program will generate a new random number every time it is run. You need to include the `time.h` file into your files to use the `time` function.

Generating a Random Number Within a Range

The `rand` function returns a random number from 0 to `RAND_MAX`, which is a constant defined by the compiler. In VC6, `RAND_MAX` is equal to `0x7FFF`, or 32,767 in decimal. Well, that's great and all—it gives me a huge range—but what if I want a random number between 1 and 6? What do I do then?

There are two ways to generate a random number within a specific range. The first method, using *modulo*, is what has been used in this book up until this point. The other method uses division.

Modulo Range Determination

There are two steps you must take to get a random number within a specified range using this method. First, you need to find out the size of the range. If you want a number from 1–6, then the size of the range is 6, because there are 6 possible outcomes: 1, 2, 3, 4, 5, and 6.

The easiest way to chop the huge number returned by `rand()` down to a range of 6 is to use the `modulo` function. For example, if you take any number and `modulo` it by 6, the result is a number from 0–5, giving you six total outcomes.

```
int x = rand() % 6;
```

After the preceding line of code is executed, x will contain a random number from 0–5. You're not quite done yet, however. Because you need a number from 1–6 and you have a number from 0–5, you just need to add 1 to the result:

```
int x = (rand() % 6) + 1;
```

Now, x will have a random number from 1–6! The entire process can be generalized into this function, which can be found in RandomNumbers.h in the \structures\ directory on the CD:

```
int RandomRangeModulo( int p_min, int p_max )
{
    int difference = (p_max - p_min) + 1;
    return (rand() % difference) + p_min;
}
```

The function takes two parameters: `p_min` and `p_max`. These will be the minimum range and the maximum range of the result. For a six-sided die, you would pass in 1 and 6.

On line 3, I calculate the difference between the min and max by subtracting `p_min` from `p_max` and adding 1. Adding the 1 is very important. If you wanted to find the difference in range from 1–6, you would end up with 5 if you didn't add the 1, which is wrong because you need six numbers, not five.

On the next line, I call `rand` and modulo it by the difference, which gives me a random number in the range of 0 through `difference - 1`. Now all that is left is to add the minimum value, and I have a random number in the correct range!

That was a big leadup to such a small function, wasn't it?

Why This Is a Bad Method

The modulo-based random number generator has a flaw in it due to the `rand` function. Even though the `rand` function returns a number with a period of 2 billion, using the modulo function reduces the period of the numbers that are generated. The method that the `rand` function uses actually creates patterns in the lower bits of the generated number that have periods that are far shorter than 2 billion. The modulo function essentially chops off the higher bits of the number, so the resulting value always has a shorter period and produces more recognizable patterns. To create a better generator that has fewer repeating patterns, you need to find a way to use the upper bits of the generated number instead of the lower bits.

Division Range Determination

Using the division operator on a random number turns out to be the easiest way to generate a number that uses the upper bits. This is the formula to use instead if you want to generate a number from 1–6:

```
number = ((6 * rand()) / (RAND_MAX + 1)) + 1;
```

You multiply the number returned by the `rand` function by the range that you want, and then divide that result by the total range possible plus one. This produces a number in the range of 0–5. Finally, 1 is added to the overall total to increase the range from 1–6.

Following is the general function for this algorithm:

```
int RandomRange( int p_min, int p_max )
{
    int difference = (p_max - p_min) + 1;
    return ( (difference * rand()) / (RAND_MAX + 1) )+ p_min;
}
```

This function has one downside, however: The range of the function cannot be more than 2^{17}, or the numbers will overflow, and you'll get weird results. This is because `rand` returns a 15-bit number, so you can't use a number more than 17 bits large. A 15-bit number × a 17-bit number potentially generates a number that is 32 bits large, so using any number that requires 18 bits will end up giving you a 33-bit number, which is too big for most computers. So just remember not to use this function when you're generating numbers with a range larger than 131,072.

> **NOTE**
> Although the division in this algorithm at first appears to make the function slower than the modulo function, in reality, it is faster. RAND_MAX + 1 in MSVC6 is a power of two, 2^{15}. The compiler knows this, and instead of dividing by that number, it shifts the number down by 15 bits (see Appendix A, "A C++ Primer," for more information on bitshifting). So this function takes up one multiply, one call to rand, one shift down, and one addition. The modulo function takes up one division (modulo is really a division), one call to rand, and one addition. Even though there is one less command in the modulo function, remember that a multiply and a shift is always faster than a single divide.

Generating Random Percents

Up until now, you've only generated random integers, which are discrete numbers.

A *discrete number* is a number with an exact integer value, such as 1, 2, 3, and so on. The area of mathematics that is involved with computers is called *discrete mathematics* because of the exact nature of computers.

Many times, you might find yourself needing a random percent, however. Percents are useful because they fall within the range of 0.0–1.0, and they can be used for many purposes.

The rand function only returns discrete numbers, though, so how do you convert the output of rand into a percent from 0.0 to 1.0? The answer is simple: Because the range of the random number is from 0 to RAND_MAX, you can take the result of rand and divide it by RAND_MAX. If rand returns RAND_MAX, then RAND_MAX/RAND_MAX is 1. Likewise, 0/RAND_MAX is 0.

You can turn this into a function:

```
float RandomPercent()
{
    return (float)rand() / (float)RAND_MAX;
}
```

The most important thing to remember is that you are dealing with floats here, so you need to convert the result from `rand` into a float and `RAND_MAX` into a float as well before you do the division, or else the compiler will think you are performing an integer division and return exactly 0 or 1, and nothing else.

Generating Random Floats

Generating a random floating-point number is very similar to the `RandomPercent` function. Because you want a random floating-point number in any given range, you'll use the `RandomPercent` function to generate a float from 0 to 1 first and then modify the result to fit in the new range.

Luckily, this algorithm is not much different than the `RandomRange` function. Say you want a random floating-point number from 0.0 to 5.0. All you need to do is multiply the result of `RandomPercent` by 5.0. Figure 22.3 shows this expansion.

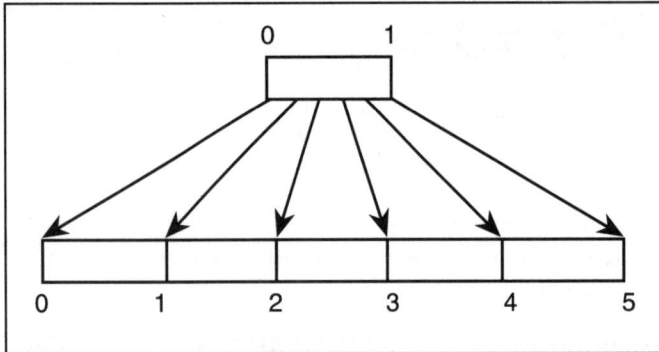

Figure 22.3

Here is how you expand a number from 0–1 to 0–5 by multiplying it by 5.

```
float x = RandomPercent() * 5.0f;
```

After the preceding line of code is executed, x will contain a random floating-point number anywhere between 0 and 5.

Now what if you want a number from 1–6? Like the integer example, all you need to do is add 1 to the final result:

```
float x = (RandomPercent() * 5.0f) + 1.0f;
```

Like the `RandomRange` function, this can be expanded into a general-purpose function:

```
float RandomRangeF( float p_min, float p_max )
{
```

```
    float difference = (p_max - p_min);
    return (RandomPercent() * difference) + p_min;
}
```

You can see that this is almost the same as the `RandomRange` function. On a test run, I received the following values when I asked for numbers from 1–6: 2.99789, 5.48180, 3.79229, 4.43303, 5.20530, and 1.21805.

Generating Non-Linear Random Numbers

Up until now, you've only generated linear random numbers. This means that every number that they generate has the same probability of being generated. If you call `RandomRange` and ask for a number from 0–4, each number will be generated approximately 20 percent of the time. There are five total numbers that can be generated, so the probability that one of them will be generated is 1/5.

Although this is a good feature to have in some cases, it doesn't make sense in other cases.

For example, say you are randomly generating the height of characters in a game, and you can choose from five sizes: very short, short, average, tall, and very tall. With a random number generator, there will theoretically be the same number of people in each category. Out of 100 people, each category will have about 20 people.

This model doesn't mimic real life, though. If you randomly pick 100 people out of a city, you'll only find 1 or 2 very short people and probably 40 or 50 average people!

Probability Distribution Graphs

There is an easy way to visualize how a random number will look. Figure 22.4 is called a *Probability Distribution Graph* because it shows how random numbers in a certain range are distributed. Figure 22.4 shows a linear distribution from 0–4. The numbers at the bottom are the possible outcomes. The bold line above the numbers represents the distribution. Because every number is distributed evenly, they all have the same value: 20 percent.

708 22. Random Numbers

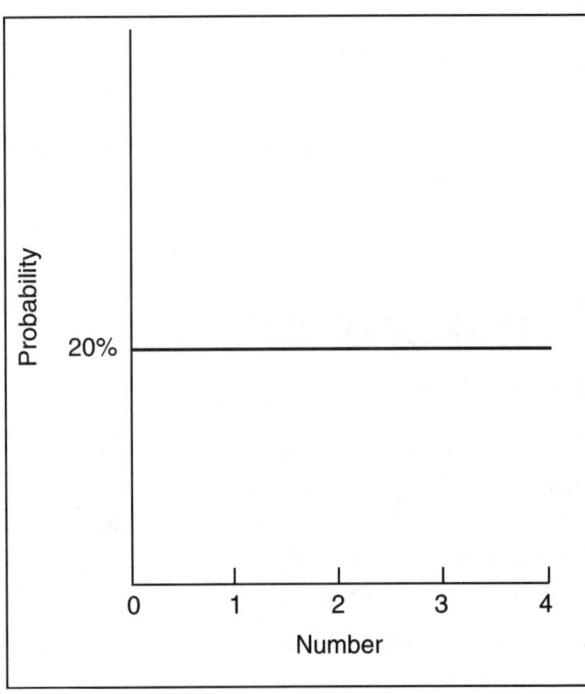

Figure 22.4

This is an even distribution graph. Every number has an equal chance of being generated if the random number generator has this distribution.

If you take the height example from the previous section in the real world, you will probably end up with a graph that looks like Figure 22.5. See how the number of average-height people far outnumbers the very tall or the very short? This is generally how the distributions work in real life, and this graph is commonly called the *bell curve*, because it looks like a bell.

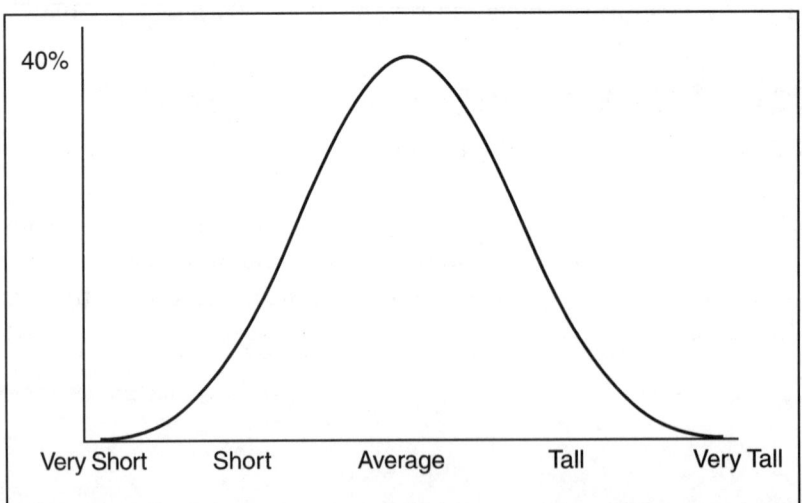

Figure 22.5

This is a bell-curve distribution graph. The middle numbers are more likely to be generated if the random number generator has this distribution.

Adding Two Random Numbers

Now you need to find a way to generate a non-linear random distribution. Luckily, the easiest way is to add two random numbers.

Say you add two random numbers, each of them ranging from 0–4, like this:

```
int x = RandomRange( 0, 4 ) + RandomRange( 0, 4 );
```

Obviously, x will contain a number from 0–8, but its distribution is no longer even. The probability that you will get a 0 is much less than the probability that you will get a 4. Why is this? You need to analyze what happens when you add two random numbers.

The first call to RandomRange will generate a random number from 0–4, and each number will have a 20 percent chance of being generated. But then another random number is generated. If the first call generates a 0, the second call could generate any number from 0 to 4.

You can easily represent the results in a 2D array, like Figure 22.6 shows.

	0	1	2	3	4
0	0	1	2	3	4
1	1	2	3	4	5
2	2	3	4	5	6
3	3	4	5	6	7
4	4	5	6	7	8

Figure 22.6

Here are the results of adding two random numbers from 0–4.

If we count the number of boxes, we get 25 total results. Note that a result of (0,1) is considered to be a different event than (1,0), even though they both add up to 1. This is important. Count how many outcomes add up to 0. There is only one: (0,0). So that means that the value 0 shows up 1/25 of the time, or 4 percent. Now count how many outcomes add up to 1. There are two this time, (0,1), and (1,0), which means that the number 1 shows up 2/25ths of the time, or 8 percent.

Table 22.1 shows the distribution of adding two random numbers from 0–4.

22. Random Numbers

Table 22.1 Probabilities of Two Random Numbers from 0–4

Result	Probability	Percent
0	1/25	4 percent
1	2/25	8 percent
2	3/25	12 percent
3	4/25	16 percent
4	5/25	20 percent
5	4/25	16 percent
6	3/25	12 percent
7	2/25	8 percent
8	1/25	4 percent

So, if you put this into a graph, you get a distribution that looks like Figure 22.7. Clearly, 4 will occur more often than any other of the numbers, but this graph isn't quite close to the bell curve yet.

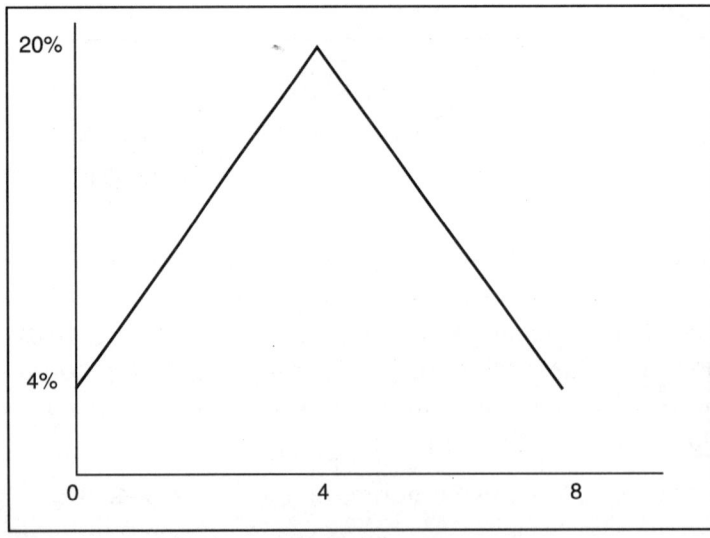

Figure 22.7

This figure shows you the distribution graph of two random numbers from 0–4. The result 4 occurs the most often (five times), and the results 0 and 8 occur the least often (one time each).

Adding Three Random Numbers

If you've ever played *Dungeons & Dragons*, you might have wondered why they require you to roll three six-sided dice for your character attributes. The reason is that adding three random numbers gives you a random distribution that is very close to the bell curve.

It is difficult to show the outcomes of three random numbers because it requires a 3D array, so I will just show you a table instead. Table 22.2 shows the probability of the results of adding three random numbers from 0 to 3.

Table 22.2 Results of Three Random Numbers from 0–3

Result	Probability	Percentage
0	1/64	1.6 percent
1	3/64	4.7 percent
2	6/64	9.6 percent
3	10/64	15.6 percent
4	12/64	18.75 percent
5	12/64	18.75 percent
6	10/64	15.6 percent
7	6/64	9.6 percent
8	3/64	4.7 percent
9	1/64	1.6 percent

Figure 22.8 shows the distribution graph of adding three random numbers from 0–3. That looks pretty close to a bell curve, doesn't it?

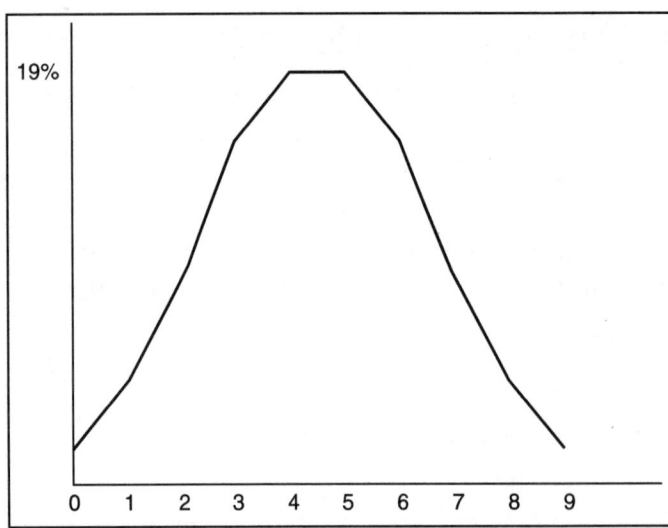

Figure 22.8

This is the distribution graph of adding three random numbers. This looks similar to a bell curve.

Graphical Demonstration: Random Distribution Graphs

I created a little program that will generate random distribution graphs for you. Figure 22.9 shows a screenshot of the program in action. The source code for this demo is on the CD in the directory \demonstrations\ch22\Demo01 - Random Distribution\.

Compiling the Demo

This demonstration uses the SDLGUI library that I have developed for the book. For more information about this library, see Appendix B, "The Memory Layout of a Computer Program."

To compile this demo, either open up the workspace file in the directory or create your own project using the settings described in Appendix B. If you create your own project, all of the files you need to include are in the directory.

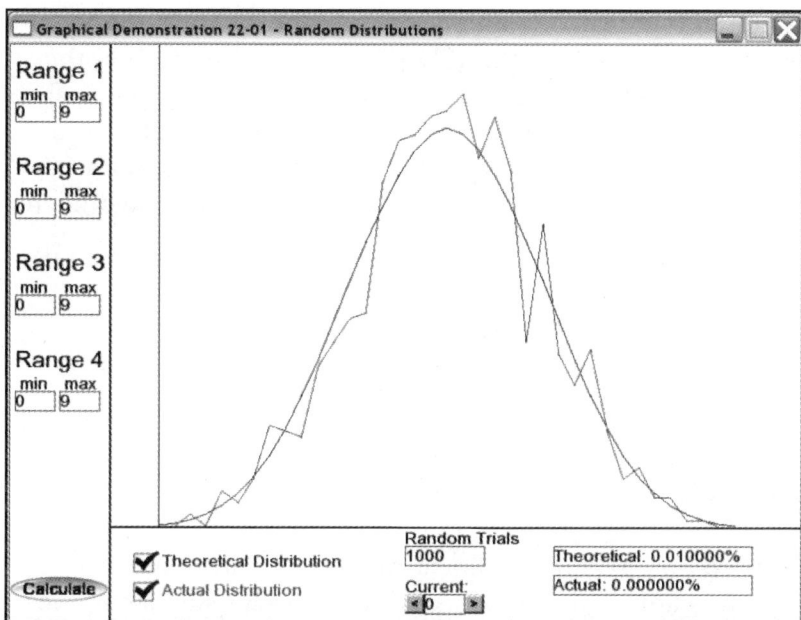

Figure 22.9

Here is a screenshot of Graphical Demonstration 22-1.

The demonstration works by adding four different random numbers together. On the left side of the screen, there are eight boxes representing the minimum and maximum values of each of the four different ranges. You can click on the boxes and type the numbers you want in them. The only thing you need to watch out for is entering very large numbers. Large numbers will cause the program to run very slowly when it calculates the graphs. A range of less than 100 for each of the four numbers is perfectly suitable for the demonstration, anyway.

At the bottom of the screen, there are two check boxes: Theoretical Distribution and Actual Distribution. This program calculates the theoretical distribution of the ranges that you create and draws it on the screen in blue (in the screenshot, it is the smooth curve).

The program also uses the `RandomRange` function to generate a graph of results that you will see in real-life programs, which is drawn in red (in the screenshot, it is the spiky curve). The program takes the number found in the Random Trials box and adds together that many numbers. The default is set to 1,000 trials, which is fine for small distributions, but you will find that the red graph gets more uneven as the range of the random numbers increases. If you increase the number of trials to a large number, then the red graph will get closer and closer to matching the blue graph.

The Current text box contains the current number. You can move this forward and backward, and the two text boxes to the right will update themselves to show the percent value of the current number. In the example in the screenshot, the chance that the number 0 will be generated is 0.01 percent, and with 1,000 random trials, it was actually generated 0 percent of the time. If I increased the number of trials or pressed the Calculate button, the number of times 0 is actually generated might be increased.

Play around with the program; it's kind of fun to see what kind of graphs you can generate using different ranges. Remember, you don't need to use the same range for all four numbers—you can create a small range for the first one and a large range for the second, or practically any combination you want!

Conclusion

In this chapter, you learned how to generate linear random numbers using the standard C library's `rand` function. This can be useful in games for simulating the unpredictability of things in real life.

You also learned how to use non-linear random number generators to generate bell-curved random numbers. This is also a useful way to generate random numbers because it gives you a little bit more stability when generating numbers.

This is only a brief glimpse into the world of random number generation. Entire books and university classes are based around this subject, so there is a lot more information to be gleaned out there. I hope you found some of this information new and interesting. Probability and statistics is one of my favorite topics.

CHAPTER 23

PATHFINDING

23. Pathfinding

At last, you have reached the final algorithm in this book: pathfinding. Pathfinding is an important topic in game programming because almost all games use some sort of map system, and they need a method to move the units around on the maps. Be it role-playing games, first-person shooters, real-time strategies, or any other game with a map, they all use some sort of pathfinding.

This chapter will teach you how to think about pathfinding and how to do intelligent pathfinding.

In this chapter, you will learn

- How to use the breadth-first search to find a path
- How to modify the breadth-first search and make it better
- How to use heuristics to make your pathfinder smarter
- How to create an even better heuristic
- How the A* pathfinder works
- How to use weighted maps within your games
- How to perform non–tile-based pathfinding

Basic Pathfinding

Look at Figure 23.1. The little guy in the middle of the map wants to get to the square with the pattern in it. How would you go about moving him toward the goal?

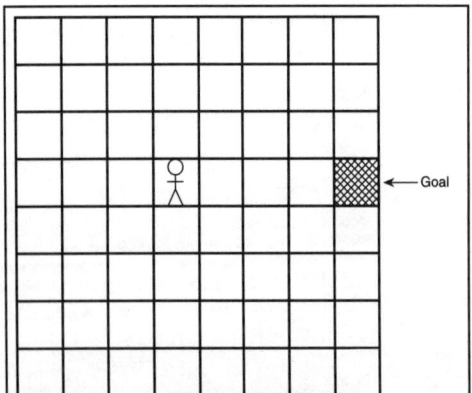

Figure 23.1

This is a simple tilemap that will be used for the pathfinding examples.

In a game, you'll know the coordinates of the goal and the coordinates of the player, too. You can figure out which direction the goal is in and move him toward it. Figure 23.2 shows this.

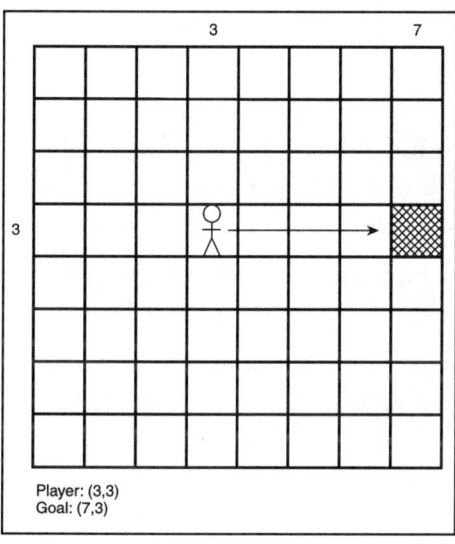

Figure 23.2

The AI is heading toward the goal.

The coordinates of the player and the goal are compared, and the computer notices that the goal has a larger x value than the player, so the player is moved in the positive x direction.

This works for the example because there are no obstacles. What happens when you add a wall into the equation, as in Figure 23.3?

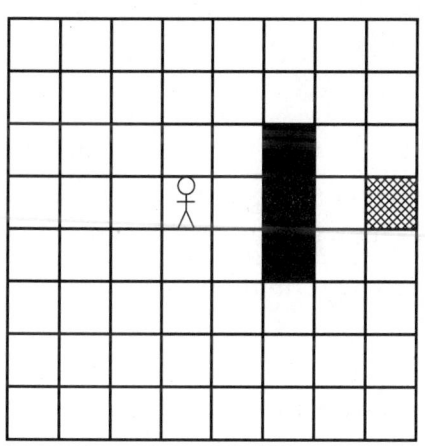

Figure 23.3

This is a more complex map, with a wall blocking the path.

718   23. Pathfinding

This time, you cannot simply move the player toward the goal because he cannot walk through the wall. You must find a better alternative.

There are many simple (simple to code, at least) ways to get around this problem, but I don't want you to spend too much time focusing on them.

Random Bouncing

This is the most basic method of pathfinding and it produces the simplest results. In fact, there is no reason for a game to use this kind of pathfinding today unless you're trying to emphasize that your AIs are kind of stupid.

The basic premise of this method is the same as before, only this time, when the player hits a wall, he moves in a random direction and then resumes toward the goal.

Unfortunately, if the wall is big, the player may spend lots of time wandering back and forth before he finally finds a way around the wall. Figure 23.4 shows the path that this kind of pathfinder takes with a wall in its path.

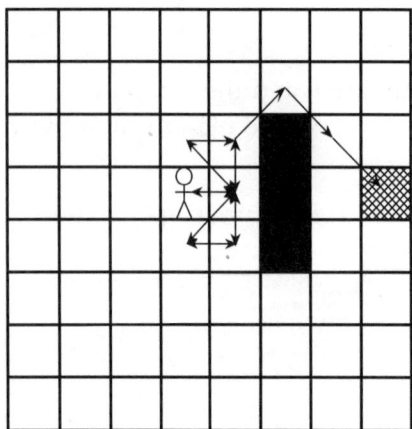

Figure 23.4

The random bouncing pathfinder tries going straight for the goal until it hits an obstacle. When that happens, the pathfinder moves one cell in a random direction and continues toward the goal.

You can't see exactly how it works from the picture, but just imagine the player bouncing up and down the wall many times until he finally finds his way past the wall.

If someone saw your AIs doing that in a game, they would think you were a very poor programmer.

Needless to say, this is a very stupid method to find paths with, and you shouldn't use it. Not only that, but the algorithm won't even work with complex maps like the one shown in Figure 23.5.

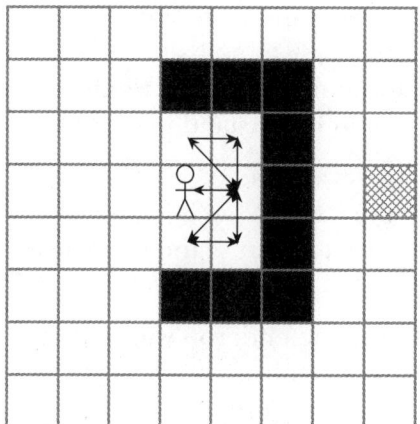

Figure 23.5

This is a map that will cause a random bouncer to become trapped.

The random bounce algorithm will never find its way out of the little cove that it is in.

Object Tracing

Have you ever tried to solve a maze before? There is an old rule that will get you through the maze every time: Follow either the left wall or the right wall, and eventually you will reach the end of the maze.

Figure 23.6 shows a sample maze.

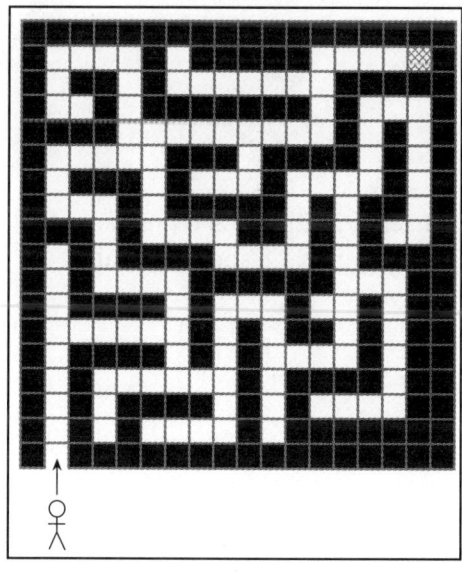

Figure 23.6

This is a maze. The cell with the cross pattern in it is the goal.

Now, imagine you're the little stick figure and you have to find your way to the square with the cross pattern in it. Although it is pretty easy to eyeball your way through this maze, think about it like a computer for a moment. How would you generate a solution for the maze that a computer would understand that would work every time?

Imagine that you put your hand on the left wall of the maze. Now, keep your hand on the maze wall and walk forward. Whenever you reach a turn in the maze, just keep your hand on the wall and follow the path.

You will end up retracing your steps a few times, but in the end, you will find the exit to the maze, which is all this algorithm is concerned with. Figure 23.7 shows the solution to the maze if you used your left hand to follow the walls.

Figure 23.7

Here is the solution to the maze if you use the left-wall tracing method.

This is exactly how object tracing works. Whenever it finds an obstacle, it traces the outline of the obstacle until it finds a way around it. Figure 23.8 shows this algorithm applied to a single obstacle.

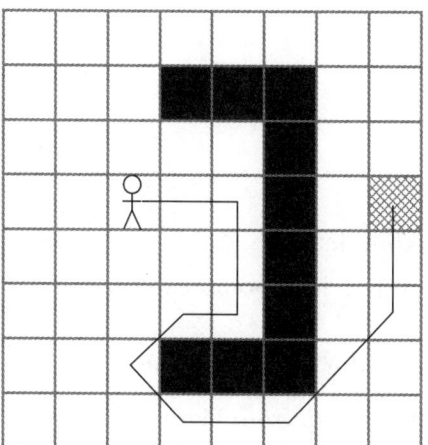

Figure 23.8

This shows how to use object tracing to get around an obstacle.

While this method seems far more useful than other methods, it is still undesirable in games these days. This is because the algorithm needs to choose which way to go whenever it hits an obstacle, and either way may end up being the longer of the two routes. About half of the time, the pathfinder will take the longer route around the object, which is usually a bad idea.

Robust Pathfinding

The previous two pathfinding algorithms were *instant* pathfinders. They determine the path that the AI will be following every time the AI moves into a new square. There are other ways that find a much more efficient path.

In games, especially real-time strategies such as *Warcraft* and all its sequels, the players expect their units to get to where they told them to go in the shortest time possible. This means that they need to find the shortest path from the beginning to the end.

The Breadth-First Search

Remember the *breadth-first search* from Chapter 17, "Graphs"? It turns out that this searching algorithm is a very basic method for searching for the shortest path through a map or a graph.

Remember, the algorithm first processes all of the cells that are one jump away from the starting cell, and then every cell that is two jumps away, and then three, and so on. To apply this to pathfinding, the algorithm stops when the goal is found.

Here is the algorithm described in pseudo-code (remember, the breadth-first search requires a queue to work). Note that the cells also require a new variable, the *previous* pointer. It tells each cell which cell pointed to it during the search. I make that clear in a moment.

1. Add the starting cell to the queue.
2. Mark the starting cell.
3. Take the first cell off of the queue.
4. If the cell is the goal, then the algorithm is complete.
5. If any of the children aren't marked, set their previous pointer to the current cell and add them to the queue.
6. Go to step 3 until the algorithm is complete or the queue is empty.

Let me take you through this algorithm on the simple map from Figure 23.8.

When a cell is added to the queue, it is turned light gray. Whenever a cell is not in the queue but is marked, it will be dark gray. Each cell in the queue will have a pointer to the previous cell.

Figure 23.9 shows the entire process of the breadth-first search, level by level.

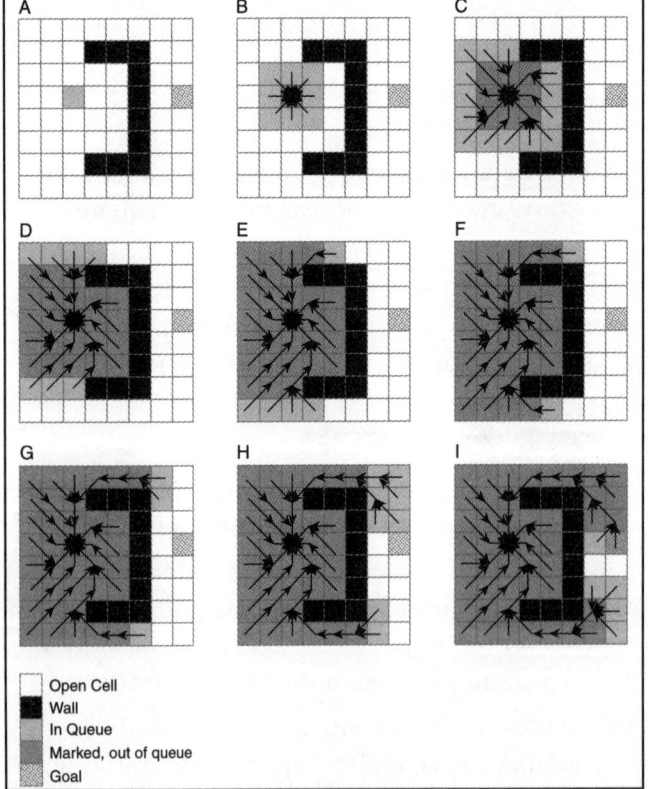

Figure 23.9

This shows the breadth-first search.

On the second iteration (see Figure 23.9.B), all eight surrounding cells of the starting cell are placed into the queue. The images don't show it, but the cells are processed in clockwise order, starting with the top-most cell.

On the third iteration (see Figure 23.9.C), the next layer of cells is processed, and so on. At the end of the last iteration (Figure 23.9.I), the goal cell is found, at which point the function terminates. Now, in order to get the path from the start to the goal, you just follow the arrows from the goal to the starting cell and reverse the order.

Figure 23.10 shows the final path.

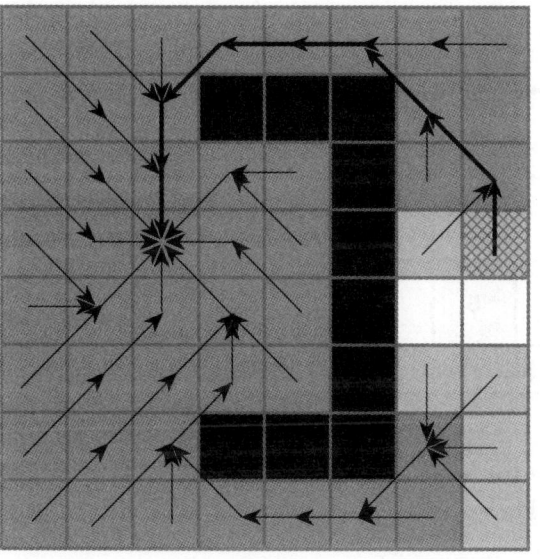

Figure 23.10

The final path is shown in bold.

Modifying the BFS Pathfinder

The plain breadth-first pathfinding algorithm has a few flaws. First of all, it treats all adjacent cells as the same distance away from the center, which is not true. Figure 23.11 clearly shows that the distance from the center to a diagonal cell is more than the distance from the center to a horizontal or vertical cell.

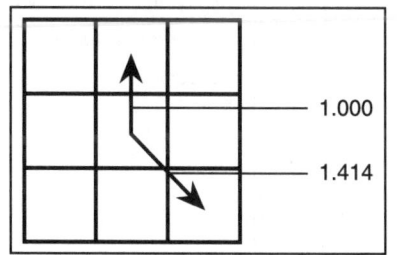

Figure 23.11

This shows the distance between cells.

Because of this flaw, the paths that a BFS pathfinder take tend to be more diagonal, because it treats all eight directions as the same length. The paths usually end up being longer and don't look as good.

There are two ways to fix this.

Modifying the Visitation Order

In the example I showed you previously, the adjacent cells are visited in clockwise order. Instead of using that method, why not change the visitation order so that the horizontal and vertical cells are added to the queue before the diagonal cells?

Figure 23.12 shows the visitation orders.

8	1	2
7		3
6	5	4

Old Order

8	1	5
4		2
7	3	6

New Order

Figure 23.12

This shows the two different visitation orders.

The benefit of this new ordering method may not be apparent to you immediately, so let me show you an example. Imagine for a moment that you have a simple 9 × 9 tile map with an AI at the center. He wants to go three squares to the right by using the breadth-first search pathfinder.

Figure 23.13 shows this scenario, computed first using the old traversal order and then using the new traversal order.

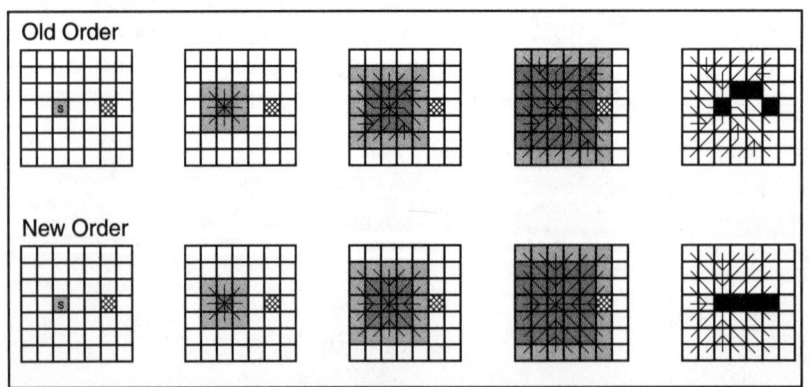

Figure 23.13

These are the two different path calculations using two different visitation orders.

The top path looks undesirable right away because it goes up and then down again. The bottom path looks much better, as it is just a straight line. The problem with this algorithm is that it sees both paths as being the same length, even though they are clearly not.

Although changing the visitation order makes things a little better, there are still places where it will run into trouble (mostly on large maps).

Therefore, another method is required.

A True Breadth-First Search

The problem with the previous method is that the algorithm still treats every cell as the same distance from the center cell. When you perform this kind of a search, you end up with a search area that is square.

What if you were able to process each cell based on the distance it takes to travel to the starting cell? For example, look at Figure 23.14. It has three 5 × 5 grids in it.

Distance From Center				
2.8	2.4	2.0	2.4	2.8
2.4	1.4	1.0	1.4	2.4
2.0	1.0	0.0	1.0	2.0
2.4	1.4	1.0	1.4	2.4
2.8	2.4	2.0	2.4	2.8

Processing Order Breadth-First				
2	2	2	2	2
2	1	1	1	2
2	1	0	1	2
2	1	1	1	2
2	2	2	2	2

Processing Order Distance-First				
5	4	3	4	5
4	2	1	2	4
3	1	0	1	3
4	2	1	2	4
5	4	3	4	5

Figure 23.14

This shows the distances of each cell from the center cell, and the orders in which the cells are visited using the two different visitation orders.

The first grid shows the approximate distance of each cell from the middle. You can see that cells that are on the same level (or are the same number of "jumps" away from the center) have varying distances. A standard breadth-first search would consider cell (0,0) the same distance away as cell (0,2), even though their actual distances from the center are quite different. The first cell is 2.8 units away from the center, and the second one is only 2.0 units away, a difference of almost an entire cell! In order to avoid confusion between these two different methods, I call the new method the *distance-first search* because it processes all of the cells with the smallest distance first.

The second grid in Figure 23.14 shows the order in which each level of cells is processed. On the first iteration, all 8 cells surrounding the center are processed, and the 16 cells on the outside are processed on the second iteration.

The third grid in Figure 23.14 shows the order in which cells are processed using their actual distance from the center. You can see that the cells are processed in a more *radial* fashion, so the pattern goes outward in a circle.

So what does this mean? It means that this method is somewhat faster than a plain breadth-first search. First of all, consider what happens when you find a horizontal path that is 64 squares away from the start. Using the standard breadth-first search, you end up searching 128^2 squares (remember, it searches in each direction, so it ends up searching 64 squares up, down, left, and right, which is a 128×128 square) before it finds the goal, which is 16,384 squares.

Using the distance-first method, you search a smaller circular area, which is approximately pi * 64^2, or 12,867 squares. So for horizontal and vertical goals, the distance-first search will do about 21 percent less searching. Hooray!

But wait! What happens when you search for a goal that is directly diagonal from the starting point, 64 units away? Well, using the distance-first algorithm, you end up searching pi * 64^2 squares, the same as for horizontal and vertical goals, 12,867. But the breadth-first algorithm gets there quicker because it searches fewer cells. Consider the number of squares the pathfinder will go through when moving 64 units diagonally, which is $64/\sqrt{2}$, or around 45 squares. So it searches 45 squares in all four directions, giving you a total of 90^2 squares searched, or 8,100 squares. This works out to be about 36 percent less searching!

How to Calculate the Number of Squares in the Search Areas

The area in a circle is a simple mathematical formula: area = pi * radius^2. In the example, the radius is 64, so you get pi * 4096, which is approximately 12867.963509. If you truncate the decimal, you get 12,867 squares that fall in a radius of 64 squares on a tilemap.

When a square is 64 units away on the diagonal, that square isn't actually 64 jumps away. Because each diagonal is actually 1.4 units long, the square that is 64 units away is 64/1.4, or 45.254834. That means that on the diagonal, the 45th square away is 64 units away. The traditional breadth-first search searches a square area, 45 units in each direction in this case, so it searches around 90 squares on each side, or 90^2, which is 8,100 squares.

All of these figures are approximate, of course, because I only wanted to give you a general idea of how many squares are searched in each method.

Figure 23.15 shows a comparison of these two scenarios.

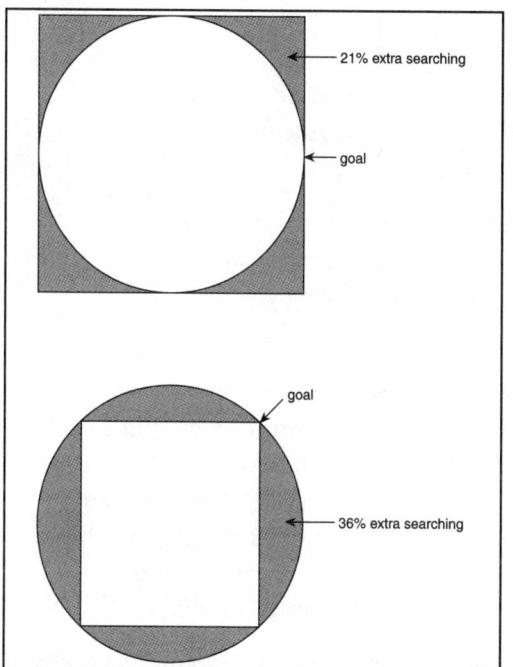

Figure 23.15

Here are the search areas of the two different pathfinders.

So which method is better? At a first glance, you can see that the distance-first search has a worse worst case than the breadth-first search, but there is one thing that the BFS neglects: *weighted cells*.

Imagine for a moment that in your game, you have two types of terrain: grass and rocks. It is easy to walk through areas of the map with grass in them, but harder to walk through the rocky areas of the map. The standard BFS search doesn't take into account how long it takes to walk through these areas, but the distance-first search does (if you pretend that walking through one rocky cell is the same as walking through two grassy tiles).

Just keep this idea in the back of your mind for now. I go over it in more detail later on.

I show you the algorithm for this pathfinder later in this chapter.

Graphical Demonstration: Distance First Pathfinder

This is Graphical Demonstration 23-1, which is on the CD in the directory \demonstrations\ch23\Demo01 - Distance First\.

> ### Compiling the Demo
>
> This demonstration uses the SDLGUI library that I have developed for the book. For more information about this library, see Appendix B, "The Memory Layout of a Computer Program."
>
> To compile this demo, either open up the workspace file in the directory or create your own project using the settings described in Appendix B. If you create your own project, all of the files you need to include are in the directory.

This demo starts off with a large grid full of white squares and four buttons. In the lower right corner, there is a square. This square contains the color of the tile that will be drawn if you move your mouse over the map and click it. You can change the color by pressing the numbers 0 through 9 on the keyboard. Each color has a different weight associated with it. For example, 0 draws a tile with a weight of 1, 4 draws a tile with a weight of 5, and 9 draws a wall, which is impassable.

Once you have drawn all the walls and tiles, you put your mouse over the place where you want to start pathfinding and press the S key. Then put the mouse over the place where you want the goal to be and press the G key. Figure 23.16 shows a screenshot.

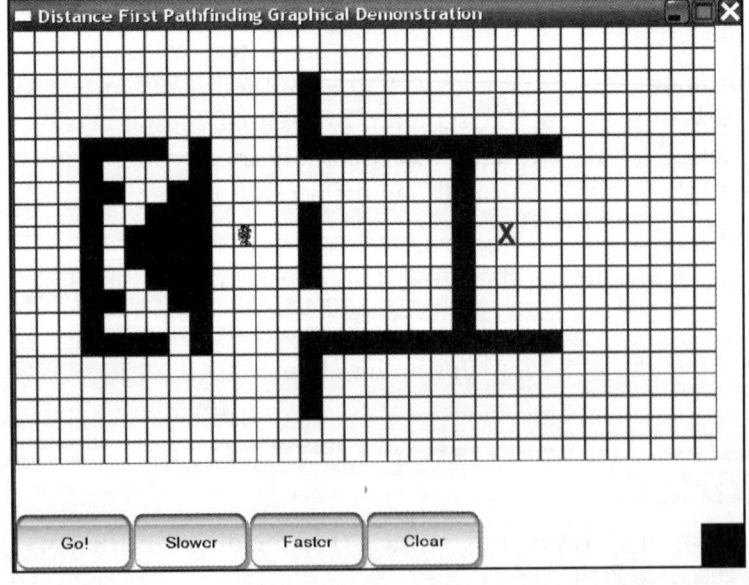

Figure 23.16

Here is a screenshot of the demo.

The little guy on the map represents the starting place, and the X marks the goal. When your map is totally set up, click the Go! button, and watch it find your path!

It's a bit slow, isn't it? Well, to fix that, click the Faster button a few times and watch it fly! If you want it to slow down again, click the Slower button.

When it is done finding the path, it will look something like Figure 23.17.

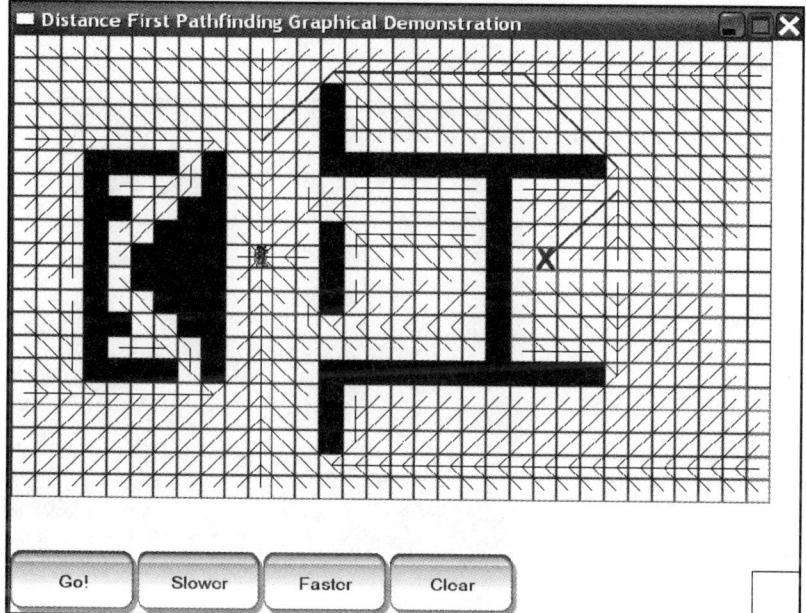

Figure 23.17

Here is a screenshot of the demo after it has calculated a path.

While the demo is calculating the path, certain cells will turn different colors. Table 23.1 shows a listing of the meanings of the colors.

Table 23.1 Cell Color Meanings

Color	Meaning
Black	Cell is unprocessed and is not in the queue.
Green	Cell is unprocessed but it is in the queue.
Blue	Cell is already processed and removed from the queue.
Red	Cell is being processed.

Play around with the demo a bit to try to get the hang of how the algorithm works. After the path has been found, it is shown with a bold red line.

Coding the Distance-First Pathfinder

This section will show you how to go about programming a distance-first pathfinder. All of the pathfinding algorithms can be found in the Pathfinding.h file in the \structures\ directory on the CD.

The Base Code

Because this section deals with many different pathfinders, it makes sense to create a base in which to test the pathfinders.

The four pathfinders in this section will all operate on 2D arrays.

The Cell Class

Because the pathfinding algorithms need to maintain information about individual cells, it makes sense to make a class that will store this data.

> **NOTE**
> Even though all of the demos and figures in this chapter show 2D top-down views, pathfinding can be applied to any game anywhere. The 2D view is only used to emphasize the basic concepts; if you were using a 3D world with heightmaps, you could easily adapt these algorithms into your game. This information won't limit you.

This is the `Cell` class:

```
class Cell
{
public:
    bool m_marked;
    float m_distance;
    int m_lastx;
    int m_lasty;
    bool m_passable;
    float m_weight;
};
```

The first item is a boolean, which is used to tell if the cell has been marked or not by the pathfinding algorithm.

Then the cell retains information about the distance it takes to travel from the starting cell to this cell.

The two integers are used as a pointer to point to the previous cell in the path.

The last two variables determine if the cell is passable (if it is not, then it has an obstruction in it, like a wall or a tree) and the *weight* of the cell. The weight is defined as the amount of work it takes to walk into a particular cell. Using the grass and rocks example, the grass would have a weight of 1.0, and the rocks would have a weight of 2.0.

If you haven't already guessed, the pathfinders will be finding paths through maps that are stored in a 2D array of this `Cell` class.

The Coordinate Class

Whenever a cell is placed in the queue for processing, the actual cell structure isn't placed in the queue. It is far easier to use a small structure that points to the cell that is in the queue instead.

Here is the class definition:

```
class Coordinate
{
public:
    int x;
    int y;
    float heuristic;
};
```

The class has the *x* and *y* coordinates of the cell in the queue and another variable, the *heuristic value* of the cell. If that word sounds familiar to you, it's because I used it in Chapter 15, "Game Trees and Minimax Trees." Remember, a heuristic is a function that tries to pick out a smart choice from all of the options it has available. The reason this variable is here will become apparent when I start explaining the actual pathfinding function.

The Comparison Function

This is a comparison function that the pathfinders will use to figure out which cell to process next.

```
int CompareCoordinatesDescending( Coordinate left, Coordinate right )
{
    if( left.heuristic < right.heuristic )
        return 1;
    if( left.heuristic > right.heuristic )
        return -1;
```

```
        return 0;
}
```

This function compares the heuristic value of two Coordinates. This is a *descending* function, so it treats lower heuristic values as if they were actually higher. Again, you will see why this is used when the pathfinding function is described.

Clearing the Cells

Whenever a pathfinder function is called, the first thing it does is go through every cell in the 2D array and clear all of the variables it is going to use for pathfinding.

```
void ClearCells( Array2D<Cell>& p_map )
{
    int x;
    int y;
    for( y = 0; y < p_map.Height(); y++ )
    {
        for( x = 0; x < p_map.Width(); x++ )
        {
            p_map.Get( x, y ).m_marked = false;
            p_map.Get( x, y ).m_distance = 0.0f;
            p_map.Get( x, y ).m_lastx = -1;
            p_map.Get( x, y ).m_lasty = -1;
        }
    }
}
```

The function performs a standard doubly-nested for-loop to go through every cell in the map. (See Chapter 5, "Multi-Dimensional Arrays," if you don't remember how this works.)

For each cell, the marked flag is set to false, the distance is reset to zero, and the previous-cell pointers are both reset to −1. Because the map starts at index (0,0), it is easy to tell whether the cell has been processed already.

The other two variables of the cell class, m_passable and m_weight, are not modified by this function. The pathfinders only look at these variables and do not modify them in any way because they define the map and are meant for you to modify.

The Distance Function

Some of the pathfinders need the ability to find the distance between two cells, so there is a function to do this easily.

```
float CellDistance( int x1, int y1, int x2, int y2 )
{
    int dx = x1 - x2;
    int dy = y1 - y2;
    dx = dx * dx;
    dy = dy * dy;
    return (float)sqrt( (double)dx + (double)dy );
}
```

This function uses the standard mathematical distance formula: distance = square root($dx^2 + dy^2$), where dx and dy are the distance between the x and the y coordinates, respectively. If you don't know how this works, don't worry about it; you can just assume that the function works properly.

The Constants

There are a number of constants defined in the file to speed up some calculations.

```
const int QUEUESIZE = 1024;
```

The first one is the queue size. Naturally, arrayed queues (specifically, heaps, but I'll get into that later) are better for these algorithms because they are faster to insert and remove items from. Because resizing the arrays during run-time is usually a bad idea, you want to start the array off at a decent size. I think 1024 cells is a decent size to use because it doesn't seem too likely that you'll have more than 1024 cells in the queue at any given time. However, if you do end up needing a larger queue size, just increase this constant, and everything will be handled automatically.

```
const int DIRTABLF[8][2] = { { 0, -1 },
                             { 1, 0 },
                             { 0, 1 },
                             { -1, 0 },
                             { 1, -1 },
                             { 1, 1 },
                             { -1, 1 },
                             { -1, -1 } };
```

Next, there is a direction table. This defines the coordinate offsets for each of the eight directions that are possible at each cell. This particular table defines north, east, south, and west first, and then northeast, southeast, southwest, and northwest. How is the data interpreted? Well, direction 0 represents north, so to go north from any given cell, you add 0 to the *x* coordinate and add −1 to the *y* coordinate. In effect, you get this code:

```
x = x + DIRTABLE[direction][0];
y = y + DIRTABLE[direction][1];
```

For the second index, 0 means *x* and 1 means *y*.

```
const float DISTTABLE[8] = { 1.0f, 1.0f, 1.0f, 1.0f,
                       1.414214f, 1.414214f, 1.414214f, 1.414214f };
```

Finally, there is a table that stores the distance from a cell to an adjacent cell. The first four distances (for the N, E, S, and W directions) all contain 1.0, and the second four distances (for the NE, SE, SW, and NW directions) all contain 1.414214, which is the distance for a diagonal cell. You'll see how this works when you get into the pathfinding algorithms.

The Distance-First Pathfinder

This is a long and complex function. It should be—it performs a long and complex task. Because it is so long, I split it up into several segments and explain what each segment does after the code listing to make it easier to understand.

```
void PathDistanceFirst( Array2D<Cell>& p_map,
                        int p_x, int p_y,
                        int p_gx, int p_gy )
{
```

First are the parameters. The function accepts an `Array2D` as the map and four integers. The integers are map coordinates; the first two are the starting position of the pathfinder, and the second two are the goal position.

```
    Coordinate c;
    int x, y;
    int ax, ay;
    int dir;
    float distance;
```

These variables are all used to cache data in the function so it doesn't have to be looked up constantly. The `c` variable is used to set up `Coordinates` that are then added into the queue. The `x` and `y` coordinates store the coordinates of the current cell that is being processed; the `ax` and `ay` coordinates store the coordinates of the current adjacent cell. The `dir` variable stores the current direction, and `distance` stores distance calculations.

```
    Heap<Coordinate> queue( QUEUESIZE, CompareCoordinatesDescending );
```

Next, the queue is defined. Note that the queue isn't a regular queue, but it is instead a priority queue heap. The heap is defined with a size of QUEUESIZE and the descending coordinate comparison function, which means that coordinates with the smallest heuristic value are always at the top of this queue.

```
ClearCells( p_map );
c.x = p_x;
c.y = p_y;
c.heuristic = 0.0f;
queue.Enqueue( c );
```

The cells of the map are all cleared using the ClearCells function, and then the starting cell in the map is placed into the queue with a heuristic value of 0.0. This value really isn't important, as you'll see in a moment.

```
while( queue.m_count != 0 )
{
    x = queue.Item().x;
    y = queue.Item().y;
    queue.Dequeue();
```

This begins the pathfinding loop. The first item is pulled off of the queue. Because there was only one item on the queue in the first loop, it is pulled off right away, so its heuristic value didn't really matter.

The coordinates of the cell are recorded in the *x* and *y* coordinates.

```
if( p_map.Get( x, y ).m_marked == false )
{
    p_map.Get( x, y ).m_marked = true;
```

This section of code makes sure that the cell that was on top of the queue wasn't already marked. If the cell was already marked, then nothing happens; the cell is discarded, and the loop starts over, pulling off another cell. If the cell wasn't marked yet, it is then marked, and the algorithm continues.

I know that sounds a little weird. "How can a cell that is already marked still be on the queue?", you might be asking. Well, the pathfinder might actually end up enqueuing a cell several times. Figure 23.18 shows how this happens.

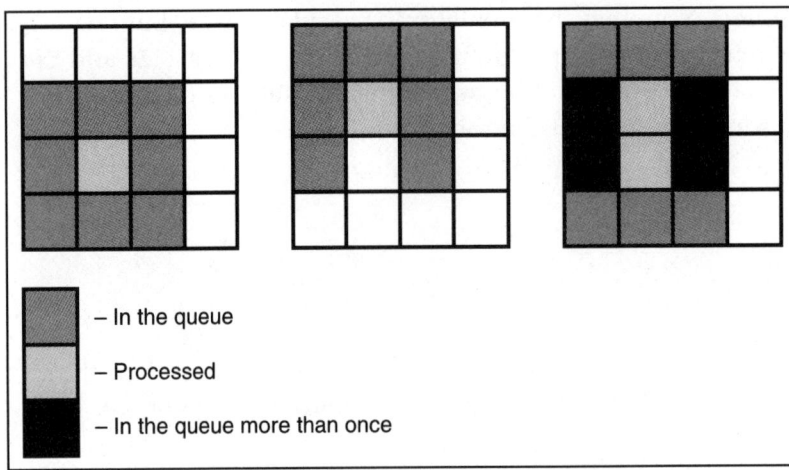

Figure 23.18

Some cells end up in the queue more than once. This is why it is important to mark them when they are removed from the queue the first time.

The leftmost grid shows the processing of one cell, and the middle grid shows the processing of the cell above it. Now, if the first cell is processed, all of the dark cells are added to the queue but not marked. Then the second cell is processed, and all of the dark cells are added to the queue again. The third grid shows which cells are in the queue twice in black.

So why does this happen? Wouldn't it be better not to add the cells again? The answer is no. When a cell is added to the queue, it points to the cell that was being processed at the time. However, this does not mean that the cell was the best choice at the time. It might turn out, later on, that when a cell is again added to the queue, there might be a shorter path leading to it. You'll see this in action in a moment. Back to the algorithm:

```
if( x == p_gx && y == p_gy )
    break;
```

If the current cell is the goal cell, the algorithm just exits out with a `break` call. There is no need to continue processing.

```
for( dir = 0; dir < 8; dir++ )
{
    ax = x + DIRTABLE[dir][0];
    ay = y + DIRTABLE[dir][1];
```

Now the function loops through all eight directions. The `ax` and `ay` variables hold the coordinates of the current adjacent cell.

```
if( ax >= 0 && ax < p_map.Width() &&
    ay >= 0 && ay < p_map.Height() &&
```

```
            p_map.Get( ax, ay ).m_passable == true &&
            p_map.Get( ax, ay ).m_marked == false )
{
```

This large `if` statement checks many things. First of all, it checks to see if the adjacent cell is within the bounds of the map. Sometimes the adjacent coordinates are invalid, so this is important.

Then it checks to see if the adjacent cell is passable. If it isn't passable, then it will not process the cell.

Finally, it checks to see if the cell is marked. This part of the algorithm ignores marked cells because those cells have already been processed.

```
            distance = p_map.Get( x, y ).m_distance +
                       p_map.Get( ax, ay ).m_weight * DISTTABLE[dir];
```

Next, the function calculates the distance to the adjacent cell. The function calculates this value by adding the distance of the current cell to the distance from the current cell to the adjacent cell. For now, just think of the weight as being 1.0. So if the adjacent cell is either horizontal or vertical, then the distance to get into that adjacent cell is 1.0. If the cell is a diagonal cell, then the distance is 1.414.

> **NOTE**
> The Pythagorean theorem states that the relationship between the three sides of a right triangle is governed by this equation: hypotenuse^2 = side1^2 + side2^2. Because both sides of a square are 1.0, the length of the hypotenuse is the square root of 1^2 + 1^2, or the square root of 2: 1.414.

```
            if( p_map.Get( ax, ay ).m_lastx != -1 )
            {
```

Now the function checks to see whether the adjacent cell has valid pointer links. If it doesn't, then this is the first time the cell is being added to the queue. If the `m_lastx` variable isn't -1, then it has been added to the queue before.

```
                if( distance < p_map.Get( ax, ay ).m_distance )
                {
```

At this point in the code, you know that the adjacent cell is in the queue at least once already. Now the function tries to figure out if it should add it to the queue again. The `distance` variable holds the distance it takes to get into the adjacent cell through the current cell, so it compares that value with the existing `m_distance` value in the adjacent cell. Remember: Because the cell is already in the queue, it has a valid distance value that was calculated by going through a different cell.

If the new distance is less than the distance through a different cell, then the function needs to add the cell to the queue again. If the new distance is more than the existing distance, then nothing happens, and the adjacent cell is not added to the queue again. (Why bother looking into that path if a better path has already been found?)

```
                p_map.Get( ax, ay ).m_lastx = x;
                p_map.Get( ax, ay ).m_lasty = y;
                p_map.Get( ax, ay ).m_distance = distance;
```

At this point, you know that the path through the current cell to the adjacent cell is shorter than a path that has already been found, so the m_lastx and m_lasty pointer links are updated, as well as the distance.

```
            c.x = ax;
            c.y = ay;
            c.heuristic = distance;
            queue.Enqueue( c );
        }
    }
```

The temporary Coordinate value is set up pointing to the adjacent cell and added to the queue. Notice what value it uses as the heuristic value: the distance it took to reach that cell. This means that the cells are processed so that the cells with the smallest distance (that is, closest to the starting point) are processed first. This gives the effect of the distance-first pathfinder, which gradually expands outward in all directions.

```
        else
        {
            p_map.Get( ax, ay ).m_lastx = x;
            p_map.Get( ax, ay ).m_lasty = y;
            p_map.Get( ax, ay ).m_distance = distance;
```

At this point in the code, you know that the adjacent cell is not in the queue at all, so you set its pointer links to point to the current node and set its distance.

```
            c.x = ax;
            c.y = ay;
            c.heuristic = distance;
            queue.Enqueue( c );
        }
    }
```

                }
            }
        }
    }
}

And finally, the adjacent node is added to the queue.

That was a very long function, but when you think about it, the function isn't really very complex. It follows the same basic formula as the 6-line description of the breadth-first search earlier in this chapter.

Making a Smarter Pathfinder

I want you to try something. Load Graphical Demonstration 23-1 again and place the starting point in the very center of the map. Then place the goal at the right-most edge of the map, on the same horizontal level as the starting point, so that it looks like Figure 23.19.

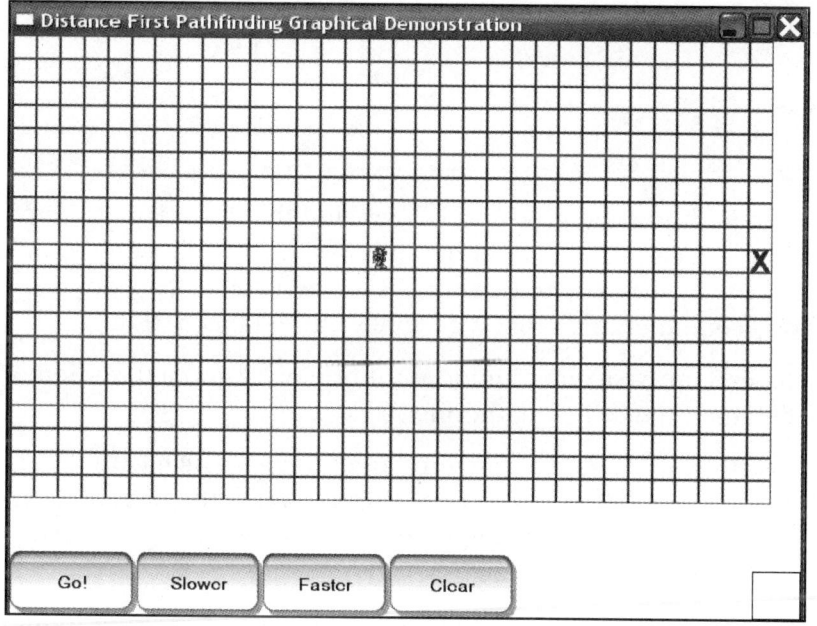

Figure 23.19

You should set up the demo like this.

Now click Go! And wait... and wait... and wait. Gee, this is slow, isn't it?

Imagine that you're playing a game and it shows you where the pathfinder is searching for the path. You notice that it is searching not only toward the goal, but in every other direction, too! Don't you just want to jump up and yell, "Hey, stupid, the goal is to your right—go that way! Don't bother searching to the left, or up, or down!"? Figure 23.20 shows a screenshot of the demo after it has found the path. Pay attention to how much of the map has been searched.

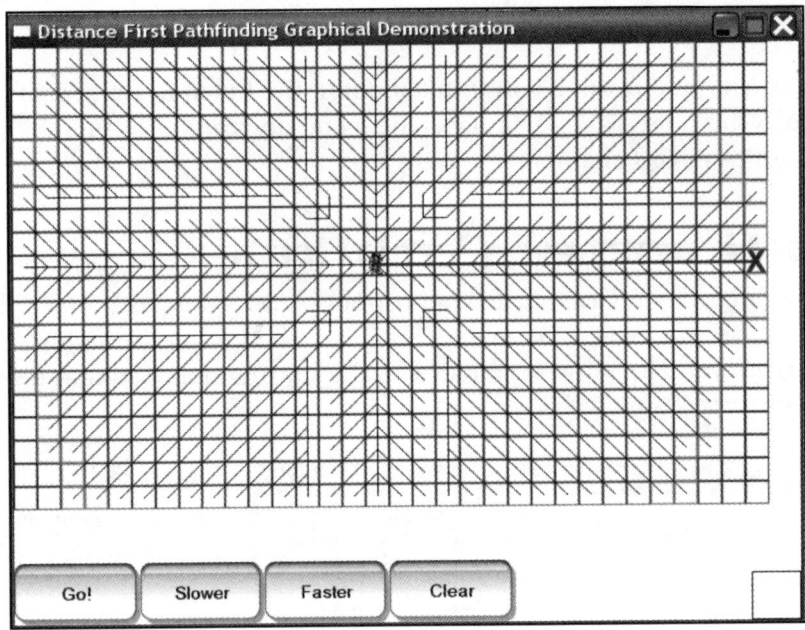

Figure 23.20

Almost all of the map is searched using this algorithm.

The distance-first pathfinder is neat because it will always find the shortest path from one point to another. But it is also stupid because it searches in every direction. As a human, you can look at a map and generally figure out the best way to get from point A to point B. For a computer to do that is generally more difficult, though.

This is where heuristic searching becomes important. I briefly mentioned it when going over the code for the distance-first pathfinder.

A *heuristic,* when applied to pathfinding, is a method used to pick which cells should be processed first. When the distance-first pathfinder picks the next node to process, it picks the closest node to the starting point that has not been processed yet. This isn't a very smart method.

What if you were to create a method that would choose nodes that are closer to the goal first rather than closer to the start?

Imagine a system that would rate a cell based on how much closer it got you toward the goal. If you got closer to the goal in the x axis, it would subtract 1, if it stayed the same, it wouldn't do anything, and if you got further away in the x axis, it would add 1 to the heuristic value. Then it would do the same thing to the *y* axis. Figure 23.21 shows this.

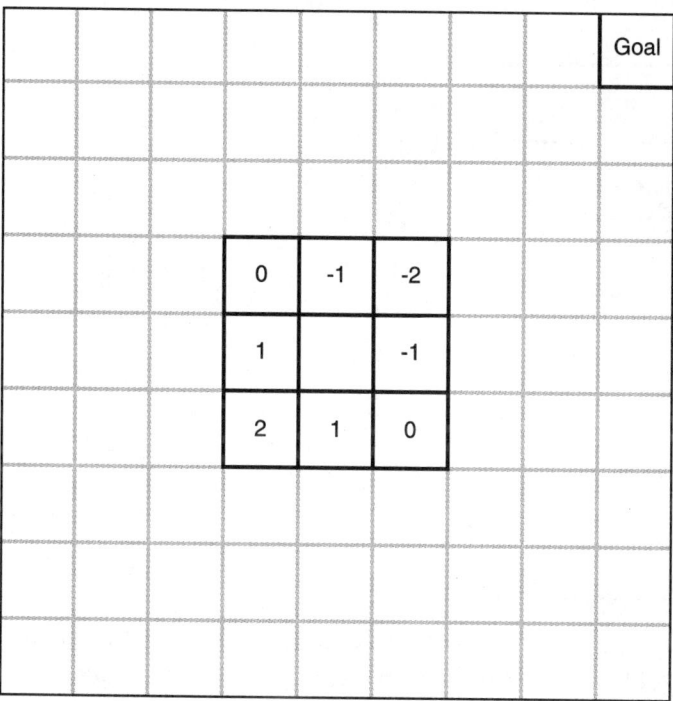

Figure 23.21

This is a smart but simple heuristic.

The center cell is the starting point. First, it processes the northern node. Because it gets closer in the y axis but the x axis stays the same, its heuristic is –1.

Then the northeast cell is processed; it gets closer in both axes, so its heuristic value is –2.

This process continues, as you can see, and all eight cells now have a heuristic value. So now all eight of these cells are in the queue. The first one it processes is the cell with the lowest value, which is the cell that got the closest to the goal.

Figure 23.22 shows the next iteration of this algorithm.

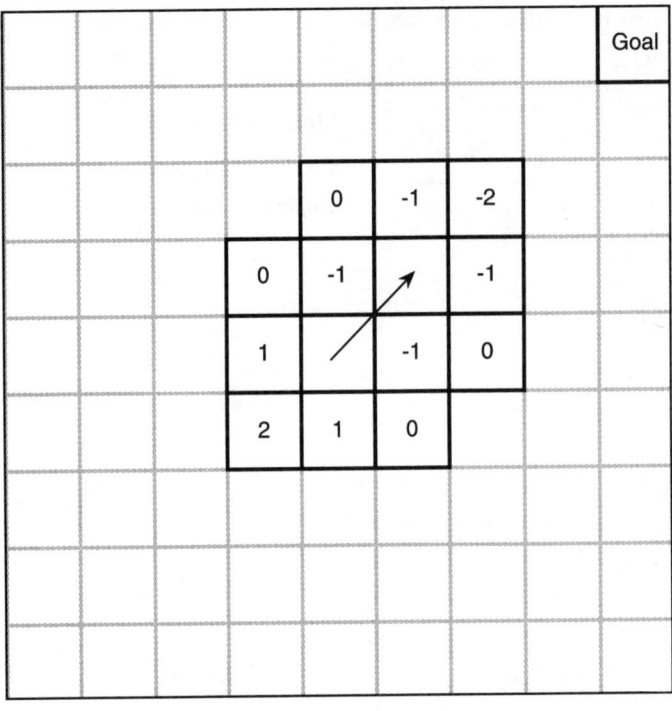

Figure 23.22

This is the second iteration of the algorithm.

Again, all the surrounding cells have their heuristic values calculated, and the cell that moved the closest to the goal is again the lowest in the queue. This process continues, and the search moves toward the goal in a straight line, not bothering to search elsewhere.

Isn't that simple? That's why I call this the *Simple Heuristic Pathfinder*.

Graphical Demonstration: Simple Heuristic Pathfinder

This is Graphical Demonstration 23-2, which you can find on the CD in the directory \demonstrations\ch23\Demo02 - Simple Heuristic\.

This demonstration is exactly the same as Graphical Demonstration 23-1, except that the Go! button now processes the map using the simple heuristic pathfinder.

Figure 23.23 shows a screenshot.

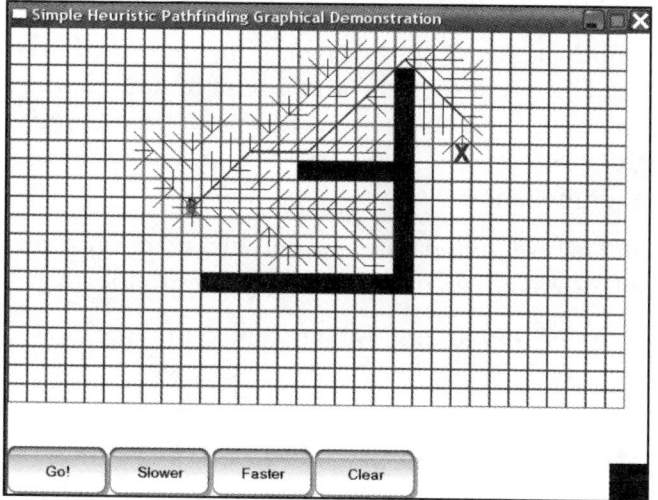

Figure 23.23

Here is a screenshot of the demo.

You can see that this pathfinding algorithm is smarter than the distance-first algorithm in terms of how much time it spends searching.

Problems with This Pathfinder

There are many problems with this pathfinder. First of all, it doesn't take into account the weight of each cell, so it will not find the shortest path from any two points. However, even on a map with no weights, it *still* won't find the shortest path. This search method focuses on making an intelligent decision on the general direction to search rather than being complete.

Figure 23.24 shows what I mean.

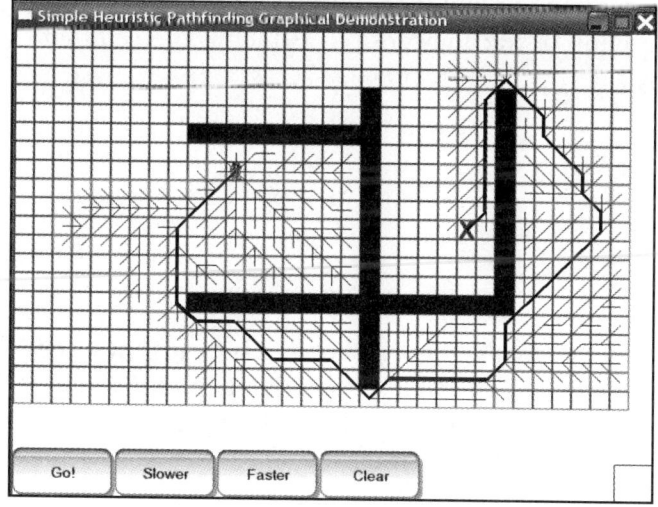

Figure 23.24

The pathfinder found a sub-optimal path that wanders all over the map.

This is what I call the *mutant-4* test—the walls look similar to a disfigured number 4. Note that the player starts off slightly higher than the goal, so the heuristic starts off trying to go south. After messing around in the little area where he started, he finds his way out around the bottom and under the goal. At this point, he is trying to find his way upward again to get closer to the goal. So he goes up again and finally gets over the top of the 4 and finds the goal.

That is clearly the long way around. However, the path was found in a relatively short amount of time because the pathfinder was always trying to move closer to the goal.

You can see that although this pathfinder is smarter, it will not always find the best path.

Coding the Simple Heuristic Pathfinder

Let me first start off by saying that coding this pathfinder is incredibly easy. In fact, the algorithm is almost the same as the distance-first pathfinder.

The Heuristic Function

The first thing you need to do is create a function that will calculate a heuristic value based on the current cell and the direction of the adjacent cell.

```
float SimpleHeuristic( int x, int y, int gx, int gy, int dir )
{
    float h = 0.0f;
    int diff1;
    int diff2;
```

The function takes five parameters: the coordinates of the current cell, the coordinates of the goal cell, and the direction of the adjacent cell (which is the cell that the heuristic is being calculated for).

```
    diff1 = gx - x;
    diff2 = gx - (x + DIRTABLE[dir][0]);
    if( diff1 < 0 )
        diff1 = -diff1;
    if( diff2 < 0 )
        diff2 = -diff2;
```

First, it finds the difference between the goal's *x* coordinate and the current *x* coordinate. Then it finds the difference between the goal's *x* coordinate and the adjacent cell's *x* coordinate. After that, it gets the absolute value of both of those values (if either of them is below zero, then it just negates them).

```
if( diff1 > diff2 )
    h -= 1.0f;
else if( diff1 < diff2 )
    h += 1.0f;
```

This is the part that determines the heuristic. If `diff1` is greater than `diff2`, the adjacent cell is closer in the *x* axis, so 1.0 is subtracted from the heuristic. If, on the other hand, `diff1` is less than `diff2`, then the current cell is closer to the goal on the *x* axis, so 1.0 is added to the heuristic because it is getting farther away.

```
diff1 = gy - y;
diff2 = gy - (y + DIRTABLE[dir][1]);
if( diff1 < 0 )
    diff1 = -diff1;
if( diff2 < 0 )
    diff2 = -diff2;
if( diff1 > diff2 )
    h -= 1.0f;
else if( diff1 < diff2 )
    h += 1.0f;
```

This process is repeated, this time for the *y* axis.

```
    return h;
}
```

Finally, the heuristic is returned.

The Simple Heuristic Pathfinder

Only two lines of code need to be changed from the distance-first pathfinder to make it use the new heuristic.

Look back to the distance-first pathfinder and find the two lines that look like this:

`c.heuristic = distance;`

Now, in order to make this use the simple heuristic, just change both lines to this:

`c.heuristic = SimpleHeuristic( x, y, p_gx, p_gy, dir );`

Now, instead of picking the cells that are closest to the starting point, the algorithm picks the cells that move closer to the goal first.

Making a Better Heuristic

I want you to try something. Open up Graphical Demonstration 23-2 again and set up the map like in Figure 23.25.

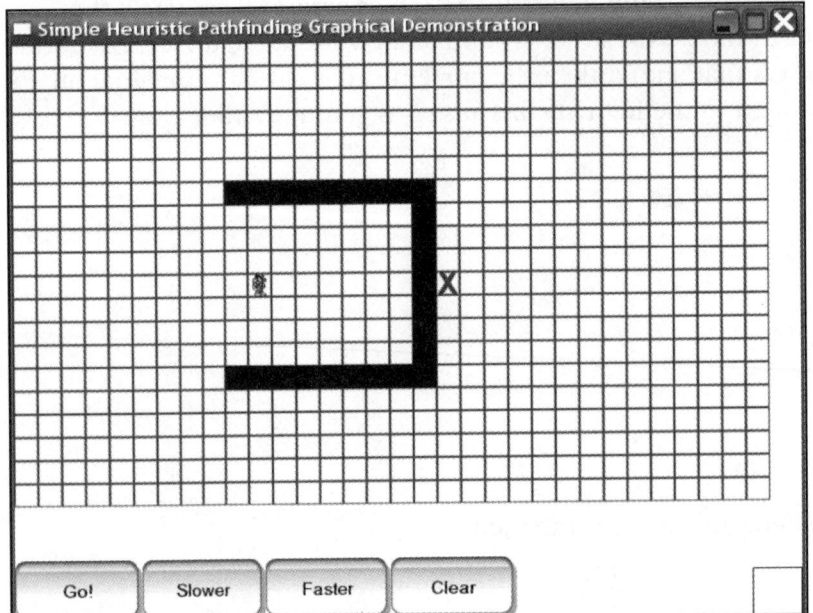

Figure 23.25

Set up the demo like this to test out the simple heuristic.

Now click the Go! button. You'll see the search start off toward the goal, which is good. Eventually it will hit the wall, so it will search out along the wall, trying to get around it. Soon, it will hit the top and bottom walls, so the algorithm backtracks, looking for a way out.

Eventually it will search every node within the little cove and then get back to the starting position. What does it do then? It searches backward, away from the goal!

Why does it do this? It does this because the heuristic thinks that going directly backward is better than going backward and upward, which is the direction that you need to take to get out of the cove. The algorithm ends up just traveling backward until it can't go backward anymore, and then it decides to go up, at which point it discovers that it can go toward the goal again.

When the algorithm is complete, you should get something similar to the screenshot in Figure 23.26.

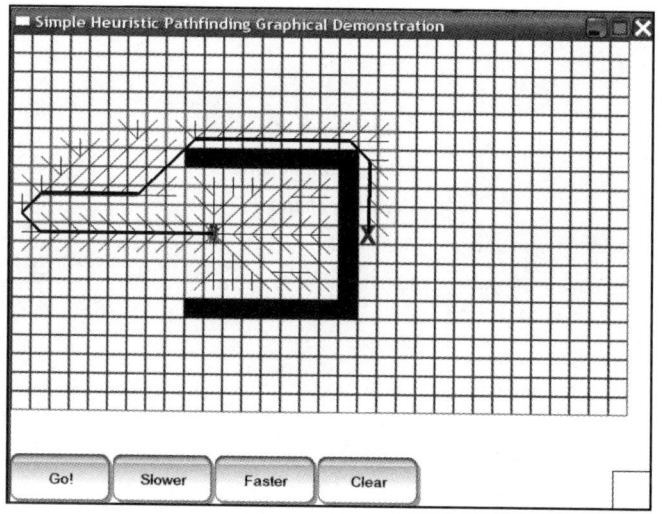

Figure 23.26

The complete path went farther than you wanted it to go.

That path looks quite dumb, don't you think? The pathfinder didn't really know any better, though.

So it looks like you need a better pathfinder. To do this, you need to create a better heuristic function.

Last time, the function judged each move based on if it got any closer to the goal or not. What if you modified the heuristic so that it judges each cell based on its distance from the goal?

Figure 23.27 shows the first calculation of this heuristic on a simple map.

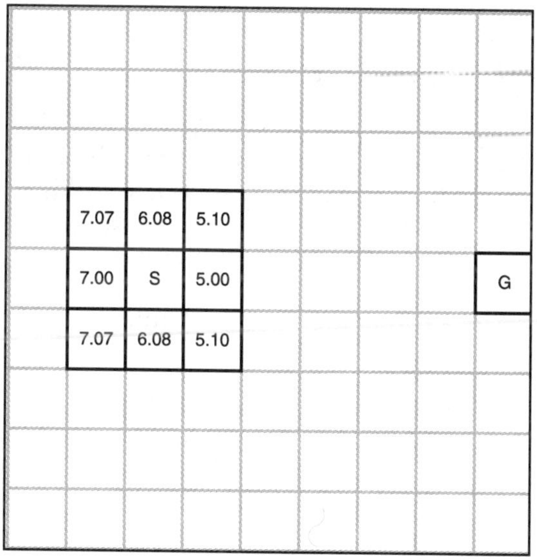

Figure 23.27

The first iteration is performed, and each cell contains the heuristic value from the more complex function.

7.07	6.08	5.10
7.00	S	5.00
7.07	6.08	5.10

(G appears to the right)

The cell with 5.00 has the lowest value, so it is processed first, creating the map in Figure 23.28.

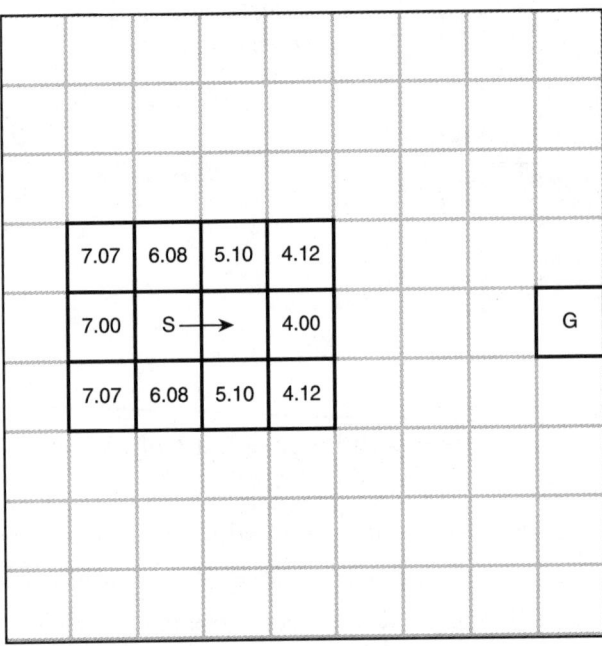

Figure 23.28

Here is the second iteration of the algorithm.

Whereas the simpler heuristic treated all moves that moved toward the goal as the same value, this heuristic treats cells that are physically closest to the goal as the best choice.

Graphical Demonstration: Complex Heuristic

This is Graphical Demonstration 23-3, which is on the CD in the directory \demonstrations\ch23\Demo03 - Complex Heuristic\. Although the heuristic function isn't very complex, I still call this a complex heuristic because it uses a more complex idea for its heuristic calculations.

The demo has the same interface as the previous two demos in this chapter, so you can just play around with it.

Figure 23.29 shows a screenshot of this demo solving the cove problem I showed you before. This pathfinder actually finds the optimal path to the goal this time, which shows that it is somewhat better than the simple heuristic pathfinder.

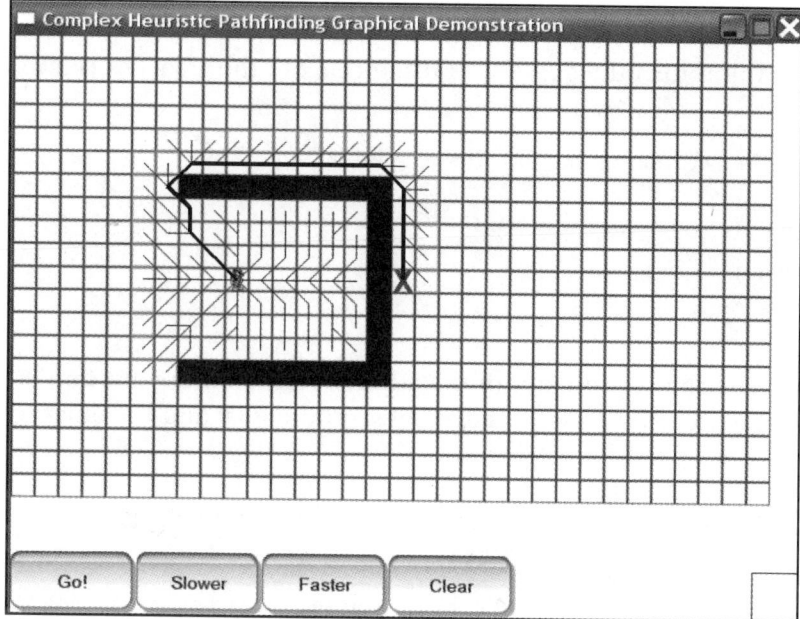

Figure 23.29

Here is a screenshot of the complex heuristic solving the cove problem.

Problems with This Heuristic

Unfortunately, this heuristic has problems as well. This one also fails the mutant-4 test and makes the path go around the 4 the long way (see Figure 23.24 for reference). This is because these two pathfinders don't take into account how long the path is when they are calculating where to go, so when the pathfinder is searching around for a path, it always thinks it is getting closer, even though it is going around the long way.

See, this algorithm doesn't consider that it might have to get farther away from the goal to find a shorter path.

If you play around with the demo, you can see that it always quickly heads for the goal, but it will not always find the shortest path.

Another problem with this pathfinder is that it doesn't factor in the weight of the paths, so it will walk through heavily weighted areas with no second thoughts. I will go into this in more depth later.

Coding the Complex Heuristic

Luckily for you, making this pathfinder work requires only one new function and two lines of code to be changed from the original distance-first search.

The New Heuristic Function

This heuristic function will return the amount of distance from the adjacent cell to the goal.

```
float ComplexHeuristic( int x, int y, int gx, int gy, int dir )
{
    x = x + DIRTABLE[dir][0];
    y = y + DIRTABLE[dir][1];
    return CellDistance( x, y, gx, gy );
}
```

The first two lines calculate the coordinates of the adjacent cell, and the last line calls the `CellDistance` function to get the distance between the goal and the adjacent cell.

The Complex Heuristic Pathfinder

Just like the simple pathfinder, this requires only two lines of code from the distance-first pathfinder to be changed.

Find the two lines of code in the distance-first pathfinder that look like this:

```
c.heuristic = distance;
```

These two lines will be replaced with this:

```
c.heuristic = ComplexHeuristic( x, y, p_gx, p_gy, dir );
```

Then the function is complete.

> **TIP**
> Whenever you see many functions using almost identical code, it's a sign that you are doing something the hard way. These pathfinders *should* have been programmed to accept the heuristic function as a parameter so that the same function could be used to find paths, but I felt that this function was already complex enough. Feel free to modify the pathfinder to take custom heuristic functions and then play around with them to see which ones work best in your games. For example, you could make a heuristic function that avoids certain cells for particular players in a game, but goes right through them for other players. The possibilities are really endless.

The A* Pathfinder

If you look at any game in existence, it probably uses the A* (pronounced *A-star*) pathfinder. This is because this pathfinder is much faster than the breadth- or distance-first pathfinders, and it doesn't have any of the problems of the other two pathfinders, either.

In games, finding the shortest path from any two points is somewhat important. Although it is usually more important to get a faster pathfinder, you also don't want it doing the stupid things that the simple and complex heuristic pathfinders did.

So now you go back to the drawing board and try to make a better heuristic function. You see that the previous heuristic was pretty smart, but got fooled easily into taking long detours because it didn't take into consideration the length of the current path, so you want to take that into account.

You want to find the *shortest* path from the start to the goal, right? So what if the heuristic value of each cell was the combination of the actual distance it took to get to that cell and the estimated distance from that cell to the goal?

Figure 23.30 shows the calculation of two different cells (the ones with the dark outline).

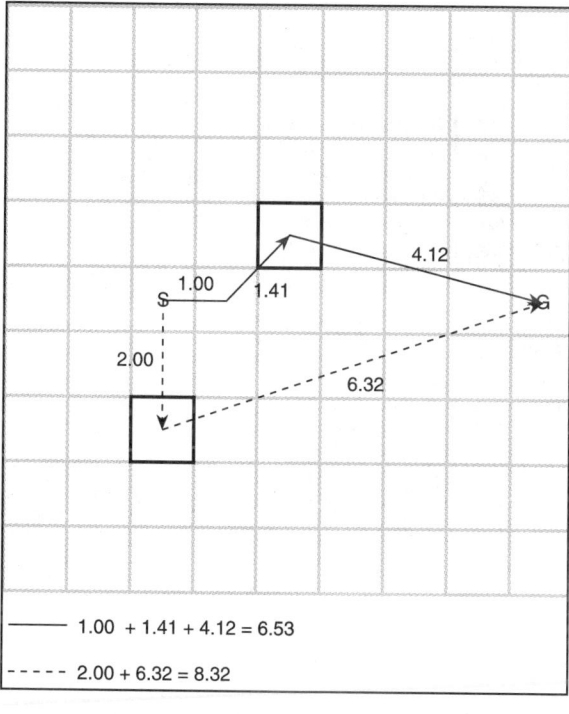

Figure 23.30

This is how the A* heuristic is calculated.

The first path is the solid black line, which takes 2.41 units to get to the cell from the starting point. The function doesn't yet know the path from that cell to the goal, so it estimates the length by using a straight line, which is 4.12 units long. So the heuristic for that cell is 6.53 units.

The second path is dotted. It only takes 2.0 units to get to that cell, so a distance-first pathfinder would prefer this cell over the first one. However, the A* pathfinder estimates that the path from that cell to the goal will take 6.32 units, which means that this cell has a heuristic of 8.32 units.

So the first cell is the winner in this case because it has a lower value. That's all there is to this pathfinder; you can see that it is just a combination of the distance-first pathfinder and the complex-heuristic pathfinder.

Graphical Demonstration: A*

This is Graphical Demonstration 23-4, which you can find on the CD in the directory \demonstrations\ch23\Demo04 - A-Star\.

This demo uses the same interface as the previous three, so I'll just show you a screenshot of this pathfinder solving the mutant-4 problem. See Figure 23.31.

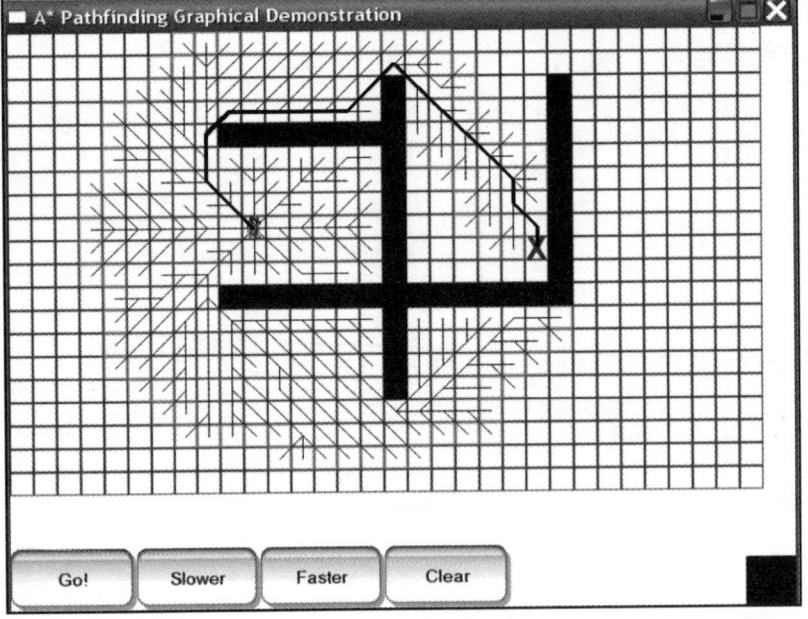

Figure 23.31

Here's a screenshot from the demo solving the mutant-4 problem.

Coding the A* Pathfinder

Believe it or not, the A* pathfinder is almost the same as the three previous pathfinders, with the exception of two lines of code.

Go to the complex-heuristic pathfinder and locate the two lines of code that look like this:

```
c.heuristic = ComplexHeuristic( x, y, p_gx, p_gy, dir );
```

To turn this into an A* pathfinder, you just need to add one thing to those lines:

```
c.heuristic = ComplexHeuristic( x, y, p_gx, p_gy, dir ) + distance;
```

And that's it. See, I told you it was easy.

Graphical Demonstration: Path Comparisons

This is Graphical Demonstration 23-5, which is on the CD in the directory \demonstrations\ch23\Demo05 - Path Comparisons\.

This demo changes the interface of the previous four demos slightly. The way you draw the maps is the same, but the speed buttons and the Go! button are now gone. Instead, there are four new buttons, each representing one of the four pathfinders, as you can see in Figure 23.32.

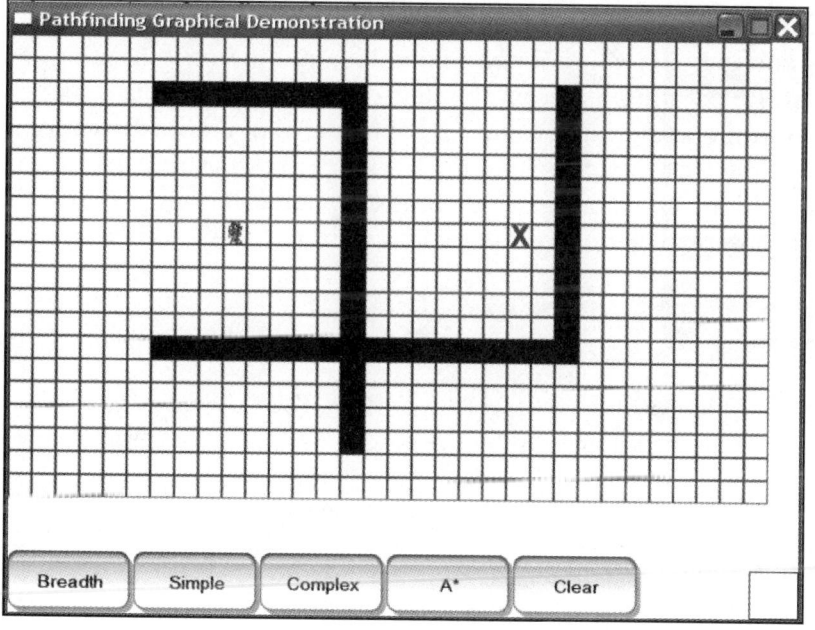

Figure 23.32

Here's a screenshot from the demo.

Just for fun, I drew up the mutant-4 problem and took screenshots of the solution for each pathfinder. See Figure 23.33.

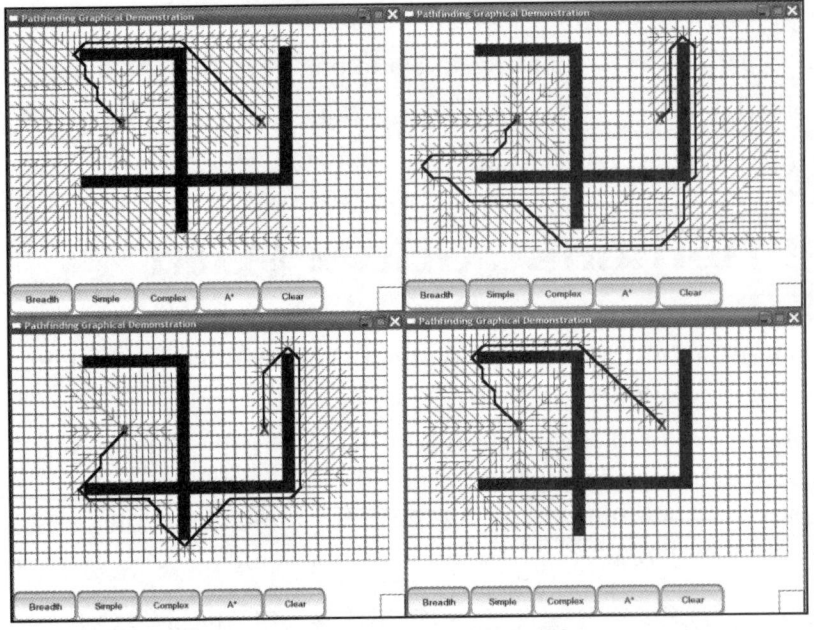

Figure 23.33

Here are the four solutions to the Mutant-4 map. At the top left is the distance-first search, at the top right is the simple-heuristic, at the bottom left is the complex-heuristic, and at the bottom right is the A* search.

Play around with this program; it will give you a good idea of the strengths and weaknesses of each of the pathfinders. From the figure, you can see that the distance-first and A* pathfinders found the same exact path, except that the distance-first pathfinder searched a lot more cells than the A*. The simple search performed lots of searching and came up with a long path, and the complex search did less searching, but still managed to go the long way around the 4.

Weighted Maps

At long last, here is the section dealing with weighted maps. You got just a hint of what weighted maps and pathfinding meant before, and now here is the whole thing.

There will be times when you want to make it harder for things in your game to go through a certain area of your map. For example, say you are making a tank game. The tank will go around the terrain and shoot at things.

So if the tank is going around on grass, dirt, or road, it can go nice and fast. However, if the tank is going to travel over rocks or shallow water, then it will go somewhat slower. And if there is a minefield on the map, it should be avoided at all costs. Figure 23.34 shows an example of what a map would look like.

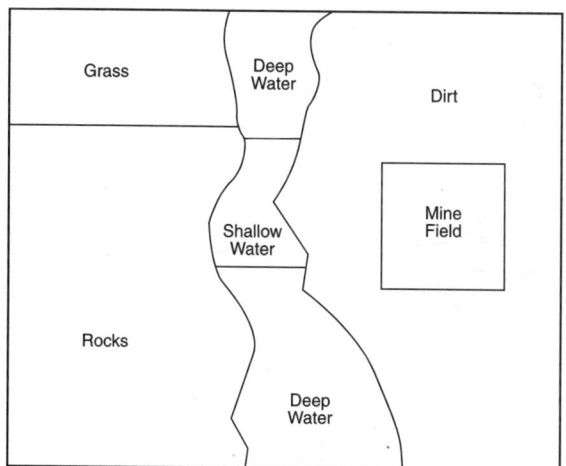

Figure 23.34

Here is an example map for a tank game.

Each of these regions would be weighted differently. The grass and dirt sections would have a weight of, say, 1.0, which is the base weight. Then, the rocks would have a weight of 2.0, which means that the pathfinder will treat moving through one rock tile as the same amount of effort as moving through two grass or dirt tiles.

Now, moving through shallow water is even tougher than going over rocks for a tank, so that should have a weight of 3.0, which means that moving through one tile of shallow water is the same as moving through three tiles of grass or dirt.

Finally, you want to avoid the minefield if possible, so you assign that a high value, like 9.0.

Figure 23.35 shows a screenshot of Graphical Demonstration 23-5 with the map set up to look like Figure 23.34.

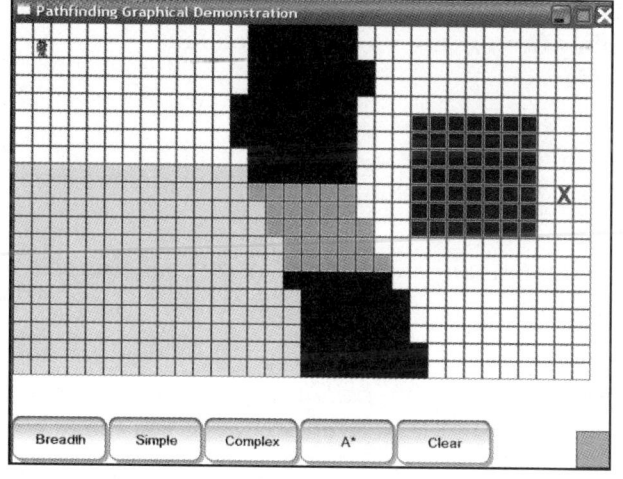

Figure 23.35

Here is Graphical Demonstration 23-5 set up to look like Figure 23.34.

Now, Figure 23.36 shows a screenshot of the path taken through that map.

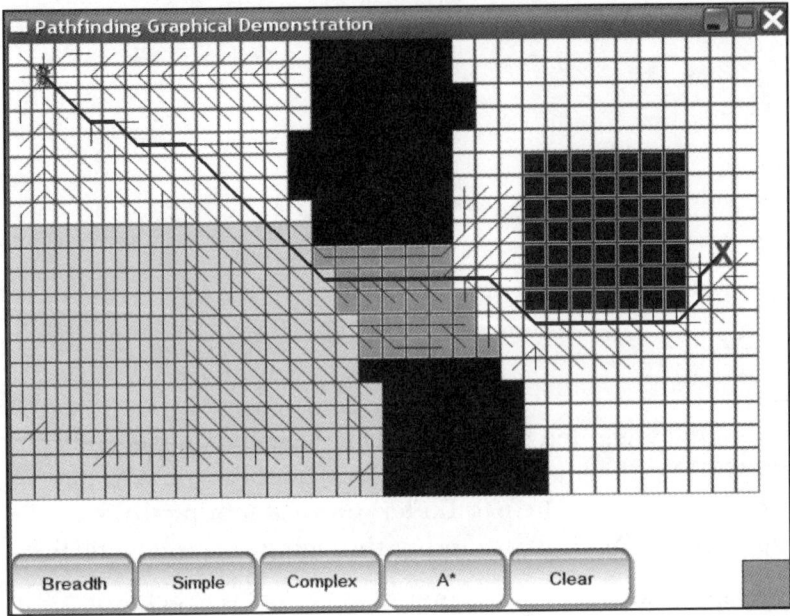

Figure 23.36

Here is the path that the pathfinder takes.

Study the path for a moment.

The path spends as much time as possible in the grassy region first, and then it cuts through a tiny area of rocks. After that, it takes the shortest straight path through the water, and then it neatly goes around the minefield and ends up at the goal.

Isn't that cool?

Weighting the tiles of your maps has thousands of applications. You can literally do anything to discourage your pathfinders from going into certain regions.

Application: Stealth

This is Game Demonstration 23-1, which is on the CD in the directory \demonstrations\ch23\Game01 - Stealth\.

You're a secret agent sent to spy on an area in a forest. Your primary concerns are to gather information and not get caught.

In the area, there are six different types of terrain: dense forest, light forest, grassland, dirt road, paved road, and stone walls. In each terrain type, you have a different chance of being seen by the enemies. You are least likely to be seen in the dense forest and most likely to be seen on the paved road. Table 23.2 shows a listing of the weights for each terrain type.

Table 23.2 Terrain Weights

Terrain	Weight
Dense Forest	4.0
Light Forest	8.0
Grassland	12.0
Dirt Road	16.0
Paved Road	20.0
Stone Wall	Impassable

To prevent being caught, you would be advised to stay in the forest areas as much as possible when moving around.

The Variables

There are a few variables used for this game demo:

```
const int MAPX            = 100;
const int MAPY            = 75;
Array2D<Cell> g_map( MAPX, MAPY );
LStack<int> g_xmovement;
LStack<int> g_ymovement;
int g_goalx = -1,
    g_goaly = -1;
int g_currentx = -1,
    g_currenty = -1;
bool g_moving = false;
```

The first two are the size of the map, which is a 100 × 75 tilemap. The second variable is the actual map, stored in a 2D array.

After that, there are two stacks. Don't worry about them now; I get into them a little later.

Then there are two sets of coordinates: the goal position and the current position of the player.

Finally, there is a boolean, which determines whether the player is moving.

Loading and Saving the Map

The map is stored on disk, so you can load it up, modify it, and then save it back to disk. Here are the routines that load and save the map to disk:

```
void SaveMap()
{
    FILE* f = fopen( "map", "wb" );
    fwrite( g_map.m_array, MAPX * MAPY, sizeof(Cell), f );
    fclose( f );
}

void LoadMap()
{
    FILE* f = fopen( "map", "rb" );
    fread( g_map.m_array, MAPX * MAPY, sizeof(Cell), f );
    fclose( f );
}
```

They directly store and load the map data from the Array2D class.

Finding the Path

When the map is loaded and the starting and goal positions are placed on the map, the program can then begin pathfinding. Here is the section of code that does this:

```
g_moving = true;
while ( g_xmovement.Count() != 0 ||
        g_ymovement.Count() != 0 )
{
    g_xmovement.Pop();
    g_ymovement.Pop();
}
```

This first part sets the moving boolean to true so that the program now knows that the player is following a path. After that, both of the stacks are emptied.

```
PathAStar( g_map, g_currentx, g_currenty, g_goalx, g_goaly );
```

Now, the A* pathfinding algorithm is called on the map, so it will trace a path from the current position to the goal. After this call, the path is stored in the map within the `m_lastx` and `m_lasty` variables of each cell.

```
x = g_goalx;
y = g_goaly;
```

Now, to convert the path into a list of coordinates, you need to reverse the path on the map into something you can use. This part just notes the last coordinates of the path and places them into the *x* and *y* variables.

```
while( x != -1 && y != -1 )
{
    g_xmovement.Push( x );
    g_ymovement.Push( y );
    t = g_map.Get( x, y ).m_lastx;
    y = g_map.Get( x, y ).m_lasty;
    x = t;
}
```

This section loops through the path, starting at the goal node, and traces it backward toward the starting node. For each new coordinate, it is pushed onto the stacks, and the next coordinate in the path is retrieved. The temporary t variable is used because you don't want to overwrite the x variable yet because it is used again on the next line.

Why use a stack? Well, remember that a stack is a *last-in first-out* data structure, and the path in the map is backward. So the last move is placed into the stack first, and the first move is placed into the stack last, which means that the first move will be removed from the stack first, essentially reversing the order of the path so that it is usable!

```
g_xmovement.Pop();
g_ymovement.Pop();
```

These lines pop off the first pair of coordinates from the stacks. This is done because the starting coordinates are pushed onto the stack last, and because the player is already at the starting position, there is really no need for them to be on the stack.

Walking the Path

Now, whenever it comes time to move to the next square, the following piece of code is executed:

```
if( g_xmovement.Count() == 0 )
{
    g_moving = false;
}
else
{
    g_currentx = g_xmovement.Top();
    g_currenty = g_ymovement.Top();
    g_xmovement.Pop();
    g_ymovement.Pop();
}
```

If the size of the stacks is zero, then the path has been traced, and the movement is halted. If not, then the current position of the player is updated by getting the next coordinates off the stack, and then both stacks are popped.

That was simple enough, wasn't it?

Playing the Game

The game is fairly simple to play. When the game starts off, the map is shown, as in Figure 23.37.

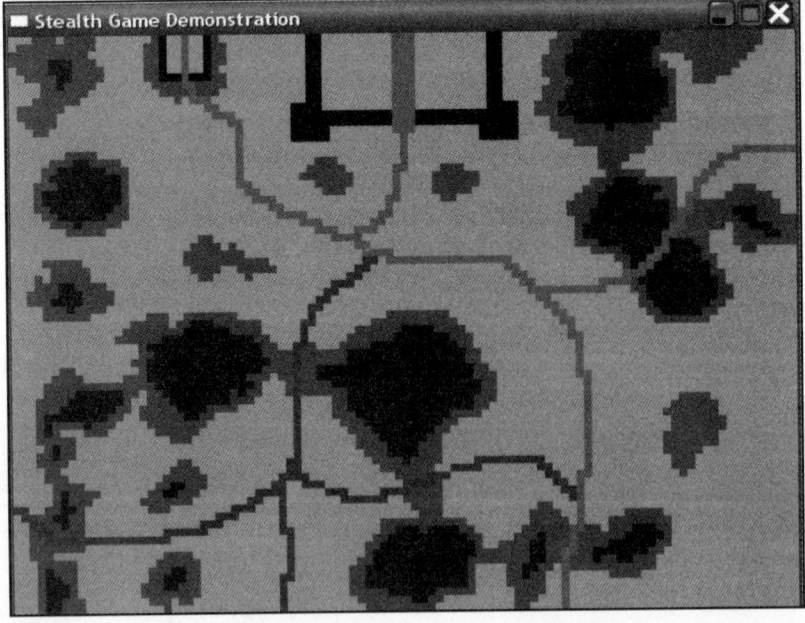

Figure 23.37

Here is a screenshot from the Stealth game demo.

Press the S key on your keyboard to place the player's start position where your mouse cursor is pointing (represented by a red square).

Press the G button on your keyboard to place the goal on the map (represented by a blue square).

To get the player moving, just press the Spacebar on your keyboard, and the player will begin his long trek toward the goal.

Table 23.3 shows the colors of each of the terrains.

Table 23.3 Colors of the Terrain Squares

Color	Terrain
Dark Green	Dense Forest
Medium Green	Light Forest
Light Green	Grass
Brown	Dirt Road
Gray	Paved Road
Black	Stone Wall

When you play around with the game, you will see that the player in general will try to stick to the forest areas and avoid the grasslands if possible.

Bonus Feature: Editing the Map

You can edit the map. By pressing D on the keyboard, you enable the drawing mode. Be careful, though; the map is saved when the game exits, so any changes you make will still be there the next time the game starts up. You can change the current tile by pressing the number keys on your keyboard. Table 23.4 shows a listing of each number.

Table 23.4 Keys

Key	Terrain
0	Dense Forest
1	Light Forest
2	Grass
3	Dirt Road
4	Paved Road
5	Stone Wall

Thinking Beyond Tile-Based Pathfinding

Lets face it; many games are not tile based. But tile-based pathfinding is so easy that it sometimes ends up deciding what kind of game engine you will use. If, however, you end up creating a game engine that doesn't handle tiles, then you'll need to learn some new pathfinding techniques. Unfortunately, I don't have room to do much but explain them, but hopefully that will be enough to get your brain running at full speed.

Line-Based Pathfinding

In many games, the players are not restricted to occupying certain tiles in a game; instead, they can go anywhere they want at any degree and speed. Pathfinding for these types of games is difficult, however, so most of the time these games use simple pathfinding methods (such as the random bounce method I mentioned at the beginning of the chapter).

Figure 23.38 shows an example of this kind of pathfinding.

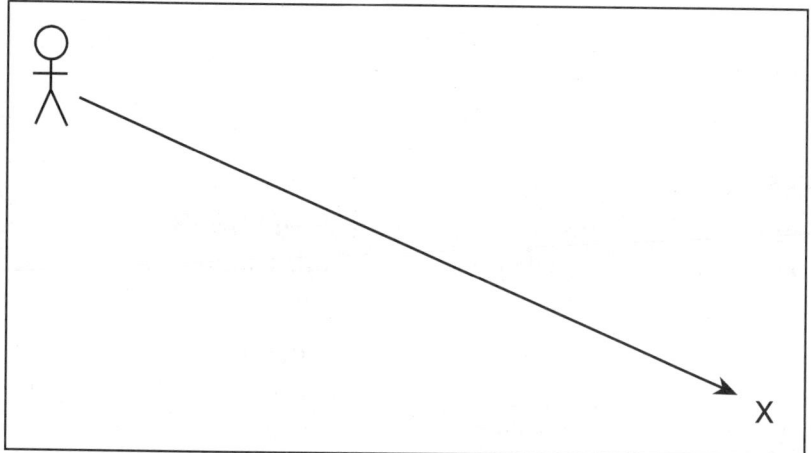

Figure 23.38

Line pathfinding tries to find a line straight to the goal.

Unfortunately, this method doesn't work for maps with obstacles. Of course, you could use a random bouncer to move around obstacles, but that doesn't usually work well.

Whenever you have an obstacle in a map like this, you could pre-generate a path around the obstacle, like in Figure 23.39.

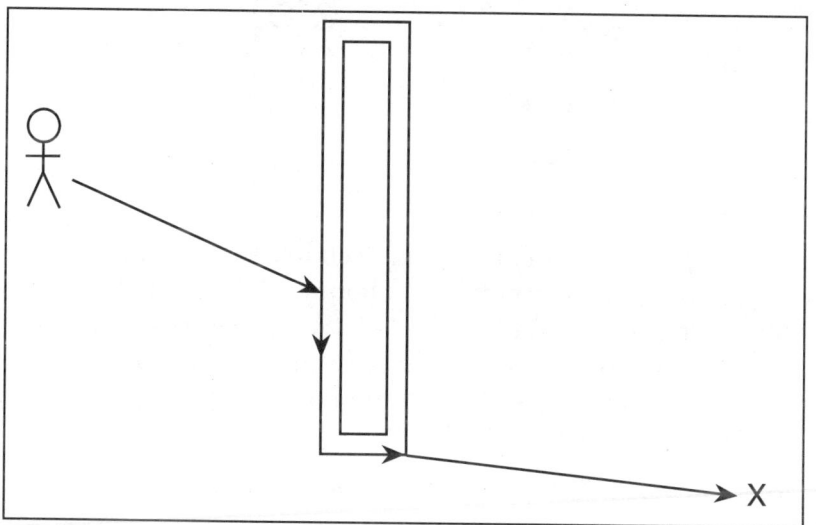

Figure 23.39

This map shows how to use a pre-generated path to get around an obstacle.

The path itself would be just an array of lines. Whenever a player gets too close to an obstacle, it would *attach* itself to the path around the obstacle. Then the player would just follow each line in the path until it finds that it can break away from the path and start getting closer to the goal again.

To optimize this method, perhaps you could also store the lengths of each line in the path and figure out which way around the path is the shortest to get to the other side.

Quadtrees

Oh, no! Not trees again! Trust me, trees are amazing wonderful structures that can do almost anything, even your laundry. Okay, maybe not your laundry, but they can still do tons of stuff.

Imagine that you have a large square game world. You split that up into four squares. Then you go to each square and split it up into another four squares. And you keep doing this over and over. This is called a *quadtree*. Figure 23.40 shows a map divided into quadtrees and the corresponding tree on the right side.

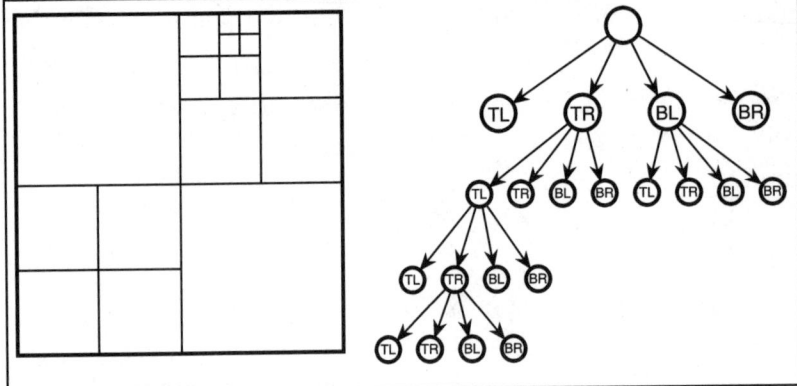

Figure 23.40

This figure shows a quadtree.

The root node of the tree represents the entire map. Each node in a quadtree has four children: the top left, top right, bottom left, and bottom right quads. The main map is divided into four quads, so the root node has four children. In this particular map, the top left and bottom right quads aren't divided any more, so those nodes are leaf nodes. However, the top right and bottom left nodes continue to subdivide, so the tree continues downward.

What does this have to do with pathfinding, though? Imagine you have a large map with a large lake in one part of it. This lake is impassable to most units in the game, so you want some way to go around it.

Now, create a quadtree out of the map so that the tree is full to a certain number of levels (3 or 4 is good). Now, for each quad on the lowest level of the tree, check the midpoint of each quad. If all four of the quad's midpoints are not obstructed, then you can remove that branch of the tree. When the lowest level is complete, go up to the next level and continue removing nodes, but only if all four branches of each node go down to the same level.

Eventually, you will end up with a quadtree that looks like the one in Figure 23.41. Now you have all these nodes that are linked together, and you can store them into a graph.

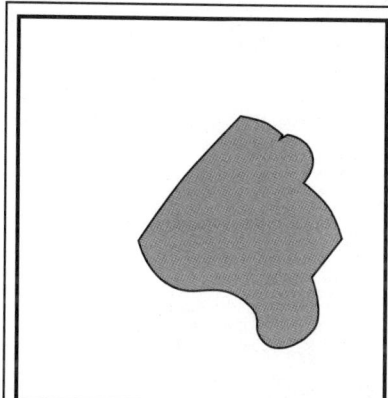 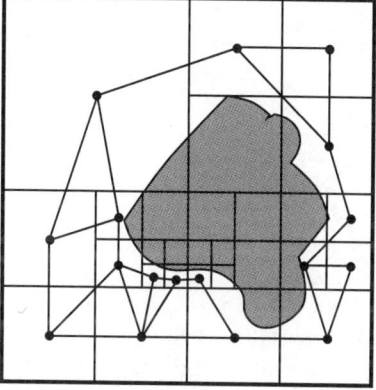

Figure 23.41

This demonstrates using quadtrees to make paths around a map for pathfinding.

How do you find the shortest path through this graph, though? I discuss that in the next section.

> **NOTE**
> There is also a 3D version of quadtrees, called *octrees*. An octree is simply a cubic volume split up into eight equally sized sub-cubes.

Waypoints

Suppose you have a map in a shooter game like *Quake*. Figure 23.42 shows this map. Each of the little dots on the map represents an item in the game—say, a weapon or a powerup or some health. It doesn't matter at this point in time; all that matters is that the points represent something.

23. Pathfinding

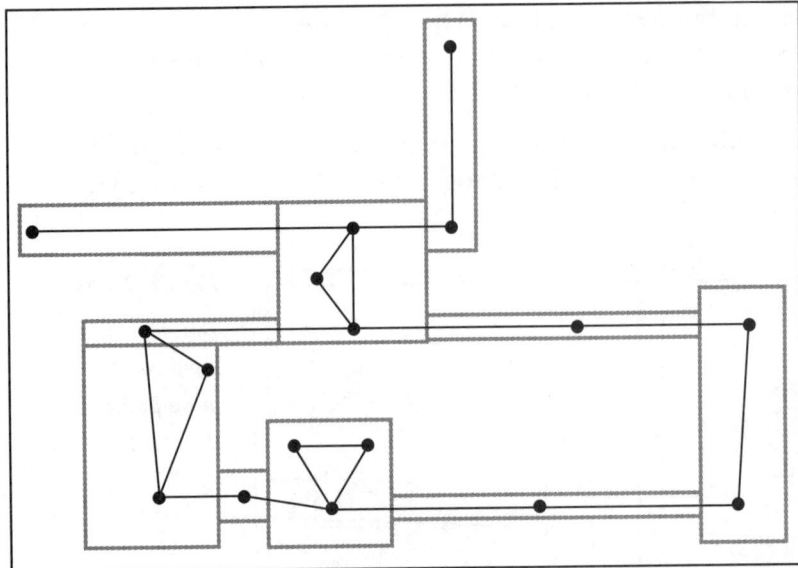

Figure 23.42

The dots in this map store item waypoints, and the AIs follow the lines to get to the item they want.

Now, all the points are connected together using lines, and a graph is formed. Each of the points on the graph is called a *waypoint*. When you want to find a path through this map, you get to the closest waypoint and then follow the lines until you get to the waypoint where you want to be.

This method is popular in shooter games because it works well with finite state machine AI (see Chapter 18, "Using Graphs for AI: Finite State Machines"). The AI decides what item it wants and then attaches itself to the graph and follows the paths until it gets to the point that has the item that it wants. If a particular AI prefers the rocket launcher, then he follows the paths toward the rocket launcher waypoint. If he needs health, then he follows the paths toward a health node.

So how does the AI know which paths to follow? Simple. The AI uses a pathfinding algorithm. The great thing about pathfinding algorithms is that they work for graphs of any type, not just tilemaps.

Here is the tilemap pathfinding algorithm:

```
TilePathfind( map, start, goal )
    Queue q
    q.Enqueue( start )
    while( q is not empty )
        current = q.Front
        q.Dequeue
        Mark( current )
```

```
        for( all 8 directions )
            if( adjacent node not marked )
                q.Enqueue( adjacent node )
                adjacent node.previous = current
            end if
        end for
    end while
end Function
```

Now, to adapt this algorithm to linked graphs, you just need to change one thing. Change this:

```
for( all 8 directions )
```

To this:

```
for( each linked node )
```

And the algorithms fit perfectly.

Conclusion

This was another large chapter packed with tons of information. Unfortunately, what I showed you was barely a glimpse into the realm of pathfinding. There are so many more algorithms out there that they could probably fit into an entire book.

Hopefully, the information I have given you has inspired you to think about smarter ways to perform pathfinding. The most important thing to learn about game programming is that there are always better ways to do things. Sure, you could have just stuck with a breadth-first search for your pathfinding needs, but why should you waste precious CPU time on an inefficient algorithm?

Even though all of the methods I showed you were 2D algorithms, you can easily adapt them to 3D games. The easiest way to do this is to treat your game world as a conceptual graph. If your game is separated into rooms, then that would be a good structure to use as your graph nodes.

Hopefully, by now you have learned a few things and are able to spot a brute-force algorithm and a smart algorithm.

CHAPTER 24

Tying It Together: Algorithms

24. Tying It Together: Algorithms

This is it! The final chapter! By now, you should be well acquainted with all of the data structures and algorithms in this book and with the *Adventure* game that is developed in Chapters 9, "Tying It Together: The Basics," 16, "Tying It Together: Trees," and 19, "Tying It Together: Graphs." This final chapter shows you how to add some of the new algorithms you've learned into the game demo.

In this chapter, you will learn

- How to add A* pathfinding to a tilemap
- How to add A* pathfinding to a directionmap
- How to optimize the game logic to use these new pathfinders

Making the Enemies Smarter with Pathfinding

When you play the *Adventure* demos from Chapters 9, 16, and 19, you may have noticed something: The AI is *dumb*. Not just dumb, but seriously digitally handicapped. Look at Figure 24.1, for instance.

Figure 24.1

Hey dummy, just walk up and then right! He won't get it; he'll stand there until you move around.

Making the Enemies Smarter with Pathfinding

The AI in the figure will stand there, like a 4-bit calculator, just looking at you. He won't go and attack you or anything else.

The `GetClosestDirection` function I implemented for those demos was simple, fast, and stupid. It just tried to figure out which direction a person should move in order to get closer to the player; it didn't care if there was a wall or another person in the way.

Now that you have gotten this far in the book, you know enough to fix this problem. In this demo, the A* pathfinding algorithm is added to the map classes to make it possible for the AIs to find their way around the map.

Unlike Chapters 9, 16, and 19, this chapter only modifies the game engine and logic. The map format stays the same, so the map editors stay the same as they were in Chapter 19.

All of the code modifications are on the CD in the directory \demonstrations\ch24\Game01 - Adventure v4\.

Compiling the Demo

This demonstration uses the SDLGUI library that I have developed for the book. For more information about this library, see Appendix B, "The Memory Layout of a Computer Program."

To compile this demo, either open up the workspace file in the directory or create your own project using the settings described in Appendix B. If you create your own project, all of the files you need to include are in the directory.

If you aren't familiar with the A* pathfinding algorithm, now is a good time to go back to Chapter 23, "Pathfinding," and read about it.

Adding Pathfinding to the TileMap Class

When I built the pathfinding functions for Chapter 23 (they are all in the file \structures\pathfinding.h), I assumed that they were going to be used on an 8-direction tilemap.

However, when I build the *Adventure* demo, the player is limited to 4-direction movement; diagonals are not allowed in the demo. Unfortunately, this means that the `PathAStar` function cannot be reused on this class, and I will need to code a new function that performs the same algorithm.

The Consequences of a Bad Design

The fact that I need to re-code the A* algorithm should be flashing warning bells in your head right now. Usually, it is a bad idea to re-code algorithms for specific purposes after they have already been coded. Chapter 2, "Templates," should have given you an idea of why re-coding is bad. So why does this large and complex algorithm need to be re-coded? This is a mixture of the function being coded for learning and bad design. When the original *Adventure* engine was created, all of the map data was stored in the `Map` class, so it was logical that the map would know how to move things around. When you actually think about real life, though, it is the *person* who decides where to go, not the map. A more flexible method would have put the pathfinder into the `Person` class and find a path through the map by using the `Map` class interface. This method has many advantages. For example, you can

- Make different pathfinders with different agendas for each of the AI types (that is, make certain pathfinders avoid certain areas of the map).
- Use the same pathfinding algorithm on every map implementation, as the map interface hides the implementation from the user.

Unfortunately, now I must deal with the consequences of this decision and implement the A* pathfinding algorithm twice.

Also, the pathfinding functions implemented in Chapter 23 were designed to show you how the algorithms actually worked, and therefore they weren't as complicated or flexible as they could be. This is why the function cannot be adapted to the `TileMap` class.

The Coordinate Class and Comparison Function

If you remember the algorithm from Chapter 23, then you also remember that I needed an extra class to store information about the cells that are in the priority queue and their current heuristic value. Also, because the `Heap` class (which is acting like the priority queue) needs to sort items inside of it, it needs a comparison function (see Chapter 14, "Priority Queues and Heaps," for more information).

Here is the `Coordinate` class:

```
class Coordinate
{
public:
    int x;
    int y;
    float heuristic;
};
```

Whenever a cell is added to the queue, its coordinates are stored in a `Coordinate`, and so is its heuristic value.

Here is the comparison function, which treats cells with lower heuristic values as "better":

```
int CompareCoordinates( Coordinate left, Coordinate right )
{
    if( left.heuristic < right.heuristic )
        return 1;
    if( left.heuristic > right.heuristic )
        return -1;
    return 0;
}
```

The New Data

You might remember from Chapter 23 that the A* pathfinding algorithm requires some extra data to be contained in each cell so that it knows which cells it has searched. Therefore, new data has been added to the `TileCell` class (in the Tilemap.h file):

```
bool m_marked;
float m_distance;
```

```
int m_lastx;
int m_lasty;
```

This data is virtually identical to the data found in the `Cell` class from \structures\pathfinding.h. Each cell knows if it has been marked, its distance from the starting cell in the map, and the coordinates of the previous cell in the path. If any of this information is unfamiliar to you, please, go back and review Chapter 23 before continuing.

The ClearCells Function

Whenever the pathfinder is called, it needs to clear all the marks, distances, and links in each cell (the data declared in the previous section). Therefore, this function was created to accomplish this:

```
void ClearCells()
{
    int x, y;
    for( x = 0; x < m_tilemap.Width(); x++ )
    {
        for( y = 0; y < m_tilemap.Height(); y++ )
        {
            m_tilemap.Get( x, y ).m_marked = false;
            m_tilemap.Get( x, y ).m_distance = 0.0f;
            m_tilemap.Get( x, y ).m_lastx = -1;
            m_tilemap.Get( x, y ).m_lasty = -1;
        }
    }
}
```

All of the marks are cleared to `false`, the distances are cleared to 0, and the last cell links are set to −1, meaning that they point to an invalid cell.

The Heuristic Function

This function finds out the coordinates of the cell adjacent to the current cell and estimates the distance from this cell to the goal. (I discussed this function in Chapter 23.)

```
float Heuristic( int x, int y, int gx, int gy, int dir )
{
    x = x + DIRECTIONTABLE[dir][0];
```

```
        y = y + DIRECTIONTABLE[dir][1];
        return Distance( x, y, gx, gy );
}
```

> **NOTE**
> The Distance function is just a small helper function, which you have seen previously in a few demos.

The AStar Function

Because this algorithm has been discussed in depth in the previous chapter, there really isn't a need to explain the entire thing again. However, this particular implementation differs a little bit from the PathAStar function (in the \structures\pathfinding.h file) to make it work with the *Adventure* map format. I will focus on pointing out these differences:

```
void AStar( Person* p_one, Person* p_two )
{
    Coordinate c;
    int x, y;
    int ax, ay;
    int dir;
    float distance;
    static Heap<Coordinate> queue( 1024, CompareCoordinates );
```

The PathAStar function (from \structures\pathfinding.h) uses a heap as the priority queue. However, it uses a local heap that is allocated and deallocated whenever the pathfinder is called. This can be quite inefficient. In this function, I have placed the static keyword in front of the heap this time (see Appendix A, "A C++ Primer," if you are unfamiliar with this keyword). This means that the queue is created when the program starts up and isn't deleted until the program ends. The static queue is sort of like a global variable because there is only one instance of it and it always exists, but it is sort of like a local variable, too, because *only* this function can access it. This will save on speed because the heap doesn't have to be created and deleted every time the function is called.

```
    queue.m_count = 0;
```

When the function starts, the queue should be empty. When the A* pathfinder finishes, there might still be cells in the queue that weren't emptied out. This line sets the count of the heap to 0, which makes the queue think that it is empty.

```
// clear the cells first.
ClearCells();
// enqueue the starting cell in the queue.
c.x = p_one->GetX();
c.y = p_one->GetY();
queue.Enqueue( c );
// start the main loop.
while( queue.m_count != 0 )
{
    // pull the first cell off the queue and process it.
    x = queue.Item().x;
    y = queue.Item().y;
    queue.Dequeue();
    // make sure the node isn't already marked. If it is, do
    // nothing.
    if( m_tilemap.Get( x, y ).m_marked == false )
    {
        // mark the cell as it is pulled off the queue.
        m_tilemap.Get( x, y ).m_marked = true;
        // quit out if the goal has been reached.
        if( x == p_two->GetX() && y == p_two->GetY() )
            break;
        // loop through each direction.
        for( dir = 0; dir < 4; dir++ )
        {
```

Note that it loops through four directions this time instead of eight.

```
            // retrieve the coordinates of the current adjacent cell.
            ax = x + DIRECTIONTABLE[dir][0];
            ay = y + DIRECTIONTABLE[dir][1];

            if( ( CanMove( x, y, dir ) &&
                  m_tilemap.Get( ax, ay ).m_marked == false ) ||
                ( ax == p_two->GetX() && ay == p_two->GetY() ) )
            {
```

Making the Enemies Smarter with Pathfinding

The previous line is somewhat important. In the `PathAStar` function from Chapter 23, the pathfinder determined if it could go through a cell solely by accessing an `m_passable` variable in each cell. Although the `TileCell` class has a similar variable (`m_blocked`), the game is generally more complex than the old pathfinder could handle. For example, there could be a person in the cell or an item that blocks the path, and so on. This means that the function now needs to check to see if it can go through a cell with more conditions. Luckily, there already is a function that can tell that: the `CanMove` function. This makes sure that a person can move into the current adjacent cell. It also makes sure that the cell isn't marked. If the cell is marked, then the function just ignores it (because the shortest path to that cell has already been found).

Unfortunately, there is a problem with the `CanMove` function. It always returns `false` when the pathfinder is trying to move into the final cell, so the pathfinder can never find a path into the cell. Therefore, I had to add a special case to the `if` statement. Whenever the current adjacent cell's coordinates are the same as the goal's coordinates (the coordinates of p_two), then the function automatically processes the cell, even though the `CanMove` function says it is blocked.

```
            // calculate the distance to get into this cell.
            distance = m_tilemap.Get( x, y ).m_distance + 1;
            // check if the node has already been calculated before.
            if( m_tilemap.Get( ax, ay ).m_lastx != -1 )
            {
                // the node has already been calculated; see if the
                // new distance is shorter. If so, update the links.
                if( distance < m_tilemap.Get( ax, ay ).m_distance )
                {
                    // the new distance is shorter; update the links.
                    m_tilemap.Get( ax, ay ).m_lastx = x;
                    m_tilemap.Get( ax, ay ).m_lasty = y;
                    m_tilemap.Get( ax, ay ).m_distance = distance;
                    // add the cell to the queue.
                    c.x = ax;
                    c.y = ay;
                    c.heuristic = distance +
                                Heuristic( x, y, p_two->GetX(),
                                        p_two->GetY(), dir );
                    queue.Enqueue( c );
                }
            }
```

```cpp
                    else
                    {
                        // set the links and the distance.
                        m_tilemap.Get( ax, ay ).m_lastx = x;
                        m_tilemap.Get( ax, ay ).m_lasty = y;
                        m_tilemap.Get( ax, ay ).m_distance = distance;
                        // add the cell to the queue.
                        c.x = ax;
                        c.y = ay;
                        c.heuristic = distance +
                                    Heuristic( x, y, p_two->GetX(),
                                            p_two->GetY(), dir );
                        queue.Enqueue( c );
                    }
                }
            }
        }
    }
}
```

The rest of the function is the same as the A* pathfinder from Chapter 23.

Modifying the GetClosestDirection Function

The modification isn't quite done yet. The last thing that needs to be done is to modify the `GetClosestDirection` function so that it calculates which direction the AI should move to get closer to the player. Now it needs to call the `AStar` function to calculate a path from the AI to the player:

```cpp
int GetClosestDirection( Person* p_one, Person* p_two )
{
    AStar( p_one, p_two );
    int lx, ly, x, y;
    x = p_two->GetX();
    y = p_two->GetY();
```

The very first thing the function does is calculate the path from the first person to the second person. After that, it declares four integers, which represent two pairs of coordinates. You'll see what they represent in a bit. One of the pairs of coordinates is initialized to the same coordinates as the goal.

```
while( x != p_one->GetX() || y != p_one->GetY() )
{
    lx = x;
    ly = y;
    x = m_tilemap.Get( lx, ly ).m_lastx;
    y = m_tilemap.Get( lx, ly ).m_lasty;
```

Remember, once the A* pathfinder is complete, you need to start at the goal and backtrack through the path. To find out which direction to move, you need to backtrack to the first cell and keep track of the cell right before the first cell in the path. This will be the cell that the AI moves into. So the loop keeps track of the previous cell in the path (lx and ly) and gets the next cell and stores in into x and y.

```
    if( x == -1 || y == -1 )
    {
        return rand() % 4;
    }
}
```

During the loop, if at any time it finds that the previous cell in the path is $(-1,-1)$, that means that there is no path from the AI to the player. If this happens, then the function returns a random number from 0–3. This has the effect of making the AI walk around like he is frustrated (or has lost his keys).

```
    if( ly < y )
        return 0;
    if( lx > x )
        return 1;
    if( ly > y )
        return 2;
    if( lx < x )
        return 3;
}
```

When the loop is done, the lx and ly variables should contain the coordinates of the first cell in the path, and x and y should contain the coordinates of the starting position. The previous code segment determines which direction the next cell lies in. If the next cell's *y* coordinate is above the first cell's, then he needs to move north (direction 0), and so forth.

Adding Pathfinding to the DirectionMap Class

Adding pathfinding to the `DirectionMap` class is similar to adding pathfinding to the `TileMap` class.

> **NOTE**
>
> Keep in mind what I said earlier about how you should be careful about duplicating code. The fact that the pathfinder for the directionmap is very similar to the one for the tilemap should tell you that there is a way to make the function more flexible. Remember, part of learning is making mistakes.

In a tilemap, it is easier to access each cell by its 2D coordinates, but in a directionmap, it is easier to use the cell's number.

The CellCoordinate Class

This is just like the `Coordinate` class used with the tilemap pathfinder; however, it has been updated to use the cell number instead of its coordinates:

```
class CellCoordinate
{
public:
    int cell;
    float heuristic;
};
```

Likewise, there is also a comparison function to use along with this when it is in the priority queue:

```
int CompareCellCoordinates( CellCoordinate left, CellCoordinate right )
{
    if( left.heuristic < right.heuristic )
        return 1;
    if( left.heuristic > right.heuristic )
        return -1;
    return 0;
}
```

The New Data
New data needs to be added to the `DirectionCell` class to use the A* pathfinder algorithm. The new data is similar to the data added to the `TileCell` class earlier, with one difference.

```
bool m_marked;
float m_distance;
int m_lastcell;
```

The two `m_lastx` and `m_lasty` variables have been replaced with just one `m_lastcell` variable.

The ClearCells Function
This function loops through each cell in the map and clears the pathfinding variables.

```
void ClearCells()
{
    int x;
    for( x = 0; x < m_rooms.Size(); x++ )
    {
        m_rooms[x].m_marked = false;
        m_rooms[x].m_distance = 0.0f;
        m_rooms[x].m_lastcell = -1;
    }
}
```

The Heuristic Function
To make things a little easier, the `Heuristic` function takes the number of the cell it will calculate the heuristic of and the number of the goal cell.

```
float Heuristic( int p_cell, int p_goal )
{
    return Distance( m_rooms[p_cell].m_x,
                     m_rooms[p_cell].m_y,
                     m_rooms[p_goal].m_x,
                     m_rooms[p_goal].m_y );
}
```

This function assumes that the cell numbers will both be valid, so if you don't check it before sending them to this function, you may end up with some bad bugs.

The AStar Function

This function is almost exactly the same as the AStar function in the TileMap class. When reading through this code, you can go back and compare it with the tilemap version. Note that the *x* and *y* coordinate references have been replaced with cell number references.

```
void AStar( Person* p_one, Person* p_two )
{
    CellCoordinate c;
    int cell;
    int adjacentcell;
```

For example, the tilemap version had four integers: x, y, ax, and ay. Those have been replaced with cell and adjacentcell.

```
    int dir;
    float distance;
    static Heap<CellCoordinate> queue( 1024, CompareCellCoordinates );
    // clear the queue.
    queue.m_count = 0;
    // clear the cells first.
    ClearCells();
    // enqueue the starting cell in the queue.
    c.cell = p_one->GetCell();
    queue.Enqueue( c );
```

Also, whenever a cell is enqueued or dequeued, its cell number is retrieved, not its coordinates.

```
    // start the main loop.
    while( queue.m_count != 0 )
    {
        // pull the first cell off the queue and process it.
        cell = queue.Item().cell;
        queue.Dequeue();
        // make sure the cell isn't already marked. If it is, do
        // nothing.
        if( m_rooms[cell].m_marked == false )
        {
            // mark the cell as it is pulled off the queue.
            m_rooms[cell].m_marked = true;
            // quit out if the goal has been reached.
```

```
        if( cell == p_two->GetCell() )
            break;
```

This is somewhat simpler in some parts, like the two lines of code listed previously. You only need to check to see if the cell number of the current cell and the goal cell are equal instead of comparing two sets of coordinates.

```
            // loop through each direction.
            for( dir = 0; dir < 4; dir++ )
            {
                // retrieve the index of the current adjacent cell.
                adjacentcell = m_rooms[cell].m_exits[dir];
                // check to see if the adjacent cell is passable
                // and not marked.
                // note that the CanMove function will return false
                // when adjacentcell is the same as the goal because there
                // is a person on that cell. Therefore, you need to make
                // a special exception to allow that cell to be processed.
                if( ( CanMove( cell, dir ) &&
                      m_rooms[adjacentcell].m_marked == false ) ||
                      adjacentcell == p_two->GetCell() )
                {
                    // calculate the distance to get into this cell.
                    distance = m_rooms[cell].m_distance + 1;
                    // check if the node has already been calculated before.
                    if( m_rooms[adjacentcell].m_lastcell != -1 )
                    {
                        // the cell has already been calculated; see if the
                        // new distance is shorter. If so, update the link.
                        if( distance < m_rooms[adjacentcell].m_distance )
                        {
                            // the new distance is shorter; update the link.
                            m_rooms[adjacentcell].m_lastcell = cell;
                            m_rooms[adjacentcell].m_distance = distance;
                            // add the cell to the queue.
                            c.cell = adjacentcell;
                            c.heuristic = distance +
                                          Heuristic( adjacentcell,
                                                     p_two->GetCell() );
                            queue.Enqueue( c );
                        }
```

```
                }
                else
                {
                    // set the links and the distance.
                    m_rooms[adjacentcell].m_lastcell = cell;
                    m_rooms[adjacentcell].m_distance = distance;
                    // add the cell to the queue.
                    c.cell = adjacentcell;
                    c.heuristic = distance +
                                    Heuristic( adjacentcell,
                                               p_two->GetCell() );
                    queue.Enqueue( c );
                }
            }
        }
    }
}
```

Overall, the code for the directionmap pathfinder is a little easier, but not by much. I've stated before that the code for both pathfinders are so similar that you would probably be better off abstracting the pathfinder from the map, but the current design would need a complete overhaul. This code demonstrates an important point: Plan for *everything* before you write a single line of code. You never know what you will add in the future.

Modifying the GetClosestDirection Function

Again, the `GetClosestDirection` function must be modified in order to take advantage of the new pathfinder that has been installed into the map.

The directionmap implementation of this function is almost the same as the tilemap implementation, but the path is now in terms of the cell numbers instead of the coordinates, so the path is traced using cell numbers:

```
int GetClosestDirection( Person* p_one, Person* p_two )
{
    // calculate the path between the two persons.
    AStar( p_one, p_two );
    int lastcell, cell, d;
    // now follow the path from the goal to the start.
```

```
    cell = p_two->GetCell();
    // loop through the path while the current cell
    // isn't the goal.
    while( cell != p_one->GetCell() )
    {
        // save the last cell number.
        lastcell = cell;
        // calculate the next cell number.
        cell = m_rooms[cell].m_lastcell;
        if( cell == -1 )
        {
            // the path is unreachable, so return a random
            // direction.
            // this makes the AI seem frustrated.
            return rand() % 4;
        }
    }
    // the path was reached, so calculate which direction the person
    // needs to move to get closer.
    for( d = 0; d < 4; d++ )
    {
        if( lastcell == m_rooms[cell].m_exits[d] )
            return d;
    }
}
```

The only thing of major difference is the loop that figures out which direction to return. This code is shown in bold in the previous code listing. Instead of figuring out which direction the function should return based on coordinates, this time it loops through each exit of the starting room. If any of the exits leads to the next cell in the path, then the current direction is returned.

Visualizing the GetClosestCell Algorithm

Sometimes it is difficult to understand just how a piece of code works unless you see it illustrated. This happens particularly often in the field of data structures, as it is a very visual subject. Now I will demonstrate the `GetClosestCell` algorithm for you. This applies to both versions of the function.

Figure 24.2 shows a simple map, which could either be a directionmap or a tilemap. It really doesn't matter at this point.

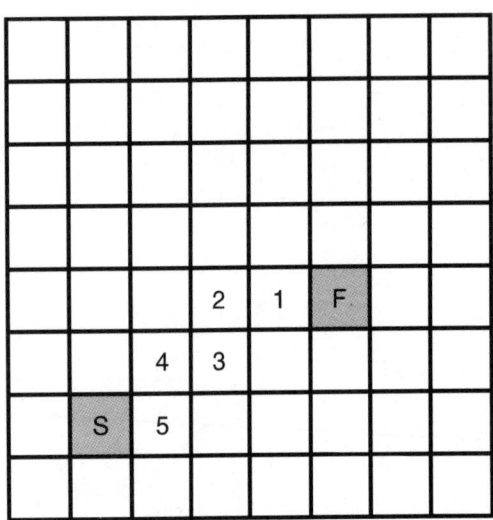

Figure 24.2

This is the process of the `GetClosestCell` *function. The path is calculated from S to F; after that happens, the function backtracks from F to S.*

After the call to `AStar` has completed, the map has the data for a path from the starting position (*F* in the figure) to the final position (*F* in the figure). Now, the function starts at *F* and follows the path backward to *S*. When the function is at cell 5, the *previous cell* pointer is pointing to *S*. Then it goes on to cell 4, and the previous cell pointer points to node 5. This continues until the current cell pointer is pointing to cell *F* and the previous cell pointer is pointing to 1. Finally, the function figures out which direction the AI needs to move in order to get into that cell and returns that direction.

Is That All?

Right about now, you might be asking, "Is that all I need to do to add pathfinding?" The answer is both "yes" and "no." True, you now have a working, fully functional smart pathfinder.

If you compile this demo right now, though, you will be greeted with a *very slow* game. "Gee, thanks, you've made me implement a slow algorithm," you might be thinking right now, and you're somewhat correct.

Making the Enemies Smarter with Pathfinding

To understand what is going on, you need to go and look at the game logic from Chapter 19 (in the file \demonstrations\ch19\Game01 - Adventure v3\g19-01.cpp). Look for the `PerformAI` function.

In that function, you will see these lines of code:

```
for( i = 0; i < g_peoplecount; i++ )
{
    if( g_peoplearray[i] != g_currentplayer )
    {
        direction =
            g_currentmap->GetClosestDirection( g_peoplearray[i],
                                                g_currentplayer );
```

This function loops through every AI on the map for every frame and calculates the closest direction for each AI to move toward the player.

This was just fine when the pathfinding function was small and simple. Now that you've implemented a rather large and complex pathfinder, though, calling this function for *every* player once *every* frame is an incredible waste of processing power.

Implementation Versus Interface

In Chapter 9, I emphasized how you can make games much more flexible by separating the *implementation* and the *interface* of your game classes. Therefore, you can swap out implementations and the rest of your game will still work properly.

Replacing the pathfinder, in this instance, exposes a flaw in this method. When you first programmed something that used an interface, you programmed it thinking that the implementation was simple. However, in this case, you ended up replacing a simple function with a complex one and ended up making the game *very* slow.

Sometimes knowing how fast an implementation works is important. It is also important to optimize your code after you know that it works. When you don't know how fast an algorithm is, always assume that it is slow and should be called as little as possible.

Instead of calling this function every frame for every person, you want to call it *only* when you need a result from it.

This requires several modifications.

The Person's Following Status

Now that you have a decent pathfinder, you will want the people in the game to act more realistically. For example, in the old version, if you came within six cells of an enemy, he would start to chase you, but it you went outside of the six-cell range, he would forget about you.

This isn't very realistic, as a real enemy would still chase you even if he couldn't see you. So now you want to add a new piece of data to the `Person` class so that the person knows if he is chasing the player or not:

```
bool m_following;
void SetFollow( bool p_follow )
{
    m_following = p_follow;
}
bool GetFollow()
{
    return m_following;
}
```

The game logic will now be able to tell if the person is following the player or not and calculate the next node in the path whenever he is following.

The New PerformAI Function

Now you are ready to modify the `PerformAI` function to make it more efficient.

```
void PerformAI( int p_time )
{
    int i;
    float dist;
    int x = g_currentplayer->GetX();
    int y = g_currentplayer->GetY();
    int direction;
    for( i = 0; i < g_peoplecount; i++ )
    {
        if( g_peoplearray[i] != g_currentplayer )
        {
```

The function starts off in much the same way as it did before by getting the coordinates of the player and storing them into x and y and starting a loop that will go through every AI in the game. It changes after that, though:

```
dist = Distance( g_peoplearray[i], g_currentplayer );
if( dist > 10.0f )
{
    g_peoplearray[i]->SetFollow( false );
}
if( dist <= 6.0f )
{
    g_peoplearray[i]->SetFollow( true );
}
```

First, the distance from the player to the current AI is calculated. Whenever the distance between the two is more than ten cells, the AI forgets about the player and stops moving. Whenever the distance goes below six cells, the AI sees the player and starts following him.

```
if( dist > 1.0f && g_peoplearray[i]->GetFollow() &&
    p_time - g_peoplearray[i]->GetMoveTime() > MOVETIME )
{
    direction =
        g_currentmap->GetClosestDirection( g_peoplearray[i],
                                            g_currentplayer );
    g_peoplearray[i]->SetMoveTime( p_time );
    g_peoplearray[i]->SetDirection( direction );
    g_currentmap->Move( g_peoplearray[i], direction );
}
```

This code segment calculates a few things. First, it makes sure that the distance from the player to the AI is greater than one (which means that the AI isn't within attacking range, so the AI should move closer), and then it checks to see if the current AI is following the player. Finally, the second line in the `if` statement checks to see if enough time has passed since the last time the AI has moved to see if he can move again.

If all of those checks pass, then the AI can move closer to the player. You can calculate the direction the AI should move now that you know that the AI is actually going to move.

After that, the movement time is reset, the AI is turned to face the right direction, and the AI is moved in that direction.

```
            if( dist <= 1.0f &&
                p_time - g_peoplearray[i]->GetAttackTime() >
                g_peoplearray[i]->GetCurrentWeapon()->GetSpeed() )
            {
                direction =
                    g_currentmap->GetClosestDirection( g_peoplearray[i],
                                                       g_currentplayer );
                g_peoplearray[i]->SetDirection( direction );
                Attack( g_peoplearray[i] );
            }
        }
    }
}
```

If the distance is less than or equal to one, then the AI is within attack range, and he should attack the player. However, it first checks to see if enough time has passed since the last time he has attacked so that he can attack again. After this, you know that the AI is going to attack, so you call the pathfinder to make the AI face the player so he can attack him, and finally, the AI attacks him.

And *that* is all that needs to be done. Congratulations! You now have a really smart AI that will hunt you down.

Efficiency

Now you need to sit back and consider how much more efficient the new pathfinding AI is. Pathfinding is a very difficult thing to implement in games, as it is a really complex and time-consuming task. Most games, such as *Diablo II*, cheat with their pathfinding. If you've ever played that game and had a computer-controlled ally following you, try outrunning him. After a few seconds, the ally will magically appear right next to you if you get too far away. This is because the pathfinding in a huge game like that would take forever if every AI had to find an individual path.

Generally speaking, the larger your maps are, the longer it will take to perform pathfinding on them. This can get to be a very large problem because most pathfinders increase at around $O(n^2)$, which means that maps twice as large will take four times longer to find a path in.

The pathfinding done in this demo isn't very complicated when using the new and improved `PerformAI` function. When you think about it, the AIs never calculate the path when they are more than 10 cells away from the player. Not only that, but each AI only calculates a path once every 750 milliseconds, which is the amount of time before each AI moves around.

Overall, the pathfinding in this demo is smart yet efficient because you really aren't searching a large area (most searches are in an area smaller than 10 cells), and searches don't happen too often.

Playing the Game

The game demo plays exactly the same as all the demos before it, so there is no need to post the instructions here. Just play around and try running away from the AIs to see how long they will chase you and what kind of obstacles they will avoid. Figure 24.3 shows a screenshot of the game in action.

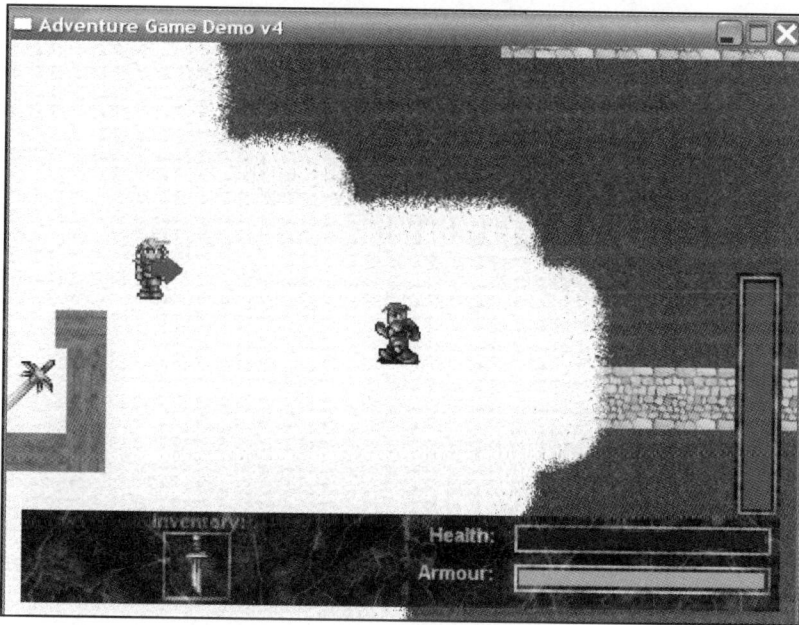

Figure 24.3

Oh, no! The enemy found his way out of his box the moment I stepped into view! Run! Run for the hills! They're chasing me!

Conclusion

Chapters 9, 16, 19, and this one all followed a single theme: creating a simple game and extending it to reinforce your understanding of the data structures and algorithms in this book. In Chapters 16, 19, and this one, I only chose one aspect/structure/algorithm to implement into the game, but don't think that these are the only extensions you can make. There are hundreds of ways you can apply the things you've learned in this book to a game. You can use stacks to create a menu system in the game, bitvectors to implement a quicksave, queues to store commands for the player, hash tables to store resource data, and so on. You could use binary trees to make a simple scripting system or add a sorting algorithm to the items in the game so you could use larger sprites that stick out of the map. I've showed you all of these concepts before, so it shouldn't be any problem for you to add these into the game.

Use your imagination; after all, that is what game programming is all about.

Conclusion

Congratulations! You have just completed the main part of this book! Do you know everything there is to know about data structures and algorithms? Well, of course not; no one does!

This book shows you only a tiny fraction of the world of data structures and algorithms. Yes, there is a lot of information that you need to absorb to fully understand this book, but there is so much more out there in the real world.

However, you should now be well on your way to understanding how data structures in games work and why it is important to study them. Some people dedicate their lives to this stuff, and you should be glad that people have already figured out most of it for you. Imagine discovering all those sorting algorithms—yuck!

Extra Topics

When I was designing this book, I had to cut out some of the less important material to make room for the stuff you will use most often in game programming. When you have mastered the things in this book, you can move on to some of the more advanced data structures and algorithms out there.

I have mentioned some of them, and others I haven't mentioned. If you're interested in expanding your knowledge in data structures and algorithms, look into the following topics:

- Red-black trees
- AVL trees
- Skip lists
- The binary search
- Minimum spanning tree algorithms
- Dijkstra's "all shortest paths" pathfinding algorithm
- Quadtrees
- Binary space partition trees

The list could go on forever, but those topics listed are immediately applicable to game programming, so that should give you a good start.

Further Reading and References

When writing this book, I referenced many other books and sources of information. I must admit, I learned quite a bit about some of the things I wrote about. This just goes to show that we are constantly learning and we should never stop.

Data Structure Books

When researching the data structures and algorithms for this book, I referenced quite a few books.

Sams Teach Yourself Data Structures and Algorithms in 24 Hours

By Robert Lafore (ISBN 0-672316-33-1)

This book was recommended to me by André LaMothe, and it is very good. My only problem with it is that the examples that come with the book are all in Java, and they take forever to run. Other than that, Lafore covers a very wide area of structures and algorithms. I had a difficult time finding this one, though. It took me a month to track down a copy, and even then, it was a used copy!

Introduction to Data Structures and Algorithm Analysis with C++

By George Pothering and Thomas Naps (ISBN 0-314045-74-0)

This was my very first data structures book, and it is an okay book. I would only look into this book if you were required to buy it for a class, like I was.

Introduction to Algorithms, 2nd Edition

By Thomas H. Cormen, Charles E. Leiserson, Ronald L. Rivest, and Clifford Stein (ISBN 0-262032-93-7)

This is one HUGE book. By huge, I mean that it is almost 1,200 pages long! This book has almost everything in it, but it takes a very academic approach to teaching data structures and algorithms, which you may not like. If you're going to school for a computer science degree, chances are that one of your classes will use this book.

The Art of Computer Programming
By Donald Knuth (ISBN 0-201485-41-9)

This is actually a set of three books, and it is considered the bible of data structures and algorithms. Again, this is a more academic book, but it contains almost everything you will ever want to know about the topics.

Effective STL
By Scott Meyers (ISBN 0-201749-62-9)

This is a great book for learning how to use STL in different situations. It's relatively cheap, too, so you can't use that as an excuse not to buy it! Meyers also has some good optimized C++ books out, including *Effective C++* and *More Effective C++*.

The C++ Standard Library: A Tutorial and Reference
By Nicolai M. Josuttis (ISBN 0-201379-26-0)

This is an excellent introduction and reference manual for the entire C++ standard library, which includes STL. If you're ever interested in learning all there is to learn about STL, this is the book to buy.

C++ Books

Here is a list of the C++ books that I referenced when writing this book. Some of them are quite well written, and I would recommend them to you.

Object Oriented Programming in C++
By Robert Lafore (ISBN 1-571691-60-X)

This is a really great C++ book that explains things in an easy-to-understand way and has good chapters on arrays, strings, and templates.

Sams Teach Yourself C++ in 21 Days
By Jesse Liberty (ISBN 0-672320-72-X)

This is the C++ book that I first learned C++ with, and it is pretty good. It separates the material into well-paced segments, and it even has a little introduction to linked lists and binary trees.

C++ How to Program
By Deitel & Deitel (ISBN 0-130895-71-7)

This is a very popular introduction to C++ programming, and it has a lot of information. Most notable about this book is that it has a large section on the STL, which is great for learning how to use it for the first time.

Game Programming Books

Of course, I can't forget to include the many game programming books out there that you might be interested in.

Game Programming All in One
By Bruno Sousa (ISBN 1-931841-23-3)

This is written by a friend of mine, and it is a very ambitious book. Basically, it is a huge introduction into game programming and everything you ever wanted to know about DirectX. It's a good read and a great reference.

Focus On SDL
By Ernest Pazera (ISBN 1-59200-030-4)

This is a complete reference to SDL, the media API that I've used throughout the book. If you're at all interested in SDL, this is the book to buy!

Focus On 3D Terrain Programming
By Trent Polack (ISBN 1-59200-028-2)

This is a book all about storing 3D terrain information and generating the information as well. Naturally, this applies to data structures and algorithms.

Focus On 3D Models
By Evan Pipho (ISBN 1-59200-033-9)

This is another book dealing with data structures, and specifically how to store 3D Model information efficiently in a computer game.

Game Scripting Mastery
By Alex Varanese (ISBN 1-931841-57-8)

This book is all about game scripting. I hinted on this subject a little bit in Chapter 12, with the arithmetic parser game demo. This book will expand upon those concepts and give you a great deal of information on game scripting, virtual machines, and all that great stuff.

AI Techniques for Game Programming
By Mat Buckland (ISBN 1-931841-08-X)

This book is mentioned earlier in the book. It looks like it will be a great book dealing with all sorts of advanced AI techniques, such as genetic algorithms and neural nets. These topics can be applied to data structures because they use bitvectors and graphs.

Web Sites

Last, there are a number of great Web sites out there with tons of information on game programming. Here are a few of my favorites:

- http://www.gamedev.net
- http://www.flipcode.com
- http://www.gamasutra.com

Conclusion

I would just like to take this time to thank you for purchasing and reading this book. As my family and friends can well attest to, I have invested a significant part of my life for the past few months writing this. I hope you understood everything that I have written, but if not, you can usually find me in the Gamedev.net chat room, which you can get to by going to this address: http://www.gamedev.net/community/chat/. I am usually there with the nickname Mithrandir. I have set up an e-mail account for this book at this address: RonPenton@Hotmail.com. Please send bug reports, errors, compliments, and free gifts to me there. Thank you once again.

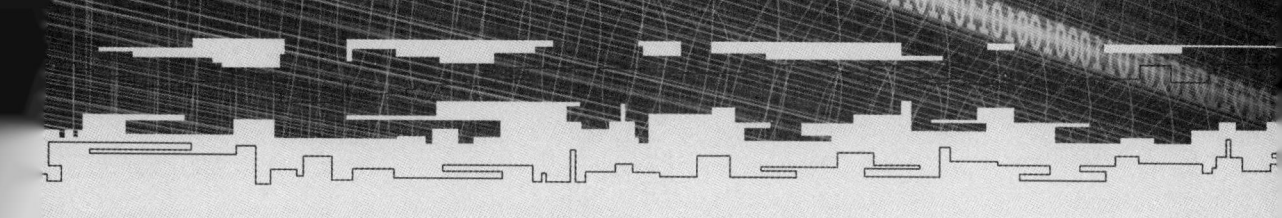

PART SIX

Appendixes

Appendix A   A C++ Primer

Appendix B   The Memory Layout of a Computer Program

Appendix C   Introduction to SDL

Appendix D   Introduction to the Standard Template Library

APPENDIX A

A C++ Primer

This is an intermediate-level book, and I use some complex features in it. You should probably know most of them, but no one is perfect, and you might have forgotten something. That is why this Appendix is here. If I use something you have forgotten how to use or something you have never learned, this Appendix will give you a little overview of it.

Basic Bit Math

Some of the chapters in this book get down to the lower levels of programming and work with the individual bits of a number in memory. Some C++ books don't really get into the nitty-gritty details though, so I'll go over the basics here.

The most basic form of storage on a computer is called the *bit*. The word bit is short for *binary digit*. When you look at a standard everyday number, it is usually in a form called *base-10*, which means that there are a total of 10 *digits*.

A digit is the name of a single number, like 0, 1, 2, 3, 4, 5, 6, 7, 8, and 9. In base-10, there are 10 digits, numbered 0–9. The binary number system is sometimes called *base-2*, because there are two digits: 0 and 1.

> **NOTE**
> Computers use binary numbers because it is much easier to build circuits that detect binary numbers. When a bit is being sent over the wires in a processor, it is really a pulse of electricity, which can either be in a high voltage state (1) or a low voltage state (0). It is much harder to make circuits that detect more than two different voltages, and more expensive as well. People have made *trinary* computers before, but they didn't really work out.

Binary Numbers

Binary numbers are different from the normal numbers you have used all of your life. Whenever I am referring to a binary number, I will postfix it with the letter b so you know that it is a binary number.

Because there are only two digits in a binary number, all binary numbers look something like this: 1,0011,1010,0101b. Most people separate binary numbers in groups of four bits, and you will see why later on.

When you think about a decimal number, what do the digits actually mean?

Take the number 1,234 for example. Start from the right. The 4 is in the *ones* column, so that represents 4 items in the real world. The 3 in the number is in the *tens* column, which represents 30 items. The 2 in the number is in the *hundreds* column, and the 1 is in the *thousands* column.

So, the number 1,234 can be treated as the same as this:

1 * 1000 + 2 * 100 + 3 * 10 + 4 * 1.

Take a look at the base value of each column (the 1, 10, 100, and 1000 numbers). Notice any relationship between them? Each base number, going from right to left, is ten times the value as the previous number. You can also represent the number 1,234 in terms of 10 (since this is base-10): $1 * 10^3 + 2 * 10^2 + 3 * 10^1 + 4 * 10^0$.

> **NOTE**
> A three-digit base-10 number can represent numbers from 000 to 999. Likewise, a three-bit base-2 number can represent binary numbers from 000b to 111b. Of course, that number doesn't mean much to you, so here's an easy way to figure out the maximum value of a binary number with n digits: max = $2^n - 1$.

> **NOTE**
> Sometimes you want to be able to store negative numbers as well. These kinds of numbers are called *signed* numbers. Due to the way binary numbers are encoded (a method called *2s complement*), a signed number can store negative numbers from -2^{n-1} to 0 and positive numbers from 0 to $2^{n-1}-1$. For example, an 8-bit signed number can store numbers from -2^7 to $2^7 - 1$, which is –128 to 127.

Converting from Binary to Decimal

A binary number can be represented in the same way as a decimal number. Take the number 1011b, for example; if you take out the 10s in the digit expansion and replace them with 2s, you get this: $1 * 2^3 + 0 * 2^2 + 1 * 2^1 + 1 * 2^0$.

The base values for each digit are 8, 4, 2, and 1, so if you expand this expression, it becomes 1 * 8 + 0 * 4 + 1 * 2 + 1 * 1, or 8 + 2 + 1. 1011b is the same number as 11.

Converting from Decimal to Binary

This is a slightly more complex procedure than converting a binary number to decimal. To do this, you must create a long string of zeros, like in Figure A.1. It helps if you write the base value of each cell underneath it, like in the figure.

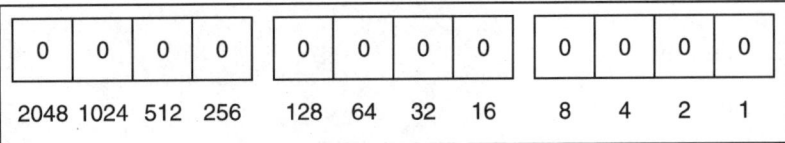

Figure A.1

This is an empty binary number. The base value for each cell is written underneath the cell.

After that, you need to first find the largest power of two that is smaller than or equal to the number. So if the number was 512, the largest power of two smaller than or equal to that is 512. However, if the number was 511, the largest power of two smaller than that is 256.

NOTE

Powers of two are numbers of the form 2^x where x is any number greater than or equal to 1.

As an example, I am going to show you how to convert the number 1,996 into binary. If you look at the base numbers in the figure (or if you have memorized them), you can see that the largest power of two that is smaller than 1,996 is 1,024. Place a 1 in the cell 1,024. After that, subtract 1,024 from 1,996, and you get 972. Now, repeat this process again, and keep repeating it until the number is 0. Figure A.2 shows this process.

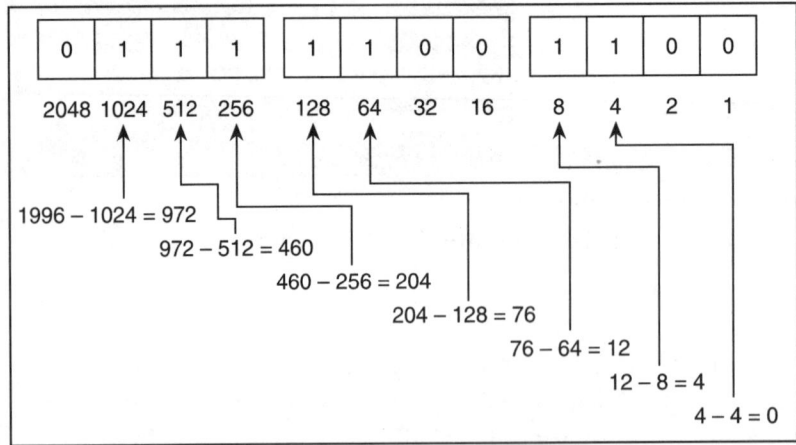

Figure A.2

This is the process of converting a decimal number into binary.

So the number 1,996 is the same as 111,1100,1100b.

Computer Storage

When dealing with computers, a single bit is usually too small to do anything useful with. So early on, computers bunched bits together in groups. First, they were grouped into bunches of four bits, and these were called *nibbles*. These could store numbers from 0–15 (remember, $2^4 - 1$ is $16 - 1$, or 15). Although they are more useful than just plain bits, only being able to use numbers from 0–15 is still quite limiting.

So then the *byte* was invented, which is a group of eight bits. They can store values from 0–255, which is a lot more useful.

> **NOTE**
> Bit, nibble, byte... get it?

There are no official names for bit-groups larger than 8 bits. However, on the Intel x86 platform, groups of 16 bits are called *words*, and groups of 32 bits are called *double words*. I don't believe there is an official name for anything past 32 bits, but the next logical expansion would be a 64-bit *quad word*. Figure A.3 shows the relative sizes of these structures.

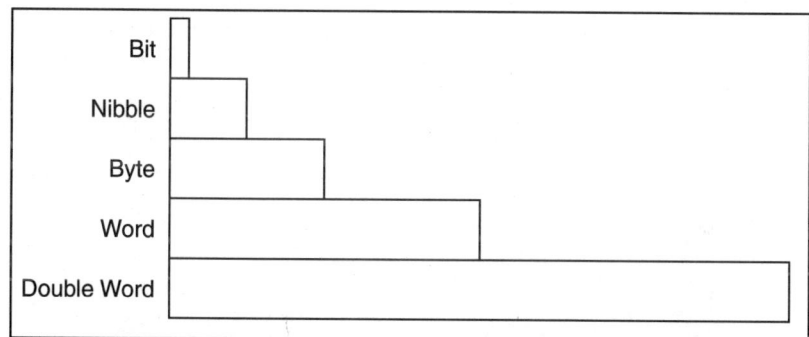

Figure A.3

Here are the relative sizes of the basic integer types.

Table A.1 shows the range of each of the types of numbers.

Table A.1 Integer Data Sizes

Type	Unsigned	Signed
Bit	0 to 1	-1 to 0*
Nibble	0 to 15	-8 to 7
Byte	0 to 255	-128 to 127
Word	0 to 65,535	-32,768 to 32,767
Double Word	0 to 4,294,967,296	-2,147,483,648 to 2,147,483,647
Quad Word	0 to 18,446,744,073,709,551,616	-9,223,372,036,854,775,808 to 9,223,372,036,854,775,807

*Negative bits aren't really useful for anything.

On x86 C++ compilers, some of these integer types correspond to built-in datatypes. Table A.2 shows you the C++ equivalents of the data sizes in Visual C++.

Table A.2 Datatype Sizes

C++ Datatype	Size
char	byte
short int	word
int	double word
long int	double word
float*	double word
double*	quad word

*floats and doubles aren't integer types, but they are stored in memory just like everything else. They just have a different encoding method. I have included them here for completeness.

Bitwise Math

There is an area of math involved with binary numbers called *Boolean math*, named after its inventor, James Boole. The math operates on bits, and there are four basic Boolean operators: *not, and, or,* and *xor*. The first one, *not*, is a *unary* operator, which means that it operates on only one bit at a time. The other three are *binary* operators, which means that they operate on two bits.

Table A.3 shows a listing of the results of the operators on different bit combinations.

Table A.3 The Not Operator

x	y	not x	x and y	x or y	x xor y
0	0	1	0	0	0
0	1	1	0	1	1
1	0	0	0	1	1
1	1	0	1	1	0

You can see from the table that the *not* operator simply flips the bit from 0 to 1 or from 1 to 0.

The *and* operator only returns 1 if both *x* and *y* are 1; it returns 0 if they are any other combination.

The *or* operator returns 1 if either *x* or *y* are 1 or if they are both 1. The only time it returns 0 is when both *x* and *y* are 0.

Finally, the *xor* operator only returns 1 when *x* and *y* are different, and it returns 0 when they are both the same.

Bitwise Math in C++

Unfortunately, because the lowest size data you have access to in C++ is a byte, using bitwise math is somewhat awkward.

When you perform a binary operator on a C++ integer type, it performs the operation on every bit of that integer. For example, if you use the *not* operator on a byte, every bit in that byte will be flipped.

Likewise, if you *and* two integers, the bits in the resulting integer will be the value of the *and* operator on each of the pairs of bits in the two original integers. Figure A.4 shows how this works.

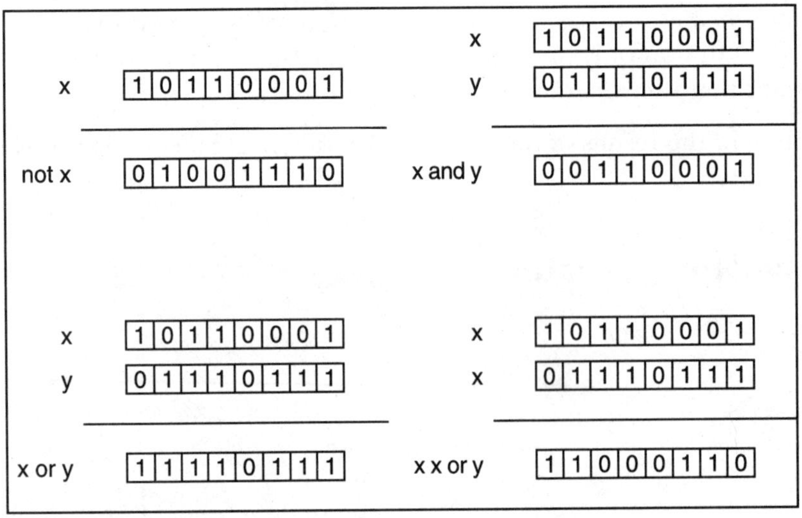

Figure A.4

Here are the four Boolean operators used on bytes in C++.

Every bit in the *not* operation is reversed. The only time any 1s appear in the result of the *and* operator are when both *x* and *y* had a 1 in the same position. Likewise, the only time any 0s appear in the result of the *or* operator is when both *x* and *y* had a 0 in the same position. Finally, the only time the result of the *xor* operator has a 1 in it is when the bits in *x* and *y* at the same positions were different.

Table A.4 shows the C++ symbols that are used for each of these operators.

Table A.4 C++ Boolean Operator Symbols

Operator	Symbol	Example
not	~	x = ~x
and*	&	x = x & y
or*	|	x = x | y
xor	^	x = x ^ y

*Do not confuse the & and | bitwise operators with the && and || logical operators used in conditional if-statements.

Bitshifting

There is one last topic that I must discuss when dealing with bits: *bitshifting*. Bitshifting is the act of taking the bits in a number and shifting them all left or right.

There are two types of bitshifting: You can either *shift left* or *shift right*. The idea behind this is amazingly simple. If you shift a number left, you just take every bit and move it to the left by one position. To shift a number right, you take every bit and move it a cell to the right.

Figure A.5 shows these operations in action.

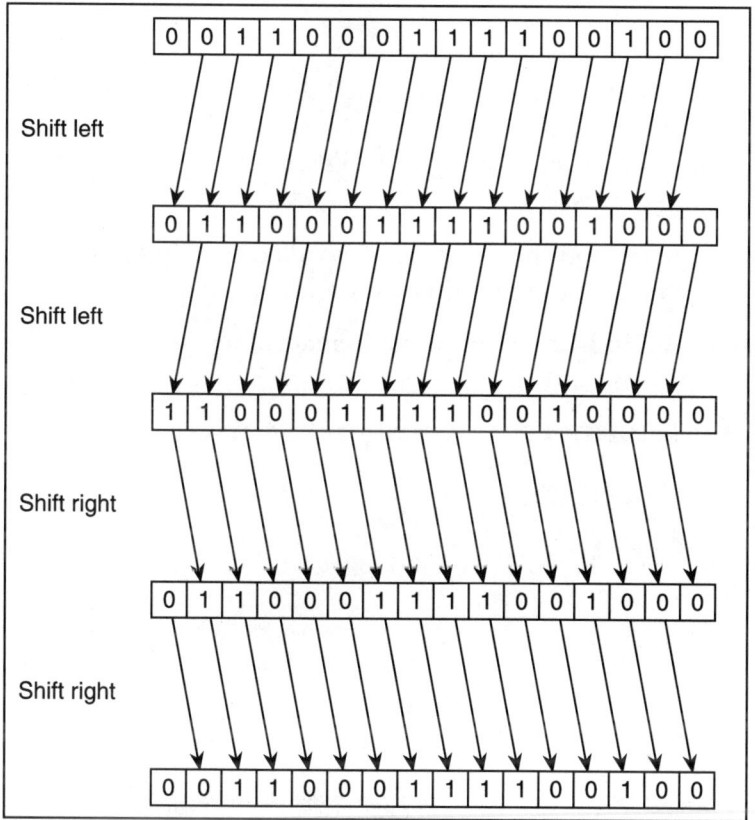

Figure A.5

This shows a number being shifted left twice and then right twice.

There are two things you need to watch out for when shifting. If there is a 1 in the left-most cell and you shift left, then that 1 is carried out and lost. The same thing happens when you shift right; the right-most bit is also shifted out and lost. This can cause some problems if you don't compensate for it.

So why would you want to bitshift numbers around? Chapter 4, "Bitvectors," uses it a lot to gain access to the individual bits in an integer. It turns out that bitshifting is also a very quick way to do some mathematical tricks, such as multiplying and dividing by powers of two.

Take the following binary number, for example: 1b. Now, shift it left by one space, and you get 10b. Shift it again, and you get 100b. These numbers in decimal are 1, 2, and 4. Each time you shift a number left by one bit cell, you multiply it by 2.

Likewise, shifting right has the effect of dividing by 2.

C++ gives you the ability to shift left and right at varying number of bits. Take the following code for example:

```
x = x << 2;
```

This is also called *shifting left*, and the << operator is called the *left shift operator*. That code takes the value of x and shifts each bit left by two places and then stores the result back into x. You can also do the same thing with right shifting:

```
x = x >> 3;
```

Likewise, this is called *shifting right*, and the >> operator is called the *right shift operator*. You can put any number you want to the right or even use a variable.

Table A.5 shows the effect of shifting a number in mathematical terms.

Table A.5 Shifting Numbers in Code and Math

Shift	Code	Mathematical
left	x = x << y	$x = x * 2^y$
right	x = x >> y	$x = x / 2^y$

So you can think of x = x << 3 as the same statement as x = x * 8 and x = x >> 5 as x = x / 32.

> **NOTE**
> Why would anyone use bitshifting for math when it is easier to type and read x = x * 4, as opposed to x = x << 2? It turns out that bitshifting is a lot faster than multiplication or division, and you can make many performance optimizations by utilizing it.

Standard C/C++ Functions Used in This Book

C/C++ is much more than just a programming language. It also comes with a huge collection of built-in functions, a lot of which I use throughout this book. I show you the most popular ones here as a quick reference guide.

All of the header files listed in this section come with your compiler and should always be accessible to you.

Basic Input/Output

None of the Examples in the book, located on the CD in the \examples\ folder, use a fancy graphical user interface. Instead, they use a plain console-based text *input and output (I/O) system*. C++ has a built-in text I/O system because when it was invented, *graphical user interfaces (GUI)* weren't very popular. Luckily for us, using this kind of I/O in C++ is very easy.

The very first thing you need to do when you want to use the I/O functions in C++ is to include the appropriate *header file*, which contains the code for the functions you want to use. This header file is called stdio.h.

> **NOTE**
> Newer revisions of the C++ standard have renamed this file to stdio, without the .h ending. The difference between these two files is that the functions and classes in stdio.h are in the *global namespace*, and everyone can access them. The functions and classes in stdio, however, are in the std namespace. If you don't know anything about namespaces, don't worry; this book doesn't use them much (only in Appendix D, "Introduction to the Standard Template Library," when using the STL). All of the Examples in this book use stdio.h, which almost every compiler supports.

Screen Output

This is a simple example that shows you how to put a piece of text on the screen:

```
cout << "Hello!" << endl;
```

The cout variable listed is defined in the stdio.h file. Previously, you've seen the << operator used in bitshifting; however, it has a completely different meaning in this case. When dealing with screen I/O, the operator is called the *stream insertion operator* instead of the *left shift operator*. That means that the program takes the string

"Hello!" and *streams* it into cout, which is just a big buffer that holds characters of text. The endl constant, when streamed into cout, tells the buffer to end the current line by inserting a *newline* character and then *flushing* the buffer. When the buffer is flushed, all of its contents are printed to the screen. If you don't flush cout with an endl, the contents of the buffer are never written to the screen.

If you just want to flush the buffer without inserting a newline character, then you can manually flush it like this:

```
cout.flush();
```

You can also print out any of the built-in datatypes, such as characters, floats, doubles, and integers, using cout:

```
float pi = 3.1415f;
int answer = 42;
char letter = (char)65;
cout << "The answer to life, the universe, and everything is ";
cout << answer << "." << endl;
cout << "The value of pi is " << pi << "." << endl;
cout << "The letter that has the ASCII value of 65 is ";
cout << letter << "." << endl;
```

When these lines of code are executed, the program will print:

```
The answer to life, the universe, and everything is 42.
The value of pi is 3.1415.
The letter that has the ASCII value of 65 is A.
```

There are a ton of formatting options available when using cout, but they aren't important for this book, so I do not cover them here.

Keyboard Input

C++ also provides an easy way to enter input by using the cin variable. Look at this example for a moment:

```
char string[64];
cin >> string;
```

This example gets a string of characters from the keyboard and puts it into the string. Input works the same way as output; cin is a buffer just like cout, and it only spits out information when it is flushed.

When you are typing into a console screen, the only time it is flushed is when you press Enter. However, using `cin` can sometimes give you unexpected results. For example, say you're executing the previous two lines of code. When the second line is executed, the program stops and waits until the input buffer is flushed. When the program stops, it just displays a blinking cursor. Say you typed in the following text:

```
Hello! How are you?
```

Normally, you would expect `string` to now contain "Hello! How are you?", but unfortunately, it will not. It will instead contain only the word "Hello!".

The `cin` variable will only flush the input buffer when you press Enter on the keyboard, but when it is executing the *stream extraction* (the opposite of stream insertion), it copies everything it has until it reaches *whitespace*. Whitespace is considered any character that is empty, such as a space, a tab, or a newline. When `cin` is copying the string over, it checks for whitespace, and when it finds some, it stops copying characters over into the string. There are ways around this, of course, but becaues console input is rarely used anymore and this book doesn't need spaces in the input strings, I do not cover that topic here.

So what happens to the rest of the string? Is it discarded and thrown away? No, the `cin` buffer keeps track of it, and whenever you try getting input again, it starts with the rest of the string.

For example, you might have this code later in the program:

```
char filename[64];
cin >> filename;
```

When the first call to `cin` was completed, the string "Hello!" was extracted from the buffer, but the buffer still contains "How are you?" After these lines of code, the `filename` string will now contain "How", which is probably not what you wanted. So, just beware that `cin` separates input by whitespace by default.

You can also use `cin` to get numbers from input, like this:

```
int x;
float y;
cin >> x;
cin >> y;
```

If you run this code with the following input:

```
10
3.1415
```

then the variables x and y will contain 10 and 3.1415, respectively. That's pretty much all you need to know for the input and output functions in this book.

File I/O

C++ provides a file library called *file stream* that is just like using `cin` and `cout`. However, I don't really like that method of file I/O, and it is usually much easier to use the file I/O functions included with C.

The C file functions and classes are located in the header file stdio.h.

The FILE Structure

The C file library has provided you with a structure that will point to a file, and it is called the `FILE` structure. Because it is just a plain structure, there really isn't much to be said about it.

Most of the time, you want to declare and use a pointer to a `FILE` structure because the C file functions all operate with pointers to the `FILE` structure. You declare one like this:

`FILE* f = NULL;`

You should always clear it to `NULL`, so that you know it isn't pointing to a file.

> **NOTE**
> Sometimes in this book, I use 0 in place of NULL. You should know that although almost every compiler in the world treats NULL as 0, they don't *have* to. In fact, some compilers could choose a random number out of nowhere and use that instead. So just be careful.

Opening a File

Opening a file is an easy task; all you need to do is call the `fopen` function. The function definition for `fopen` looks like this:

`FILE* fopen( const char* filename, const char* mode );`

You can see from the definition that it returns a pointer to a `FILE` structure and takes two strings as parameters. The first string is the name of the file, and the second string is the mode in which the file should be opened.

> **NOTE**
> The `const` keyword before both parameters says that the function will not modify the strings.

The list of different modes is listed in Table A.6.

Table A.6 fopen Modes

Mode	Meaning
r	This opens the file for reading. The fopen function will return 0 if the file cannot be found.
w	This opens the file for writing. If a file already exists with the same name, the file is destroyed and its contents are overwritten. This is a very dangerous option, and you should be careful using it so you don't accidentally overwrite anything important.
a	This opens the file for appending, which means that it will start writing data at the end of the file. If the file does not exist, then it will create it automatically.
r+	This opens the file for reading and writing. The fopen function will return 0 if the file does not exist.
w+	This mode is like the r+ mode, but it will create the file if it doesn't exist.
a+	This opens the file in reading and writing mode, but when you start writing to the file, it will write at the end of the file.
b*	This opens the file in *binary* mode.

*This mode can be combined with any of the first six modes. For example, you can combine this and reading mode by typing rb.

There are two types of files that the C file library supports: *ASCII* files and *binary* files. I rarely use ASCII files, and I don't know anyone who uses them often either, so it is somewhat confusing to me that ASCII mode is the default for fopen. When a file is in ASCII mode and you write out a newline character (ASCII value of 10), it will actually write out two characters to disk: a linefeed (10) and a carriage return (13). These two characters are pretty much useless in modern computers, but they are still supported. (Don't ask me why!)

> **NOTE**
> The linefeed/carriage return combination is a holdover from the bad old days when the very first computers were created and they used advanced typewriters to print their output (there weren't any monitors!). Whenever you wanted to advance to the next line of output, you had to do two things: you had to move the roller so that the paper would be moved up by one line (the linefeed command) and then you had to move the printing head, also known as a carriage, back to the left (the carriage return command). Now you know why ASCII is like this, and knowing is half the battle.

In binary mode, the data that is written to disk is the same as it is in the computer memory.

Perhaps the number one cause of file I/O errors is people accidentally opening their files in ASCII mode when they needed binary mode instead. Be careful when opening your files and make sure they are opened in the correct mode.

Writing to Disk

The `fwrite` function writes data to disk. Here is the function header:

```
size_t fwrite( const void* buffer, size_t size, size_t count, FILE* stream );
```

This function takes four variables and returns a piece of data of the type `size_t`, which is a built-in `typedef` for an integer.

The first parameter is a pointer to the place in memory where the function should start reading data that is going to be written to disk. The second parameter is the size of the type of data that is being written. For example, if you are writing integers, then you should pass `sizeof(int)` into that parameter.

The third variable is the number of items that you are saving to disk. If you're saving an array of integers, you should pass how many integers you're saving into the function.

Finally, the last function is a pointer to the file that the files will be written to.

The function returns the number of items that were actually written to disk. If the number is 0, or less than the `count` variable that you passed in, then that might mean you ran out of disk space

This function is demonstrated in a lot of the chapters in this book, most notably Chapters 3, "Arrays," 4, "Bitvectors," and 21, "Data Compression."

Reading from Disk

If you want to read data from the disk, you can use the `fread` function, which has the same interface as `fwrite`:

```
size_t fread( void* buffer, size_t size, size_t count, FILE* stream );
```

All of the parameters have the same meaning. The only difference is that the function reads data in from the file and stores it into the buffer.

This function returns the number of items that were read from the disk; if that number is smaller than you expected, you may be dealing with an incomplete file.

Closing the File

Finally, when you are done working with a file, you should close it so that other programs can use it.

> **NOTE**
>
> What actually happens when you try reading or writing to an open file from a different program varies from operating system to operating system. Some operating systems won't allow you to open a file that is already open, and others will let you only open it for reading. In general, it is a bad idea to try messing around with a file that is already open.

For this, you must use the `fclose` function. Here is the function header:

```
int fclose( FILE* stream );
```

This function simply closes the file and returns 0 if it was successfully closed. I'm really not sure that this can fail because I've *never* had it return anything but 0 before, but it is always wise to check for an error anyway.

Math Functions

C++ comes with a really large math library, which is quite useful, considering that most games use lots of math. All of the math functions are located in the math.h file.

Table A.7 lists most of the popular functions.

Table A.7 Math Functions

Function Name	Function Purpose
abs(int x)	Computes the absolute value of x. Basically converts negative numbers to positive and leaves positive numbers alone.
pow(double x, double y)	Computes the power of two numbers, x^y.
sqrt(double x)	Computes the square root of x.
sin(double x)	Computes the sine of x.
cos(double x)	Computes the cosine of x.
tan(double x)	Computes the tangent of x.
asin(double x)	Computes the arcsine (or inverse sine) of x.
acos(double x)	Computes the arccosine (or inverse cosine) of x.
atan(double x)	Computes the arctangent (or inverse tangent) of x.
exp(double x)*	Computes the exponential of x, which is e^x. (e is a mathematical constant equal to 2.718282...)
log(double x)*	Computes the natural logarithm of x, which is $\log_e x$. Note that you can compute the $\log_y x$ of any number by doing this: `log( x ) / log( y )`.
log10(double x)	Computes the base-10 logarithm of x, which is $\log_{10} x$.

*The mathematical constant e is used frequently in calculus equations and really doesn't have much to do with anything in this book. I mention base-2 logarithms a few times in the Tree chapters, so it might help to know how to calculate the value of a base-2 logarithm.

The Time Function

A few times throughout the book, I mention the `time` function that comes with the C standard library. This function is located in the file time.h, and here is its function header:

```
time_t time( time_t* timer );
```

The function takes a pointer to a `time_t` structure and fills it in with the current time. It also returns the same value, which is kind of redundant. This is why I always pass 0 into the function whenever it is called.

The `time_t` structure is really just a `typedef` for an integer. This return value from this function is the number of seconds that have passed since midnight on January 1, 1970.

The Random Functions

The random number generation functions are stored in the stdlib.h file. Two of them are used throughout the book, and Chapter 22, "Random Numbers," focuses on them exclusively.

> **NOTE**
> The `time_t` type is a `signed long int`, which is 32 bits. Normally, a 32-bit number can hold up to four billion seconds, but because this is signed, it can hold only up to two billion seconds. Why did they make `time_t` signed? I don't know, maybe they wanted to be able to go back in time or something. Unfortunately, this poses a very large problem, one that will probably cause more problems than the Y2K scare of 2000. Two billion seconds represent a span of time that is 68 years long, and because the counting started in 1970, that time is almost half over already. In the year 2038, the standard system timer for most computer programs will roll over and reset itself.

The srand Function

The `srand` function is short for *seed random generator*. I cover random seeds in Chapter 22, so here I will just show you the function header:

```
void srand( unsigned int seed );
```

The function takes a number and sets that as the random seed. The most popular seed value is the value you get from the `time` function discussed previously.

The rand Function

The `rand` function is also discussed completely in Chapter 22, so I will only post the header here:

```
int rand( void );
```

This function returns a random integer from 0 to `RAND_MAX`, which is a constant defined by the compiler.

Exceptions and Error Handling

Although I don't use exceptions anywhere in the book, they are mentioned quite a few times in reference to error checking code.

Before exceptions came along, you had two basic methods to check for errors in your programs. You could use the ASSERT debug macro, or you could have your functions return an error code.

Assertions

When you use an assert macro, your code will look like this:

```
ASSERT( condition );
```

This line of code is only executed in *debug* mode in most compilers, which is a special compiling mode that allows you to debug the program. Most compilers ignore this line of code when they are in *release* mode.

Whenever this line is executed and the condition evaluates to false, the program ends, and it usually spits out a message like "debug assertion error in file blah.cpp at line 345."

This method can be useful sometimes because it halts right when it detects an error. Of course, it is also a pain in the butt because many times you cannot repeat the circumstances that caused the assertion to fail.

Return Codes

Sometimes when you detect an error, you don't want the program to just shut down. So you want to tell the function that called the current function that an error occurred. Usually, this looks like this:

```
if( error )
    return error_code;
```

This method is quite popular, mainly because it was the only flexible method to detect errors for a very long time.

Unfortunately, it has big problems. First of all, you need to make your functions so that they can return error codes. What happens if you're returning integers from a function? Do you set one number aside as the error code? What happens if the function accidentally generates that same number as its result and did not mean it as an error?

Also, you end up with huge gobs of ugly code, 90 percent of which is dedicated to checking for errors:

```
if( function() == error )
    // handle error
if( anotherfunction() == error )
    // handle error
if( yetanotherfunction() == error )
    // handle error
if( thelastfunction() == error )
    // handle error
```

If you've ever programmed in DirectX, you will be very familiar with this method because every DirectX function returns a code, which can be an error or a success code.

Exceptions

Finally, *exceptions* allow you to code in a cleaner fashion. An exception is sort of like an error code, except that you don't return it. Let me show you an example:

```
void function()
{
    // do stuff
    if( error )
        throw exception();
    // continue to do stuff
}
```

When the exception is thrown, the function immediately halts and returns to the function that called it. What happens then? The function that called function will probably look like this:

```
try
{
    // do lots of stuff
    function();
    // do more stuff
}
catch( exception )
{
    // handle error
}
```

There are two new keywords defined that deal entirely with exceptions: the `try` keyword and the `catch` keyword. When you start a `try` block, the code inside of the block is monitored for exceptions. If any of the code inside throws an exception, the execution immediately jumps to the `catch` block, which will then handle the error.

The benefits of this method are many, because it allows you to execute all the code within the `try` block and assume that it will all work correctly. If anything fails, it is handled by a separate piece of code.

One more thing needs to be noted: The `exception` used in the examples is actually a class, defined in the file `exception` (it has no extension, and it should come with your compiler). C++ allows you to create your own exception classes that store custom information about what kind of error occurred and throw them instead of the standard `exception`. In the previous line of code, `throw exception()`, you may have wondered about the parentheses after the class name. Those are there because you're really calling the constructor of the `exception` class.

When you catch an exception, you can catch specific types of exceptions. For example:

```
catch( exception e )
{
    // handle regular exception
}
catch( userexception u )
{
    // handle custom exception
}
```

This code catches two types of exceptions. If you throw an exception of type `exception`, the first segment will execute. If you create your own `userexception` class and throw that, the second segment will execute.

A final thing to note is that the `e` and the `u` in the previous code segment are optional (the `e` wasn't in the first catch block you saw). The `e` and the `u` are the actual instances of the exception, and you can use them to get data about what happened. If you don't put a name for the exceptions in there, like in the first catch example, then you only know what kind of exception was thrown, and you cannot access any of the data in the exception.

> **NOTE**
> If you don't have a try block in a function and something it calls causes an exception to be raised, then the exception is passed up along the hierarchy until it is caught or the program exits. This is called *stack unwinding* (see Appendix B, "The Memory Layout of a Computer Program," for more information on the function-call stack). I'm sure you've seen an error in a program before that looks just like this: `Unhandled exception in module blah`.

Why C++?

Let me tell you, C++ is one of the most controversial programming languages in the industry at the moment. Everyone seems to have a strong opinion on it, and most of them fall into one of two categories: You either love C++ or hate C++.

So why is C++ so controversial? It has to do with its origins. C++ didn't just magically appear one day. The creator wanted to take the most popular programming language of the day, which was C, and apply some of the new object-oriented concepts to it. The end result is that C++ is essentially the same language as C, but with many features added to it.

However, many people who program never want to change their ways and stuck to C when C++ was unveiled, and still do so today. Of course, there are places where programming in C is preferred, such as low-level systems programming, but niches like that are becoming few and far between.

Unfortunately, C++ is a pretty complex language. No single person could learn the entire language inside and out in a reasonable amount of time. This is probably the largest factor of keeping people away from C++. I'll admit, some of this stuff is pretty darn hard to learn. In fact, one of the largest problems with C++ is that most of the basic stuff in the language doesn't even begin to make sense until you've learned the more complex things. C++ is definitely a big-picture language. There really is no easy way to start at the bottom and work your way up. Luckily for you, however, I will not focus on any of the really deep features of C++. This is a data structures book, after all. I will only use what I think is important to get the points across to you in the easiest way possible.

Up until very recently, the realm of game programming has stayed mostly with C. After all, they had good reasons to:

- C compilers were generally faster than the relatively new C++ compilers.
- C is a tried-and-true language.
- C allowed you to interface more efficiently with low-level hardware.
- C++ is complex. C is much easier to learn.
- Older games were simple and didn't need much organization.

Look at some recent games, however. Games are no longer little one-man projects that keep a person entertained for a few hours. Games are beginning to become entire life simulators! Companies spend millions of dollars on games nowadays, and they want a return on their investment. Programming teams are made up of a dozen or more people, and thus, an efficient method of programming must be utilized.

C++ is generally considered one of the best languages to program in group settings, and that is the main reason many people are switching to C++. However, that is not the main reason I want to use C++ in this book.

Data structures are an object-oriented concept. C++ is an object-oriented language. Thus it seems perfectly natural to use a language that was designed for objects to describe objects to you.

Class Topics

You should already know something about classes if you're reading this book, but some class features used in this book are a little complex, and you might not be entirely familiar with them.

Constructors

Every class has a special function called a *constructor*, which *constructs* the object. The main reason for this is to assure that your classes always have correct data in them.

For example, if you've ever declared a new integer in a release-mode project and then printed its contents, you may notice that it contains a seemingly random number. When memory is deleted, the program really doesn't do anything with it; it just tells the operating system that the memory is now free and can be used for something else. When you ask the system for memory again, it gives you that memory, but it still contains the information that was in it before it was deleted.

So the program calls a constructor implicitly whenever you create a new object (the only exceptions are the built-in numerical types, like `int`, `float`, and `char`).

The compiler automatically creates a default constructor for you, which does absolutely nothing. Take the following class, for example:

```
class Foo
{
public:
    int x;
};
```

Now, whenever this class is constructed like this, nothing happens:

```
Foo f1;
Foo* f2 = new Foo();
Foo f3 = Foo();
```

All three of these functions are valid, and the second two make reference to a constructor call, even though there isn't one. C++ says that every class will have a constructor, so it just pretends that there is one and doesn't do anything.

Now, later on, you want to add a constructor to the class Foo:

```
class Foo
{
public:
    Foo() { x = 42; }
    int x;
};
```

Now that there is a constructor, all three of the Foo declarations above will call it. All three Foos will have their x value set to 42. This is called an *implicit* constructor because it is called implicitly whenever the class is created.

There are other types of constructors available, too—ones that take parameters:

```
class Foo
{
public:
    Foo() { x = 42; }
    Foo( int y ) { x = y; }
    int x;
};
```

This class has added a new constructor, one with a parameter. Now you can construct the class in many different ways:

```
Foo f1;
Foo* f2 = new Foo();
Foo f3 = Foo();
Foo f4( 5 );
Foo* f5 = new Foo( 5 );
Foo f6 = Foo( 42 );
```

The first three methods call the first constructor, and the second two methods call the second constructor.

> **NOTE**
> Note that most compilers treat the constructor lines of f1 and f3 as the same thing. The same goes with the constructor lines of f4 and f6.

There is another form of syntax used in constructors. Here is an example:

```
class Foo()
{
public:
    Foo()
        : x( 42 ) {};
    int x;
}
```

The colon after the constructor name starts something that is called an *initializer list*. This is just a list, separated by commas, that calls the constructors of the member variables. This is the only way you can initialize *references* inside a class, and it is also the only way to initialize a member class that doesn't have a default constructor. This is used a few times in the book, like in Chapter 8, "Hash Tables," and Chapter 14, "Priority Queues and Heaps."

Destructors

A *destructor* is a special function of a class that is called whenever an object goes out of scope or is deleted. Most of the time, you will probably have complicated classes that allocate memory when they are constructed (the Array class from Chapter 3 is one example), so when the class itself goes out of scope or is deleted, you want the memory it has allocated to be deleted as well. Here is an example of a class that allocates something in a constructor and then deletes it in the destructor:

```
class Foo
{
public:
    Foo() { x = new int; }
    ~Foo()  { delete x; }
```

```
    int* x;
};
```

The class now has a pointer to an integer, and when it is created, a new integer from the free store is allocated and stored into x. (See Appendix B for more information about the free store.)

When the object goes out of scope or is destructed, the destructor is called, and it deletes the integer. Look at the following code:

```
void function()
{
    Foo f1;                     // constructor called on f1
    Foo* f2 = new Foo();        // constructor called on f2
    delete f2;                  // destructor called on f2
}                               // destructor called on f1
```

When the function ends, the destructor for f1 is automatically called because it is a local variable.

Operator Overloads

A neat new addition to C++ is the ability to create your own custom operator functions. This is a pretty cool feature, but it has the ability to be abused quite easily.

Say you create your own fractional number class, with a numerator and a denominator:

```
class Fraction
{
public:
    int numerator;
    int denominator;
};
```

Now, you can create fractions using this class, but it is a little bit difficult to use the standard mathematical operations using it. You can't, for example, do this:

```
// one, two, and three are all Fractions:
three = one * two;
```

Normally, you'd want that to multiply those two fractions together and store the result into the third one. Unfortunately, this code will not work. Operator overloads can fix this, though. This next function is an operator overload that will over load the * operator of the Fraction class so that the compiler will automatically call the function whenever it sees one * two.

```
Fraction& operator* ( const Fraction& p_frac )
{
    Fraction result;
    result.numerator = numerator * p_frac.numerator;
    result.denominator = denominator * p_frac.denominator;
    return result;
}
```

> **NOTE**
> The operator function, to work correctly in its present form, must be defined inside the class definition. If you wanted to define it outside of the class, you would need to add a Fraction:: in front of the operator*.

The function takes a single fraction reference as its parameter (see Appendix B as to why you should always try to pass references into functions), and the result is a reference to another fraction.

Whenever the compiler sees this code in the program:

```
three = one * two;
```

It automatically treats that as this:

```
three = one.operator*( two );
```

The call to operator* is made on the object on the left, and the parameter is passed into the function, which returns a new fraction.

Almost every operator in the C++ language can be overloaded, and Table A.8 has a list of them.

Table A.8 Operators That Might Be Overloaded

+	-*	/	%	
+=	-=	*=	/=	%=
&	|	^	>>	<<
&=	|=	^=	>>=	<<=
&&	||	!	!=	==
<	>	<=	>=	=
,	~	[]	()	->
->*	new	delete	++	--

Some operators have two meanings. They are the -, +, *, and & operators. As unary operators, they don't have a parameter, and they are the *negate operator, positive operator, dereference operator,* and *address-of operator*. When they have a parameter, they become unary operators and are the *subtraction operator, addition operator, multiplication operator,* and *binary-and operator*.

There are some operators that you may never use in real life, such as the comma operator and the unary+ operator. I included them only to be complete.

Conversion Operators

Conversion operators are another neat feature of C++ that allows you to expand upon classes and treat them as other classes implicitly. Say, for example, you create your own string class.

```
class String
{
public:
    char m_string[64];
};
```

Later on in the program, you want to copy the string over into a regular char* array, using the strcpy function. So you type in the following lines of code and hit compile:

```
String string1;
char string2[128];
strcpy( string2, string1 );
```

Bzzzt! Error! The compiler has no idea how to convert a String into a char*, so that last line will cause an error.

This can be fixed, and you can tell the compiler how to convert a String into a char* using a conversion operator:

```cpp
operator char* ()
{
    return m_string;
}
```

The syntax is: operator <typename> (). Because the string in the class is really a char* to begin with, all you need to do is return the string, and the strcpy function will automatically use that as its parameter!

The This Pointer

There is a special pointer that is available in every class function, called the this operator. It essentially returns a pointer to the current class that the function is in.

For example, look at this piece of code:

```cpp
class Foo
{
public:
    Foo() { this->x = 42; }
    int x;
};
```

The this pointer is just a pointer to the current class.

Inline Functions

When programming, the word *inline* has two meanings. The first meaning is when you define a function within the class definition:

```cpp
class Foo
{
public:
    void DoSomething() { x = 10; }
    int x;
};
```

The DoSomething function is defined inline.

However, there is another meaning to the word: the `inline` keyword in the C++ language.

When a function uses the `inline` keyword, it looks like this:

```
inline int Function()
{
    return 50;
}
```

The meaning of the word *inline* here is completely different. In this case, it is telling the compiler that this function is pretty small and should be directly inserted into code that uses this function. For example, if the compiler sees this code later on:

```
x = Function() * y;
```

It will automatically turn it into this:

```
x = 50 * y;
```

The `inline` keyword essentially tells the compiler that the function is so small that it really shouldn't be a function, but it is used so often that you don't want to copy and paste it into a hundred different places in your program.

This has the effect of removing the function-call overhead that you get with un-inlined functions (see Appendix B for more information about function call overhead) and usually makes things faster.

There is one caveat, however. The compiler only takes the `inline` keyword as a *suggestion*. It doesn't have to actually inline the function. If the compiler thinks that the function is too large to be inlined (inlining is only really beneficial when the function is really small), then it will ignore your command and implement it as a regular function.

> **TIP**
>
> Most of the small accessor functions in C++ classes (the ones you learn about in Chapter 9, "Tying It Together: The Basics") should be inlined. The number one argument against accessor functions is that they are slower than direct access to variables, but inlining them effectively destroys that argument. None of the data structures in this book have inlined functions, but if you decide to use them on your own, you may want to add the `inline` keyword to the smaller functions.

Function Pointers

Function pointers are one of those features in C++ that are life savers, but they will also cause you to start cussing at your compiler. The idea of a function pointer is simple: It is simply a pointer that points to a function, rather than a variable.

Using function pointers, you can have a variable that keeps track of a function and then replace it with a different function while the program is still running. I use function pointers quite a bit in this book in Chapters 8, 13, 14, and 20.

Unfortunately, their syntax is *ugly*. The basic structure of a function pointer declaration looks like this:

```
returntype ( *functionname )( parameters );
```

Although this doesn't look so ugly now, it does get worse. Let me show you an example of how to use function pointers. Pretend that you are developing a game that uses a lot of advanced features on the newest video cards, but you also want the game to run on regular video cards. Here are the two different drawing functions:

```
void DrawNormal();
void DrawAdvanced();
```

Now, during the game, you have a choice. You might do this every time you draw a new frame:

```
if( videocard == advanced )
    DrawAdvanced();
else
    DrawNormal();
```

This isn't a very good idea because you know that the video card will not change in the middle of a game, so you will always be calling one function all the time. Instead, you can create a function pointer at the beginning of the game:

```
void (*DrawFunction)( void );
if( videocard == advanced )
    DrawFunction = DrawAdvanced;
else
    DrawFunction = DrawNormal;
```

Then, during the game, all you need to do is this:

DrawFunction();

Isn't that neat? There are a few rules, however. A function pointer has a fixed return type and argument list, so it can only point to functions that have the same return type and argument list.

Also, regular function pointers can only point to global functions; they cannot point to functions inside of a class. Function pointers that point inside of a class are an entirely different topic. In fact, the syntax for function pointers within classes is even uglier. Because I don't use them at all in this book, there isn't a need to go over them here.

Conclusion

As I have stated many times before, C++ is a complicated language. This is an intermediate level book, so it is assumed that you know most of the C++ that I use in this book. However, it is reasonable to assume that you might have forgotten how to use some of the features in this appendix. While writing this book, I had to look up syntax for some of the features many times (I can never remember the syntax for function pointers!), so don't feel bad if you keep flipping back to this appendix to look something up.

APPENDIX B

The Memory Layout of a Computer Program

B. The Memory Layout of a Computer Program

To fully understand how a program works, you must first understand how it is structured. This is one topic that is almost always lacking in computer books, yet I consider it very important. Knowing how a program is structured is essential to understanding how to optimize a program, and this is especially important for game programming.

The Memory Sections

I will be dealing with four main memory sections in this appendix:

- The code memory
- The global memory
- The stack
- The free store

When a program is run by the operating system, the operating system creates the first three sections of memory for the program automatically. Every program in memory has its own code memory, global memory, and stack memory. The free store is a separate area of memory that is shared by all programs at the same time, depending on the operating system. Conceptually, the free store takes up all of the memory that isn't being used by the other segments and the operating system memory. See Figure B.1 for a diagram showing the memory of a computer that is running two programs.

> **NOTE**
> Different operating systems handle the free store in different ways. For example, in Windows, the operating system gives each program its own little free store, and if the program fills it up, it gives more memory to the program (if it is available). However, it is much easier to think of the free store as a gigantic area in memory that all programs have access to.

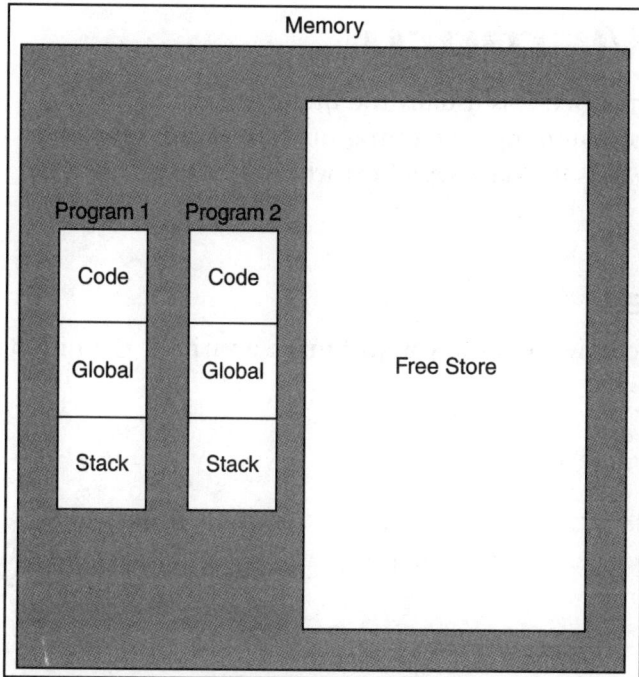

Figure B.1

This is a sample memory layout for a computer that has two programs running.

The Code Memory

When you write a program in C++, it is just text stored in a .cpp file. The computer has no idea that this is a program. To make this text into a program, you tell your compiler to convert the program into commands that the processor understands. When the operating system runs the program, it loads the program code into the code memory (also known as the *code segment*).

When the program is running, the computer copies portions of the code from the code segment into the instruction cache (a little memory chip on the processor), which is the place the processor runs the code from.

Because the code is stored in memory, you can do some neat (and potentially dangerous) tricks with it and modify the code manually while the program is running! Of course, to do something like this, you need to use assembly language. I wouldn't recommend trying to do something like this, however, unless you are an assembly language master, but even then you have a chance of messing up the code so that it does something malicious. I only mention this ability here to show you that the program is actually stored in memory.

The Global Memory

Everyone is familiar with global memory. It is usually the first place you store data in memory when you first start programming. Each program has its own global memory section (sometimes known as the data segment) where all the global data of a program is stored.

Global Variables

When you define a global variable in a program, you just make a variable definition outside of any class or function:

```
int g_integer = 5;
char g_text[] = "012345678";
```

A global variable is then accessible by every function in the program, as Figure B.2 illustrates. Every time g_integer is referenced in the program, the computer looks at the same variable in global memory.

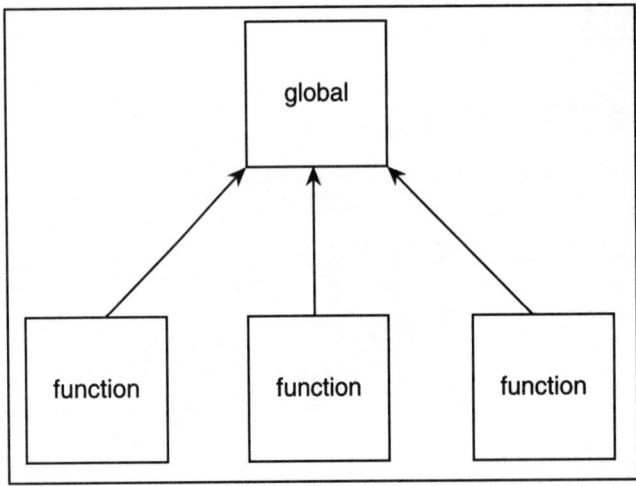

Figure B.2

Any function or class has direct access to global variables.

When you compile a program with global variables, the compiler actually creates a whole area in the file where the values of the global variables are placed. Figure B.3 shows how the actual program file is laid out (different implementations might use different formats, but the concepts are all the same).

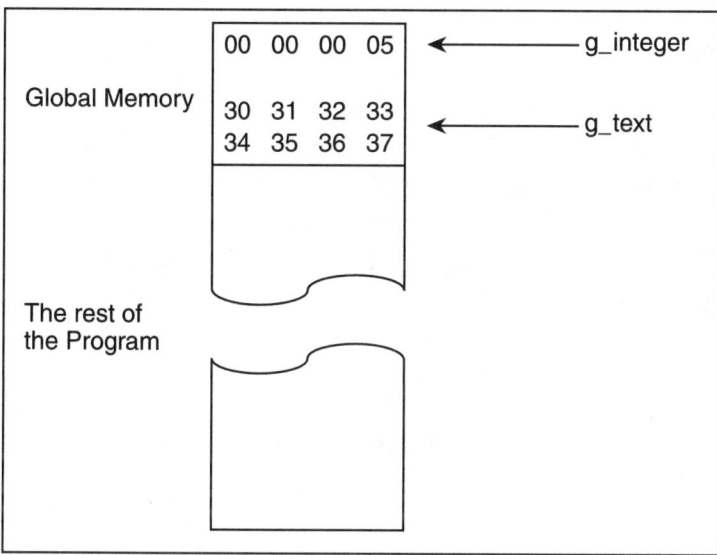

Figure B.3

This is the file layout of a program that uses `g_integer` and `g_text`. All numbers are in hexadecimal. The hexadecimal value 30 is the ASCII equivalent of the character 0, and so on.

So the operating system creates the global memory section when it loads a program, and it loads all the global data from the file and places it into the global memory section.

> **NOTE**
>
> When you don't initialize a global variable, some compilers will still make room for them in the compiled program file anyway. I remember using an uninitialized global array that was about 4 megs in size once, and I could not understand why my program files ended up being 4 megs! Of course, I didn't find this out until much later, so I'm hoping to alert you on this little occurrence. Some compilers have an option that allows you to prevent this from happening.

Static Variables

When you define a static variable within a function, it is also placed in the global memory section. Although static variables reside in the global memory section, they can only be accessed by the function that they are defined in. This is a C++ feature. With some assembly hacks, you should be able to access static function data outside of the function it is defined in, but I would recommend against that because it defeats the purpose behind static data and you have no guarantees that the static data will be where you think it will be.

The Stack

Up until now, the memory sections have been simple and straightforward. The stack in a computer program is probably the most complex part, though. If you are unfamiliar with how a stack works, please familiarize yourself with Chapter 7, "Stacks and Queues," first.

Every program has a stack, but it hasn't always been this way. Back in the bad old days, when memory was scarce, people did whatever they could to conserve memory.

Local Variables

Old languages used to store local function variables in the global memory section. What does this mean? Consider the following example:

```
void function()
{
    int variable;
    variable = 5;
    // do stuff with variable here
    function();
}
```

Although this is a stupid example that leads to an infinite loop, you need to examine what actually happens. The local `variable` is stored in global memory and then set to 5. Pretend that the function does other things to `variable` where the comment is. Now, the function calls itself, and then it resets `variable` back to 5, because the function references the same exact place in memory. Without a stack, this function works exactly as if `variable` was static. Obviously, this would cause a lot of problems with recursive algorithms (see Chapter 10, "Recursion," if you are unfamiliar with recursion), so you need a way to be able to have many copies of the variable at the same time.

Because there is no way for a program to be able to determine how many times `function` will be called at the same time, you need some sort of flexible memory. The stack data structure comes to your rescue.

When a function is called and it is told to create a local variable, like the `function` example, the computer puts the local variables onto the stack. Figure B.4 shows the stack local variable stack for the `function` example.

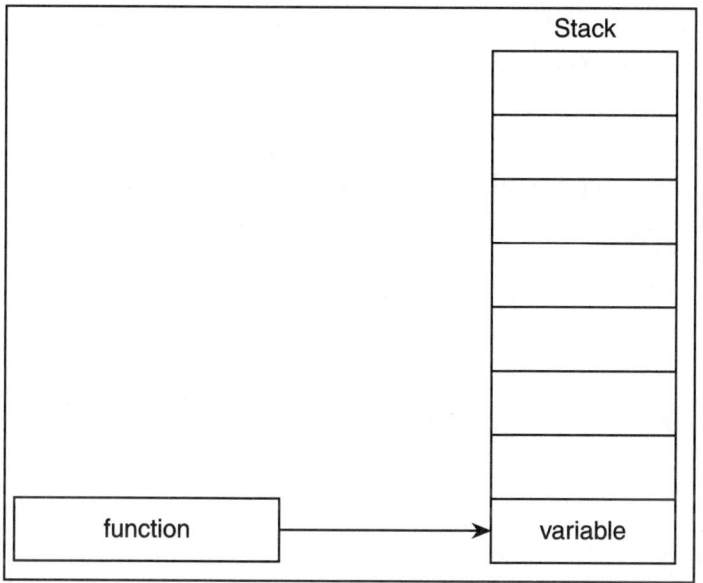

Figure B.4

The local variable is placed on the current top of the stack. Because this particular stack is empty, it is placed on the bottom.

Now, whenever `variable` is referenced, the computer accesses that particular place on the stack. The neat stuff happens when you call `function` within itself: A different version of `variable` is placed on top of the stack. Figure B.5 shows this.

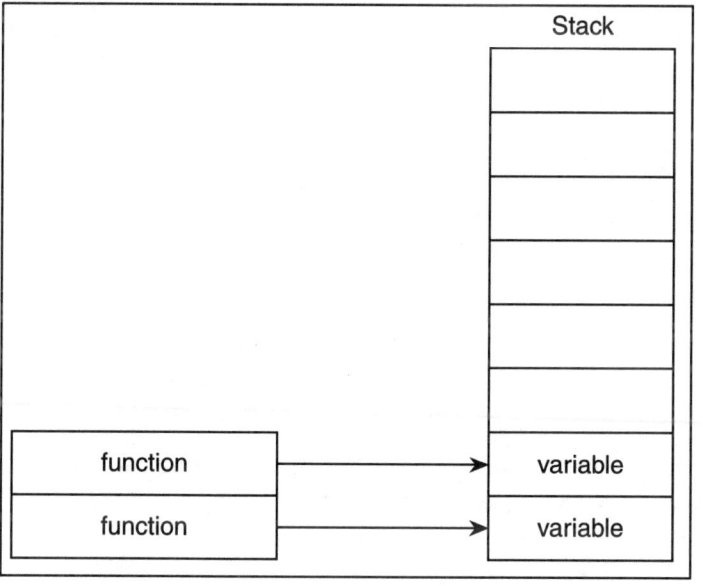

Figure B.5

When `function` is called again, it creates another instance of `variable` on the stack.

Now each instance of the function can use its local variables without worrying about modifying global data.

When the second function exits, its version of variable is popped off of the stack, and the end result looks exactly like Figure B.4.

Parameters

Parameters to functions are also placed on the stack. They are pushed onto the stack before the local variables are. Consider the following function:

```
void function( int parameter )
{
    int local;
}
```

When this function is called, the program places the parameter on the stack, and then it places the local variable on the stack, like Figure B.6 shows.

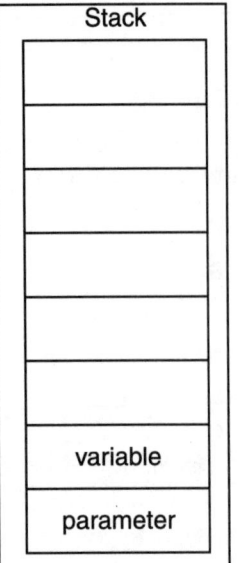

Figure B.6
This shows a parameter and a local variable on the stack.

When a function exits, the local variables are popped off first, before the parameters.

> **TIP**
> When you pass a large structure into a function using the pass-by-value method, the entire structure is copied onto the stack. If you call this function a lot, the computer is forced to do tons of work just moving data around. This is the main reason why pass by reference is much more efficient for large structures. When you pass by reference, the only thing that is copied onto the stack is a pointer to the structure, which is much smaller than the entire structure.

Return Values

When a function returns a value from a function, it is also placed onto the stack. However, the return value is placed on the stack even before the parameters are placed on the stack. The computer makes space on the stack for the return value, even though the value won't be filled in until the function returns.

Take the following function, for example:

```
int function( int parameter )
{
    int local = 3;
    return 6;
}
```

When this function is called, these events occur:

1. An empty integer placeholder is pushed onto the stack (return value).
2. The parameter is pushed onto the stack.
3. The local value is pushed onto the stack.
4. The value 6 is placed into the return value cell on the stack.
5. The local variable and the parameter are popped off the stack.
6. The calling function can use the return value because it is on top of the stack.

Figure B.7 illustrates this process, using the value 4 as the parameter.

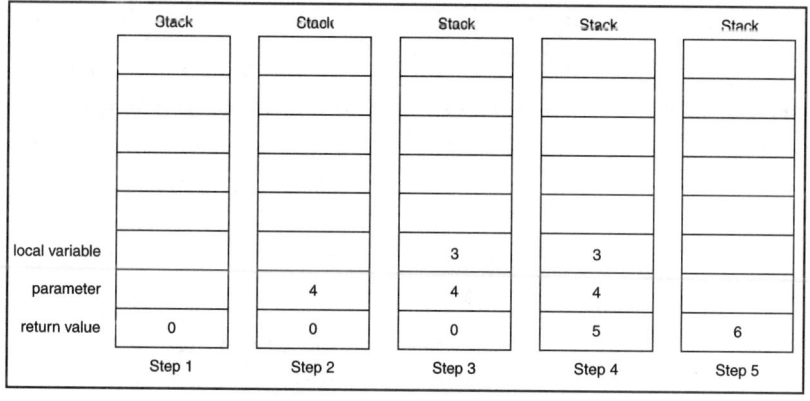

Figure B.7

This is an example of calling a function with a return value, a parameter, and a local variable.

> **CAUTION**
> What happens when you try returning a pointer or a reference to a local variable or a parameter? You end up with some big bugs! If you try to return a pointer to a local variable, the pointer will not be valid, because the computer pops off the local variables when it returns. So you end up with a pointer to memory that isn't valid anymore!

> **NOTE**
> There are other things that go on the stack besides the local variables and parameters shown, such as the return address of the function that called the current function. These things are different for every system, and you should only be concerned about them if you are programming in assembly language. For high-level programming, you only need to know that local variables, parameters, and return values are placed on the stack.

The Free Store

Sometimes this section of memory is known as the *heap*, but I don't want to confuse this with the data structure of the same name (they are totally unrelated).

Whenever you use dynamic memory (created with either `malloc` or `new`), the computer places this memory on the free store. The *free store* is basically just a huge area of memory that can be used for anything you want it to.

The free store acts just like global memory, except that you can create new data and then delete it later, whereas you cannot create or delete globals while the program is running.

You should be aware of a few things about the free store. First of all, allocating memory takes time. The computer needs to find a place in memory where it can fit what you want, and this doesn't happen instantly.

> **TIP**
> Don't allocate and delete memory rapidly; this is a very slow operation.

The other thing you need to worry about is memory leaks. When you allocate memory from the free store and then never delete it, you end up with a memory leak. The computer will think that you're using the memory, even if you aren't, and this will cause large problems if the program slowly leaks all of its memory.

> **CAUTION**
> Always delete memory that you allocate from the free store.

Conclusion

If you didn't know much about how memory is arranged in a computer, hopefully you know now. This is an important topic when you're trying to optimize how a computer works. Quite often, someone will pass a huge data structure into a function that is called many times in a program, and not even know that this is going to slow down the computer.

You should walk away from this appendix remembering the following three points:

- Function calls take time to complete because they need to put all of the parameters and other data on the stack.
- Never pass entire classes into a function. Use pointers or references instead.
- Remember to delete all memory that you allocate in the free store.

APPENDIX C

Introduction to SDL

When I was trying to figure out how to demonstrate the examples for this book, I had originally just planned on making everything use the text-based console. How boring!

I quickly realized that I needed to use a graphical API to demonstrate the nifty demonstrations you see throughout the book. I am very familiar with DirectX, but DirectX is a fairly complex and low-level API.

OpenGL is even worse because it has no 2D portion.

Then, along comes my pal Ernest Pazera, and he introduces me to a little game API called the *simple directmedia layer*, or *SDL* for short.

SDL is separated into many different components, such as graphics, sound, input, network, and so on. Only three of these components are used in this book: the video component, the input component, and the timer component.

The Licensing

SDL is a free open-source API that is licensed using the *GNU Lesser General Public License (LGPL)*. You can find this license at the URL http://www.gnu.org/copyleft/lgpl.html.

You can always find the newest version of the SDL library at the URL http://www.libsdl.org/ and a whole collection of add-on modules at http://www.libsdl.org/libraries.php.

To use the SDL library in your own projects, you must comply with the LGPL license, which states:

> *To comply with this license, you must give prominent notice that you use the Simple DirectMedia Layer library, and that it is included under the terms of the LGPL license. You must include a copy of the LGPL license.*
>
> *You must also do one of the following:*

1. Include the source code for the version of SDL that you link with, as well as the full source or object code to your application so that the user can relink your application,
2. Include a written offer, valid for at least three years, to provide the materials listed in option 1, charging no more than the cost of providing this distribution,
3. Make the materials listed in option 1 available from the same place that your application is available.

The most common way to comply with the license is to dynamically link with SDL, and then include the SDL source code and appropriate notices with your application.

This basically states that you must include the source code of SDL with all of your projects, as well as the text of the LGPL license. In addition, you need to make available your source code or, if you don't want to include your source code, the object code that your compiler produces (all those .o files that appear when your compiler compiles your project) is okay, too. As long as people can re-link your project, you comply with the license.

Setting Up SDL

You can always download the newest version of SDL on the SDL Web site. During development of this book, I used SDL Version 1.2.3, but a new version was developed halfway through (Version 1.2.4). Version 1.2.4 is the version I've included on the CD for you.

The Files

Table C.1 shows the directories on the CD where the SDL files are located and what is located in those directories.

Table C.1 SDL Files on the CD

Directory	Contents
\Source Code\	This holds all of the source code to SDL in .zip format.
\Development Libraries\	This holds all of the files you need to develop SDL applications.
\Development Libraries\BeOS\	The development library for BeOS.
\Development Libraries\Linux\	The development libraries for Linux, which includes three versions: one for PowerPC processors, one for x86 processors, and one for the PlayStation 2 Linux development kit.
\Development Libraries\MacOS\	The development libraries for the Macintosh Operating System prior to OS X.
\Development Libraries\MacOSX\	The development libraries for the Macintosh Operating System X.
\Development Libraries\Win32\	The development libraries for the Windows32 platform. There are two libraries: one for Microsoft Visual C++ and one for MinGW, which is another Windows compiler.

All of these directories are inside the \goodies\SDL\ directory.

There are two ways to install SDL. The first method is to use the source code of SDL directly, but technically this is a violation of the LGPL because your projects will not be re-linkable with newer versions of SDL. Because of this, I don't cover how to set it up this way.

The other way is the most popular method, and I show you how to set it up for Visual C++.

Setting Up the Files

The first thing you need to do is go into the CD and navigate to this directory: \goodies\SDL\Development Libraries\Win32\. After you get there, you can unzip the SDL-devel-1.2.4-VC6.zip file onto your hard drive in a place where you keep your libraries. For example, I keep mine in the directory D:\programming\SDL\. You can put yours wherever you want.

In that directory, you should have three subdirectories and a bunch of files; it should look like the screenshot in Figure C.1.

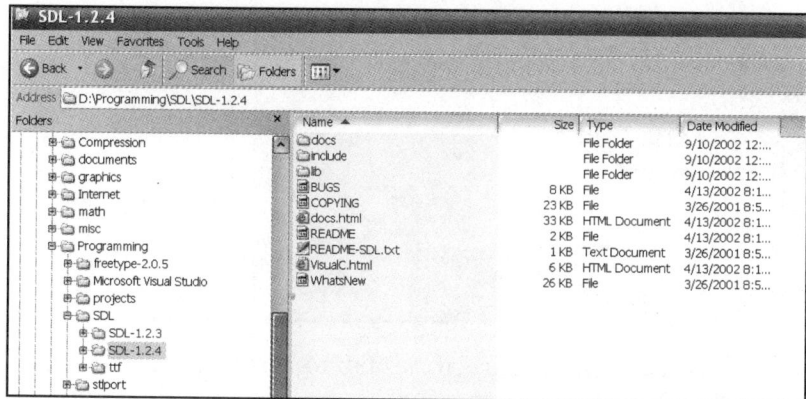

Figure C.1

Here are the files that should be in your SDL directory.

There are three directories, one containing the documentation for SDL in HTML format. The \include\ directory has all of the header files for SDL in it. The \lib\ directory contains the Visual C++ library files for SDL and the SDL.DLL file, which you need to include with every program you create in SDL.

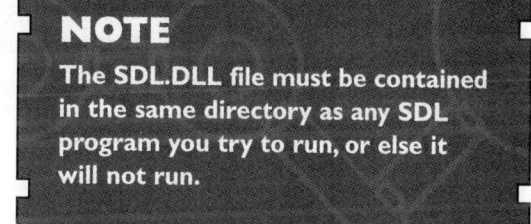

NOTE

The SDL.DLL file must be contained in the same directory as any SDL program you try to run, or else it will not run.

The rest of the files contain information about bugs, a copy of the LGPL license (in the file COPYING), and information about setting up Visual C++ for SDL.

Setting Up Visual C++

After you do all that, you are ready to set up Visual C++ to use SDL. The first thing you need to do is set up your library and header paths so that you use the SDL libraries. To do this, you must open up Visual C++ and choose Tools, Options. Figure C.2 shows this.

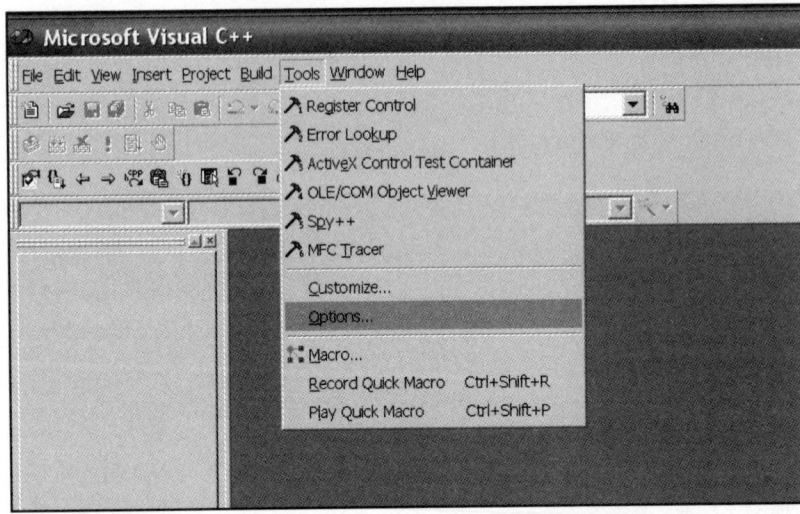

Figure C.2
Here is the Tools, Options menu.

After you choose Tools, Options, click the Directories tab to bring up a screen that looks like Figure C.3.

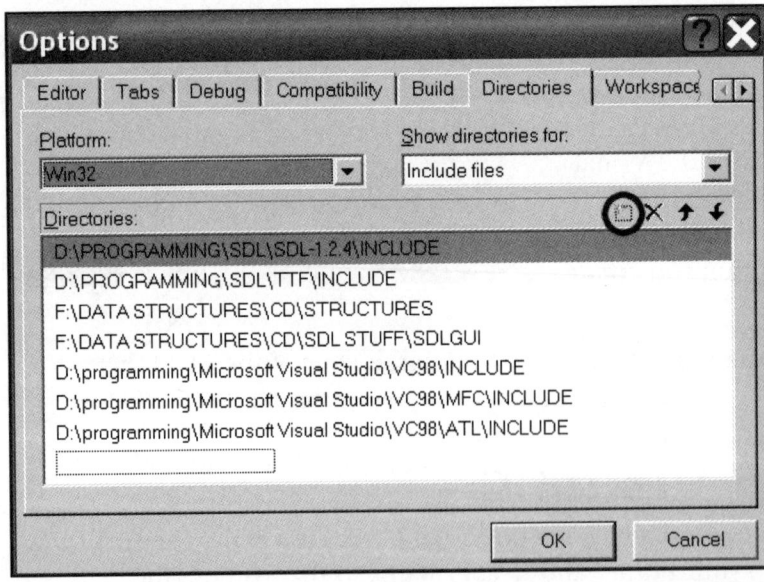

Figure C.3
Here is the Directories tab.

Now that you have the window open to the Directories tab, make sure that the Platform drop-down list says Win32 and the Show directories for drop-down list says Include files. Click the dotted square button that is circled in the figure. A new box appears below the last entry of the list. In this box, type the location of your SDL include directory. In my case, this is D:\PROGRAMMING\SDL\SDL-1.2.4\INCLUDE.

After you have entered the name, press Enter, make sure your SDL include directory is highlighted, and then click the up-arrow button (next to the X in the figure) until your include directory is at the top of the list.

Next, go to the Show directories for drop-down list and select Libraries this time. Now you will add another new directory to the list, but this time it will point to the SDL lib folder. In my case, this is D:\PROGRAMMING\SDL\SDL-1.2.4\LIB.

> **NOTE**
> Visual C++ looks for the header files that you've included in the directories listed in that box. It searches each directory until it finds a match for the filename and then uses that. By putting the SDL include directory at the top, it will search there first, in case you have header files with the same name in any of the other directories.

Now Visual C++ is set up to use SDL! Hooray!

Setting Up Your Project

Unfortunately, you're not quite done yet. You still need to set up each project you create to use SDL. To do this, you must first create a project. SDL projects are created just like you would create a normal Win32 project; you go to the File menu and choose the first option, New. A window pops up, as shown in Figure C.4.

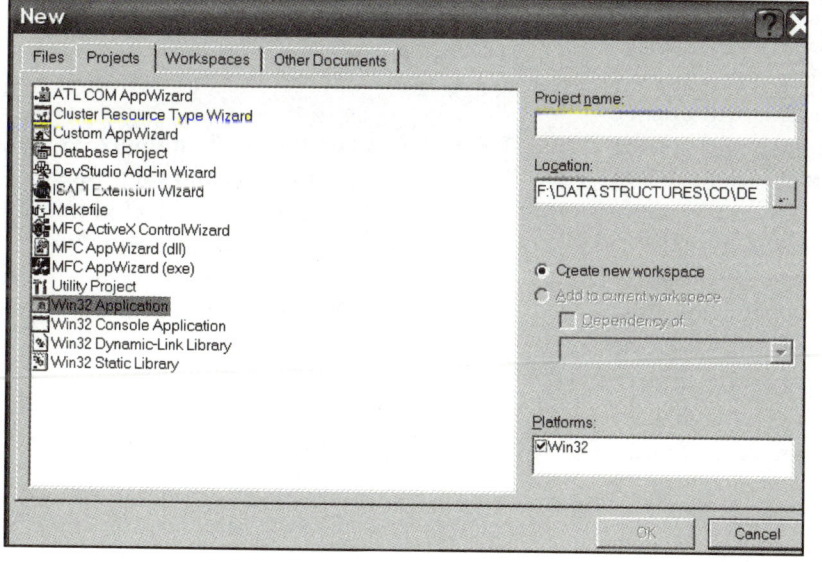

Figure C.4

Here is where you create a new project.

In this window, enter the name of your project in the Project name box and enter the directory it will be in in the box directly below it. Then select Win32 Application from the list on the left and click OK, and you're almost there!

When the window pops up asking you what kind of project you want to create, select An empty project and click Finish.

Now, choose Project, Settings. The window shown in Figure C.5 appears.

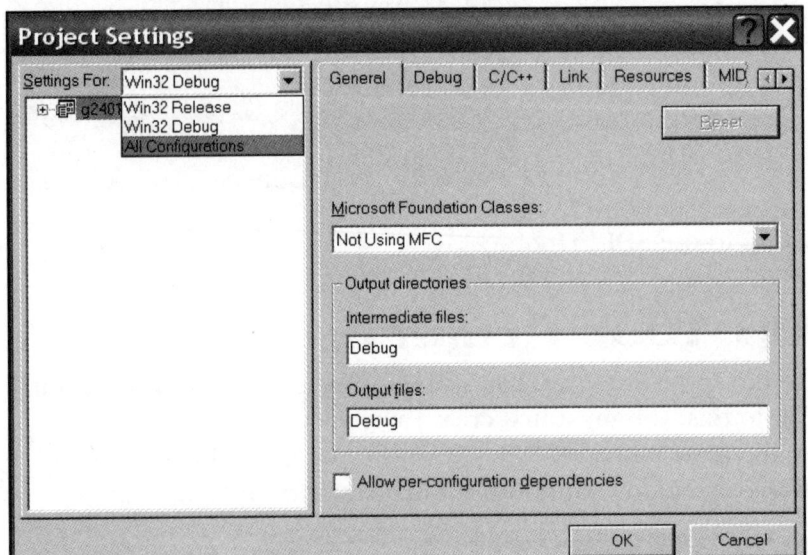

Figure C.5

This is the Project Settings window.

Go to the Settings For box and select All Configurations. This will ensure that you set both debug and release modes up to use SDL.

Now click on the C/C++ tab and move the category box down to Code Generation. After you do that, select Multithreaded DLL in the Use runtime library box. This is the only runtime library that works with SDL, so this is a very important step. Figure C.6 shows a screenshot of this.

> **TIP**
>
> There have been times when I only set SDL up for debug mode, and then when I switch to release mode, it won't compile. This is frustrating because you don't immediately know what is wrong on a large project. So make sure you set up SDL for all configurations.

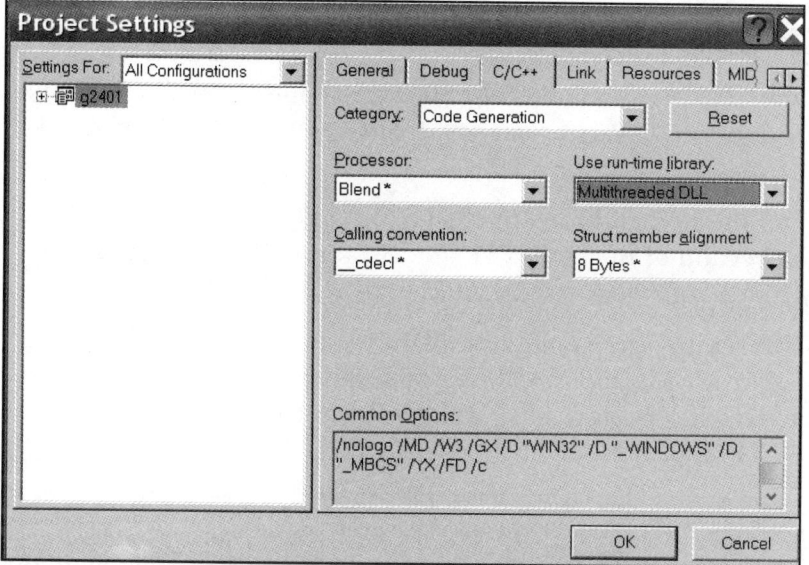

Figure C.6
Here are the code generation settings.

Now that you have set the code generation settings, you must do one more thing. Go to the next tab over, Link. Go to the Object/library modules text box and enter the names of the two SDL library files, sdl.lib and sdlmain.lib. Figure C.7 shows this.

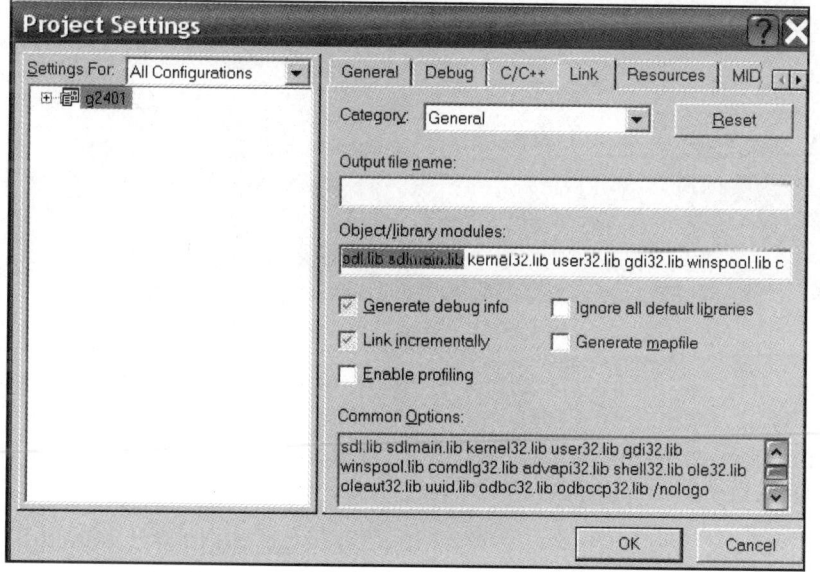

Figure C.7
Here are the link settings.

Now click OK. Your project is set up to use SDL.

Setting Up SDL_TTF

Unfortunately, SDL doesn't have a built-in font library, so you cannot display text unless you build your own font library or use one that someone has already developed.

I have chosen the latter method and used the SDL_TTF add-on library. You can always find the newest version of the SDL_TTF library on the SDL Web site at this address: http://www.libsdl.org/projects/SDL_ttf/.

The SDL_TTF library is set up just like the base SDL library was set up. The Web page has links to the source code and development libraries available to download. As of this writing, the newest version is 2.0.5, which is included on the CD in the directory \goodies\SDL_TTF\.

> **NOTE**
> If you know what you're doing, you can set up your program so that you can use the source code provided in the \goodies\SDL_TTF\Source Code\ directory to build your application and link it statically without needing to use the SDL_TTF.DLL file. However, this is again a violation of the LGPL, so I wouldn't recommend doing it. If you do decide to statically link your project, you need to use the FreeType Font Library because this is what the SDL_TTF library is built on top of. You can find the newest version of FreeType at http://www.freetype.org/, and Version 2.1.2 is included on the CD for your use (\goodies\FreeType\). Be warned, though: FreeType is difficult to set up, and you should only use it if you really want to mess around with it. It is better to just use the SDL_TTF library in the way that this appendix explains instead. I don't discuss how to statically link FreeType, SDL_TTF, or SDL itself.

There are several different SDL_TTF development libraries available using the same platforms as the SDL base libraries, with two exceptions: There is no PlayStation 2 SDL_TTF development library, nor is there a MinGW library. The libraries are all in their appropriate directories on the CD in \goodies\SDL_TTF\Development Libraries\.

I am covering the installation and setup of the Win32 development library, which is on the CD in the directory \goodies\SDL_TTF\Development\Libraries\Win32\ in the file SDL_ttf-devel-2.0.5-VC6.zip. You should unzip this file into a directory where you store all of your libraries. For example, I like to keep this library unzipped into the same directory where I unzipped the base SDL library: D:\Programming\SDL\. After you unzip it, your directory should look something like Figure C.8.

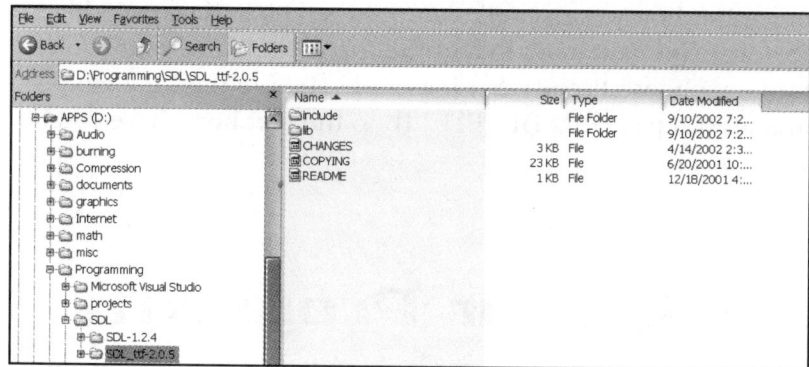

Figure C.8

Here are the files in your SDL_TTF library directory after unzipping it.

After you have done that, you need to set up Visual C++ to recognize your SDL_TTF directory. This is done the same way as when you set up Visual C++ to recognize your base SDL directory. Go to the Tools, Options menu and select the Directories tab.

Figure C.9 shows how you set up the include file directory by making it point to the \include\ directory inside of the directory where you unzipped SDL_TTF. You must also do this for the library file, which is located in the \lib\ subdirectory of your SDL_TTF directory.

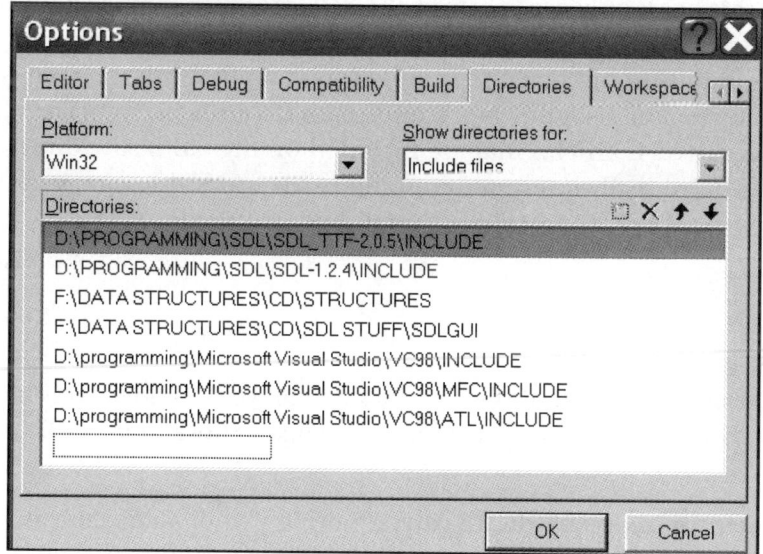

Figure C.9

This is where you add the TTF directories to your compiler's path.

Now Visual C++ recognizes the SDL_TTF library, but you have one more step to do.

This next step must be performed for every project you create that uses the SDL_TTF library. Remember how you needed to add the sdl.lib and sdlmain.lib files to your project before? Now you need to add the sdl_ttf.lib file to your project. When your project is open, choose Project, Settings and switch to the Link tab. When you have done that, you just add SDL_TTF.LIB to the text box where you added the other two library files.

Now your project is ready to use SDL_TTF.

Distributing Your Programs

When you have the compiler set up and you actually compile some programs, you need to include both the SDL.DLL file and the SDL_TTF.DLL file with your programs to make them run. They will not run if they cannot find the DLLs.

The DLLs come with the Win32 development libraries, and they are both located in the \lib\ directory of each library where you unzipped them. Just copy the DLL and paste it into the same directory as your EXE, and you're ready to go.

Using SDL

As I have stated before, this book only uses a few of the SDL modules. This section gives you a very brief introduction to them and how to use them. It isn't a very comprehensive overview, but it should be enough to get you familiar with the common functions and structures. For a slightly more informative approach, you can take a look at Ernest Pazera's SDL articles that are included on the CD in the directory \goodies\articles\. If you're really interested in some hard-core SDL usage, you should also check out his new book *Focus On SDL*, published by Premier Press (ISBN 1-59200-030-4).

SDL_Video

The component of SDL that handles all of the graphics is called SDL_Video. It is a fairly easy component to use, which is one of the main reasons I chose to use SDL with this book.

The SDL_Video component supports hardware video drawing if your video card is capable, but even if it isn't, SDL_Video supports a software drawing mode that will work no matter what you have installed on the computer as far as hardware goes.

The Structures

There are several structures that are used frequently with the SDL_Video component.

First, there is the `SDL_Surface`, which is really just a bitmap. These structures can hold bitmaps in any format, and the SDL drawing routines will draw them correctly.

Then there are `SDL_Rect`s, which are rectangles. These are often used in the drawing functions to define the source and destination areas. They have four variables: an *x* and a *y* coordinate and a width and a height.

There is also an `SDL_PixelFormat` structure, which defines the exact format that a surface is in, in case you ever need to do any image editing or converting.

Finally, you have `SDL_Color`, which is a simple structure that stores a single color value.

You will see how these structures are used in the next few sections.

Initializing the Video

Setting up video in SDL takes three easy steps. You need to initialize the video library, set the video mode, and set the window caption. You should note that the third step is optional.

```
SDL_Surface* g_window;
SDL_Init( SDL_INIT_VIDEO );
g_window = SDL_SetVideoMode( WIDTH, HEIGHT, 0, SDL_ANYFORMAT );
SDL_WM_SetCaption( PROGRAM_NAME, 0);
```

In the first step, the video module is initialized. This must be performed before the other two steps.

Then, the `SDL_SetVideoMode` function is called with the width, the height, and the bitdepth of the surface (use 0 if you want to use the default depth, which varies based on the system) and the format of the video mode. In this example, I have passed in the `SDL_ANYFORMAT` flag, which means that SDL should use the best format it can find. This assures that it will work on pretty much every system out there. The `g_window` variable is just a regular `SDL_Surface` pointer, and you will use it whenever you draw anything on the screen.

Finally, the caption of the window is set to a name, and the second parameter is a string of the name of the icon to use (a filename of a .bmp, I suppose. I'm not sure because I never needed to play around with it, and the docs don't really specify it anyway).

Loading and Drawing Bitmaps

If you've ever played around with the windows .bmp file format, you know how difficult and awkward it is to work with. Not only is the data stored in BGR format (when almost everyone else uses RGB), but the bitmap is also stored upside-down!

SDL is really a lifesaver in this respect; it does everything for you. Look at this code, for example:

```
SDL_Surface* bitmap = SDL_LoadBMP( "bitmap.bmp" );
```

Now, wasn't that easy? SDL automatically loads the bitmap and creates a new surface for you. You can instantly draw it to any other surface that you want, too.

Here is how you would blit onto the screen:

```
SDL_Rect sourcerect = { 0, 0, 64, 64 };
SDL_Rect destrect = { 32, 32, 64, 64 };
SDL_BlitSurface( bitmap, sourcerect, g_window, destrect );
SDL_UpdateRect( g_window, 0, 0, 0, 0 );
```

The first two lines declare two rectangles. When SDL draws surfaces onto other surfaces, it needs two rectangles. The source rectangle determines what part of the source bitmap it is going to copy over. The destination rectangle determines where on the destination the source will be drawn. Look at Figure C.10 for example.

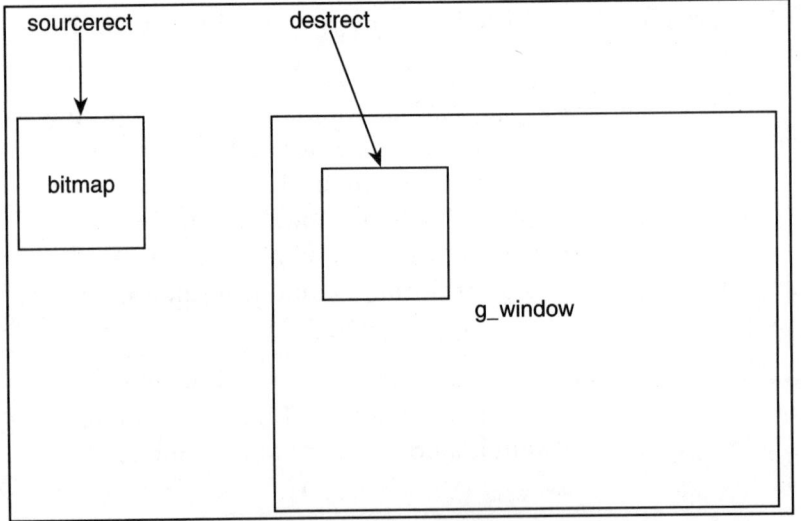

Figure C.10

This shows the source and destination rectangles.

Say, for example, that the `bitmap` surface is 64 × 64 pixels. The source rectangle starts at coordinates (0, 0) and has a size of 64 × 64, which means that the entire surface is going to be drawn. Then, the destination rectangle is set up. This time, its coordinates start at (32, 32), but the size still stays at 64 × 64. This means that you want the entire source rectangle drawn on the destination at (32, 32).

The third line of the code snippet actually performs the drawing. Although the bitmap is now drawn on the screen surface, it won't actually show up on your screen. You need to do one more thing: update the surface. When you draw to the screen surface, the data isn't actually sent to the video card until you call this function. So `SDL_UpdateRect` function updates a rectangle on the screen. You can pass in four coordinates (x, y, width, and height variables), or you can pass in all 0s. If you pass in all 0s, the entire screen is updated, and any changes you made now appear on the monitor.

That's pretty much all there is to drawing stuff.

Freeing Surfaces

When you are done with a surface, you should always free the surface to clear the memory. Here is how you do it:

```
SDL_FreeSurface( bitmap );
```

SDL Event Handling

This is the SDL module that takes care of program events and user input. It works very similarly to the windows message pump, if you've ever worked with that before.

There really isn't much to the system. Pretty much everything that occurs in SDL is considered an event. If the user presses or releases a key, moves the mouse, or clicks, an event is generated. The `SDL_Event` structure is designed to store information about an event.

Your game loop should check to see if an event has occurred fairly frequently. I prefer to check for events every loop, like this:

```
SDL_Event event;
while( 1 )
{
    if( SDL_PollEvent( &event ) )
    {
        // handle the event here
```

```
        }
        // handle the game logic here
    }
```

The `SDL_PollEvent` function fills in an `SDL_Event` structure with event information if an event has occurred and returns 1 if there are any events or 0 if there haven't been any events. So if there were any events, then the function starts handling the input; otherwise, it just processes the game logic as usual.

You want to check for events as often as possible because if you let events get piled up in the queue while the game is busy doing other things, it will look like the input is lagging, and the users don't like that.

There are a few events that I usually check for, and here is a listing of how to check for them:

```
if( event.type == SDL_QUIT )
    break;
if( event.type == SDL_MOUSEBUTTONDOWN )
{
    // handle mouse button down
}
if( event.type == SDL_MOUSEBUTTONUP )
{
    // handle mouse button up
}
if( event.type == SDL_KEYDOWN )
{
    // handle keyboard down
}
```

The first event is important; it is a signal from the program that it is shutting down. So you should always detect the `SDL_QUIT` event. Because this loop is within the `while( 1 )` loop I showed you previously, a `break` call will literally break you out of the `while`-loop.

The other events detect some of the more common events in a game. You can add code to handle these easily.

For example, you can use the `SDL_GetMouseState` function to get the coordinates of the mouse on the window like this:

```
SDL_GetMouseState( &x, &y );
```

The function gets the mouse coordinates and stores them into two integers. Note that you must pass pointers into the function because the function physically modifies the integers that are passed in.

You may also detect what key was pressed or released like this:

```
if( event.key.keysym.sym == SDLK_ESCAPE )
```

SDL has a whole mess of key defines that you can use, all of which are defined in the sdl_keysym.h file (this is located in the \include\ directory wherever you have installed SDL).

SDL_Timer

The SDL_Timer component is pretty small and simple to use. You initialize it like this:

```
SDL_Init(SDL_INIT_TIMER );
```

When you have initialized the timer component, you have access to the SDL_GetTicks function, which returns the number of milliseconds that have passed since the program was started.

Because the function uses 32-bit integers to store the time, the timer will reset itself every 49 days.

SDL_TTF

The very first thing you must do in order to use the SDL_TTF library is to initialize it with this function:

```
TTF_Init();
```

After it is initialized, you can use the functions in the library to create fonts and text.

The main structure in the SDL_TTF library is the TTF_Font structure. Fonts are amazingly easy to open, and you can do so with just one function call:

```
TTF_Font* font = TTF_OpenFont( "arial.ttf", 16 );
```

This line of code opens the TrueType font file arial.ttf at 16 points.

> **NOTE**
> The *point size* of a font is the vertical size of a font. Traditionally, on paper, there are 72 points per inch vertically. However, every computer system uses a different measure to convert them to actual pixels, so you have to experiment with font sizes to see what is the best one to use.

> **CAUTION**
> Many TrueType font files are copyrighted, so you should be sure to get permission from the copyright holder before distributing one with your game.

You can change the style of a font file after it's been opened, but you cannot change its size. This is the function you would use to set the style of a font:

```
TTF_SetFontStyle( font, TTF_STYLE_BOLD );
```

This example makes the font bold. There are a total of four different flags you can use: `TTF_STYLE_NORMAL`, `TTF_STYLE_BOLD`, `TTF_STYLE_ITALIC`, and `TTF_STYLE_UNDERLINE`. The last three styles may be combined using the binary-or operator, like this:

```
TTF_SetFontStyle( font, TTF_STYLE_BOLD | TTF_STYLE_ITALIC );
```

This makes the font bold and italic.

Now, you can finally create text using a font. The font library renders text onto a new surface, so you need to be careful. This is a cool feature and a pain in the butt at the same time. You can keep the text rendered onto a surface so that you can quickly draw it whenever you want it, but don't forget to free it, or you will end up with large memory leaks.

Here's how you render text:

```
bitmap = TTF_RenderText_Shaded( font, "Hello!", BLACK, WHITE );
```

This is only one of the font rendering functions. There are two more: `TTF_RenderText_Solid` and `TTF_RenderText_Blended`.

The solid function is the fastest; it draws plain solid-edged text onto a surface, but this can look bad sometimes, especially with small text.

The shaded function is slightly slower, but it draws the font with anti-aliasing, which smoothes out the edges so that it looks better to your eyes. Figure C.11 shows a screenshot of the letter C. On the left is a solid font; compare it to the anti-aliased font on the right.

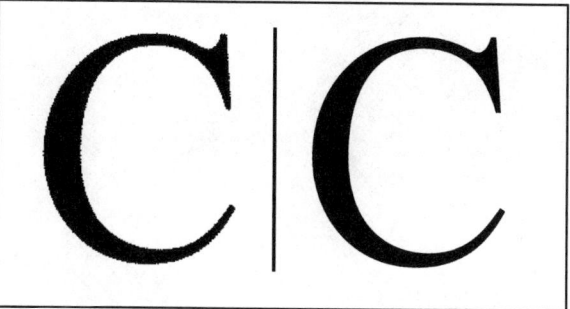

Figure C.11

The C on the left is drawn normally. You can easily see the sharp edges on a computer screen. The C on the right is drawn with anti-aliasing; the font blends into the background and makes it easier to read.

The blended font function apparently uses alpha blending to achieve some cool blending effects, but I've never been able to get it working properly (probably because I never really tried).

The render function renders a piece of text with the supplied font and then uses two `SDL_Color` structures to determine the foreground and the background colors. The solid rendering function only uses a foreground color because it doesn't need to blend the edges of the font.

> **NOTE**
>
> The `BLACK` and `WHITE` color structures are defined in my own `SDLHelpers` library, which I show you in a little bit. They are not part of SDL, but I found it easier to have a few pre-defined colors to use.

When you are done using a font, you should close the font, like this:

`TTF_CloseFont( font );`

And finally, when you are completely done with the font library, you can shut it down like this:

`TTF_Quit();`

That's pretty much all of the font functions that are used in the demos for the book.

The SDLHelpers Library

When I started developing demos for this book, I realized that SDL is great for bitmapped graphics, but it is somewhat lacking in the vector graphics department.

So I decided to make my own functions that would automate some of the most common things that I needed to do in SDL.

> **NOTE**
> Because these functions are somewhat long and they don't have any direct relation to the book besides the fact that they are used in the graphical demos to demonstrate the data structures, I left the source code out. I am showing you the function definitions so you can understand what they do if you see them used in the book. If you're really interested in how these functions work, you can always look at the source code. I've commented it all to make it easy to understand.

The SDLHelpers library is contained in two files, SDLHelpers.h and SDLHelpers.cpp. You can find both of these files on the CD in the \structures\SDLHelpers\ directory. They also appear wherever they are needed in the demonstration directories.

The first function I created was a function to draw pixels on a surface.

```
void SDLPoint( SDL_Surface* p_surface, int x, int y,
               SDL_Color p_color );
```

The function draws a point of the specified color at the given *x* and *y* coordinates on the surface.

The next function draws a line of a specific color on a surface:

```
void SDLLine( SDL_Surface* p_surface, int x1, int y1,
              int x2, int y2, SDL_Color p_color );
```

Then there is a function that draws an arrow line, which has optional arrows at each end:

```
void SDLArrowLine( SDL_Surface* p_surface, int x1, int y1,
                   int x2, int y2, int r1, int r2,
                   bool arrow1, bool arrow2, SDL_Color p_color );
```

The function adds four new variables to the regular line function: two radiuses and two booleans. The booleans determine if an arrow should be drawn or not at each end. The radiuses take a little more explanation, though. This function is designed to be drawn so that the arrows can be pointing to circles. See Figure C.12 for reference.

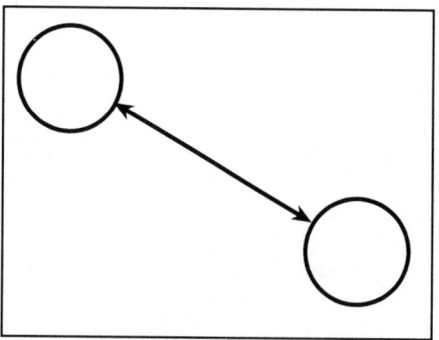

Figure C.12

Here is an example of the SDLArrowLine function.

In the figure, a line is drawn between two circles. Both pairs of coordinates lie directly in the center of the circles, and the radius variables contain the size of the radius of each circle. The function automatically figures out how far away from the center of the circle it should be drawn and then adds the arrowheads on after that.

If you don't want to constantly be setting up rectangles just to draw things in SDL, you can use this function instead. It automatically sets up the rectangle structures for you and draws the entire bitmap at the requested coordinates:

```
void SDLBlit( SDL_Surface* p_source, SDL_Surface* p_dest, int x, int y );
```

Finally, you may want to draw solid boxes on surfaces to clear out parts of the surface. The SDL rectangle-fill function also uses lots of rectangle structures, so I made this function to make things easier for you:

```
void SDLBox( SDL_Surface* p_surface, int x, int y,
             int width, int height, SDL_Color p_color );
```

Finally, I have defined preset colors that you can use in any of the SDL functions. They are WHITE, BLACK, RED, BLUE, GREEN, YELLOW, ORANGE, CYAN, DCYAN, PINK, GREY, LTGREY, DKBLUE, DKRED, and DKGREEN.

The SDLFrame

I have created a very basic framework file for you to use with the SDLHelpers library. A lot of the Game Demonstrations in the book are based on this framework. It is located on the CD in the directory \structures\SDLHelpers\, in the file SDLFrame.cpp. Here is a listing of the file:

```
#include "SDL.h"
const char PROGRAM_NAME[]    = "INSERT PROGRAM NAME HERE";
const int WIDTH              = 640;
```

C. Introduction to SDL

```c
const int HEIGHT         = 480;
// this is the main window for the framework
SDL_Surface* g_window = 0;

// main function
int main( int argc, char* argv[] )
{
    // declare coordinates.
    int x, y;
    // declare event holder
    SDL_Event event;
    // initialize the video system.
    SDL_Init( SDL_INIT_VIDEO | SDL_INIT_TIMER );
    // set our at exit function
    atexit( SDL_Quit );
    // set the video mode.
    g_window = SDL_SetVideoMode( WIDTH, HEIGHT, 0, SDL_ANYFORMAT );
    SDL_WM_SetCaption( PROGRAM_NAME, 0);

    // the main game loop
    while( 1 )
    {
        //look for an event
        if( SDL_PollEvent( &event ) )
        {
            //an event was found
            if( event.type == SDL_QUIT )
                break;
            if( event.type == SDL_MOUSEBUTTONDOWN )
            {
                // get the mouse state.
                SDL_GetMouseState( &x, &y );
            }
            if( event.type == SDL_MOUSEBUTTONUP )
            {
                // get the mouse state.
                SDL_GetMouseState( &x, &y );
            }
            if( event.type == SDL_KEYDOWN )
            {
```

```
                // a key was pressed.
                if( event.key.keysym.sym == SDLK_ESCAPE )
                {
                    // if ESC was pressed, quit the program.
                    SDL_Event quit;
                    quit.type = SDL_QUIT;
                    SDL_PushEvent( &quit );
                }
            }
        }  // end event loop.
        // do all game-related stuff here.
        // update the entire window.
        SDL_UpdateRect( g_window, 0, 0, 0, 0 );
    }
    // do game cleanup here
    // done
    return 0;
}
```

The SDLGUI Library

The SDLHelpers library is great, but it is not really useful for lots of complex GUI-type stuff, like the stuff you see in all of the Graphical Demonstrations in this book, so I went ahead and created a new object-oriented GUI library to use.

Like the SDLHelpers library, I don't show the code in the book. It is simply too large to show in this book, and it has little to do with the actual subject matter anyway. As always, the source code is freely available on the CD, fully commented and ready for you to use on your own.

In this section, I show you how to set up and use the GUI just like it is used in the Graphical Demonstrations throughout the book.

All of the files you need are located on the CD in the directory \structures\SDLGUI\.

The SDLGUI Class

The main class you will be using in this library is the SDLGUI class, located in the SDLGUI.h and SDLGUI.cpp files.

The GUI class keeps track of every button, label, text box, and check box in the GUI, as well as all the fonts it will use. When you construct one, here is what it looks like:

```
SDLGUI g_gui( 800, 600, 32, WHITE );
```

This constructs a GUI with a size of 800 × 600 that can hold a maximum of 32 GUI items (buttons and so on) and has a background color of white.

The GUI class can have a total of 16 different fonts loaded at any given time, and you must load them through the GUI by using this function:

```
const int ARIAL = 0;
g_gui.SetFont( "arial.ttf", ARIAL, 16, TTF_STYLE_NORMAL );
```

Note the constant integer declaration that comes first; when accessing the fonts through the GUI, you must use an index, but using a number to refer to a font can get ugly quickly. So now you have defined the constant ARIAL to be the index 0. Whenever you want to access that font from the GUI from now on, instead of typing 0, you type ARIAL instead. It makes your programs much more legible.

The last two parameters are the point size of the font and the style of the font (see the SDL_TTF section).

The GUI Objects

Now that you've got your GUI and a font created, you want to add elements to it. You can do so by using a few functions. For example, the following function adds a button to the GUI:

```
void AddButton( int p_x, int p_y,
                const char* p_up,
                const char* p_down,
                const char* p_text,
                int p_font,
                SDL_Color p_fore,
                SDL_Color p_back,
                void (*p_func)(void) );
```

You pass in the coordinates of the button and then the names of the bitmaps you want to represent the up and down states of the button. After that, you pass in the text that will be shown on the button and then the font index number. Then, there are two colors: the foreground and background colors of the text on the button. Finally, there is a function pointer to a *callback function*. Whenever this button is pressed, it will call that function. This allows you to create buttons that will call whatever function you want (as long as it takes no parameters and doesn't return anything) whenever the button is pressed!

The other object types are all similar, with minor differences:

```
void AddCheckbox( int p_x, int p_y,
                 const char* p_up,
                 const char* p_down,
                 const char* p_text,
                 int p_font,
                 SDL_Color p_fore,
                 SDL_Color p_back,
                 void (*p_func)(void) );
```

The `AddCheckBox` function has the same parameters and will call its callback function every time it is clicked on. There is no immediate way to retrieve the current status of the check box, so you must store a boolean yourself that keeps track of the state of the check box. By default, check boxes are unchecked.

```
void AddLabel( int p_x, int p_y,
               const char* p_text,
               int p_font,
               SDL_Color p_fore,
               SDL_Color p_back );
```

A label is just a piece of text that sits on the screen and does nothing.

```
void AddTextBox( int p_x, int p_y,
                 int p_w, int p_h,
                 char* p_string,
                 int p_length,
                 int p_font,
                 SDL_Color p_fore,
                 SDL_Color p_back,
                 bool p_enabled,
                 void (*p_func)(void) );
```

The most complex GUI item is the text box. It adds a height and a width, as it is not based on a graphic. Also, the string that you pass in to the `p_string` parameter is the string that this text box will display and modify. The `p_length` variable determines the maximum length of the text box in case you want to limit the number of characters the user can input. Finally, the `p_enabled` boolean determines if the box can be edited or not. If this is false, then the text box cannot be edited.

All of these functions create the appropriate classes and add them to the GUI. All four GUI objects inherit from a class called `SDLGUIItem`.

The Drawing Function Wrappers

The GUI class doesn't allow you to easily access the main surface, so I have included a few wrapper functions into it that use the standard SDLHelper drawing functions: `Point`, `Line`, `ArrowLine`, `Blit`, and `Box`. These functions are essentially the same as their regular counterparts except that they assume that the destination surface is the screen and therefore don't have the `p_surface` parameters.

The Utility Functions

There are a few utility functions included in the GUI class in order to get information about it.

The first function is the `GetFont` function, which gets a pointer to the `TTF_Font` at the index that you requested:

    TTF_Font* GetFont(int p_index);

Then there is a function that gets a pointer to the requested GUI item:

    SDLGUIItem* GetItem(int p_item);

All of the GUI items are stored in an array, so the very first item you added to the GUI is number 0, the next item is 1, and so on. I will show you how to use these item pointers later.

After that, there is a function to get a pointer to the screen surface:

    SDL_Surface* GetScreen();

Finally, there is a function to set the *focus* of the GUI. The GUI can be focused on an item, but this really only matters with the text box items. When you are typing on the keyboard, the text is sent to the item with the focus. Obviously, sending text to labels, buttons, or check boxes does nothing, but sending text to a text box will add the letters to the box or, if you press Delete, delete letters from the box.

    void SetFocus(int p_item);

The Event Functions

Whenever an event happens in an SDL program, you want the GUI to know about it as well. You need to send messages to the GUI yourself, as the GUI doesn't automatically control the SDL event loop.

Whenever the mouse is pressed, you should call this function:

```
void MouseDown( int p_x, int p_y );
```

The two parameters are the coordinates of the mouse when the mouse was pressed down. Likewise, there is a command that should be called whenever the mouse button is released:

```
void MouseUp( int p_x, int p_y );
```

Finally, there is a function that should be called whenever a key on the keyboard is pressed:

```
void KeyDown( SDLKey p_key, SDLMod p_mod, Uint16 p_char );
```

The first parameter is the `SDLKey` code for the key that was pressed (i.e., `SDLK_ENTER` and so on). The second parameter is an instance of the `SDLMod` structure. This structure tells you what keyboard modifier buttons are pressed (Shift, Alt, Control). The last parameter is a `Uint16`, which is an SDL typedef meaning *unsigned integer that is 16 bits long*. This is the *Unicode* representation of the key that was pressed.

> **NOTE**
> Unicode (also known as UTF-16) is a 16-bit character encoding format that is meant to replace standard ASCII characters. ASCII can only represent 256 different letters, but UTF-16 can represent 65,536 different letters. This may seem to be enough for every language in the entire world, but it really isn't. This means that a new Unicode format, called UTF-32, needed to be created. This new format can represent 4 billion characters! That's enough for every language on this planet, I think. The UTF-32 spec is so large that they even have a whole range of letters that represent the Klingon Alphabet from *Star Trek*!

The Unicode representation of the key that was pressed varies depending on what keys were pressed. For example, pressing Shift and Z gives you the letter Z, whereas leaving off Shift will give you z.

These three parameters can be gotten from the `SDL_keysym` structure, which you can find in the event structures when an event occurs in SDL. I will show you an example of how to do this later.

The Display Functions

The GUI also has two functions that you use to make it display itself on the screen. The first is the `Draw` function:

```
void Draw();
```

This function, when called, will clear the background of the screen to the color that you set in the GUI's constructor. Then it will go through every item in the GUI and draw each of them onto the screen surface. However, nothing will display on the screen if you only call this function. Therefore, the GUI also has a function that will actually display the contents of the screen surface on your monitor:

```
void Update();
```

The SDLGUIItem Class

Whenever you add items to the GUI or retrieve them, you're dealing with the SDLGUIItem class. This is a *virtual base class* for the four different kinds of items. If you're not familiar with inheritance, Chapter 9, "Tying It Together: The Basics," introduces you to this concept and why it is useful. For now, if you don't know what a virtual base class is, all you need to know is that every single GUI item supports the functions that are contained within this class. The code for this class is contained within the SDLGUIItem.h file. Because this is a virtual class, there isn't a .cpp file accompanying it.

The Visibility Functions

Every GUI item has a *visibility* status. You can make certain items visible or invisible. When an item such as a button or a check box is invisible, you cannot click it with the mouse. Here are the functions to set and get the visibility status:

```
void SetVisibility( bool p_vis );
bool Visible();
```

The Position Functions

There are two functions that deal with the position of the item on the screen. The first one moves the item to a different set of coordinates:

```
void Move( int x, int y );
```

The second one determines if a set of coordinates is over the item (used to detect if the mouse is over an item):

```
bool IsOver( int p_x, int p_y );
```

The Input Functions

There are four user input functions for each item. The first two tell the item that a mouse button was clicked on or released when the mouse cursor was over the button:

```
void ClickDown();
void ClickUp();
```

The next function is called whenever a key is pressed and the item is the one that the GUI is currently focused on:

```
void KeyPress( SDLKey p_key, SDLMod p_mod, Uint16 p_char );
```

These parameters are the same as in the `KeyDown` function in the `SDLGUI` class. Whenever that function is called, it finds out what item currently has the focus and sends the key information to that item.

The last function is a crude hack I made because my GUI system doesn't support mouse-movement events:

```
void ResetOnUp();
```

This function is called for every item every time the mouse button is released. This has to do with the way buttons are implemented. When you click a button, it goes into the down state and stays that way until you release the button. However, if you move the mouse off of the button and then release it, a release-button event is never sent to the button, so it still thinks you're pressing on it, and it looks stupid. This function says to every item that a mouse button was released and it should reset its state if needed.

Focus Functions

There are two functions that deal with the focus of an item.

```
bool CanGetFocus();
```

First, the GUI must be able to find out if an item can actually get the focus before it decides to focus on it. Therefore, this function will return true if it can get the focus or false if not. Currently, the only items that can get the focus are text boxes.

```
void GetFocus( bool p_focus );
```

Then this function tells an item if it has gotten (true) the focus or lost (false) the focus.

The Drawing Function

The last function an item has is a function to draw itself on a surface:

```
void Draw( SDL_Surface* p_dest );
```

Considering that an item doesn't know where the surface is, and you might want to draw items on other surfaces in the future anyway, you need to pass the surface in as a parameter.

The SDLGUI Items

I don't post how to use any of the specific GUI items here because they aren't really used directly in the Graphical Demonstrations throughout the book; the GUI class manages them for you. If you're interested, though, you can find the source code in these files: SDLButton.h, SDLButton.cpp, SDLCheckBox.h, SDLCheckBox.cpp, SDLLabel.h, SDLLabel.cpp, SDLTextBox.h, and SDLTextBox.cpp. From their names, you can tell what classes are contained within each file.

The SDLGUIFrame

I have included a simple framework to use with the SDLGUI library. In fact, every Graphical Demonstration was built from this framework, which is located in the file SDLGUIFrame.cpp. Here is a listing of the code:

```cpp
#include "SDLGUI.h"

const char PROGRAM_NAME[]    = "INSERT PROGRAM NAME HERE";
const int WIDTH              = 640;
const int HEIGHT             = 480;
const int ITEMS              = 32;

SDLGUI* g_gui;

int main( int argc, char* argv[] )
{
    // declare coordinates.
    int x, y;
    // declare event holder.
    SDL_Event event;
    // set the at exit function.
    atexit( SDL_Quit );
    // initialize systems
    SDL_Init( SDL_INIT_VIDEO | SDL_INIT_TIMER );
    TTF_Init();
```

```cpp
// create the GUI and set the caption.
g_gui = new SDLGUI( WIDTH, HEIGHT, ITEMS, WHITE );
SDL_WM_SetCaption( PROGRAM_NAME, 0);

// add your GUI items here.

// main message loop.
while( 1 )
{
    // look for an event.
    if( SDL_PollEvent( &event ) )
    {
        // an event was found.
        if( event.type == SDL_QUIT )
            break;
        if( event.type == SDL_MOUSEBUTTONDOWN )
        {
            // get the mouse state.
            SDL_GetMouseState( &x, &y );

            // tell the GUI that a button has been pressed.
            g_gui->MouseDown( x, y );
        }
        if( event.type == SDL_MOUSEBUTTONUP )
        {
            // get the mouse state.
            SDL_GetMouseState( &x, &y );

            // tell the GUI that a button has been released.
            g_gui->MouseUp( x, y );
        }
        if( event.type == SDL_KEYDOWN )
        {
            // a key was pressed.
            if( event.key.keysym.sym == SDLK_ESCAPE )
            {
                // if ESC was pressed, quit the program.
                SDL_Event quit;
                quit.type = SDL_QUIT;
                SDL_PushEvent( &quit );
            }
```

```
                // tell the GUI that a key was pressed.
                g_gui->KeyDown( event.key.keysym.sym, event.key.keysym.mod );
            }
        } // end event loop.

        // do all game-related stuff here.

        // tell the GUI to redraw itself.
        g_gui->Draw();

        // DO ALL YOUR RENDERING HERE.

        // tell the GUI to update itself.
        g_gui->Update();
    }

    // do game cleanup here.

    // done.
    return 0;
}
```

Conclusion

This concludes my small introduction to SDL and the two libraries I've developed to make those pretty demos that accompany each chapter. I hope I've given you enough information so that you can compile any of the demos in this book on your own.

If you are interested in more SDL, there are two articles on the CD written by Ernest Pazera about setting up SDL and using the SDL_Video component. They are quite thorough and do a good job of explaining everything you would ever want to know about SDL_Video. If you're *really* interested, then you can pick up his new book that I mentioned, *Focus On SDL*. It's bound to be great.

APPENDIX D

Introduction to the Standard Template Library

This book has three primary goals:

- To teach you about the various data structures that exist
- To show you how to code the data structures for yourself so you get hands-on experience seeing how they work
- To instruct you on applying these data structures directly to computer games

Most other data structures books only focus on one of those goals; I have books that teach you how data structures work but have no code examples. I have books that teach you how to code the data structures, but don't use them in any applications. I also have books that teach you only how to use data structures. These last books usually use something called the *standard template library (STL)*, which is a container library that is included into the C++ standard.

I chose not to use the STL for general use in this book for several reasons:

- It is a complex library, using lots of complex template features.
- It only covers about half of the structures and algorithms in this book.
- Every compiler has a different version, and not all of them are standard.
- STL only defines an *interface*, not an *implementation*. To understand data structures better, you must be shown an implementation.

The last point is the most important. STL only defines an interface for each of the classes and a general performance rating for each operation on them. Every STL implementation is different, and I can't really teach you how data structures work under the hood with STL.

This appendix is meant to be read after you have read the rest of the book because it references many of the chapters within.

STLPort

Unfortunately, every version of STL is different in its own little way, and this can cause problems. The STL implementation that comes with Microsoft Visual C++ 6 is generally considered by most to be a slow and incomplete version (it was

Microsoft's first try, after all) of the STL. (Apparently the STL in Microsoft Visual C++ .NET is much better; however, I have not had a chance to test it.)

So, most of the time, people like to replace the compiler's version of STL with a better and more standard version. The most popular of these is STLPort, which is a totally free version of STL based on the SGI version. The Web site is located at http://www.stlport.org, and the newest version can always be downloaded from the page http://www.stlport.org/download.html. I have included the newest version that was available at the time of writing this on the CD. STLPort version 4.5.3 is located on the CD in the directory \goodies\stlport\ in the STLport-4.5.3.zip file.

If you want to install STLPort for Visual C++, you must follow a process similar to that of installing SDL and SDL_TTF, which I explain in Appendix C, "Introduction to SDL." First, unzip your file onto your hard drive somewhere, preferably the place where you keep all of your libraries and things. For example, I keep mine in the directory D:\Programming\STLport-4.5.3\.

Figure D.1 shows a screenshot of the directory after you've unzipped it.

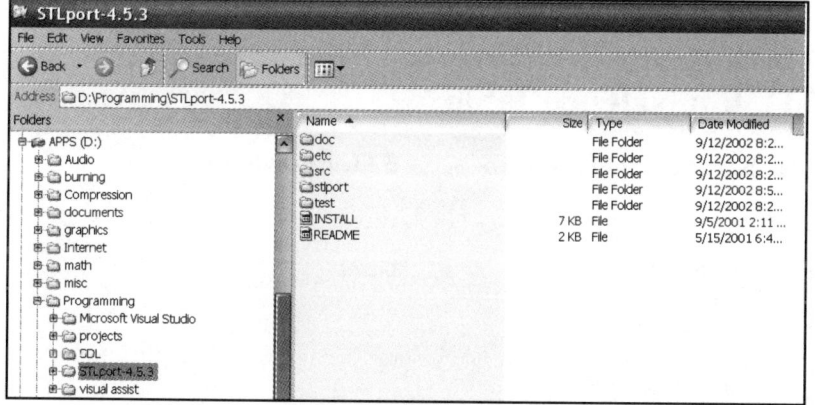

Figure D.1

This shows the contents of your STLPort directory.

There are a number of directories that contain documents, source code, header files, and test files. You want to add the file that has all of the headers in it to your compilers path list, which is \stlport\. You can do this by choosing Tools, Options, Directories and entering the path of that directory into the box. Make absolutely certain that the STLPort directory is moved to the top so that whenever you use the STL headers, the compiler will use the STLPort versions and not its own.

After you have done that, you are almost ready to use STLPort. To get STLPort working to use just the structures and algorithms, you need to disable the IOStream portion that comes with STLPort. If you don't disable it, you need to actually build the IOStream portion into a compiled library file in order to use it, and quite frankly, that is a very complicated task that I still haven't figured out how to do yet.

So, to disable the IOStream portion, you need to go into the \stlport\ directory and find the file stl_user_config.h. When you find it, open it up and search for a line that looks like this:

`// #define _STLP_NO_OWN_IOSTREAMS   1`

You need to remove the comment slashes from this line and save the file. After you do that, you can use STLPort!

STL Versus This Book

This book has covered many data structures and algorithms, some of which the STL implements as well. Table D.1 shows a listing of all the data structures and algorithms covered in this book and their equivalent STL structures and algorithms.

Table D.1 STL Equivalence Table

Chapter	Data Structure/Algorithm	STL Equivalent
3	Array	vector
4	Bitvector	bitset
5	2D Array	*
5	3D Array	*
6	Linked List	list
7	Stack	stack
7	Queue	queue**
8	Hash Table	*
11	Tree	*
12	Binary Tree	*

Chapter	Data Structure/Algorithm	STL Equivalent
13	Binary Search Tree	set/multiset/map/multimap***
14	Heap	priority_queue
15	Game Tree/Minimax Tree	*
17	Graph	*
20	Bubble Sort	*
20	Heap Sort	make_heap/sort_heap
20	Quick Sort	sort
20	Radix Sort	*
21	RLE Compression	*
21	Huffman Compression	*
22	Random Number Generation	*
23	Breadth First Pathfinder	*
23	Heuristic Pathfinder	*

*There are no STL equivalents to these.

**There is an STL structure known as the *deque*, which is often used as an arrayed queue, somewhat similar to the circular queue, but not quite the same.

***These usually use a variant of the BST called a *red-black tree*.

As you can see from the table, STL doesn't cover about half of what I showed you in the book. At first glance, this may appear as if the STL is a tiny library, but this is incorrect. In this book, I focus on a lot of advanced data structure and algorithms. The STL has a different focus, though. The STL has an absolutely huge library of small functions that are used all the time for things like searching, moving, and copying data structures.

Namespaces

There is one final thing that you need to know about STL before I dive into explaining it: Everything within the STL exists within the std namespace.

Namespaces are a new feature in C++. They allow you to place variables, functions, and classes within a certain space so they don't cause name collisions.

For example, say you accidentally create two functions that do two totally different things, but they both have the same name: DoSomething. Normally, C++ will spit out an error at you when you try to compile this, so you need to rename one of them. If you just programmed that function, that shouldn't be too difficult, but imagine this situation:

You're trying to create a brand-new game, and you want to combine parts from two games that you've already made before, so you include the header files from each project into your new one, and you forget that they both have some functions with the same names.

There are two ways you can fix this. The first way is the old way; just rename every conflicting function, find out where they are referenced, and change them. This can get ugly quickly, and there is a better way to do this.

The other way is to place each of the game libraries into a namespace. The easiest way is to create a new header file (like gameone.h) and put this in it:

```
namespace gameone
{
    // #include all of game one's header files here
}
```

This places everything defined in the header files into a namespace called gameone. Now you can do the same thing with the second game's headers in a file called gametwo.h:

```
namespace gametwo
{
    // #include all of game two's header files here
}
```

> **CAUTION**
>
> Make sure that if you use the method of including the header files into a new namespace, you only include the gameone.h or gametwo.h files into the new project. If you include any of the actual files (the ones that are commented out), they will be treated as part of the global namespace again.

Figure D.2 shows how the namespaces are separated from each other.

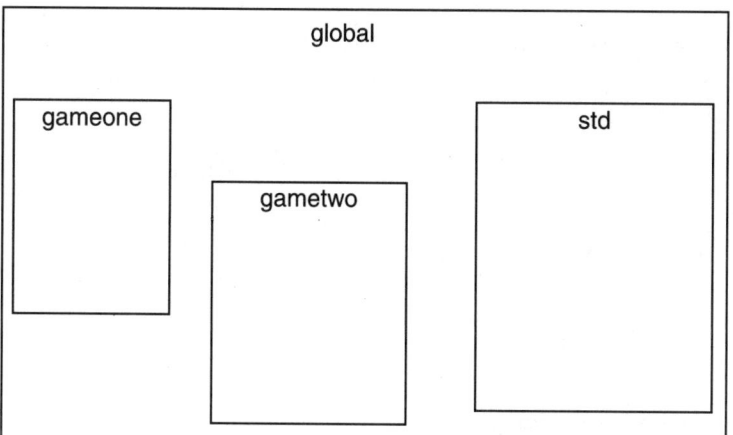

Figure D.2

This is the orientation of namespaces; everything is in the global namespace by default, but putting something in a namespace separates it from the rest of the project.

Now, whenever you want to access the function DoSomething from either of the libraries, you can do this:

```
gameone::DoSomething();
gametwo::DoSomething();
```

This calls both of the functions, specifying which library to call them from.

Unfortunately, having to continuously type the name of the namespace in front of every class, function, or variable can get quite cumbersome.

Therefore, C++ allows you to set a *default* namespace. Take the following code, for example:

```
void Function()
{
    using namespace gameone;
    DoSomething();         // same as gameone::DoSomething();
}
```

Now, inside that function, you can use anything within the gameone namespace as if it were part of the global namespace.

The Organization of STL

STL is organized into two major sections: the *structures* and the *algorithms*. STL uses a unique approach to data structures and tries to separate the algorithms from the structure as much as possible so that the algorithms are usable on as many data structures as possible.

STL achieves this by using *iterators* extensively; I introduce the concept in Chapter 6, "Linked Lists." STL has five categories of iterators related in the hierarchy shown in Figure D.3.

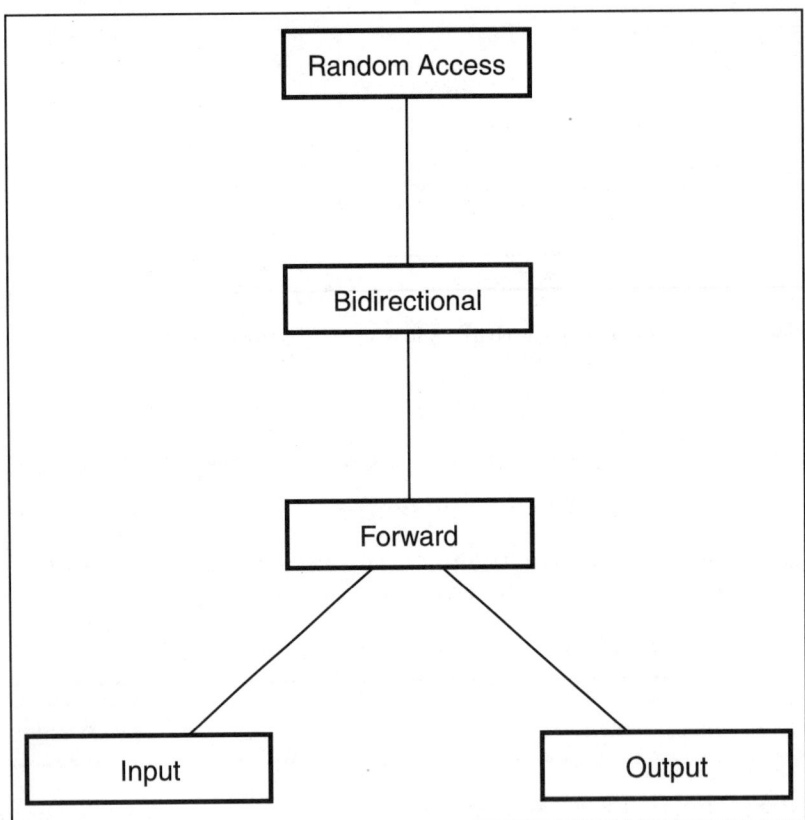

Figure D.3

This shows the relative flexibility of the different iterator categories. The iterators on the top are the most flexible.

The iterator on the top, the random access iterator, is the most flexible and can do the most. Likewise, the iterators on the bottom are the least flexible and can do the least. Table D.2 shows the iterator categories and what they can do.

Table D.2 Iterator Categories

Category	Purpose
Input	These iterators can only be used to get data from a container. You cannot write data into an input iterator, and they can only move in one direction.
Output	These iterators can only write data into a container. You cannot read data from an output iterator, and they can only move in one direction.
Forward	These iterators combine the features of input and output iterators: They can both read and write data to a container, but still can only move in one direction.
Bidirectional	These iterators have all the functionality of a forward iterator, and they can be moved backward as well.
Random Access	These iterators are the most flexible; they have all the features of a bidirectional iterator and can also skip around the container to access cells based on an index.

The categories of iterators aren't actually real classes. Most structures in STL have iterators, and their iterators are rated with a certain category. The algorithms in STL operate on iterators of a certain category as well.

For example, the vector class in STL has iterators that are rated as random access. The STL sort algorithm requires iterators that are rated as random access. This means that you can use the sort algorithm on the vector data structure. However, the list data structure has iterators that are only rated as being bidirectional. Because the sort algorithm requires a random-access iterator, you cannot sort a list with it.

Here's another example. STL has a function called `remove`, which will go through a container and remove the item that you tell it to. This algorithm requires a forward iterator. This means that you can use both the list structure and the vector structure with it because they both have higher-class iterators. Table D.3 shows the relationship between the structure's iterator categories and the algorithms you can use on them.

Table D.3 Structure-Algorithm Support

Category Relationship	Can Structure Use Algorithm?
Structure has higher iterator class than algorithm	Yes
Structure has same iterator class as algorithm	Yes
Structure has lower iterator class than algorithm	No

STL separates the structures it has into several different categories as well. There are *sequence* containers, which are basically one-dimensional containers. There are *associative* containers, which have no defined structure but are designed to have very quick search times. There are container *adapters*, which encapsulate a different class and change the way you access things in it. Finally, there are the *miscellaneous* structures, ones that don't fit in any of the previous categories.

Table D.4 shows a listing of the STL container classes, their structure categories, and their iterator categories, if available.

Table D.4 STL Containers and Their Categories

Container	Category	Iterator Category
vector	sequence	random access
deque	sequence	random access
list	sequence	bidirectional
set/multiset	associative	bidirectional
map/multimap	associative	bidirectional
stack	adapter	none
queue	adapter	none
priority_queue	adapter	none
bitset	miscellaneous	none
string	miscellaneous	none

Note that the only iterators in the table are bidirectional and random access; there are more classes in the STL that use the different iterator types (mainly IOStreams), but I don't cover them at all in this book.

Containers

Every container class has a certain set of functions in STL. Table D.5 shows a listing of what they are and their purpose.

Table D.5 Container Functions

Function	Purpose
Constructor	Constructs the container.
Copy Constructor	Copies the contents of the current container into a new container of the same type. Uses a shallow value-copy so that if the container holds pointers, pointers in the new container will point to the same items.
operator=	Same as copy constructor.
Destructor	Destroys every item in the container. If container contained pointers, then you may end up with a memory leak.
size	Returns the number of items in the container.
max_size	Returns the largest possible size of the container.
empty	Returns true if container is empty, false if not.
swap(C)	Swaps the contents of the container with container C.
begin	Returns an iterator pointing to the very first item in the container.
end	Returns an iterator pointing past the end of the container. This does not point to a valid item.

There are also three other general classes of containers: *forward* containers, *reversible* containers, and *random access* containers. Table D.6 shows the functions that each of these container classes has.

Table D.6 Forward, Reversible, and Random Access Container Functions

Container Type	Function	Purpose
forward	operator==	Determines if the contents of two containers are equal and in the same order.
forward	operator<	Determines if the contents of the left container are less than the contents in the right container.
reversible	rbegin	Returns a reverse iterator starting at the back of the container. These iterators, when moved forward, actually move backward through the container.
reversible	rend	Returns a reverse iterator pointing to an invalid position before the start of the container.
random access	operator[I]	Returns the element at index I.

Sequence Containers

There are three sequence containers. You should be familiar with two of them, but the third one is a structure that I haven't used at all in this book, the deque (pronounced *deek*). All sequence containers have the same functions listed in Table D.5, plus the additional ones listed in Table D.7.

Table D.7 Sequence Functions

Function	Purpose
front	Returns the first item in the container.
insert(I, D)	Inserts new data D into the container before iterator I.

Function	Purpose
insert(I, N, D)	Inserts N copies of D into container before iterator I.
erase(I)	Removes the item in the container pointed to by iterator I.
erase(S, E)	Removes the items starting at iterator S and ending with iterator E (but not including E).
clear	Totally erases everything in the container.
resize(N, D)	Resizes container so that it contains N items. If any new items are needed, they are placed at the end of the array and are copies of item D.
resize(N)	Resizes container so that it contains N items.

Additionally, there are two more types of sequence containers, called *front insertion* and *back insertion* sequences. Table D.8 shows a listing of the functions these containers add.

Table D.8 Insertion Sequences

Type	Function	Purpose
front	push_front(D)	Adds data D at the front of the container.
front	pop_front	Removes the first item from the container.
back	back	Returns the last item in the container.
back	push_back(D)	Adds data D to the end of the container.
back	pop_back	Removes the last item from the container.

The Vector

The vector structure (stored in the vector file) is just another name for the data structure you know and love so much: the array. However, a vector is more than just an array; it is a smart array, even smarter than the Array class I developed in

Chapter 3, "Arrays." A vector can automatically resize itself when you insert items into it. The STL vector class belongs to the *back insertion sequence container* category and also the *random access container* category, so that means it supports all of the functions for those two classes, as well as the *sequence* and *container* class functions.

Furthermore, the vector class adds two new functions, shown in Table D.9.

Table D.9 Vector Functions

Function	Purpose
capacity	Returns the actual size of the vector, not how many items are currently in it.
reserve(N)	Resizes the array, but unlike the sequence resize function, it does not construct any of the new items created by resizing.

Here is an example of the vector class in use:

```
using namespace std;            // use the std namespace.
vector<int> v;                  // declare an int vector.
v.push_back( 10 );              // add 10 to the end of the vector.
v.push_back( 20 );              // vector automatically resizes
v.push_back( 30 );              // whenever you add items to it.
v[0] = v[2];                    // copy 30 into 10.
v.pop_back();                   // erase the last item.
int s = v.size();               // s should be 2.
v.resize( 32 );                 // make array hold 32 items.
```

I think you can get the point from those functions how a vector is used. Now, let me show you how to use iterators with the vector class:

```
vector<int>::iterator itr = v.begin(); // get an iterator.
int i = *itr;                   // get value that iterator points to.
++itr;                          // move to the next item.
i = *itr;                       // get that item.
--itr;                          // move back to the first item again.
*itr = 10;                      // put 10 back into the first index.
sort( v.begin(), v.end() );     // sort the vector.
```

As you can see, the iterator for a vector acts exactly as if it were a pointer into an array, so you can move it forward and backward, and dereference it.

Also, take a look at the last line, the one that calls sort. The sort algorithm takes two random-access iterators and sorts everything between them, not including the item that the end iterator points to. So you can call the begin and end functions of the vector and pass them into sort, and it will automatically sort everything in the array for you.

The Deque

The deque (stored in the deque file) is a strange vector-like structure that is random access, but it provides $O(c)$ insertion to the front of the container as well as the back. If you remember how an array or a vector works, you can easily insert items at the back of the container in $O(c)$ time, but inserting anywhere else in the container is $O(n)$—much slower. The deque structure fixes that and provides very quick insertion to either the back or front of the container and $O(n)$ insertion in the middle.

> **NOTE**
> The deque structure is usually implemented in a series of linked memory *chunks*. Whenever you add an item to the end of a full chunk, a new chunk is allocated, and the data is placed into the beginning of the new chunk. Likewise, if you add an item to the front of a full chunk, then a new chunk is created, and the data is placed at the end of the new chunk. Although this means that inserting to the beginning is now an O(c) algorithm and accessing items is still O(c), it is slower than a vector when accessing indexes because it needs to find the right chunk first and then locate the index within the chunk.

> **NOTE**
> Most implementations of the deque do not deallocate chunks when they are emptied, so you might end up wasting a lot of space sometimes. For example, if you continuously insert items at the back of a deque and remove them from the front, you will end up with a constant number of items in the deque, but the place of the items inside will slowly travel from chunk to chunk, and you will end up with lots of empty chunks at the beginning of the deque.

The `deque` class does not add any new functions, so it is the same as the vector but it is missing the capacity and reserve functions and has access to the *front insertion sequence* functions `push_front` and `pop_front`.

Here is some code demonstrating deques:

```
using namespace std;
deque<int> d;
deque<int>::iterator i;
// create a deque containing 70, 60, 50, 40, and 30:
d.push_front( 50 );
d.push_back( 40 );
d.push_front( 60 );
d.push_back( 30 );
d.push_front( 70 );
// multiply each item in the deque by 2.
for( i = d.begin(); i != d.end(); ++i )
{
    (*i) *= 2;
}
// sort the deque.
sort( d.begin(), d.end() );
```

The List

The STL list class (stored in the list file) is a doubly linked list, just like the `DLinkedList` class from Chapter 6. However, it is usually implemented as a *circular* linked list, which I only mentioned and did not actually show you. However, it doesn't matter; the way the list works internally doesn't make a difference to you when you're using this class.

The list is a sequence, and it is bidirectional, but it is not random access. Table D.10 shows a listing of all of the new functions that the list class adds.

Table D.10 List Functions

Function	Purpose
splice(I, L)	All items inside of list L are removed from L and placed into the current list in front of iterator I.
splice(I, L, F)	This removes the item pointed to by iterator F inside of list L and inserts it into the current list before iterator I.
splice(I, L, F, L)	This removes every item in list L between the iterators F and L (not including L) and places them into the current list before iterator I.
remove(D)	This removes all instances of D within the list.
unique	This goes through the entire list and removes all but the first item in any group of repeated items.
merge(L)	This performs one iteration of the mergesort algorithm and merges list L with the current list. Both lists must be sorted first, and list L will be completely emptied.
sort	This will sort the list. No algorithm is specified, but it runs in $O(n\log_2 n)$ time, so it could be a quicksort or a mergesort.

The only way you can access items inside of a linked list is by using iterators or the front and back functions defined by the *sequence* and *front insertion sequence* containers.

Here is some code demonstrating lists:

```
using namespace std;
list<int> l;
list<int>::iterator i;
// fill the list so that it has 20, 10, 50, 40:
l.push_back( 50 );
l.push_back( 40 );
l.push_front( 10 );
l.push_front( 20 );
// this next line wont work, since the list class doesn't have
// random access iterators:
// sort( l.begin(), l.end() );
// instead, do this:
```

```
l.sort();
// multiply each item by 2:
for( i = l.begin(); i != l.end(); ++i )
{
    (*i) *= 2;
}
```

Associative Containers

Associative containers differ from the sequence containers. All four of them have bi-directional iterators, but you cannot insert items into an associative container like you can with sequential containers. Due to space restraints, I don't have time to go over them here, but they are similar to some of the structures I've shown you in the book.

For example, the set and multiset structures (contained in the file set) are designed to store data like the `BinarySearchTree` from Chapter 13, "Binary Search Trees," does; it stores the data directly in the structure.

The map and multimap structures (contained in the file map), on the other hand, store data like the `HashTable` class from Chapter 8, "Hash Tables," with a key and data associated with that key.

Of course, they aren't actually BSTs or hash tables, I was just using examples to show how each structure manages data. In reality, almost every implementation of all four classes uses a *red-black tree* underneath, which is a variant of the binary search tree.

Container Adaptors

There are three container adaptors: the stack (in the file stack), the queue, and the priority_queue (both contained in the queue file).

The `stack` and the `queue` classes are the easiest to use:

```
using namespace std;
stack<int> s;
queue<int> q;
int i;
// push 10 and 20
s.push( 10 );
s.push( 20 );
i = s.top();        // i should be 20
```

```
s.pop();           // pop off 20
i = s.top();       // i should be 10
s.pop();           // pop off 10
// put 10 and 20 into the queue
q.push( 10 );
q.push( 20 );
i = q.front();     // i should be 10
q.pop();           // pop off 10
i = q.front();     // i should be 20
q.pop();
```

Now, both the stack and the queue in this example use a deque as their base, but you can change that. The whole point of the adapter classes is to allow you to adapt another container into the same interface.

Remember how I showed you how to create a linked stack and then an arrayed stack? That took two different classes, but the STL version only uses one class:

```
using namespace std;
stack< int, vector<int> > vs;
stack< int, list<int> > ls;
stack< int, deque<int> > ds;
```

This creates three stacks: one using a vector, one using a list, and one using a deque. You can do this with a queue also:

```
using namespace std;
queue< int, vector<int> > vq;
queue< int, list<int> > lq;
queue< int, deque<int> > dq;
```

The stack and queue adapters can use any sequence container.

The other adapter, the priority_queue, doesn't work with all sequence containers, though, so it needs random access containers because it usually uses a heap implementation underneath (see Chapter 14, "Priority Queues and Heaps").

```
using namespace std;
priority_queue< int > pq;                          // vector priority queue
priority_queue< int, vector<int> > vpq;            // vector priority queue
priority_queue< int, deque<int> > dpq;             // deque priority queue
```

As you can see from the example, the default implementation of a priority_queue uses vectors, but you can explicitly state that it should use vectors or deques. The priority queue class supports all of the stack functions: push, top, and pop. I guess they used top instead of front because you're accessing the top of the heap.

> **NOTE**
> STL priority queues by default use the less-than operator of the datatype that is stored in the container, so this means that pointers do not work correctly in priority queues. However, you can change this by creating something called a `functor`, which is like the function pointers I used for the Heap class. In reality, a functor is a class that overloads `operator()` so that you can use it like a function. This is a somewhat advanced topic, so I don't explain it in this book, but any book dedicated to STL will explain this for you. The `functor` class is usually a static class with no data, and it is passed in as the third template parameter of the priority_queue.

The Miscellaneous Containers

The two main miscellaneous structures are the bitset and the string. Strings aren't covered in depth in this book, so I will only show you how to use the bitset class.

The bitset structure is contained within the bitset file and acts very much like the `Bitvector` class from Chapter 4, "Bitvectors." There are a few differences, though.

First of all, a bitset cannot be resized. When you create it, it must be a certain size, like this:

```
using namespace std;
bitset<64> b;
```

This creates a bitset with 64 bits in it. You can do many things with a bitset:

```
b = 100;            // set the bitset to 100, which is 1100100
b |= 1;             // set the first bit to 1
b |= 15;            // set the first 4 bits to 1
b &= 31;            // chop off every bit past the 5th bit
int i = b[4];       // get bit 4
b[4] = 1;           // set bit 4 to 1
b <<= 2;            // shift the bitset up by 2
```

```
b >>= 3;              // shift the bitset down by 3
b = ~b;               // flip every bit
```

The bitset also has other functions, which make your programs cleaner to read:

```
b.reset();            // clear every bit to 0
b.set();              // sets every bit to 1
b.flip();             // flips every bit
b.set( 10 );          // sets bit 10
b.set( 10, 0 );       // clears bit 10
b.reset( 10 );        // clears bit 10
b.flip( 10 );         // flips bit 10
i = b.size();         // gets the size of the set (64 in this case)
i = b.count();        // gets the number of bits that are 1
bool a = b.any();     // a is true if any bits are set
a = b.none();         // a is true if no bits are set
a = b.test( 10 );     // a is true if bit 10 is 1, false otherwise
```

That's pretty much all you need to know to use a bitset.

> **NOTE**
>
> Remember back to the bitvector implementation from Chapter 4, where I showed you that you could use the operator[] to access bits, but not write them? The STL bitset, however, lets you do things like this: b[5] = 1;. How is this possible, considering that you cannot return a reference to an individual bit? The STL uses a clever hack called a *proxy class*. It doesn't actually return a reference to a bit, but a class that has an overloaded operator= and a pointer to the bit. So when you call b[5], it returns a new proxy class. When you put the = 1 after it, it calls the assignment operator of the proxy class, and this in turn sets the bit. As you can imagine, this adds a lot of overhead to the whole operation, so this is usually a bad way to set bits. It is usually a better idea to just use the set function instead.

Conclusion

The material contained within this Appendix is just the tip of the iceberg; the STL is a *huge* library, and it takes a long time to master it. Luckily, there are also lots of resources for STL. For example, the most complete online documentation is on SGI's Web site at http://www.sgi.com/tech/stl/. Beware, however, because it includes documentation on non-standard containers that SGI has added in their version of the STL. The conclusion section of this book also contains a listing of helpful STL books.

Index

Symbols

#define macros, 35
2D arrays. *See also* arrays
   data storage, 116-117
   defined, 108-110
   graphical demonstration, 111-112
   initializing, 113
   tilemaps, 131-136
3D arrays. *See also* arrays
   data storage, 117-118
   defined, 108-110
   tilemaps, 136-144
4D arrays, 117-118

A

A* pathfinding, 750-752
   code, 752-753
   DirectionMap class, 780-785
   graphical demonstration, 752
   Tilemap class, 771-779
abstract classes, 252
access operator, 89-91
accessing
   multi-dimensional arrays, 115-116
   static arrays, 44-46
accessor functions, 247
adaptors (containers), 896-898
Add function, 20, 72-74
AddArc function, 503, 508-509
AddButton function, 870
AddCheckbox function, 871
addition, digit (hash tables), 221-222
AddLabel function, 871
AddNode function, 506
AddTextBox function, 871
adjacency tables (graphs), 486-488
Adventure
   AI, 304-305
   designing, 266-269
      troubleshooting, 772
   directionmaps, 567
      A* pathfinding, 780-785
      DirectionCell class, 568-569
      DirectionMap class, 570-579, 780-785
      game logic, 580
      image sets, 580
      LoadFromFile function, 572-574
      LoadMap function, 581-582
      map functions, 574-579
      MapEntry class, 569
      playing, 582
      tilesets, 580
   game logic, 299-309, 470-472
      speed, 787-790
   gameplay, 309-310
   interfaces, 269-275
   loop, 308-309
   MakePerson function, 297-299
   pathfinding, 770
   Person class, 290-297
   Tilemap class (A* pathfinding), 469, 771-779

Index

tilemap editor, 310-314
tilemaps, 275-290
trees
    game logic, 470-472
    Item class, 467-468
    Map class, 468-469
    map editor, 473-475
    maps, 464, 465-466
    Player class, 469-470
    TileMap class, 469
AI (Artificial Intelligence), 304
    Adventure, 304-305
    finite state machines, 530-532
        AI class, 552
        attackers, 548
        complex, 533-534
        conditional events, 541-546
        constants, 550-551
        defenders, 548
        DFAs, 538
        enumerations, 551
        Event function, 555-556
        graphical demonstration, 537, 546-547
        implementing, 535-536
        initializing, 554-555
        Intruder, 547-560
        linked ranges, 544-545
        multi-dimensional arrays, 542-544
        multiplying states, 538-541
        ProcessAI function, 557-559
        pure, 538
        state transition tables, 535-536
        trees, 545-546
    high-level, 530
    intelligence (game logic), 788-790
    priority queues, 425
    recursion, 319

AI class, 552
algorithms. *See also* functions
    Array class, 59-68
    asymptotic analysis, 11
    doubly linked lists, 172-174
    functions, 9-10
    graphical demonstration, 10-11
    linked lists, 184-185
    O notation, 4-9
    parsing binary trees, 381-382
    recursion, 319
        Towers of Hanoi, 320-328
    STL, 885-889
    walk down (heaps), 414
    walk up (heaps), 411
analysis
    arrayed stacks, 199
    arrays, 77-80
    bitfields, 105
    bitvectors, 105
    linked lists, 184
    multi-dimensional arrays, 144-145
    singly linked lists, 169
    stacks, 196
and operator, 91-93
API (SDL). *See* SDL
Append function, 156-157
AQueue class, 209-212
arcs
    cost, 484
    graphs, 482
ArcType datatype, 501
arithmetic expressions, 376-377
Array class, 27-32
    algorithms, 59-68
    constructor, 59-60
    conversion operators, 63-64

data, 59
destructor, 60
inserting items, 64-65
intarray operator, 62-63
removing items, 65-66
Resize function, 60-61
size, 67-68
Array2D class, 121
   constructor, 122
   data, 122
   destructor, 123
   Get function, 123
   Height function, 125
   parameters, 122
   Resize function, 123-125
   Size function, 125
   Width function, 125
Array3D class, 127-130
arrayed binary trees, 363-366
   graphical demonstration, 366-368
   size, 364-366
   traversing, 365-366
arrayed heaps, 411
arrayed queues, 207-212
arrayed stacks, 196-199
arrays. *See also* 2D arrays; 3D arrays
   analysis, 77-80
   bitvectors. *See* bitvectors
   Boolean, 84
   bounds checking, 29
   classes, 243-245
      parameters, 30-31
   declaring, 72
   defined, 40-41
   dynamic, 49-59
      calloc function, 51
      deleting, 53-54
      exceptions, 52

      free function, 53
      malloc function, 50-51
      memory leaks, 53-55
      new function, 52
      pointers, 53
      realloc function, 54-57
      size, 54-57
   functions (templates), 15-16
   graphical demonstration, 41-43
   inserting, 80
   loading, 68-71
   memory cache, 77-80
   multi-dimensional
      analysis, 144-145
      branch predictors, 142-144
      finite state machines, 542-544
      performance, 142-144
      pipelining, 142-144
      size, 144
      speed, 142-144
   reading, 70-71
   removing, 80
   size, 80
   sorting. *See* sorts
   static, 43-49
      accessing, 44-46
      declaring, 43-44
      fencepost errors, 44
      initializing, 48
      passing to functions, 46-48
      pointers, 47-48
      reading, 45-46
      size, 48
      troubleshooting, 45-46
      writing, 45-46
   storing, 68-71
   storing data, 71-77
   writing, 69-70

Artificial Intelligence. *See* AI
ASM (assembly languages), 243
assembly languages (ASM), 243
ASSERT macro, 820
assignment operator, 344
associative containers, 896
AStack class, 197-199
AStar function, 775-784
asymptotic analysis, 11
attackers (finite state machines), 548
Averagetype data type, 25
AVL BSTs, 395

B

bad alloc exception, 61
balance (binary trees), 362
base 2 radix sorts, 633-635
base 4 radix sorts, 636
base 16 radix sorts, 636
base case (recursion), 319
base numbers (minimax trees), 441
bi-directional graphs, 483-491
bin sorts, 630
binary and operator, 90-91
binary math rules, 91
binary numbers, 802-804
binary search trees. *See* BSTs
binary trees
    arrayed, 363-366
        graphical demonstration, 366-368
        size, 364-366
        traversing, 365-366
    balance, 362
    BSTs. *See* BSTs
    code, 368-371
    defined, 360-361
    dense, 361-362
    full, 361
    game demo, 386-388
    heaps. *See* heaps
    left, 361
    linked, 362-363
    parsing, 374-376
        algorithms, 381-382
        arithmetic expressions, 376-377
        code, 382-384
        executing, 384-386
        recursive descent, 377-386
        scanning, 378-379
        tokenizing, 378-379
        tokens, 377-378
        variables, 378
    right, 361
    structure, 362-366
    traversing, 371-374
        graphical demonstration, 373-374
BinarySearchTree class, 397-401
BinaryTree class, 368-371
bins (radix sorts), 633
bit maths, 802-810
    binary numbers, 802-804
    bitshifting, 809-810
    bitwise, 807-808
    datatype sizes, 805-806
    integer data sizes, 805-806
bitfields
    analysis, 105
    declaring, 103
    defined, 102-103
    using, 103-105
bitshifting math, 809-810
Bitvector class, 86
    access operator, 89-91
    binary and operator, 90-91
    ClearAll function, 93

constructor, 87
data, 87
destructor, 87-88
ReadFile function, 94-95
Resize function, 88-89
Set function, 91-93
SetAll function, 93-94
WriteFile function, 94
bitvectors
   analysis, 105
   arrays, 98-99
   defined, 84-85
   graphical demonstration, 85-86
   memory caching, 101
   saving players, 96-102
bitwise math, 807-808
blue ray DVD, 646
books
   C++, 796-797
   data structures, 795-796
   game programming, 797-798, 858
Boolean arrays, 84
bouncing, 718-719
bounds checking, 29
branch predictors (multi-dimensional arrays), 142-144
branching data structures, 41
BreadthFirst function, 511-512
breadth-first pathfinding, 721-727
breadth-first searches, 495-499
brute force sorts, 600
BSTs (binary search trees), 390
   AVL, 395
   code, 397-401
   data
      finding, 394
      inserting, 391-394
      removing, 394
   defined, 390-391
   graphical demonstration, 395-397
   red-black, 395
   rotations, 395
   rules, 394
   sorts, 638
   splay, 395
   storing resources, 402-405
   sub-optimal, 395
bubble sorts
   code, 605-609
   comparison functions, 606
   defined, 600-602
   graphical demonstration, 602-604
   optimizing, 604-605
Bubblesort function, 605-609
buffers (z-buffers), 639
building
   priority queues, 424-430
   trees, 347
busses (data compression), 647-648

C

C++
   books, 796-797
   controversy, 823-824
   SDL, 851-853
cache
   arrays, 77-80
   memory (bitvectors), 101
Calculate function, 215
CalculateMiniMax function, 449
CalculateMiniMaxValue function, 450-452
CalculateTree function, 446-448, 680-682
calculating (pathfinding), 726
calloc function, 51
catch keyword, 821-823

Index

Cell class, 730-731
CellCoordinate function, 780
CellDistance function, 732-733
Central Processing Unit (CPU), 647-648
Check function, 75-77
checkers
    game trees, 456-459
    minimax trees, 442, 456-459
chess, 442
children (classes), 249
cin variable, 812-814
circular queues, 207
class keyword, 17
classes
    abstract, 252
    AI, 552
    AQueue, 209-212
    Array, 27-32
        algorithms, 59-68
        constructor, 59-60
        conversion operators, 63-64
        data, 59
        destructor, 60
        inserting items, 64-65
        intarray operator, 62-63
        removing items, 65-66
        Resize function, 60-61
        size, 67-68
    Array2D, 121
        constructor, 122
        data, 122
        destructor, 123
        Get function, 123
        Height function, 125
        parameters, 122
        Resize function, 123-125
        Size function, 125
        Width function, 125

Array3D, 127-130
arrays, 243-245
    parameters, 30-31
AStack, 197-199
BinarySearchTree, 397-401
BinaryTree, 368-371
Bitvector, 86
    access operator, 89-91
    binary and operator, 90-91
    ClearAll function, 93
    constructor, 87
    data, 87
    destructor, 87-88
    ReadFile function, 94-95
    Resize function, 88-89
    Set function, 91-93
    SetAll function, 93-94
    WriteFile function, 94
Cell, 730-731
CompareNodes, 678
constructors, 824-826
conversion operators, 829-830
Coordinate, 731-773
Coordinates, 213-214
data storing, 243-245
destructors, 826-827
DirectionCell, 568-569
DirectionMap, 570-579
    A* pathfinding, 780-785
DLinkedList, 196
Factory, 426
functions
    inline, 830-831
    pointers, 832-833
Graph, 501, 504-512
GraphArc, 501-502
GraphNode, 502-504
HashEntry, 228-229

HashTable, 229-233
Heap, 418-424
Huffman, 678-691
HuffmanFrequency, 677
HuffmanNode, 676-677
inheritance, 248-260
　children, 249
　down-casting, 263
　Object class, 260-265
　parents, 249
　types, 256-258
Item, 256, 290, 467-468
LStack, 196
Map, 468-469
MapEntry, 569
Menu, 201-204
Monster, 72
Object, 250-255
　inheritance, 260-265
overloading operators, 827-829
Person, 258-260, 290-297, 788
Player, 97, 469-470
pointers, 252-254
private, 246-248
public, 245-246
Resource, 402
RLE, 656-665
RLEPair, 656
RockState, 443-445
　global variables, 445-446
SDLFrame, 867-868
SDLGUI, 869-874
SDLGUIFrame, 876-878
SDLGUIItem, 874-876
Sector, 523
SListIterator, 162-163
SListNode, 151-152

Append function, 156-157
　constructor, 155
　destructor, 155-156
　encapsulating, 154-155
　InsertAfter function, 152-153
　iterators, 153-154
　Prepend function, 158
　RemoveHead function, 158-160
　RemoveTail function, 160-161
String, 236-237
templates, 19-24
　declaring, 23
　instances, 23
this pointer, 830
TileCell, 773-774, 781
TileMap
　A* pathfinding, 771-779
　Adventure, 469
Tree, 338
　constructor, 340
　Count function, 342
　Destroy function, 341-342
　destructor, 340-341
　structure, 339
TreeIterator, 342
　assignment operator, 344
　constructor, 343-344
　Down function, 346
　horizontal functions, 346
　ResetIterator function, 344-345
　Root function, 345
　structure, 343
　Up function, 345-346
Clear function, 30
clear functions, 91
ClearAll function, 93, 101
ClearCells function, 732, 774, 781

ClearMarks function, 510
ClickRock function, 452-453
clipping, 519
code
   binary trees, 368-371
      parsing, 382-384
   BSTs, 397-401
   Huffman trees, 677-692
   memory, 837
   pathfinding
      A* pathfinding, 752-753
      distance-first pathfinding, 730-739
      heuristics, 744-745, 749-750
   return codes, 820-821
   sorts
      bubble sorts, 605-609
      heap sorts, 613-616
      quicksorts, 623-627
      radix sorts, 633-637
collisions (hash tables), 221
commands
   fseek, 100
   fwrite, 101
   queues, 212-216
Compare function, 640
CompareCellCoordinates function, 780
CompareCoordinateDescending function, 731-732
CompareCoordinates function, 773
comparefloat function, 607
compareint function, 607
compareintreverse function, 607
CompareInts function, 397-398
CompareNodes function, 678
CompareUnits function, 427
comparison functions, 606
complex finite state machines, 533-534
ComplexHeuristic function, 750

Compress function, 682-684
compression. *See* data compression
compressor (RLE), 656-665
conditional events
   finite state machines, 541-546
   graphical demonstration, 546-547
const keyword, 814
constants (finite state machines), 550-551
constructors
   Array class, 59-60
   Array2D class, 122
   Bitvector class, 87
   classes, 824-826
   SListNode class, 155
   Tree class, 340
   TreeIterator class, 343-344
containers, 898-899
   adaptors, 896-898
   associative, 896
   categories, 888-889
   functions, 889-890
   sequence, 890-896
conventions
   multi-dimensional arrays, 118
   STL, 882-883
conversion operators, 63-64, 829-830
Convert function, 689-691
converting maps, 583-584
ConvertTreeToArray function, 688-689
Coordinate class, 731, 773
coordinates (multi-dimensional arrays), 118
Coordinates class, 213-214
cost (arcs), 484
Count function, 195, 199, 370
   Tree class, 342
cout variable, 811-812
CPU (Central Processing Unit), 647-648

crashes, memory, 55
CreateLookupTable function, 691
CreateRLE function, 657-659
culling, 519

D

data
  Array class, 59
  Array2D class, 122
  Bitvector class, 87
  BSTs
    finding, 394
    inserting, 391-394
    removing, 394
  compression. *See* data compression
  sorting. *See* sorts
  sparse, 218-219
  storing
    2D arrays, 116-117
    3D arrays, 117-118
    4D arrays, 117-118
    arrays, 71-77
    classes, 243-245
data compression, 646
  busses, 647-648
  CPU, 647-648
  encryption, 693
  fractal, 694
  GPU, 647-648
  Huffman trees, 665
    code, 677-692
    decoding, 665-667
    frequency tables, 667-668
    graphical demonstration, 674-676
    lookup tables, 691
    priority queues, 668-674
  Internet, 649

  Pentiums, 647
  RLE, 649-651
    compressor, 656-665
    decompressor, 656-665
    graphical demonstration, 651-655
    sprites, 655
  test files, 692-693
  wavelets, 694
  XBox, 648
data structures
  books, 795-796
  branching, 41
  linear, 41
  random-access, 41
  STL, 885-889
    deque, 893-894
    list, 894-896
    vector, 891-893
data types
  ArcType, 501
  Averagetype, 25
  NodeType, 501
  references (functions), 62
  sizes, 805-806
  Sumtype, 25
  template parameters, 24-26, 29
declaring
  arrays, 72
  bitfields, 103
  multi-dimensional arrays, 112-115
  static arrays, 43-44
  template classes, 23
decoding (Huffman trees), 665-667
Decompress function, 684-685
decompressor (RLE), 656-665
defenders (finite state machines), 548
#define macros, 35
defining Monster class, 72

delete operator, 54-57
deleting dynamic arrays, 53-54
dense binary trees, 361-362
dense heaps, 411
depth-based sorts, 638-642
    z-buffers, 639
DepthFirst function, 510-511, 522
depth-first searches, 493-495
depth-limited depth-first searches (DLDFS), 521-522
deque data structure, 893-894
Dequeue function, 206-207, 422
design
    Adventure, 266-269
    troubleshooting, 772
Destroy function, 341-342
destructors
    Array class, 60
    Array2D class, 123
    Bitvector class, 87-88
    classes, 826-827
    SListNode class, 155-156
    Tree class, 340-341
determinism (random integers), 699-700
DFAs (deterministic finite automatons), 538
dice (random integers), 698-699
digit addition (hash tables), 221-222
direction tables
    dungeons, 512-518
    graphs, 488-489
    portal engines, 518-527
DirectionCell class, 568-569
DirectionMap class, 570-579
    A* pathfinding, 780-785
directionmaps
    Adventure, 567
        DirectionCell class, 568-569

DirectionMap class, 570-579
    game logic, 580
    image sets, 580
    LoadFromFile function, 572-574
    LoadMap function, 581, 582
    map functions, 574-579
    MapEntry class, 569
    playing, 582
    tilesets, 580
identification numbers, 566, 583
map editor, 584-593
    loading maps, 588-590
    saving maps, 590-593
    tiles, 586-588
maps
    converting, 583-584
    formats, 564-567
    memory leaks, 573
directory (STLPort), 880-882
discrete games, 432
distance-first pathfinding, 725-727
    code, 730-739
    graphical demonstration, 727-730
distributing programs (SDL), 858
DLDFS (depth-limited depth first) searches, 521-522
DLinkedList class, 196
documenting templates, 33
double hashing, 222
doubly linked lists, 169
    algorithms, 172-174
    graphical demonstration, 170-171
    inserting nodes, 172-173
    node structure, 171-172
    ReadFromDisk function, 175-176
    removing nodes, 173-174
    SaveToDisk function, 174-175
Down function, 346

down-casting, 263
DrawMap function, 514-516
DrawTile function, 587
DrawTilemap function, 135
dungeon direction tables, 512-518
DVD Consortium, 646
dynamic arrays, 49-59
  calloc function, 51
  deleting, 53-54
  exceptions, 52
  free function, 53
  malloc function, 50-51
  memory leaks, 53-55
  new function, 52
  pointers, 53
  realloc function, 54-57
  size, 54-57
dynamic multi-dimensional arrays, 121-131

E

editors
  maps
    Adventure, 473-475
    directionmaps, 584-593
    loading, 588-590
    saving, 590-593
    tiles, 586-588
  tilemap, 310-314
    upgrading, 594-595
efficiency
  heaps, 416-417
  pathfinding, 790-791
Empty function, 445
encapsulating (SListNode class), 154-155
encryption, 693
Enqueue function, 420

enumerations (finite state machines), 551
equivalence operator, 445
error handling, 820-823. *See also* troubleshooting
fencepost errors (static arrays), 44
Evaluate function, 384-386
Event function, 555-556
events
  conditional
    finite state machines, 541-546
    graphical demonstration, 546-547
  handling (SDL), 861-863
exceptions, 820-823
  bad alloc, 61
  dynamic arrays, 52

F

Factory class, 426
fclose function, 817
fencepost errors (static arrays), 44
Fibbionacci series, 318
FILE pointer, 69
file streams (I/O), 814-817
FILE structure, 814
files
  data compression test, 692-693
  SDL, 849-851
  STLPort directory, 880-882
FillArray function, 659-660
FILO (First In, Last Out), 191
Find function, 400-401
finding data, 394
finite state machines
  AI, 530-532
  AI class, 552

attackers, 548
complex, 533-534
conditional events, 541-546
constants, 550-551
defenders, 548
DFAs, 538
enumerations, 551
Event function, 555-556
graphical demonstration, 537, 546-547
implementing, 535-536
initializing, 554-555
Intruder, 547-560
linked ranges, 544-545
multi-dimensional arrays, 542-544
multiplying states, 538-541
ProcessAI function, 557-559
pure, 538
state transition tables, 535-536
trees, 545-546
floats (random), 706-707
fopen function, 69-70, 814-816
formats (directionmaps), 564-567
Forth function, 163
fractal compression, 694
fread function, 70, 817
free function, 53
free store, 836, 844-845
frequency tables (Huffman trees), 667-668
Front function, 207
fseek command, 100
full binary trees, 361
functions. *See also* algorithms
   accessor, 247
   Add, 20, 72-74
   AddArc, 503, 508-509
   AddButton, 870
   AddCheckbox, 871
   AddLabel, 871

AddNode, 506
AddTextBox, 871
algorithms, 9-10
Append, 156-157
AStar, 775-784
BreadthFirst, 511-512
Bubblesort, 605-609
Calculate, 215
CalculateMiniMax, 449
CalculateMiniMaxValue, 450-452
CalculateTree, 446-448, 680-682
calloc, 51
CellCoordinate, 780
CellDistance, 732-733
Check, 75-77
clear, 91
Clear, 30
ClearAll, 101
   Bitvector class, 93
ClearCells, 732, 774, 781
ClearMarks, 510
ClickRock, 452-453
Compare, 640
CompareCellCoordinates, 780
CompareCoordinateDescending, 731-732
CompareCoordinates, 773
comparefloat, 607
compareint, 607
compareintreverse, 607
CompareInts, 397-398
CompareUnits, 427
comparison, 606
ComplexHeuristic, 750
Compress, 682-684
containers, 889-890
Convert, 689-691
ConvertTreeToArray, 688-689

Index

Count, 195, 199, 370
　Tree class, 342
CreateLookupTable, 691
CreateRLE, 657-659
data types, 62
Decompress, 684-685
DepthFirst, 510-511, 522
Dequeue, 206-207, 422
Destroy, 341-342
Down, 346
DrawMap, 514-516
DrawTile, 587
DrawTilemap, 135
Empty, 445
Enqueue, 420
Evaluate, 384-386
Event, 555-556
fclose, 817
FillArray, 659-660
Find, 400-401
fopen, 69-70, 814-816
Forth, 163
fread, 70, 817
free, 53
Front, 207
fwrite, 69, 816-817
GameInit, 98
Get, 123
GetArc, 503-504, 509
GetClosestDirection, 778-779, 784-785
GetFollow, 788
GetFont, 872
GetItem, 872
GetIterator, 163
GetMouseState, 214
GetScreen, 872
hash tables, 221-224
HeapWalkDown, 614

Height, 125
Heuristic, 449-450, 774-775, 781
horizontal, 346
identity, 91
inline, 830-831
Inorder, 372-373
Insert, 64-65, 399-400
　singly linked lists, 164-167
InsertAfter, 152-153
Item, 163
KeyDown, 873
Load, 313, 588-590, 595
LoadData, 661-662, 687-688
LoadFromFile, 572-574
LoadMap, 302-303, 581-582
LoadTree, 686
MakePerson, 297-299
malloc, 50-51
map, 574-579
math, 817-818
MedianOfThree, 623-624
MiniMax, 449
MouseDown, 873
MouseUp, 873
new, 52
OpponentMove, 453-454
ParseArithmetic, 382-384
passing
　multi-dimensional arrays, 119-121
　static arrays, 46-48
PathAStar, 775-778
PathDistanceFirst, 734-739
PerformAI, 787-790
PickUp, 471
pointers, 832-833
Pop, 195, 198
Postorder, 350-351, 372
Preorder, 348-350, 372

Prepend, 158
ProcessAI, 557-559
Push, 194-195, 198
queues, 206
QuickSort, 624-627
rand, 700-702, 819
random integers, 700-702
RandomPercent, 705-706
RandomRange, 704-705
RandomRangeF, 706-707
RandomRangeModulo, 702-704
ReadFile, 70-71
   Bitvector class, 94-95
ReadFromDisk, 175-176
realloc, 54-57
recursion, 318
   base case, 319
Remove, 65-66, 74-76, 504
   singly linked lists, 166-168
RemoveArc, 509
RemoveHead, 158-160
RemoveNode, 506-508
RemoveTail, 160-161
ResetIterator, 344-345
Resize
   Array class, 60-61
   Array2D class, 123-125
   Bitvector class, 88-89
ResourceCompare, 403
return values, 843
Root, 345
Save, 312, 590-595
SaveData, 661, 686-687
SavePlayers, 100-101
SaveToDisk, 174-175
SaveTree, 686
SDLArrowLine, 866
SDLBlit, 135, 867

SDLBox, 867
SDLLine, 866
SDLPoint, 866
set, 91
Set, 91-93
SetAll, 93-94
SetFocus, 872
SetFollow, 788
SetFont, 870
SetLife, 99
SetNewMap, 302-303, 471-472
SimpleHeuristic, 744-745
Size, 67-68
   Array2D class, 125
srand, 700-702, 819
stacks, 193
Start, 162
strcat, 663
StringHash, 223-224
switch, 516-517
templates. *See* templates, 24
TilePathfind, 766-767
time, 818-819
Top, 195, 198
Up, 345-346
Valid, 163
virtual, 251-255
WalkDown, 422-424
WalkUp, 420-422
Width, 125
WriteFile, 69
   Bitvector class, 94
fwrite command, 101
fwrite function, 69, 816-817

G

Game Demos
  Game Demo 3-1, 71-77
  Game Demo 4-1, 96-102
  Game Demo 5-1, 131-136
  Game Demo 5-2, 136-144
  Game Demo 6-1, 176-180
  Game Demo 6-2, 180-183
  Game Demo 7-1, 199-204
  Game Demo 7-2, 212-216
  Game Demo 8-1, 235-239
  Game Demo 9-1, 266-314
  Game Demo 11-1, 352-358
  Game Demo 12-1, 386-388
  Game Demo 13-1, 402-405
  Game Demo 14-1, 424-430
  Game Demo 15-1, 442-456
  Game Demo 16-1, 466-475
  Game Demo 17-1, 512-518
  Game Demo 17-2, 518-527
  Game Demo 18-1, 547-560
  Game Demo 19-1, 567-583
  Game Demo 19-2, 584-593
  Game Demo 20-1, 638-642
  Game Demo 23-1, 756-762
game programming books, 797-798, 858
game trees
  checkers, 456-459
  defined, 432-434
  game logic, 470-472
  limited depth algorithms, 460
GameInit function, 98
games. *See also* game trees
  discrete, 432
  gameplay (Adventure), 309-310
  logic
    Adventure, 299-309, 580
    AI, 788-790
    speed, 787-790
    trees, 470-472
  MMO, 105
  states, 439-442
Get function, 123
GetArc function, 503-504, 509
GetClosestDirection function, 778-779, 784-785
GetFollow functions, 788
GetFont function, 872
GetItem function, 872
GetIterator function, 163
GetMouseState function, 214
GetScreen function, 872
global memory, 838-839
global variables, 838-839
  RockState class, 445-446
GPU (Graphics Processing Unit), 647-648
Graph class, 501-512
GraphArc class, 501-502
graphical demonstration
  2D arrays, 111-112
  A* pathfinding, 752
  algorithms, 10-11
  arrayed binary trees, 366-368
  arrays, 41-43
  binary trees, 373-374
  bitvectors, 85-86
  BSTs, 395-397
  conditional events, 546-547
  distance-first pathfinding, 727-730
  doubly linked lists, 170-171
  finite state machines, 537, 546-547
  graphs, 492-493
    traversals, 500-501
  hash tables, 226-228
  heaps, 417-418

Huffman trees, 674-676
minimax trees, 437-439
pathfinding, 753-754
    heuristics, 742-744, 748-749
queues, 204-205
quicksorts, 621-622, 627-630
radix sorts, 631-633
Random Distribution Graphs, 712-714
RLE, 651-655
singly linked lists, 149-150
sorts
    bubble sorts, 602-604
    heap sorts, 611- 613
stacks, 192-193
Towers of Hanoi, 327-328
trees, 333-338
    traversing, 351-352
weighted maps, 755-756
graphics (SDL), 858-861
    vector, 865-867
Graphics Processing Unit (GPU), 647-648
GraphNode class, 502-504
graphs
    adjacency tables, 486-488
    arcs, 482
    bi-directional, 483, 489-491
    clipping, 519
    culling, 519
    direction tables, 488-489
        dungeons, 512-518
        portal engines, 518-527
    directionmaps. *See* directionmaps
    graphical demonstration, 492-493
    implementing, 486-491
    linked, 489-491
    linked lists, 480-481
    networks, 484
    nodes, 482
    Probability Distribution Graphs, 707-708
    sectors, 519-522
    tilemaps, 485-486
    traversals, 493
        breadth-first searches, 495-499
        depth-first searches, 493-495
        graphical demonstration, 500-501
        marking nodes, 495
        stacks, 495
    trees, 480-481
    uni-directional, 483-484, 491
    weighted, 484
GUI (SDL), 869-878

H

hash tables
    collisions, 221
    digit addition, 221-222
    double hashing, 222
    graphical demonstration, 226-228
    hashing functions, 221-224
    implementing, 228-233
    keys, 218-219
    linear overflow, 224-225
    linked overflow, 225-226
    overview, 219-221
    quadratic overflow, 225
    resources, 235-239
    searching keys, 226
    strings, 223-224
    using, 233-235
HashEntry class, 228-229
HashTable class, 229-233
header files (I/O), 811
Heap class, 418-424

heap sorts, 609-611
  code, 613-616
  graphical demonstration, 611-613
heaps
  arrayed, 411
  defined, 410-411
  dense, 411
  efficiency, 416-417
  graphical demonstration, 417-418
  items
    inserting, 411-414
    removing, 414-416
  linked, 411
  memory, 844-845
  walk down algorithm, 414
  walk up algorithm, 411
HeapSort function, 615
HeapWalkDown function, 613-614
Height function, 125
Heuristic function, 449-450, 774-775, 781
heuristics (pathfinding), 739-742, 746-748
  code, 744-745, 749-750
  graphical demonstration, 742-744, 748-749
high-level AI, 530
horizontal functions, 346
Huffman class, 678-691
Huffman trees
  data compression, 665
    code, 677-692
    decoding, 665-667
    frequency tables, 667-668
    graphical demonstration, 674-676
    lookup tables, 691
    priority queues, 668-674
HuffmanFrequency class, 677
HuffmanNode class, 676-677

I-J

identification numbers (maps), 566, 583
identity functions, 91
image sets, 580
implementing
  finite state machines, 535-536
  graphs, 486-491
  hash tables, 228-233
  queues, 206-212
  speed, 787
  stacks, 193-199
  templates, 34-35
  tilemaps, 275-290
index variable, 16
inheritance (classes), 248-265
  children, 249
  down-casting, 263
  parents, 249
  types, 256-258
initializing
  2D arrays, 113
  finite state machines, 554-555
  multi-dimensional arrays, 113-114
    non-symmetrical, 114
    variable length, 114-115
  static arrays, 48
inline functions, 830-831
inline keyword, 247, 830-831
Inorder function, 372-373
input. *See* I/O
Insert function, 64-65, 399-400
  singly linked lists, 164-167
InsertAfter function, 152-153
inserting
  arrays, 80
  data (BSTs), 391-394

items (heaps), 64-65, 411-414
nodes (doubly linked lists), 172-173
insertion sorts, 637
instances (template classes), 23
intarray operator, 62-63
integers. *See also* numbers
   bitfields. *See* bitfields
   data sizes, 805-806
   random, 698-699
      determinism, 699-700
      functions, 700-702
      linear congruency, 700
      non-constant values, 702
      ranges, 702-705
      repeating patterns, 699-700
interfaces
   Adventure, 269-275
   speed, 787
Internet data compression, 649
Intruder (finite state machines), 547-560
inventories (linked lists), 176-180
I/O (input/output), 811-814
   file streams, 814-817
   header files, 811
Item class, 256-290
   trees, 467-468
Item function, 163
items
   inserting, 64-65
      heaps, 411-414
   removing, 65-66
      heaps, 414-416
iterators
   singly linked lists, 164
   SListNode class, 153-154
   STL, 886

K

KeyDown function, 873
keys
   hash tables, 218-219
   searching, 226
keywords
   catch, 821-823
   class, 17
   const, 814
   inline, 247, 830-831
   template, 17
   try, 821-823

L

left binary trees, 361
libraries, SDL. *See* SDL
licensing SDL, 848-849
LIFO (Last In, First Out), 191
limited depth algorithms
   game trees, 460
   minimax trees, 460
linear congruency (random integers), 700
linear data structures, 41
linear overflow, 224-225
line-based pathfinding, 762-764
linked binary trees, 362-363
linked graphs, 489-491
linked heaps, 411
linked lists
   algorithms, 184-185
   analysis, 184
   doubly, 169
      algorithms, 172-174
      graphical demonstration, 170-171
      inserting nodes, 172-173

node structure, 171-172
ReadFromDisk function, 175-176
removing nodes, 173-174
SaveToDisk function, 174-175
graphs, 480-481
inventories, 176-180
nodes, 148-149
singly linked lists
analysis, 169
Append function, 156-157
constructor, 155
destructor, 155-156
encapsulating, 154-155
graphical demonstration, 149-150
Insert function, 164-167
InsertAfter function, 152-153
iterators, 153-154, 164
Prepend function, 158
Remove function, 166-168
RemoveHead function, 158-160
RemoveTail function, 160-161
SListIterator class, 162-163
SListNode class, 151-152
structure, 150
size, 185-186
speed, 187-188
tilemaps, 180-183
trees, 332
linked overflow, 225-226
linked queues, 206-207
linked ranges (finite state machines), 544-545
linked stacks, 194-196
list data structure, 894-896
lists. *See* linked lists
Load function, 313, 588-590, 595
LoadData function, 661-662, 687-688
LoadFromFile function, 572-574
loading
arrays, 68-71
directionmaps, 588-590
LoadMap function, 302-303, 581-582
LoadTree function, 686
local variables, 840-842
logic, 580
lookup tables (Huffman trees), 691
loop (Adventure), 308-309
LStack class, 196

M

macros
ASSERT, 820
#define, 35
MakePerson function, 297-299
malloc function, 50-51
Map class, 468-469
map editor
directionmaps, 584-593
loading, 588-590
saving, 590-593
tiles, 586-588
tilemaps, upgrading, 594-595
trees, 473-475
map functions, 574-579
MapEntry class, 569
maps
directionmaps
converting, 583-584
format, 564-567
loading, 588-590
saving, 590-593
identification numbers, 566, 583
tilemaps, upgrading, 594-595
trees, 464-466

weighted, 754-755
    graphical demonstration, 755-756
    pathfinding, 758-759
    terrain, 756-762
marking nodes, 495
Massively Multiplayer Online games, 105
math
    bit math, 802-810
        binary numbers, 802-804
        bitshifting, 809-810
        bitwise, 807-808
        datatype sizes, 805-806
        integer data sizes, 805-806
    functions, 817-818
    math rules (binary), 91
mazes (pathfinding), 719-721
mean (statistics), 618
median (statistics), 618
median-of-three (quicksorts), 618
MedianOfThree function, 623-624
memory
    arrays
        cache, 77-80
        size, 80
    caching (bitvectors), 101
    code, 837
    crashes, 55
    free store, 836, 844-845
    global, 838-839
    leaks
        directionmaps, 573
        dynamic arrays, 53- 55
        troubleshooting, 168
    overhead, 185-186
    sections, 836-837
    speed, 105
    stack, 840-844
Menu class, 201-204

menus (stacks), 199-204
merge sorts, 637
Microsoft XBox data compression, 648
min variable, 61
MiniMax function, 449
minimax states (tic tac toe), 439-442
minimax trees
    base numbers, 441
    checkers, 442, 456-459
    chess, 442
    defined, 434-437
    game states, 439-442
    graphical demonstration, 437-439
    limited depth algorithms, 460
    recursion, 446-448
    Rock Piles, 442-456
MMO (Massively Multiplayer Online)
    games, 105
mode
    wb, 69
    statistics, 618
modulo, 703-704
Monster class, 72
monsters Game Demo, 71-77
MouseDown function, 873
MouseUp function, 873
multi-dimensional arrays. *See also* 2D arrays;
    3D arrays
    accessing, 115-116
    analysis, 144-145
    branch predictors, 142-144
    conventions, 118
    coordinates, 118
    declaring, 112-115
    defined, 108-110
    dynamic, 121-131
    finite state machines, 542-544

initializing, 113-114
  non-symmetrical, 114
  variable length, 114-115
passing functions, 119-121
performance, 142-144
pipelining, 142-144
size, 144
speed, 142-144

N

namespaces (STL), 883-885
naming conventions (STL), 882-883
network graphs, 484
new function, 52
nodes
  graphs, 482
  doubly linked lists
    inserting, 172-173
    removing, 173-174
    structure, 171-172
  linked lists, 148-149
  marking, 495
NodeType datatype, 501
non-constant values (random integers), 702
non-linear random numbers, 707-714
non-symmetrical multi-dimensional arrays, 114
nonvariable length symmetrical multi-dimensional arrays, 114-115
notation. *See* algorithms
numbers. *See also* integers
  base (minimax trees), 441
  binary, 802-804
  random, non-linear, 707-714

O

O notation, 4-9
Object class, 250-255
  inheritance, 260-265
object tracing, 719-721
OOP (object-oriented programming), 243
operators
  access, 89-91
  and, 91-93
  assignment, 344
  binary and, 90-91
  conversion, 63-64, 829-830
  delete, 54, 57
  equivalence, 445
  intarray, 62-63
  or, 91-93
  overloading, 827-829
  sizeof, 48
OpponentMove function, 453-454
optimizing bubble sorts, 604-605
or operator, 91-93
output. *See* I/O
overflow
  linear, 224-225
  linked, 225-226
  quadratic, 225
overhead (memory), 185-186
overloading operators, 827-829

P

parameterized types, 17
parameters
  classes
    Array2D class, 122
    arrays, 30-31

templates
  data types, 24-29
  values, 27-32
parents (classes), 249
ParseArithmetic function, 382-384
parsing binary trees, 374-376
  algorithms, 381-382
  arithmetic expressions, 376-377
  code, 382-384
  executing, 384-386
  recursive descent, 377-386
  scanning, 378-379
  tokenizing, 378-379
  tokens, 377-378
  variables, 378
passing functions
  multi-dimensional arrays, 119-121
  static arrays, 46-48
PathAStar function, 775-778
PathDistanceFirst function, 734-739
pathfinding
  A*, 750-752
    code, 752-753
    DirectionMap class, 780-785
    graphical demonstration, 752
    Tilemap class, 771-779
  Adventure, 770
  breadth-first, 721-727
  calculating, 726
  distance-first, 725-727
    code, 730-739
    graphical demonstration, 727-730
  efficiency, 790-791
  graphical demonstration, 753-754
  heuristics, 739-748
    code, 744-745, 749-750
    graphical demonstration, 742-744, 748-749
  line-based, 762-764
  object tracing, 719-721
  overview, 716-718
  quadtrees, 764-765
  random bouncing, 718-719
  speed, 786-790
  waypoints, 765-767
  weighted maps, 758-759
patterns (random integers), 699-700
Pentium data compression, 647
percents (random), 705-706
PerformAI function, 787-790
performance (multi-dimensional arrays), 142-144
performing quicksorts, 618-621
Person class, 258-260, 290-297, 788
PickUp function, 471
pipelining multi-dimensional arrays, 142-144
pivots (quicksorts), 616-618
Player class, 97
  trees, 469-470
players, saving, 96-102
playing Adventure, 582
plotlines (trees), 352-358
pointers
  classes, 252-254
  dynamic arrays, 53, 55
  FILE, 69
  functions, 832-833
  memory leaks, 55
  static arrays, 47-48
  strong type-checking, 51
  this, 830
Pop function, 195, 198
popping stacks, 191
portal engines, 518-527
Postorder function, 350-351, 372

postorder traversal, 449
powers (recursion), 319-320
Preorder function, 348-350, 372
Prepend function, 158
priority queues
   AI, 425
   building, 424-430
   defined, 408-410
   Huffman trees, 668-674
private classes, 246-248
Probability Distribution Graphs, 707-708
ProcessAI function, 557-559
programs, distributing, 858
projects (SDL), 853-855
public classes, 245-246
pure finite state machines, 538
Push function, 194-195, 198
pushing
   stacks, 191

Q

quadratic overflow, 225
quadtrees, 764-765
queues
   arrayed, 207-212
   circular, 207
   commands, 212-216
   defined, 204
   functions, 206
   graphical demonstration, 204-205
   implementing, 206-212
   linked, 206-207
   priority queues. *See* priority queues
QuickSort function, 624-627
quicksorts, 616
   code, 623-627
   graphical demonstration, 621-622, 627-630
   median-of-three, 618
   performing, 618-621
   pivots, 616-618

R

radix sorts, 630-631
   base 2, 633-635
   base 4, 636
   base 16, 636
   bin size, 633
   code, 633-637
   graphical demonstration, 631-633
rand function, 700-702, 819
random bouncing, 718-719
Random Distribution Graphs graphical demonstration, 712-714
random floats, 706-707
random integers, 698-699
   determinism, 699-700
   functions, 700-702
   linear congruency, 700
   non-constant values, 702
   ranges, 702-705
   repeating patterns, 699-700
random non-linear numbers, 707-714
random percents, 705-706
random-access data structures, 41
RandomPercent function, 705-706
RandomRange function, 704-705
RandomRangeF function, 706-707
RandomRangeModulo function, 702-704
ranges
   linked, 544-545
   random integers, 702-705

ReadFile function, 70-71, 94-95
ReadFromDisk function, 175-176
reading
    arrays, 70-71
    static arrays, 45-46
realloc function, 54-57
recursion
    AI, 319
    algorithms, 319
    defined, 318-319
    Fibbionacci series, 318
    functions, 318
        base case, 319
    minimax trees, 446-448
    powers, 319-320
    Towers of Hanoi, 320-328
        graphical demonstration, 327-328
    trees, 332
recursive descent (binary trees), 377-386
red-black BSTs, 395
references (data types), 62
registers (arrays), 77-80
Remove function, 65-66, 74-76, 504
    singly linked lists, 166-168
RemoveArc function, 509
RemoveHead function, 158-160
RemoveNode function, 506-508
RemoveTail function, 160-161
removing
    arrays, 80
    data (BSTs), 394
    items, 65-66, 414-416
    nodes (doubly linked lists), 173-174
repeating patterns (random integers), 699-700
ResetIterator function, 344-345
Resize function
    Array class, 60-61

Array2D class, 123-125
    Bitvector class, 88-89
Resource class, 402
ResourceCompare function, 403
resources
    hash tables, 235-239
    storing (BSTs), 402-405
return codes, 820-821
return values (functions), 843
right binary trees, 361
RLE (Run Length Encoding)
    compressor, 656-665
    data compression, 649-651
    decompressor, 656-665
    graphical demonstration, 651-655
    sprites, 655
RLE class, 656-665
RLEPair class, 656
Rock Piles (minimax trees), 442-456
RockState class, 443-445
    global variables, 445-446
Root function, 345
rotations (BSTs), 395
RTTI (Run Time Type Information), 261-263
rules (BSTs), 394
Run Length Encoding. *See* RLE
Run Time Type Information (RTTI), 261-263

S

Save function, 312, 590-595
SaveData function, 661, 686-687
SavePlayers function, 100-101
SaveToDisk function, 174-175
SaveTree function, 686

saving
    directionmaps, 590-593
    players, 96-102
scanning (binary trees), 378-379
SDL (simple directmedia layer), 848
    C++, 851-853
    distributing programs, 858
    event handling, 861-863
    files, 849-851
    graphics, 858-861
    GUI, 869-878
    licensing, 848-849
    projects, 853-855
    SDL TTF, 856-858, 863-865
    setup, 849-855
    text, 856-858, 863-865
    timer, 863
    using, 858
    vector graphics, 865-867
    video, 858-861
SDL TTF, 856-858, 863-865
SDLArrowLine function, 866
SDLBlit function, 135, 867
SDLBox function, 867
SDLFrame class, 867-868
SDLGUI class, 869-874
SDLGUIFrame class, 876-878
SDLGUIItem class, 874-876
SDLHelpers library, 865-867
SDLLine function, 866
SDLPoint function, 866
searches
    breadth-first, 495-499
    depth-first, 493-495
    DLDFS, 521-522
    keys, 226
    pathfinding. *See* pathfinding
Sector class, 523

sectors (graphs), 519-522
sequence containers, 890-896
Set function, 91-93
set functions, 91
SetAll function, 93-94
SetFocus function, 872
SetFollow function, 788
SetFont function, 870
SetLife function, 99
SetNewMap function, 302-303, 471-472
setup (SDL), 849-855
shell sorts, 637
simple directmedia layer. *See* SDL
SimpleHeuristic function, 744-745
singly linked lists
    analysis, 169
    Append function, 156-157
    constructor, 155
    destructor, 155-156
    encapsulating, 154-155
    graphical demonstration, 149-150
    Insert function, 164-167
    InsertAfter function, 152-153
    iterators, 153-154, 164
    Prepend function, 158
    Remove function, 166-168
    RemoveHead function, 158-160
    RemoveTail function, 160-161
    SListIterator class, 162-163
    SListNode class, 151-152
    structure, 150
size
    arrayed binary trees, 364-366
    arrays (memory), 80
    bins (radix sorts), 633
    datatype sizes, 805-806
    dynamic arrays, 54-57
    integer data sizes, 805-806

linked lists, 185-186
multi-dimensional arrays, 144
static arrays, 48
Size function, 67-68
Array2D class, 125
sizeof operator, 48
SListIterator class, 162-163
SListNode class, 151-152
Append function, 156-157
constructor, 155
destructor, 155-156
encapsulating, 154-155
InsertAfter function, 152-153
iterators, 153-154
Prepend function, 158
RemoveHead function, 158-160
RemoveTail function, 160-161
sorts
bin, 630
brute force, 600
BSTs, 638
bubble
code, 605-609
comparison functions, 606
defined, 600-602
graphical demonstration, 602-604
optimizing, 604-605
depth-based, 638-642
z-buffers, 639
heap, 609-611
code, 613-616
graphical demonstration, 611-613
insertion, 637
merge, 637
quicksorts, 616
code, 623-627
graphical demonstration, 621-622, 627-630

median-of-three, 618
performing, 618-621
pivots, 616-618
radix, 630-631
base 2, 633-635
base 4, 636
base 16, 636
bin size, 633
code, 633-637
graphical demonstration, 631-633
shell, 637
statistics
mean, 618
median, 618
mode, 618
sparse data, 218-219
speed
culling, 519
game logic, 787-790
linked lists, 187-188
memory, 105
multi-dimensional arrays, 142-144
pathfinding, 786-790
speed variable, 247
splay BSTs, 395
sprites (RLE), 655
srand function, 700-702, 819
stacks
analysis, 196
arrayed, 196-199
analysis, 199
defined, 190-192
FILO, 191
functions, 193
graphical demonstration, 192-193
graphs (traversals), 495
implementing, 193-199
LIFO, 191

Index   927

linked, 194-196
memory, 840-844
menus, 199-204
popping, 191
pushing, 191
standard template library. *See* STL
Start function, 162
state transition tables, 535-536
states
   FSM. *See* Finite State Machines
   games, 439-442
static arrays, 43-49
   accessing, 44-46
   declaring, 43-44
   fencepost errors, 44
   initializing, 48
   passing to functions, 46-48
   pointers, 47-48
   reading, 45-46
   size, 48
   troubleshooting, 45-46
   writing, 45-46
static variables, 839
statistics, 618
STL (standard template library), 880
   algorithms, 885-889
   containers, 898-899
      adaptors, 896-898
      associative, 896
      categories, 888-889
      functions, 889-890
      sequence, 890-896
   data structures, 885-889
      deque, 893-894
      list, 894-896
      vector, 891-893
   iterators, 886
   namespaces, 883-885
   naming conventions, 882-883
   STLPort directory, 880-882
STLPort directory, 880-882
storing
   data
      2D arrays, 116-117
      3D arrays, 117-118
      4D arrays, 117-118
      arrays, 68-77
      classes, 243-245
      resources (BSTs), 402-405
stray pointers (dynamic arrays), 53
strcat function, 663
String class, 236-237
StringHash function, 223-224
strings (hash tables), 223-224
strong type-checking, 51
structure
   binary trees, 362-366
   doubly linked lists, 171-172
   singly linked lists, 150
   Tree class, 339
   TreeIterator class, 343
   trees, 332-333
structures. *See* data structures
sub-optimal BSTs, 395
sum variable, 16
Sumtype data type, 25
switch function, 516-517

T

tables. *See also* hash tables
   adjacency, 486-488
   direction, 488-489
   frequency tables, 667-668

lookup tables, 691
state transition tables, 535-536
template keyword, 17
templates
   classes, 19-24
      declaring, 23
      instances, 23
   documenting, 33
   functions, 15-19
   implementing, 34-35
   overview, 14-15
   parameters
      data types, 24-26, 29
      values, 27-32
   troubleshooting, 32-33
   Visual C++, 34-35
terrain (weighted maps), 756-762
   pathfinding, 758-759
test files (data compression), 692-693
text (SDL), 856-858, 863-865
this pointer, 830
tic tac toe, 440-442
TileCell class, 773-774, 781
TileMap class
   A* pathfinding, 771-779
   trees, 469
tilemap editor, 310-314
tilemaps
   2D arrays, 131-136
   3D arrays, 136-144
   Adventure, 275-290
   graphs, 485-486
   linked lists, 180-183
   map editor, upgrading, 594-595
TilePathfind function, 766-767
tiles (directionmaps), 586-588
tilesets, 580
time function, 818-819

timer (SDL), 863
tokenizing (binary trees), 378-379
tokens (binary trees), 377-378
Top function, 195, 198
Towers of Hanoi, 320-328
   graphical demonstration, 327-328
tracing objects, 719-721
traversals
   graphs, 493
      breadth-first searches, 495-499
      depth-first searches, 493-495
      graphical demonstration, 500-501
      marking nodes, 495
      stacks, 495
   postorder, 449
traversing
   arrayed binary trees, 365-366
   binary trees, 371-374
      graphical demonstration, 373-374
   trees, 347-351
      graphical demonstration, 351-352
Tree class, 338
   constructor, 340
   Count function, 342
   Destroy function, 341-342
   destructor, 340-341
   structure, 339
TreeIterator class, 342
   assignment operator, 344
   constructor, 343-344
   Down function, 346
   horizontal functions, 346
   ResetIterator function, 344-345
   Root function, 345
   structure, 343
   Up function, 345-346
trees
   Adventure

game logic, 470-472
Item class, 467-468
Map class, 468-469
map editor, 473-475
maps, 464-466
Player class, 469-470
TileMap class, 469
binary. *See* binary trees
BSTs. *See* BSTs
building, 347
defined, 330-332
finite state machines, 545-546
game trees. *See* game trees
graphical demonstration, 333-338
graphs, 480-481
heaps. *See* heaps
Huffman. *See* Huffman trees
linked lists, 332
minimax trees. *See* minimax trees
plotlines, 352-358
quadtrees. *See* quadtrees
recursion, 332
structure, 332-333
traversing, 347-351
    graphical demonstration, 351-352
troubleshooting. *See also* error handling
bad alloc exception, 61
design, 772
memory crashes, 55
memory leaks, 55, 168
    directionmaps, 573
    dynamic arrays, 53
speed (pathfinding), 786-790
static arrays, 45-46
templates, 32-33
try keyword, 821-823
type-checking (pointers), 51
types. *See* data types

U

uni-directional graphs, 483-484, 491
Up function, 345-346
upgrading tilemaps, 594-595
using
    bitfields, 103-105
    hash tables, 233-235
    SDL, 858

V

Valid function, 163
values
    non-constant, 702
    return, 843
    templates (parameters), 27-32
variables
    cin, 812-814
    cout, 811-812
    global, 838-839
        RockState class, 445-446
    index, 16
    local, 840-842
    min, 61
    parsing, 378
    speed, 247
    static, 839
    sum, 16
vector data structure, 891-893
vector graphics (SDL), 865-867
video (SDL), 858-861
virtual functions, 251-255
Visual C++ templates, 34-35

W-Z

walk down algorithm (heaps), 414
walk up algorithm (heaps), 411
WalkDown function, 422-424
WalkUp function, 420-422
wavelets (data compression), 694
waypoints (pathfinding), 765-767
wb mode, 69
Web sites, 798, 881
weighted graphs, 484
weighted maps, 754-755
   graphical demonstration, 755-756
   pathfinding, 758-759
   terrain, 756-762
Width function, 125
WriteFile function, 69, 94
writing
   arrays, 69-70
   static arrays, 45-46
XBox data compression, 648
z-buffers, 639

TAKE YOUR GAME TO THE XTREME!

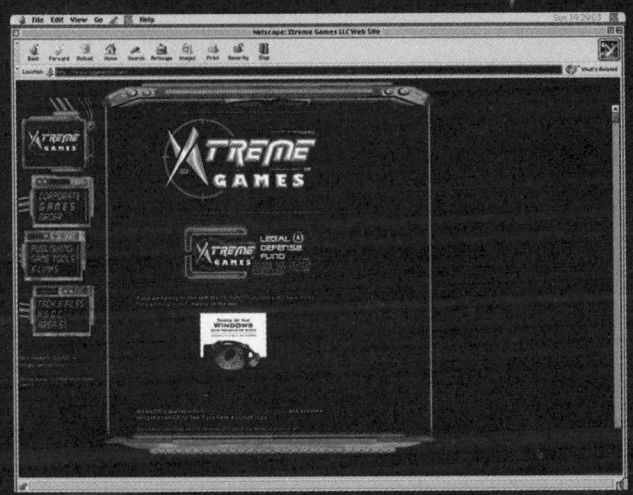

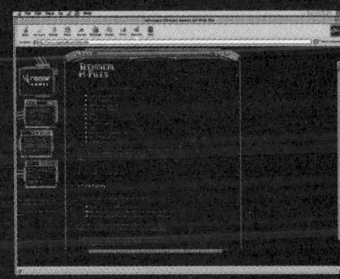

Xtreme Games LLC was founded to help small game developers around the world create and publish their games on the commercial market. Xtreme Games helps younger developers break into the field of game programming by insulating them from complex legal and business issues. Xtreme Games has hundreds of developers around the world, if you're interested in becoming one of them, then visit us at **www.xgames3d.com**.

www.xgames3d.com

GAME DEVELOPMENT.
IT'S SERIOUS BUSINESS.

"Game programming is without a doubt the most intellectually challenging field of Computer Science in the world. However, we would be fooling ourselves if we said that we are 'serious' people! Writing (and reading) a game programming book should be an exciting adventure for both the author and the reader."

—André LaMothe,
Series Editor

Premier Press, Inc.
www.premierpressbooks.com

Gamedev.net
The most comprehensive game development resource

The latest news in game development
The most active forums and chatrooms anywhere, with insights and tips from experienced game developers
Links to thousands of additional game development resources
Thorough book and product reviews
Over 1000 game development articles!
Game design
Graphics
DirectX
OpenGL
AI
Art
Music
Physics
Source Code
Sound
Assembly
And More!

OpenGL is a registered trademark of Silicon Graphics, Inc.
Microsoft, DirectX are registered trademarks of Microsoft Corp. in the United States and/or other countries.

License Agreement/Notice of Limited Warranty

By opening the sealed disc container in this book, you agree to the following terms and conditions. If, upon reading the following license agreement and notice of limited warranty, you cannot agree to the terms and conditions set forth, return the unused book with unopened disc to the place where you purchased it for a refund.

License:
The enclosed software is copyrighted by the copyright holder(s) indicated on the software disc. You are licensed to copy the software onto a single computer for use by a single user and to a backup disc. You may not reproduce, make copies, or distribute copies or rent or lease the software in whole or in part, except with written permission of the copyright holder(s). You may transfer the enclosed disc only together with this license, and only if you destroy all other copies of the software and the transferee agrees to the terms of the license. You may not decompile, reverse assemble, or reverse engineer the software.

Notice of Limited Warranty:
The enclosed disc is warranted by Premier Press, Inc. to be free of physical defects in materials and workmanship for a period of sixty (60) days from end user's purchase of the book/disc combination. During the sixty-day term of the limited warranty, Premier Press will provide a replacement disc upon the return of a defective disc.

Limited Liability:
THE SOLE REMEDY FOR BREACH OF THIS LIMITED WARRANTY SHALL CONSIST ENTIRELY OF REPLACEMENT OF THE DEFECTIVE DISC. IN NO EVENT SHALL PREMIER PRESS OR THE AUTHORS BE LIABLE FOR ANY OTHER DAMAGES, INCLUDING LOSS OR CORRUPTION OF DATA, CHANGES IN THE FUNCTIONAL CHARACTERISTICS OF THE HARDWARE OR OPERATING SYSTEM, DELETERIOUS INTERACTION WITH OTHER SOFTWARE, OR ANY OTHER SPECIAL, INCIDENTAL, OR CONSEQUENTIAL DAMAGES THAT MAY ARISE, EVEN IF PREMIER AND/OR THE AUTHORS HAVE PREVIOUSLY BEEN NOTIFIED THAT THE POSSIBILITY OF SUCH DAMAGES EXISTS.

Disclaimer of Warranties:
PREMIER AND THE AUTHORS SPECIFICALLY DISCLAIM ANY AND ALL OTHER WARRANTIES, EITHER EXPRESS OR IMPLIED, INCLUDING WARRANTIES OF MERCHANTABILITY, SUITABILITY TO A PARTICULAR TASK OR PURPOSE, OR FREEDOM FROM ERRORS. SOME STATES DO NOT ALLOW FOR EXCLUSION OF IMPLIED WARRANTIES OR LIMITATION OF INCIDENTAL OR CONSEQUENTIAL DAMAGES, SO THESE LIMITATIONS MIGHT NOT APPLY TO YOU.

Other:
This Agreement is governed by the laws of the State of Indiana without regard to choice of law principles. The United Convention of Contracts for the International Sale of Goods is specifically disclaimed. This Agreement constitutes the entire agreement between you and Premier Press regarding use of the software.